INVESTIGATING
THE ISSUES
OF
READING
DISABILITIES

INVESTIGATING THE ISSUES OF READING DISABILITIES

GEORGE D. SPACHE

Professor Emeritus
University of Florida

Allyn and Bacon, Inc.   Boston · London · Sydney

Library of Congress Cataloging in Publication Data

Spache, George Daniel, 1909–
 Investigating the issues of reading disabilities.

 Includes bibliographies and indexes.
 1. Reading disability. I. Title.
LB1050.5.S62   428′.4′2   75-40271

ISBN 0-205-05408-0

Fifth printing . . . August, 1977

contents

preface

The purpose of *Investigating the Issues of Reading Disabilities* is to provide in depth the background knowledge essential for practice in the field of remedial reading. In general, the parts of the book are arranged to parallel those of the core text, *Diagnosing and Correcting Reading Disabilities.* If both texts are used concurrently, the student or practitioner will be enabled to move directly from the research summarized here for each etiological area to everyday clinical practices. Since common diagnostic tools are also critically evaluated in Parts One and Two of this book, the remedial specialist will be helped to make more effective uses of these instruments.

In Part Two the strengths and limitations of both formal and informal reading tests are reviewed, and a guide for the user's evaluation of other such tests is provided. Part Three analyzes many innovative approaches to remediation and their results. Part Four emphasizes integration of diagnosis with remediation, the reading of reading research critically, and factors that influence the outcomes of remedial programs.

This is not a how-to-do-it book for the remedial practitioner, like many of its kind. Rather it explores the "why" and "what good is" questions that should be considered by everyone engaged in any aspect of diagnosis and remediation. Specific suggestions for detailed testing and treatment procedures are reserved for the core text, which can function as a daily guide.

This author has often been accused of being hypercritical of many of the current practices in our field of remedial reading. And, at the same time, he has been criticized for not telling his audiences just what they should do in every diagnosis or treatment, what tests to use, and what steps to follow. These parallel texts make it plain that there are many unanswered problems both in diagnostic testing and in the relative efficacy of various treatments. These cannot be disposed of by following stereotyped patterns of procedure. In our opinion, only an intensive review of every major facet of our practice will prepare the reading specialist to make these decisions. This text offers such a review to prepare the reader to understand, and perhaps to follow, the practical suggestions of the parallel book.

To stimulate learning, we offer a preview of each chapter and a learning activity based on the concepts offered. Reading in order to answer provocative questions and then the carrying out of relevant activities are well-recognized techniques for enabling students to understand and to implement their knowledge. We hope that these aids will provide meaningful, firsthand experiences with this field.

The use of *she/he* in this book is for convenience and clarity only, with *she* indicating the teacher and *he* the pupil.

Sarasota, Florida   George D. Spache

acknowledgments

We are indebted to a number of sources for permission to use some of the matter and illustrations of this book. We are grateful to:

The National Reading Conference, the University of Chicago Press, and the American Journal of Orthopsychiatry for permission to adapt certain of our earlier articles that appeared in their publications.

The Educational Testing Service of Princeton, N.J., for the privilege of reproducing certain tables from their *Short-Cut Statistics for Teacher-Made Tests*.

Dr. Paul B. Diederich, Senior Research Associate of Educational Testing Service, for permission to use his personal letter offering suggestions for a rapid method of computing reliability of a test.

Dr. Arthur S. McDonald of the Department of Education, Halifax, Nova Scotia, and the University of Chicago Press for permission to use his paper presented at the University of Chicago Reading Conference of 1964.

Dr. Milton H. Hodge of the University of Georgia and the American Psychological Association for permission to use his letter to the editor of the *American Psychologist*.

We are also appreciative of the following illustrations:

The Minnesota Percepto-Diagnostic Test, by Dr. Gerald B. Fuller.

Illustrative designs from the Graham-Kendall Memory for Designs Test, supplied by Dr. Carol H. Ammons of Psychological Test Specialists.

A specimen performance on the Benton Visual Retention Test supplied by Dr. Arthur L. Benton of the University of Iowa.

Several eye-movement analysis records and graphs, supplied by Mrs. Helen Morris, Senior Editorial Consultant of Educational Developmental Laboratories.

Several tests of auditory abilities by Joseph M. Wepman and Anne Morency of Language Research Associates.

INVESTIGATING
THE ISSUES
OF
READING
DISABILITIES

part one

ETIOLOGICAL AREAS

1
Reading and Visual Perception Tests

Visual perception and its significance for success in early reading has been receiving tremendous emphasis in recent years. As is so often the case in a new area of interest, we see a proliferation of new tests, new terms, and conflicting definitions of the field. Literally hundreds of measuring devices have suddenly appeared, often with only the author's logic to support their use. When even the dimensions of visual perception are being debated and the components claimed are identified and measured in dozens of different ways, it is difficult for a reviewer of the field to offer a coherent, objective overview, as you will recognize.

As you read this mass of uncoordinated data about visual perception and relevant tests, we suggest that you use these questions to aid in organizing your impressions of the field.

1. Compare your previous concept of visual perception with the many facets currently being talked about. Do these help you gain a clearer idea of the nature of visual perception? How would you finally define it?

2. Which elements of perception seem logically to be related to learning to read? Does the research support this logic strongly? How important do you believe any of the elements of visual perception are in early reading?

3. How do the factors of chronological age, mental age, experiential background, and socioeconomic status affect performance on tests of visual perception? Can you conceive of any method of controlling these influences when we are attempting to interpret the child's test performances?

I N AN AREA as confused as perception and its relation to reading, we might well begin by an attempt to define as precisely as possible the nature of perception. Various schools of psychology attempt to define perception as the result of stimulating sense organs (including the resulting action, according to some); or the interpretation of sensory data as based on past experiences extracted from mental storage; or the ability to recognize messages from the environment and to decipher them (26); or the process of maintaining stability with respect to the environment by immediate discriminative responses whether reflex, motor, or conscious acts (7). Some definitions emphasize the indivisibility of the sensory stimuli and the conscious response such as reflexes and gestures. Others separate the sensory data from the response into categories of sensation and perception. Test Makers seem to use the terms *discrimination* and *perception* interchangeably and to define operationally their labels by the nature of the subtests that they construct for instruments (such as a readiness, a visual, or an auditory discrimination test, or some other measure, as we shall point out). It is apparent that definitions of perception extend over a continuum from classic to popular to operational. The concept is further beclouded if we recognize the physical, emotional, and intellectual factors that influence the responses called perception.

FACTORS INFLUENCING VISUAL PERCEPTION

Some biologists propose a sensory-tonic theory of perception involving a reciprocal relation between sensory and postural factors. Body posture has been shown to affect tactile sensitivity and orientation to visual directions. These scientists stress the importance of visual feedback for readjustments of visual-motor coordination. A simple example of this sensory-tonic interaction is the apparent distortion of even simple geometric figures (and the consequent perceptual errors) arising from their presentation in different visual planes, or because the viewer varies his posture with respect to the form. Squares may not be experienced or reproduced as squares when they or the viewer are tilted, for example.

Perceptual readiness to make a response (or perceive) is influenced by motivational aspects of the stimulus such as the "goodness" or "badness" of the figure; the frequency and recency of exposure to it or similar forms; and its anxiety-provoking properties. Visual skills of the viewer as fusion, refractive error, and accommodation to distance can readily affect perception, as can the dimensions of the retinal area stimulated, the light intensity, the contrast of the object with its background, the duration of the stimulus, the state of adaptation to light of the eye of the perceiver, and his eye movements during viewing (38, 81).

In form perception, there is ample evidence that both the physical properties of the target and variables internal to the viewer are significant. Among such factors are contour, grouping, figural after-effects, distance, time intervals, and fluctuations of attention, not to mention the experiential elements of continuity, completion, closure, and meaningfulness (22, 81). The role of meaningfulness was demonstrated back in 1886, for example, in the finding that we can recognize three to four letters, two disconnected words as long as twelve letters, or a sentence of four words, in exposures as brief as .01 of a second.

Set or attention determines that the total amount of the field that can be attended to is constant; if only a small part receives attention, little will be perceived in other areas. Conversely, if attention is diffused over a large area, no one part or detail may be clearly perceived. The work of Piaget (67) and Gesell (33) has emphasized the developmental stages of progression from attention to wholes to gradual discrimination of details. The Goins study (35) demonstrated the importance of ability in detailed as well as wholistic attention for early reading.

Recently identified aspects of intelligence as cognitive "styles" or patterns of thinking are now recognized as related to perception. Analytic versus synthetic methods of perceiving complex stimuli, objective and subjective perceivers, as well as field dependent–field independent types are gradually being identified and their patterns of behavior in reading explored (44, 79). Other differences in perceptual behavior have been reported among neurotics and psychotics, obsessional persons, cases of anxiety and hysteria, and other personality deviates—all of them showing variations in perception differing from those of normal persons.

THE DIMENSIONS OF VISUAL PERCEPTION

In the efforts to utilize concepts of perception in the field of reading for diagnostic and predictive purposes, we find the studies limited to definition by test labeling and then further confounded by factor analyses of these same tests. It is a question whether the sophisticated procedure of analysis of the intercorrelations of a group of "perception" tests can prove the validity of such tests or reveal, as it claims to, the chief components of perception. Factor analysis can only reveal the common factors in the instruments examined. It does not prove their ability to measure the aspects implied in their titles and does not tell any more about the nature of perception. Factor analysis tells us no more than the common components of the tests tossed into the analysis. These would be synonymous with the dimensions of perception only if we assumed that the tests include all possible elements or all possible tests of perception. Since we do not know all these elements, the results of the factor analysis are significant only with respect to the tests analyzed, which represent an unknown portion of the total of perception.

A. Jean Ayres (4) offers a factor analysis of thirty-five instruments labeled as perception tests. Among 100 children with suspected deficits (identified how?), Ayres found factors that she labeled as follows:

1. Developmental apraxia—motor planning and eye-hand relations
2. Perceptual dysfunction—form constancy and space relations
3. Tactile defensiveness—hyperactivity, distractibility
4. Lack of integration—inability to discriminate between sides of body
5. Perceptual dysfunction—figure-ground discrimination

Gordon and Hyman (37), analyzing fourteen tests, found these factors:

1. Mimicry of sounds
2. Age and using a pencil
3. The Seguin Form Board
4. Multiple-choice visual discrimination tests
5. Matching visual discrimination tasks
6. The Wepman Auditory Discrimination Test, oral sequencing, and form rotation tests

In our opinion, Gordon and Hyman's results illustrate our point that we can extract as factors only the peculiar tests that we place in the analysis.

Dunsing (23) found six factors in the Purdue Perceptual-Motor Survey that he called organization of movements in space, ocular control, dynamic balance, rhythmic writing and postural stability, form perception, and motor planning and mobilization. He also followed up these factors to determine their predictive values during the primary grades, thus offering some implications for training programs.

Extensive lists of tests purported to measure visual perception are offered by McAninch (63). In fact, the list of current tests in this area is almost endless. Groffman,* for example, lists eighty-three tests of single visual

*Sidney Groffman, "Optometric Utilization of Objective, Standardized Perceptual Tests," *American Journal of Optometry and Archives of American Academy of Optometry,* 48 (October 1971), 825–33.

perception elements and twenty-one multiple test batteries, all of which are freely available, often without inspection of the technical qualifications of those purchasing them. We have not attempted to review all these tests, for many are of unknown validity and are unstandardized. Rather we shall cover many of the familiar commercial instruments in wide use, along with a number of informal tests offered by various researchers in the course of their experiments.

Tests of Perception

Part-Whole These are the tasks requiring the matching of parts of a whole or completing the whole by drawing, or recognizing or assembling the whole from its incomplete parts. The Gestalt Completion test, which asks the viewer to recognize the whole by mental closure of its parts (for example, a face or a word), is one such test. The Picture Integration Test of Elkind (24) was used to identify children in need of perceptual training on nonverbal exercises in this ability, with consequent gains in the test and two measures of reading. The Goldstein-Scheerer Cube Test, originally offered for the study of the effects of brain damage, is also of this type. Thurstone's Pattern Copying was one of the first tests of this type, created in 1944. In the First Grade Reading studies (13), this test yielded correlations with paragraph meaning from .34 to .46 in experiments in various methods of beginning instruction.

Visual Memory for Designs The ability to reproduce geometric designs of varying complexity is undoubtedly the most widely accepted type of perceptual test. Among those in wide use, whose validity we shall analyze in a later section, are the Bender Visual Motor Gestalt Test, the Benton Visual Retention, the Graham-Kendall Memory for Designs, the Beery Developmental Test of Visual-Motor Integration, the Minnesota Percepto-Diagnostic, and the Winter Haven Perceptual Achievement Forms. Despite the obvious influence of the factor of memory recall, of variations in ways of administration, of skill or familiarity with the use of a pencil, and of the fact that some of these tests were created primarily to detect brain damage among persons older than school beginners, they continue to have wide use in predicting probable success in reading in the early school years. Other than Beery (8), few authors of this type of test have attempted to justify it as a measure of visual-motor integration, a label frequently used. Few authors of this type of test, other than Beery (8) and Benton (10), appear to recognize that failure to reproduce geometric forms may reflect the data in Table 1–1.

TABLE 1–1

poor visual acuity or poor experiential background	as shown by comparing matching with reproducing
motor difficulties or lack of experience with paper and pencil	as evidenced in inability to trace forms or to draw lines composing them in terms of shape or direction
immediate visual memory	when child can copy or match but not reproduce from memory
intelligence	as shown by correlations with mental age and inferior performances by mentally retarded
personality variables	as perfectionism, compulsiveness, autism, hostility, paranoia, and the like

Figure-Ground

The test usually requires the recognition of a drawing, picture, or design obscured by or embedded in a confusing background. As Kaufman has said, the seven or eight forms of this test are not identical or perhaps even related (45). The Frostig battery uses intersecting figures; Kephart, simple geometric forms; Cruikshank, pictures embedded in a highly structured background; while Strauss and Lehtinen use marble board designs against a background. Satterly (73), using a test called Embedded Figures, found no relationship with reading achievement among primary children. In contrast, Stuart (79) reports that above-average readers in the seventh and eighth grades were superior to poor readers in this same test. Elkind (24, 25) calls his test one of Decentering of Perception, using Piaget's terminology, and has found some relationship with reading success in primary and intermediate grades.

Form Discrimination

Second in popularity only to the visual memory for designs are the tasks of matching visually or by cutouts of various geometric shapes. The task forms range from simple circles, squares, and rectangles to complex versions of these with many internal details. The Weigl-Goldstein-Scheerer Color Form Sorting test involves separate color or form matching of plastic pieces. The Pictorial Test of Intelligence employs picture parts. Informal tests of this type by Birch and Lefford (12), Nelson and Bartley (64), Lila Ghent (34), the Haeussermann Preschool Inventory, and the Minnesota Preschool Scale use visual matching of forms. The Chicago Test of Visual Discrimination employs a multiple-choice matching of forms similar to those in the Bender and has discontinued the reproduction part of the test because of the relative lack of relationship of the latter to reading (84). The stick test of the Goldstein-Scheerer battery and the block design matching in the Raven Progressive

Matrices (15) are other examples of types of form discrimination. Thurstone's Identical Forms, matching a given design to one of five, yielded *r's* of .27 to .40 with paragraph meaning taught by various methods in the large-scale First Grade Reading studies(13).

Form Constancy The task is that of recognizing a form or shape despite rotations or reversals. Ardis and Fraser (2) have built such a test, and one is included in the Frostig battery. Using a shape somewhat like a lamb-chop, Wechsler and Hagin (83) report that good readers made fewer errors when viewing the rotated figure around vertical and horizontal axes. Scribble patterns caused more errors in discrimination among poor readers at the age of ten, according to Whipple and Kodman (87).

Letter and Word Discrimination Tests involving matching, recognizing, or crossing out letters or digits in pied material (series of mixed letters), or of matching words are becoming common in readiness tests, because of their recognized relationships with success in first-grade reading. Apparently the ability to deal with letters or words prior to exposure to school instruction in reading reflects some influential factors in the child's background that may be cultural status, intelligence, parental tutoring, preschool learning, or some combination of these (3, 7, 72).

Miscellaneous Tests A number of relatively unique instruments are offered for visual perception testing. These include one sampling children's recall of the temporal order of presentation of meaningful and meaningless figures devised by Bakker (5). Poor readers were no worse than good with meaningless figures, but significantly poorer in this measure—of what some might call visual attention span—in recalling the presentation order of meaningful figures. The author interprets his results as an indication of a deficiency with verbal clues. Scott (74, 75) has conducted several studies with a seriation test, of arranging forms in size or pattern by pasting them in a given order in a booklet or by marking the forms on a page. Using both seriation tests in the kindergarten yielded significant but slight correlations with reading scores later in the second grade (Test I, *r* of .48; Test II, .58; Total, .59). Designating children scoring .3 of a grade above grade level as advanced readers in the second grade (a deviation probably well within the standard error of the reading test) and .3 below grade level as poor readers (apparently while ignoring the mental age, socioeconomic status, or other factors that might have influenced the achievements), Scott found that his seriation tests discriminated well between these groups. A second study of Scott's reports that his tests, although correlated well with the Metropolitan Readiness test, predicted third grade reading much more poorly for black children ($r = .19$) than for whites ($r = .46$), while the commercial readiness test yielded correlations of .42 and .53 for the blacks and whites respectively. These results may indicate that the seriation test also samples a cultural or experiential factor. Snyder and Freud (78) report on the Spiral After-Effect Test, a measure of ability to report an after-effect and its duration after viewing a spinning spiral. Bender Gestalt and readiness scores were higher for those who perceived an after-effect, which the authors interpret as an indication of superior readiness among first graders.

Reed used the drawing of a Greek cross as a perceptual test. He identified twenty-eight very poor and twenty-eight good performers on this test, finding that these groups differed in mean score in the Gates Primary Reading Test in paragraph meaning by one month. Yet the r between the drawing test (which, incidentally, is widely accepted) and reading was .45. However, when intelligence quotient was held constant, this r dropped to as low as .26 (WISC total IQ). These relationships were consonant with Reed's prediction that many perception test makers have not controlled the factor of intelligence; and that they do not realize that the relationships of their tests with reading are, in all probability, largely the result of variations in the pupils' intelligence (68).

In an early study (35) in 1958, Goins, employing fourteen tests of visual perception, found their order of validity in predicting reading to be Pattern Copying; Reversals—discrimination of identical or reversed pictures; Figures—matching designs with a given design; Picture Squares—matching two identical objects in a square composed of nine; Pattern Completion; Identical Pictures—matching a given picture or stylized pictures; Cancellation—of digits or letters; Visual Memory—for pictures presented among a group; Picture Comparison—detecting missing parts in a pair of almost identical pictures; Pictures—marking pictures containing a given pictured object; Controlled Association—marking pictures having a common element; Street Gestalt Completion—attempting to recognize incomplete pictures (35). Of these tests, Goins's analysis indicated that the Pattern Copying, Pattern Completion, and Reversals were the most closely interrelated and predictive of reading. Other studies support Goins's tests as predictive of reading success in elementary school children. Leider (59) for example, found r's of .677 for a combined score on the Reversals and Pattern Copying tests with word recognition and .699 with total reading score. However, correlation with mental age for this same combined test score was .707, implying that much of the relationship of these tests to reading is related to the intelligence factor.

Unfortunately, Goins's tests were never made generally available, and her effort to determine several significant tests of visual perception was never followed up. It would seem logical for researchers who followed Goins to have continued to validate their own tests by comparison with those that she identified. Thus, conceivably, additional components of perception could have been identified and perhaps new and better tests found. But it is apparent from the studies cited that each new author seems to feel a need to devise his own unique instrument and to ignore the previous research. Even in the factor analysis studies mentioned, practically all the tests involved were, again, unique to their authors and therefore of unknown validity, insofar as this might be determined by comparison with existing instruments such as those of Goins.

Are we now any closer to understanding what perception is? Or may we conclude that perception seems to include a large number of behaviors, some of which seem related to each other while some do not; some of which show a degree of relationship to early reading, while others seem irrelevant to reading. Critiques of these attempts to measure "perception" in some fashion or other are numerous. It might be profitable to review these prior to evaluating some of the better-known perception tests, in order to permit the reader to deal more analytically with their authors' claims.

Many of the tests enumerated above have been characterized as having low predictive values, being unclear in their interrelations and overlap, and almost irrelevant to an attempt to diagnose children's needs. Other criticisms are that the tests are often based on post hoc ergo propter hoc reasoning; that is, if a child is poor in visual perception in the third grade, this explains his learning failures in the first and second grades. There is very loose interpretation of correlations of the test with reading achievement, with authors often accepting statistically significant but minute correlations as indications of validity. For example, the r's of .27 to .40 of the Thurstone Identical Forms test with paragraph meaning in the First Grade studies cited above were probably statistically significant. But they meant that the ability to match forms accounted for 7 to 16 percent of the variance in reading scores. In other words, under various instructional methods, 84 to 93 percent of the factors helping children learn to read had nothing to do with matching forms; and this is one of the most positive findings in the literature regarding this type of test!

Reviewers' comments on some of the batteries of tests (including some that we shall analyze later) indicate the authors' belief that the weights they give to subtest scores, perhaps derived from multivariate regression equations, are applicable from one sample of children to any other—a false assumption. Correlations among subtests, from which scoring weights are derived, may vary with cultural background, race, intelligence, and age. Sometimes the reliabilities of subtests are ignored in assembling the battery;

and moreover, labels for these tests are completely arbitrary and hence misleading or confusing. (See discussion of Frostig and de Hirsch batteries later in this chapter.)

The fact that disadvantaged children usually do much more poorly on these tests than do middle-class pupils is usually either ignored or deemphasized. If freely recognized, these social-class results would have to be interpreted as indicating that most lower-class children are "perceptually handicapped" to use the test makers' common terminology. Or the contrasting results would have to be interpreted as indicating that whatever the test is measuring is readily learned in favorable environments and is not a "developmental lag" or some deficit in perceptual-motor functions.

Mann and Phillips (61) deplore the fractionation of behavior or the attempts to identify specific areas of function and dysfunction—and then to develop remedial programs directed at the supposed specific disabilities. They cite the lack of theoretical support for fractionation of perception into bits and pieces, the lack of validating research on most of the tests, and the proffered remedial programs. Ralph M. Reitan (69), who has specialized in the study of the brain-damaged (an area from which many perception tests have been borrowed), criticizes many of these tests. The reproduction of forms tests, for example, is influenced by a half-dozen environmental factors, as fatigue, depression, poor instructions, or lack of interest on the part of the testee, Reitan points out. We might also add that this commonest of all perception tests is certainly affected by the child's experience with a pencil, and even by the child's basic ability to draw the lines composing the figure that he is supposed to be perceiving. But few have made any attempt to determine the effects of these fundamental abilities that influence the child's "perception." It is apparently sufficient for them to find that their test (for undetermined reasons) shows some sort of relationship with reading success.

CRITIQUES OF CERTAIN PERCEPTION TESTS

Purdue Perceptual-Motor Survey

This battery of eleven tests is designed to detect errors in perceptual motor development. Its parts are predicated upon the authors' theory of the interrelationships of laterality, directionality, and perceptual-motor matching. In reporting the results, the authors group the tests as follows: (a) Balance and posture—walking board, jumping; (b) Body image and differentiation—identification of body parts, obstacle course, imitation of movements, the two Kraus-Weber physical fitness tests of raising head and shoulders or feet from floor when prone on face, and the Angels-in-the-Snow test of moving arms or legs as directed when lying on the back; (c) Perceptual-motor match—drawing on the chalkboard and rhythmic writing; (d) Ocular control—the ocular pursuits tests; and (e) Form Perception—the Winter Haven visual achievement form reproduction test.

The standardization of the test contained some rather unusual features. Fifty children were selected from each of the first four grades of a small midwestern city, but race was ignored and not reported. All children were achieving at or above grade level. For checking reliability and validity, a nonachieving group of ninety-seven children referred to a clinic was matched in age and grade level with the normative group. Five of the possible thirty test items failed to show normal growth in scores through the grades, but were retained in the battery. The Visual Achievement Forms (as administered here without timing or scoring of individual form reproductions), when scored grossly for form and organization of drawings on the page, failed to discriminate between achievers and nonachievers; but the items were retained in the final test. No reliability data are reported for the separate tests.

Dunsing (23) made a factor analysis of this battery of perceptual motor tests that resulted in a grouping very different from that suggested by its authors. For example, the chalkboard and Angels-in-the-Snow formed a factor called Organization of Movements in Space; the walking beam and obstacle course formed a Dynamic Balance factor; the Kraus-Weber physical fitness tests and the rhythmic writing were labeled Rhythmic Writing and Postural Stability; the jumping, identifying body parts, and imitation of movements were called Motor Planning and Mobilization. Only the ocular pursuits tests and the Winter Haven forms were identified as they had been by the authors. Dunsing also offered a follow-up of the predictive values of the factors that he identified in primary grades. But we shall reserve discussion of these to the section dealing with training programs that follow this rationale of visual perception.

A sidelight on the validity of the Purdue Perceptual-Motor Survey is offered in a master's thesis from Cardinal Stritch College (86). Matching thirty-eight pairs of pupils in sex, age, mental age, and socioeconomic status, Margaret Werner found that superior readers excelled poor readers in part of the walking beam test, in jumping, and in the two Kraus-Weber tests. The differences were in favor of the *poor* readers in the identification of body parts, imitation of movements, Angels-in-the Snow, and the chalkboard tests, although total scores did favor the superior readers.

In our opinion, the Purdue Perceptual-Motor Survey is really in its preliminary stages as a measuring instrument. Results are undoubtedly influenced by such factors as intelligence and socioeconomic status, as shown in the case of the latter by the authors' own data. While some of these perceptual-motor behaviors may have significance (as shown later) in training programs, the authors' attempt to create a diagnostic test for these elements is still in a very formative stage.

Bender Visual Motor Gestalt

First introduced in 1938, the Bender Gestalt, as it is popularly known, has slowly grown to be one of the most preferred tools of clinical psychologists. The nine geometric forms of the test were adapted from Gestalt psychology studies to form a visual motor test by Lauretta Bender. She offered the test as a measure of growth pattern and maturation level of an individual and as a tool for determining the presence of organic or functional pathological states. Although she illustrated the reproductions of children from three to eleven years of age, Bender offered no objective scoring system.*

Dissatisfaction with the reliability of intuitive and clinical interpretations of the Bender soon led to a number of attempts to devise scoring schemes. Of these, the Pascal-Suttell system of 1951† for ages fifteen to fifty was most widely accepted. Interestingly enough, the Pascal-Suttell interpretation of the Bender was as a measure of ego-strength or positive emotional adjustment, with the magnitude of the Bender score being related to the severity of the emotional disturbance. Use with children was a natural extension, and scoring systems for children's performances soon appeared, under the authorship of Koppitz in 1964 (52), Keogh and Smith in 1965 (50), and, most recently, by Lambert (56) in 1970, to mention only the more widely used scoring approaches. Among the applications of the Bender were attempts to screen for school readiness, to predict school achievement, to diagnose learning disabilities, to evaluate emotional difficulties, to diagnose brain injury, and to measure intelligence or study mental retardation. It is also used as a projective test of personality (52).

It is probably superfluous to point out again, as Koppitz has done, that interpretations of deviations in children's performances seem to have any of a half-dozen implications to different investigators, that is, a sign of brain injury or emotional problems or perceptual handicap, or, more simply, immaturity or mental dullness. As Koppitz asks: "Can one deviation indicate all these things? And if this is so, how can one tell which interpretation is the correct one at a given time?" (52, p. 4). Obviously more validation studies like those

---

*Lauretta Bender, *Bender Motor Gestalt Test.* New York: American Orthopsychiatric Association, 1946.
†G. Pascal and B. Suttell, *The Bender-Gestalt Test.* New York: Grune and Stratton, 1951.

of Koppitz (52) and Lambert (56), identifying the meaning of various signs or deviations, are greatly needed. It is no surprise that reviews of the Bender and the results of various studies vary markedly in their support of the uses of the test.

Relationship of the Bender to Readiness and Reading Achievement

Although it is perhaps an oversimplification of the pertinent data, we shall summarize by Table 1-2 some of the studies of the relationships of the Bender to readiness and reading achievement tests. For contrast, the data on readiness tests versus reading achievement, and the Bender versus teacher ratings are included.

TABLE 1-2   RELATIONSHIPS OF THE BENDER TO READINESS
AND READING ACHIEVEMENT

Grade Level N. of Cases	Bender— Readiness	Bender— Reading Achievement	Readiness— Reading Achievement	Bender—Teachers' Ratings
I 53 (53)	−.64[1]	−.67	.67	Low in
I 56	−.30	−.37	.42	kindergarten
I 40	−.21	−.41	.54	and fourth
I 26	−.33	−.58	.40	grade; significant
I 34	−.54	−.61	.67	in I, II
Total 199	−.61	−.68	.66	and III.
I 31	−.73	−.71	.63	
I 42	−.41	−.29	.66	
Total 73	−.59	−.58	.59	
II 141 (53)		−.53		
I 145 (53)		−.54		
III 127 (126)		−.23 to −.27[2]		
VI 73 (127)		.51[3]		
K 149 (148)	.51			.54
I 149 (148)		.39		.42
I–II 50 (120)	.61	.37		
IV 67 (41)		.16		
II 50 (107)		.39, .46[4]		
III 50 (107)		.32, .29[4]		
III 74 (50)		−.41		

[1]Correlations are negative since Bender is scored only in terms of errors in some scoring systems.
[2]Partial correlation with intelligence held constant.
[3]Kindergarten Bender with reading achievement in VI.
[4]For low and high scoring groups in Bender, respectively.

These correlations are almost all statistically significant, according to their authors, but this does not necessarily mean that they are indicative of great values for the Bender Gestalt as a predictor of early readiness or reading achievement. Correlations below .40 are usually considered low; .40 to .60 as moderate; and above .60 as marked interrelationships. According to the table above, three correlations of the Bender with commercial readiness tests are low, four are in the moderate range, and four are high. We could conclude that the Bender does seem to relate to whatever is measured in readiness tests. But intelligence is an important component of readiness tests, as we note in the analysis of such tests in chapter 6. And the Bender Gestalt is also definitely influenced by the intellectual factor, as evidenced by its use as an intelligence test per se in some studies. For example, for a population of 239 children aged five to ten, Koppitz (52) reports r's of the Bender with I.Q. from .48 to .79, leading her to recommend the Bender as a short, nonverbal intelligence test at these ages! How much, then, of the relationship between the Bender and readiness is due to the common factor of intelligence? In other words, would the Bender improve our predictions if used as a supplement to an intelligence or readiness or both tests?

The values of the Bender in predicting reading achievement are offered in the third column. They range from .16 to .71, with ten in the low range, eight moderate, and four ranking high, a somewhat poorer showing than in the Bender—Readiness test column. The lowest correlations are those reported in the fourth grade by Hafner (41) and in the third grade by Keogh (50), who statistically subtracted the intelligence factor in the Bender (and reading achievement). Collectively, this column indicates, as Koppitz has admitted, that the Bender fails to differentiate good and poor readers beyond the age of nine. And, as Koppitz and many other psychologists have not recognized, the Bender is a poor predictor of reading, even in primary grades, when its intelligence factor is held constant.

The fourth column reports a number of correlations between readiness and reading tests. Sometimes these are appreciably higher than the Bender versus reading test r's for the same children; one or two are probably significantly lower. In terms of magnitude, they are fairly typical of other such predictions. We might conclude from these data that the Bender is about as good a predictor of reading achievement as is a readiness test given in the beginning of the first grade.

Another way of interpreting these correlations, in order to ascertain their educational significance, is in terms of the overlap or variance, as it is called, in the correlated tests. This variance is indicated by the square of the correlation; that is, an r of .40 indicates that the tests overlap 16 percent, or, in other words, 16 percent of the tests is a common element (and 84 percent is something else). Quickly reviewing the columns again, the Bender and readiness tests overlap from 4 percent to 53 percent in various classroom samples. The Bender and reading tests overlap in primary grades from 5 percent to 50 percent, while readiness and reading tests overlap from 16 percent to 45 percent. (We omitted the Hafner sixth grade *r* of .16 between the Bender and reading, since the Bender admittedly does not really function at this level.) To summarize then, from 47 to 96 percent of whatever is measured in readiness tests is not sampled by the Bender; 50 to 95 percent of what is measured by primary reading tests is not sampled by the Bender. Finally, readiness tests fail to sample from 55 to 84 percent of whatever primary reading tests measure.

Since the Bender and readiness tests appear reasonably equally effective in predicting reading achievement, the argument is often offered that both should be used in the first grade. But Keogh's results indicate that much of what the Bender might add to the prediction is due to its intelligence testing component. Since this factor, which certainly does influence reading success, is more thoroughly measured by any of a number of primary verbal intelligence tests (and verbal intelligence is certainly more closely related to reading achievement than the nonverbal intelligence measured by the Bender), what really would be contributed by using the Bender?

Much the same conclusions are offered by Cellura and Butterfield (18), who found no significant difference in the Bender among mildly retarded adolescents who differed in reading achievement; by Connor (20), who reported poor Bender scores as often among good or poor second-grade readers; and by Henderson, Butler, and Goffeney (42), who discovered that the WISC predicted reading much better among seven-year-olds than did the Bender, which added very little to the prediction when intelligence was held constant. Kelly and Amble (46) also observed that the Bender added nothing to prediction of reading based on the WISC intelligence test results in the third grade.

Keogh (49), who has made numerous studies with the Bender, has concluded that the test has negligible value in predicting reading achievement in the first grade when intelligence is held constant; and in the third grade only half of the good achievers were identified correctly while a poor Bender signified nothing (48). Keogh and Smith (51) gave repeated Benders in the kindergarten with very poor reliability coefficients from one testing to the next. Lambert (55, 57) has reported several attempts to improve the reliability of the Bender by validating separately each sign or scoring item and apparently has succeeded in establishing a scoring scheme to distinguish emotionally disturbed or neurologically handicapped from normal children. But the reliability coefficients that she reports (.54 to .71) are not much better than Koppitz's (.55 to .66) or Keogh and Smith's (.55 to .65), reliabilities that many would consider much too low for predictions regarding individual pupils. These and other critical evaluations of the Bender are amply reviewed by Tolor and Shulberg (80).

There are some who would argue that in the hands of a psychologist the Bender can be of value in evaluation of primary children and prediction of their success. To agree, we need to assume that information about the ego strength or personality or emotional disturbance or possible brain damage or whatever the psychologist derives from his testing would be meaningful to, and could be implemented by, the average primary teacher. Our own fourteen years of experience as a school psychologist working closely with classroom teachers lead us to believe that this is a grandiose assumption regarding teachers' training and skills with children. Bender results may be useful in some psychologists' practice, but its relevance to reading success even in primary grades is questionable both in validity and reliability in our opinion.

Frostig Test of Developmental Perception

This battery of tests is widely used in primary grades to detect "perceptually handicapped" children and to introduce the author's training program for such. The five subtests are as follows:

1. Eye-Motor Coordination—drawing lines between printed boundaries varying in direction, and from point to point.
2. Figure-Ground—perception of intersecting figures against confusing backgrounds.
3. Constancy of Shape—recognition of geometric forms when varied in size, shading, and position in space.
4. Position in Space—discriminating reversals and rotations of figures in series.
5. Spatial Relationships—copying simple forms and patterns using dots as guide points.

According to the authors, the test "seeks to measure five operationally-defined perceptual skills" (62). Norms are offered for ages three to nine with sex-differentiated norms only for the kindergarten. The standardization population was drawn almost exclusively (93 percent) from southern California middle-class white children. In the 1963 edition this population is cited as

2,116 children, but no evidence is presented to clarify whether there is an accumulation of cases from the several editions or an actual restandardization. The authors (27) and other researchers have suggested that the test may also function as a measure of classroom adjustment by citing some moderate correlations between the test and classroom behavior scales (30). But Gazley's study did not find significant relationships in a similar exploration (32).

A good deal of statistical data about the 1963 Frostig is offered in a brochure distributed with the test (62). These data provide some interesting and unusual information regarding this battery. From a test construction standpoint, it is illuminating to discover that subtest 5 in spatial relationships apparently does not function below the age of five; to overcome this lack, the authors suggest that at such ages children be credited with an additional score, as though they had actually obtained some score on this test. The arbitrary score awarded for failure on this test is equivalent to normal performance for five-year-olds. It is not very clear just why the test should be given to four-year-olds when the norms indicate that they are not expected to be able to do any of it. This same strange practice of awarding scaled scores for absolute failures on subtests is repeated throughout the tables for converting raw to scaled scores. Just how meaningful would a total score based on five absolute failures—a possibility if we use the authors' norm tables—be? Why do the authors fail to admit that their battery, like any other test, has limits in applicability and discrimination?

Reliability data supplied by the authors are also intriguing. We note that test-retest reliability for total score drops from .98 when the test was administered individually by a trained psychologist; to .80 in groups in the hands of one trained, one untrained psychologist; to .69 when test was given to groups by examiners who were trained and supervised in procedures but were not psychologists. What will the reliability be in the hands of an ordinary teacher or reading supervisor, who is neither trained nor supervised in the testing?

Reliability of the subtest scaled scores in a kindergarten varied from .29 to .74 (subtest 3 reliability exceeding that of the total score). In a first grade, reliability r's ranged from .39 to .67 (total score .69). In these data, only subtest 3 in the kindergarten and 3 and 4 in the first grade exhibited reliabilities above .60, a minimal reliability for the comparison of groups and, in our opinion, far too low for individual diagnosis. How can we justify the use of such unreliable test scores for a diagnosis of the child's perceptual difficulties, if indeed that is what the tests measure?

In the data of Corah and Powell (21), these subtests exhibited greater intercorrelations in some instances (test 1-2, 1-4, 1-5, 2-5, and 4-5) than did the *subtest reliabilities* reported by the authors. When the overlap between subtests is as great as the overlap between two administrations of the same subtest, how can the authors claim to be measuring different aspects of perception? Similarly, the authors report correlations of their battery with the Goodenough as high as .460 in the kindergarten, .318 in the first grade, and .366 in the second. Again, these correlations are as large as some of the reliability *r*'s for several of the Frostig subtests, raising the question of the overlap between them and intelligence. These questions could be answered by a factor analysis of the authors' own data, but they choose not to attempt such an analysis.

Validity of the Frostig battery in predicting reading achievement, a crucial question in view of the authors' claims, is reported for only one statistical study in the authors' data, as between .4 and .5. In other words, 75 to 84 percent of the variance in reading scores in this group was unrelated to the children's Frostig scores. Further evidence of the validity of this test and its parallel training program will be offered later.

TABLE 1-3   THE FROSTIG AND READING ACHIEVEMENT

Grade Level and N. of cases	Frostig— Reading Achievement	Readiness— Reading Achievement
I 60 (8)		
Subtest 1	.361	
Subtest 2	.24*	
Subtest 3	.445	
Subtest 4	.206*	
Subtest 5	.313*	
Total	.615	
I ? (119)		
Subtest 4	.30	
Subtest 5	.38	
Total-word recognition	.41	.55
Total-sentence meaning	.39	.55
Total-paragraph meaning	.41	.58
I 108 (32)		
Subtest 1	.12*	
Subtest 2	.27	
Subtest 3	.49	
Subtest 4	.31	
Subtest 5	.32	
K–II 382 (57)		
Subtest 2 Boys	.38	
Girls	.14*	

Grade Level and N. of cases	Frostig— Reading Achievement	Readiness— Reading Achievement
Subtest 4[1]		
K 50 Boys	.48	
	.55	
K 68 Girls	.43	
	.08*	
I 71 Boys	−.03*	
	.06	
I 54 Girls	.35	
	−.05*	
II 69 Boys	.26	
	.16*	
II 56 Girls	.06*	
	.37	
Subtest 5 (1)		
K 50 Boys	.28	
	.43	
K 68 Girls	.35	
	.15*	
I 71 Boys	.38	
	.47	
I 54 Girls	.22*	
	.23	
II 69 Boys	.20	
	.05*	
II 56 Girls	−.20	
	.01*	
II 121 (140)		
Total—vocabulary	.44	
Total—comprehension	.35	
Total—paragraph meaning	.32	
Total—word recognition	.42	

*Correlations not significantly different from 0.
[1]Leibert's two correlations for each group of children were with tests of word matching and phrase matching respectively.

It is quite apparent that the skills tested in the various subtests of the Frostig show little relationship with measures of reading achievement. Fifteen of thirty-eight correlations are statistically insignificant and thus useless for prediction. Only seven of these thirty-eight correlations achieve a level indicating a moderate relationship (.40 to .60), and none reaches the marked relationship level (above .60). As for the total score on the Frostig, of the eight correlations with reading only one reaches the upper range of usefulness. To interpret these correlations from another viewpoint, total scores in the Frostig account for from 10 to 38 percent of the variance in reading scores, while subtests account for anywhere from 0 to 30 percent of the variance in reading. Despite its labels and variety of subtests, the Frostig appears less relevant to reading achievement than does even the Bender Gestalt single measure.

Pertinent comments on the Frostig are offered by the authors whose data we have cited above, as well as several other researchers, if we may be permitted to paraphrase their observations, as follows:

Benger (9) reported no significant differences between good and poor readers on Frostig subtests 2 and 4; and doubtful on subtest 5. Maximum scores and hence no discriminative power in these subtests by the end of the first grade. Only the skills of Eye-Motor Coordination and Constancy of Shape seem significant enough to try to improve them by training.

Bryan (16) found the Frostig better than an intelligence test in predicting reading success in the first grade (in tests of word recognition). In the second grade, the Frostig total was better for predicting reading comprehension; the intelligence test for reading vocabulary. In the third grade, the intelligence test was better than the Frostig for predicting both reading skills.

Gazley (32) reports girls significantly higher on all subtest scores except Eye-Motor Coordination and considers subtests 4 and 5 (see her data in table) as the best predictors of reading of all the subtests.

Goldstein et al. (36) indicated that the Constancy of Shape Subtest was the only useful predictor in a multiple regression equation combining a readiness test and a visual-motor sequencing subtest of the ITPA, although even this formula did not differentiate good and poor readers in the low I.Q. group. Distributions of scores were so widely spread and overlapping, however, that they could not even establish cutoff scores to distinguish pupils who would need some specific training if failure in reading was to be prevented.

Leibert and Sherk (58) built special reading tests of letter, word, and phrase matching in order to parallel as closely as possible the skills presumably measured by the Frostig. Even in these tests, only Frostig subtests 4 and 5 differentiated low from high achievers; and even this discrimination was successful only at the kindergarten level, and much poorer in first and second grades.

Olson (66) discovered that the Constancy of Shape and Figure Ground subtests had minimal significance for reading in the second grade. His overall results led him to conclude that the Frostig was of little value in predicting specific reading abilities.

Anderson (1) reviewed the Frostig and observed that, in his opinion the directions were confused and unclear with terms such as "draw around" and "mark" used interchangeably. He questioned the low weights given some of the most difficult items, as in items 5 and 9 of subtest 1, as illogical, and the lack of clear description of the standardization population. Other reviews with the same source deplore the rigidity of scoring directions in the Eye-Motor Coordination test and the subjectivity of the scoring of the Constancy of Shape as well as the inadequate sampling of children, particularly at the preschool levels.

Apparently the authors of the Frostig test have never submitted the intercorrelation matrix of the subtests to factor analysis in order to identify the basic components of the test. Other researchers have, however, with interesting results. Boyd and Randle (14) and Olson and Johnson* found only one basic factor in all five tests, and concluded that the subtests were not measuring different fundamental perceptual abilities, as claimed. Corah and Powell (21) identified only two factors—general intelligence and developmental changes in perception. Ohnmacht and Olson (65) found only one common factor in the first grade in all five tests. Rosen and Ohnmacht (71) combined readiness, reading, and intelligence tests with the Frostig. Their factor of reading achievement did not include any of the Frostig tests; isolated the Figure-Ground subtest as unique and unrelated to all the other tests; identified the Eye-Motor Coordination test as a function of age for boys; and found a factor of perceptual readiness for girls that included the Position in Space and Spatial Relationship subtests only, with several subtests of the commercial readiness measure. For boys, the three subtests of the Frostig, Position in Space, Constancy of Shape, and Spatial Relationships combined with the readiness tests to form a different factor, labeled perceptual readiness. Rosen and Ohnmacht concluded that the specific tests of the Frostig (as well as those of the readiness test) make limited contributions to the prediction of reading achievement.

Minnesota Percepto-Diagnostic Test

By selecting from the forms of the Bender-Gestalt those most likely to be rotated in the testee's reproduction, Fuller (28) has developed a test to assess visual perception and visual motor abilities. Two of the Bender figures, rotated or framed by rectangles or diamonds for a total of six test forms, constitute the test. Reproduction of each form in turn requires a total of two to eight minutes at ages five to twenty. Corrections of the score according to

---

*A. V. Olson and C. I. Johnson, "Structure and Predictive Validity of the Frostig Developmental Test of Visual Perception in Grades One and Three," *Journal of Special Education*, 4 (1970), 49–52.

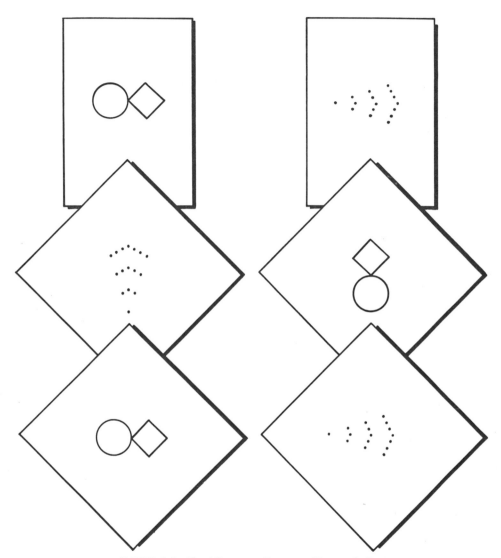

FIGURE 1–1   The Minnesota Percepto-Diagnostic Test

the testee's I.Q. are made to remove the intelligence factor as well as corrections for the age factor. Such corrections assume, of course, that the relationships of CA and MA in Fuller's test are similar in all populations, a questionable assumption.

The author's rationale for his test is that errors in rotating the forms during reproduction, above the age of eight, are a significant deviation from normal performance and may indicate brain damage, emotional disturbance, psychosis, or mental deficiency. Therefore, with the aid of a protractor, the degrees of rotation of each figure from its base line are measured. Designs rotated more than 25 degrees receive a raw score of 25; for all others, the number of degrees of rotation becomes the raw score. Cutoff scores are offered by the author to distinguish normals from emotionally disturbed, schizophrenic, and brain-damaged. These cutoff scores, according to his data, will identify correctly 79 to 84 percent of the causative factors, or, conversely, will falsely identify from 16 to 21 percent of the cases. Similarly, good readers can be differentiated from primary disability (no neurological or perceptual problems), secondary type poor readers (result of emotional disturbance), and organic poor readers (result of brain damage). Accuracy in this discrimination is reported to be as high as 89 percent by the author (28). An early study by the author failed to establish criteria to distinguish brain-damaged children among mentally retarded pupils. A new scoring for distortions and separations in the drawings seemed more successful in making this distinction among mental retardates, at least in the initial population. Studies in predicting reading scores among junior high pupils gave relatively poor results, while another study indicated that culturally deprived achievers obtain practically the same mean score on this test as do more advantaged children (29).

Kreitman (53) reports that the test successfully distinguished correctly 82 percent of emotionally disturbed from organic dysfunction cases; and Krippner (54) claimed that the MPD classified all but two of twenty-four cases (92 percent) previously identified as primary, secondary, or organic readers by clinical opinion. Test-retest reliabilities for normals is reported as .85; as .82 for emotionally disturbed; as .74 for brain-damaged; and as .81 for schizophrenics (28).

Although most of the basic data on the MPD appear favorable to its use in reading diagnosis, there are a number of questions yet to be answered. Validating the test on clinical groups ranging from ages five to twenty-one makes us wonder whether the test is equally efficient at all these ages. How well would the test work during the period from kindergarten to second or third grade when prevention of reading failure might be attempted? The cutoff score for brain-damaged and schizophrenics is the same. The author suggests that schizophrenics can recognize and correct errors in reproducing the designs, while brain-damaged cannot; also that the distortions and separations of drawings can aid in this distinction. But how does the school decide on the basic cause and treatment? In a normal school population, how many cases would be thus identified, and the school expected to refer for neurological and psychiatric diagnosis? In other words, granted that the test may discriminate among previously identified psychiatric groups, and even among some types of poor readers, how does it function when applied to a normal school population? Could its indications be taken at face value and economically implemented?

Reviewers of the first edition of the MPD (17) questioned the effects of intelligence, age, and education upon test performances—influences that the author now tries to minimize by his scoring procedure. Other reasons for great caution in using the MPD scores are the facts that rotations are affected by personality variables and by the type and location of brain damage. In a general population (as that of a class in school, for example), the test probably will not display the same degree of efficiency as it does in research groups. In such a population symptoms are not as clear-cut; very few true organic cases are likely to be encountered, and most cases so diagnosed by the test would be likely to be false positives; discrimination of mild brain damage from schizophrenia would be questionable if based simply on this test; detection of minimal or very mild brain damage is not probable.

Graham-Kendall Memory for Designs Test

The examinee is asked to reproduce each of fifteen geometric forms after five seconds of exposure to each. The test is offered for ages eight and a half to sixty as a sensitive detector of brain injury of many types. Accuracy in classifying patients ranges from 43 to 90 percent in various studies (17), while the reported reliabilities range from .72 to .90. Some studies seem to show a relation between the scores and reading (60, 82), while others do not. There is

FIGURE 1–2 Illustrative designs from the Graham-Kendall Memory for Designs Test (Drawings supplied by Psychological Test Specialists for the Graham-Kendall Memory for Designs Test, copyright 1962.)

also the influence of the intelligence factor upon reading predictions, as shown in an *r* of −.60 with WISC Full Scale I.Q.'s in Lyle's study of children of six and a half to twelve and a half (60).   Some studies indicate that the Graham-Kendall is superior to other tests for organicity, while others find it inferior, particularly in the mildly impaired cases (17).   Recognizing the inherent influence of the memory factor, the authors tried to add a simple copying of designs task to the test but found it too easy to be discriminative.

It appears that the Graham-Kendall may function reasonably well in distinguishing severely damaged organic cases from normals and in avoiding the influence of emotional disorders upon test performances.   Whether it will aid in predicting reading failure; or identify children with perceptual-motor handicaps; or find children whose reading difficulties are due to mild brain damage and distinguish these reading cases from those due to emotional disturbance, psychosis, or mental deficiency remains to be demonstrated.

Winter Haven Perceptual Forms Test

In a group or individual administration, the child is asked to reproduce seven geometric forms and, on the reverse side of the test paper, to finish incomplete versions of the same forms(88).   Speed and memory factors are eliminated by allowing the testees to view each form until they finish their reproductions.   The test is sponsored by the Lions Club of Winter Haven, Florida, who have supported the research on it since 1953.   Early studies indicated significant relationships of the test with school achievement in the primary grades only.   The simplicity of the task does not support adequate discrimination above the ages of eight or nine(17).   Although it is mentioned frequently in conjunction with reading predictions, independent studies indicate that the test functions best in predicting general achievement.   Helen M. Robinson (70) in one of several studies, reports correlations of .24 to .44 with reading and a partial *r* with intelligence constant of .34.   Training programs based on templates of the same geometric forms are offered by the authors and are reported in chapters 15 and 16.

As a simple instrument for identifying primary children who are likely to experience school failure, the test may be useful as a supplement to other measures of readiness.   There are certainly merits in its ease of administration and scoring and its control of the speed and memory factors that distort many other comparable tests.   Moreover, the provision of a corrective or preventive training program, which can be directly applied on the basis of the test scores, appeals strongly to pragmatic classroom teachers.   Later in chapters 15 and 16, we shall consider whether this training program is effective.

Beery Developmental Test of Visual-Motor Integration

The test requires children to copy twenty-four geometric forms, each on a separate sheet of paper on which the design to be reproduced is printed at the top of the page. The test is administered in groups, and the reproductions scored as a total up to the point of three consecutive failures. Test-retest reliabilities range from .80 to .90 for periods as great as six months. Correlations with intelligence are quoted as .59, .37, and .38 in the first, fourth, and seventh grades respectively, and as high as .70 among mentally retarded. The author acknowledges that the relationships with intelligence are probably higher than with chronological age, even though the test is standardized as an age scale. Correlations with word knowledge of .33 to .50, with word discrimination of .36 to .48 at the first-grade level, are cited by the author, with the best relationships in the low socioeconomic groups. In the same groups, r's with intelligence ranged from .36 to .48 in word knowledge, from .38 to .45 in word knowledge, and from .37 to .50 with Beery's VMI test.

Beery is to be commended for his thoroughly detailed manual and the extensive work with his test(8). The careful validation of the test forms and the testing procedure along with the control of the speed and memory factors, are strong points of the author's work. His efforts to establish the test as a measure of visual-motor integration (rather than as a sampling of just one of these processes) and to distinguish the test from others of auditory or auditory-visual functions contrast greatly with the information offered by many other test makers. As a measure of the child's integration of visual impressions and motoric responses, the test appears to be useful in identifying children who may benefit from some types of sensory-motor training. Whether the test has any greater direct relationship to reading success than to general school achievement and its values in this use above the first grade are as yet unknown. We should also mention that Beery rejects the use of his test as a neurological diagnostic instrument, as in identifying brain-damaged children, by teachers and psychologists. He feels that such an application must be in the context of a complete neurological study only.

The Revised Visual Retention Test

Arthur L. Benton (10) offers his test as a measure of visual perception, visual memory, and visuoconstructive abilities. It consists of three forms of the test, Forms C, D, and E, consisting of ten designs each. Four means of administration are used: (1) ten-second exposure of each design with reproduction from memory; (2) five-second exposure with reproduction from memory; (3)

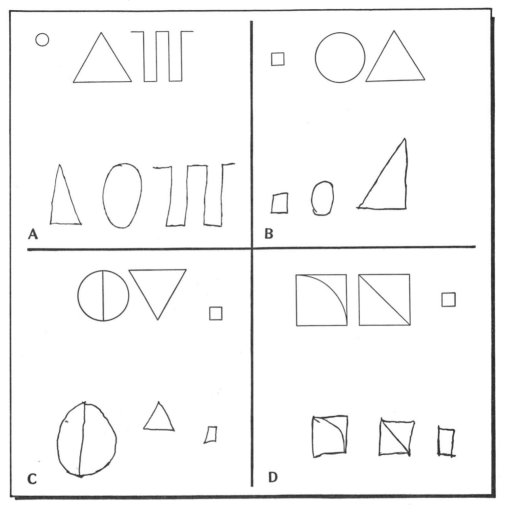

FIGURE 1–3   Reproduction from memory of some of the designs of the Benton Visual Retention Test by a nine-year-old brain-damaged child.   Note the neglect of the relative size of the figures in all the reproductions, the reversal of the figures in *A,* and the rotation in *C.*

copying of the designs; and (4) ten-second exposure with reproduction from memory after a delay of fifteen seconds.   Retest reliability for the first type of administration as estimated by the correlations between forms is about .85. Two systems of scoring—one by a total of correct reproductions; the other, a count of errors—correlate about .85.   The latter, of course, permits qualitative analysis of a subject's performance in such errors as omissions, distortions, perseverations, rotations, misplacements, and size errors (assuming that the examiner can interpret these). Samples of correct and incorrect reproductions and of common errors in various designs are supplied in the Manual.

Norms for adults for the first three ways of testing are given for ages approximately fifteen to sixty-four and for children ages eight to fourteen for the first type of administration only. The influence of intelligence upon the scores is recognized by equating them to I.Q. levels, rather than age levels, in the norms for both adults and children. Benton suggests that a number correct score of 3 points or more (three incorrect designs) below the expected level in terms of the adult patient's intelligence is considered indicative of brain damage. Accuracy in identifying cases with brain pathology using the cutoff score vary from 50 to 57 percent in various studies cited by the author. False positives, that is, normals identified by test score as brain-damaged, varied from 4 to 6 percent.

Explorations in use of the test to ascertain the locus of a brain lesion and to identify errors characteristic of the brain-diseased by various administrative procedures are described by the author as preliminary researches needing much wider study. Testing of children who were either emotionally disturbed or brain-damaged successfully identified 28 percent of the latter, while yielding 4 percent of false positives. The question of the relationship of the test performance to reading disability was explored in a study of twenty children of average intelligence, ages nine to eleven. Only two of these showed defective performance on the Visual Retention Test, perhaps, as the author notes, because of their age. The test might be more valuable (or less) with younger children who experience, or are about to experience, reading failure.

Recognizing the possible influence of visual, memory, or motoric factors upon test performances, Benton suggests use of his different methods of administration in child cases in which the evidence from this and other measures of the child's abilities are inconsonant. He further discusses this clinical approach to puzzling cases; to the mentally deficient, schizophrenic, and depressed; to persons simulating brain injury; to the aged; and to cases of defective immediate or delayed memory through the study of both types of scoring, as in the timed versus the untimed procedure, or the responses to the immediate versus the delayed reproduction. The Visual Retention Test has probably had more study and research, particularly among the brain-damaged, than many of its competitors have. A more flexible test, it offers several types of administration and interpretation, and it has been lengthened and improved in the restandardization. Reviewers (17) point out, however, that its effectiveness in discriminating between groups of normal and brain-damaged is weak in several of the studies cited by the author; they consider the test improved but still experimental.

The Predictive Index Tests

De Hirsch, Jansky, and Langford (43) offer a series of ten tests for identifying kindergarten children who are likely to be unsuccessful in school achievement in the first two school grades. They include in the battery measures of pencil use, the Bender, the Wepman Auditory Discrimination, the number of words used in a story, a categories and a reversal test, a word-matching test, two word recognition tests, and a word reproduction measure. Their study began with a total of thirty-seven tests selected for their predictive values in a group of fifty-three children, yielding the ten final Predictive Index Tests that had a 91 percent efficiency in this group, according to the authors. Criticizing this study for the minute size of the population and the faulty procedure of selecting a few measures from among many in a small group, Zaeske (90) tried to replicate the study with 259 first-grade children. Using the Predictive Index Tests, the Metropolitan Reading Readiness, and Peabody Picture Vocabulary tests, Zaeske determined their predictive values in terms of end-of-year measures of teacher judgment, a word recognition test, and the Metropolitan Reading Test.

The results indicated that the Predictive Index Tests predicted thirty-three failures, of which fifteen were incorrect, while eighteen predicted as successful were indeed failures. In contrast, the Metropolitan Readiness erred only in overpredicting for twenty-eight who subsequently failed. Zaeske concluded that there was little difference in the predictive values of the two sets of tests, except that the Metropolitan was more conservative. Correlations for the Predictive Index with teacher judgment, the word test, and the Metropolitan Reading were .55, .61, and .63 respectively, while the corresponding r's for the readiness test were .73, .67, and .68; those for the Peabody, .44, .33, and .37. The difference between the two predictions of teacher judgment was significantly better for the Metropolitan test.

In the ten subtests of the Predictive Index battery, r's with the total Predictive Index Score ranged from .39 to .70. If we interpret these data correctly, they are r's of subtests with a total score derived from the same tests and are thus artificially inflated. In conclusion, Zaeske felt that his larger-scale study demonstrated the preferability of the Metropolitan readiness test in predicting early reading success, while the de Hirsch-Jansky-Langford battery was better in predicting failures, even though it overpredicted such. If this overprediction resulted in a stronger readiness program for such children, Zaeske believed it worthwhile as a preventive measure and probably less costly than a remedial program for the failures that such a test as the Metropolitan might fail to detect.

A study by Trimble* of the validity of the de Hirsch battery gives a different picture of its values. Using seven of the de Hirsch tests and two additional measures to predict reading failure or success in the first grade, Trimble discovered that the battery heavily overpredicted failure. About 60 percent of the children who were supposed to fail in reading, according to the de Hirsch scores, actually succeeded. In contrast, only 5 percent of those predicted to succeed failed in reading at the end of the first grade. This larger study of 417 kindergarten–first-grade children raises strong doubts about Zaeske's support of the de Hirsch battery. The false predictions for more than 60 percent of the population hardly argues for use of this battery.

In another article, Zaeske (89), offering a critique of the de Hirsch battery, enumerated many flaws, most of which he did not explore in the data available in his replicative study described above. Zaeske deplored the size of the de Hirsch population, the interpretations of correlations as cause-effect relationships, and the failure to realize that in eliminating tests from the initial battery of thirty-seven measures, it would be well within the mathematical probabilities to find a small number that appeared to function predictively. He further criticized the de Hirsch scoring and administrative procedure as confusing and almost impossible to follow; but he gives no indication whether he followed these impossible (?) instructions in his own study.

We might also point out the statistical naiveté of the authors of the de Hirsch battery in expecting such data as subtest intercorrelations, or subtest correlations with the criterion, or the weights given to the scoring of the subtests to be similar in any other population to the data in their group of fifty-three children. It is also true that these authors tended to ignore the reliabilities of the separate tests, thus including some of very doubtful value; and they also failed to submit their final data to factor analysis to eliminate overlapping subtests. Certainly we can expect test makers of today to explore these factors thoroughly and also to inform us of the inherent effect of the intellectual and socioeconomic influences upon the validity of their instruments.

Birch and Lefford's Perception Tests

Like Benton (10), Birch and Lefford (12) approach the problem of visual perception at several levels of function. They distinguish between recognition of two dimensional forms, and analysis and synthesis. Recognition is the

---

*A. C. Trimble, "Can Remedial Reading Be Eliminated?" *Academic Therapy,* 5 (1970), 207–13.

well-known ability to identify and make gross discriminations among forms; analysis is multifaceted and includes ability to respond to selected aspects of a whole figure, as in finding hidden figures, forms within forms, and identifying a line or segment of a complete form.   Discriminations between identical forms varied in spatial orientation as *b-d,* and separating elements of a given Gestalt to be used in another arrangement are other aspects of analysis. Synthesis in visual perception implies the ability to reorder fragments or subwhole segments into a whole figure.

The Birch-Lefford series begins with Visual Discrimination of a test form from among twelve other geometric forms, a task easy enough for young children and hence used as an introduction or warm-up to the other tests. This test is similar to the form discrimination test at the four-year level of the Stanford-Binet.   Visual Motor tasks demand the drawing (copying) of triangles and diamonds, four freehand, four on a dot grid, four on a line grid.   The final four are done freehand from a model in which each junction of lines (or angle) is marked by a dot in the angle.

Visual Analysis tasks require the children to identify in turn each line or segment, as printed on a separate card, of an entire triangle or diamond shown.   Six segments of each of two forms are displayed, which the child identifies by tracing or by pointing with his finger to the corresponding portion of the whole figure.   Visual Synthesis tasks involve a multiple-choice selection of sets of three or four vertical or horizontal lines which would form the model triangle or diamond when rearranged mentally.   The final tests of the series require the drawing of lines to reproduce the model figure by connecting the four dots representing the outline of the triangles or diamonds, and, lastly, tracing over a line drawing of each of the four model figures.   All tests use the same four geometric figures: an isosceles triangle, apex up; another with apex down; a vertical diamond, and an equiangular (square) diamond.

Birch and Lefford tried out their tests on a group of 145 children, ages five to eleven.   In the Visual Motor tests, each of the six attempts to draw a triangle or diamond under different conditions was scored on the criteria of relative size, vertical and horizontal spatial orientation, angle formation, and straightness of lines.   Each criterion was given a weight of 1, thus permitting a score of 5 for each drawing.   Rescoring correlations or reliabilities were all greater than .90.   The tracing task was easiest for all four figures, the connecting dots next most difficult, the grid background tasks next, and the freehand drawings hardest for all ages.   The increase in scores was greatest from age five to six, and as great as that from six to eleven.

In the Visual Analysis tests, the children's identification of the segments of the triangle or diamond increased in accuracy from about age five to eight with little improvement from nine to eleven. In the Visual Synthesis tests, the task proved to be quite difficult for five-year-olds, their scores being not much better than a chance score in the multiple choice situation. Beyond five, scores increased fairly regularly and interindividual variability decreased. Synthesis of the elements of a triangle was consistently more difficult than in dealing with a diamond.

Correlations between analysis and reproducing freehand for ages five to eight range from .073 to .219; between synthesis and drawing, from .124 to .353, which are at best weak relationships. On the other hand, when helped by a line grid, the correlations between analysis and drawing range from .399 to .526, being significant at the six- and seven-year-old levels; while r's between synthesis and drawing while using the line grid become −.008 to .551, significant only at the seven-year-old level. Combined scores in synthesis and analysis correlate with drawing on a line grid at .467 at six, .650 at seven, and .204 at eight years; the first two being significant. Similarly, the gains in children's scores when moving from freehand drawing to a line grid are significantly correlated with visual synthesis of synthesis and analysis scores combined. In summary, these data indicate that, beginning at the age of six, children become increasingly capable or using visual information as a facilitator in their drawings. Analysis and synthesis, as measured in this study, however, do not show significant associations at the ages tested with the ability to reproduce from a visual model, unless the child is aided by such visual information as a line or dot grid.

In an earlier study, Birch and Lefford (11) investigated intersensory integration, a report we shall consider later in greater detail. The tests involved matching geometric blocks in view (visual) with those felt behind a screen (haptic) or those traced by a stylus guided by the examiner's hand through an indented track (kinesthetic). Eight identifications through each cross-modality (visual-haptic, visual-kinesthetic, haptic-kinesthetic) were tested. Correlations of freehand drawing with intersensory integrative ability were significant for visual-kinesthetic functioning at ages five to seven. Correlations of errors in the intersensory tests with perceptual analysis or synthesis tended to be significant, particularly above age five, for visual-kinesthetic ability. To summarize these two studies, we may make the following conclusions:

1. Tests of tracing, reproducing freehand, reproducing on a dot or line grid, or analyzing or synthesizing components of a geometric form are not equivalent measures of perception.

2. In terms of the difficulty of visual motor tasks, tracing forms is easiest,

connecting dots next, drawing on a grid background next, and freehand drawings hardest.

3. As measured here, visual analysis of forms increased most from ages five to eight, with little increment from nine to eleven.

4. As measured here, visual synthesis was almost too difficult for five year-olds, but the ability increased regularly from six to eleven. Synthesis of the elements of a triangle was consistently more difficult than the same for a diamond.

5. Visual analysis and synthesis do not show marked relationships with freehand reproduction unless the drawing is aided by a line grid, and then only at ages six to seven.

6. Intersensory integrative ability, as measured here, particularly of the visual-kinesthetic type, tends to be markedly related to visual analysis and synthesis, and freehand drawing at ages five to seven.

7. Visual analysis and synthesis are only weakly related to visual motor functioning as measured in freehand reproduction. But intersensory integration of the visual-kinesthetic type is markedly related to perceptual analysis and synthesis and visual motor tasks.

8. These interrelationships may imply that (a) intersensory development is founded upon motor capacity or (b) that intersensory processing underlies improvement in motor skill, and visual analysis and synthesis. Citing other neurophysiological studies, Birch and Lefford (11) are inclined to accept the second hypothesis, implying that kinesthetic and muscular feedback tend to influence visual motor experience.

9. This interaction is, of course, a reciprocal process in which intersensory integration itself is modified by the sensory experiences and the feedback from voluntary action.

In our view, the significant implications to be drawn from Birch and Lefford's studies are that visual motor skill, commonly measured by freehand reproduction in "perception" tests, is not a unitary, independent trait. Such visual motor performances are a reflection of long-term interaction (reciprocal input and feedback) or visual-kinesthetic intersensory integration and motor skill. In other words, the ability to reproduce geometric forms cannot be evaluated without reference to the interrelated motor-visual-kinesthetic experiences of the individual.

To pursue the implications further, other common tests of "perception"—such as those involving visual analysis of overlapping figures (figure-ground) or rotated figures (position in space); or visual motor tasks of drawing figures on a dot grid (spatial relationships?) and drawing lines between boundaries—are not independent of the intersensory integration status of the individual.

What does all this information regarding the factors that influence perception imply? Simply that form perception, as we think of it in the field of reading, is not an all-or-none process. Children are not either good or poor in form perception, but rather their perceptions of forms are influenced by a host of factors. When they are tested for form perception by being required to reproduce or match forms, or to recognize similarities and differences among forms, or to remember a form exposed momentarily and then to match or reproduce it, many factors influence their performances. They may fail to' reproduce because their short-term memory is poor; their familiarity with paper and pencil may be slight; the forms may be unfamiliar and hence confusing; or, subconsciously, the shapes presented may be frightening. Other elements in the testing situation that may be reflected in children's performances are these: the form may be presented in a different visual plane, such as vertical, when the paper on which it is to be reproduced is horizontal (and even tilted a little); or the child may not really see forms that he is supposed to match or reproduce in their actual shape because his visual errors of fusion double them, or his astigmatism blurs part of them, or his accommodative powers are inadequate to bring the forms into sharp focus at the distance at which they are displayed. Owing to his lack of experience with similar testing situations or his inability to control his attention, the duration of exposure of the test form may be too brief for his perception. Or the lack of training in responding to time pressure in his cultural background may make him unready for tachistoscopic or timed exposures of test forms. For lack of interest or motivation, his attention may well fluctuate and his performance vary accordingly. His experiences in reacting to forms and shapes may have fitted him to respond only to gross wholes or outlines with consequent omission of details. Or his basic cognitive style of attacking such a problem may cause him to attend to certain parts of the figure rather than its totality, to attempt to analyze it in detail and fail because of the short term of exposure, or to attend to the outer limits of the form and fail to react to its internal details. Can we, then, always be certain that our measures of perception are measuring just that function? Is it possible that their predictive relationships to reading are due in large part to the factors of attention, motivation, cultural training, visual and cognitive skills, and the like, that they are sampling?

DiLorenzo, Salter, and Hayden* provide another interesting viewpoint on tests of visual perception as predictors of reading comprehension. By reviewing some twenty-one studies of such predictors, these authors were able to collate data for comparing nine readiness factors. Visual design memory and recall—the factor stressed frequently in the tests that we have

---

*Louis T. DiLorenzo, Ruth Salter, and Robert Hayden, "Empirical Bases for a Prekindergarten Curriculum for Disadvantaged Children," Paper presented at Educational Research Association of New York State, November 7, 1968.

TABLE 1–4 THE SCOREBOARD ON VISUAL PERCEPTION

| TEST | VALIDITY FOR READING | RELIABILITY | CONTROL OF | | |
			SPEED	MEMORY	INTELLIGENCE
Bender	−.16 to −.71	.54 to .71	None	None	None .48 to .79
Frostig	.32 to .615 total −.03 to .49 subtests	.69 to .98 total .29 to .74 subtests	Yes	Yes	None .318 to .460
MPD	uses cutoff scores; r's not known	.74 to .85	Yes	Yes	Yes (?) Norms corrected for I.Q.
Graham-Kendall	Unknown	.72 to .90	None	None	Yes (?) −.60
Winter Haven	.24 to .44	Unknown	Yes	Yes	None
Beery	.33 to .50	.80 to .90	Yes	Yes	None .37 to .70
Benton	Unknown	ca .85	Yes	Yes	Yes Norms corrected for I.Q.
de Hirsch	.55, .63		Yes	Yes	None

reviewed—was the poorest predictor of all, with an average *r* with reading comprehension of .30. Figure and pattern copying, in contrast, ranked 3.5 among the nine readiness factors, yielding an average *r* or .46 with reading comprehension. Figure and pattern matching ranked seventh with an *r* of .36 with reading comprehension. When the opinions of fourteen leading reading authorities were collated by questionnaire, visual design memory and recall was ranked seventh; figure and pattern copying, sixth; and figure and pattern matching, fourth, among the same nine readiness factors in this same study. Reading experts are apparently aware of the limitations of tests of visual design memory and recall; but they tend to underestimate the value of figure and pattern copying and, like workbook writers, overestimate the contribution of figure and pattern matching.

WHERE ARE WE IN PERCEPTUAL TESTING?

Our review of the factors influencing visual perception—and of its dimensions as evidenced by factor analysis and the content of perceptual tests—certainly argues that this area is extremely complex. Despite the claims of test makers and publishers, it is apparent that most current tests leave a great deal to be desired. Of the eight that we examined in detail, none is entirely satisfactory if we consider their validity in predicting readiness or reading achievement; the test reliability; the control of the speed, memory, and intelligence factors; and their possibilities for alternative administrations to analyze the child's performances. We still need a test that predicts reading as well (or better) than do the Bender, the Frostig total, or the de Hirsch total. We need a perceptual test with the higher reliabilities of the Beery or the Benton or the Graham-Kendall (none of which appears greatly related to reading achievement). We need a test that controls the speed, memory, and intelligence factors, as only the Benton or perhaps the MPD do. Finally, we need a test that permits alternative administrations, perhaps in the manner of the Benton test. Only then can we compare the child's ability to trace, to match, to reproduce at sight, and to reproduce from memory, thus determining, perhaps, whether the child has a perceptual difficulty or simply lacks certain underlying visual or motor abilities.

Furthermore, Birch and Lefford's studies and the related neurophysiological research tell us that we cannot consider a single perception test of any type as an adequate sample of this entire area of development. Intersensory integration, of the visual-kinesthetic type at least, is interlinked with the visual motor performances that we sample in perception tests. Yet not one of the tests currently in wide use attempts to provide information on this visual-motor-intersensory integration interaction.

LEARNING PROJECT

Obtain a copy of one of the simpler tests of visual perception. Read the Manual and the directions for administering and scoring. Then give the test to a pupil of appropriate age.

What does the test tell you about this pupil that may be significant in his efforts to learn to read?

Does the author offer any suggestions for corrective steps for pupils who do poorly on his device? What do you think of these recommendations? Would you follow them?

Does the Manual clarify the significance of this test for early reading? What relevance do you see, if any, to learning to read?

If you see relevance in certain parts or all of the test for the act of reading, can you suggest a training program relevant to the pupil's performances? In other words,

what do you think should be done to help this pupil, assuming that his test results indicate some needs? After you finish outlining your ideas of a corrective program, compare it with those programs described in chapters 15 and 16.

REFERENCES

1. Anderson, James M., "Review of the Frostig Developmental Test of Visual Perception, Third Edition," pp. 855–56 in *Sixth Mental Measurements Yearbook,* Oscar K. Buros, editor. Highland Park, N.J.: Gryphon Press, 1965.
2. Ardis, Amorj, and Fraser, Elizabeth, "Personality and Perception: The Constancy Effect and Introversion," *British Journal of Psychology,* 48 (February 1957), 48–54.
3. Ashlock, P., "Visual Perception of Children in Primary Grades and Its Relation to Reading Performance," in *Reading and Inquiry,* J. Allen Figurel, editor, Proceedings International Reading Association, 10 (1965), 331–33.
4. Ayres, A. Jean, "Patterns of Perceptual-Motor Dysfunction in Children: A Factor Analytic Study," *Perceptual and Motor Skills,* 20 (April 1965), 335–68.
5. Bakker, D. J., "Temporal Order, Meaningfulness and Reading Ability," *Perceptual and Motor Skills,* 24 (1967), 1027–30.
6. Barrett, T. C., "The Relationship between Measures of Pre-reading Visual Discrimination and First Grade Reading Achievements: A Review of the Literature," *Reading Research Quarterly,* 1 (Fall 1965), 51–76.
7. Bartley, S. Howard, "Some Misconceptions Concerning Perception," *American Journal of Optometry and Archives of American Academy of Optometry,* 47 (April 1970), 259–65.
8. Beery, Keith E., *Developmental Test of Visual-Motor Integration.* Chicago: Follett Publishing, 1967.
9. Benger, Kathlyn, "The Relationships of Perception, Personality, Intelligence and Grade One Reading Achievement," in *Perception and Reading,* Helen K. Smith, editor, Proceedings International Reading Association, 12, No. 4 (1968), 112–23.
10. Benton, Arthur L., *The Revised Visual Retention Test.* New York: Psychological Corporation, 1963.
11. Birch, Herbert G., and Lefford, Arthur, "Intersensory Development in Children," *Monographs of the Society for Research in Child Development,* 28 (May 1963), 3–48.
12. Birch, Herbert G., and Lefford, Arthur, "Visual Differentiation, Intersensory Integration, and Voluntary Motor Control," *Monographs of the Society for Research in Child Development,* 32, No. 2 (1967), 1–87.
13. Bond, Guy L., and Dykstra, Robert, "The Cooperative Research Program in First-Grade Reading Instruction," *Reading Research Quarterly,* 2 (Summer 1967), 5–142.
14. Boyd, Larry, and Randle, Kenneth, "Factor Analysis of the Frostig Developmental Test of Visual Perception," *Journal of Learning Disabilities,* 3 (May 1970), 253–55.
15. Bradley, Betty Hunt, "Differential Responses in Perceptual Ability Among Mentally Retarded Brain-Injured Children," *Journal of Educational Research,* 57 (April 1964), 421–24.

16. Bryan, Quentin R., "Relative Importance of Intelligence and Visual Perception in Predicting Reading Achievement," *California Journal of Educational Research,* 15 (January 1964), 44–48.
17. Buros, Oscar K., editor, *Sixth Mental Measurements Yearbook.* Highland Park, N.J.: Gryphon Press, 1965.
18. Cellura, A. R., and Butterfield, E. C., "Intelligence, the Bender-Gestalt Test and Reading Achievement," *American Journal of Mental Deficiency,* 71 (1966), 60–63.
19. Chang, T. M. C., and Chang, Vivian A. C., "Relation of Visual Motor Skills and Reading Achievement in Primary-Grade Pupils of Superior Ability," *Perceptual and Motor Skills,* 24 (1967), 51–53.
20. Connor, James, "The Relationship of Bender Visual-Motor Gestalt Test Performance to Differential Reading Performance of Second Grade Children," *Dissertation Abstracts,* 28 (August 1967), 491–92A.
21. Corah, N. L., and Powell, B. J., "A Factor Analytic Study of the Frostig Developmental Test of Visual Perception," *Perceptual Motor Skills,* 16 (1963), 59–63.
22. Craig, Eugene A., "Exposure Time and the Perception of Complex Forms," *American Journal of Optometry and Archives of American Academy of Optometry,* 47 (November 1970), 887–91.
23. Dunsing, Jack D., "Perceptual-Motor Factors in the Development of School Readiness: An Analysis of the Purdue Perceptual-Motor Survey," *American Journal of Optometry and Archives of American Academy of Optometry,* 46 (October 1969), 760–65.
24. Elkind, D., Horn, J., and Schneider, G., "Modified Word Recognition, Reading Achievement and Perceptual Decentration," *Journal of Genetic Psychology,* 107 (1965), 235–51.
25. Elkind, David, Larson, Margaret, and Van Doorminck, William, "Perceptual Decentration Learning and Performance in Slow and Average Readers," *Journal of Educational Psychology,* 56 (February 1965), 50–56.
26. Forrest, Elliott B., "Perception and Human Communication," *American Journal of Optometry and Archives of American Academy of Optometry,* 47 (August 1970), 640–43.
27. Frostig, Marianne, Lefever, Welty, and Whittlesey, John, "Disturbances in Visual Perception," *Journal of Educational Research,* 57 (November 1963), 160–62.
28. Fuller, Gerald B., *The Minnesota Percepto-Diagnostic Test* (Revised). Brandon, Vt.: Clinical Psychology Publishing, 1969.
29. Fuller, G. B., and Ende, R., "The Effectiveness of Visual Perception, Intelligence and Reading Understanding in Predicting Reading Achievement in Junior High School Children," *Journal of Educational Research,* 60 (1967), 280–82.
30. Gamsky, Neal Richard, and Lloyd, Faye W., "Relationship of Classroom Behavior to Visual Perceptual Difficulties," *Psychology in the Schools,* 8 (1971), 60–61.
31. Gaunt, Jean Campbell, and Hayes, Patricia Collis, *An Investigation of Visual-Motor Disabilities in First-Grade Children.* Project P.L. 89–10 FY 67–69, Pinellas County Public Schools, Clearwater, Florida, 1969.
32. Gazley, Mary M., Homsey, Edward B., Lethbridge, Horace J., and Stewart, Robert E., "The Frostig Developmental Test of Visual Perception as a Predictor of Reading Difficulties," unpublished paper, Longridge School, Rochester, N.Y., 1968.
33. Gesell, Arnold, et al., *The First Five Years of Life.* New York: Harper, 1940.

34. Ghent, Lila, "Perception of Overlapping and Embedded Figures by Children of Different Ages," *American Journal of Psychology,* 69 (December 1956), 575–87.

35. Goins, Jean Turner, *Visual Perceptual Abilities and Early Reading Progress.* Supplementary Educational Monographs No. 87. Chicago: University of Chicago Press, 1958.

36. Goldstein, H. A., Whitney, G., and Cawley, J. F., "Prediction of Perceptual Reading Disability among Disadvantaged Children in the Second Grade," *Reading Teacher,* 24 (October 1970), 23–28.

37. Gordon, George, and Hyman, Irwin, "The Measurement of Perceptual-Motor Abilities of Head Start Children," *Psychology in the Schools,* 8 (1971), 41–48.

38. Graham, Clarence, et al., *Vision and Visual Perception.* New York: Wiley, 1965.

39. Graham, Frances K., and Kendall, Barbara S., *Memory for Designs Test.* Missoula, Mont.: Psychological Test Specialists, 1960.

40. Gredler, Gilbert R., "Performance on a Perceptual Test with Children from a Culturally Disadvantaged Background," in *Perception and Reading,* Helen K. Smith, editor, Proceedings International Reading Association, 12, No. 4 (1968), 86–91.

41. Hafner, Lawrence E., Weaver, Wendell W., and Powell, Kathryn, "Psychological and Perceptual Correlates of Reading Achievement Among Fourth Graders," *Journal of Reading Behavior,* 2 (Fall 1970), 281–90.

42. Henderson, Norman B., Butler, Bruce V., and Goffeney, Barbara, "Effectiveness of the WISC and Bender-Gestalt Test in Predicting Arithmetic and Reading Achievement for White and Non-White Children," *Journal of Clinical Psychology,* 25 (July 1969), 268–71.

43. de Hirsch, Katrina, Jansky, Jeanette J., and Langford, William S., *Predicting Reading Failure.* New York: Harper, 1966.

44. Kagan, J., et al., "Information Processing in the Child," *Psychological Monographs,* 78, No. 1 (1964).

45. Kaufman, Maurice, "Figure-Ground in Visual Perception," in *Reading Disability and Perception,* George D. Spache, editor, Proceedings International Reading Association, 13 (1969), 119–126.

46. Kelly, Thompson J., and Amble, Bruce R., "I.Q. and Perceptual Motor Scores as Predictors of Achievement Among Retarded Children," *Journal of School Psychology,* 8 (1970), 99–102.

47. Keogh, Barbara K., "The Bender Gestalt as a Predictive and Diagnostic Test of Reading Performance," *Journal of Consulting Psychology,* 29 (February 1965), 83–84.

48. Keogh, Barbara K., "Form Copying Tests for Prediction of First Grade Reading," in Twenty-seventh Yearbook, *Claremont Reading Conference* (1965), 141–44.

49. Keogh, Barbara K., "School Achievement Associated with Successful Performance on the Bender Gestalt Test," *Journal of School Psychology,* 3 (Spring 1965), 37–40.

50. Keogh, Barbara K., and Smith, Carol E., "Visuo-Motor Ability for School Prediction: A Seven-Year Study," *Perceptual and Motor Skills,* 25 (1967), 101–10.

51. Keogh, Barbara K., and Smith, Carol E., "Changes in Copying Ability of Young Children," *Perceptual and Motor Skills,* 26 (1968), 773–74.

52. Koppitz, Elizabeth Munsterberg, *The Bender Gestalt Test for Young Children.* New York: Grune and Stratton, 1964.

53. Kreitman, Leon, "A Note on the Use of the Minnesota Percepto-Diagnostic Test," *Journal of Clinical Psychology,* 22 (April 1966), 196.

54. Krippner, Stanley, "Diagnostic and Remedial Use of the Minnesota Percepto-Diagnostic Test in a Reading Clinic," *Psychology in the Schools,* 3 (April 1966), 171–75.

55. Lambert, Nadine M., "The Development and Validation of a Process for Screening Emotionally Disturbed Children," Coop Research Project 1186. Sacramento: California State Department of Education, 1963.

56. Lambert, Nadine M., "An Evaluation of Scoring Categories Applicable to Children's Performance on the Bender Visual Motor Gestalt Test," *Psychology in the Schools,* 7 (1970), 275–87.

57. Lambert, Nadine M., "An Item Analysis and Validity Investigation of Bender Visual Motor Gestalt Test Score Items," *Psychology in the Schools,* 8 (1971), 78–85.

58. Leibert, Robert E., and Sherk, John K., "Three Frostig Visual Perception Sub-tests and Specific Reading Tasks for Kindergarten, First and Second Grade Children," *Reading Teacher,* 24 (November 1970), 130–37.

59. Leider, Alice B., "Relationship of Visual Perception to Word Discrimination," pp. 104–108 in *Clinical Studies in Reading III,* Helen M. Robinson, editor. Supplementary Educational Monographs No. 97. Chicago: University of Chicago Press, 1968.

60. Lyle, J. G., "Errors of Retarded Readers on Block Designs," *Perceptual and Motor Skills,* 26 (1968), 1222.

61. Mann, Lester, and Phillips, William A., "Fractional Practices in Special Education: A Critique," *Exceptional Children,* 33 (January 1967), 311–17.

62. Maslow, Phyllis, Frostig, Marianne, Lefever, D. Welty, and Whittlesey, John R. B., "The Marianne Frostig Developmental Test of Visual Perception, 1963 Standardization," *Perceptual and Motor Skills,* 19 (October 1964), 463–99.

63. McAninch, Myrene, "Identification of Visual Perceptual Errors in Young Children," in *Vistas in Reading,* J. Allen Figurel, editor, Proceedings International Reading Association, 11, Part I (1966), 507–12.

64. Nelson, Thomas N., and Bartley, S. Howard, "Various Factors Playing a Role in Children's Response to Flat Copy," *Journal of Genetic Psychology,* 100 (June 1962), 289–308.

65. Ohnmacht, F. S., and Olson, Arthur, "Canonical Analysis of Reading Readiness Measures and the Frostig DTVP," Paper presented at AERA, Chicago, 1968.

66. Olson, A. V., "Relation of Achievement Test Scores and Specific Reading Abilities to the Frostig Development Test of Visual Perception," *Perceptual and Motor Skills,* 22 (1966), 179–84.

67. Piaget, J., and Inhelder, B., *The Child's Conception of Space.* London: Routledge and Kegan Paul, 1956.

68. Reed, James C., "Children's Figure Drawing—A Clue to Reading Progress," *Reading Teacher,* 23 (November 1969), 132–36, 143.

69. Reitan, Ralph M., "A Research Program on the Psychological Effects of Brain Lesions in Human Beings," pp. 153–218 in *International Review of Research in Mental Retardation,* Vol. I, N. R. Ellis, editor. New York: Academic Press, 1966.

70. Robinson, Helen M., et al., "An Evaluation of the Children's Visual Achievement Forms at Grade I," *American Journal of Optometry and Archives of American Academy of Optometry,* 35 (1958), 515–25.

71. Rosen, Carl L., and Ohnmacht, Fred, "Perception, Readiness and Reading Achievement in First Grade," in *Perception and Reading,* Helen K. Smith, editor, Proceedings International Reading Association, 12, No. 4 (1968), 33–39.

72. Samuels, S. J., "Word Recognition and Beginning Reading," *Reading Teacher,* 23 (November 1969), 158–161, 177.

73. Satterly, D., "Perceptual, Representational and Conceptual Characteristics of Primary School Children," *British Journal of Educational Psychology,* 38 (1968), 78–82.

74. Scott, Ralph, "Perceptual Readiness as a Predictor of Success in Reading," *Reading Teacher,* 22 (October 1968), 36–39.

75. Scott, Ralph, "Perceptual Skills, General Intellectual Ability, Race and Later Reading Achievement," *Reading Teacher,* 22 (April 1970), 660–70.

76. Smith, Carol E., and Keogh, Barbara K., "The Group Bender-Gestalt as a Reading Readiness Screening Instrument," *Perceptual and Motor Skills,* 15 (1962), 639–45.

77. Smith, Carol E., and Keogh, Barbara K., "Developmental Changes on the Bender Gestalt Test," *Perceptual and Motor Skills,* 17 (1963), 465–66.

78. Synder, R. T., and Freud, S. L., "Reading Readiness and Its Relationship to Maturational Unreadiness as Measured by the Spiral Aftereffect and Other Visual-Perceptual Measures," *Perceptual and Motor Skills,* 25 (1967), 841–54.

79. Stuart, I. R., "Perceptual Style and Reading Ability," *Perceptual and Motor Skills,* 24 (1967), 135–38.

80. Tolor, Alexander, and Shulberg, Herbert C., *An Evaluation of the Bender-Gestalt Test.* Springfield, Ill.: Charles C. Thomas, 1963.

81. Vernon, Magdalen D., *Perception Through Experience.* New York: Barnes and Noble, 1970.

82. Walters, C. Etta, "Reading Ability and Visual-Motor Function in Second Grade Children," *Perceptual and Motor Skills,* 13 (December 1961), 370.

83. Wechsler, David, and Hagin, R., "The Problem of Axial Rotation in Reading Disability," *Perceptual and Motor Skills,* 19 (1964), 319–26.

84. Weiner, Paul S., "A Revision of the Chicago Test of Visual Discrimination," *Elementary School Journal,* 68 (April 1968), 373–80.

85. Weiner, Paul S., Wepman, Joseph M., and Morency, Anne S., "A Test of Visual Discrimination," *Elementary School Journal,* 65 (March 1965), 330–37.

86. Werner, Margaret Lillian, "A Study of the Perceptual-Motor Development of Superior and Retarded Readers in the Primary Grades," Master's thesis, Cardinal Stritch College, 1967.

87. Whipple, C. I., and Kodman, F., "A Study of Discrimination and Perceptual Learning with Retarded Readers," *Journal of Educational Psychology,* 60 (1969), 1–5.

88. Winter Haven Lions Research Foundation, *Perceptual Achievement Forms.* Winter Haven: Winter Haven Lions Club.

89. Zaeske, Arnold, "The Diagnosis of Sensory-Motor Disabilities," in *Reading Disability and Perception,* George D. Spache, editor, Proceedings International Reading Association, Part 3 (1969), 52–58.

90. Zaeske, Arnold, "The Validity of Predictive Index Tests in Predicting Reading Failure at the End of Grade One," pp. 28–33 in *Reading Difficulties: Diagnosis, Correction and Remediation,* William K. Durr, editor. Newark, Del.: International Reading Association, 1970.

2
The Role of Visual Defects in Reading Disabilities

The role of visual defects in reading disabilities is an equivocal one, in the opinion of many reading experts. While freely admitting that a severe visual defect would probably hinder reading progress, some writers in this field touch very lightly on this etiological area. Even some vision specialists dismiss visual deviations as significant contributors to reading difficulties in any great number of cases. In fact, in devoting several chapters to the role of vision in reading disabilities, the present writer is thought by some of his colleagues to be overemphasizing the relationship.

It will become apparent, as the reader completes this chapter, that the research evidence regarding the interaction of vision and reading is conflicting and often confusing. If the reader expects to find that certain visual defects are peculiar to, or perhaps even dramatically more frequent among, poor readers than good, he will be disappointed. Most researchers in this area who had made that assumption discarded their results as almost meaningless when their expectations were unfulfilled. There are numerous flaws in this line of reasoning, but the basic fallacy is the illusion that each visual function tested is independent of all the others and that, alone, it has a direct effect upon reading. Rather, we shall see that these functions are linked and that it is in these interactions that we find effects upon reading.

As you attempt to understand these many studies of vision and reading, try to formulate some generalizations in answer to these questions.

1. Do groups of poor readers necessarily show greater incidence of visual difficulties than do good readers in most of the studies cited? Why not?

2. When tested alone, the evidence that each type of visual deviation affects reading is weak. But certain combinations of deviations do appear significant. What are some of these interacting functions?

THOSE WHO HAVE REVIEWED the literature on the significance of visual defects in reading disabilities, such as the present author (54), have experienced difficulty in reaching very definite conclusions. Even when using the same screening instruments, studies often give contradictory results, while those employing different tests certainly vary in their conclusions. This or that visual defect appears relevant in some researches and insignificant in others. Yet most reading clinicians persist in examining the vision of retarded readers in the belief that this may be a contributing factor in the pupil's difficulty.

There are several very good reasons for the variations in the research results. First, vision tests purporting to measure the same visual function do not yield precisely the same indications. For example, the half-dozen targets used to measure visual acuity are not equally discriminative. A pupil's performance may well vary greatly from one of these tests to another. Because of this variance in the physical aspects of screening tests and in their discriminative values, similar results from different testing batteries would be quite unlikely. When we realize that two batteries of vision screening tests may differ in as many as six or eight subtests, the point becomes obvious.

Second, most of the current vision tests are very brief and hence not very reliable. Most require but a few seconds of attention to the targets and are hardly a true sample of a continuous visual function. As we shall point out later, this limitation of screening tests definitely influences their relationship to sustained reading performances.

A third flaw inherent in the attempts to reconcile vision studies is the fact that the ages or visual development of the populations studied are not comparable. To illustrate, Eames (20) found a high incidence of hyperopia, or farsightedness, in a group of young elementary school pupils showing reading problems. Because the incidence exceeded that in other large groups, Eames concluded that farsightedness probably contributed to the reading failures. In direct contradiction, among college students retarded in reading, Stromberg (61) and Swanson and Tiffin (62) found a low incidence and drew the opposite

Adapted from George D. Spache, "The Role of Visual Defects in Reading and Spelling Disabilities," *American Journal of Orthopsychiatry,* 10 (April 1940), 229–38. Reprinted with permission from the *American Journal of Orthopsychiatry;* copyright 1940 by the American Orthopsychiatric Association, Inc.

conclusion. In all three studies, the developmental nature of vision—the changes in vision normally appearing as life progresses—was ignored. As we shall point out later in a brief review of the common natural changes in vision, these studies were simply reporting a condition that was normal for the ages of their respective populations, not actually uncovering a relationship between hyperopia and reading retardation.

A fourth factor that complicates an attempt to relate visual dysfunctions to reading success is the resilience of the individual in learning to live with his visual equipment. Even children sometimes learn to adjust to, or compensate for, a defect and to achieve normally. The very same dysfunction to the same degree may seriously retard one child and have no apparent effect upon another one of similar age and ability. A personal example is present in the writer's own family in which he and two of three daughters exhibit an hereditary marked lateral imbalance. Only the second daughter ever showed any ill effects, developing a temporary loss of binocular coordination, which was soon overcome after a period of corrective training. Despite the imbalance that would be expected to cause fusional difficulties, no member of this family was hindered in academic efforts extending through the graduate level. Apparently the effects of visual defects differ from one individual to another, as well as from type of work situation to another. This latter is shown by the differential results in vocational testing at Purdue University in the standardization of the Ortho-Rater battery designed by Bausch and Lomb.

Finally, many directors of vision studies treat their results as though each visual function was independent of the others. They attempt to show the significance of a solitary subtest result by correlating the test score with that from a reading test. Or they compare groups of poor and good readers according to their performance on this single vision test, usually with no conclusive results. These practices reflect an atomistic concept of vision as being composed of a number of disparate, unrelated skills. However, as we shall point out later in recounting the indications of Kelley's comprehensive study, the various visual functions are interdependent (37). Only when clusters of skills are recognized as interacting functions can we expect to determine the true relationships with reading, as in the studies of Robinson (46) and Silbiger and Woolf (52).

The review of these four factors, which complicate the interpretations of studies trying to discover the effects of visual defects, was not intended to discourage the reader from accepting any research conclusions. Rather, the review was meant to aid in anticipating contradictions and inconsistencies and in understanding how these conflicting results can arise.

GENERAL SURVEY OF THE LITERATURE

Generalizing from the data of numerous school surveys of the early part of this century, Terman and Almack (64) estimated that 20–30 percent have defects in vision. Of these, astigmatism accounted for more than half, or more than hyperopia and myopia (nearsightedness) combined. Fusional or phoria imbalances affect about 2 percent of all children, according to Terman and Almack's summary. When considering the extent of all types of visual defects combined into the category of defective vision, Berkowitz's data indicated slightly higher incidence among pupils retarded academically in Camden, N.J., and Philadelphia (2); Smedley reported similar findings for the city of Chicago (53). Interestingly, in his study of genius children, Terman (63) discovered a slightly higher incidence of defective vision among gifted children than among average. His finding may have reflected, of course, a greater tendency to myopia among his gifted population, which may have been induced by their concentration upon reading and other near-point school work.

Negative studies that failed to show very significant relationships between vision and reading were conducted by Stromberg (61), Swanson and Tiffin (62), Fendrick (24), and Imus, Rothney, and Bear (36). In contrast, Witty and Kopel's data (68) indicated a higher incidence of defects among poor readers (although these authors did not realize it), as did one of Eames's studies (19).

Support for the belief that defects hinder progress in reading may be deduced from the results when these defects are corrected. Eames (15) reports that a reading disability group gained 7.8 months in a seven-months' period following visual corrections, while a control group without corrections gained on the average only 5.33 months in the same period. Individual cases in which similar gains appeared after vision corrections are recounted by Dearborn and Comfort (13), Eames and Peabody (22), Carter (6), and Gates (26), to mention only a few of those in the literature. Imus, Rothney, and Bear (36) categorized their college students according to the defect present, finding that the remedial groups with no defects gained more than the defective groups, except for one small group of corrected aniseikonics. To summarize, in a speech at the Annual Forum on Visual Problems in Schools in Chicago in 1957, Charles B. Huelsman, Jr., reported on his review of fifty-eight studies of vision and reading. He found that thirty-five indicated definite relationships between vision and school success, nineteen evidenced no relationship, and four were equivocal in their results.

Perhaps the most carefully planned study of vision ever reported is that by Kelley (37), a research known as the North Carolina Study. He completed four years of longitudinal testing of first, fifth, and ninth graders, reexamining each of the groups of seventy-five pupils each year with nineteen measures of vision and thirteen tests of achievement, personality, and intelligence. Kelley's repeated tests indicated that far-point acuity declines sharply while near-point acuity increases. Myopia rose particularly from the fifth to eighth grade and was related to good grades and good reading. In contrast, hyperopic pupils with distinct phorias tended to show retardation in reading. In near-point measures, only esophoria (tendency to overconverge) seemed negatively related to school success.

There was a marked increase in the number of fusional difficulties during the high school period. This defect showed little relationship to pupil performances on brief reading tests, but on longer tests these poor fusion cases showed slower rate and poorer comprehension. Cases with no fusion at all (suppressing vision in one eye) showed normal speed and comprehension, since their one-eyed reading caused no confusion in images of words.

Good depth perception performances were accompanied by good acuity, good fusion, and good lateral balance test results or convergence. But good depth perception scores were not associated with above-average reading performances. On the other hand, very poor depth scorers made below-average scores on almost all nonvision tests. Exophoric or underconverging pupils did badly in depth perception, as also did hyperopic cases with convergent squint or cross-eyes.

Poor convergence, or exophoria at near-point cases, tended to show poor fusion, low depth, and poor visual acuity, but these symptoms were not accompanied by poor reading scores. Esophoria, or overconvergence at both near and far, was related to poor reading; as it developed, school grades went down.

The interaction among visual functions is readily shown in Kelley's results. We see that poor reading is related to farsightedness when that is linked to the phorias; and to depth perception, which, in turn, is linked to exphoria and to hyperopia with squint. Esophoria showed consistent harmful influence upon reading at both near-point and far-point. Another observation possible from Kelley's data is the nonlinear relationship between some defects such as depth perception and reading. Depth perception is not consistently related to reading, as is assumed in correlating scores in this area with reading scores in many studies. Only poor depth perception scores are significant in influencing test scores in reading as well as in other areas. As we suggested earlier, this North Carolina longitudinal study reveals some of the unsuspected flaws in other vision studies that result in their inconsistent results. To secure a clear picture of the nature of vision, though, we shall review the studies of each separate function.

SPECIFIC VISUAL FUNCTIONS

Visual acuity may be defined as the efficiency or keenness of vision. Three tests are usually made, one of left-eye acuity, one of right-eye, and one of the two eyes or binocular acuity. These tests should be repeated at near or reading distance and again at far-point. There is a marked tendency for visual acuity, as measured by the Snellen Chart, to be the same in both eyes, as evidenced by a correlation of $+.73\pm.003$ between vision in each eye for 9,245 cases reported by Collins (9). This correlation is probably lowered by including children who were defective in one or both eyes, for the correlation between vision in each eye was only $+.34\pm.01$ for 3,429 children with defects in acuity. It appears that there is a marked tendency for similar acuity in both eyes among children with good acuity, while the tendency is distinctly less among children with poor acuity in one or both eyes. However, near-point and far-point acuity are not closely related, as several large-scale studies show.

Better visual acuity in one eye than the other frequently causes the child to read more with the good eye. This may result in an undue strain on the better eye and perhaps, some loss in the poorer eye through disuse. Gray (27) reports a case in which the left eye read 16 percent more content in a given time than the right eye did and 9.3 percent more than both eyes did. The left eye read with fewer errors than both eyes did. In fact, there were 27.7 percent fewer errors in reading with the left eye. In a series of articles, Spache (56, 57, 58) has shown the interrelationships among differences in acuity of the two eyes, reading performances, and eye preferences. In testing oral reading, Robinson (45) takes this tendency into account by having the child read one of the Gray Standardized Oral Reading Paragraphs with each eye and a third paragraph with both eyes. The time, number, and types of error of each reading are then compared. Spache (57) offers a number of case studies in one-eyed and two-eyed reading based on the Binocular Reading Test, an instrument that he devised to measure a reader's use of both eyes in the act of reading.

This situation may be further complicated if the child, because of eye preference, does the major part of his reading with the poorer eye. Spache (56), Gahagan (25), and Coons and Mathias (10) have shown that eye prefer-ence and visual acuity are not necessarily related. In other words, the dominant eye that the child favors for sighting and reading may not be the better eye in terms of vision. Tests of eye preference, as well as of visual acuity, must be used before attempting to correct the student's dependence upon one eye.

Comparison between the visual acuity of groups of good and poor readers have been made by Monroe (42), Fendrick (24), C. T. Gray (27), Wagner (65), Eames (17), and Witty and Kopel (68, 70) on the elementary school level and by Swanson and Tiffin (62) and Stromberg (61) on the college level. Russell (48) compared the visual acuity of good and poor spellers. Of these writers, all except Fendrick report insignificant differences between the groups. Fendrick's tests showed reliably better right-eye, left-eye, and binocular acuity among good readers at both reading and far distances. It may be noted that of all these groups only Fendrick's and Eames's were tested by those professionally trained in eye examinations.

In more recent studies, Starnes (60) found no general interaction between visual acuity and reading, although his good readers tended to be nearsighted, his poor readers farsighted. Silbiger and Woolf's college students who were poor in reading differed significantly from the good readers in visual efficiency in the better and worse eyes (52). A later study by Silbiger (51) also revealed poor college readers to be poorer in acuity of the poorer eye at near-point only.

When the eyes differ in acuity, the condition is called anisometropia, and, as we might expect from the earlier discussion of the interaction of eye preference, reading, and visual acuity, this condition is unfavorable to reading success. Eames's study in 1964 (21) and that by Spache and Tillman (59) confirm the negative effect of anisometropia. Retarded readers often fail near-point acuity tests, showing differences in acuity of the two eyes and low near-point acuity in the left eye, according to this last study.

In this area of visual acuity, it appears that group comparisons between good and poor readers tend to be inconclusive. But when variations between the acuity of the two eyes are investigated and this is related to independent reading with either eye or with both, interactions with reading appear.

Refractive Errors

Refractive errors are those due to irregularities in the shape of the eyeball, according to some authorities, Hyperopia, or farsightedness, is the result of the eyeball being too short from cornea to retina. It may cause excessive fatigue by blurred vision and discomfort in reading. Muscular compensation may occur for lesser degrees of the condition, but this is also conducive to fatigue.

Myopia, or nearsightedness, is due to too great length of the eyeball. Low degrees of the defect are not unfavorable to reading if the far-point of clear vision is not closer to the eyes than reading distance. Astigmatism, or the lack of clearness of image, is due to unequal curvature of the cornea or lens of the eye. In severe cases the images of words are blurred and distorted, and eye-strain results.

These definitions of refractive dysfunctions in terms of eye structure are only one way of viewing these conditions. Another interpretation, deemphasizing the importance of structural differences, suggests that refractive errors are a matter of the development of vision in response to environmental pressures. These experts point out that myopia gradually increases during the school year, diminishes during the summer vacation, and increases markedly in incidence only during the school years (34). As remarked earlier, genius children (63) and high-ability groups show greater incidence of myopia (29) in this country and others. Myopia is beginning to increase sharply among Eskimo children since schooling has become available (73), while it is virtually nonexistent among older Alaskan Eskimos who had little or no schooling. In almost every available survey of school children in any country, myopia grows rapidly during the school years (35). Children lose their farsightedness, which is characteristic of almost 90 percent at school entrance ages, and begin to develop better near-point functioning. Above-average performers tend to develop myopia sooner, while below-average pupils maintain emmetropia (freedom from myopia or hyperopia) or show mild hyperopia (37). From the viewpoint of a reading specialist, these facts seem to imply that myopia is, perhaps, a result of close work, and that those children who develop this condition are more likely to succeed academically, while retention of the early hyperopia would appear to be unfavorable to such achievement. These conclusions are, of course, directly contradictory to the philosophy underlying vision screening of school children with the Snellen Test. Only those developing myopia are regularly referred in such programs, while those retaining farsightedness in the testing at 20 feet are usually *not referred.*

These interpretations of myopia were reviewed quite thoroughly in a recent article by Lanyon and Giddings.* They acknowledge the effect of heredity, especially in severe cases, and of the elongation of the axial length of the eye as basic elements in the development of myopia. But, at the same time, they support the role of excessive near-point work in the widespread appearance of myopia during the school years. They cite additional studies

---

*Richard I. Lanyon and John W. Giddings, "Psychological Approaches to Myopia: A Review," *American Journal of Optometry and Physiological Optics*, 51 (April 1974), 271–81.

from Japan indicating a parallel trend to that in the United States of increase in myopia from 27 percent at grade three, to 44 percent among boys and 48 percent among girls in high school and 67 percent among both sexes at college age. (Apparently not all Japanese are nearsighted, as we Occidentals often think!)

Lanyon and Giddings suggest that, if the lessened acuity of myopes is thus environmentally induced, its correction may be possible by psychological techniques, as operant conditioning. Preliminary studies that they conducted were successful in producing temporary and small increases in visual acuity. The development of myopia does seem linked to the near-point demands of school. And its absence in primitive, unschooled societies implies that it is not a normal developmental change with increasing maturity. In view of these facts, we shall welcome further experiments with psychological treatments, in addition to the current treatments of plus lenses and visual training.

Hyperopia was present in greater proportion in mixed age groups of poor readers by Blake and Dearborn (4) and Eames (14, 19). The present writer has determined from Eames's data that in both studies the hyperopia was significantly greater in either eye among poor readers. Farris (23) found that in matched junior high school groups hyperopia was associated with less than normal progress in reading, and that corrected cases made greater achievement than did uncorrected.

Myopia was associated with better than normal progress in reading at the junior high school level, according to Farris (23). A group wearing glasses to correct myopia did not make greater achievement than did an uncorrected group, according to the same author. Eames's unselected group (14) showed significantly greater incidence of left-eye myopia than did the reading-disability group. These findings of greater incidence of myopia among good readers are in accord with the earlier statement that nearsightedness is not necessarily a barrier to normal progress. It appears that moderate myopia may even be favorable to reading success in some instances.

The data of Fendrick (24) and Blake and Dearborn (4) indicate greater frequency of astigmatism among poor readers. Eames (17) does not report similar differences. In fact, hyperopic and myopic astigmatism were more frequent among unselected children than among the reading-disability cases. The differences, however, were unreliable. These findings are supported in a further study by Eames (14). Again there was unreliably greater hyperopic astigmatism among the 143 unselected cases. The frequency of myopic astigmatism was unreliably greater among the reading-disability cases.

Farris's results (23) indicate that myopic astigmatism is associated with more than normal progress and that corrected groups do not achieve more than uncorrected groups do. Swanson and Tiffin (62), Stromberg (61), and Witty and Kopel (68) report no real differences in frequency of hyperopia, myopia, or astigmatism among good and poor readers. Russell's good and poor spellers (48) and Imus, Rothney, and Bear's college freshmen (36) were not differentiated by tests of such visual defects.

The evidence on the significance of refractive errors is not entirely clear-cut. Hyperopia appears to be associated with less than normal progress and to be more frequent among disabled readers. Myopia is equally frequent among good and poor readers and in some samples is associated with more than normal progress. Astigmatism of both hyperopic and myopic nature is not always more frequent among poor readers or spellers and may be associated with normal or more than normal success.

Fusion or Phoria Dysfunctions

Muscular imbalance is often attributed to a defect of one of the muscles controlling the movements of the eyes. One or both of the eyes may have a tendency to turn inward as in strabismus (cross-eyes) or to turn outward as in the condition known as cast or cock-eye. The tendency to turn inward is called esophoria and is associated with nearsightedness. The tendency to turn outward is called exophoria and is associated with farsightedness. These phorias may be present in a vertical, horizontal, or oblique plane. It may be obvious to the observer (heterophoria) as in strabismus or cock-eye, or it may be latent and undiscovered without test (heterotropia).

The results of the phorias, like all the other visual defects, are determined to a large extent by the degree to which the pupil can compensate for the handicap. In many cases the child receives blurred images (lack of fusion) or even two distinct images (diplopia). Loss of fusion produces mixing of letters and small words, jumbling of words, loss of place, and some inability to follow a line of print, according to Eames (16). The child may meet the situation by alternating from one eye to the other (alternating vision) or by squinting or even suppressing the vision of one eye entirely (suspenopsia). Spache (58) and Crider (11, 12) confirm this tendency to suppress the vision in the affected eye in their studies of elementary school children. Some vision specialists point out that these divergences also arise in cases of marked difference in visual acuity between the eyes or the refraction of the eyes. Thus they may represent the individual's attempt to achieve clear vision by unconsciously turning one eye until its image does not interfere, rather than being a true muscle imbalance. Lipton, a psychoanalyst, recounts a case in which strabismus appeared as a result of threat to the child's ego, and was spontaneously remitted when insight was conveyed to the patient (39).

Significant differences in phorias have been reported between groups of good and poor readers by a number of writers. Selzer (50) found imbalance in 90 percent of a group of thirty-three reading disability cases and only 9 percent of 100 unselected children, a wholly reliable difference. Eames (14) reports exophoria at reading distance among 114 reading disability cases to an extent six times the S.D. of the difference above than among unselected children. In another comparison by Eames (17), there was a reliably greater incidence of exophoria among poor readers. In esophoria in these same groups, there was an insignificant difference. Farris (23) showed that strabismus and poor binocular coordination were associated with less than normal progress in reading among junior high school pupils. Blake and Dearborn (4) discovered that a larger proportion of their college freshmen poor readers showed poor binocular coordination, although measurement of the phorias did not clearly differentiate the groups. Eames (16) found lower fusion convergence in eighty-eight reading disability cases than in fifty-two controls in grades two to four. Among Witty and Kopel's poor readers, the incidence of slow fusion was significantly greater than among the normals (71). Louttit (40) describes in detail the case of a boy retarded in reading because of fusional difficulties resulting from strabismus.

Clark (7, 8) matched two groups of college students in sex, reading comprehension, and linguistic ability. One group evidenced marked exophoria, the other slight or none. Photographing the eye movements of the groups revealed no real differences in the mechanics of eye movements in reading other than a tendency for the students with marked exophoria to make a greater number of divergence movements. Clark believes that these movements probably cause enough fatigue to be of considerable importance.

Fendrick (24), Witty and Kopel (69, 71), Swanson and Tiffin (62), Stromberg (61), and Russell (48) failed to find wholly reliable differences in the phorias in groups of good and poor readers or spellers. Although not wholly reliable, the greatest differences between Wagner's groups were in lateral imbalance (esophoria at far-point) and fusion at near-point (65).

Further evidence that such defects may be important in individual cases is given in the studies of Eames and Peabody (22), Selzer (50), Farris (23), and Witmer (67). Witmer's case of diplopia, Eames's nonreader, and Selzer's two cases of lateral imbalance showed striking improvement in reading after visual corrections. Eames's reading disability cases (15) gained more in a seven-months' period after correction than did uncorrected cases. Farris reports greater achievement in reading among corrected strabismatics than among uncorrected groups.

It is also apparent from this review that we are not discussing a single phenomenon but rather a variety of conditions relevant to the individual's ability to achieve fusion or single, clear, identical images in both eyes simultaneously. We have not even mentioned the accommodation-convergence function, the posturing of the eyes and adjustment of the lens, as the viewer attempts to achieve focus and fusion at different distances. This function also changes with age, maturing at about the age of six and beginning to fail to function in middle or old age. The inability to shift from point to point and see clearly, presbyopia, is common at later ages as we begin to need bifocal lenses. Some see its absence before school age as a strong argument against preschool reading instruction (49). Other vision specialists deplore our lack of attention to the accommodation-convergence function in school screening, for, as they point out, anomalies are not uncommon in this ability among school children.

In the early 1940s this writer became greatly interested in the effects of fusional difficulties upon reading. As a result, we undertook a series of studies, invented the Binocular Reading Test to measure the participation of both eyes in the reading act, and reported a number of observations (55, 56, 57, 58). We found that about 27 percent of school children showed a definite eye preference in the presumably two-eyed act of reading. About one in three of those with strong eye preference differed significantly in reading skill from one eye to the other. These results were confirmed in the independent study by Robinson (45). The effects of differences in visual acuity of the two eyes upon single-eye reading skill were confirmed in these studies, while fusional difficulties revealed in vision tests produced such variances in reading skill in about three out of five cases.

We have referred to these personal explorations of fusional problems and reading simply to reinforce the obvious conclusion from the relevant literature that this is a significant interaction.

Stereopsis and Binocular Coordination

Under ordinary conditions, vision is achieved by coordinated action of the two eyes. This coordination or fusion of images results in the ability to perceive depth or to achieve tridimensional vision. One interpretation of stereopsis suggests that because the eyes focus upon an object at slightly different angles we are able to perceive thickness or depth. Other experts add that, of course, the ability to interpret depth is also based on firsthand muscular experiences with tridimensional objects. With this experience, some individuals can demonstrate depth perception even when lacking perfect fusion or binocular coordination. Stereopsis, or depth perception, may not be required per se for reading, but the degree of visual fusion necessary for its achievement contributes to the acquiring of good reading habits. The significance of fusional difficulties has already been demonstrated in the preceding section.

Unfortunately, when one eye is defective, loss of coordinated or binocular vision is quite common. In this situation, one eye assumes the dominance and the other is suppressed, often to the extent that the suppressed eye appears to decrease in sensitivity. Another concomitant of defect in one eye is alternating of vision. Children lacking binocular vision are often free from apparent difficulties until attempts are made to reestablish coordinated action. Then they may experience headaches, fatigue, tension, and the like, because of the necessary readjustments (36).

Farris (23) and Blake and Dearborn (4) give data showing the greater proportion of children with poor binocular coordination among poor readers. Farris further demonstrates that the difficulty is associated with less than normal progress in reading. Crider (11, 12) attempted to determine the relationship between eye preference and imbalance. His data strongly suggest that in the presence of an imbalance the major part of reading is apt to be done with the normal eye. This is confirmation of the tendency to suppress vision in a defective eye and hence to lose binocular coordination.

It appears that the loss of binocular coordination (and, in turn, of depth perception and hence of facility in spatial orientation) may be caused by the presence of a gross defect such as deficient visual acuity, a phoria, and so on. The loss in coordination may also be reflected in fusional difficulties and the suppression of vision in one eye, both of which have important concomitants for reading and spelling success.

Aniseikonia

A relatively unfamiliar visual defect is that of aniseikonia, or a condition in which the images formed in the two eyes are unequal in size or shape. Unfortunately, the defect is not detected by the tests in ordinary use. Like other dysfunctions, aniseikonia has different effects upon different individuals. It has been reported that 60 percent of the cases suffered from headaches or car-train-sea sickness, difficulty in reading, supersensitivity to light, or combinations of these symptoms (36).

This defect was found in a greater number of the poor than the good readers of Blake and Dearborn's college students (4). The reading disability cases of Dearborn and Comfort (13) suffering from aniseikonia were materially aided by correction. However, reading ability was not significantly related to aniseikonia in a large group of college freshmen according to Imus, Rothney, and Bear (36). There was no consistent evidence from the testing of thirty-eight students whose aniseikonia was corrected that such correction resulted in improved reading speed or comprehension, although twenty-nine of the students felt that they had been helped by the corrections.

It appears that the presence of aniseikonia—at least in mature students such as college freshmen—may not prove an insurmountable barrier to reading achievement. It is quite possible that sufficient adjustment or compensation has occurred to overcome any marked influence of the defect in these subjects. In the younger subjects of Dearborn and Comfort (13), the defect was apparently a hindrance. Further evidence is offered in the fact that the college students in whom aniseikonia was corrected gained more than did any of the other remedial reading groups (36). This is indirect evidence that the defect was a hindrance and that correction enabled the group to make the greater gains of which they were capable.

A recent report by Rosenbloom (47) indicated that 25 percent of the poor readers and 17.5 percent of the controls had a clinically significant amount of aniseikonia. Using the Spache Binocular Reading Test revealed that these pupils tended to suppress vision in one eye to compensate for the defect. The incidence of this defect was not significantly different in the groups compared, but was much higher in both than the experimenter expected. Perhaps this dysfunction is much more common than we have discovered, for it is seldom tested in ordinary visual examinations. The implication that a test to discover aniseikonia should be included in assessing poor readers (and perhaps in testing all children) is obvious.

Visual Fields

Early studies in diagnosis of reading problems tended to place strong emphasis upon limitations in the visual field. Often, as we shall point out in reviewing these studies, these limitations were interpreted as a basic cause of retardation in reading. We later learned a good deal more about the actual size of the visual field used in the act of reading. We know, for example, that at reading distance the reader brings into sharp focus only about two inches of a line of print. Letters and words beyond this area cannot be seen clearly enough to distinguish them. Limitations of the visual field do tend to narrow the visual area but hardly to the degree necessary to interfere with a fixation in reading. The individual would have to be literally blind before a common limitation of the visual field would affect reading. But the early writers who thought that the usual span of distant vision was present in the act of reading naturally assumed that any limitation in this field would affect reading.

One of the earliest studies regarding the significance of losses in the visual field is that offered by Hinshelwood (33).   He reported that several of his word-blind cases, as he called them, exhibited homonymous hemianopsia, or loss of the same half of the field of vision in both eyes.   This condition would indicate severe brain damage in the visual field in one of the cerebral hemispheres of these patients, but Hinshelwood did not seem to recognize this possibility.   Hincks (32) claimed that most of her reading cases had limited peripheral vision, which she felt might explain the pupils' reading problems.

Monroe (42) found that deficiencies in peripheral vision were present in 1 to 2 percent of her reading disability cases.   Despite the insignificance of this proportion, she felt that the visual field limitations might contribute to reading disability.   Eames (17) reports a tendency for educational disability cases to have a smaller visual field than unselected children.   Treatment resulted in improvement in these cases, but Eames does not show whether better reading resulted.   Brombach (5) found several retarded readers with abnormally large foveal blind spots as a result of heterophoria or strabismus.   His treatment improved the condition, resulting in more efficient vision.   There is the possibility that Brombach failed to realize that in strabismus cases the eye is often turned away so far that images fail to fall on the most sensitive parts of the retina.   Hence the person cannot really resolve images, and measurements of his visual acuity are very low.   As the strabismus is corrected, the alignment of the pupil orifice and the retina is improved, and acuity appears to be regained.   In contrast, Ong et al. (43) found no difference in peripheral visual fields in fast or slow, powerful or weak readers, or in high or low I.Q. groups.

Recent studies in this area of the visual field have moved on to a recognition that each eye has two hemifields, which in turn are divided in function into quarter fields.   The studies have been concerned with differences in recognition of stimuli presented to these hemifields.   Both Barton et al. (1), Koetting (38), and Overton (44) noted significantly more recognition of words presented tachistoscopically by the right field of each eye whether the student read Hebrew or English.   Koetting noted the high score in the nasal field of the left eye, which is directly connected with the left cerebral hemisphere, the site of language learning.   In several studies Harcum (30, 31) also noted the superiority of the right hemifield when normal words and normal or scrambled word sequence was offered.   When word sequence was reversed, the left hemifield was superior, confirming his hypothesis that the hemifields differ in varied situations.

Winnick and Dornbush (66) felt that their experiments demonstrated that the prereading set of the pupil outweighs any neurological differences that might exist in the hemifields.   Obviously more research in this area is needed to clarify the role of the hemifields of each eye, as well as the function of the quarter fields, if any, in the reading act.

This review of vision functions and reading success covers a span of more than seventy years in the studies it has cited. This breadth of coverage of the literature was deliberate in attempting to help the reader realize the importance that has been attached to this area. The problems caused by visual defects are a source of concern to members of a number of disciplines, as psychology, optometry, and ophthalmology, as well as to reading specialists. Occasionally one of these scientists who is not really well read in his field will dismiss vision difficulties as a causal factor in reading or learning disabilities. We hope that the wealth of evidence brought together here helps the teacher or reading specialist to have an informed view on this subject and, in working with retarded readers, to give proper emphasis to children's visual deviations.

LEARNING PROJECT

Study the manual for administration of one of the more complete vision screening tests. Then arrange to give the test to a poor reader for whom records on oral reading tests are available. If the pupil's test performances indicate no vision difficulties, repeat your vision testing with another such pupil. Then discuss the vision and oral reading test results with your instructor to seek answers to these questions.

1. What effects upon oral reading are the visual deviations of the pupil likely to produce? Are these interactions present? Or are the deviations not likely to produce effects upon the reading?

2. Is there any apparent relationship between the oral reading errors and the pupil's vision deviations?

3. If there appears to be an interaction of the pupil's vision and his reading errors, what are some of the corrective steps that may be taken?

REFERENCES

1. Barton, M. I., Goodglass, H., and Shai, A., "Differential Recognition of Tachisto-scopically Presented English and Hebrew Words in Right and Left Visual Fields," *Perceptual and Motor Skills*, 21 (1965), 431–47.
2. Berkowitz, J. H., "The Eyesight of School Children," *Education Bulletin*, 65 (1919). Washington, D.C.: Government Printing Office.
3. Betts, Emmett A., *The Prevention and Correction of Reading Difficulties.* Evanston, Ill.: Row, Peterson, 1936.

4. Blake, Mabelle D., and Dearborn, Walter F., "The Improvement of Reading Habits," *Journal of Higher Education*, 6 (February 1935), 83–88.

5. Brombach, T. A., *Blind Spot Measurements and Remedial Reading Problems.* Southbridge, Mass.: American Optical Co., 1936.

6. Carter, Homer L., "A Case in Reading," *Educational Research Bulletin*, Ohio State University, 9 (October 8, 1930), 385–90.

7. Clark, Brant, "The Effect of Binocular Imbalance on the Behavior of the Eyes During Reading," *Journal of Educational Psychology*, 26 (October 1935), 530–38.

8. Clark, Brant, "Additional Data on Binocular Imbalance and Reading," *Journal of Educational Psychology*, 27 (September 1936), 473–75.

9. Collins, S. D., "Eyesight of the School Child as Determined by the Snellen Test," *Public Health Reports*, November 28, 1924.   Washington, D.C.: Government Printing Office.

10. Coons, J. C., and Mathias, R. J., "Eye and Hand Preference Tendencies," *Pedagogical Seminary and Journal of Genetic Psychology*, 35 (December 1928), 629–32.

11. Crider, Blake, "Certain Visual Functions in Relation to Reading Disabilities," *Elementary School Journal*, 35 (December 1934), 295–97.

12. Crider, Blake, "Ocular Dominance: Its Nature, Measurement and Development," Doctoral dissertation, Western Reserve University, 1934.

13. Dearborn, Walter F., and Comfort, F. D., "Difference in the Size and Shape of Ocular Images as Related to Defects in Reading," unpublished, as quoted by Betts (3).

14. Eames, Thomas H., "A Comparison of the Ocular Characteristics of Unselected and Reading Disability Groups," *Journal of Educational Research*, 25 (March 1922), 211–15.

15. Eames, Thomas H., "Improvement in Reading Following the Correction of Eye-Defects of Non-Readers," *American Journal of Ophthalmology*, 17 (April 1934), 324–25.

16. Eames, Thomas H., "Low Fusion Convergence as a Factor in Reading Disability," *American Journal of Ophthalmology*, 17 (August 1934), 217–19.

17. Eames, Thomas H., "A Frequency Study of Physical Handicaps in Reading Disability and Unselected Groups," *Journal of Educational Research*, 29 (September 1935), 1–5.

18. Eames, Thomas H., "Restrictions of the Visual Field as Handicaps of Learning," *Journal of Educational Research*, 29 (February 1936), 460–65.

19. Eames, Thomas H., "The Ocular Conditions of 350 Poor Readers," *Journal of Educational Research*, 32 (September 1938), 10–16.

20. Eames, Thomas H., "Comparison of Eye Conditions Among 1000 Reading Failures, 500 Ophthalmic Patients and 150 Unselected Children," *American Journal of Ophthalmology*, 31 (June 1948), 713–17.

21. Eames, Thomas H., "The Effect of Anisometropia on Reading Achievement," *American Journal of Optometry and Archives of American Academy of Optometry*, 41 (December 1964), 700–702.

22. Eames, Thomas H., and Peabody, Robert W., "A Non-Reader Reads," *Journal of Educational Research*, 28 (February 1935), 450–55.

23. Farris, L. P., "Visual Defects as Factors Influencing Achievement in Reading," *California Journal of Secondary Education*, 10 (October 1934), 50–51.

24. Fendrick, Paul, *Visual Characteristics of Poor Readers.* Contributions to Education, 656, Teachers College, Columbia University, 1935.

25. Gahagan, L., "Visual Dominance–Visual Acuity Relationships," *Journal of General Psychology,* 9 (October 1933), 455–59.

26. Gates, Arthur I., *Psychology of Reading and Spelling with Special Reference to Disability.* Contributions to Education, 129, Teachers College, Columbia University, 1922.

27. Gray, C. T., *Types of Reading Ability as Exhibited Through Tests and Laboratory Experiments.* Supplementary Educational Monographs 1, No. 5. Chicago: University of Chicago Press, 1917.

28. Gray, C. T., "Problems of Reading Disabilities Requiring Scientific Study," *Elementary English Review,* 12 (April 1935), 96–100.

29. Grosvenor, Theodore, "Refractive State, Intelligence Test Scores and Academic Ability," *American Journal of Optometry and Archives of American Academy of Optometry,* 47 (May 1970), 355–60.

30. Harcum, E. Rae, "Visual Hemifield Differences as Conflicts in Direction of Reading," *Journal of Experimental Psychology,* 72 (1966), 479–80.

31. Harcum, E. Rae, "Hemifield Difference in Visual Perception of Redundant Stimuli," *Canadian Journal of Psychology,* 22 (1968), 197–211.

32. Hincks, Elizabeth M., *Disability in Reading and Its Relation to Personality.* Harvard Monographs in Education, 7. Cambridge: Harvard University Press, 1926.

33. Hinshelwood, James, *Congenital Word-Blindness. London: H. K. Lewis, 1917.*

34. Hirsch, Monroe J., and Wick, Ralph E., *Vision of Children: An Optometric Symposium.* Philadelphia: Chilton, 1963.

35. Holmes, Jack A., "Visual Hazards in the Early Teaching of Reading" *Perception and Reading,* Helen K. Smith, editor, Proceedings International Reading Association, 12, No. 4 (1968), 53–61.

36. Imus, H. A., Rothney, J. W. M., and Bear, Robert M., *An Evaluation of Visual Factors in Reading.* Hanover, N.H.: Dartmouth College, 1938.

37. Kelley, Charles R., *Visual Screening and Child Development: The North Carolina Study.* Raleigh, N.C.: Department of Psychology, North Carolina State College, 1957.

38. Koetting, James F., "Word Recognition as a Function of Locus in the Four Lateral Visual Fields: The Iota Phenomenon," *American Journal of Optometry and Archives of American Academy of Optometry,* 47 (January 1970), 56–65.

39. Lipton, Edgar L., "A Study of the Psychological Effects of Strabismus," *The Psychoanalytic Study of the Child,* 146–74. New York: International Universities Press, 1970.

40. Louttit, C. M., *Clinical Psychology.* New York: Harper, 1936.

41. Mann, Gloria T., "Reversal Reading Errors in Children Trained in Dual Directionality," *Reading Teacher,* 22 (April 1969), 646–48.

42. Monroe, Marion, *Children Who Cannot Read.* Chicago: University Press, 1932.

43. Ong, Jin, Schneider, Kenneth, and Moray, Kenneth, "Reading Ability and Perimetric Visual Field," *California Journal of Educational Research,* 11 (March 1960), 61–67.

44. Overton, W., and Wiener, M., "Visual Field Position and Word Recognition Threshold," *Journal of Experimental Psychology,* 71 (1966), 249–53.

45. Robinson, Helen M., "Visual Efficiency and Reading," in *Clinical Studies in Reading I*. Supplementary Educational Monographs No. 68. Chicago: University of Chicago Press, 1949.
46. Robinson, Helen M., "Visual Efficiency and Reading Status in the Elementary School," pp. 49–65 in *Clinical Studies in Reading III*. Supplementary Educational Monographs No. 97. Chicago: University of Chicago Press, 1968.
47. Rosenbloom, A. A., "The Relationship between Aniseikonia and Achievement in Reading," pp. 109–16 in *Clinical Studies in Reading III*. Supplementary Educational Monographs No. 97. Chicago: University of Chicago Press, 1968.
48. Russell, David H., *Characteristics of Good and Poor Spellers: A Diagnostic Study*. Contributions to Education No. 727. New York: Teachers College, Columbia University, 1937.
49. Rutherford, W. L., "Vision and Perception in the Reading Process," in *Vistas in Reading*, J. Allen Figurel, editor, Proceedings International Reading Association, 11 (1966), 503–507.
50. Selzer, Charles A., *Lateral Dominance and Visual Fusion*. Harvard Monographs in Education No. 12. Cambridge: Harvard University Press, 1933.
51. Silbiger, Francene, "Visual Test Score Differences between High and Low Reading Achievement Groups among College Freshmen," *College and Adult Reading*, D. M. Wark, editor, Yearbook of the North Central Reading Association, 5 (1968), 134–45.
52. Silbiger, Francene, and Woolf, D., "Perceptual Difficulties Associated with Reading Disability," *Proceedings College Reading Association*, 6 (1965), 98–102.
53. Smedley, F. W., "Report of Department of Child Study and Pedagogical Investigation," *Annual Report*, Board of Education, Chicago, 1899–1900.
54. Spache, George D., "The Role of Visual Defects in Reading and Spelling Disabilities," *American Journal of Orthopsychiatry*, 10 (April 1940), 229–38.
55. Spache, George D., "A Binocular Reading Test," *Journal of Applied Psychology*, 27 (February 1943), 109–13.
56. Spache, George D., "Eye Preference, Visual Acuity and Reading Ability," *Elementary School Journal*, 43 (May 1943), 539–43.
57. Spache, George D., "Case Studies in Binocular Reading," *American Journal of Orthopsychiatry*, 13 (October 1943), 723–26.
58. Spache, George D., "One-Eyed and Two-Eyed Reading," *Journal of Educational Research*, 37 (April 1944), 616–18.
59. Spache, George D., and Tillman, Chester E., "A Comparison of the Visual Profiles of Retarded and Non-Retarded Readers," *Journal of Developmental Reading*, 5 (Winter 1962), 101–109.
60. Starnes, D. R., "Visual Abilities vs. Reading Abilities," *Journal of the American Optometric Association*, 40 (1969), 596–600.
61. Stromberg, E. L., "Relationship of Measures of Visual Acuity and Ametropia to Reading Speed," *Journal of Applied Psychology*, 22 (February 1938), 70–78.
62. Swanson, D. E., and Tiffin, J., "Betts' Physiological Approach to the Analysis of Reading Disabilities as Applied to the College Level," *Journal of Educational Research*, 29 (February 1936), 433–38.
63. Terman, Lewis M., "Genetic Studies of Genius," *Mental and Physical Traits of 1000 Gifted Children*. Stanford: Stanford University Press, 1925.

64. Terman, Lewis M., and Almack, John C., *Hygiene of the School Child.* Boston: Houghton Mifflin, 1929.

65. Wagner, Guy W., "The Maturation of Certain Visual Functions and the Relationship between These Functions and Success in Reading and Arithmetic," *Psychological Monographs,* 48, No. 3 (1937), 108–46.

66. Winnick, Wilma, and Dornbush, Rhea L., "Pre- and Post-Exposure Processes in Tachistoscopic Identification," *Perceptual and Motor Skills,* 20 (February 1965), 107–13.

67. Witmer, Lightner, "A Case of Chronic Bad Spelling—Amnesia Visualis Verbalis Due to Arrest of Post-Natal Development," *Psychological Clinic,* March 1907, 53–68.

68. Witty, Paul, and Kopel, David, "Factors Associated with the Etiology of Reading Disability," *Journal of Educational Research,* 29 (February 1936), 449–59.

69. Witty, Paul, and Kopel, David, "Heterophoria and Reading Disability," *Journal of Educational Psychology,* 27 (March 1936), 222–30.

70. Witty, Paul, and Kopel, David, "Causation and Diagnosis of Reading Disability," *Journal of Psychology,* 2 (1936), 161–91.

71. Witty, Paul, and Kopel, David, "Studies of Eye-Muscle Imbalance and Poor Fusion in Reading Disability: An Evaluation," *Journal of Educational Psychology,* 27 (December 1936), 663–71.

72. Wold, R. M., "The Santa Clara County Optometric Society's Perceptual-Motor Survey," *Optometric Weekly,* 60 (1969), 21–26.

73. Young, Francis A., et al., "The Transmission of Refractive Errors within Eskimo Families," *American Journal of Optometry and Archives of American Academy of Optometry,* 46 (September 1969), 676–85.

Perhaps because it was an expensive machine and because many reading teachers are prejudiced against such devices, the eye-movement camera has had a varied history of acceptance in reading diagnosis. Some opponents claimed that it did not duplicate or measure the normal act of reading, that it was not very reliable, and even that it really did not measure the effects of training. Gradually, however, during the first half of this century, as eye-movement photography was refined, it began to reveal a great many facts about what actually takes place in the visual medium in the act of reading.

This accumulation of basic facts about the role of eye movements in reading happened to coincide with the period in which a host of reading training devices appeared on the market. The claims of many of the distributors of these gadgets and the evidence from eye-movement photography were often absolutely contradictory. The camera did not show that visual span could be materially increased or that regressions would be eliminated, as some manufacturers claimed. Similarly, eye-movement records did not support the claims of those teaching "speed reading" at astronomical rates. Yet in spite of these conflicts in data and the bias against using mechanical devices in diagnosis, eye-movement photography continues to make its own objective contribution to our comprehension of the reading act and the evaluation of training programs.

As you learn about this approach to diagnosis and evaluation of reading training, try to answer these questions.

1. Why has widespread use of eye-movement photography shown such slow progress?

2. How has eye-movement photography contributed basic facts about the reading act, speed reading, and the results of using reading machines?

3. What are some specific contributions to diagnosis that eye-movement photography only can make?

3
Eye-Movement Photography in Reading Diagnosis

E YE MOVEMENTS IN THE ACT of reading have been the object of scientific study since the early part of the nineteenth century; even before that time, efforts were made to study the behavior of the eye during reading by such methods as simple observation, ordinary cameras, mirrors, and using a peephole in the printed materials. Early efforts to attach a kymograph to the eye (an instrument that records movements on a smoked drum) and spectacles with side mirrors (to reflect eye movements to an observer standing behind the reader) were tried but found uncomfortable and ineffectual. The idea of having someone watch a pupil's eye movements through a pinhole in the printed page has persisted in some textbooks on diagnosis, however, despite its invalidity. The flaw in most of the schemes involving direct observation of the eye movements of one person by another is the fact that when the observer's eyes move to follow those of the reader he is temporarily out of focus, as any human being is when shifting focus from one point to another. No accurate count of the fixations, regressions, or other eye movements of a pupil is possible, since the movements of the observer's own eyes prevent him from following precisely those of the reader.

Eventually in about 1907, Raymond Dodge (8) devised the corneal reflection method, which has proved to be the most practical approach to the recording of eye movements. Briefly, the corneal reflection method involves bouncing a beam of light off the eye and directing the reflection into a camera with moving film. Thus the light ray produces a streak on the film depicting accurately every movement of the eye. The film, which is commonly called a graph, shows fixations and regressions in a stair-step image, moving down and across the film from left to right. Since the film moves vertically in the camera, each horizontal movement of the eyes is recorded as a vertical light-streak on the film. Each fixation is reproduced in a short vertical line on the film, the duration of the fixation being indicated by the length of the line. Saccades, or jumps from one point to another on the line of reading, show as short horizontal lines connecting the fixations. Regressions show as saccades from right to left, breaking the stair-step pattern of the usual progression from left

Adapted from George D. Spache, "Evaluation of Eye-Movement Photography in Reading Diagnosis and Reading Training," in *Research and Evaluation in College Reading*, Ninth Yearbook National Reading Conference, 1959, by permission of the copyright owner, the National Reading Conference.

to right. Return sweeps to the next line show as relatively long, almost horizontal streaks moving from right to left.

During the twenty-five years following Dodge's discovery of the corneal reflection approach, a number of cameras using this method were built at various universities and reading centers. One constructed at the University of Minnesota by Miles A. Tinker, for example, was about ten feet long and five feet high (32). Monster though it was, this camera—the basis of many research studies by Tinker and his colleagues—was instrumental in discovering most of the basic facts about eye movements (33, 34, 35). In 1932 the designing by Earl A. Taylor of the Ophthalmograph, a smaller semiportable eye-movement camera, opened the way to widespread use of this reading diagnosis tool. The Ophthalmograph was a camera mounted on a heavy iron base that limited its portability. And, unfortunately, the film could not be extracted for development until it had been used in its entirety. Since each application used only a foot or so of film, analysis of each pupil's graph was thus delayed until some twenty to twenty-five cases had been photographed. Despite these physical limitations, the Ophthalmograph received wide use, which persisted even after production of the instrument ceased in 1939.

In 1960 a new eye-movement camera, called the Reading Eye, was produced by Educational Developmental Laboratories of Huntington, New York. This simplified, completely portable camera was designed by Stanford E. Taylor, the son of the inventor of the Ophthalmograph. ·The camera could easily be carried from place to place, and individual portions of the film could be extracted immediately after the testing to be developed and analyzed.

In 1969, Reading Eye II, an improved model of the device was offered. The corneal reflection technique was replaced by a photocell monitoring procedure. The photographic film was replaced by heat-sensitive graph paper that issues directly from the camera as it operates. Thus the new recording procedure obviates the problems of development of the film and the consequent time lag between testing and diagnosis. This Reading Eye II yields a record of the number of fixations and regressions and of gross reading time but not of the duration of single fixations, according to reviewers.

The Eye Movement Monitor is another device for observing and recording eye behavior in a variety of viewing situations including reading. Using a photoelectric technique, it records both horizontal and vertical eye movements. Sensors are attached to spectacle frames, and these transmit to an instrument case that records the eye movements or presents them visually on an oscilloscope. It is offered by Space Sciences, Inc., of Waltham, Massachusetts.

68

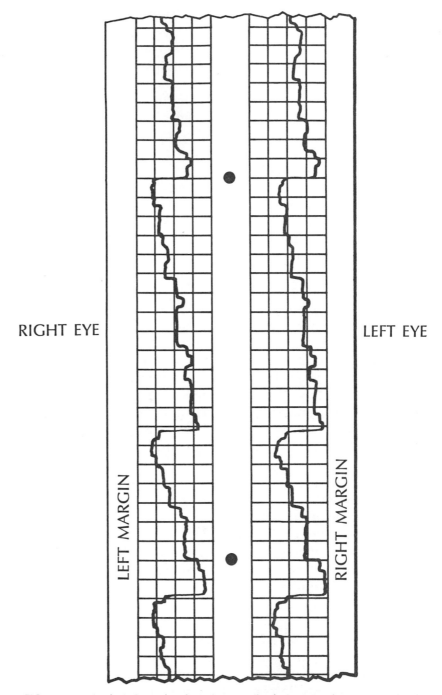

FIGURE 3–1   Analysis Record and Reading Graph of a Poor Reader (Reprinted with permission from *Controlled Reading Study Guide* for Series GH-MN by Stanford E. Taylor, Helen Frackenpohl Morris, et al. New York: McGraw-Hill, Inc., 1963.)

EYE-MOVEMENT ANALYSIS RECORD
for the EDL/Biometrics Reading Eye® II

Name _____ *Robin* , _____ *Red* _____
     Last   First   Age   Sex

School/Organization/Group _____   Class/Division _____

Address _____
        Street   City   State   Zip

TESTING DATES

1	2	3

GRADE PLACEMENT

1	2	3

Record actual grade placement in years and months.

A. READING PERFORMANCE PROFILE

DATA			Component Grade	Part 1[1] 1	2	3	4	5	6	7	8	9	10	11	12	Col.	Part 2[2] Adv. 1	Adv. 2	Adv. 3	Adv. 4	Adv. 5
136			Fixations/100 w.	224	174	155	139	129	120	114	109	105	101	96	94	90	77	65	57	48	44
36			Regressions/100 w.	52	40	35	31	28	25	23	21	20	19	18	17	15	11	8	5	4	2
.73			Av. Span of Recog.	.45	.57	.65		.78	.83	.88	.92	.95	.99	1.04	1.06	1.11	1.30	1.53	1.75	2.08	2.27
.34sec.	sec.	sec.	Av. Dur. of Fix.	.33	.30	.28	.27	.27	.27	.27	.27	.27	.26	.26	.25	.24	.23	.23	.22	.22	.22
111wpm	wpm	wpm	Rate With Comp.	80	115	138	158	173	185	195	204	214	224	237	250	280	340	400	480	560	620
80%	%	%	Comprehension																		
			Card Level & No.																		

[1] Part 1 is taken from "Grade Level Norms for the Components of the Fundamental Reading Skill," by Stanford E. Taylor, Helen Frackenpohl, and James L. Pettee, EDL Research and Information Bulletin No. 3, Educational Developmental Laboratories, 1960.

[2] Part 2 represents typical reading performance characteristics for trained readers, accumulated from various reading centers employing instrument training techniques and using eye-movement photography as an evaluative procedure.

B. RELATIVE EFFICIENCY

GRADE EQUIVALENT

2.5		

$$\text{Relative Efficiency} = \frac{\text{Rate } (111)}{\text{Fix. } (136) + \text{Reg. } (36)} = .64 \text{ Grade Level}$$

C. DIRECTIONAL ATTACK

% of Regressions

27%	%	%

$$\text{Use formula: } \frac{\text{Regressions } (36)}{\text{Fixations } (136)} = 27\%$$

R. E. Scale

R. E.	Grade Level
.29	1.0
.41	1.5
.54	2.0
.63	2.5
.73	3.0
.83	3.5
.93	4.0
1.01	4.5
1.10	5.0
1.18	5.5
1.28	6.0
1.34	6.5
1.42	7.0
1.50	7.5
1.57	8.0
1.64	8.5
1.71	9.0
1.79	9.5
1.87	10.0
1.97	10.5
2.07	11.0
2.16	11.5
2.25	12.0
2.40	12.5
2.66	13.0
2.77	13.5
2.95	14.0
3.86	Adv. 1
5.48	Adv. 2
7.74	Adv. 3
10.77	Adv. 4
13.48	Adv. 5

VALIDITY AND RELIABILITY OF EYE-MOVEMENT PHOTOGRAPHY

From time to time reading diagnosticians have seriously questioned the values of eye-movement photography. They questioned whether the graph was really a valid measure of reading test results. Some of their studies did not indicate high correlations between eye-movement data and certain reading tests. This observation really did not mean very much, however, for comparative studies of reading tests themselves do not disclose high correlations even between tests supposedly measuring the same skills (9). Luther C. Gilbert, who has been active in eye-movement studies for many years, has produced strong evidence that eye-movement photography is measuring the manner in which reading functions in other life situations (13, 14, 15, 16). Miles A. Tinker (33), reaching the same conclusions, cited correlations of .87 and .90 between rate at or away from the camera, when comparable reading materials were used. There is now little doubt among experienced reading diagnosticians that the camera does accurately reflect an individual's reading habits.

Variations between camera and reading test results can, of course, be expected when the type or content or length of the reading selections differ materially. But these variations reflect the interaction among the directions for the test, the reader's purpose, the difficulty of the selection, and the reader's response in terms of rate of reading. These varying results do not indicate that the eye-movement camera is offering a false or inaccurate report, for they are also present in the comparison between almost any two reading tests available. Other proofs of the values of eye-movement photography in reading diagnosis will appear as we discuss below the various studies made with it.

The reliability of the Ophthalmograph was strongly attacked in the report of Imus, Rothney, and Bear (19) in their study of the reading of college students. They suggested that the test selections used in the camera were much too brief for good reliability. This criticism was met in designing the testing materials for the Reading Eye camera, though. Carefully graded test selections were created, and a test of comprehension was devised for each. Several trial tests are given with these selections off the camera until an appropriate reading level for the testee in terms of adequate comprehension is established. This pretesting insures that the test selections used on camera are suitable for the pupil. If later these are read with poor comprehension in the camera, the individual is retested with simpler selections that he can read comprehendingly. Subsequent research studies have confirmed the values of this careful testing procedure in obtaining reliable eye-movement data (31). Taylor found correlations of .83 at the fourth and seventh grades and .91 at the tenth grade between rate of reading at the camera and in a rate of reading test. When selections of the appropriate grade level of reading were used in the camera, as determined by the pretesting procedure, there was little variation in the pattern of eye movements because of differences in the content of the selections or their degree of interest to readers.   These studies also showed that the most accurate results were obtained by the camera when the directions to the testee stressed reading for comprehension, not reading for speed.   Other studies by Laycock (20) and Siebert (23) confirm these observations.

BASIC FACTS ABOUT EYE MOVEMENTS

Early in the history of the study of eye movements by a camera, a number of fundamental facts were discovered. It was learned that one does not just move his eyes across a line of print but rather that the eyes hop or glide from one stop or fixation to the next. During the glide or saccade the eyes relax or diverge slightly and are momentarily out of focus; vision is, in a sense, suspended. These fixations occupy only a fraction of a second, averaging from one-half to one-third of a second, actually; and it is during this brief interval of pause that comprehension occurs. If a difficult word or thought is encountered in the reading, the usual left-to-right progression of fixations may be interrupted. The eyes may then move backward in a regression from right to left, to permit the reader a second look, as it were. When, after a series of fixations, the end of the line is reached, the reader's eyes make a return sweep to the beginning of the next line, fixate somewhere near the beginning of the line, and then move progressively on across the line. Span of each fixation is determined by dividing the number of words read by the number of fixations (1, 4, 11, 32).

Photographing the eye movements of poor readers has shown that they usually exhibit a number of deviations from the expected patterns. Poor spellers also tend to show many of the same difficulties, as these:

1. An unusual number of fixations overall
2. Periods of confusion with regressions and forward movements intermixed
3. Numerous regressions throughout the reading
4. Extra-long durations of fixations, or a mixture of long and short durations

5. Inaccuracies in the return saccade to the next line, as frequent regressions at this point or fumbling with the first or second fixation (1, 11, 34)

These deviations among poor readers or spellers have often led to training programs intended to eradicate them, under the belief that better reading would inevitably ensue. We have seen many instances of training to eradicate regressions and to reduce the number of fixations by increasing the recognition span; these and many others are all based on the assumption that better eye-movement patterns will result in improved reading (5). The elimination of regressions, however, would be most undesirable unless present in an excessive degree, for it is by these extra movements that the reader completes analysis of puzzling words and clarifies his comprehension. Obviously, if a pupil were to read with few or no regressions, he would perforce be reading most superficially without any attempt at dealing with vocabulary problems or depth of comprehension.

As for span of recognition, this is determined, first of all, by the size of the sensitive area of the retina (which cannot be altered) and, second, by the difficulty of the reading material. Easy material is simpler to comprehend; hence fewer fixations are needed, and the span appears to be larger. Moreover, the actual number of words seen in a fixation is limited by the size of the area of the printed page that can be brought into sharp focus, about one and one-half to two inches of the printed line. This area is determined by the extreme convergence of the eyes as they are brought to a point of focus on the page, a much narrower span of vision than in looking across a room with the eyes in a parallel, unconverged posture.

Yet we frequently see classroom practice in reading ever-widening printed columns of words or phrases, machines to practice with similar material, flash devices such as the tachistoscope, or even flash cards made by the teacher, all of which are supposed to increase the eye-span. Some methods of teaching rapid or speed reading also claim to avoid the physiological limits of the eye in the act of reading and thus induce the reader to read a whole line or even a whole page in one fixation. Our earlier description of the basic functions of eye movements in reading, and of the limits inherent in the structure and functioning of the eye indicate the fallacy in these span training efforts (25, 27, 28, 29, 30).

When the eye-movement camera is employed to analyze reading span behavior, it is shown that even when skimming at rates from 600 to 1,380 words per minute, the readers studied by Grayum (18) averaged a span of only 2.65 words per fixation. Other studies indicate that after prolonged instrument training or tachistoscopic work, the span even for an exceptionally good reader averages only 2.5 words. If greater rate of reading appears after what is thought to be span training, it is revealed by the camera that the gain has been achieved simply by a small decrease in the number of fixations and, even more significantly, by shortening the duration of fixations. Since fixation pauses occupy about 90 percent of the reading time, it is apparent that a change as small as a fractional part of a second will result in sizeable gains in rate of reading. Machine or other types of training intended to increase span may also force the reader to greater use of minimal clues to word recognition and to more dependence upon the context than formerly, with consequent increase in rate, but no changes in span. Perhaps the only situations in which some sort of training intended to increase span would be justified are those cases of high school, college, or adult readers who are found to have a span of only a few letters or a half a word (if their condition is not caused by extreme nearsightedness). The final argument against span training is present in the negative results of all the experiments planned to achieve an increase, of which only a few need to be cited (2, 4, 6, 10, 17, 24).

It is apparent from the publication dates of these studies that the use of the eye-movement camera to determine the actual outcomes of training programs intended to increase span of recognition has not persisted into recent years. The great bulk of the relatively recent studies of reading improvement have been satisfied to report gains on a reading test, particularly in rate of reading, and to assume significant changes in eye-span and other aspects of the eye movements. There are reasons for this diminution in use of the eye-movement camera by reading instructors, which must be recognized although we may deplore them.

The early studies of reading improvement evaluated by camera records occurred largely in university settings where such equipment was readily available. But the cost of the camera and the time required for analysis of its records tended to limit its use in reading improvement work in other educational settings. Besides, many reading instructors who were recruited from the field of English and from classroom teaching were inclined to look with disfavor upon interpretation of reading in mechanistic terms, as in the use of the camera. In contrast, many reading tests were available, were easy to administer, and apparently yielded valid measures of gains. In the eyes of the average reading instructor, these group reading tests appeared to measure broader and more significant aspects of the reading process than does the camera. Thus, use of the camera to measure outcomes of reading improvement programs is not common today except, perhaps, in some clinics.

As its use diminished, general knowledge of the basic facts about eye movements and their implications for training also tended to disappear. As a result, reading improvement programs often became structured to produce results that eye-movement data indicate are impossible. An example of this is the trend toward emphasis upon speed reading or reading at very high rates. Another trend in reading courses has been toward the widespread use of a variety of machines to produce great gains in rate of reading, or so their manufacturers claimed and reading instructors believed.

Among the few recent studies of eye-movement behavior is that of Stennett et al.* The experimenters were desirous of separating simple oculomotor skill of the eyes from the complex process of reading and determining the development of this skill in young children. Using rows of digits read as fast as possible, they found little variation in fixations, regressions, or duration of fixations in the first four grades. In a second study of canceling and copying of letters, there was again little variation in fixations and regressions with age. Some change in the duration of fixations was attributed to reduction in recognition time or, in other words, to the development of cognitive skills.

In a third study, the factor analysis of nine subtests of reading, age, sex, and teacher ratings of oral reading indicated that most of the reading tests, age, teacher ratings, motor speed, and canceling formed the main factor. The eye-movement and motor tasks were not related to the ratings or reading tests. In fact, the eye-movement measures formed an independent factor. The authors concluded that simple oculomotor skill in reading is overlearned by the time that children are taught to read and does not account for much of the variance in reading performances. Variations in reading abilities, they believe, are the result of differences in perceptual and cognitive abilities rather than of oculomotor skill. They conclude that their studies support Tinker's statement that efficient eye movements are a result, not a cause, of good reading.

The impression that a reader of this research is likely to receive is that eye-movement behaviors are not related to reading success. Hence, it is implied, records of the variations of individuals in these behaviors are not essential or useful in determining the possible reasons for poor reading. These implications are not accurate, as we shall point out later, and they are not justified on the basis of Stennett's results. Their studies did show that primary children, on the average, could move their eyes from one target to the next in a noncognitive task. Under these conditions, there did not appear to be any great variation by age levels from the first to fourth grades, except in duration of fixations. From these studies we could conclude that primary

---

*R. G. Stennett, P. C. Smythe, June Pinkney, and Ada Fairbaim, "The Relationship of Eyemovement Measures to Psychomotor Skills and Other Elemental Skills Involved in Learning to Read," *Journal of Reading Behavior,* 5 (winter 1972–73), 1–13.

children do have a fundamental oculomotor skill, which is well developed when they enter school and does not show much of a developmental trend thereafter.

But reading is a complex cognitive task demanding much more than simple oculomotor skills. Moreover, eye-movement behaviors differ in reading and simple noncognitive tasks. The lack of relationship of their eye-movement measures to reading in this study reflects the fact that these measures were obtained in nonreading tasks. Many studies, including some of Tinker's, indicate that eye-movement behavior in the act of reading is affected by cognitive processes such as the difficulty of comprehension, the reader's purpose for reading, and the set for speed or comprehension of the reader. When, as in true reading, the task involves cognitive processes, eye-movement behavior is related to reading measures.

WHAT ARE THE LIMITS OF SPEED TRAINING?*

Many recent newspaper and magazine articles have featured claims that speed training can readily produce reading rates of several thousand words per minute. For example, one author quotes such rates as 1,500, 3,500, and 6,000 words per minute as being characteristic of good readers (3). Even a rate of 25,000 words per minute is mentioned in a popular Sunday supplement as the result of a special training course (21). These various articles suggest that such speeds are obtained by reading straight down the page, gulping whole paragraphs or whole pages at a single glance. If these claims are credible, they imply a serious lack of effectiveness in the methods employed by most reading teachers and clinics, for none of the published reports of such clinics has been able to find these astronomical speeds among their pupils.

The real problem of interpreting these grandiose claims is, unfortunately, one of semantics. This author uses the term *reading* in the common sense of meaning the act of reading most of the words on the page. If this is the speed reading teachers' meaning (and there is little doubt of this intention), it is appropriate to point out that it is impossible to read faster than 800 to 900 words per minute.

A few simple figures will suffice to demonstrate this fact. First, the shortest fixation during which reading usually occurs requires one-sixth to one-fifth of a second. Second, the sweeping movement to each new fixation

---

*This section is adapted from George D. Spache, *Toward Better Reading* (Champaign, Ill.: Garrard Publishing, 1963).

requires one-thirtieth to one-twenty-fifth of a second, and the return sweep to the next line necessitates a similar amount of time. Third, the maximum number of words that the eye can possibly read with a single fixation during continuous reading is between two and one-half and three words. Thus the minimum essential time to read a ten-word line of four inches is approximately .66 of a second, assuming that each span is the largest possible, while its duration is the shortest possible (see Table 3–1).

In this illustration we are suggesting that it takes 3.3 fixations to cover a ten-word line, if we grant the largest possible span of three words per fixation. We are aware that by using the context clues a reader can skip several words and thus may need fewer than 3.3 fixations. But it is also true that the span of a fixation is not constantly at its maximum, as we are assuming it to be in this illustration. For the sake of this discussion, we are hypothesizing that the reader is reading practically all the words on the line and that his span is at the maximum possible.

To perform three and one-third fixations, the reader would have to make at least two and a fraction saccades or sweeps from one fixation to the next. This is a fixed behavior not influenced by any characteristic of the reader or the material. Again we have credited this reader with the fastest possible saccade. Similarly, the reader must make a return sweep to the next line in order to continue reading. There is no other efficient way of returning to the beginning of the line.

We have also credited this reader with no regressions, which would, of course, have increased the time to read the ten-word line. Almost no one reads with no regressions, but we are pretending that this reader is most unusual, as the teachers of speed reading seem to think that their pupils are.

This illustration has been criticized by some who claim that we have described reading behavior in terms of average performances. They would insist that some supernormal readers can read more rapidly than our hypothetical case does. Careful reading of the data that we have cited, however, reveals that we are not discussing average performances and interpreting these as the fastest possible. Each figure used represents the fastest performance

TABLE 3–1 READING A TEN-WORD LINE

	TIME IN SECONDS
3 words per fixation = 3.3 fixations at .166 sec. each	.547
2.5 saccades at .033 sec. each	.083
1 return sweep at .033 sec. each	.033
Total	.663

on record.   In fact, they represent a performance in span and duration of fixation (and no regressions) that probably no one could achieve for sustained periods.

These data were confirmed by Javal's studies in 1878 and many other more recent studies of eye movements. Walton, for example, has shown that even when practically no comprehension is demanded in the reading task, the fastest average time for a fixation was one-sixth of a second (37).   Gilbert's study, using tachistoscopic procedures that permit a larger span than at a reading distance, shows that the shortest possible fixation in reading a two-word phrase is at least one-fifth to one-fourth of a second (15).

Translating reading ten words in two-thirds of a second or fifteen words per second into a rate of reading yields a maximum rate of 900 words per minute. Assuming that a reader performs constantly with the best possible pattern of eye movements known and reads most of the words on a page—as he must in challenging material—his rate of reading cannot normally exceed 900 words per minute.

Thus it is apparent that the speeds of reading suggested in the various newspaper and magazine articles could not possibly describe the act of reading, as that act is commonly understood. Those speeds must refer to performances such as skimming, scanning, previewing, or other rapid reading techniques in which relatively large portions of the reading matter are omitted. Tinker similarly concludes from his review of eye-movement studies that "any rate of over 800 words per minute can only mean that the reader is skimming rather than reading all the material" (35).

One other misleading implication is present in the popular articles that we have cited—the suggestion that some readers can read large portions or even whole pages at a single fixation.   It is true that most readers trained in the art of skimming depart somewhat from the usual line-by-line procedure. Skimming, or scanning for a single fact on a page without reading the page, as in a telephone directory, does involve a tendency to use many vertical eye movements.   These are used to skip from line to line or from one part of a page to another.   Eye-movement records of individuals who are skimming at high rates of speed are not numerous.   But a group of such records was analyzed in a recent article (27).   The records showed approximately one fixation per line.   At the same time, there was some intermittent horizontal reading, for the group averaged a few left-to-right fixation movements per page.   These records demonstrate that skimming does *not* permit reading large portions at a single fixation, but rather a reduced number of fixations per page, largely in the vertical direction but interspersed with normal reading. Large amounts of reading material can be dealt with by skimming, for these students covered an average of 2,500 words per minute by this process.   But our point is that this rapid reading technique cannot be confused with the normal act of reading and its physiological limits.

It is significant also to note that the comprehension of these skimmers was no better than 50 percent, a chance performance in the true-false questions employed.

READING MACHINES AND EYE MOVEMENTS

It is interesting to note that the users of pacers and controllers offer different explanations for the success of their devices in improving rate of reading. The proponents of controllers claim that the machine reduces the number and duration of fixations, the brief rests of the eye during which reading actually occurs. They also claim that their devices increase the span of recognition, or the number of digits, words, or phrases read during one fixation. Proponents of pacers usually claim that their devices produce gains in speed by pushing the reader until he acquires the habit of reading faster. Users of both pacers and controllers claim to eliminate or reduce the number of regressions or backward movements of the eye while reading. Both types of devices do produce gains in reading speed for some individuals, but not entirely for the reasons claimed. Reviews of the extensive research on machine training agree that it achieves its primary goal of increasing speed, but they do not all agree that the method markedly modifies eye movements or the span of recognition or produces permanent changes in eye-movement characteristics (25, 33, 34, 36, 38).

It is true that regressions and the number of fixations decrease as speed in reading grows. The duration of fixations also decreases slightly, but there is very little evidence that any of these changes results only from machine training (25, 38). These changes also occur among readers trained by any recognized method for improving reading, with or without machines. Nor is there tremendous change in the span of recognition as a result of machine training, for this is very similar among both good and poor readers. Thus there is still some debate regarding the way in which machines actually produce gains in rate of reading.

Perry and Whitlock, who helped produce the original Harvard Reading Films, suggest that machines may be effective because of their motivational influence (22). Reading with the machine may inspire self-confidence, concentrate attention, and provide a set or attitude toward comprehension at higher rates. Spache and Westover both offer the explanation that the machines may be successful because they contribute to improvement in habits of perception and organization, or to the reduction of cues needed for word recognition (25, 38). In their opinion, the reader using a machine is helped to read faster by indirect training in more efficient perception and discrimination rather than by very great modification of his eye movements.

A recent reading improvement program conducted at the junior high school level illustrates some of the difficulty of interpreting the results of machine training (7). Two groups of eighth graders received twenty-one sessions of reasonably comparable training in rate, comprehension, and vocabulary. The instrument group used the Controlled Reader for the reading selections (read by both groups) and the Tach-X for tachistoscopic training. In most other respects, the training in both groups was similar.

The results indicated an average mean gain of 2.52 years on the Iowa Silent Reading Test for the instrument group, and 1.26 years for the noninstrument group. The changes, as measured by eye-movement camera records, are shown in Table 3–2.

The instrument group did reduce the number of fixations per 100 running words by about 12 percent, while the control group decreased in this respect by less than 3 percent. Regressions decreased in the instrument group about 5 percent, while *increasing* in the other group by 25 percent. This result raises the interesting speculation that perhaps some types of improvement training increase tension and insecurity in the reader, leading him to a poorer eye-movement pattern than before training. Increases in span of recognition, as we predicted, were very minute in both groups, although they were significant in the instrument group when we consider the average changes from year to year during the school career.

TABLE 3–2

COMPONENT	INSTRUMENT GROUP				NON-INSTRUMENT GROUP			
	OCT.	JAN.	DECREASE OR INCREASE	CHANGE IN GRADE PLACE-MENT	OCT.	JAN.	DECREASE OR INCREASE	CHANGE IN GRADE PLACE-MENT
Fixations/100 words	117.1	102.9	14.2 dec.	3.0	126.9	123.3	3.6 dec.	0.3
Regressions/100 words	22.8	21.6	1.2 dec.	0.5	25.1	31.5	6.4 inc.	−2.0
Span of Recog. (in words)	.85	.96	.11 inc.	2.5	.79	.81	.02 inc.	0.8
Duration of fix. (sec.)	.269	.216	.053 dec.	6.0	.271	.243	0.028 dec.	3.5
Rate with Comprehension	190.2	268.5	78.3 inc.	6.0	173.5	200.5	27.0 inc.	3.0
Comprehension	74.5	81.3	5.9 inc.	...	81.0	81.5	.5 inc.	...

From "A Concentrated Junior High School Reading Program," *EDL Newsletter,* No. 14. Huntington, N. Y.: Educational Developmental Laboratories.

Duration of fixations was reduced by .053 seconds in the instrument group, a gain equivalent to six years of growth among normal junior high school pupils. Even the decrease of .028 seconds in the noninstrument group is significant, since it equals a four-year growth in the standards for eye movements. The gain in rate in words per minute was about 40 percent in the instrument group and about 15 percent in the control group. On the eye-movement camera, these gains are equivalent respectively to six years and three years.

It is apparent that the instrument group showed consistently greater gains in eye-movement characteristics. But it will be noted that these changes are, for the most part, very minute, since they involve measurements that are extremely small. Those who are skeptical about machine training will ask: "How much of this apparent six-grade change will be permanent? How much of this is a real change not due to chance, to regression to the mean, or to the unreliability of a brief test? Might not changes as minute as these frequently appear in two successive reading tasks that differ somewhat in difficulty for the reader? How much are these results due to the novelty or motivational effect of the machines themselves?"

The consistency of the results in the instrument group certainly implies that it made greater gains than did the noninstrument group. All gains were in the expected direction of the reduction of fixations and regressions. But even the directors of this study cannot answer all the questions that the skeptics raise. Like their critics, the authors also recognize the inherent motivation of a mechanical device, for they observed that the lack of devices in the noninstrument group failed to provide the same constant motivation and support. Without the machines, many of the students were not convinced that they could increase their speed without losing comprehension. Thus the experiments cannot prove beyond question whether the gains were due to the methods of presentation implicit in the devices used, or to the sheer motivational impact of using a mechanical device. Moreover, their data do not permit them to prove that the gains were permanent or that equal gains could not have been achieved by a more highly motivated noninstrument program.

This argument about machine training could continue indefinitely, perhaps, without convincing the most rabid proponents on either side. In our opinion, there is ample evidence that machines do produce relatively permanent gains in rate of reading for some students, even though they may not know exactly how they accomplish this goal.

The answer given by research on this question is that gains in reading rate or speed of word recognition can be achieved equally as well by ordinary motivated practice or by carefully planned classroom activities. Machines add variety, additional motivation, economy in dealing with large groups, and a certain attitude toward improvement for those who read slowly simply because of habit, lack of confidence, or perfectionism. They will help some students to read faster when other methods fail to provide sufficient motivation or impetus. But, like all other methods, they are not successful with all students and cannot be used indiscriminately.

WHY PHOTOGRAPH EYE MOVEMENTS?

If, as we argue, eye-movement behavior is not amenable to training, some may ask why, then, is it profitable to make a photographic record? If we cannot change the pattern, why bother to spend this time and money on an expensive camera and the analysis of its record? In answer, we shall attempt to point out what we think are the very real values of eye-movement photography in reading diagnosis. Eye-movement graphs, which are obtained from the camera, serve four basic purposes:

1. To survey the individual's mechanical functioning in the reading act. Because it provides a completely objective record of visual behavior in reading, eye-movement records can function as a survey technique in classifying subjects according to their needs for remediation. They can also identify those who would experience difficulties in dealing with large amounts of reading or studying in school or industry. They can assist in classifying individuals according to their aptitude for various work situations such as inspection, gauge reading, and other detailed work.

Wide-scale testing with the camera would be relatively expensive and time-consuming. It could not economically be defended, if used as frequently, for example, as reading tests are. On the other hand, its use in clinics with practically all cases admitted, and as a diagnostic and predictive tool during the primary grades and again perhaps at some later date in the school career, could conceivably be justified. The records would be extremely helpful in many cases in educational and vocational guidance, and in planning and evaluating the results of corrective or remedial instruction, as we shall point out.

2. To obtain indications of the need for specific types of corrective instruction. In a sense, the eye-movement records reveal the maturity of reading skill in terms of durations of fixations, number of fixations or regressions, and span of recognition. Gilbert's studies (13) lead him to conclude that all pupils do not naturally mature or improve in these characteristics simply because they are exposed to the usual reading program. Many pupils who exhibit fairly normal performances on standardized tests of comprehension, and who apparently can read materials appropriate to their educational status, employ ineffectual or even harmful mechanical habits in reading. They may consistently show excessive regressions, abnormal duration of fixations, a very large number of fixations, or a small recognition span. We may suspect some of these difficulties from extremely slow rate on a reading or word recognition test, but the exact nature of the reader's deviation from normal eye movements would not be so apparent.

For example, some readers compensate for narrow recognition spans and many fixations by shortening the duration of fixations. Therefore, their rate of reading as usually measured in words per minute appears normal. But reading in this fashion may be accompanied by a high degree of tension, excessive energy demands, rapid onset of fatigue, and often a consequent dislike for sustained reading. With the shortened fixation time, the process of comprehension is also abbreviated, which will be manifest in a lengthy reading test. Without an eye-movement record, we would be suspicious of the symptoms of variations in comprehension, fatigue, tension while reading, and poor attitude toward reading in what seems to be a normal reader. But we would never discover the underlying reasons for this puzzling behavior pattern until the eye-movement pattern was analyzed.

Another type of reading difficulty revealed only by the eye-movement camera is the reader's adequacy of directional attack. Some pupils habitually regress at certain points of every line regardless of the difficulty of the reading material. Others show a lack of accurate return sweep, with visual fumbling at the beginning of each line or even no true return sweep at all. They may actually return to the beginning of the next line by a series of regressions from right to left. Poor directional attack may also be shown by an excessive proportion of regressions when compared with total fixations.

The only symptoms observable by the teacher in these cases of directional attack may be slow rate, a good deal of fumbling in reading across the line, and perhaps a tendency to reversals in word order or frequent repetitions of words or phrases. These are, of course, common behaviors of very poor readers and are often interpreted as indicating poor phonic skill or sight vocabulary deficiency, which may not be correct diagnoses.

We could cite other types of reading disability cases in which a true diagnosis cannot be made without using an eye-movement camera. But these two kinds may suffice to support our earlier statement of the essential need for this diagnostic approach in all cases of severe reading retardation.

3. To give indications of difficulties in visual functioning. The eye-movement camera is not primarily intended to explore the visual functions of the reader; thus it cannot serve as a substitute for a complete vision screening. But because the camera does record the exact behavior of the eyes during reading, it may provide a basis for referral to professional vision specialists. We are well aware that some professionals denigrate the importance of vision in reading despite the research published by colleagues in their own branch of vision science. And, if they have heard about it, they will probably disparage use of the eye-movement camera, particularly if the record is used by nonmedical persons to refer pupils for visual examination. Despite this negative attitude, we have presented a mass of evidence elsewhere in this book supporting the importance of the interaction of visual difficulties and reading success. It is also possible to find further evidence of this relationship in eye-movement camera records.

Three types of functional visual deviations are readily observed in the camera record. The first type includes inadequate binocular coordination and vergence problems. Normally both eyes perform alike in the act of reading, and the records of each are exactly duplicate and parallel. When binocular coordination is lacking, for any of a half-dozen reasons, the movements of one eye may be less pronounced or even different from those of the other eye on the film or printed record. One eye may not make the same interfixational saccades as the other does, or may make them to a lesser degree. The saccades on the record may appear as curves rather than as straight lines for one eye, or they may be shorter or longer than those recorded by the other eye. Accuracy in reading is almost impossible when the eyes do not successively fixate on precisely the same spot in a series of fixations. In effect, the reader may be trying to read different words with each eye, with consequent frequent reading errors.

In the return sweep, vergence or coordination deficiencies can cause one eye to overshoot the edge of the next line with resulting fumbling for a single fixation, inaccurate focus on the beginning words of the line, several regressions in an effort to fixate, and obvious confusion for the reader. The reasons for these faulty reading behaviors are not apparent to the teacher or clinician listening to the pupil read aloud.

A second type of functional visual deficiency is lack of vertical or lateral balance of the eyes. Because of deviations in exactly parallel posturing of the eyes, with one tending to turn in or out, up or down, again both eyes may fail to perform similarly in the reading act. Symptoms such as overshooting the return sweep with the eye, regressions to achieve focus, or random movements of one eye are all clearly reproduced in the camera record. When the problem is severe, we sometimes see records in which the parallel records of the eyes gradually diverge more and more until one eye record moves off the recording surface. Reading symptoms may include losing place, frequent omissions or repetitions, and slow reading rate, all of which are common enough to be considered normal malfunctioning among poor readers.

84

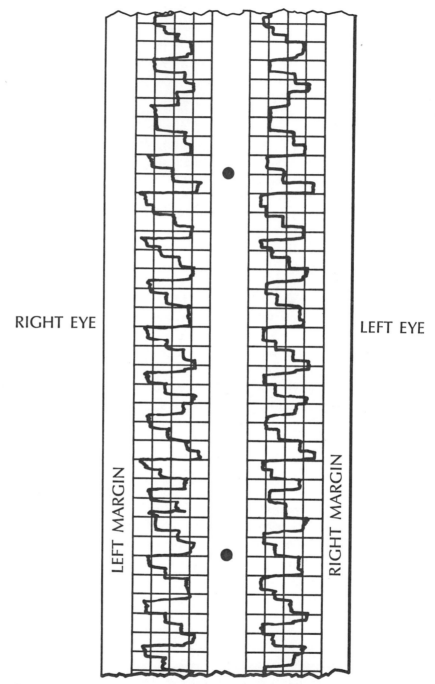

RIGHT EYE

LEFT EYE

LEFT MARGIN

RIGHT MARGIN

FIGURE 3–2 Analysis Record and Reading Graph of a Good Reader (Reprinted with permission from *Controlled Reading Study Guide* for Series GH-MN by Stanford E. Taylor, Helen Frackenpohl Morris, et al. New York: McGraw-Hill, Inc., 1963.)

EYE-MOVEMENT ANALYSIS RECORD
for the EDL/Biometrics Reading Eye® II

Name _____ *Doe*, _____ *John* _____

Last   First   Age   Sex

School/Organization/Group _____ Class/Division _____

Address _____

Street   City   State   Zip

TESTING DATES

1	2	3

GRADE PLACEMENT

1	2	3

Record actual grade placement in years and months.

A. READING PERFORMANCE PROFILE

DATA			Component Grade	1	2	3	4	5	6	7	8	9	10	11	12	Col.	Adv. 1	Adv. 2	Adv. 3	Adv. 4	Adv. 5
41			Fixations/100 w.	224	174	155	139	129	120	114	109	105	101	96	94	90	77	65	57	48	44
6			Regressions/100 w.	52	40	35	31	28	25	23	21	20	19	18	17	15	11	8	5	4	2
2.44			Av. Span of Recog.	.45	.57	.65	.72	.78	.83	.88	.92	.95	.99	1.04	1.06	1.11	1.30	1.53	1.75	2.08	2.27
*.25*sec.	sec.	sec.	Av. Dur. of Fix.	.33	.30	.28	.27	.27	.27	.27	.27	.27	.26	.26	.25	.24	.23	.23	.22	.22	.22
*511*wpm	wpm	wpm	Rate With Comp.	80	115	138	158	173	185	195	204	214	224	237	250	280	340	400	480	560	620
80%	%	%	Comprehension																		
			Card Level & No.																		

Part 1[1]   Part 2[2]

[1] Part I is taken from "Grade Level Norms for the Components of the Fundamental Reading Skill," by Stanford E. Taylor, Helen Frackenpohl, and James L. Pettee, EDL Research and Information Bulletin No. 3, Educational Developmental Laboratories, 1960.

[2] Part 2 represents typical reading performance characteristics for trained readers, accumulated from various reading centers employing instrument training techniques and using eye-movement photography as an evaluative procedure.

B. RELATIVE EFFICIENCY

GRADE EQUIVALENT

ADV. 4		

$$\text{Relative Efficiency} = \frac{\text{Rate } (511)}{\text{Fix. } (41) + \text{Reg. } (6)} = 10.85 \text{ Grade Level}$$

C. DIRECTIONAL ATTACK

% of Regressions

15%	%	%

Use formula: $\dfrac{\text{Regressions } (6)}{\text{Fixations } (41)} = 15\%$

R. E. Scale

R. E.	Grade Level
.29	1.0
.41	1.5
.54	2.0
.63	2.5
.73	3.0
.83	3.5
.93	4.0
1.01	4.5
1.10	5.0
1.18	5.5
1.28	6.0
1.34	6.5
1.42	7.0
1.50	7.5
1.57	8.0
1.64	8.5
1.71	9.0
1.79	9.5
1.87	10.0
1.97	10.5
2.07	11.0
2.16	11.5
2.25	12.0
2.40	12.5
2.66	13.0
2.77	13.5
2.95	14.0
3.86	Adv. 1
5.48	Adv. 2
7.74	Adv. 3
10.77	Adv. 4
13.48	Adv. 5

Another type of visual problem often uncovered by the camera is in the area of visual acuity. For example, prolonged durations of fixation are often present in myopia, or they may be observed when astigmatic errors prevent rapid, accurate focusing. Disturbances of the convergence-accommodation balance often give rise to many of the symptoms mentioned earlier. Hyperopia—farsightedness—may be detected by the presence of a repeated regression in the first or second fixation at the beginning of each line, thus reflecting a focusing problem. Cases of monocular or binocular nystagmus, an uncontrollable constant movement of the eye, yield, as we might expect, very unusual records. Severe suppression of the vision in one eye is shown by lack of parallel movements or by irregularity in the behavior of the suppressed eye on the camera record. Thus, in a number of ways, eye-movement photography not only reveals certain visual deficiencies but also makes apparent the effect of these on the reading act.

4. To observe the reader's adjustment to the reading situation. Evidence of nervous tension and discomfort in reading are often recorded by the camera. Pupils with these problems show less definite or distinct patterns of eye movements. Their fixations are more irregular and more frequent; they evidence uncontrollable head movements that distort the record; the duration of their fixations is often variable. Sometimes the record is speckled rather than in solid lines because of the tremors or vocalization or frequent blinking.

We have tried to show that eye-movement photography can play a significant role in reading diagnosis, in revealing reading behavior in unique ways, and in guiding more intelligent training programs.

LEARNING PROJECT

Secure the Manual for an eye-movement camera and familiarize yourself with its administration and the interpretation of the graph. If a camera is available, arrange to use it with several pupils. Try to interpret the results and discover what the testing reveals about these pupils. Use these questions to evaluate this experience.

1. What abnormalities or deviations appeared in these records? What is their probable meaning?

2. What did you discover about the pupils that would not have been revealed by a silent or an oral reading test? Are these facts of significance in diagnosis or treatment? How?

3. Based on this brief experience, how do you think that eye-movement photography should be used in schools or clinics?

REFERENCES

1. Abernethy, Ethel M., "Photographic Records of Eye Movements in Studying Spelling," *Journal of Educational Psychology,* 20 (November 1929), 695–701.
2. Anderson, Irving H., "Studies in the Eye-Movements of Good and Poor Readers," *Psychological Monographs,* 48 (1937), 1–35.
3. Bass, Raply, "You *Can* Read Faster," *Coronet,* 50 (June 1961), 49–53.
4. Buswell, Guy Thomas, *How Adults Read.* Supplementary Educational Monographs No. 45. Chicago: University of Chicago Press, 1937.
5. Center, Stella S., and Persons, Gladys L., *Teaching High School Students To Read.* New York: Appleton-Century, 1937.
6. Clark, Brant, "The Effect of Binocular Imbalance on the Behavior of the Eyes During Reading," *Journal of Educational Psychology,* 26 (October 1935), 530–38.
7. "A Concentrated Junior High School Reading Program," *EDL Newsletter,* No. 14. Huntington, N.Y.: Educational Developmental Laboratories.
8. Dodge, Raymond, "An Experimental Study of Visual Fixations," *Psychological Monographs,* 8 (1907), 1–95.
9. Eurich, Alvin C., *The Reading Abilities of College Students.* Minneapolis: University of Minnesota Press, 1931.
10. Freeburne, Cecil Max, "The Influence of Training in Perceptual Span and Perceptual Speed Upon Reading Ability," *Journal of Educational Psychology,* 40 (October 1949), 321–52.
11. Gilbert, Luther C., "An Experimental Investigation of Eye Movements in Learning to Spell Words," *Psychological Monographs,* 43 (1932), 1–75.
12. Gilbert, Luther C., "The Effect on Silent Reading of Attempting to Follow Oral Reading," *Elementary School Journal,* 40 (April 1940), 614–21.
13. Gilbert, Luther C., "Functional Motor Efficiency of the Eyes and Its Relation to Reading," *University of California Publications in Education,* 11 (1953), 159–232.
14. Gilbert, Luther C., "Speed of Processing Visual Stimuli in Reading," *Journal of Educational Psychology,* 50 (February 1959), 8–14.
15. Gilbert, Luther C., "Saccadic Movements as a Factor in Visual Perception in Reading," *Journal of Educational Psychology,* 50 (February 1959), 15–19.
16. Gilbert, Luther C., and Gilbert, Doris W., "Reading Before the Eye Movement Camera versus Reading Away From It," *Elementary School Journal,* 42 (February 1942), 443–47.
17. Glock, Marvin D., "The Effect upon Eye Movement and Reading Rate at College Level of Three Methods of Training," *Journal of Educational Psychology,* 40 (February 1949), 93–105.
18. Grayum, Helen S., "What Is Skimming? What Are Its Uses at Different Grades?" *Reading Teacher,* 7 (December 1953), 11–14.
19. Imus, Henry A., Rothney, John W., and Bear, Robert M., *An Evaluation of Visual Factors in Reading.* Hanover, N.H.: Dartmouth College Publications, 1938.
20. Laycock, Frank, "Motor and Perceptual Skill in 'Reading' Material Whose Meaning Is Unimportant," *Journal of Experimental Education,* 23 (June 1955), 320–30.

21. Mitchell, Curtis, "She Can Teach You to Read 2500 Words a Minute," *Family Week*, February 5, 1961, 18–19.
22. Perry, William G., and Whitlock, Charles P., "A Clinical Rationale for a Reading Film," *Harvard Educational Review*, 24 (Winter 1954), 6–27.
23. Siebert, Earl W., "Reading Reactions for Varied Types of Subject Matter," *Journal of Experimental Education*, 12 (September 1943), 37–44.
24. Sisson, E. Donald, "Eye-Movement Training as a Means of Improving Reading Ability," *Journal of Educational Research*, 32 (September 1938), 35–41.
25. Spache, George D., "A Rationale for Controlled Reading," in *Reading for Effective Living*, J. Allen Figurel, editor, Proceedings International Reading Association, 3 (1958), 190–93.
26. Spache, George D., "Evaluation of Eye-Movement Photography in Reading Diagnosis and Reading Training," in *Ninth Yearbook National Reading Conference*, 1960, 98–106.
27. Spache, George D., "Is This a Breakthrough in Reading?" *Reading Teacher*, 15 (January 1962), 258–66.
28. Spache, George D., "Rate of Reading—The Machine Approach," pp. 255–72 in *Toward Better Reading* by George D. Spache. Champaign, Ill.: Garrard Publishing, 1963.
29. Spache, George D., "Reading Rate Improvement or Success for the Wrong Reasons," *Journal of Developmental Reading*, 7 (Autumn 1963), 2, 5–6.
30. Spache, George D., "Reading Rate Improvement: Fad, Fantasy, or Fact?" in *Improvement of Reading Through Classroom Practice*, J. Allen Figurel, editor, Proceedings International Reading Association, 9 (1964), 28–31.
31. Taylor, Stanford E., "A Report on Two Studies of the Validity of Eye-Movement Photograph as a Measurement of Reading Performance," in *Reading in a Changing Society*, J. Allen Figurel, editor, Proceedings International Reading Association, 4 (1959), 240–44.
32. Tinker, Miles A., "Apparatus for Recording Eye-Movements," *American Journal of Psychology*, 43 (January 1931), 115–18.
33. Tinker, Miles A., "The Role of Eye-Movements in Diagnostic and Remedial Reading," *School and Society*, 39 (February 3, 1934), 147–48.
34. Tinker, Miles A., "Eye-Movements in Reading," *Journal of Educational Research*, 39 (December 1936), 241–77.
35. Tinker, Miles A., "The Uses and Limitations of Eye-Movement Studies of Reading," in *Psychology of Reading Behavior*, Eighteenth Yearbook National Reading Conference, 1969, 4–8.
36. Traxler, Arthur E., "Value of Controlled Reading: Summary of Opinion and Research," *Journal of Experimental Education*, 11 (June 1943), 280–92.
37. Walton, Howard N., "Vision and Rapid Reading," *American Journal of Optometry and Archives of American Academy of Optometry*, 34 (February 1957), 73–82.
38. Westover, Frederick L., *Controlled Eye-Movement versus Practice Exercises in Reading*. Contributions to Education No. 917. New York: Teachers College, Columbia University, 1946.

Attention to the auditory abilities of poor readers has markedly increased in the past few years, and the exploration of this aspect of reading has broadened considerably. Here we examine the relationships of acuity, discrimination, synthesis, span, and other minor auditory abilities to reading success. Because they have grown out of the interest in auditory skills, a survey of intersensory integration and the learning modalities of pupils is included.

Despite efforts by a number of researchers in the auditory field, there has not been great success in showing that the various subabilities have a major effect upon reading. Rather, as the evidence accumulates, it begins to appear that these auditory performances are often interlinked with each other and with other traits such as an articulation, dialect, and speech development. Because they also tend to interact with instructional

4 Auditory Perception, Intersensory Integration, and Learning Modalities

method, we may expect their significance to vary from one classroom to another. Thus, those proposing specific training exercises for each auditory trait may experience difficulty in justifying their programs except under limited conditions.

Although reading probably involves the integration of data from several sensory channels, it has been challenging to devise measures that simulate this integration and assess it in children. If successful, these explorations might enable us to understand and train cross-modality transfer of information and to refine our reading instruction in this respect. If we can learn to evaluate pupil learning through each and/or several modalities, we could again direct our instruction more efficiently toward the preferred modality.

Keep these questions in mind as you review this diagnostic area.

1. Which of the auditory abilities seem to have logical relationships to reading achievement? How might they influence reading performances under various conditions? In which cases does the research really support these logical relationships?

2. What are some of the problems being encountered in the research on intersensory integration and learning modalities?

T HE STUDY OF THE RELATIONSHIP of auditory abilities to reading achievement has, in recent years, broadened into an exploration not only of the basic characteristics of acuity and discrimination but also of the significance of intersensory integration, as well as the attempt to identify the particular sensory modality through which the child may learn best. As we might expect, the broadening of the field has brought with it a flood of new terms, new tests, and new theories.

SPECIFIC AUDITORY FUNCTIONS

Auditory Acuity

The influence of the facility of the learner in hearing pitches of different levels and loudness upon reading achievement is seldom questioned. The hard-of-hearing and deaf show distinct retardation in reading and in a number of other language skills. Losses in acuity that involve the high tones affect the learner's ability to deal with consonant sounds and blends, although he retains the ability to hear vowel sounds. It is apparent that such children are severely handicapped in responding to the usual phonic sequence that begins with an emphasis upon consonants, blends, and digraphs. As a result, these children hear words in a muffled, indistinct fashion, and they tend to fail in the primary grades, at least (28, 34). In low-tone losses, the child has difficulty with vowel sounds and with *r, g, b, h,* and their blends. Since the words of the primary reading vocabulary (and most words) are not distinguished so much by their vowels as by their consonant sounds, low-tone losses are not a great obstacle to learning to read. Several American dialects, such as that of the Southeast, make weak distinctions among vowel sounds; yet children of this region learn, in general, to read as well as other children do. Although the use of a watch (with a loud tick) or a whisper test of hearing are sometimes recommended, these are unreliable measures of auditory acuity. No true standards for judging the child's hearing can be enunciated for these two measures, for the results will vary from one room to another because of its acoustic qualities, from one teacher to another, and from one watch to the next. Auditory acuity can be determined only by a carefully calibrated audiometric screening test with controlled pitch and loudness reproduction, and then perhaps only at the hands of a relatively experienced examiner.

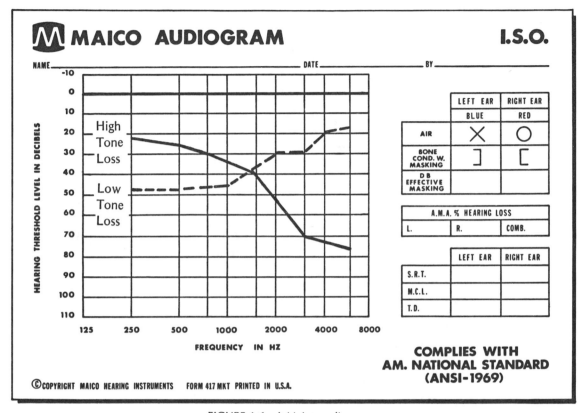

FIGURE 4–1   A Maico audiogram

Auditory Discrimination

By common definition, auditory discrimination is the ability to hear similarities and differences among the sounds of letters. Unfortunately, this concept can be interpreted in a dozen ways, and the measures claiming to test auditory discrimination vary with their author's views. For example, Dykstra (27) compared seven such tests taken from popular readiness and reading tests. Among the tasks proposed were matching a pictured object with a spoken word beginning with the same sound as the name of that object; blending mentally a group of given sounds to match the name of a pictured object: comparing three pronunciations of the name of a pictured object (varying usually in the vowel sound); determining whether given words rhyme; choosing one of several similar words as appropriate to a given context; and, finally, listening to a list of pairs of words to distinguish whether they were identical or dissimilar, when the pair sometimes varies in a single sound as in the Wepman Auditory Discrimination Test (87). Other tests are listed in the References for this chapter (14, 33, 44, 47, 69, 73). It is almost superfluous to point out that Dykstra discovered that these tests of auditory discrimination varied greatly in their intercorrelations, even when they superficially appeared to be somewhat similar.

Another that has recently come upon the market is the Goldman-Fristoe-Woodcock *Test of Auditory Discrimination* (Circle Pines, Minn.: American Guidance Service). It varies from the others in using taped directions to which the pupil reacts by pointing to pictures.

The variations in test content and predictive values tend to yield different implications for the significance of auditory discrimination in early reading success in different research studies. To illustrate, Dykstra's data indicated weak correlations of the tests he analyzed with reading, with even combinations of five or six of the tests accounting for only 36 percent of the variance in first-grade reading (that is, a multiple coefficient of about .60). He concluded that an intelligence test was as good a predictor as any of the auditory tests. In contrast, Thompson (84) claimed that such scores were "highly" prognostic of reading levels in the second grade; and, after reviewing a number of studies, Di Lorenzo (25) ranked auditory discrimination as fifth in value among ten readiness predictors. The experts whose opinions he solicited ranked this ability as second among the same ten. Beery (8) used a test of pure tone discrimination rather than words, finding it a better predictor than the Wepman in a middle socioeconomic group, but only equal to this test in the low socioeconomic population. Correlations of Beery's test with academic achievement in reading and spelling varied from .30 to .51; the Wepman, from .32 to .46.

At fourth grade, Reynolds (67) reported negligible *r*'s between various auditory tests and silent reading abililies. Kerfoot (43) seemed to agree with Dykstra and Beery in his finding that auditory discrimination tests were inferior in general in predictive efficiency to visual discrimination measures, and that intelligence test results were as good as either of these readiness measures in primary grades. Wheeler and Wheeler* likewise found no significant relationship between a test of auditory discrimination and reading in the intermediate grades.

Apparently the importance of a difficulty with auditory discrimination is greater at primary reading levels (because of the phonics demand in the

---

*L. R. Wheeler, and V. D. Wheeler, "A Study of the Relationship of Auditory Discrimination to Silent Reading Abilities," *Journal of Educational Research*, 48 (1954), 103–13.

program?) and varies with sex and socioeconomic status, although it is not a highly significant factor in reading success at any level or in any population. Despite these implications of research, we find many researchers greatly emphasizing the extent of poor auditory discrimination among minority or disadvantaged pupils. For example, this difference was present in the study of Mexican-American primary pupils in Arnold's study (2); and among economically disadvantaged Head Start children, according to Clark and Richards (20). It is cited in many studies of black ghetto children (24). Among low socioeconomic primary children, there appear to be significant differences between good and poor readers in this ability according to Deutsch (24); Oakland (63); and Goetzinger, Dirks, and Baer (30), to mention a few of the typical studies. As a result of their findings, most of these authors demand intensified training in this area for low socioeconomic children, despite the low reliability of such tests in this population.*

In contrast, Venezky and some other language specialists† feel very strongly that the weight of evidence is against poor auditory discrimination as a cause of poor reading among dialect users. The poor reading could as well be attributed to deficiencies in attention and in cognitive development, these experts argue. Venezky points out that most auditory discrimination tests are based on standard English. Thus they demand distinctions not present in dialectal speech. The same version of English is used, of course, in our readers, making these a more difficult and complex task linguistically speaking for the dialect user. But the discriminations demanded in auditory discrimination tests are not inherent in reading or listening because the context supplies such powerful cues. Thus auditory discrimination is poorer for dialect speakers, but only in the usual isolated word pairs—not in context. Moreover, this poor performance on word pairs is not related to the reading comprehension of these pupils.

The weak relationship between auditory discrimination and reading success that we have observed, along with Venezky's cogent arguments, certainly raises doubts regarding special emphasis on this auditory ability for children using dialects.

Morency, Wepman, and Hass (56) have explored the significance of auditory discrimination in its relationship to articulation and reading. In one study, Morency (56) demonstrated that, even in a white middle-class population of first graders, certain speech sounds were not yet developed, as *l, sh,* voiced *th, v, s, z, j,* and *r.* The error ratio on these sounds corresponded to

---

*H. Alan Robinson, "Reliability of Measures Related to Reading Success of Average, Disadvantaged and Advantaged Kindergarten Children," *Reading Teacher,* 20 (December 1966), 203–209.

†R. L. Venezky, *Nonstandard Language and Reading* (Madison: Wisconsin Research and Development Center for Cognitive Learning, 1970.)

the known developmental sequence in children's speech. Furthermore, these errors declined rapidly during the three-year primary period, without any special training. She concludes that speech therapy (and auditory discrimination training?) seems pointless at this time. In a second study, Wepman (87) found the mean reading scores of a group with adequate articulation and auditory discrimination (adequate for their age, in all probability) to be superior to a group low in both these same abilities. But there were no differences between these groups and those of adequate articulation and poor auditory discrimination. We interpret these studies to imply that auditory discrimination is related to articulatory development; that both are not completely developed until about the age of eight or nine (and perhaps later for children in a language-deprived environment); that inaccuracies in either ability are not necessarily a defect but rather a reflection of the child's rate of development; and, finally, since this dual development spontaneously reaches adequacy in the course of time, therapy to correct inaccuracies does not appear needed.

Before the reader accuses us of a laissez-faire attitude toward auditory discrimination training, let us consider the results of such programs. In an apparently uncontrolled study, Lissitz and Cohen (49) affirm the values of auditory discrimination training because it produced gains on a posttest of that ability! Silvaroli and Wheelock believed their taped, programmed material to be very helpful, again because it increased scores on one of two relevant tests (77). Duggins (26) describes a two-year program for black children, with demonstrated effect upon reading achievement. In view of the facts that auditory discrimination plays a very minor role in early reading success, that its development may be intertwined with that in articulation, and that special training programs have not succeeded in showing a strong effect upon reading success (although they may improve auditory discrimination), how much emphasis shall we place upon its development in the primary reading program? Pragmatically, probably only as much as the child needs to deal with the phonics program that is a part of the developmental reading plan. As Jean Robertson has cautioned (70), we must expect variations in the development of articulation and discrimination of sounds, with lesser ability among boys; we must recognize that there is a difference between the abilities to mouth (or apparently hear differences in sounds) and the ability to use these learnings in obtaining meaning from the printed page by the use of phonic analysis.

Auditory Synthesis

In one sense, auditory recognition—or word recognition in reading—demands a synthesis of a series of sounds into a recognizable whole word. In the phonics curriculum, most systems, but not all, attempt to teach children to blend sounds into whole words. In fact, this is the only basic justification for the teaching of letter sounds, although not all phonics series authors are aware of it. This ability to synthesize auditorily is approached in several instruments. Chall, for example (19), was able to show some relationship to certain reading skills of a phoneme-blending test. More recently, Rosner and Simon (72) constructed an Auditory Analysis Test asking the child to repeat a spoken word and then to repeat it again without a specified element, as a beginning, medial, or ending sound. Correlations with reading achievement ranged from .53 in first grade to .84 in the third grade, but decreased to .59 by the sixth grade. When I.Q. was held constant, the respective figures were .40 to .69 (first to third), dropping to .10 in the sixth grade. These results suggest replication of the study in some other than a suburban, white, middle-class population for a fuller evaluation of its merits. If valid in other populations, the test may well serve to indicate those children in need of special help in learning to synthesize and blend sounds during phonics training, at least in the manner tested by Rosner and Simon.

To be as realistic as possible, testing of auditory synthesis must also include evaluation of the child's ability to blend letters together to form a whole word, as he normally does in the phonic analysis of an unknown word in the act of reading. In other words, both analysis-identification and execution of the separate portions of a word, for example, $f + a + t$ equals *fat,* as well as synthesis, *fat* minus *f* equals *at,* should be tested. This testing may well be extended to measuring the child's ability to write a given sound; to listen to several sounds, blend them, and write the resulting word; and to listen to nonsense words and then write them. Additional tests in giving the name of the letter representing a given sound, as well as the usual test of giving a common sound for each grapheme, should be included in this analysis.

There are multiple linkages between letters and sounds that function both in reading and spelling, as we have tried to indicate above, and in an earlier article (80). Perhaps all of these should be explored before attempting to use training programs such as that offered by Rosner.*

Auditory Span

As early as the 1930s, Arthur I. Gates included tests of auditory span as diagnostic instruments in reading disabilities. He dropped their use later because his data never seemed to show consistent differences between poor and good readers. By 1941, when we reviewed causal factors in reading and

---

*J. Rosner, *Phonic Analysis Training and Beginning Reading Skills* (Pittsburgh: Learning Research and Development Center, University of Pittsburgh, 1971).

spelling disabilities (80), the bulk of the evidence seemed to indicate that, although auditory span might be significant in extreme cases, its general relationship with reading success was minimal.   But the authors of many books in diagnostic and remedial reading continue to recommend the use of auditory span measures, such as the digit span of the WISC and the WAIS, the Schuell test (76), the relevant subtests of the Detroit Learning Aptitude battery, and, more recently, the auditory sequencing test of the ITPA battery.   Alone, the digit span test of the WISC may or may not discriminate between good and poor readers (59, 81).   Factor analysis of the WISC indicates that the Arithmetic and Digit Span tests are loaded with what might be termed attention or concentration, and their results should be considered in combination rather than singly.   As for the auditory sequencing (repeating digits) test of the ITPA, studies vary in finding any differences between good and poor readers in this task (17, 15, 39).   Moreover, two studies, at least, indicate that auditory span ability interacts, as we might expect, with instructional method and intelligence (17, 62).

Belle Ruth Witkin's research* indicates considerable interrelationship among auditory discrimination, synthesis, and span.   Her data indicate that apparent defects in auditory discrimination are influenced by deficits in auditory span and synthesis.   She raises the question of the validity of auditory discrimination as a unitary trait.   Witkin also made the observation that variability in various tests of auditory perception is present not only among learning disability cases but also among minimal or mild cerebral dysfunction and among normal pupils.   How, then, do we interpret this variability: as the causes of learning difficulties, as the results of brain damage, or simply as a manifestation of individual differences?   As we did earlier, Witkin remarks also upon the many studies in which auditory memory span tests of various types are found to be related to mental age.

Selma G. Sapir† investigated tests of auditory discrimination from a different viewpoint.   She raised the question of the use of true words versus nonsense syllables and the testing of auditory discrimination by varying initial, medial, or final sounds in the contrasting pairs of words.   She demonstrated that discrimination between words or syllables varying in the initial sound was much easier than hearing differences in ending sounds among kindergartners. Fortunately for many of the current tests, Sapir also showed that there were no significant differences in children's ability in tests using true words or non-

---

*Belle Ruth Witkin, "Auditory Perception—Implications for Language Development," *Journal of Research and Development in Education,* 3 (Fall 1969), 53–71.
†Selma G. Sapir, "Auditory Discrimination with Words and Nonsense Syllables," *Academic Therapy, 7* (Spring 1972), 307–14.

sense syllables. She noted that discrimination between certain sounds was usually not completely mastered by young children, as *v-th* gave a relatively high incidence of errors among the kindergarten population. This observation and Morency's earlier comment on the relationship between articulation development and auditory discrimination should cause some doubts about the validity of the same test for young and older pupils.

Various Auditory Abilities

Auditory reaction time in relation to reading has been explored in at least one study with inconclusive results (3); there does not seem to be any logical reason for expecting it to be significant. Another group of so-called tests of auditory abilities is offered in the Slingerland battery (78). According to the author, these unnormed, unvalidated instruments of unknown reliability will select those children suffering from a "specific language disability." The author offers tests of writing letters and phrases at dictation, writing the letter corresponding to the beginning or ending sound, repeating polysyllabic words, and so on, in this rather unique instrument of unknown merits.

A quick review of our discussion of auditory abilities may well leave the reader with the impression that, except for absolute hearing losses, they are relatively unimportant in children's reading success. Statistically the point is probably true, but in many classrooms this will not be the case. If the instruction places a heavy emphasis upon phonics and teaches children to equate reading with letter-sound analysis, those with poor auditory discrimination or synthesis will indeed be likely to fail, unless they are given intensive training to accelerate their development of these abilities. It is also true that some children with weak auditory skills and articulatory errors do learn to read, and that some children manifesting these deviations because of dialect also learn to read adequately. But in certain reading programs this success is achieved only by tremendous effort and in spite of the handicap imposed by the instructional program. Thus, training in these auditory abilities becomes essential if we wish to make the learning less traumatic in reading programs with strong phonic or oral reading biases. Furthermore, toward the end of the primary ages, if the child's articulation of speech sounds has not adequately developed, speech therapy to accelerate this development would seem indicated. While one may misarticulate sounds and still learn to read, these errors are carried over into spelling and children tend to spell as they pronounce. Correct articulation and discrimination of letter sounds is probably more crucial to spelling than to reading, particularly in the intermediate grades. Thus in many classrooms, training in auditory discrimination and synthesis *is* essential if it can be shown that the children can be helped in these areas.

INTERSENSORY INTEGRATION

In chapter 1, "Reading and Visual Perception Tests," we made reference to the work of Birch and Lefford in their attempts to show the interaction or coordination of various senses in perception (11). We noted that their studies indicated a marked relationship between visual-kinesthetic perception and visual analysis, synthesis, and freehand drawings. Among the implications drawn from these observations, there was the hypothesis that kinesthetic and muscular feedback influence visual motor experience in a reciprocal relationship and thus bear an indirect relationship with reading.

It has been recognized for some time that the visual, oculo-motor, proprioceptive (stimuli arising from within the organism as skeletal or muscular impulses), and motor systems of the human being are integrated in the interpretation of sensory stimuli. The beginnings of visual-haptic integration are manifest as early as twenty weeks of age when the infant reaches to touch an object within his visual field. Some writers believe that the kinesthetic and visceral senses develop first, with the visual and auditory systems serving merely as background or reinforcement for responses. When, eventually, the visual and auditory systems become dominant, the interior systems then serve as reinforcements. Birch and Lefford suggest that visual-haptic integration occurs earlier than haptic-kinesthetic, which, in turn, precedes visual-kinesthetic integration. Other authors suggest that visual-motor integration precedes all other types in the development of man (8). Among the facets of intersensory integration currently being explored (in addition to the work of Birch and his coworkers) are studies of the effects of tilt of the head and body in opposite directions upon errors in perception of the vertical; matching body posture with the direction of sound or light; visual and haptic perception as related to spatial position and orientation of objects; visual and auditory sequential pattern perception; and the interaction of head-eye position and size perception, and so on, as reviewed by Pick and Ryan (65).

Relationships with Reading

Ontogenetically, reading is a late development in man, and we may expect that by the time it is acquired, the development of the various integrative systems is far advanced and very complex. While we may be able to chart the development of each integrative system during infancy and preschool ages, by the time the child reaches school age her integrative systems have become united with each other in subordinate and superordinate relationships of infinite variety. Sorting out the significance of each system for the act of reading, as well as devising developmental or corrective measures, will be a very challenging task. Hence the researches we can cite are obviously preliminary studies.

Jean A. Ayres (4) factor-analyzed sixty-four test scores and believed that she identified the components of sensory integration as auditory language functions, sequencing, reading achievement, and one factor that might possibly reflect hand-hemisphere dominance discrepancy. Hurley (36) in analyzing three tests of short-term memory, three spatial, and four intersensory integration tests, identified five factors. But, as in the Ayres study, reading was a separate factor, and there was no main effect of reading on his measures of intersensory integration.

Among those investigating intersensory integration and reading, a number of studies have employed the Birch-Belmont test of converting visual dot patterns to tapping patterns. With this test, Birch and Belmont (9, 10) found that retarded readers performed more poorly than good readers did in two studies, as did Judith W. Beery (7). The least adequately nourished children in the Cravioto, Gaona, and Birch study (22) performed less well in this same test. Other intersensory tests of colored light stimuli–pure tone are reported to be performed much more poorly among a small group of black poor readers by Katz and Deutsch (40), and a similar pattern was present among British poor readers of average intelligence by Lovell and Gorton (50). But, using the same procedure, Busby and Hurd (18) identified no significant relationships to reading or intelligence, sex, race, or socioeconomic status in a small population, finding rather that the performance simply decreased with age.

Despite its relatively wide use, the Birch and Belmont dot-tapping test has been severely criticized for lack of reliability (reported as .62 for a ten-item test) and for being highly influenced by the factor of intelligence (28, 66). In one of their own studies, Birch and Belmont (10) recognized that the correlations of their test with reading achievement were largely the result of the intelligence factor at primary grade levels. Their correlations with reading were marked (.70) only in the first grade, where the *r* with I.Q. of their test was .56. Correlations with reading dropped to .42 in the second grade and even lower in third and fourth, where the test proved undiscriminative, as the correlations between reading and intelligence increased from .27 at fourth to .83 at sixth. Kahn likewise discovered that, with intelligence held constant, the *r*'s of the dot-tapping test became insignificant for most reading skills in grades two to six (38).   Ford reports that some types of oral reading errors were related to this test, but they dwindled to insignificance when intelligence was held constant (29).

Because of these findings, several experimenters have modified the Birch-Belmont visual-auditory approach.   Among these are Muehl and Kremenak (57), who varied it to permit testing of auditory-visual, visual-visual, visual-auditory, and auditory-auditory performances.   The auditory-visual was most closely related to reading among first graders, but some scoring high in the test performed poorly in reading.   Blank and Bridger (12) changed the test to a temporal-spatial integration—the matching of light flashes to dot patterns—and found no differences in this integrative matching between good and poor readers.   In verbalizing the light patterns, however, poor readers were inferior.   This may have reflected poorer cognitive skill in categorizing as much as it did any deficit in intersensory integration.   Sabatino and Hayden* included the Birch-Belmont in a battery of tests of reading, perception, behavior, and intelligence.   Factor analysis revealed the Birch-Belmont, auditory perception, and arithmetic achievement as one of the factors of the battery.   But this factor did not include reading.   A second study by the same authors analyzed and contrasted factors by dividing this group into a young (7-7 mean CA) versus an older group (mean CA 11-4).   The A-V factor was present in both groups, although in the older group it shifted from perceptual to language tests as major contributors.   Academic achievement was again a separate factor relatively independent of the A-V factor.   These three studies seem to imply that there is an A-V integration factor as measured by the Birch-Belmont, but that its relevance to reading—and even its nature—varies with different samples and ages.

Another approach to analysis of audio-visual integration was attempted by Dombush and Basow.†   Two sets of digits ranging from three to five in number were presented at different rates.   Children were told to write down first the visual or auditory set or vice versa of the two number series presented simultaneously.   The results indicated that more items were retained from the channel reported first rather than second.   Modality and rate interacted as visual recall increased with rate of presentation.   Auditory recall did not vary with rate and was consistently higher than visual.   There were, though, no significant differences in this study of auditory and visual short-term memory for good and poor readers.

---

*D. A. Sabatino, and D. L. Hayden, "Psycho-educational Study of Selected Behavioral Variables with Children Failing the Elementary Grades," *Journal of Experimental Education,* 38 (1970), 40–57.

†Rhea L. Dombush, and Susan Basow, "The Relationship between Auditory and Visual Short-term Memory and Reading Achievement, *Child Development,* 41 (1970), 1033–44.

Rodenborn* used an auditory memory digit span test, a visual memory measure of matching capital letters (exposed for two seconds) to a multiple-choice set of answers, and lengthened the Birch-Belmont dot-tapping test to twenty-four items, using a pure tone to replace the pencil taps. The reliabilities for his tests appeared to be exceptionally good: .92 for the tone-dot patterns; .87 for the digit span, and .92 for the visual memory measure. He found that scores on the auditory-visual test increased in almost a straight line from the first to sixth grade in keeping with chronological or mental age. He noted the absence of the plateau in performances in this performance, in contrast to the studies cited above. Scores on this test also increased with oral accuracy on the Gilmore Oral Reading Test up to grade scores at the sixth-grade level, although he does not cite a correlation between these variables.

Intercorrelations among Rodenborn's tests were fairly low, ranging from .40 between the auditory-visual and auditory memory to .53 between auditory-visual and visual memory. The fact that these intercorrelations are so much lower than the separate test reliabilities implies that the abilities are relatively distinct and independent. Moreover, results of any of these three tests added to mental age did little to increase the prediction of oral reading accuracy. Rodenborn has demonstrated that the dot pattern-tone test can be improved and helped to function over a wider range of ages to enable us to discover the significance of this ability for certain types of reading performances.

In several studies, Sterritt and his coworkers were unable to find significant relationships of the Birch-Belmont test with reading (82). They suggested that the critical intersensory factor in reading might well be auditory pattern perception rather than the ability to transpose stimuli from visual to auditory or vice versa. They conceive of auditory-visual integration as a temporal-spatial relationship (like Blank and Bridger) in which there is involved the auditory recognition of a sequence in time and a visual recognition of a sequence of objects in space. They consider their interpretations analogous to translating speech (auditory sequences) into visual sequences (printed speech). Moreover, they recognize subprocesses such as auditory sequence perception, visual sequence perception, temporal sequences, and spatial sequences, as well as auditory-visual and temporal-spatial integration. With this analysis in mind, Sterritt et al. (82, 83) designed nine new tests as well as a modified Birch and Belmont test, administering these to forty third graders.

---

*Leo V. Rodenborn, Jr., "The Importance of Memory and Integration Factors to Oral Reading Ability," *Journal of Reading Behavior*, 3 (Winter 1970), 51–59.

They hypothesized the order of difficulty of these tests drawing upon the earlier work, but discovered that this order was due largely to the difficulty of the modality of the first pattern rather than following a logical sequence or reflecting presumed cross-modality difficulties. Only two of their tests yielded significant r's with reading, the visual-temporal–auditory-temporal correlating .41 with a reading test; the auditory-temporal–auditory-temporal giving an r of .55 with the phonics subtest of the Stanford. The visual-spatial test was easier than the auditory-temporal or the visual-temporal, according to this study.

The Sterritt group was unable to interpret logically the variations in the difficulty and relationships to reading of their subtests. They could not understand why tests requiring translation from one modality to another were not even so hard as some without a cross-modality transfer, or why none of the six types of tests was materially more significantly related to reading than any other type. These frank admissions of puzzlement over their own results are certainly refreshing, however, and perhaps a reassurance of continued research in this area. It is greatly to be desired that these studies will continue to refine their definitions and instruments, to explore the many intersensory relationships that exist, and to try to define the significance of these for reading success. We cannot see any justification at this time for practices in administering some test or other labeled as a measure of intersensory integration, categorizing those children who do poorly as learning disability cases, and subjecting them to some special treatment that may seem logical but has unknown validity in affecting reading.

In the study mentioned earlier, Selma G. Sapir offered some observations regarding current thinking about intersensory integration. She disagrees with Blank and Bridger (12) that verbal mediation or reacting to the meanings of the test words is a factor in auditory discrimination. And she does not see this verbal mediation as an essential stage within the auditory modality before the child can develop the ability to handle stimuli from both visual and auditory modalities as in the act of reading, as some researchers claim. Sapir feels that the ability to integrate stimuli, or to establish equivalences within a modality between words and auditory or visual presentations, and the child's use of verbal mediation have different relevance to the individual child.

Sapir is intimating that the findings that some poor readers seem unable to integrate stimuli from two modalities may represent a difficulty in auditory discrimination, or in the visual modality, or the auditory, or in verbal mediation. She recommends approaching remediation more specifically in one of these four areas of possible deficit rather than assuming an intersensory difficulty.   At this stage in the development of our knowledge about intersensory integration, we are inclined to agree with Sapir that diagnoses of intersensory integration deficits may be ignoring other developmental variations.

John Paul Jones* has recently reviewed this area in detail, describing many of the experiments that we have cited.   He appears to draw the conclusion that intersensory transfer, although highly related to intelligence, appears to be related to word recognition, at least among primary pupils.   The relationship to comprehension does not seem to be as significant, in the studies cited by Jones.

Jones also cites several studies of perceptual shifting, for example, reaction time in response to random arrangements of light or tone stimuli.   Of the five investigations he cites, only one with black boys found significant differences in cross-modal shifting between good and poor readers.   Another study uncovered the fact that children whose reaction times were less affected by the shifts in stimuli appeared to have larger sight vocabularies.   Since sight vocabulary is so often acquired at the primary levels by repetitive drill as with flash cards or blackboard drills or seatwork matching drills, the implications of this last study apparently has some logic.   Those children who can react quickly and consistently to these varied drills do succeed better in learning the sight vocabulary, this study seems to be telling us.   Perhaps we should explore the child's reaction time to cross-modal shifting (or to varied types of presentations of words) before selecting an appropriate instructional procedure.

LEARNING MODALITIES

Long before the inception of intersensory research, reading clinicians accepted a modality concept of learning implying that some children learn better when taught to read by instruction keyed to one sense, as visual, auditory, or kinesthetic.   We can all remember, for example, the impact of the teachings of Grace Fernald, who sponsored her own version of a kinesthetic approach to academic learning.   Reasoning perhaps that more of the same idea was even better, many present-day remedial workers stress a VAKT–visual-auditory-kinesthetic-tactile method as the best possible approach, simply because it is multimodal (58).   Sensory modality approaches are currently being recom-

---

*John Paul Jones, *Intersensory Transfer, Perceptual Shifting, Modal Difference and Reading*, ERIC/CRIER and IRA Reading Information Series (Newark, Del.: International Reading Association, 1972).

mended in particular for the economically disadvantaged child, although why the concept is more essential here than with other children is not clear (68). In a later discussion of innovative approaches in chapter 13, we allude to the Neurological Impress method of reinforcing children's reading by reading along with them, a crude application of the multimodal concept. Hagin, Silver, and Hersh (31) have evolved their own version of modality emphasis with the avowed purpose of overcoming what they identify as deficits among poor readers. Their system moves from visual matching, copying, and recall to intersensory matching of input of one modality to another to final training at the verbal level with oral and written language. The public market now offers many multimodal devices, such as Borg-Warner's System 80 of a combined filmstrip and record presentation, and General Electric's Project Life programmed filmstrip projector with response buttons. At first glance, it appears that this latter device purports to teach reading by requiring nonverbal responses.

Two testing instruments are now available, although not widely known, for attempting to relate preferred modality to mode of reading instruction. Both the Mills Learning Methods Test and the experimental Peabody Differential Learning Test (56, 60) measure the child's actual learning of real words—or those in an artificial language in the case of the Peabody—in comparative classroom lessons emphasizing each single possible mode. Field trials of these tests have demonstrated certain facts that ought to be known to all teachers of reading:

1. Children do differ in their learning from one modality to another.
2. The most effective modality can be established for many but not all children (the modality seeming to be of little importance among children of high mental ability, and the auditory seeming to be least effective among low-ability pupils).
3. Despite the common assumption to the contrary, a multimodal approach is not generally superior in producing learning but rather is more effective only for some children.
4. These instruments are of high reliability and validity for reading instruction.

The ITPA has been recommended by some for modality testing, despite the criticisms of inconsistency between theoretical description and actual subtests, restricted norms, low reliability for subtests, some tendency to measure cognitive rather than psycholinguistic skills (51, 86), and deviations in the profile of subtest scores even in the standardization population (5). The tendency of writers to refer to the subtests of this battery by any of a half-dozen names according to their peculiar interpretations of the test functions is also an irritation to reviewers of the literature.   There is little consistency in the results of the attempts to find significance for reading in the ITPA subtests or the modalities or intersensory functions that they purport to measure.   For example, in a factor analysis of this battery and the WISC, McLeod (52, 53) identified what he calls an Integrative-Sequencing factor that included the auditory-vocal-automatic, visual-motor-sequential, and auditory-vocal-sequential ITPA subtests, as well as the digit-span of the WISC, a factor that made the greatest contribution to reading of those he was able to sort out.   Other WISC and ITPA tests were not so discriminative as this with respect to reading.   In contrast, Brown and Rice (15) report only the auditory-vocal-sequential subtest as predictive of achievement among low I.Q. children; Kass (39) found the auditory-vocal-automatic, visual-motor-sequential distinguished poor from good readers; and Bruininks, Lucker, and Gropper (17) found that children who learned poorly with the i.t.a. approach were poorer in auditory decoding, auditory-vocal-automatic, auditory-vocal-association, and auditory-vocal sequencing.   If taught by traditional methods, the inferiorities of those children who failed in reading well were present in the auditory-vocal-association and visual-motor-association subtests only.   In two studies, Slobodzian (79) discovered contradictory results with respect to the auditory-vocal-association and the visual-decoding tests and their significance for reading success.   As a result, she concluded that the ITPA was of doubtful value as a predictor of reading achievement, but still recommends its use as a diagnostic tool to guide remediation (despite its inconsistencies?).

Margaret M. Clark's* study of Scottish primary children who persisted in reading failure through the first three years despite average intelligence is relevant here.   She found little differentiation among the seventy persistent failures in the subtests of the ITPA.   In fact, the automatic sequential tests, which several of the other studies have cited as differential, were the best performances of the Scottish children.   This brief review of the criticisms of the ITPA and the research in relation to the modality concept does not seem to indicate that this instrument is a very consistent or effective tool in this area.

There are a number of isolated research studies that are concerned with the modality concept.   Among these are Arnold's (1) teaching-testing experiment (in the Mills fashion) with twelve retarded readers.   The number of words learned in sixteen sessions was more dependent upon initial reading level than upon method.   No method evidenced greater efficiency; the kinesthetic was the least effective.   King and Muehl (45) contrasted word-

---

*Margaret M. Clark, *Reading Difficulties in Schools.* (Baltimore: Penguin Books, 1970).

picture, saying word to child, picture plus auditory, auditory plus child echoing the word, and picture plus auditory plus echoic. The most effective presentation for similar words was the picture or the echoic; for dissimilar words, auditory was only slightly more effective than other modes were. In other words, if we translate this study into common classroom procedures, no one method or multimodal presentation is generally superior for a group in learning a list of dissimilar words.

Using nonsense syllables and three-letter nouns to be paired with a single letter, Cooper and Gaeth (21) found visual presentation superior in general at all levels from grades four to twelve, but nouns were learned more readily through the visual at four to six, and by auditory presentation at ten and twelve. Otto (64) also found that the patterns of learning aptitude vary with age and show individual growth patterns among both good and poor readers. Working with adults, Johnson and Cortright (37) demonstrated that a visual-auditory (matching word heard to that just seen) was their most significant cross-modality for learning, but that, as adult reading ability increased, visual-visual matching became a more effective mode. Morency's longitudinal study in primary grades (55) indicated variations in the rate of growth of preferred modalities, development of some but not others for some children, and little relationship to reading achievement in the first grade. Collectively this group of studies appears to imply that, although learning does differ in varying modalities from one learner to another, these modality preferences exhibit some developmental changes in time and in response to growing reading ability.

Prospective purchasers of some of the new programmed auditory devices might profit from the reading of several evaluations of this approach. Hill and Hecker (35) and Keislar and McNeil (42) both explored the learning of words from tapes. Hill and Hecker contrasted this mode with visual recognition of line drawings of words; Keislar and McNeil with auditory-echoic (child repeats words after tape). In both experiments, there appeared to be little transfer from the pure auditory taped presentation to visual recognition. Mary H. Neville (61, 62) reports two relevant studies of learning modality. In one, a group of new words were inserted in a story that children either (a) read aloud twice, then once silently, (b) heard the teacher read, then read the story aloud and again silently, (c) read twice silently, then listened as a child read the story. Learning of the new words was better under (b) than (a) for lower-level children, while fluency of oral reading was better after (b) than (a) for upper-level readers. Auditory span was negatively related to learning ($-.463$) for the (c) group. In her second study, Neville's children (a) read silently, (b) read orally, or (c) were read to. In accuracy of later oral reading of the selection, there were no treatment differences; but the listening presentation was significantly better for the learning of new words and for comprehension of the selection. These four studies may indicate that the learning of new words is greater among primary children when auditory presentation in context is reinforced by an echoic or silent reading reinforcement.

Another interpretation of a multisensory method of learning to read is offered in an article by Linn and Ryan.* First graders were taught the names and sounds of letters through tracing and vocalizing plus visual study, as part of the word recognition program. The group was divided into seventy-two matched pairs equated in I.Q. for the experimental and control groups. End-of-the-year testing favored significantly the children given the multisensory training in both reading and spelling at all I. Q. levels. It is not entirely clear which component of the multisensory training really produced the superior reading and spelling. A heavy emphasis upon synthetic phonics often produces similar test results; hence we are not certain whether tracing or vocalizing—or the combination of all three activities—or the phonics alone was responsible for the outcomes.

The experiment of Linder and Fillmer (48) may have been influenced by the selection of poor black readers. In sequential recall, the auditory (calling off names of objects) was poorer than visual or auditory-visual for objects, digit span, and colors. Blau and Blau (13) take an unusual stance in this problem area by suggesting that the visual modality may actually interfere with learning! They prefer what they call a nonvisual VAKT presentation in which the word to be learned is traced on the back of a blindfolded child and spelled aloud, letter by letter, by the teacher. The child traces three dimensional letters and arranges these to spell out the word, looks at it, then writes it. We hope that these authors will answer the many questions that can be raised about this technique and the apparent contradiction of its rationale by the negative evidence regarding the role of letter recall in word recognition.

Two other studies of cross-modality teaching are relevant here. Pick, Pick, and Thomas† found that distinctive feature training in one modality seemed to transfer to other sense modalities. Transfer was present from touch to vision in tracing blocks with raised letters to printed words in their experiment. Just what this study means is not entirely clear. Is it a justifica-

---

*J. R. Linn, and T. J. Ryan, "The Multi-Sensory-Motor Method of Teaching Reading," *Journal of Experimental Education*, 36 (1968), 57–59.

†A. Pick, H. Pick, Jr., and M. Thomas, "Cross-Modal Transfer and Improvement of Form Discrimination," *Journal of Experimental Child Psychology*, 3 (1966), 279–88.

tion for multimodality training? For which types of children will it be helpful, and how do we discover the aptitudes of these children? What sequences in multimodality will be most effective in general and for different children? What part does sheer memory play in this apparent transfer? Are we simply reinforcing memory or actually providing multimodal associations for the pupils?

In another article, Pick and Ryan (65) point out that when two normally corresponding sources of information—such as the printed page and the narration from a tape recorder—are incongruent (as when the child fails to keep pace with the recorder in his silent reading), the conflict is called biasing. One or the other of the modalities tends to function better.

Our observations of children attempting to read while following a taped version of the same material justify this caution of Pick and Ryan and make us wonder whether many multimodal presentations are really functioning in the intended manner. Other questions inherent in this multimodal research are the lack of information on the significance of the modality preferences of the learners; the possibility of interference of modality preference in a multimodal presentation, that is, a tuning out of one mode; and whether the redundancy of a multimodal presentation results in cue summation or cue reduction.

Teaching to Modalities

There are only a few experimental studies that have tried to explore the ultimate outcomes of directing instruction toward a particular learning modality. We recognize, of course, that these studies are handicapped by the lack of proven validity of the instruments used to determine the preferred modalities of their subjects. There is also the modifying fact that teaching to a modality is still a theoretical hypothesis. At this stage in the development of research in the area, we cannot be certain exactly what the diagnostic tests that we employ are measuring, how stable the phenomenon we observe really is, or for how long the indications of the tests should be followed in reading instruction.

Several attempts have been made to relate instruction to the apparent preferred learning modality of children. Bateman (6) and Harris (32) tried the practice with first graders, and in his doctoral dissertation Bruininks (16) attempted to relate modality to mode of presentation. Bateman and Bruininks used the ITPA to identify the preferred modality but, like Harris, could find no interaction among modality, mode of presentation, and the learning of words. These results are not encouraging, but, of course, they do not thoroughly refute the inherent logic of teaching to modality.

Jones mentions several other relatively inconclusive studies testing the hypothesis that teaching to the child's apparent preference would produce greater learning.   Helen M. Robinson* found no differences among high visual–high auditory, high visual–low auditory, or low visual–low auditory groups in silent or oral reading when taught by a sight (basal reader) or phonic method.   The low visual–high auditory group did, however, show greater silent reading achievement under the phonic method.   Ringler, Smith, and Cullinan† used a New York University Modality Test to identify learning preferences of 128 first-grade children.   In learning a list of fifty words, there were no relationships apparent between modality preference, mode of presentation, and learning.

Using the Mills test to determine preferred learning modality for nonsense syllables rather than words, Cooper‡ found that modality preference appeared to be an individual matter and more important for good than for poor readers.   Good readers learned significantly better in all modalities except the visual, in which they did not differ from poor readers.   Good readers retained significantly better in the kinesthetic and combination modalities than did poor readers.   Variation in learning and ultimate retention after twenty-four hours was greater among poor than among good readers.

Bruininks§ identified twenty pupils of high visual–low auditory abilities, matching them with a similar number with the reverse pattern.   Six tests of visual and auditory abilities were used for this identification in this low socioeconomic group.   Each type was then taught fifteen unknown words by a visual and again by an auditory approach, as in the Mills test.   The group averaged eight years of age and 90 in I.Q.   Bruininks found no differences in learning according to method, the child's dominant modality, or the order of the lessons.   Repeated trials of this effort to relate pupil learning to dominant modality would have been more conclusive, of course, than was this one comparative trial.   But the general results are consonant with those of longer studies.

As Wolpert¶ has implied perhaps the reason that many attempts to

---

*Helen M. Robinson, "Visual and Auditory Modalities Related to Two Methods for Beginning Reading," *AERA Paper Abstracts, 1968,* 74–75.

†L. H. Ringler, I. L. Smith, and B. E. Cullinan, "Modality Preference, Differentiated Presentation of Reading Tasks, and Word Recognition of First-Grade Children" (Paper presented at the International Reading Association Convention, 1971).

‡J. David Cooper, "A Study of the Learning Modalities of Good and Poor First Grade Readers," in *Reading Methods* and *Teacher Improvement,* Nila Banton Smith, editor. (Newark, Del.: International Reading Association, 1971).

§R. H. Bruininks, "Teaching Word Recognition to Disadvantaged Boys," *Journal of Learning Disabilities,* 3 (1970), 28–37.

¶Edward M. Wolpert, "Modality and Reading: A Perspective," *Reading Teacher,* 24 (April 1971), 640–43.

relate various tests of intersensory integration or learning modality to reading have been inconclusive is the fact that such tests have not paralleled the reading process. Tests of pure tone, light dots, reaction time, digits, objects, pictures, and the like, often deal with relatively nonverbal learning. Can such nonreading tasks actually predict the best learning modality for the child in the task of word recognition? Moreover, the response to a printed word is, and must be, an intersensory or multimodal act of visual recognition, auditory sensations, and voco-motor kinesthetic sensations in the speech mechanism. Wolpert questions whether it is realistic to speak of an auditory, or a visual, or a kinesthetic approach to word recognition as though they stressed unimodal learning.

Reviewers of the studies in modality research attribute the contradictory results to four other variables. First, there is the factor of practice or the previous experience of the learner with a particular mode. Second, age appears to be related both to modality performance and practice. Auditory presentations, for example, may be superior to visual for young children, but this difference diminishes with age (and practice). The third variable is the type of material to be learned. The mode of presentation appears less significant when meaningful materials are the learning task than when disconnected or meaningless materials are offered.

A fourth variable is the mode of apprehension, the manner in which the learner translates the task during attempts at storing it. The learner may readily translate the material to be learned into other terms than those by which it is presented. Hence the modality employed for the presentation may often be less important than the mediating processes of the learner.

We suggest adding several other variables that have obviously influenced the results of attempts to teach children by presentation through a seemingly preferred modality. We are not certain that many of the tests used to ascertain the preferred modality are very valid or efficient. Sensory defects, as of vision or auditory abilities, have not been assessed among the subjects in most experiments on modality teaching. Finally, we are not at all certain that learning to read a word is or can be presented as a unimodal experience, as Wolpert has already suggested.

Multimodal Learning

In an earlier discussion, we expressed the view that teaching to a preferred modality may not be as logical as it appears. The learning of words is certainly dependent upon much more than the particular mode of presentation employed in a reading lesson, if there is anything at all to the concept of intersensory integration. A word is more than a visual or auditory or even kinesthetic image that will be recognized readily in new contexts after a certain number of reinforcements through one or the other modality. A word is probably a whole group of visual, auditory, muscular, visual-motor, and cross-modality associations. In other words, it has depth of meaning, in the intersensory sense. Why, then, should we expect to find that presenting the word a number of times through only one modality is more likely to result in its permanent retention?

We cite the studies of Samuels (74) and Wittrock (75) and Rohwer (71) on the role of meaningful associations among words in their learning. These studies again demonstrate that there are meaningful semantic and syntactic relationships among words, as adjective-noun, noun-verb-noun, and experiential associations as moon-sky-light-star. How would teaching through one modality capitalize on these syntactic, semantic and experiential associations for words?

The results of the studies of the effectiveness of modality teaching and of these in linguistic and experiential relationships among words seems to lead us toward trying a multimodal approach to teaching word recognition. Psychological theories of cue summation imply that learning increases with the number of available cues. The stimulus generalization principle implies that information gain increases as a testing situation becomes more similar to the media presentation system. In contradiction, there is the observed phenomenon of cue reduction in which the learner presented with multiple cues to word recognition (as in experiments employing color as an aid) tends to select one cue to retain—which may be the word or the color. Opinions regarding the values of multichannel instruction are likewise quite contradictory (85), with some writers defending, others flatly rejecting such an approach. In our opinion, we must answer these questions of the relative effectiveness of a modality emphasis or a multimodal presentation or the usual eclectic teaching of words, if we are going to spend our instructional time and our budget for teaching devices wisely. It is apparent that tests of learning modality and intersensory integration need revision. To be meaningful to reading instruction, such tests probably must become more closely identical with the verbal task of learning words, perhaps in the manner of the Mills and Peabody tests that we mentioned earlier. Perhaps then future researchers will sort out the role of the various sensory modalities in the multimodal act of word recognition.

LEARNING PROJECT

Read the research report on auditory discrimination in *Reading Research Quarterly*, 1 (Spring 1966), 5–34.   To clarify your thinking about the role of auditory discrimination in reading disabilities and its proper place in remediation, answer these questions as you read this research.

1. What appear to be the implications of the research prior to Dykstra's in (a) comparisons of good and poor readers; (b) correlations between auditory discrimination and reading achievement?

2. In Dykstra's correlation analysis, (a) is chronological age highly related to auditory discrimination; (b) is intelligence highly related; (c) are the various auditory tests closely related?

3. In the use of the regression equations, which predictor was consistently the best for word recognition?   Which of the auditory tests were consistently good predictors, and which were the poorest?

4. Which predictor was the best for paragraph reading?   Was this the same as in word recognition?

5. Why do you suppose that two tests as similar as the Making Auditory Discriminations and the Discrimination of Beginning Sounds are so different in effectiveness?

6. Why are even the largest correlations between any of the auditory discrimination tests and either word recognition or paragraph reading so low?   Under what circumstances might these correlations be somewhat higher and more significant?

7. What does Dykstra finally conclude about the values of testing auditory discrimination among beginning first graders?   What alternative does he suggest?

REFERENCES

1. Arnold, Richard D., "Four Methods of Teaching Word Recognition to Disabled Readers," *Elementary School Journal*, 68 (1968), 269–74.
2. Arnold, Richard D., and Wist, Anne H., "Auditory Discrimination Abilities of Disadvantaged Anglo- and Mexican-American Children," *Elementary School Journal*, 70 (March 1970), 295–99.
3. Auxter, David, "Reaction Time of Children with Learning Disabilities," *Academic Therapy*, 6 (Winter 1970–71), 151–54.
4. Ayres, Jean A., "Deficits in Sensory Integration in Educationally Handicapped Children," *Journal of Learning Disabilities*, 2 (1969), 160–68.
5. Bateman, Barbara, "A Reference Line for Use with the ITPA," *Journal of School Psychology*, 5 (Winter 1967), 128–35.

6. Bateman, Barbara, "The Efficacy of an Auditory and a Visual Method of First Grade Reading Instruction with Auditory and Visual Learners," *Curriculum Bulletin,* School of Education, University of Oregon, 23 (1967), 6–14.

7. Beery, Judith W., "Matching of Auditory and Visual Stimuli by Average and Retarded Readers," *Child Development,* 38 (1967), 827–33.

8. Beery, Keith E., *Visual-Motor Integration Monograph.* Chicago: Follett Publishing, 1967.

9. Birch, Herbert G., and Belmont, Lillian, "Auditory-Visual Integration in Normal and Retarded Readers," *American Journal of Orthopsychiatry,* 34 (October 1964), 852–61.

10. Birch, Herbert G., and Belmont, Lillian, "Auditory-Visual Integration, Intelligence and Reading Ability in School Children," *Perceptual Motor Skills,* 20 (February 1965), 295–305.

11. Birch, Herbert G., and Lefford, Arthur, "Visual Differentiation, Intersensory Integration, and Voluntary Motor Control," *Monographs of the Society for Research in Child Development,* 32, No. 2 (1967), 1–87.

12. Blank, Marion, and Bridger, W. H., "Deficiencies in Verbal Labeling in Retarded Readers," *American Journal of Orthopsychiatry,* 36 (1966), 840–47.

13. Blau, Harold, and Blau, Harriett, "A Theory of Learning to Read," *Reading Teacher,* 22 (November 1968), 126–29, 144.

14. *Boston University Speech-Sound Discrimination Picture Test.* Boston: W. Pronovost, Department of Speech, Boston University.

15. Brown, Louis F., and Rice, James A., "Psycholinguistic Differentiation of Low I.Q. Children," *Mental Retardation,* 5 (February 1967), 16–20.

16. Bruininks, R. H., "Relationship of Auditory and Visual Perceptual Strengths to Methods of Teaching Word Recognition Among Disadvantaged Negro Boys," doctoral dissertation, George Peabody College for Teachers, 1968.

17. Bruininks, R. H., Lucker, William G., and Gropper, Robert L., "Psycholinguistic Abilities of Good and Poor Reading Disadvantaged First-Graders," *Elementary School Journal,* 70 (April 1970), 378–86.

18. Busby, W. A., and Hurd, D. E., "Relationships of Auditory and Visual Reaction Time to Reading Achievement," *Perceptual and Motor Skills,* 27 (1968), 447–50.

19. Chall, Jeanne, and Roswell, N., *The Roswell-Chall Auditory Blending Test.* New York: Essay Press, 1963.

20. Clark, Ann D., and Richards, Charlotte J., "Auditory Discrimination among Economically Disadvantaged and Non-disadvantaged Preschool Children," *Exceptional Children,* 33 (1966), 259–62.

21. Cooper, J. C., Jr., and Gaeth, J. H., "Interactions of Modality with Age and Meaningfulness in Verbal Learning," *Journal of Educational Psychology,* 58 (1967), 41–44.

22. Cravioto, Joaquin, Gaona, Carlos Espinosa, and Birch, Herbert G., "Early Malnutrition and Auditory-Visual Integration in School-Age Children," *Journal of Special Education,* 2 (1967), 75–82.

23. Denison, Joseph W., "Perceptual Influences in the Primary Grades: An Alternative Comparison," *Journal of School Psychology,* 7 (1968–69), 38–46.

24. Deutsch, Cynthia P., "Auditory Discrimination and Learning Social Factors," *Merrill-Palmer Quarterly of Behavior and Development,* 10 (July 1964), 277–96.

25. DiLorenzo, Louis T., Salter, Ruth, and Hayden, Robert, "Empirical Bases for a Prekindergarten Curriculum for Disadvantaged Children," paper presented at Educational Research Association of New York State, November 7, 1968.
26. Duggins, Lydia A., *Auditory Perception in the Beginning Reading Program.* Special Education Clinic, Research Report Bulletin No. 1. Hammond: Southeastern Louisiana College, 1956.
27. Dykstra, Robert, "Auditory Discrimination Abilities and Beginning Reading Achievement," *Reading Research Quarterly,* 1 (Spring 1966), 5–34.
28. Evans, James R., "Auditory and Auditory-Visual Integration Skills as They Relate to Reading," *Reading Teacher,* 22 (April 1969), 625–29.
29. Ford, Marguerite P., "Auditory-Visual and Tactual-Visual Integration in Relation to Reading Ability," *Perceptual and Motor Skills,* 24 (1967), 831–41.
30. Goetzinger, C. P., Dirks, D. D., and Baer, C. J., "Auditory Discrimination and Visual Perception in Good and Poor Readers," *Annals of Otology, Rhinology and Laryngology,* 69 (1960), 121–36.
31. Hagin, Rosa A., Silver, A. A., and Hersh, Marilyn P., "Specific Reading Disability: Teaching by Stimulation of Deficit Perceptual Areas," in *Reading and Inquiry,* J. Allen Figurel, editor, Proceedings International Reading Association, 10 (1965), 368–70.
32. Harris, Albert J., "Individualizing First-Grade Reading According to Specific Learning Aptitudes," Research Report, Office of Research and Evaluation, Division of Teacher Education, City University of New York, 1965.
33. Haspiel, George, and Bloomer, Richard H., "Maximum Auditory Perception (MAP) Word List," *Journal of Speech and Hearing Disorders,* 26 (May 1961), 156–63.
34. Henry, Sibyl, "Children's Audiograms in Relation to Reading Achievement," *Pedagogical Seminary and Journal of Genetic Psychology,* 70 (June 1947), 211–13; 71 (September 1947), 3–63.
35. Hill, Suzanne D., and Hecker, E., "Auditory and Visual Learning of a Paired-Associate Task by Second Grade Children," *Perceptual and Motor Skills,* 23 (1966), 814.
36. Hurley, O. L., "Perceptual Integration and Reading Problems," *Exceptional Children,* 35 (1968), 207–15.
37. Johnson, Raymond L., and Cortright, Richard W., "Auditory and Visual Word Recognition in Beginning Adult Readers," pp. 298–305 in *Reading Goals for the Disadvantaged,* J. Allen Figurel, editor. Newark, Del.: International Reading Association, 1970.
38. Kahn, D., "The Development of Auditory-Visual Integration and Reading Achievement," doctoral dissertation, Columbia University, 1965.
39. Kass, Corrine E., "The Psycholinguistic Abilities of Retarded Readers," *Kansas Studies in Education,* 18 (1968), 35–47.
40. Katz, Phyllis A., and Deutsch, M., "Relation of Auditory-Visual Shifting to Reading Achievement," *Perceptual and Motor Skills,* 17 (1963), 327–32.
41. Katz, Phyllis, and Deutsch, M., *Visual and Auditory Efficiency and Its Relationship to Reading in Children.* Cooperative Research Project No. 1099. Washington, D.C.: Office of Education, 1963.
42. Keislar, Evan R., and McNeil, John D., "Oral and Non-Oral Methods of Teaching Reading," *Educational Leadership,* 25 (May 1968), 761–64.

43. Kerfoot, James Fletcher, "The Relationship of Selected Auditory and Visual Reading Readiness Measures to First Grade Reading Achievement and Second Grade Reading and Spelling Achievement," doctoral dissertation, University of Minnesota, 1964.
44. Kimmel, G. M., and Wahl, J., "Screening Test for Auditory Perception," *Academic Therapy,* 5 (1970), 317–19.
45. King, Ethel M., and Muehl, S., "Different Sensory Cues as Aids in Beginning Reading," *Reading Teacher,* 19 (1965), 163–68.
46. Kirk, S. A., McCarthy, J. J., and Kirk, W. D., *Illinois Test of Psycholinguistic Abilities.* Urbana: University of Illinois Press, 1968.
47. *Lindamood Auditory Conceptualization Test.* Boston: Teaching Resources.
48. Linder, Ronald, and Fillmer, Henry T., "Auditory and Visual Performance of Slow Readers," *Reading Teacher,* 24 (October 1970), 17–22.
49. Lissitz, Robert W., and Cohen, Sidney L., "A Brief Description and Evaluation of the Syracuse Oral Language Development Program," *Reading Teacher,* 24 (October 1970), 47–50.
50. Lovell, K., and Gorton, A., "A Study of Some Differences Between Backward and Normal Readers of Average Intelligence," *British Journal of Educational Psychology,* 38 (1968), 240–48.
51. McCarthy, James J., "Notes on the Validity of the ITPA," *Mental Retardation,* 3 (April 1965), 25–26.
52. McLeod, John, *Dyslexia in Young Children: A Factorial Study with Special Reference to the ITPA,* University of Illinois IREC Papers in Education, 1966.
53. McLeod, John, "Some Psycholinguistic Correlates of Reading Disability in Young Children," *Reading Research Quarterly,* 2 (Spring 1967), 5–32.
54. Mills, Robert E., *The Learning Methods Test Kit.* Fort Lauderdale: Mills Educational Center, 1970.
55. Morency, Anne, "Auditory Modality, Research and Practice," in *Perception and Reading,* Helen K. Smith, editor, Proceedings International Reading Association, 12, No. 4 (1968), 17–21.
56. Morency, Anne, Wepman, Joseph M., and Hass, Sarah K., "Developmental Speech Inaccuracy and Speech Therapy in the Early School Years," *Elementary School Journal,* 70 (January 1970), 219–24.
57. Muehl, Siegmar, and Kremenak, Shirley, "Ability to Match Information Within and Between Auditory and Visual Sense Modalities and Subsequent Reading Achievement," *Journal of Educational Psychology,* 57 (August 1966), 230–39.
58. Naylor, Marilyn J., "Reading Instruction Through the Multi-Station Approach," *Reading Teacher,* 24 (May 1971), 757–61.
59. Neville, Donald D., "A Comparison of WISC Patterns of Retarded and Non-Retarded Readers," *Journal of Educational Research,* 54 (January 1961), 195–97.
60. Neville, Donald D., *Peabody Differential Learning Test.* Nashville: the author (George Peabody College for Teachers), 1970.
61. Neville, Mary H., "Methods of Teaching Reading to Beginners," *Alberta Journal of Educational Research,* 12 (1966), 131–39.
62. Neville, Mary H., "Effects of Oral and Echoic Responses in Beginning Reading," *Journal of Educational Psychology,* 59 (1968), 362–69.
63. Oakland, Thomas D., "Auditory Discrimination and Socio-Economic Status as

Correlates of Reading Disability," *Journal of Learning Disabilities,* 2 (June 1969), 326–29.

64. Otto, Wayne, "The Acquisition and Retention of Paired Associates by Good, Average and Poor Readers," *Journal of Educational Psychology,* 52 (October 1961), 241–48.

65. Pick, Herbert L., Jr., and Ryan, Sarah M., "Perception," in *Annual Review of Psychology,* 22 (1971), 164–92.

66. Powell, William R., "Review of Strang's Reading Diagnosis and Remediation," *Reading Research Quarterly,* 4 (Summer 1969), 560–65.

67. Reynolds, Maynard Clinton, "A Study of the Relationships Between Auditory Characteristics and Specific Silent Reading Abilities," *Journal of Educational Research,* 46 (February 1953), 439–49.

68. Riessman, Frank, *The Culturally Deprived Child.* New York: Harper and Row, 1962.

69. *Robbins Speech-Sound Discrimination and Verbal Imagery Type Tests.* Magnolia, Mass.: Expression Company.

70. Robertson, Jean, "Kindergarten Perception Training: Its Effect on First Grade Reading," in *Perception and Reading,* Helen K. Smith, editor, Proceedings International Reading Association, 12, No. 4 (1968), 93–98.

71. Rohwer, W. D., Jr., "Constraint, Syntax and Meaning in Paired-Associate Learning," *Journal of Verbal Learning and Verbal Behavior,* 5 (1965), 541–47.

72. Rosner, J., and Simon, D., *The Auditory Analysis Test: An Initial Report.* Pittsburgh: Learning Research and Development Center, University of Pittsburgh, 1970.

73. *Rush Hughes Phonetically Balanced Lists.* St. Louis: Technisonic Studios, 1951.

74. Samuels, S. Jay, "Effects of Word Associations on Reading Speed, Recall and Guessing Behavior on Tests," *Journal of Educational Psychology,* 59 (1968), 12–15.

75. Samuels, S. Jay, and Wittrock, Merlin C., "Word Association Strength and Learning to Read," *Journal of Educational Psychology,* 60 (1969), 248–52.

76. Schuell, E., "A Short Examination for Aphasia," *Neurology,* 7 (1957), 625–34.

77. Silvaroli, Nicholas J., and Wheelock, Warren H., "An Investigation of Auditory Discrimination and Training for Beginning Readers," *Reading Teacher,* 20 (December 1966), 247–51.

78. Slingerland, Beth H., *Screening Tests for Identifying Children with Specific Language Disability.* Cambridge, Mass.: Educators Publishing, 1964.

79. Slobodzian, Evelyn B., "Use of the Illinois Test of Psycholinguistic Abilities as a Readiness Measure," in *Reading Diagnosis and Evaluation,* Dorothy L. DeBoer, editor, Proceedings International Reading Association, 13, No. 4 (1970), 43–48.

80. Spache, George D., "Spelling Disability Correlates II—Factors That May Be Related to Spelling Disability," *Journal of Educational Research,* 35 (October 1941), 119–37.

81. Spache, George D., "Intellectual and Personality Characteristics of Retarded Readers," *Psychological Newsletter,* 9 (September 1957), 9–12.

82. Sterritt, Graham M., Martin, Virginia E., and Rudnick, Mark, "Sequential Pattern Perception and Reading," in *Reading Disability and Perception,* George D. Spache, editor, Proceedings International Reading Association, 13, No. 3 (1969), 61–71.

83. Sterritt, Graham M., and Rudnick, Mark, "Auditory and Visual Rhythm Perception in Relation to Reading Ability in Fourth Grade Boys," *Perceptual and Motor Skills,* 22 (1966), 859–64.

84. Thompson, B. B., "A Longitudinal Study of Auditory Discrimination," *Journal of Educational Research,* 56 (1963), 376–78.

85. Travers, Robert M. W., *Studies Related to the Design of Audio-visual Teaching Materials.* U.S. Office of Education, No. 3-20-003. Salt Lake City: Bureau of Educational Research, University of Utah, 1964.

86. Weener, Paul, Barritt, Loren S., and Semmel, Melvyn I., "A Critical Evaluation of the Illinois Test of Psycholinguistic Abilities," *Exceptional Children,* 33 (February 1967), 373–80.

87. Wepman, Joseph M., "Auditory Discrimination, Speech and Reading," *Elementary School Journal,* 60 (1960), 325–33.

88. Wepman, Joseph M., *Auditory Discrimination Test.* Chicago: Language Research Associates, 1972.

At the risk of alienating the feelings of many of his readers, the author points out ways that teachers and school practices may actually be contributing to reading problems. He criticizes, for example, teachers' common grouping practices, the way that they use instructional materials, and other aspects of school life. He claims that preservice training of teachers in the area of reading instruction is often inadequate or even faulty. He seems to believe that teachers are perhaps the most important element in pupils' successes and failures.

Try to keep these questions in mind as you read to assist in crystalizing your reactions to these criticisms.

1. Do you basically agree with the author's arguments that teachers may sometimes promote pupil reading problems? Which of his points do you accept and with which do you disagree?

2. Have you witnessed classroom incidents in which children's progress or even their attitudes toward what they are reading were harmed by a teacher's practices? Are such harmful practices really fairly common?

3. If you accept some of the author's criticisms and perhaps add one or two of your own, what changes in teacher preparation and school policies would you suggest to eradicate these poor or unsound practices?

5
Do Teachers Create Reading Problems?

I S IT CONCEIVABLE that competent and well-meaning teachers actually create cases of retardation among their pupils? Is it true that many pupils become retarded in reading simply because of what happens or fails to happen in the classroom? Are the majority of reading failures free from obvious handicaps in vision, hearing, intelligence, personality, and the like? Many experienced reading clinicians and supervisors will probably give an emphatic affirmative answer to these questions. Moreover, the statistics emanating from remedial programs of all types point an accusing finger at classroom practices as causes of reading failure. Diagnosticians find relatively few children for whom the obvious cause of retardation is found solely in physical or psychological areas. The majority of retarded readers are normal or average in these causal areas, or, at least, they were normal in most respects during the early stages of reading instruction. What happens in classrooms to cause almost one out of every four pupils to fall seriously behind his age group at some time during his school career?

As shown by the extensive discussion of contributing factors elsewhere in this text, we are not ignoring the fact that several causes enter into almost every case of reading retardation. Classroom teachers' practices alone are not the sole cause of most reading failures. But they are a major contribution to failure among children, whether handicapped or normal and well-adjusted. To prove this point, we shall examine some of the classroom practices and teacher behaviors that we believe produce pupil reading failures.

METHODS AND MATERIALS

The American classroom teacher commonly bases her instruction on some set or group of commercial instructional materials. Each such piece embodies a concept of the process of learning to reading, and a continuum of skills development that will guide both teacher and pupils toward the authors' objectives. Each reading skill is practiced to a degree in keeping with the authors' emphasis upon it as a basic part of the process of learning to read. No one really knows what the most effective skill sequence is, nor whether all the skills taught are essential for most children to read comprehendingly. But all these plans are offered for groups or total class instruction, as though they were the best possible system for most or all pupils. As a result, the average teacher tends to employ a system or method of teaching reading without really questioning its relevance to the individual differences among her pupils.

The fact that some reading methods are based on, let us say, unique or esoteric definitions of the reading process is often ignored. To some, learning to read is a matter of first learning the sounds of individual letters or letter combinations and then blending these sounds into words in isolation or in patterned sentences that keep repeating certain combinations of sounds in almost meaningless phrases. To others, learning to read is the process of associating printed words with common meaningful auditory and vocal experiences, while letter sounds are only a minor aid in pronouncing a momentarily unfamiliar word. To still other authors, learning to read is the process of recognizing written words and sentences drawn almost entirely from the child's own oral language, with minor emphasis upon letter sounds or other approaches to word recognition. Does the average teacher recognize the contradictions among these and other methods? Is she aware of their dependence upon the auditory and visual abilities and experiential backgrounds of children for their success? Is she aware that no authors of any system have been able to show that their system was more effective than others for most pupils exposed to it?

Our obvious point is that methods and materials are often adopted and used indiscriminately for large masses of pupils. And, as a result, those pupils who, for any reason, cannot profit from a system are condemned to failure. Every reading program in the American market produces a sizeable number of reading failures when it is used in total class or even large-group instruction. The proportion of failures, like the average achievement, may vary greatly from one class to another or, in other words, from one teacher to the next. But this is a reflection of differences among teachers—a point we shall discuss later—not a reflection of relative superiority of the method. And, no matter how gifted, few teachers produce 100 percent reading success for their pupils, irrespective of what method they employ.

The differences in the success of various systems as measured by the averages of reading test scores are affected greatly by the attitude of the teacher toward each system. Some teachers, welcoming a new approach, enter into its presentation with great vitality. Others, having doubts or negative feelings about any new method, grudgingly offer it with little expectation. In short-term experiments, these contrasting attitudes produce the kind of reading performances that the individual teacher expects. She has succeeded in conveying to her students her feelings about the new approach, and they tend to respond accordingly. In fact, the teacher manipulates the expectations and achievements of her class when she is teaching according to any program, old or new. Even individual children, as well as the class averages, tend to confirm at the end of the year the teacher's predictions as made after a few weeks of the term. We realize, of course, that teachers are not always responsible for the selection of the reading materials or, hence, the method to be employed. But we also know that almost any system can be made reasonably effective if presented enthusiastically.

Why are teachers' predictions so often more accurate than prognostic tests? Is it possible that she limits or promotes pupil development in keeping with her early estimates of pupil potential? Does she actually hold some pupils back and impel others onward in terms of her expectations? In all probability she does treat them according to her evaluations, although we doubt that she differentiates in this fashion simply to prove the accuracy of her predictions.

The reaction of teachers to pupil potential, as they see it, is subtly expressed in her instructional practices. To illustrate, children who are thought to be slow learners are directed at a painstakingly slow pace through the reading materials. Whole semesters are occupied with the reading and rereading line by line, page by page, of a simple book often less than a hundred pages in length. The assumption is made that these weaker pupils can learn to read only by extensive repetition of a small vocabulary. Often these pupils are given intensive drill in phonic skills over long periods of time, even when there is evidence that they seem unable to profit. After all, the skill sequence in the program must be mastered step by step or the children will not learn to read, she thinks. Finally, these low-expectation pupils are permitted almost no choice of reading matter in the classroom or the library. They do not read very well, and besides they have not demonstrated complete memorization of the vocabulary of the program. How can they read recreationally? Thus, with perhaps the best intentions in mind, reading becomes drudgery, a disliked and unsuccessful activity accompanied by negative feelings. The possibility that learning might progress somewhat more rapidly by deviating from the stipulated program with word games, dramatics, simple recreational reading materials, teacher-made seatwork, or other enriching activities seldom seems considered. These pupils are fortunate if they complete even the minimum materials offered for the grade level and if they score only moderately below the class average. Multiply this discouraging experience by about 180 days for each school year for several years, and the resulting end product is, in all probability, a pupil of low self-concept and low reading achievement—a candidate for remedial reading.

GROUPING PRACTICES

After pupil potential has been estimated, a common classroom practice tending to produce reading failures is that of assuming about three levels of reading ability in the class and utilizing three corresponding levels of the program materials for these groups. Despite the evidence offered by reading test scores or the spontaneous reading interests of the children, the average teacher operates as though there were only three grade levels of reading performance among her pupils. And once these groups have been designated, there are hardly any shifts of pupils for the rest of the year (3). In actuality, school surveys commonly show that there are more than three grade levels of ability in classrooms at every grade level except perhaps the first. Even the first grade exhibits at least four or five levels of ability ranging from nonreading through beginning third grade by the end of the year. In fact, some schools, using a nongraded program, differentiate as many as eleven reading levels in the primary grades.

Using the fifth grade as an example, we may assume that the at-grade-level group ranges six months to a year above and below their exact grade placement. Since a fifth grade often encompasses six or more grades of reading ability, this implies that some of the best readers may be capable of handling seventh–eighth grade materials, while some of the worst group may be functioning at a second–third grade level or even lower. What, then, is the experience of pupils repeatedly assigned to the poor reading group? Month after month, year after year, some of them are attempting to deal with instructional materials for which their sight vocabulary and word-attack skills are inadequate. With these handicaps, their attempts in the reading group are excruciatingly slow, and the daily experience brings only discouragement and frustration. What happens to the self-concept of the members of the poor reading group who must struggle with materials too difficult for their weak skills, year after year? The answer is obvious.

TEACHER SELF-CONCEPT

It has been suggested that teachers entertain certain concepts of their professional role and hence create corresponding social climates in the classroom. One such self-concept is that of the businesslike dispenser of information. A teacher is supposed to fill those little minds with facts, keep those little hands busy and out of mischief, and keep those little bodies under her control. In keeping with this orientation, the teacher creates an authoritarian climate with practically all activities directed by the teacher, evaluated by the teacher, and understood only by the teacher. Some insecure, anxious pupils or those who lack self-direction or personal organization profit under this climate, but all children are not of these types. The highly intelligent, the creative, or those with strong self-concepts and self-insight chafe under the restrictions, resist the constant directions, and, in protest, fall far below their potential levels of achievement. A few children, feeling threatened by the teacher's constant demands, become more and more disorganized, with consequent mental health or behavioral disturbances as well as reading failure.

A contrasting teacher self-concept is that of a social worker or helper. From this viewpoint, the teacher's function is to help children to help themselves learn. Planning of activities, evaluation, and insight into their goals is a joint effort of both teacher and pupils. As one of our former students used to phrase it in greeting children who came for remedial help, "What do you think you ought to work on today to help yourself read better?" The democratic atmosphere created by this approach involves children in the process of learning; promotes self-insights into one's own needs, strengths, and goals; and emphasizes competition with self rather than with peers. As a result, learning is a real part of life and advances farther than under constant teacher direction. Some children, of course, who need the directiveness of the authoritarian climate do not progress well in this setting.

A third teacher self-concept may be compared with the role of a baby-sitter. For both, the primary function is to stay with children for a certain period of time, making sure that they do not harm themselves or others. But little planning or direction is present, and pupils are almost free to follow their own devices. Activities are suggested and pupil effort is encouraged, but no real direction or limits are obviously set to guide pupils, other than those related to bodily harm. In effect, the teacher's behavior evidences lack of real involvement with her function. She resembles a paraprofessional called into work with pupils for a certain number of hours rather than a true professional. She busies herself and the pupils with distributing bits and pieces of work, but she and the pupils are not conscious of the real purposes of the busywork or the functional nature of the skills presumably developed. More attention is paid to record keeping (to make the central office happy) and to keeping pupils busy than to actual, planned instruction. If pupils show progress in learning to read in this climate, it is solely because they become personally involved with their own efforts, not because of the small amount of instruction offered.

TEACHER PREPARATION

The program of studies in the teacher training program varies from one college or state to another. Some states require a college course in methods of teaching reading, while others do not. Some of the former credit an education major with such a course when he takes the so-called methods block, a multicredit arrangement that touches upon methods in a number of areas. The depth of instruction in reading instruction teaching techniques varies in the block, of course, from one college to another, and even from one year to another as the staff for the block changes.

Stimulated by the surveys of teacher training practices of Mary Austin and her coworkers (1), many studies of the professional knowledge of teachers have been conducted.

Phonics instruction has been explored more than have other aspects of the reading program, such as comprehension, critical reading, reading in the content areas, and others. But even these few studies indicate a lack of depth in teacher preparation. In promoting the development of comprehension, for example, teachers are only beginning to learn the questioning techniques that stimulate more reaction and thinking than does the common emphasis upon immediate recall (2, 4). Similarly, the techniques and materials to foster those reading skills demanded by each content field have only recently become familiar in preservice training and classroom instruction.

As for the skills of diagnosis of pupil needs, even teachers admit that their preparation in this area is very poor. And the recent promotion of use of an informal reading inventory has not really improved this deficit, in our opinion, particularly in phonics and word analysis instruction. These studies tend to reveal that the average teacher's preparation for this area of reading instruction varies widely, although it is generally poor. Many teachers begin their professional work knowing less here than their pupils do. They learn more about the subject as they teach it (with the aid of the teacher's manual) especially if they work with primary grades. Above the primary levels, teacher knowledge of word attack skills tends to diminish at successive grade levels (6).

Let us illustrate the impact of these gaps in teacher preparation in an area about which we are personally concerned, namely, the teacher's understanding of the process of learning to read. We consider her concepts of the process of paramount importance, for they influence every aspect of her instructional practices. To the average primary teacher and to many at intermediate grades, the process that she is teaching the children is the pronouncing of printed words, learned largely through repetition, with some assistance from phonic, structural, and contextual clues. She demonstrates this concept of the process of learning to read in many ways such as these:

1. Daily oral reading lessons in a circle emphasizing almost exclusively correct recognition of words
2. Vocabulary exercises making no distinction between words that are meaningful and those that function only to give structure to sentences
3. Flash cards and other exercises that drill on all types of words out of context

4. Questions emphasizing immediate recall of the words just read to the exclusion of interpretation of the thought

5. Drill on letter sounds and letter combinations in isolation from words or in relatively meaningless words

6. Practice in phrase reading from cards displayed at far-point, as though the span was similar to that at reading distance

7. Judgment of progress of children based largely on their success in reading orally, that is, in pronouncing words

8. Emphasis upon oral reading as though it were similar to, or foundational to, silent reading

9. Slavishly leading pupils through each successive page of the material in the belief that this practice controls the number of new words and that the vocabulary offered is fundamental to future reading

10. Coaching on new words at the chalkboard prior to actual reading for fear that the initial misreading of these words would prevent their eventual learning

We are aware that in the beginning stages the problem of word recognition or building a sight vocabulary is a very real one. But the emphasis upon word learning throughout the entire reading program—as though reading were simply a word recognition task—hinders the development of what we consider to be a meaning-getting process. Comprehension is not obtained by the simple recognition of successive words, for the reader often cannot recall exactly how the thought was phrased, even when he can understand it. Meaning of a sentence is obtained by an amalgamation of the associative thinking of the reader, calling upon his stored memories and the idea of the sentence—not by the simple pronunciation of the words offered in the book. Meaning can be obtained even when some words are unknown, if the reader can supply probable meanings for these from his own associative thinking (5).

The concept of reading as a word recognition task makes great demands upon auditory discrimination and visual short-term memory, erroneously assuming that words pass from short-term to long-term memory sheerly by repetition, not because of their meaningful associations. Owing to the simplicity of the content, many children apparently make good progress during the primary grades only to fail abysmally in later grades because they have not learned to read for ideas. The high proportion of children who are first referred for remedial help during the fourth and fifth grades supports this argument. Nor does the phonics taught them earlier prove helpful, since it functions only in recognition of words familiar auditorily, not for the technical vocabulary of the content fields. In our opinion, gaps in the teacher's preparation—as in phonics and content fields and lack of depth of understanding of the multifaceted nature of the reading process—contribute to pupil failures.

OTHER SCHOOL PRACTICES

The classroom teacher is not the only member of the school staff to contribute to pupil failure. Principals and reading supervisors may make arbitrary decisions in selection of materials of instruction, their appropriateness for various grades, and the range of materials needed. School librarians may create schedules and regulations that make it almost impossible to give children access to a wide variety of reading matter or to stimulate reading interests. For lack of leadership, communication between teachers is often poor; detailed reports of pupil strengths and weaknesses to be passed along are not required; and reports to parents and school records are frozen into a numerical or letter-grading system that really reveals almost nothing to parents or to teachers. Finally, the importance of pupil ages is overemphasized in contrast with intelligence and readiness at school entrance and in ignoring reading ability in grouping children by grade levels. Most of these school practices militate against the recognition of individual differences and the differentiation in instruction that, at critical stages in the pupil's development, might make the difference between success and failure.

LEARNING PROJECT

Try to recall the details of an incident that you have witnessed or even experienced in a classroom which may have hindered the reading progress of the pupils or damaged their self-concept as readers. Describe the incident.

In your opinion, what was wrong with the teacher's behavior or teaching procedure? How was it unsound psychologically or pedagogically?

What should the teacher have done in these circumstances that would have been more positive and constructive?

How do you suppose our educational system can prevent recurrences of these harmful experiences for children? What would you suggest as preventive measures in teacher preparation? What school policies need to be changed if we want to eliminate these happenings?

REFERENCES

1. Austin, Mary C., *The Torch Lighters*. Cambridge: Harvard University Press, 1961.
2. Bartolme, P. I., "Teachers' Objectives and Questions in Primary Reading," *Reading Teacher,* 23 (October 1969), 27–33.
3. Groff, Patrick J., "A Survey of Basal Reading Grouping Practices," *Reading Teacher,* 15 (January 1962), 232–35.
4. Guszak, Frank J., "Teacher Questioning and Reading," *Reading Teacher,* 21 (December 1967), 227–34.
5. Samuels, S. Jay, "The Psychology of Language," *Review of Educational Research,* 37 (April 1967), 109–19.
6. Spache, George D., and Baggett, Mary E., "What Do Teachers Know about Phonics and Syllabication?" *Reading Teacher,* 19 (November 1965), 96–99.

Because of the recognized significant relationship between intelligence and reading achievement at all ages, it has long been the practice of reading teachers to use intelligence test results in their diagnosis. There is little doubt that knowledge of a pupil's performance on an appropriate mental test can be of some use in this fashion. But, as we shall point out, many faulty practices and assumptions have gradually appeared in this apparently simple comparison of mental and reading ages.

Typical of these naive assumptions regarding the degree of relationship between each pupil's mental age and his reading achievement are the over-simplified formulas offered to predict the expected reading achievement. If we accept these formulas, about all we have to know about the child is his I.Q. and the number of years he has been in school to predict what his reading achievement should be (or will be, if we give a bit of help). Obviously such formulas ignore the possible influences of socioeconomic status, race, native language, instructional method, personality disorders, any physical handicaps, or any of the other recognized obstacles to pupil achievement.

6 The Intellectual Factor— Estimating Potential

To counteract this tendency, the author reviews the detailed uses that can be made in diagnosis of the information obtained from a number of individual and group intelligence tests. Other prognostic approaches, as tests of listening comprehension, the ITPA, and associative learning measures, are also examined in the light of their values for predicting reading success or potential. Other readily available data that may be significant for planning remediation, such as age, grade level, initial status, and degree of disability, are briefly reviewed.

As you review this area of diagnosis, consider these questions.

1. How do the author's suggested uses of intelligence test data really differ from the common simple comparison of mental and reading ages?

2. What are some of the factors that should be considered in selecting a verbal versus a nonverbal mental ability test in assessing a particular pupil?

3. Which of the many approaches to evaluating the pupil's potential for improving his reading would you use as a supplement to an intelligence test? Why?

ONE OF THE BASIC STEPS in diagnosis is the estimation of the pupil's intelligence. From this estimate, it is usually assumed that we can decide these crucial questions: Is the pupil really retarded in reading? Is he a good candidate for remedial treatment, or, in other words, what sort of gain is he likely to make if treated? Some diagnosticians even try to use the intelligence test results as direct clues to the type of remedial treatment. Some consider the test results as a measure of potential and interpret the mental age as indicating that level at which the pupil can function in reading when his skills are improved to the utmost. A few highly experienced clinicians emphasize observation of the pupil's test behavior more than the precise results. They look for interferences in attention and concentration, thinking disorders such as loose conceptual thinking, overconcreteness, poor judgment, verbalism in place of logic, and difficulties with abstract reasoning (2). They look for the effects of test anxiety and tension upon performances as well as indications of the subject's self-concept and persistence in the presence of failure. Other insights that may be gained by the trained observer are comparisons of the pupil's verbal and nonverbal abilities involving learning, or his success in verbal and nonverbal thinking, as well as some ideas about his basic personality traits.

In contrast to those who believe that intelligence testing of a suspected retarded reader is both essential and informative, there are some who would reject such tests entirely. Neisworth (106), for example, emphasizes (and properly so) that the test is a description, not an explanation, of the pupil's behavior. Its results are not, he says, genetically predetermined or of permanent significance but are a result of the interaction between the original mental abilities of the individual and his environment. For this reason, Neisworth insists that such tests cannot reveal capacity or potential and cannot be used to match students with educational treatments. Basically his argument for interactionism is sound, for measured intelligence is certainly an amalgam of genetic equipment and environmental opportunities; and there are many other limitations and difficulties in its interpretation, as we shall point out. But, pragmatically speaking, the prognosis works when cautions are taken to allow for these limitations. Knowledge of the pupil's present performance on an appropriate mental test can and does aid the planning of remedial operations.

PROBLEMS IN USING INTELLIGENCE TESTS

The most widespread misinterpretation of the I.Q. test is the assumption that the relationship between mental age and reading is a one-to-one continuum, that is, each child can and should read at a grade level equal to his mental age. Actually the statistical relation between reading and mental age is a very moderate one at primary levels and only later increases with grade level to a marked level. For example, Louttit (87) cites a median correlation in forty-five comparisons between group tests of intelligence and reading of .75; of the Stanford-Binet and reading of .56. In the large-scale First Grade reading studies, however, the correlation was .45 at the end of the first grade and .48 in the second grade (18). Individual studies vary, of course, above and below these large-scale comparisons, but the general trend is still present (27, 122). The point is that reading grades and mental ages do not consistently parallel each other, except in the very gross sense that reading is somewhat dependent upon intelligence.

Neisworth's stand for interactionism is well supported in the studies of intelligence testing among minority groups (8, 44, 53, 96, 149). In the same tests, blacks often test lower than whites; urbans test higher than rurals; differences both positive and negative appear among Jews, non-Jews, blacks, and Orientals; bilinguals tend to test lower than monolinguals; and high socioeconomic score better, particularly in verbal tests, than do low socio-economic. Even some tests claimed to be culture-free or culture-fair are depressed by racial and cultural factors (149). Nor is the problem solved by using nonreading or nonverbal intelligence tests, as Anastasi has pointed out (6), for interests, work habits such as speed, and problem-solving attitudes may reflect cultural differences and affect test performances. Because of these cultural influences some school systems have abandoned the use of intelligence tests entirely. But we believe that there is sufficient data for many of the common mental tests to enable the careful examiner to make allowances or corrections in interpreting results with a minority subject. The solution is not simple, for it is evident that the allowances must take into consideration the quality of the schooling that the pupil has had and the length of residence in an urban setting, for I.Q.'s of Southern black children (82) increase with length of residence in the cities of the North.

Other factors making it impossible to expect that reading grade and mental age will usually be similar are the following:

There are variations in the relevance of the content of different intelligence tests to the mental processes involved in reading. Some mental tests are purely vocabulary measures; others sample quantitative and spatial thinking. Only a few sample the types of reasoning that are required in the reading act. In fact, the more factors of intelligence sampled, the less the test parallels the reading act. Obviously different tests cannot be equally predictive of reading ability or potential.

Some intelligence tests are given to groups of children under conditions that are not conducive to eliciting the pupils' maximum performances. Their results do not yield comparable estimates as found by an individual test administered by a trained, empathetic examiner (16). Nor does averaging of several group and individual tests yield a more meaningful estimate. Unless they make no demand for reading, group tests are apt to function poorly for readers below fourth-grade level (108).

Even in individual testing, the race and sex of the examiner, along with the halo effect upon his scoring of his expectancy for the pupil, have been shown to influence the final estimates (125).

Progress in reading is more often influenced by the instructional method and the degree of personalized attention given pupils than by their actual mental ages, as Gates's study clearly demonstrated more than thirty years ago (56). There is no essential mental age for beginning reading, under ideal conditions. Nor will pupils with the same mental ages necessarily make similar progress under any given method or methods.

Inherent in the expectation that mental age and reading should be parallel is the false assumption that all cognitive processes or skills develop at approximately the same rate (that indicated by the I.Q.). In other words, school administrators think that children's performances in vocabulary, rate, comprehension, and word-attack skills should all mature similarly and be equal to the child's mental age. To the contrary, longitudinal studies indicate that variability, not similarity, is the usual developmental pattern in the cognitive processes. Variations in subtest scores, not equality, is the normal expectation.

The commonest mistake in comparing mental ages with reading levels is the tendency to ignore the errors of estimate present in both scores. Some reading authorities suggest that differences as small as .5 a year or a full year or two above elementary grades between mental and reading ages are evidence of retardation. Many reading and mental tests have a probable error of at least five or six months, and these errors increase with age. Since the difference between two scores should be at least twice the probable error of estimate to be significant, it is apparent that at most levels differences would have to be much greater than the recommendations of these writers, before we can suspect retardation.

Bond and Tinker's data (20) indicate that the only points at which mental age and reading really tend to agree are between 90 and 110 I.Q. Above this point, mental age tends to exceed reading; and below 90, mental age is often *below* reading performance. Jensen and Rohwer (74) have made this point in a different manner. They show that individuals of the same mental age do not show the same learning rate. Low I.Q.'s are slower, but low I.Q. low socioeconomic children showed faster learning rates than did low I.Q. middle socioeconomic pupils. Arthur S. McDonald (96) is certainly accurate when he says that our use of the terms *overachiever* and *underachiever* are simply excuses for imperfect predictions.

Yet, despite these problems in precise interpretation of the meaning of an intelligence test, we believe that it is an essential part of diagnosis. Its values may not lie in prediction of the reading level that the pupil could or should achieve as much as in the variety of observations possible of the pupil's cognitive strengths and weaknesses, his attitudes and performances in challenging tasks, and some insights into his self-concept and personality. We shall try to show how these goals may be accomplished in the later discussion of the tests in common use.

USING FORMULAS TO PREDICT READING ABILITY

Many others have recognized some of the limitations cited concerning the sole use of a mental test in predicting what a pupil can do in reading. Perhaps the first attempt to arrive at an indication of potential by using a combination of factors was that used by Monroe (103). In her early clinical study of poor readers, she used a combination of the chronological age, the mental age, and the arithmetic computation grade score to derive her predictions. All three items were expressed in grade equivalents and divided by three to weight them equally. Then a reading index or quotient was found by dividing the pupil's reading grade by the expectancy grade obtained from the index. If the reading quotient was below 90, reading disability was supposedly present.

Monroe apparently assumed that performance in arithmetic computation, unlike many mental tests, was relatively free from the influence of reading skills. Thus, combining the arithmetic score with chronological age—which was also considered independent of reading ability—would, in Monroe's opinion, counteract the contamination present in the reading element in the mental test. Her logic was partially correct in that many pupils do vary distinctly in their reading and arithmetic computation scores. But verbal ability, reasoning, and quantitative thinking are recognized factors in both mathematics and mental tests. And poor readers do not necessarily show better achievement in computation than in reading, possibly because of the commonality of the cognitive processes in both.* Hence her reading

---

*See later discussion of WISC subtest scores for proof that poor readers are often also poor in arithmetic computation.

index does not really achieve its intention of combining independent measures to give a more accurate prediction. Moreover, the decline in popularity of the use of quotients to express the relationship between actual and expected reading performance militated against the continued use of Monroe's approach.

Bond and Tinker (20) use a formula in which the number of years the child has been in school is multiplied by his I.Q. and one is added to this figure. To illustrate, a child who has been in school three years with an I.Q. of 150 is expected to read at the 5.5 grade level (3 years × 1.50 = 4.50 + 1 = 5.5). The one added to the formula is to account for the first grade. Bond and Tinker make the assumption, obviously, that any pupil makes progress in school in direct relation to his I.Q. This formula has been uncritically accepted as a method of predicting reading expectancy in a number of studies (58) despite the fact that it ignores all the factors in the school or the pupil's environment that influence his reading progress. In fact, as we have already cited, data offered by Bond and Tinker in the same text in which this expectancy formula is proposed contradict its validity. I.Q.'s and reading levels tend to agree only in the 90–110 I.Q. range, according to these same authors.

Alfred S. Lewerenz (85) also tried to avoid the overdependence upon mental age in a formula that averaged twice the mental plus the chronological age. The expected age was thus thought to weight the experiential background of the child and his intellectual growth in an estimate of his functional reading level. Thus Lewerenz hoped to combine measures of ability and interest (as reflected by chronological age) into a predictive formula. Unfortunately, however, studies of the reading interests of bright and dull students indicate more similarity than difference. Dull students may read fewer books, but the maturity of their interests and the types selected are similar to those of their brighter peers.

Torgerson and Adams (155) refined the combining of mental and chronological ages to predict reading by varying their formula for different ages. At ages 6 to 8-5, they simply averaged MA and CA; 8-6 to 9-11, three times MA plus twice CA divided by five; at 10-0 to 11-11, twice MA plus CA divided by three; and above 12-0, three times MA plus CA divided by four.* The justification for this variable weighting is obscure, particularly since applying any one of the formulas to the same child's data gives practically

---

*The weighting of MA does reflect the increase in correlations between mental age and reading as age increases. But these formulas also reflect trends in a particular school system using specific tests and may not be applicable generally.

the same results. For example, a pupil with an MA of 10.5 and a CA of 8.5 has respective reading expectancies by each of the four formulas of 9.5, 9.7, 9.8, and 10.0. When the probable error in the mental test or the reading test is perhaps five or six months, how real are the differences among these scores?

Apparently unaware of its existence, Harris (66) offers precisely the same formula as Lewerenz did in 1939, that is, twice the mental age plus the chronological age divided by three. This Reading Expectancy is then compared with the pupil's reading age (his reading grade score plus 5, added to allow for preschool years). We have already pointed out the limitations of this approach.

Bruininks, Glaman, and Clark (26) recently reviewed several of the formulas offered for predicting reading achievement. They offer a body of comparative data to show that these various formulas vary considerably in estimating potential both at different I.Q. levels and at various ages. In applying the formulas at third and sixth grades, and considering one and two years below expectancy as indicating retardation, these authors found wide variations in the number of children supposed to show reading retardation. The numbers varied not only according to the particular formula used but also according to the use of a verbal or a nonverbal intelligence test as the measure for obtaining mental ages. The authors point out several problems in interpreting such formulas, such as the variations in the definition of a retarded reader; the low reliability of difference scores in comparisons of reading and intelligence test scores; and the failure of most formula writers to recognize that the same degree of retardation, such as a year, does not have the same significance to classroom performance at increasing ages.

Attempting to apply one or several of these formulas in predicting expected reading performance or in deciding whether the pupil is retarded in reading becomes confusing, as Pescosolido and Gervase (113) have demonstrated. In comparing nine hypothetical cases scored by four of these formulas, these authors found agreement in only two cases for all estimates. In some cases, the same child was rated anywhere from above average to disabled. Which formula, if any, can be used to secure a realistic estimate of potential or the need for remedial treatment? As Neisworth would say, this type of thinking is an excellent example of the genetic predeterminism school of thought that completely ignores the interaction of intelligence and environment. Any single study in the literature of the school achievement of economically disadvantaged, racial minority, and socially or emotionally maladjusted groups contradicts this predeterministic philosophy.

SELECTING AND INTERPRETING INDIVIDUAL INTELLIGENCE TESTS

The use of individual intelligence tests in reading diagnosis represents an attempt to overcome some of the limitations inherent in group testing. The influence of the pupil's reading ability should be minimized by the examiner's skill in observation and interpretation of the variety of tasks included in such a measurement. In part, this assumption is possible, for an experienced examiner can, in some individual mental tests, omit or discount test items obviously dependent upon reading. And she certainly can modify the interpretation of the sections biased against poor readers in her overall estimate of ability. The judgment and clinical experience of the examiner can be utilized to overcome the depressing effect of the pupil's poor reading ability. By appropriate stimulation and personalized attention, the skilled examiner can also evoke the maximal effort of the examinee in order to assess his mental abilities to their limits. Thus there may be distinct advantages in an individual intelligence testing to estimate potential not present in group testing. At the same time, certain individual tests require training not possessed by the average teacher. This limitation may be met by employing some of the individual tests to be described that are not highly complex or demanding of examiner's skills.

Stanford-Binet

Binet and Simon were commissioned by the French educational authorities in 1904 to construct some instrument that would permit distinctions between normal and mentally retarded pupils. This was not the first attempt to measure intelligence in a formal way, but the Binet-Simon Scale was widely accepted and adapted almost everywhere because of its validity in distinguishing classes or types of intelligence. Lewis M. Terman made an American translation of the Binet-Simon in 1912 and subsequently standardized a similar instrument, the Stanford Revision of the Binet-Simon Tests in 1916. Other measurement experts made similar adaptations of the French work, but Terman's received the greatest use. Subsequent revisions of the test were made in 1937, when two parallel forms were devised, and again in 1960 and 1964 (152).

For many years, the Stanford-Binet was considered the best and most effective individual intelligence test that could be used in reading diagnosis. But questions arose about its bias against poor readers and its overemphasis upon the verbal factor as tending to depress the results for retarded readers.

As early as 1933, Donald D. Durrell (49) demonstrated that poor readers tended to be underestimated by the scale. Bond and Fay (19) pointed out many differences in the performances of good and poor readers on various items. Factor analysis of the 1960 version indicated that most of the performance was due to a single verbal factor, although other factors were present in the ages of four to six, where the items are more varied (116). The repeated test of digit span penalized poor readers, according to Rose (123), even though the performances varied from one child to another. Studies like that of Spache (145) found correlations between the single vocabulary test and either full- or short-scale testings ranging from .78 to .92, indicating the potency of the verbal factor in the total test. Although estimates based on the vocabulary section tend to overestimate among normal pupils, some even recommend its substitution for the entire scale when testing time is limited (151). Still other studies seem to contradict this implication in a finding that poor readers test significantly higher in the Stanford-Binet than on certain group intelligence tests. If we consider how much the test result is dependent upon the pupil's reading ability in some group tests, Bleismer's report may certainly be accurate. But this does not show that, although tending to be higher than certain group tests, the Stanford-Binet does not also yield an underestimation for retarded readers (16).

Like most current tests, the Stanford-Binet is not a culture-free test, particularly because of its highly verbal factor. Deutsch and Brown (44) have shown that, at each socioeconomic level, black children score lower than do white. Other studies, including a large-scale sample of Southern black pupils, indicate that the average I.Q. for this group is about 80, and similar deviations have been noted in other minority or linguistically different groups or low socioeconomic groups.

These limitations could conceivably be overcome and the Stanford-Binet continue to be used in reading diagnosis. A short form eliminating items known to be influenced by reading ability or by cultural or linguistic background might be employed, if it could be shown that this version yielded accurate and valid results. Although many different short forms have been offered, none yet devised meets these criteria, to our knowledge (144).

Wechsler Intelligence Scale for Children

David Wechsler produced his individual intelligence test for ages five to fifteen in 1949* after having established a similar battery of tests for adults a few years

---

*Our discussion refers, of course, to the 1949 edition of the WISC, not to the 1974 edition.

earlier. Unlike the Stanford-Binet, which varies from item to item within each year level, the ten WISC tests are scales of similar items administered consecutively. Five tests of Information, Comprehension (social judgments), Arithmetic (oral problems mostly), Similarities (common properties or characteristics), Vocabulary (by oral definitions), and a supplementary Digit Span are offered to sample verbal intelligence and to yield a Verbal Scale I.Q. Five others, Picture Completion (detecting missing parts), Block Design (assembling according to a given design), Object Assembly (four wooden puzzles), Coding (associating symbols with given numbers), and an alternate test, Mazes (seven paper and pencil mazes) sample nonverbal thinking and yield a Performance Scale I.Q. The Verbal and Performance I.Q.'s may then be combined in a Full Scale I.Q. The separate subtest raw scores are converted into comparable scaled scores, which are summed and translated into the various I.Q.'s.

In many quarters, the WISC has replaced the Stanford-Binet because of its greater ease in administration and scoring and the many comparisons that apparently can be made among subtest scores and I.Q.'s. The validity of the WISC is indicated in correlations ranging from .70 to .90 with the Stanford-Binet, although its results are generally lower than the latter, particularly in the Performance I.Q. These correlations are much lower among five- to six-year olds, .48 to .64; at this level some examiners continue to prefer the Stanford-Binet.

The validity of the WISC in predicting reading ability varies considerably from one study to the next (22, 23, 41, 153, 69), with most studies emphasizing the significance of subtest scores and the difference between the Verbal and Performance I.Q.'s as predictive measures. Pattern analysis by subtest scores in an attempt to identify types of cases, as retarded readers, brain-damaged, psychopaths, delinquents, and so on, is almost a popular pastime for some psychologists.

P. versus V.   The primary symptom of a retarded reader is indicated, some believe, by a Performance I.Q. that exceeds the Verbal I.Q. When this difference is present, it is often interpreted as indicating that the Verbal and perhaps the Full I.Q. are underestimating the true potential of the pupil as this is indicated by the Performance I.Q. Unfortunately for this assumption, deviations between the V. and P. I.Q.'s are as apt to be in either direction in any large sample; and, in fact, exact equality in the two measures is probably quite rare, according to Beck (13). We have checked this comparison as reported in some fifteen studies of retarded readers. Ten report higher Performance I.Q.'s; five found no significant differences. Neville (107) reports that four of seven studies comparing the P. and V. I.Q.'s found the P. higher for poor readers. The evidence seems slightly in favor of accepting this symptom as characteristic of poor readers.   Yet Dahlke's study of true gain from remedial instruction (41) indicated no meaning to this I.Q. difference in terms of predicting improvement.   Tillman (153) found the P. and V. equally significantly related to true gain in Oral Reading, while the V. I.Q. predicted gain in Word Recognition better than the Performance result did.   Reed (119) demonstrated that the predictions from either V. or P. scales were related to the manner of matching the experimentals and controls.   When matched on Full Scale, good readers did better in a variety of tasks, while poor readers were apparently deficient in most of these.   When matched in V. I.Q., poor readers equaled the performances of good pupils in most tests.   When matched in P. I.Q., the differences were all small but favored the good readers.   Reed's point is that those selected as poor readers vary greatly, depending upon which I.Q. is used and its relationship to the test tasks.   In a second study of 248 first- and 233 fifth-grade children, Reed (118) found no differences in reading corresponding to differences in P. versus V. I.Q.'s.   In the fifth grade, the High V., low P. were better readers than the others; and the V. I.Q. gave a better prediction than did the P. or Full I.Q.'s.   Reed surmises that lower V. I.Q.'s do not necessarily result in poor reading but rather that rapid development in reading may lead to superior verbal skills.   We might summarize this argument regarding the significance of the P. I.Q. in predicting reading ability by pointing out that in twelve of fifteen studies that we have reviewed, including one of our own (146), P. excelled V. for either *normal or poor* readers and in fact appears to do so in the original standardization population for the WISC (131).

Neville (107) and Farr (54) have offered summaries of pattern analysis studies on the WISC subtest scores of poor readers.   We have added a number of other reports to these as presented in Table 6–1.

McDonald has shown,* as we might expect from the similarity of content, that subtest patterns in the adult WAIS are similar to those above. Poor readers were low in Info. Arith., Digit Span, and Digit Symbol (Coding); high in Comp., P.C., P.A., B.D., and O.A.

It seems that poor readers perform badly in the Information, Arithmetic, Digit Span, and Coding tests and may be weak on the Vocabulary subtest. Poor readers excel in Picture Completion, Block Design, Picture Arrangement, and (in some groups) the Object Assembly and Comprehension tests.   The

---

*Arthur S. McDonald, "Intellectual Characteristics of Disabled Readers at the High School and College Levels," *Journal of Developmental Reading,* 7 (Winter 1964), 97–101.

TABLE 6–1   PATTERNS OF WISC SUBTEST SCORES AMONG POOR READERS

	INFO.	COMP.	ARITH.	SIMIL.	D.S.	VOCAB.	P.C.	B.D.	P.A.	O.A.	COD.
Graham (60)	L#	H#	L	H	L	L	H	L		H	L
Burks and Bruce (29)	L	H	L					H	H		L
Altus*	L		L								L
Richardson*	L		L			L	H		H	H	L
Spache (146)		H	L	H			H		H	H	L
Hirst (70)			L		L		H		H		L
Neville (107)	L		L		L			H	H		
Kallos (78)	L		L					H			L
Dockrell (45)	L		L				H	H	H		L
Paterra*		H	L	H		L	H				
McDonald*	L	H	L		L		H	H	H	H	L
Robeck (121)	L	H	L	H	L	H	H	H			L
Coleman and Rasof (36)		H						H	H		
McLean**	L		L		L		H				L
McLeod (98)	L		L		L	L	H				L
Muir**	L	H	L			L	H	H		H	L
Reid and Schoer (120)			L	L	L		H				
Richardson**	L		L		L		H		H	H	L
Sheldon**	L		L				H	H		H	L
De Bruler (43)			L				H				L
Dudek and Lester (46)	L		L		L						
Huelsman (72)	L		L								L
Lewis (86)	L	L	L	L	L	L					L
Beck (13)		H	L	H	L	H	H				L
Corwin (38)	L		L		L						L
Schiffman (127)	L		L		L						L

*As cited by Neville (109)
**As cited by Farr (54)
#L = Poor readers significantly lower than good.
#H = Poor readers significantly higher than good.

bases of these comparisons vary from one writer to another: some comparing mean scores of matched or unmatched groups; some allowing for the probable errors of estimate, while others ignore these; some considering almost any variation among subtest scores as significant, while others compared each pupil's subtest score with his own average as a correction.   The table of significant differences among subtest scores offered by Newland and Smith (111) has been carefully ignored in most of these reports. Yet there is considerable agreement in these analyses of patterns. The question is what this pattern of poor and good subtest scores among poor readers really means. Does it provide clues to the cognitive strengths and weaknesses that tend to produce poor reading? Does it provide clues to remedial treatment in reading or training in cognitive skills? Or, as Reed has implied, do these differences reflect environmental stimulation, as from reading itself?

Some authors are quite positive in their belief that pattern analysis leads directly to prescriptive teaching. For example, Wills and Banas (160), using their own interpretation of the meanings of the subtests, distinguish and prescribe for four types:

> 1. The Normal—little or no deviations in subtest scores
> 2. The Vulnerable (Dyslexic)—high in Comprehension, Similarities, and Block Design; low in Coding, Picture Completion, Digit Span, Arithmetic, and Information
> 3. The Fragile (Specific Language Disability)—high in Vocabulary, Information, Digit Span, Picture Completion and Object Assembly; low in Similarities, Picture Arrangement, Block Design, and Mazes
> 4. The Enchanted Prince (neurologically impaired)—low in all except Similarities; lowest in Arithmetic; Information, Digit Span, and all of the Performance tests

Bannatyne (10) similarly seems to have observed certain groups of interrelated tests, which then can be interpreted into remedial prescriptions. One group is termed spatial: Picture Completion, Block Design, and Object Assembly. Another grouping of Comprehension, Similarities, and Vocabulary reflects conceptualizing ability, Bannatyne says. A third group, Digit Span, Picture Arrangement, and Coding, samples sequencing abilities. This author suggests summing the three scaled subtest scores for each group and comparing these means to make the decision regarding treatment.

The interpretation of the meanings of the subtests of the WISC and the variations in patterns has proliferated ever since the author, David Wechsler, first suggested such an approach (with his own meanings for the tests, of course). The extremely wide use of the test with a great variety of types of populations has furthered this theorizing, despite the criticisms of some observers. Belmont and Birch (14) criticize it for pattern analysis based on clinical populations rather than on a true sample of the entire population; for use of groups not homogeneous in age or sex; and, in the comparisons of good and poor readers, for selection of cases from different schools, different social classes, and different ages. Charting and analyzing subtest scores in terms of personality types, and the like, has been called meaningless by Bijou (15). He considers pattern analysis useful only in the comparisons of equated groups. Huelsman's review of twenty studies of pattern analysis and his own data indicate the inconsistency of the performances of children supposed to fit into a certain pattern (72). Deal (42) summarizes fifteen reports on pattern analysis dating since 1945, without reaching very definite conclusions.

In our opinion, the meanings of the subtests and their interrelationships can be arrived at most logically by factor analysis. Cohen's study indicates the following factors and their components (35):

Verbal Comprehension I—Information, Arithmetic, and Similarities (and Vocabulary)

Verbal Comprehension II—Comprehension, Picture Completion

Perceptual—Block Design, Object Assembly (and at some ages, Picture Arrangement, Picture Completion and Mazes)

Freedom from Distractibility—Digit Span, Arithmetic

Specific Unique Factors—Coding or Coding plus Picture Arrangement

It appears that the verbal and performance scales are not really independent measures or factorially pure. This is evident particularly in Cohen's factor Verbal Comprehension II, which includes one subtest from each of the two scales. It is further shown in the fact that the factor analysis did not find the verbal tests to form a distinctly different group than the performance. Even when age groups at 7-10, 10-6, and 13-6 years of age are so analyzed, the same five factors appear; these factorial findings are similar to those identified in the adult WAIS by Cohen. In the unique factor, the only consistent test is Coding, although Picture Arrangement loads on this factor in the two older groups. In Verbal Comprehension II, Vocabulary is included in this factor at ages 7-6 and 10-6 but drops out at 13-6. Cohen's interpretations of his factors are offered as follows:

Verbal Comprehension I—school learning (or opportunity)

Verbal Comprehension II—application of verbal judgment to new situations

Perceptual—perceptual organization of visually perceived materials under time limits

Freedom from Distractibility—attention or concentration (or, in some instances, anxiety)

Cohen offers no psychological interpretation of the Specific Factor that includes Coding and, at the older age groups, Picture Arrangement. Although this Coding test is widely thought of as a measure of learning—and performance in it considered very significant in the case of retarded readers—some observers have pointed out that it can be performed by sheer copying of the symbol attached to each number. No learning may actually be present, as can be shown by asking the pupil to reproduce the symbols for each number from memory after he has finished the test, a task many subjects cannot do. Thus the Coding may well be simply a perceptual-motor speed sample rather than associative learning. This interpretation may account for the test's being unique and different from any of the factors found, as well as for the frequency of poor performance in it by poor readers, who often do tend to lack perceptual-motor speed.

Let us return to the indications of the patterns of subtest scores for poor readers, contrasting them with the groups identified by Cohen. Using his interpretations of these factors and the observed patterns among poor readers, we obtain the following indications:

Poor readers are apt to be weak in these:

School Learning—Information, Arithmetic (and sometimes in Vocabulary)

Attention or Concentration—Digit Span, Arithmetic

Perceptual-motor Speed—Coding.

Poor readers are not usually weak in these:

Perceptual Organization—Block Design, Object Assembly (or Picture Arrangement)

Verbal or Social Judgment—Comprehension, Picture Completion

In our opinion, an approach to decisions regarding remedial treatment, as well as to further exploration of the pupil's school and family history, can be defensibly based on Cohen's findings. When the poor reader's pattern follows expectations, the clinician must certainly explore further before making plans. If low scores are present in the School Learning factor, he must determine the quality of previous schooling, the history of attendance and particularly long absences, and the mobility in moving from school to school, along with trying to secure the comments of previous teachers regarding this pupil. Other influential factors in this area may well be found in the cultural, linguistic, or racial backgrounds. If low scores are present in the Attention factor, the clinician must consider this in planning frequency and duration of remedial sessions, as well as in programming their difficulty. Since both tests in this area were measures of auditory attention, some exploration of other auditory abilities may be essential, before any decisions about emphasizing phonics in the remedial program are made. If the Perceptual-Speed factor is weak, perhaps further testing in visual perception, writing at dictation, and handwriting may be needed to guide remediation. These are, of course, only the most obvious desirable steps in clarifying the meaning and possible contributing courses for poor performances in these factors identified by Cohen.

Like most standardized tests, the Wechsler is not culture-free or independent of the socioeconomic background of the pupil (13, 69, 120). Whites tested higher on the WISC in the samples reported by Henderson, Butler, and Goffeney (69) and by Lewis, Bell, and Anderson (85). In the latter, black students were significantly lower in Picture Completion, Object Assembly, Coding, and the Performance I.Q. In his dissertation, Ekwall (53) found bilinguals (Mexican-American) higher in Coding and Arithmetic but lower in Information and Vocabulary than the Anglo-American monolinguals. Seashore (131) has pointed out that children of professional and semiprofessional status will usually have Verbal I.Q.'s greater than Performance, as we might expect, if we accept the interactionism concept of the development of intelligence. This difference, however, does not seem to appear in other occupational groups or in contrasts of rural versus urban children. In other words, using Cohen's group factors as a basis for interpreting the probable meanings of the subtests, we then begin an exploration of the pupil's history and background to discover probable reasons for his performances and the relevance of these contributing factors to a remedial plan.

Pattern analysis does not identify a subject as a disabled reader, from which conclusion we then move into remediation in areas of *our* competence in remedial reading. Pattern analysis by group factors indicates cognitive strengths or weaknesses in the child's development in his environment. We must try to see the interrelationships among his previous environment and his subtest patterns in mental ability and reading skills before deciding which areas we shall attempt to modify. As we shall point out later in chapter 9, remedial reading alone is often not the answer to permanent improvement in reading.

Peabody Picture Vocabulary Test

Because the WISC and Stanford-Binet demand a period of supervised training before they can be administered with accuracy, many have sought a simpler verbal measure of intelligence. We shall discuss a number of these later but, because of its wide acceptance, shall begin with the Peabody Picture Vocabulary Test. The test consists of a spiral-bound book containing 150 plates of four large drawings each. The examiner simply names one of the four objects (or the action depicted) and asks the pupil to point to the corresponding picture. The test is applicable from two years, six months to eighteen years, and two forms are available in the one set of plates, each form requiring ten to fifteen minutes of testing time.

The standardization was based on 4,012 cases with about 100–375 pupils at each age level. Interform reliability coefficients range from .67 to .84 for a single age level, with a median of .77. Standard errors of measurement for the I.Q. ranged from 6.00 to 8.61, with a median of 7.2. The Manual published in 1965 offers a summary of many of the studies of the PPVT since its publication date of 1958. On the whole, these report reliability coefficients similar to those offered by the author with the expected variations due to the differences in homogeneity of the groups. Later studies such as those by Costello (39), Kahn (77), and Silberberg and Feldt (135) confirm these estimates.

Validity comparisons with the WISC give reasonable correlations according to Fitzgerald's review of twenty-two such contrasts (55). Correlations with the WISC Full Scale showed a median of .63; with the Verbal, .69 and with the Performance, .54, in Fitzgerald's review. Most of these studies were concerned with relatively homogeneous groups of pupils exhibiting school or social maladjustment, and the correlations are consequently depressed. The tendency was present in these and other samples for the PPVT to yield higher I.Q.s than did the WISC and the Binet, in some groups (38, 75, 135, 138, 154).

For our purposes as reading clinicians, the PPVT does offer the advantages of an easy verbal test, with reasonable validity and reliability particularly if both forms are used; and one free from the depressing effects of the pupil's reading ability. The question of the predictive efficiency of the PPVT in the area of reading is crucial, however. In the Manual, Dunn (48) cites several correlations with reading among small and atypical groups, such as cerebral-palsied, deaf, and emotionally disturbed. In these groups, the PPVT compared favorably with other picture type intelligence tests, but tended to yield lower correlations with reading than the WISC did. Similar results are reported by several other authors (73, 75, 61). Jerrolds, Callaway, and Gwaltney compared the PPVT, the WISC, and the Ammons Quick Test as measures of potential for reading. In their judgment, the PPVT was as adequate a measure of intelligence, for the purposes of quick diagnosis, as the WISC or the Quick Test if the examiner is cognizant that wide individual variations may be present among the results of these three tests.

Since it is apparently a measure almost purely of vocabulary, the results of the PPVT can reflect the effects of socioeconomic or cultural disadvantage. Like most such tests, the I.Q. obtained is probably depressed for bilinguals, low socioeconomic, and other such groups. Ali and Costello (3, 39) attempted to modify this limitation of the PPVT by eliminating certain items and by supporting the child by verbal reinforcement. Using only a seventy-item version of the PPVT, their test-retest correlations for two samples of disadvantaged preschool children were slightly higher than for the entire test (.86 and .87 versus .77). In the testing of pupils whose backgrounds would be likely to affect the results, this abbreviated version might well be preferable to the original test. We are not certain that it necessarily yields a more accurate I.Q. for such children, but this version does yield a higher I.Q. and is certainly satisfactory in reliability despite its abbreviated length.

Other Picture Vocabulary Tests

In 1948, Ammons and Ammons (4) offered a Full Range Picture Vocabulary Test and then abbreviated this in 1962 in the Quick Test (5). Both of these versions and the PPVT are similar to the Van Alstyne Picture Vocabulary Test first offered in 1929 (156) but now out of print.

The Full Range Picture Vocabulary contains only eighty items in the range from preschool to adult, although its reliability for the standardization groups gave a median of .81. Correlations with the WISC and Stanford-Binet were in the .80s according to the author. Other samples, such as that by Silverstein and Hill (138), have yielded validity coefficients with the Binet or the WISC much lower (.48), in a sample of mentally retarded pupils. These authors, in comparing the Full Range, the PPVT, and the Van Alstyne, found the PPVT most acceptable both in relationships with the WISC and Binet and in terms of testing time.

The Quick Test, the fifty-item version of the Full Range instrument, is offered in three forms, using the same set of plates. Critics have pointed out that the standardization group for a range from preschool to adult of 458 cases is inadequate; that the drawings are poorly done; and that the higher I.Q.'s and much greater variability of test results hardly justify its use as a substitute for the WISC or Stanford-Binet (112). Test-retest coefficients between forms average .60 or below, implying that two or three forms must be used for adequate reliability. Despite the greater discrepancies between the I.Q.'s from the Quick Test and the WISC or PPVT in their own data, Jerrolds et al. (75) feel that the Quick Test can be used with reasonable confidence, a viewpoint we cannot share. Moreover, neither the Full Range nor the Quick Test are free from cultural influences, as with Mexican-American children, and no adaptations of these instruments have been made to minimize this factor, as has been done for the PPVT. This latter test also has the added advantage of better discrimination because of its greater number of items particularly at the lower age levels.

NONVERBAL TESTS OF POTENTIAL

The realization that most verbal intelligence test results are depressed for minority or bilingual groups has stimulated the search for nonverbal instruments that might be free of this effect. Among those that have found wide use in this effort are the 1926 Goodenough Drawing of a Man, the Goodenough-Harris Drawing Test (67) of 1963, the Raven Progressive Matrices (117), and the Porteus Maze Test (114).

Goodenough-Harris Drawing Test

Since this test has largely supplanted the original version by Goodenough, we shall not review the older test. The Harris version of the task of drawing a man enlarged the test by adding the drawing of a woman. Items scored in the tasks were increased to seventy-three and seventy-one respectively and selected on the basis of their discrimination in terms of the pupils' ages, total scores, and their relation to other measures of intelligence. The standardization sample numbered 2,975 children between the ages of five and fifteen drawn from a representative sample of the occupational distribution of the U.S. in 1950.

The child is asked first to draw a picture of a man, then a woman, and then one of himself, in that order. Each drawing is scored, and the first two scores are averaged for greater reliability. The drawing of self is intended as a projective device for the possible study of personality, rather than as a measure of intelligence. Both the Man and Woman scales may be assessed for quality, by comparing them with a series of scaled sample drawings.

Most of the data on validity, reliability, and relationship to other intelligence tests is taken from the many studies of the original test. But the careful construction of Harris's version, the broad standardization, and other features argue that it is even superior to its parent. Correlations with the Binet, for example, range from .36 to .74 in various samples, and reliabilities are usually over .90.

The simplicity of the administration of this test and its scoring—thanks to the detailed directions given by Harris—has promoted its wide use in attempts to sample intelligence. The one drawback from the viewpoint of the reading teacher is that there is little known of its correlation with reading achievement or, in other words, its predictive values, although it is undoubtedly a measure of conceptual thinking. Shipp and Loudon (134) cite correlations of .42 with reading comprehension and .30 with vocabulary in a small scale first-grade study, one of the few available in the literature. In situations in which testing time is limited or an additional assessment is desired, or rapport in verbal testing is difficult to achieve, the Goodenough-Harris can be very useful. Moreover, the test can be administered as a group or individual measure.

The Raven Progressive Matrices

This series of tests requires the subject to choose, from multiple-choice answers, the design or design part that best fits an incomplete design. The answer may involve simple completion of the given design, or completing an analogy, or recognizing sequences. The tests have been under revision since their inception in 1938 in attempts to update norms, to extend the ages of applicability, to introduce the use of color in the designs, and to make other refinements.

The Standard Progressive Matrices are offered for ages eight to sixty-five; the Coloured Progressive Matrices for ages five to eleven; and the Advanced Progressive Matrices for gifted adolescents and adults. These arrangements have had wide use in Britain, where they originated, and in other countries, since they require no real communication between the examiner and the testee other than the basic instructions. Cross-cultural testing, as in Eskimo, Indian, and white groups in Canada (93), indicated no major differences among the groups on this instrument. Another Canadian study found the Matrices as effective as group intelligence tests in predicting reading achievement in a third-grade sample (97). A British study found that the Raven was not influenced by socioeconomic status as was the Stanford-Binet (92). Other studies contrasting the results with black and white pupils in America support the view that the test is relatively free of the verbal, time pressure, and experiential background factors that enter into many group intelligence tests (132). A factor analysis study of the 1947 version of the Matrices indicated that they were free of the verbal factor, that is, relatively culture-free (91), yet measured the general type of intelligence that enters into reading.

Reviews of the various versions of the Matrices criticize them for lack of differentiation of cognitive abilities, for a confusing Manual, and for equivocal results in validity and reliability, while recommending them for use with special groups such as the deaf, cerebral palsied, bilingual, culturally disadvantaged, and the like. If a group (or individual) test of general mental ability, relatively free of the influence of socioeconomic and racial background, is desired, the Raven Matrices are a possibility.

The Porteus Maze Test

In 1914 Stanley D. Porteus devised a series of paper and pencil mazes to function as a measure of nonverbal mental ability. The Vineland Revision of these tests now offered was completed in 1933 (114). The basic material consists of twelve mazes for years three to twelve, one for age fourteen, and one for adults. The task is simply to try to mark a way through the mazes without entering a cul-de-sac or lifting the pencil. The series has probably had more usage in various racial and ethnic groups than any other single test for it has been a favorite tool of anthropologists, social psychologists, and other scientists.

Early in its history, users of the test became interested in its values in studying social competence and adjustment. Since a degree of planning enters into the solution of the mazes, its application as a predictor of the ability to make judgments and to sustain oneself in the community has been widely explored and demonstrated. The Manual recounts many such studies of delinquents, psychopaths, incarcerated, and mentally retarded individuals for whom the test appeared to be quite discriminative. To cite but a single example, Cooper (37) found the Porteus Maze Test markedly superior to the WISC, the Ammons, or the Revised Binet in differentiating the socially competent from the intellectually defective in a population of academically retarded black adolescents.

Validity coefficients with other tests of intelligence range from .40 to .70 in various samples. There is little doubt that this measure of nonverbal mental ability is a culture-free instrument that is not influenced by the background or reading ability of the student. In fact, in a small-scale study reported by Eakin and Douglas (52), poor readers in the fourth–fifth grades scored higher in the Porteus than did average to good readers. The administration and scoring of the instrument is quite simple in the measurement of mental ability. The supplementary scoring for the judgment of social competence or judgment is also feasible for one reasonably experienced in test administration.

Critics of the test point out that the standardization and reliability data in the Manual is inadequate; that there seems to be a tendency for males to score higher than females in some studies; and that the norms applying in each type of population are not clearly delineated. Again, however, the Porteus may be a preferred choice for a measure of mental ability in many instances when more common tests are contraindicated because of linguistic, cultural, racial, or personality handicaps.

OTHER TESTS
The Slosson Intelligence Test

Many of those dealing with disabled readers would like to use a simple test of verbal ability that does not require great skill on the part of the examiner. By many, the Slosson Intelligence Test is accepted as an answer to this problem. There is little doubt of the validity of this instrument in terms of its resemblance to the Binet or the WISC, for correlations with these criteria are high: .75 to .90 with the Stanford-Binet, and .60 to .90 with the WISC Full Scale (65). In a sample of over 200, Armstrong and Mooney (7) report r's with Stanford of .93 and .94, with a ten-point average difference in I.Q. With poor readers, the Slosson was shown to be a better instrument than the Quick test in preliminary screening by Houston and Otto (71). With fifty-one clinic cases, Jerrolds, Gwaltney, and Callaway (76) found the Slosson gave an average I.Q. five points higher than the WISC Full Scale on the average. The correlations with the Full Scale were higher than with the Performance I.Q. These authors cautioned, though, that there may be considerable individual variations among these I.Q. findings.

There seems to be little doubt that the Slosson test is easily administered, is simple to score, has a range of applicability from preschool to adult level, and can function in the hands of a relatively untrained examiner as a substitute for the Stanford-Binet. However, the high correlations with this test and the Verbal scale of the WISC imply that the test is highly verbal, which may mean that it is probably culturally biased and, in many instances, may thus discriminate against poor readers. It has the advantages of brevity (about twenty minutes), simplicity of scoring, and relative ease of administration; and the many supporting studies justify its use certainly with normal children and with mentally retarded. But there is no evidence that the test functions as well with high validity for atypical groups that differ in racial, socioeconomic, linguistic, or cultural backgrounds, which are affecting their reading achievement.

Detroit Tests of Learning Aptitude

Because of its unusual nature, this battery of tests has had wide acceptance in the study of disabled readers or learning disabilities. The battery comprises nineteen subtests usable from age three to adult. Each test is a scale of similar items of increasing difficulty. The latest Manual (9), dated 1968, offers clear norms and directions and detailed information on the test. It is obvious from their titles why many of the subtests can find use in reading or learning disability diagnosis: pictorial absurdities, verbal absurdities, pictorial opposites, verbal opposites, motor speed and precision, attention span for unrelated words and for syllables, oral commissions, social adjustment (two such tests), visual attention span tests for objects and for letters, orientation, free association, memory for designs, number ability, broken pictures, oral directions, and likenesses and differences.

Each subtest yields a mental age, and the median mental age from the ten or more tests chosen to be administered is used as the final result. Because of their range, simplicity, and independence, any group of the scales may be used to supplement another test such as the PPVT, the Porteus Mazes, the Goodenough-Harris, or others. Thus a broader sampling of cognitive abilities may be obtained, and special areas may be explored more fully. We are not suggesting the averaging of mental ages but rather the comparisons to obtain more information about the pupil's cognitive abilities. Some of the tests will be helpful in reading diagnosis, while others are not particularly relevant (63, 110).

Critics of earlier editions of the test objected to the authors' identification of the specific mental abilities being tested, without any supporting data; the inadequacy of the standardization data; the inappropriateness of the materials for older adolescents and adults; and the lack of sufficient reliability and validity data. Most of these flaws have been corrected in the current edition, which has had thirty years of previous experience to collect such information.

SOME RELEVANT GROUP TESTS

Since individual testing is time-consuming, there have been many efforts to produce group intelligence tests that are appropriate for testing disabled readers and persons of varied ethnic and racial backgrounds. These efforts have not always been successful, as we shall note in describing certain of these tests.

California Test of Mental Maturity, 1963 (California Test Bureau). Both the regular and the Short Form of this test yield a language and a non-language I.Q. While the validity and reliability of the tests are acceptable, studies of the predictive values for reading potential vary from study to study (73, 97). The range of the test is from kindergarten to adults, with different forms being offered for various levels. Critics of the California M.M. praise its format, norms, and ease of administration, while they condemn the lack of supporting information for the grouping of subtests into certain factors, the lack of reliability data for the Long Form, the use of time limits for each subtest, and the content bias reflecting white, middle-class backgrounds (30, 31).

Pintner-Cunningham Primary Mental Test, 1965 (Harcourt Brace Jovanovich). This is a verbal group test presented entirely pictorially with oral directions. It is applicable from kindergarten to grade two. Its correlations with the Stanford-Binet and other verbal tests are quite acceptable, as is its reliability. Being basically a measure of verbal intelligence, it is a fair predictor of reading success at these primary levels where high correlations are not really expected.

SRA Primary Mental Abilities Test, 1962 (Science Research Associates.) Six levels of tests are offered, ranging from kindergarten to adult levels, each yielding five–six scores in verbal meaning, number facility, reasoning, spatial relations, perceptual speed, and total score. The perceptual speed test is present only in the form for kindergarten–first grade. The original tests were established by an early factorial analysis of many tests by L. L. Thurstone, and, on the whole, they have been maintained in their original forms through various revisions. Since the reliabilities are acceptable and the tests are presumably factorially separate, a comparison of subtest abilities is possible when the limited number of factors sampled is relevant to the diagnosis.

Critics point out the lack of sex norms that might logically be expected to differ; the weak reliability coefficients for some of the factors, particularly in the perceptual and spatial groups; the poor prediction of reading vocabulary compared with word recognition at the first-grade level; the use of time limits for subtests; and the lack of factorial analysis of the tests at the kindergarten–first grade level (30). Stablein, Willey, and Thompson (149) have demonstrated that Spanish-American children achieve lower mean scores on this test than do Anglo-American children, implying that the instrument is not culture-free.

There are, of course, many other individual and group tests of intelligence that might be reviewed here, if space permitted. But our purpose was to critique only the most commonly used tests that reading specialists could perhaps administer or those likely to be mentioned in reports from psychologists or other professional examiners.

OTHER PROGNOSTIC APPROACHES

The problems inherent in using formulas or intelligence tests to predict potential reading ability have stimulated a variety of other approaches. Among these are tests of listening comprehension, the use of the ITPA, and tests that simulate the learning situation or the ability to associate words and symbols.

Listening Comprehension

Various tests of listening are included in the individual diagnostic reading tests that we have reviewed in the parallel text, *Diagnosing and Correcting Reading Disabilities.* In addition, a number of group tests are available for different educational levels. We shall review these briefly, since all are based on the premise that any individual can learn to read adequately at a level equal to what he demonstrates in a measure of listening comprehension.

Botel Reading Inventory

The Word Opposites Test is also offered as a listening test by its author. After having attempted to match the opposites in a silent reading, the same test is read aloud to the pupil as a measure of listening comprehension. If the listening performance is higher than the silent reading, Botel assumes that this indicates higher reading potential than present reading comprehension performance. He gives no information regarding the expected magnitude of a significant difference, nor any supporting validity data for the use of the test for this purpose (21).

Durrell Analysis of Reading Difficulty

This battery includes a Listening Comprehension Test for first to "above sixth" grade. Originally an oral reading test in earlier editions of Durrell's kit, it was adapted by moving the oral reading paragraphs downward one grade level to form the listening comprehension selections. The author gives no data to support use of the former oral reading as a measure of listening comprehension, or any explanation of the reason for assuming that at any grade level listening is a more difficult task than oral reading. No data on validity or reliability of this supposed measure of reading potential are offered (50).

Individual Reading Placement Inventory

Smith and Bradtmueller suggest that reading their selections at the levels above the last successful oral performance of a subject constitutes a measure of language potential. Since their selections extend only to the fifth grade, and this battery is intended for use with adults, there may be many instances in which no selection is really available for testing language potential. Moreover, under any circumstances, no potential performance higher than sixth grade can be assessed by this instrument. The authors offer no evidence of the validity of their approach to measuring potential for reading (141).

Standard Reading Inventory

At the end of his Manual, McCracken offers a group of stories for measuring listening comprehension. In answering the questions, the standards are much more demanding than those for the oral and silent selections of the same battery, for obscure reasons. The author assumes that these are a viable sample of reading potential and that there will be differences, in favor of the listening test, in most or all cases. No information regarding the magnitude of the differences or their significance, or the validity or reliability of this subtest is offered (95).

Classroom Reading Inventory

Silvaroli offers a supplementary set of reading selections, in addition to those for oral and silent testing, for use if the teacher chooses to do so. The selections parallel those for oral or silent reading extending from preprimer to sixth grade. The author suggests that they may be used as oral, silent, or hearing capacity level measures, without offering any validity or reliability data or suggestions for interpreting the series when used as a hearing capacity measure, other than the unsupported statement that a higher performance than the instructional (oral) level indicates that reading skills may be improved through instruction to that level (137).

Diagnostic Reading Scales

Following the test of oral and silent reading in successive selections of increasing difficulty, Spache suggests that the next most difficult paragraphs above the pupil's silent reading level be read to him. Comprehension is measured as in the oral and silent reading selections, and the reading to the pupil continues at increasing levels until he fails in meeting the comprehension norm.

As evidence of the validity of the Scales as measures of potential, the author cites correlations ranging from .35 to .83 for predicting end-of-year performance on a group reading test by primary pupils, and r's of .40 to .81 in predicting end-of-year oral reading performances for the same children (148). These are correlations between testing of potential by listening comprehension at the beginning of the school year with performances in group and individual reading tests at the end of the year. Other studies cited by the author report correlations of .66 of potential with true gain (corrected for regression) after remedial work, an r of .73 of potential with true gain in silent reading, and of .62 with true gain in word recognition after remedial training.

Reliability coefficients for the primary pupils cited above over a five-month interval for the potential measurement were .94 in grade one, .67 in two, and .90 in three. A reliability coefficient for a six-grade range for the potential measure of .99 is cited in the Manual. This was a correlation between one-half of the reading selections (which are usually employed in the initial testing) and the parallel second half of selections, which are recommended for retesting.

To our knowledge, these are the only individual diagnostic batteries that claim or attempt to measure potential for reading through the medium of listening comprehension. The idea that an individual's future performance in reading can be so easily assessed by reading him a series of graded passages is certainly appealing, especially after having read about all the problems inherent in using intelligence tests for this purpose. Yet, it is apparent from our brief review of the individual diagnostic batteries that this is, except in the case of the Diagnostic Reading Scales, an unproven assumption. And, even with this test, predictions are variable from one population to another and in predicting different types of reading performances. Duker reviewed fourteen correlations between listening and reading test scores to find a median r of .61, not a very impressive figure. To state his results another way, 37 percent of reading performances, now or in the future, are sampled by a listening comprehension test. This approach to measuring potential is a feasible one, of moderate significance, as Duker's review of some six studies and the data for the Diagnostic Reading Scales show. In conjunction with a measure of verbal intelligence, or even one of nonverbal intelligence, the additional information gained from the listening comprehension test is useful. From these two or three measures, we can gain some concept of the possibilities for improvement in the case of a retarded reader.

Even these estimates, though, may become erroneous under varying circumstances. The correlations between reading and listening comprehension do not imply a one-to-one continuum, as in making a table to predict one score from the other. Children who make gains in reading do not necessarily test significantly higher in listening than in comprehension. In fact, they may show gains when the opposite test comparison is present. These contradictory but human performances were present in a report by Crowley and Ellis (40). Using the simple procedure of comparing the score in silent reading on one form of a test with that in listening comprehension in a parallel form, these authors tried to predict gains in a small group. A difference of two stanines in the two testings was considered a significant indication of potential for growth in reading. But two of the pupils showed loss in yearly testing despite this difference. Of thirteen, who scored three or more stanines higher in listening, four made more than one stanine growth, five made one stanine, and four made only normal yearly gains in reading or, in other words, retained the same relative position among their peers. As in the case of using intelligence test results to predict potential for improvement in reading, measures of listening comprehension give tentative clues, not highly accurate estimates.

For those who are interested, this is a brief list of group tests of listening comprehension. Before ordering any of these, we recommend that one consult the reviews offered in Buros's *Mental Measurement Yearbooks* (30) or his *Reading Tests and Reviews* (31) for critical evaluation.

Brown-Carlsen Listening Comprehension Test, 1955 (Harcourt Brace Jovanovich). For grades nine to thirteen.

Durrell Listening-Reading Series, 1970 (Harcourt Brace Jovanovich). Different forms for grades one to nine

Sequential Tests of Educational Progress, Listening, 1956 (Educational Testing Service). Separate forms for grades four to fourteen

Diagnostic Reading Tests, Auditory Comprehension, 1957 (Committee on Diagnostic Reading Tests). For grades seven to thirteen

Durrell-Sullivan Reading Capacity and Achievement Tests, 1944 (Harcourt Brace Jovanovich). Parallel reading and listening tests for grades two to six

The ITPA

The Illinois Test of Psycholinguistic Abilities was first published in 1961 and revised in 1968 (82). It is a battery of ten tests, plus two supplementary tests, based on a model of cognitive abilities that distinguishes channels of communication as auditory, visual, vocal, and motor; psycholinguistic processes such as the receptive, the expressive, and the central mediating or organizing process; and levels of organization, as the representational and the automatic. Actually, the authors were unable to implement all permutations of this model for various reasons.

Since the titles and meanings of the various subtests are used very loosely by many who employ them, let us repeat the authors' descriptions:

Receptive Process (Decoding)

Auditory Reception or *Auditory Decoding**—Simple sentences are read to the child to be answered by "yes" or "no" or a movement of the head. Fifty items of gradually increasing difficulty.

Visual Reception or *Visual Decoding*—Matching a given picture with one of a group of four. Forty items.

Organizing Process (Association)

Auditory-Association—An incomplete analogy is read to the child. Forty-two items.

Visual-Association—A stimulus picture is surrounded by others from which the child is to choose which "goes with" the central picture. At upper levels, the presentation takes the form of an analogy in which the examiner points to two related pictures and asks the child to indicate two others similarly related. Total of forty-two items.

Expressive Process (Encoding)

Verbal Expression or *Vocal Encoding*—To sample the child's ability to express his own concepts verbally, he is shown five familiar objects, one at a time, and urged to tell all about each one. The score is the number of

---

*The titles used in the early edition of the ITPA are given in italics.

discrete, approximately factual responses, which may be elicited by spontaneous response and by further questioning by the examiner.

Manual Expression or *Motor Encoding*—Fifteen pictures of common
objects are shown, and the child is asked to demonstrate physically the way
that the object is used.

Automatic Level

Closure or *Grammatic Closure*—An incomplete statement accompanies a picture portraying the action. The child is to complete the sentence
in thirty-three such tasks.

Visual Closure—In each of four pictures an object is partially visible in
fourteen or fifteen places. The child is to point to as many of these as he
can in thirty seconds.

Auditory Closure—Segments of thirty words are spoken, and the child
is expected to fill in the missing parts, as in airpla/   . This and the next test
are considered supplementary and need not be given to all pupils, except
those showing actual or potential problems in reading.

Sound Blending—The sounds of a word are given at half-second
intervals, and the child is asked to say the word. Pictures are used to aid
younger children, while nonsense words are used at the upper levels.

Sequential Memory

Auditory Sequential Memory—Two to eight digits are repeated at the
rate of two per second, and the child is expected to repeat the series after
the first or second trial.

Visual Sequential Memory—The examiner demonstrates a sequence of
small chips with symbols marked on them. Then, the child is asked to
reproduce the sequence, after a five-second look at a printed model.

Age and scaled score norms are given for ages two to ten and also a
composite age norm, omitting the two supplementary tests. The standardization group was composed of approximately 1,000 children, who were selected
as being of average mental and school achievement ability, socioeconomic
status, and sensory development. In other words, the group did not represent a true cross-section of the population but rather the average, or perhaps
middle-class segment; for example, the midwestern children sampled included only minute samples of nonwhite, non-Anglo-American cases. No reliability or validity coefficients are cited in the Manual, but the authors do
suggest comparisons among the scaled scores and indicate that differences of
7 or more scaled points between the median scaled score and an individual
subtest is significant. They also suggest making a diagnosis of the pupil's
needs by observing the specific areas or levels in which the child scores
poorly, as, for example, the automatic group.

This type of interpretation of the ITPA assumes that each group of tests forms a relatively independent factor or that each group designated as representing an input or output channel, or a level of functioning, is closely interrelated, in a manner that distinguishes the group from the other tests. Use of the ITPA as a diagnostic instrument to identify areas of deficit, which are then responsive to remediation, is also assumed by the authors. First of all, however, factor analyses of the nine tests of the first edition, such as that by McLeod (98), do not group the tests in the same manner as do the authors. McLeod identified what he called a visual motor factor composed of visual motor association (now called visual association), and the WISC Block Design and Object Assembly. Motor encoding (now called Manual Expression) had a low loading on this factor. McLeod's second factor, termed Integrative-Sequencing, included the auditory-vocal automatic (Grammatic Closure), the visual motor sequential, auditory-vocal sequential (Auditory Sequential Memory), and the digit span of the WISC. This factor was related to reading achievement, while the visual motor factor did not predict reading very well.

Smith and Marx's analysis of the original matrix for the standardization group indicated that general linguistic or verbal ability accounted for 80 percent of the variance in test scores, while expressive ability formed a second small factor. The general linguistic factor included subtests from both the representational and automatic groups, and both receptive and organizing processes. Smith and Marx (143) considered this factor tantamount to general intelligence. They also identified three other factors, as follows: Rote Auditory Memory—auditory sequential memory and sound blending; Mediated Memory—auditory association, visual association, visual sequential memory, and the WISC I.Q.; Representational Expression—verbal expression and manual expression.

Smith and Marx offered a number of comments on the subtests, based on their data, as the following:

1. All the nine subtests give significant correlations with WISC I.Q.'s, and the *r* in the case of "Psycholinguistic Age" is .63. (In the ITPA Manual, it is acknowledged that the instrument is a measure of molar intelligence.) Are we then to consider psycholinguistic abilities as facets of intelligence or of language development? What is the ITPA adding to our knowledge about the child if it is, in effect, largely a measure of verbal intelligence, other than perhaps new names for old subtests of intelligence?

2. Many of the subtest classifications can be questioned. For example, Auditory Reception may demand organizing rather than receptive processes; Visual Reception involves both memory and conceptual thinking and may be verbal as well as visual; Visual Sequential Memory may be representational rather than simply automatic rote reproduction of non-meaningful material, and so forth.

3. The groupings suggested by the authors or the use of the profile for diagnosis of areas of deficit are hardly supported by the relationships among the tests indicated by the factor analysis.

In his review (30) John B. Carroll strongly questions the description of the battery as a measure of psycholinguistic abilities. Only about half of the tests actually involve use of language, or the language of the examiner; that is, they are nonlanguage measures. Carroll also cites several factor analyses of the ITPA that appear to indicate much the same ideas as Smith and Marx, namely, the verbal comprehension or verbal intelligence factor, an immediate memory span factor, and a factor of auditory processing found only in the data for lower-class children (which may indicate the extent to which these children understood the dialect of the examiner). Carroll also criticizes the authors' interpretations of each subtest; the high correlations of the scaled scores with the Stanford-Binet; the excessive testing time and complexity of administration of the tests; and the use of a "normal" standardization group as a basis for a test offered for use with disabled or handicapped or mentally retarded children, for whom no comparative data are offered. Other critics of the ITPA (94, 158) offer parallel comments regarding validity, reliability, labeling, and other features.

The disagreement between the authors' grouping of tests, as into the visual or auditory channel, and the factor analyses that we have cited immediately raises the question of the validity of the ITPA in distinguishing preferred learning modalities of children. While the authors may not make a specific claim that their instrument makes this distinction, it is certainly implied in the labeling of the tests; and the battery has been widely used for this purpose. The use of the profile to identify areas of deficit as recommended by the authors tends to promote this type of interpretation, if accepted at face value. Yet Barbara Bateman (12), who has written extensively on the ITPA, rejects the use of the profile or scaled scores, preferring the mean age on the subtests as a point of reference. To support her criticism, she points out that even the original standardization group for the earlier edition varied above and below their mean age by significant amounts in auditory decoding (Auditory Reception). Six-year-olds tended to score below mean language age in visual decoding (44 percent) and motor encoding (48 percent) and in auditory visual sequencing (44 percent); while eight-year-olds were on the average a year below the mean language age (72 percent) in verbal expression, according to Bateman. We do not know whether these same inconsistencies in the norms are present in the newest edition, since the necessary data are not offered in the Manual.

Patterns of subtest scores do seem to appear for educable mental retardates, trainable mental retardates, the deaf, and the receptive aphasic (but not for the expressive aphasic) in a number of studies (57, 105). But the question whether suspected deficits are remediable does not seem to have been answered conclusively. Kirk and Bateman, who speak strongly for the ITPA in diagnosis and remediation of learning disabilities (81), support this claim by recounting the gains after remedial work in two areas of one of three siblings. The two untrained did not show such gains. As Gentile (57) has pointed out, this result does not really prove the validity of the diagnosis, since almost any remedial program even without testing for areas of weakness may well have produced such gains. We might add that this sort of evidence for gain on a retest as proof of validity of diagnosis resembles many of the studies with the Frostig program that we reviewed in chapter 1. Gain on a retest after some sort of remedial intervention does not prove the relevance of the test to reading improvement, in the case of the Frostig, or in psycholinguistic development, in the case of the ITPA.

To cite but a single other study in futility, let us refer to Smith's efforts with a group of sixteen matched pairs of educable mental retardates, ages seven to ten (142). A special program three times a week in encoding, decoding, and associating symbols was given the experimental group. The matched controls received no such training. Retest after three months gave a significant increase in mean total psycholinguistic ages for the trained group, compared with the others. But when thirteen of the sixteen pairs were retested nine months later, that gain on the ITPA did not persist (102). Does the ITPA really yield diagnostic information that can lead to successful prescriptive treatment?

In our context here, the crucial question is the relevance of the ITPA to reading development. As a clue to the answer, we have assembled about a dozen studies that attempted to identify patterns characteristic of poor readers. Most of these studies were pursued with the earlier editions, and thus we lack data on the two new supplementary tests and the new Visual Closure test. Most of these reports used the subtest titles offered in the older editions, all of which have been changed in the current version. Since some of our readers may wish to read these original reports, we shall give both titles for the subtests to aid in their relating the studies to Table 6–2.

The consistency with which poor readers exhibit a particular subtest pattern of deficit is obviously not very great. Only the Auditory Sequential Memory (digit span) appears as an area of weakness in half of these reports. Two other tests that the authors characterize as employing the auditory channel—Auditory Reception and Grammatic Closure—appear to distinguish good and poor readers, as does the Visual Sequential Memory. Considered as

TABLE 6-2 PATTERNS OF ITPA SUBTEST SCORES AMONG POOR READERS

NEW TITLES	VISUAL RECEP.	AUDITORY ASSN.	VISUAL ASSN.	VERBAL EXPRESS.	MANUAL EXPRESS.	GRAMMATIC CLOSURE	AUDITORY SEQUEN. MEMORY	VISUAL SEQUEN. MEMORY	AUDITORY RECEP.
Brown and Rice (24)							L*		
Bruininks (28) i.t.a group		L				L	L		L
Bruininks (28) basal group		L	L						
Goldstein et al. (59)								L	
Kass (79,80)	H*	L				L		L	
McLeod (98,99)		L				L	L	L	L
Sheperd (133)							L		
Slobodzian (139)	L	L					L		
Slobodzian (139)							L		
Washington (157) and Treska		L				L			
Bateman (11)						L	L	L	
Guthrie (63)				L				L	
Sears (130)									

Old titles of these same tests, in order, are Visual Decoding, Auditory-Vocal Association, Visual-Motor Association, Vocal Encoding, Motor Encoding, Auditory-Vocal Sequencing, Visual-Motor Sequencing, and Auditory Decoding. New tests, as Visual Closure, Auditory Closure, and Sound Blending, have not yet been reported in such studies.

*L = Poor readers significantly lower than good; H = poor readers significantly higher.

a group called Integrative-Sequencing by McLeod (99), the Grammatic Closure, Auditory Sequential Memory, and Visual Sequential Memory offer what some would consider a typical pattern for those with learning or reading disabilities.

In contrast, Margaret Clark of Glasgow found that the Auditory Sequential Memory was the best performance among the Scottish children who showed persistent failure in reading during the first three years of school (34). Moreover, several studies have shown the interaction between this particular type of auditory memory for digits and the method of reading instruction. Bruininks, Lucker, and Gropper (28) found the test significantly related to failure in reading under the American i.t.a. system but irrelevant to success in a common basal reader system. Using the similar auditory span test of the Detroit Learning Aptitude battery, Neville (110) noted the interaction of span and method when comparing the effectiveness of combinations of oral, silent, and echoic learning sessions.

This auditory memory span test has been used in intelligence testing since the time of Binet-Simon; it appears in both the Stanford-Binet and WISC as well as in other widely known intelligence tests. Arthur I. Gates used such a measure in his early reading diagnostic tests of 1936 but dropped it in later editions because of inconsistent diagnostic significance. Thus, although the Auditory Sequential Memory appears, as if by chance, in half of the pattern analyses of poor readers, it is certainly a questionable measure of language development (or psycholinguistic abilities) and may indeed appear significant only under certain methods of teaching reading.

The Grammatic Closure and the Auditory Association yielded significant relationships with academic achievement in the Washington and Treska report (157), alone among all the other ITPA tests. And the correlation between Stanford-Binet MA's and ITPA total scores was .85 in a population of preschool and elementary pupils largely drawn from the disadvantaged group.

Cicirelli et al. (33) studied the profiles of various ethnic and racial groups of disadvantaged pupils. These children tended to be below average in all tests in all age groups except for Visual Sequential Memory in second and third grades. Profiles for white, black, and Mexican-American children were similar in the second and third grades. Auditory Reception and Auditory Association correlated best with the readiness and the reading test, with Grammatic Closure next most significant. The correlation of Auditory Association with the readiness test in the first grade (.613) was as great as that between the total scores on ITPA and readiness. Two observations, at least, are possible from this study of about 1,500 disadvantaged children: except for two subtests, the ITPA does not appear to be culture-free; and the validities of various subtests in predicting readiness or reading achievement seem to vary considerably from one study to the next. Moreover, the pattern analysis of this group of children who might be expected to show language difficulties and low reading achievement does not agree with the typical pattern of poor readers tentatively identified by McLeod and in our summary of various reports.

For those active in the diagnosis of reading and learning disabilities, the significant question is how or whether to use the ITPA as part of the diagnostic procedures. The relationships with reading achievement of the various ITPA subtests are certainly not anywhere as consistent as the WISC patterns. Nor is there yet strong evidence of the predictive value of the battery in attempting to estimate potential for reading performance. Most of the subtests are affected by socioeconomic status, as we would expect for an instrument standardized on a population drawn from various levels of the middle class.

Perhaps the ITPA can serve as a supplementary test when the diagnostician wishes more information in certain areas. This does not mean, however, that the subtests can be used at face value in terms of their labeling. As in the case of the WISC, the subtests used as supplementary diagnostic measures should probably be interpreted in terms of the indications of the factor analyses rather than the authors' groupings. Following McLeod's factors (98), we might sample the child's abilities in the following:

> Visual Motor Factor—Visual Association
> Manual Expression
> Integrative Sequencing—Grammatic Closure
> Visual Sequential Memory
> Auditory Sequential Memory

Or, following Smith and Marx's findings:

> Rote Auditory Memory—Auditory Sequential Memory
> Sound Blending
> Mediated Memory—Auditory Association
> Visual Association
> Visual Sequential Memory
> Representational Expression—Verbal Expression
> Manual Expression

In another report on a factor analysis of the ITPA, McLeod (99) distinguished a different group of factors:

> 1. Sequencing Integrative—Auditory Sequential Memory
> Auditory Association
> 2. Encoding Factor—Manual Expression
> Visual Reception

3. Visual Motor Factor—Manual Expression
   Visual Association
4. Auditory Language Input Capacity—Auditory Reception
5. Planning Factor—WISC Arithmetic and Mazes

In this particular analysis, McLeod included the subtests of the WISC, the Wepman, the Northwestern University Auditory Test, his Dyslexia Schedule, and measures of reading by the tachistoscope and of the auditory reproduction of words in context. Some of these other tests were included in various factors, but we have not given all the details, since they are not significant to the question of how to use the ITPA.

Associative Learning Predictors

Since the problem of predicting reading potential has been with us since formal reading diagnosis first began, we have had many approaches to a solution. For example, associative learning measures of the child's ability to form a relationship between words and symbols were used by Arthur I. Gates in his diagnostic battery of 1936. Basically the attempt was made to determine the number of trials required for a child to associate a geometric symbol on one side of a card with a word on the other side. Obviously, poor readers do not do well in associative learning of this type (else they would not be poor readers). Gates dropped the test in later editions, probably because it did not really give any diagnostic information. But the idea has persisted in various forms even to the present day. The findings of an experiment like that of Woodcock (159), who pretested beginning readers in a lesson of learning artificial symbols and words, with better predictive results than an individual intelligence test, has helped keep the idea of testing associative learning alive.

Present-day psychologists call such experiments paired associate learning and use the procedure to ferret out many facts about learning. Among these are the values of colored letters in the words to be learned, colored backgrounds, and the relative merits of a presentation by picture-printed word; picture-spoken word; elaboration of the association (by the spoken sentence), that is, "the *knife* cuts the *cake*" or by simulating the elaboration by the action in the picture; and various combinations of these procedures. Other paired associate learning experiments explore the influence of the order of the list of words, of clang or meaningful relationships among the list, or ordination and superordination relationships among the words, and so on.

In effect, paired associate experiments are trials in learning reading that do parallel some types of classroom presentations. Since this is so, many clues as to how children learn words as well as how well they learn under certain circumstances can be uncovered. Also, because paired associate learning seems to be free from the influence of socioeconomic or racial grouping, several authors have suggested that a paired associate learning test is the best instrument for prediction of potential for learning to read (62, 84). Actually what these authors are telling us is that a trial or two in learning to associate words or words and symbols will tell us how well the kindergartner or first grader is likely to do in subsequent reading lessons. This is undoubtedly true, but what information of diagnostic or preventive nature will such an approach yield? All we shall learn is that the child is or is not likely to respond successfully to the particular kind of presentation that we used in the paired associate learning test. What if this procedure does not exactly parallel later reading lessons? What other types of presentations might be more successful for the child?

The question that we really should be trying to answer is that of identifying a kind of presentation most likely to promote progress in early reading of each individual child. In our opinion, it seems much more practical to utilize some prereading test such as the Mills Learning Methods Test (101), which will give us some significant clues as to the types of presentations that the child is most likely to respond to. Like any other method of testing for the preferred learning modality, the Mills Test gives a clue to a desired emphasis upon an input channel, which we need to explore in depth to refine our teaching sessions for insuring reasonable progress of the subject.

Other Predictors

Ever since case studies began to be utilized to study individuals who were disabled readers, it has become apparent that a number of factors in the school and family backgrounds are related to the disability. We shall consider some of these factors in other sections of this text in discussing social, environmental, educational, and personality factors in reading disability. Here we shall briefly look at certain predictors ordinarily derived from basic data about the subject and the common diagnostic tests. Some of the reports on the results of remedial work or those following up cases after remediation have explored a variety of data to determine which facts best predicted gain or retention of gain. As we might expect, the size and homogeneity of the groups, their ages, and the nature of the remedial treatment varies from one report to another. But we shall attempt to summarize and reconcile the findings.

Grade Level   It appears that, in most studies, upper elementary children respond more favorably to intensive remediation than do younger pupils (17, 41, 153). Only Lytton reports that his secondary pupils lost more in a retest about sixteen months after remedial treatment than did those still in primary schools (90). In contrast, Evelyn W. Stone (150) followed up at five to ten-year intervals both elementary and secondary pupils treated in a university reading center. Among the elementary and the secondary pupils the delayed test indicated performances within one standard deviation of the mean for present age and grade level. In fact, those treated during their secondary school period exhibited higher scores than the elementary pupils did. This difference was present even when the difference in school grades completed and hours of tutoring were equated.

Age

Age is, of course, practically synonymous with grade level and bears the same relationship to gains from remedial work or posttraining retention of gains.

Initial Status

The results of the reading tests administered in the course of diagnosis are positively related to the pupil's gains from remedial work. The higher the reading test scores (even though these are significantly below grade level), the greater the gains, in general, according to Bluestein (17) and, in particular, in silent reading, according to Dahlke (41), who accepted only true gains as relevant. Tillman (153), who also emphasized only true gains, found that initial status in word recognition, oral reading, and silent reading were significantly related to each true gain in each of the three areas.

Degree of Disability

The tendency for extremely low scorers to regress toward the mean, after any sort of remediation, leads many to assume that the greater the degree of disability, the more gains from treatment, as in Bluestein's report (17). But when this regression and the reliability of the test are controlled and only true gain is measured, the degree of disability is not significant as a predictor of gains, as in the dissertations of Dahlke and Tillman (41, 153).

Duration of Remediation

The actual number of hours spent in remediation, assuming a reasonable period such as twenty to forty hours, is not positively related to the degree of gains (17, 151, 153). Nor is the apparent progress of the student while undergoing treatment a good predictor of the final improvement, according to Lovell, Johnson, and Platts (88). As these observers noted, there were many children who showed little progress during remediation but who did improve spontaneously later, as well as many who showed the opposite trends. Good progress during remediation and gain in the posttraining test were not consistent predictors of reading status a year later in this study. Progress during remediation is an indicator of what is probably happening during the remedial sessions, and of the gains that may appear in a test immediately after the training, but these observations apparently have little long-range validity.

Intelligence   As we remarked before, the direct use of an I.Q. such as that derived from the WISC does not consistently indicate the degree of gain or retention of gain from remediation.   Lytton (67) and Bond and Tinker (20) seemed to observe that those with higher I.Q.'s made greater gains and retained those gains, at least in Lytton's follow-up.   Tillman (153) found all three WISC I.Q.'s related to true gains in oral reading, but of little practical importance in prediction. Dahlke (41) found neither the I.Q.'s, the P. versus V., or the subtest scores of the WISC significantly related to gains in any area of reading.   Lovell et al. report *r*'s from .12 to .38 between I.Q. and reading in their follow-up study (88), relationships that are hardly useful.

Despite his acceptance of intelligence as a predictor of gains, Lytton decries the use of an Achievement Quotient (RA/MA) as a predictor, for it was not a better predictor than teacher judgment (89, 90).

Reading Interests   Although they may be helpful in selecting appropriate reading materials during the remedial treatment, one study reported that a reading interest inventory did not predict gains for primary children (1).

Listening Comprehension   Bluestein (17), Dahlke (41), and Tillman (153) reported that measures of listening comprehension were useful as predictors of gain from remedial work.   Dahlke noted a significant correlation of listening comprehension and true gain in silent reading, while Tillman found the measure related to posttraining true gains in word recognition, listening comprehension, and silent reading, although this relationship was marked only in word recognition and silent reading.   Thus all these three studies that evaluated listening comprehension as a predictor agreed that it was most closely related to crude or true gains in silent reading, as we might logically expect.   None of the authors, however, recommended listening comprehension to be used alone, or independently of some of the other predictors discussed earlier.

LEARNING PROJECT

Select several of these means of estimating pupil ability that might be combined into a multifaceted assessment.   Choose those that supplement each other in offering additional information, rather than duplicating.   Try to sample the pupil's cognitive abilities as thoroughly as possible, without requiring excessive testing time.

Then justify your selection by constructing a chart showing (a) in the first column, the names of the tests and the cognitive abilities sampled; (b) in the second

column, the probable implications of each ability for remedial planning; (c) in the third column, the sources you might use for corroborative information, as various records, interviews, observations, and so on.

REFERENCES

1. Aaron, Ira E., Callaway, B., Hicks, R., and Simpson, Hazel D., "Reading Achievement in a Summer Reading Program," *Elementary English,* 64 (December 1967), 875–77, 882.
2. Abrams, Jules C., "Psychotherapy and Learning Problems: The Role of the Clinical Psychologist," in *Multidisciplinary Aspects of College-Adult Reading,* George B. Schick and Merrill M. May, editors, Seventeenth Yearbook National Reading Conference, 1968, 84–89.
3. Ali, Faizuniza, and Costello, Joan, "Modification of the Peabody Picture Vocabulary Test," *Developmental Psychology,* 5 (July 1971), 86–91.
4. Ammons, Robert B., and Ammons, Helen S., *Full Range Picture Vocabulary Test.* Louisville: Southern Universities Press, 1948.
5. Ammons, Robert B., and Ammons, C. H., *The Quick Test.* Missoula, Mont.: Psychological Test Specialists, 1962.
6. Anastasi, Anne, "Culture-Fair Testing," *Education Digest,* 30 (April 1965), 9–11.
7. Armstrong, R. J., and Mooney, R. F., "The Slosson Intelligence Test: Implications for Reading Specialists," *Reading Teacher,* 24 (January 1971), 336–40, 368.
8. Backman, Margaret E., "Patterns of Mental Abilities: Ethnic, Socioeconomic and Sex Differences," *American Educational Research Journal,* 9 (Winter 1972), 1–12.
9. Baker, Harry J., and Leland, Bernice, *Detroit Tests of Learning Aptitude.* Indianapolis: Bobbs-Merrill, 1968.
10. Bannatyne, Alex, "Diagnosing Learning Disabilities and Writing Remedial Prescriptions," *Journal of Learning Disabilities,* 1 (April 1968), 239–46.
11. Bateman, Barbara, "Reading and Psycholinguistic Processes of Partially Seeing Children," pp. 70–86 in *Selected Studies on the Illinois Tests of Psycholinguistic Abilities.* Urbana: University of Illinois Press, 1963.
12. Bateman, Barbara, "A Reference Line of Use with the ITPA," *Journal of School Psychology,* 5 (Winter 1967), 128–35.
13. Beck, Frances, "Performance of Retarded Readers on Parts of the Wechsler Intelligence Scale for Children," pp. 91–103 in *Clinical Studies in Reading III,* Helen M. Robinson, editor. Supplementary Educational Monographs, No. 97. Chicago: University of Chicago Press, 1968.
14. Belmont, Lillian, and Birch, H. G., "The Intellectual Profile of Retarded Readers," *Perceptual and Motor Skills,* 6 (1966), 787–816.
15. Bijou, Sidney W., "The Psychometric Pattern Approach as an Aid to Clinical Analysis—a Review," *American Journal of Mental Deficiency,* 46 (January 1942), 354–62.
16. Bliesmer, Emory P., "A Comparison of Results of Various Capacity Tests Used with Retarded Readers," *Elementary School Journal,* 56 (March 1956), 400–402.

17. Bluestein, V. W., "Factors Related to and Predictive of Improvement in Reading," *Psychology in the Schools,* 4 (1967), 272–76.
18. Bond, Guy L., "Diagnostic Teaching in the Classroom," in *Reading Diagnosis and Evaluation,* Dorothy L. DeBoer, editor, Proceedings International Reading Association, 13, No. 4 (1970), 126–38.
19. Bond, Guy L., and Fay, Leo C., "A Comparison of the Performance of Good and Poor Readers on the Individual Items of the Stanford-Binet Scale, Forms L and M," *Journal of Educational Research,* 43 (February 1950), 465–79.
20. Bond, Guy L., and Tinker, Miles A., *Reading Difficulties—Their Diagnosis and Correction.* New York: Appleton-Century-Crofts, 1967.
21. Botel, Morton, *Botel Reading Inventory.* Chicago: Follett Publishing, 1962.
22. Brown D. A., "Variables Predictive of Success in Learning to Read," in *Reading and Realism,* J. Allen Figurel, editor, Proceedings International Reading Association, 13 (1969), 794–97.
23. Brown, D. A., "Intelligence of Adult Illiterates," in *Reading: Process and Pedagogy,* George B. Schick and Merrill M. May, editors, Nineteenth Yearbook National Reading Conference, 1971, 94–98.
24. Brown, Louis F., and Rice, James A., "Psycholinguistic Differentiation of Low I.Q. Children," *Mental Retardation,* 5 (February 1967), 16–20.
25. Bruininks, Robert H., "Relationship of Auditory and Visual Perceptual Strengths to Methods of Teaching Word Recognition among Disadvantaged Negro Boys," Doctoral dissertation, George Peabody College for Teachers, 1968.
26. Bruininks, Robert H., Glaman, Gertrude M., and Clark, Charlotte R., "Issues in Determining Prevalence of Reading Retardation," *Reading Teacher,* 27 (November 1973), 177–86.
27. Bruininks, Robert H., and Lucker, William G., "Change and Stability in Correlations Between Intelligence and Reading Test Scores among Disadvantaged Children," *Journal of Reading Behavior,* 2 (Fall 1970), 295–305.
28. Bruininks, Robert H., Lucker, William G., and Gropper, Robert L., "Psycholinguistic Abilities of Good and Poor Reading Disadvantaged First-Graders," *Elementary School Journal,* 70 (April 1970), 378–86.
29. Burks, H. F., and Bruce, P., "The Characteristics of Poor and Good Readers as Disclosed by the Wechsler Intelligence Scale for Children," *Journal of Educational Psychology,* 46 (December 1955), 488–93.
30. Buros, Oscar K., *Seventh Mental Measurements Yearbook.* Highland Park, N.J.: Gryphon Press, 1972.
31. Buros, Oscar K., *Reading Tests and Reviews.* Highland Park, N.J.: Gryphon Press, 1968.
32. Callaway, Byron, "Factors Related to Reading of Children Referred to a University Reading Clinic," pp. 61–66 in *Reading Difficulties: Diagnosis, Correction and Remediation,* William K. Durr, editor. Newark, Del.: International Reading Association, 1970.
33. Cicirelli, Victor G., Granger, Robert, Schemmel, Denny, Cooper, William, and Holthouse, Norman, "Performance of Disadvantaged Primary-Grade Children on the Revised Illinois Test of Psycholinguistic Abilities," *Psychology in the Schools,* 8 (July 1971), 240–46.
34. Clark, Margaret M., *Reading Difficulties in Schools.* Baltimore: Penguin Books, 1970.

35. Cohen, J., "Factorial Structure of the WISC at Ages 7–10, 10–6 and 13–6," *Journal of Consulting Psychology,* 23 (1959), 285–99.

36. Coleman, James C., and Rasof, Beatrice, "Intellectual Factors in Learning Disorders," *Perceptual and Motor Skills,* 16 (1963), 139–52.

37. Cooper, G. David, et al., "The Porteus Test and Various Measures of Intelligence with Southern Negro Adolescents," *American Journal of Mental Deficiency,* 71 (March 1967), 787–92.

38. Corwin, Betty Jane, "The Relationship between Reading Achievement and Performance on Individual Ability Tests," *Journal of School Psychology,* 5 (Winter 1967), 156–57.

39. Costello, Joan, and Ali, Faizuniza, "Reliability and Validity of Peabody Picture Vocabulary Test Scores of Disadvantaged Preschool Children," *Psychological Reports,* 28 (June 1971), 755–60.

40. Crowley, H. L., and Ellis, Bessie, "Cross Validation of a Method for Selecting Children Requiring Special Services in Reading," *Reading Teacher,* 24 (January 1971), 312–19.

41. Dahlke, Anita B., "The Use of WISC Scores to Predict Reading Improvement after Remedial Tutoring," doctoral dissertation, University of Florida, 1968.

42. Deal, Margaret, "A Summary of Research Concerning Patterns of WISC Subtest Scores of Retarded Readers," *Journal of Reading Specialist,* 4 (May 1965), 101–11.

43. De Bruler, Ralph Miles, "An Investigation of Relationships between Subtest Scores on the WISC and Reading Ability," *Dissertation Abstracts,* 29 (1968), 143–44A.

44. Deutsch, Martin, and Brown, Bert, "Social Influences in Negro-White Intelligence Differences," *Journal of Social Issues,* 20 (April 1964), 24–35.

45. Dockrell, W. B., "The Use of Wechsler Intelligence Scale for Children in the Diagnosis of Retarded Readers," *Alberta Journal of Educational Research,* 6 (June 1960), 86–91.

46. Dudek, S. Z., and Lester, E. P., "The Good Child Facade in Chronic Underachievers," *American Journal of Orthopsychiatry,* 38 (1968), 153–59.

47. Duker, Sam, "Listening and Reading," *Elementary School Journal,* 65 (March 1965), 321–29.

48. Dunn, Lloyd M., *Expanded Manual Peabody Picture Vocabulary Test.* Circle Pines, Minn.: American Guidance Services, 1965.

49. Durrell, Donald D., "The Influence of Reading Ability on Intelligence Measures," *Journal of Educational Psychology,* 24 (September 1933), 412–16.

50. Durrell, Donald D., *Durrell Analysis of Reading Difficulty.* New York: Harcourt Brace Jovanovich, 1955.

51. Durrell, Donald D., Hayes, Mary T., and Brassard, Mary B., *Durrell Listening-Reading Series.* New York: Harcourt Brace Jovanovich, 1969.

52. Eakin, Suzanne, and Douglas, Virginia I., "Automatization and Oral Reading Problems in Children," *Journal of Learning Disabilities,* 4 (January 1971), 26–33.

53. Ekwall, E. E., "The Use of WISC Subtest Profiles in the Diagnosis of Reading Difficulties," doctoral dissertation, University of Arizona, 1966.

54. Farr, Roger, *Reading: What Can Be Measured.* Reading Review Series, ERIC/CRIER. Newark, Del.: International Reading Association, 1969.

55. Fitzgerald, Bernard J., Pasewark, Richard A., and Gloeckler, Ted, "Use of the Peabody Picture Vocabulary Test with the Educationally Handicapped," *Journal of School Psychology,* 8 (1970), 296–300.

56. Gates, Arthur I., "The Necessary Mental Age for Beginning Reading," *Elementary School Journal,* 37 (March 1937), 498–508.
57. Gentile, J. Ronald, "In Search of Research: Four Children's Tests," *Journal of School Psychology,* 5 (Autumn 1966), 1–13.
58. Glavin, John P., and Annesley, Fred R., "Reading and Arithmetic Correlates of Conduct-Problem and Withdrawn Children," *Journal of Special Education,* 5 (Fall 1971), 213–19.
59. Goldstein, H. A., Whitney, G., and Cawley, J. F., "Prediction of Perceptual Reading Disability among Disadvantaged Children in the Second Grade," *Reading Teacher,* 24 (October 1970), 23–28.
60. Graham, E. E., "Wechsler Bellevue and WISC Scattergrams of Unsuccessful Readers," *Journal of Consulting Psychology,* 16 (1952), 268–71.
61. Graubard, Paul S., "The Use of the Peabody Picture Vocabulary Test in the Prediction and Assessment of Reading Disability in Disturbed Children," *Journal of Educational Research,* 61 (September 1967), 3–5.
62. Green, Richard B., and Rohwer, William D., "SES Differences on Learning and Ability Tests in Black Children," *American Educational Research Journal,* 8 (November 1971), 601–609.
63. Guthrie, John T., Goldberg, Herman K., and Finucci, Joan, "Independence of Abilities in Disabled Readers," *Journal of Reading Behavior,* 4 (Spring 1972), 129–38.
64. Hafner, Lawrence E., Weaver, Wendell., and Powell, Kathryn, "Psychological and Perceptual Correlates of Reading Achievement among Fourth Graders," *Journal of Reading Behavior,* 2 (Fall 1970), 281–90.
65. Hammill, Donald, "The Slosson Intelligence Test as a Quick Estimate of Mental Ability," *Journal of School Psychology,* 7 (1968–69), 33–37.
66. Harris, Albert J., *How to Increase Reading Ability.* New York: David McKay, 1970.
67. Harris, Dale B., *Goodenough-Harris Drawing Test.* New York: Harcourt Brace Jovanovich, 1963.
68. Hatch, Eric, and French, Joseph L., "The Revised ITPA: Its Reliability and Validity for use with EMR's," *Journal of School Psychology,* 9 (1971), 16–23.
69. Henderson, Norman B., Butler, Bruce V., and Goffeney, Barbara, "Effectiveness of the WISC and Bender-Gestalt Test in Predicting Arithmetic and Reading Achievement for White and Non-White Children," *Journal of Clinical Psychology,* 25 (July 1969), 268–71.
70. Hirst, Lynne., "The Usefulness of a Two-Way Analysis of WISC Sub-tests in the Diagnosis of Remedial Reading Problems," *Journal of Experimental Education, 29* (December 1960), 153–60.
71. Houston, Camille, and Otto, Wayne, "Poor Readers' Functioning on the WISC, Slosson Intelligence Test and Quick Test," *Journal of Educational Research,* 42 (December 1968), 157–59.
72. Huelsman, Charles B., Jr., "The WISC Subtest Syndrome for Disabled Readers," *Perceptual and Motor Skills,* 30 (1970), 535–50.
73. Ivanoff, John M., and Tempero, Howard E., "Effectiveness of the Peabody Picture Vocabulary Test with Seventh-Grade Pupils," *Journal of Educational Research,* 58 (May–June 1965), 412–15.
74. Jensen, Arthur R., and Rohwer, William D., "Mental Retardation, Mental Age and Learning Rate," *Journal of Educational Psychology,* 59 (December 1968), 402–403.

75. Jerrolds, B. W., Callaway, Byron, and Gwaltney, W., "A Comparative Study of Three Tests of Intellectual Potential, Three Tests of Reading Achievement, and the Discrepancy Scores between Potential and Achievement," *Journal of Educational Research,* 65 (December 1971), 168–72.

76. Jerrolds, B. W., Gwaltney, W., and Callaway, Byron, *A Study Comparing the Slosson Intelligence Test for Children and the Wechsler Intelligence Scale with Disabled Readers.* Athens: College of Education, University of Georgia.

77. Kahn, Harris, "Evidence for Long-Term Reliability of the PPVT with Adolescent and Young Adult Retardates," *American Journal of Mental Deficiency,* 70 (May 1966), 895–98.

78. Kallos, G. L., Grabow, J. M., and Guarino, E. A., "The WISC Profile of Disabled Readers," *Personnel Guidance Journal,* 39 (1961), 476–78.

79. Kass, Corinne E., "Some Psychological Correlates of Severe Reading Disability (Dyslexia)," doctoral dissertation, University of Illinois, 1962.

80. Kass, Corinne E., "The Psycholinguistic Abilities of Retarded Readers," *Kansas Studies in Education,* 18 (1968), 35–47.

81. Kirk, S. A., and Bateman, B. D., "Diagnosis and Remediation of Learning Disabilities," *Exceptional Child,* 29 (1962), 73–78.

82. Kirk, S. A., McCarthy, James J., and Kirk, Winifred D., *The Illinois Test of Psycholinguistic Abilities: Examiner's Manual.* Revised edition. Urbana: University of Illinois Press, 1968.

83. Klineberg, Otto, "Negro-White Differences in Intelligence Test Performance: A New Look at an Old Problem," *American Psychologist,* 18 (April 1963), 198–203.

84. Lambert, Nadine M., "Paired Associate Learning, Social Status and Tests of Logical Concrete Behavior as Univariate and Multivariate Predictors of First Grade Reading Achievement," *American Educational Research Journal,* 7 (November 1970), 511–28.

85. Lewerenz, Alfred S., "Selection of Reading Materials by Pupil Ability and Interest," *Elementary English Review,* 16 (April 1939), 151–56.

86. Lewis, Franklin D., Bell, D. Bruce, and Anderson, Robert P., "Reading Retardation: A Biracial Comparison," *Journal of Reading,* 13 (March 1970), 433–36, 474.

87. Louttit, C. M., *Clinical Psychology.* New York: Harper, 1936.

88. Lovell, K., Johnson, E., and Platts, D., "A Summary of a Study of the Reading Ages of Children Who Had Been Given Remedial Teaching," *British Journal of Educational Psychology,* 32 (1962), 66–71.

89. Lytton, H., "An Experiment in Selection for Remedial Education," *British Journal of Educational Psychology,* 31 (1961), 79–92.

90. Lytton, H., "Follow-up of an Experiment in Selection for Remedial Education," *British Journal of Educational Psychology,* 37 (1967), 1–9.

91. MacArthur, R. S., "The Coloured Progressive Matrices as a Measure of General Intellectual Ability for Edmonton Grade III Boys," *Alberta Journal of Educational Research,* 6 (June 1960), 67–75.

92. MacArthur, R. S., and Elley, W. B., "The Reduction of Socioeconomic Bias in Intelligence Testing," *British Journal of Educational Psychology,* 33 (June 1963), 107–19.

93. MacDonald, H. A., and Netherton, A. H., "Contribution of a Nonverbal General

Ability Test to the Educational Assessment of Pupils in the Cross-Cultural Setting of the Canadian North," *Journal of Educational Research,* 62 (1969), 315–19.

94. McCarthy, James J., "Notes on the Validity of the ITPA," *Mental Retardation,* 3 (April 1965), 25–26.

95. McCracken, Robert A., *Standard Reading Inventory.* Klamath Falls, Ore.: Klamath Printing, 1966.

96. McDonald, Arthur S., editor, "Research for the Classroom: Reading Potential; Appraisal or Prediction," *Journal of Reading,* 8 (November 1964), 115–19.

97. McDonnell, M. W., "The Prediction of Academic Achievement of Superior Grade Three Pupils," *Alberta Journal of Educational Research,* 8 (June 1962), 111–18.

98. McLeod, John, *Dyslexia in Young Children: A Factorial Study with Special Reference to the ITPA.* University of Illinois IREC Papers in Education, 1966.

99. McLeod, John, "Some Perceptual Factors Related to Childhood Dyslexia," pp. 167–77 in *Reading Instruction: An International Forum,* Marion D. Jenkinson, editor. Newark, Del.: International Reading Association, 1967.

100. McLeod, John, "A Comparison of WISC Subtest Scores of Preadolescent Successful and Unsuccessful Readers," *Australian Journal of Psychology,* 17 (1965), 220–28.

101. Mills, Robert E., *Learning Methods Test.* Fort Lauderdale: The Mills Educational Center, 1970.

102. Moe, Iver A., "Auding Ability as a Measure of Reading Potential among Pupils in Primary Grades," doctoral dissertation, University of Florida, 1957.

103. Monroe, Marion, *Children Who Cannot Read.* Chicago: University of Chicago Press, 1932.

104. Mueller, Max W., "Comparison of Psycholinguistic Patterns of Gifted and Retarded Children," *Journal of School Psychology,* 3 (Spring 1965), 18–25.

105. Mueller, Max W., and Smith, J. O., "The Stability of Language Age Modification over Time," *American Journal of Mental Deficiency,* 68 (1964), 537–39.

106. Neisworth, John T., "The Educational Irrelevance of Intelligence," pp. 30–46 in Robert M. Smith, *Teacher Diagnosis of Educational Difficulties.* Columbus: Charles E. Merrill, 1969.

107. Neville, Donald D., "A Comparison of WISC Patterns of Retarded and Non-Retarded Readers," *Journal of Educational Research,* 54 (January 1961), 195–97.

108. Neville, Donald D., "The Relationship between Reading Skills and Intelligence Scores," *Reading Teacher,* 18 (January 1965), 257–62.

109. Neville, Donald D., "Learning Characteristics of Poor Readers as Revealed by the Results of Individually Administered Intelligence Tests," in *Vistas in Reading,* J. Allen Figurel, editor, Proceedings International Reading Association, 11 (1966), 554–59.

110. Neville, Mary., "Effects of Oral and Echoic Responses in Beginning Reading," *Journal of Educational Psychology,* 59 (1968), 362–69.

111. Newland, T. E., and Smith, P. A., "Statistically Significant Differences between Subtest Scaled Scores on the WISC and the WAIS," *Journal of School Psychology,* 5 (1967), 122–27.

112. Otto, W., and McMenemy, R. A., "An Appraisal of the Ammons Quick Test in a Remedial Reading Program," *Journal of Educational Measurement,* 2 (1965), 193–98.

113. Pescosolido, John, and Gervase, Charles, *Reading Expectancy and Readability.* Dubuque: Kendall Hunt Publishing, 1971.

114. Porteus, Stanley D., *The Porteus Maze Test.* New York: Psychological Corporation, 1965.

115. Quereshi, Mohammed Y., "Patterns of Psycholinguistic Development during Early and Middle Childhood," *Educational and Psychological Measurement,* 27 (Summer 1967), 353–65.

116. Ramsey, Phillip H., and Vane, Julia R., "A Factor Analytic Study of the Stanford-Binet with Young Children," *Journal of School Psychology,* 8 (1970), 278–84.

117. Raven, J. C., *Progressive Matrices.* New York: Psychological Corporation, 1938.

118. Reed, James C., "Reading Achievement as Related to Differences between WISC Verbal and Performance I.Q.'s," *Child Development,* 38 (1967), 835–40.

119. Reed, James C., "The Deficits of Retarded Readers—Fact or Artifact?" *Reading Teacher,* 23 (January 1970), 347–52, 393.

120. Reid, W. R., and Schoer, L. A., "Reading Achievement, Social-Class and Sub-test Pattern on the WISC," *Journal of Educational Research,* 59 (1966), 469–71.

121. Robeck, Mildred C., "Effects of Prolonged Reading Disability," *Perceptual and Motor Skills,* 19 (August 1964), 7–12.

122. Rodenborn, Leo V., Jr., "The Importance of Memory and Integration Factors to Oral Reading Ability," *Journal of Reading Behavior,* 3 (Winter 1970), 51–59.

123. Rose, Florence C., "The Occurrence of Short Auditory Memory Span Among School Children Referred for Diagnosis of Reading Difficulties," *Journal of Educational Research,* 51 (1958), 459–64.

124. Sandstedt, Barbara, "Relationship between Memory Span and Intellect of Severely Retarded Readers," *Reading Teacher,* 17 (January 1964), 246–50.

125. Saunders, Bruce T., and Vitro, Frank T., "Examiner Expectancy and Bias as a Function of the Referral Process in Cognitive Assessment," *Psychology in the Schools,* 8 (1971), 168–71.

126. Sawyer, Rita I., "Does the WISC Discriminate between Mildly Disabled and Severely Disabled Readers?" *Elementary School Journal,* 66 (December 1965), 97–103.

127. Schiffman, Gilbert, "Dyslexia as an Educational Phenomenon: Its Recognition and Treatment," pp. 45–60 in *Reading Disability: Progress and Research Needs in Dyslexia,* J. Money, editor. Baltimore: Johns Hopkins Press, 1962.

128. Schiffman, Gilbert, "Diagnosing Cases of Reading Disability with Suggested Neurological Impairment," in *Vistas in Reading,* J. Allen Figurel, editor, Proceedings International Reading Association, 11 (1966), 513–21.

129. Schonell, Fred J., *The Psychology and Teaching of Reading.* New York: Philosophical Library, 1961.

130. Sears, Charles Richards, "A Comparison of the Basic Language Concepts and Psycholinguistic Abilities of Second Grade Boys Who Demonstrate Average and Below Average Levels of Reading Achievement," doctoral dissertation, Colorado State College, 1969.

131. Seashore, Harold, "Difference between Verbal and Performance I.Q.'s on the WISC," *Journal of Consulting Psychology,* 15 (February 1951), 62–67.

132. Semler, Ira J., and Iscoe, Ira, "Structure of Intelligence in Negro and White Children," *Journal of Educational Psychology,* 57 (December 1966), 326–36.

133. Sheperd, G., "Selected Factors in the Reading Ability of Educable Mentally Retarded Boys," *American Journal of Mental Deficiency,* 71 (1967), 563–70.
134. Shipp, Donald E., and Loudon, Mary Lou, "The Draw-a-Man Test and Achievement in the First Grade," *Journal of Educational Research,* 57 (July–August 1964), 518–21.
135. Silberberg, Norman E., and Feldt, Leonard S., "The Peabody Picture Vocabulary Test as an I.Q. Screening Technique for Primary Grade Referral Cases," *Journal of School Psychology,* 5 (Autumn 1966), 21–30.
136. Silberberg, Norman E., and Feldt, Leonard S., "Intellectual and Perceptual Correlates of Reading Disabilities," *Journal of School Psychology,* 6 (Summer 1968), 237–45.
137. Silvaroli, Nicholas J., *Classroom Reading Inventory.* Dubuque: William C. Brown, 1965.
138. Silverstein, A. B., and Hill, T. V., "Comparability of Three Picture Vocabulary Tests with Retarded School Children," *Training School Bulletin,* 64 (1967), 58–61.
139. Slobodzian, Evelyn B., "Use of the Illinois Test of Psycholinguistic Abilities as a Readiness Measure," in *Reading Diagnosis and Evaluation,* Dorothy L. DeBoer, editor, Proceedings International Reading Association, 13, No. 4 (1970), 43–48.
140. Slosson, Richard L., *The Slosson Intelligence Test.* East Aurora, N.Y.: Slosson Educational Publications, 1963.
141. Smith, Edwin H., and Bradtmueller, Weldon G., *Individual Reading Placement Inventory.* Chicago: Follett Publishing, 1969.
142. Smith, J. O., "Group Language Development for Educable Mental Retardates," *Exceptional Child,* 29 (1962), 95–101.
143. Smith, Phillip A., and Marx, Ronald W., "The Factor Structure of the Revised Edition of the Illinois Test of Psycholinguistic Abilities," *Psychology in the Schools,* 8 (July 1971), 349–56.
144. Spache, George D., "The Short Form of the Revised Stanford-Binet Scale Form L in the Test Range II to XIV," *Journal of Consulting Psychology,* 6 (March 1942), 102–104.
145. Spache, George D., "The Vocabulary Tests of the Revised Stanford-Binet Scale as Independent Measures of Intelligence," *Journal of Educational Research,* 36 (March 1943), 512–16.
146. Spache, George D., "Intellectual and Personality Characteristics of Retarded Readers," *Psychological Newsletter,* 9 (September 1957), 9–12.
147. Spache, George D., "Estimating Reading Capacity," pp 15–20 in *Evaluation of Reading,* Helen M. Robinson, editor. Supplementary Educational Monographs No. 88. Chicago: University of Chicago Press, 1958.
148. Spache, George D., *Diagnostic Reading Scales.* Monterey: California Test Bureau, 1972.
149. Stablein, John E., Willey, Darrell S., and Thompson, Calvin W., "An Evaluation of the Davis-Eells (Culture-Fair) Test Using Spanish and Anglo-American Children," *Journal of Educational Sociology,* 35 (October 1961), 73–78.
150. Stone, Evelyn W., "A Follow-up Study of Off-Campus Students Who Attended the University of Florida Reading Laboratory and Clinic," doctoral dissertation, University of Florida, 1967.

151. Strang, Ruth, *Reading Diagnosis and Remediation.* ERIC/CRIER Reading Review Series. Newark, Del.: International Reading Association, 1968.

152. Terman, Lewis M., and Merrill, Maud, *Stanford-Binet Intelligence Scale, Third Revision.* Boston: Houghton Mifflin, 1964.

153. Tillman, Chester Earl, "Crude Gain vs. True Gain: Correlates of Gain in Reading after Remedial Tutoring," doctoral dissertation, University of Florida, 1969.

154. Throne, Frances M., Kaspar, Joseph C., and Schulman, Jerome L., "The Peabody Picture Vocabulary Test in Comparison with Other Intelligence Tests and an Achievement Test in a Group of Mentally Retarded Boys," *Educational and Psychological Measurement,* 25 (Summer 1965), 589–95.

155. Torgerson, Theodore, and Adams, Georgia, *Measurement and Evaluation for the Elementary Teacher.* New York: Holt, 1954.

156. Van Alstyne, Dorothy, *Van Alstyne Picture Vocabulary Test.* New York: Harcourt Brace Jovanovich, 1961.

157. Washington, E. D., and Treska, J. A., "Correlations between the Wide Range Achievement Test, the California Achievement Tests, the Stanford-Binet, and the Illinois Test of Psycholinguistic Abilities," *Psychological Reports,* 26 (1970), 291–94.

158. Weener, Paul, Barritt, Loren S., and Semmel, Melvyn I., "A Critical Evaluation of the Illinois Test of Psycholinguistic Abilities," *Exceptional Child,* 33 (February 1967), 373–80.

159. Woodcock, Richard W., "An Experimental Prognostic Test for Remedial Readers," *Journal of Educational Psychology,* 49 (February 1958), 23–27.

160. Wills, I. H., and Banas, Norma, "Prescriptive Teaching from WISC Patterns," *Academic Therapy,* 7 (Fall 1971), 79–83.

The contributing role of neurological defects such as brain injuries to school difficulties has been recognized since before the last century. Such obvious effects as aphasia, cerebral palsy, mental retardation, and motor disturbances have been dealt with in a number of specialized fields, as neurology, special education, speech pathology, rehabilitative medicine, and physical therapy, to mention only a few. But, within the past two decades, the emphasis upon brain damage as a possible cause of reading disabilities has broadened tremendously. Brain damage is being accepted as the primary etiological cause in thousands of pupils who not only show none of the classic massive symptoms but who also, neurologically speaking, may not show any real signs of cerebral dysfunction. To some observers, it appears that almost any failure to learn to read is now being interpreted, by some medical and/or reading specialists, as proof of the presence of brain damage or dysfunction.

7 Neurological Factors— What Is Dyslexia?

To clarify this trend in diagnosis, we here review the definitions, signs, and symptoms of this supposedly hereditary disease, dyslexia, and the role of brain damage in reading disability. Signs, symptoms, and treatment of truly or only suspected brain-damaged poor readers are contrasted. Chemotherapy, as symptomatic treatment for the hyperactivity supposed to characterize the brain-damaged, is also reviewed. Cerebral dominance, laterality, and lateral awareness, which are often claimed to be related to reading, have been widely studied, and a large number of these reports is summarized.

The question in your mind as you read this material should *not* be, "Can brain damage cause reading disability?" Obviously, if it can produce such conditions as the almost total loss of language ability, as in some aphasias, massive brain damage could make learning to read impossible or very difficult. The question to be answered is rather, "What kind or type of brain damage are these specialists talking about?" Are they assuming, without answering the preceding question, that any type or degree or place of brain damage must be the explanation for reading disabilities? Are they hypothesizing a reading center in the brain that may have been damaged or failed to mature, a center that no one else has yet been able to identify?

I F AN AUTHOR may be permitted a personal note, we must say that this is one chapter that we were loath to write. The looseness with which descriptive terms are applied to what we have called reading disability for some thirty years; the rapidity with which even newer terms are being coined; and the multiplicity of symptoms that are supposed to characterize this new disease "dyslexia" make an author feel that he does not want to touch the subject. Stanley L. Rosner has termed this new trend a Word Game and remarks:

> The term dyslexia at one time was used in a highly specific fashion and was understood to designate youngsters with a most severe disability . . . Currently this term has been so broadly applied as to render it virtually useless for communicating with anyone unless, prior to using the word, a conference is held to establish one's definition of dyslexia (92, p. 331).

With tongue in cheek, Edward Fry (44) has offered a double column of some of the terms currently being used. He has suggested that the reader may join this word game by combining any two of the terms to create his own terminology, since everyone else seems to be doing just this. S. Jay Samuels (95, 96) and other writers see little humor in these new developments and are much more critical. They emphasize primarily the reverse reasoning processes in which signs and symptoms present among children who have failed to learn to read well are accepted as the original causes of the difficulty, thus assuming facts not proven by longitudinal studies of pupil development. Terminal behaviors or deviations are often assumed to have been causes or prognostic signs. Jules C. Abrams (1) is amused by the pendulum swings or fads in diagnosis of reading difficulty from "personality conflict" to "organicity" to "perceptual handicap" to "dyslexia"; diagnoses that ignore the interplay among organic, functional, and environmental factors. We could cite many other interesting reactions to this area, but these will be more relevant in the later context. Perhaps the best way to provide an overview of this subject will be an attempt to give some of the definitions and signs and symptoms of dyslexia in the literature.

outcomes of treatment are determined in large part by emotional, intellectual potential, and socio-cultural factors (46).

We might add to the observations these facts: many actually brain-damaged children learn to read well; brain damage at birth is seldom significant at maturity; intelligence, if one thinks of it as learning capacity, is not necessarily depressed by brain damage (7).   Furthermore, we feel that it is quite illogical to conceive that reading progress is directly related to a specifically localized brain defect or insult when it is obvious that the act of reading involves integration of a number of brain areas, as the visual, the auditory, the speech motor, the spatial, the kinesthetic, the reasoning, and so on—all of which play a constant part in word recognition and reading.   This view is shared by such writers as Kurt Goldstein (48), in his book on the treatment of soldiers' brain injuries; by Delwyn G. Schubert (99); and by others.

Speaking of the concept of minimal brain damage, which is often mentioned in definitions of dyslexia, Robert Cohn (24) points out that a relationship between signs of neuropathology and actual minimal brain pathology has not been demonstrated, while the groups of clinical signs derived from various psychological tests often reflect nothing more than the tests selected and their interpretation by a particular examiner.   Ralph M. Reitan, who is considered an expert on brain function, criticizes common testing procedures in attempting to establish brain damage as follows:

> 1. The reproduction of forms tests may reflect a half-dozen environmental factors, as fatigue, depression, poor instructions or lack of interest.   (We would add that such tests also reflect effects of timing, plane of exposure, posture of viewer, dependence upon memory and intelligence, as well as perception, and so on.)
> 2. The so-called signs derived from tests may be true for adults but are seldom true among children because of their variability of performance.
> 3. Differential scores, as in the WISC, are pointless, for they do not imply any type of brain lesion when any particular profile or pattern is present.
> 4. None of these tests, or others, alone can substantiate a diagnosis of brain damage.   For this both neurological and psychological diagnosis must be combined (87).

Despite this introductory questioning of the common conepts of the role of brain damage in reading disability, the reader is entitled to make his own judgments.   For this reason, we shall now summarize a number of reports on the signs and symptoms of this relationship as these are expressed by various sources.

SIGNS AND SYMPTOMS OF BRAIN DAMAGE

Behavioral Abrams notes problems in impulse control, hyperactivity, hyperdistractibility, impulsivity, disinhibition; highly narcissistic and egocentric, defective self-concepts (3). In another article, Abrams cites higher P. than V. I.Q., general retardation in verbal skills, except arithmetic reasoning and digit span, lowest in coding in WISC performance tests, association difficulty with letters and words as symbols, hearing comprehension better than reading comprehension because of difficulties with word recognition (2). At the same time, Abrams notes that hyperactivity and distractibility have never been proven to be related to defective neural transmission or specific brain cell malfunction (1, p. 65).

Motor Development Using the Lincoln-Oseretsky Motor Development Test of thirty-six measures of motor coordination and control, N. Dale Bryant et al. (17) found 76 percent of a sample of twenty-five male poor readers below norms for their ages in the mean score, and significantly below on half of the subtests. They concluded that this general impairment seems to accompany the disability and that these cases may be exhibiting a slow development or dysfunction in the broad neurological sense. In a study of 100 junior high pupils, Lewis et al.* confirm this lower motor development among poor readers in the same instrument.

Other Tests Reed, Reitan, and Klove (84) found brain-damaged children inferior in practically all their tests including the WISC, trail-making, category, and speech perception. The brain-damaged group averaged 84 in WISC Full Scale I.Q.; the controls, 106; a difference that might explain these test results. Reitan and Klove (88) criticize Halstead's Impairment Index, his Trail-Making Test, and the aphasia screening batteries of Halstead and of Wepman as being of little value. These often-used instruments are not recommended in reading diagnosis, by these authors, because they are technical and not sufficiently refined. As in the general criticism of the validity of such tests cited above, Reitan and Klove repeat the caution that only a combination of neurological and psychological tests will suffice for this diagnosis.

Grassi has offered an adaptation of the Block Design test that requires the subject to reproduce a design tridimensionally, that is, on top, bottom, and

---

*F. D. Lewis, D. B. Bell, and R. P. Anderson, "Reading Retardation: A Bi-racial Comparison," *Journal of Reading,* 13 (1970), 433–36, 474–78.

outer edges of the blocks. He has presented preliminary evidence of the validity of this test as a measure of brain damage (49). Other tests often used in the attempt to detect brain damage include most of the form reproduction tests such as the Bender, Graham-Ellis, and others. These tests are reviewed in our treatment of visual perception and reading. See also Graham and Berman* for comments on these tests.

Brain Wave Testing

Conners, in studying a family of poor readers, found that four children and the father gave an attenuated visual-evoked response in their left parietal areas on the EEG (electroencephalogram). The mother, a normal reader, had a normal EEG. The author concluded that, because of these alterations in the information-processing capability, the reading disability was genetically determined (26). To our knowledge, this result has not been replicated in any other study.

Knott et al. (64) claim that the most common abnormalities reported for poor readers in EEG testing are slow rhythm from the posterior area when subject is awake and the presence of 14 and 6 CPS positive spikes when the subject is asleep. The exact meaning of these abnormal signs was not clarified, however.

Woody (119) matched thirty-five children, ages eight to thirteen, who had been referred as behavior problems to a psychological clinic with an equal number of well-behaved pupils. He found no differences at all in the EEG's of the two groups and no relationship between EEG and subtest variations on the WISC or differences between the V. and P. I.Q.

It should be noted that EEG's presumably reflecting abnormal brain activity and negative EEG's giving no such signs are not highly reliable indications of the true condition of the brain, according to many EEG specialists.

Minimal Brain Damage

Myklebust (76) says that children with this condition may have serious difficulties when the learning task entails interrelated functions, as both auditory and visual learning. Like Johnson (58), cited above, he recommends avoiding intrasensory or multisensory stimulation to avoid a breakdown in the neurological processes.

Wepman (117), in one sense, seems to agree with Myklebust and Johnson in emphasizing that the reading teacher should try to establish the

---

*F. Graham and P. Berman, "Current Status of Behavior Tests for Brain Damage in Infants and Preschool Children," *American Journal of Orthopsychiatry*, 31 (1961), 713–37.

preferred sensory modality of the child (that showing the fastest development in primary children) and then teach to that modality. In remedial work, Wepman suggests that it be directed toward development of the weaker modality, or, if unsuccessful in this approach, to the stronger modality, although he admits that matching instruction to modality in either of these ways may or may not produce positive results. Our chapter 4, which touched on this question of teaching to learning modalities, presented ample evidence for Wepman's equivocation regarding the effectiveness of the concept.

Barbara D. Bateman* sees no educational implications, no clues for treatment, in a diagnosis of minimal brain damage. She feels that the term does not help the educator to discover the specific strengths and weaknesses in learning of the pupil. Moreover, she cites a study that found no significant relationship among the neurological examinations, the EEG's, and the final diagnosis among 100 children suspected of minimal brain damage. Such findings lead Bateman to declare that minimal brain damage is not a set of behavioral characteristics or even a relationship among diagnostic indices.

With respect to hyperkinesis as a basic symptom of minimal brain damage, Bateman rejects this hypothesis because of the inconsistent findings. Many such children, in fact, may be hypokinetic rather than hyperkinetic, and neither type has been shown consistently to be minimally brain-damaged. She makes the same point in discussing the often-related symptoms of short attention span and perseveration.

Bateman emphasizes that the prescriptive treatments offered for the diagnosis of minimal brain damage have not been found effective or even relevant to educational goals. Rather, she suggests that we must try to find out precisely what the child can and cannot do in his efforts to read. Then with teaching objectives defined, instruction would be constantly monitored for child progress while working toward those goals.

Friedman (43) declares that the concept of minimal brain damage has little utility, even to the school psychologist, for its definition is unclear and its diagnosis through psychological tests is equivocal; moreover, differential treatment programs appear to be of questionable value. He quotes a British physician, D. Pond,† as saying that there are "no absolutely unequivocal signs, psychological tests or physiological tests that can prove a relationship between brain damage and any particular aspect of disturbed behavior."

---

*Barbara D. Bateman, "Educational Implications of Minimal Brain Dysfunction," *Reading Teacher,* 27 (April 1974), 662–68.

†D. Pond, "Psychiatric Aspects of Epileptic and Brain Damaged Children," *British Medical Journal,* 2 (1961), 1377–82, as quoted by Friedman (43).

Finger Localization and Right-Left Discrimination

Croxen and Lytton (33) compared third-year junior school English pupils (nine–ten years old) with reading quotients below 80 with a control group with quotients above 80. They employed several tests of finger localization of visual, tactual, and tactual pairs (in these tests the child identifies the finger touched while his hand is visible or hidden). The control boys and girls were superior. Right-left discrimination in an undescribed test was lower for poor readers. However, finger localization correlated with R-L discrimination .408 and with I.Q. partialed out, .356, implying that the similarity in these measures amounted to an overlap of only 13 percent, a much smaller relationship than that commonly assumed in these supposedly parallel measures of brain damage.

Macdonald Critchley, the British expert on dyslexia who formerly accepted tests of finger localization or its lack, finger agnosia, dysgraphia, dyscalculia (writing and arithmetic distortions), and R-L disorientation as symptoms of dyslexia, has withdrawn his statements on this subject. Like Arthur Benton, who pioneered in this testing area, he rejects the Gerstmann syndrome, which is composed of these signs, as relevant and now even doubts whether such a syndrome exists at all (29, 30).

Reed (85) found no relationship between finger localization and reading achievement at age six but significantly more right-hand errors among poor readers at age ten, compared with good readers. He feels that the test is not a measure of brain lesions but can reflect some sort of disturbance in the left cerebral hemisphere.

It is not clear on just what evidence Reed assigns this behavior to the left hemisphere, other than perhaps the natural desire to link it to language functions that are present in that hemisphere. As a matter of fact, motor activity and sensations to one side of the body are processed in the opposite hemisphere, not in both.

French (42) criticizes Money's Test of Direction Sense (in a road map) for insufficient evidence of validity and reliability. This test has been used by some as a measure of right-left orientation.

Rhythmic Ability

Charles Drake is apparently sincere in declaring: "Almost without exception when I observe a child having difficulty reproducing the handclapping patterns

I am teaching it turns out later that the pupil is also poor in the language symbolization areas" (36, p. 203). He goes on to claim that some neurological malfunction in the central nervous system interferes with the ordered reception, storage, and reproduction of sequential elements and that this affects also the centers that control all fine output, including oral reading, spelling, and handwriting.

Birth History

Kawi and Pasamanick (60) compared 372 male, white poor readers with a similar number of controls. They found maternal toxemias, bleeding during pregnancy, and premature births among poor readers significantly greater than among the controls; they suggest that these prenatal and paranatal occurrences, which may result in brain damage, may influence subsequent reading development. In a study of fifty-three poor first-grade readers in Sweden, Eve Malmquist (71) found significantly more premature births and very low birth weights than among normal readers.

Lyle (70) was not able to establish that actual brain injury at birth, or birth weight, tended to predict reading difficulties. For this prediction, epileptiform symptoms and early speech defects, in combination, were the best, although together they accounted for only 31.4 percent of the variance.

In this collection of signs and symptoms of brain damage, we see many that overlap with those supposed to characterize dyslexia. Thus, at first reading, the claim that reading disability or dyslexia arises from a specific brain malfunction seems to be supported. We still reject this belief, however, on the grounds that even the most common symptoms that are supposed to indicate brain damage, as hyperactivity and distractibility (a) have not been proven to be related to neural pathology; (b) may actually reflect disturbances in ego or self-concept development; (c) may or may not be present in comparative studies of good and poor readers or, in other words, are not consistent symptoms. The concept that a multisensory process like reading is related to a localized brain malfunction in a certain area is completely untenable. The evidence for the various tests and other so-called signs of brain damage is similarly unacceptable.

TREATMENT OF BRAIN-DAMAGED POOR READERS

Many adjustments to the instructional setting have gradually appeared in the work with brain-damaged children. Prominent among these are the reduction of any sort of realia ordinarily present in displays, decorations, or even instruction; the use of cubicles or space dividers to provide isolated work areas; emphasis upon individual or, at most, only small-group activities; deemphasis upon intrapupil competition; and, recently, operant conditioning training to reduce hyperactivity. Perceptual-motor training stressing coordination, body image, and form perception is also popular in many schools. It is apparent that, for the most part, these are logical treatments for the frequent symptoms of distractibility, hyperactivity, and difficulties in form perception that tend to accompany *some* types of true brain damage. These practices, whether validated or not, are being adopted in many quarters for the treatment of poor readers under the assumption that these pupils must also be brain-damaged. The following are examples of this trend, and, in some reports, are the outcomes of this transfer of practices used with the brain-damaged to remedial reading instruction.

General Studies in Treatment of the Brain-Damaged

Abrams (1, 2) recommends the reinforcement of learning by kinesthetic or tactile approaches, particularly in words drawn from the child's own language, as in the language experience approach. The purpose of this reinforcement is not, as some believe, to induce other undamaged areas of the brain to take over the reading task but to develop more adequate ego functioning or self-concept through successful experiences.

Drake (36), in keeping with his preoccupation with rhythmic hand-clapping ability as a primary diagnostic sign, recommends rhythmic training combined with remedial reading techniques.

Rost and Charles (93) adopted the use of cubicles but found them no more effective than ordinary classroom arrangements for brain-damaged and hyperactive pupils at ages eight and eleven.

Gallagher (45), after giving intensive form perception training for a year to his brain-damaged, mentally retarded pupils, found gains in the verbal area and in verbal I.Q. But these gains disappeared in the second year, when no training was given; and the controls without such training were then equal to the experimental group in these scores.

Balow (7) rejects such visual perception programs as those offered by Frostig, Delacato, Kephart, and others on the grounds that they have not been proved beneficial for children with reading disabilities or brain damage or both. These programs, he believes, may have values in terms of physical activities and positive attention from adults, as well as for training in following directions and for motor and visual skills. Thus he feels that they may generate behavior of positive significance for school success, but they are not specifically related to reading improvement.

Zedler (122) recommends oral language therapy, phonics, sentence patterns, and the development of auditory comprehension, largely by constantly reading their assignments to these pupils. In a group of pupils with "medically confirmed cerebral dysfunction," her program produced twice as much gain in educational achievement as in a control group. She makes no mention, however, of any way in which the Hawthorne effect inherent in these special procedures was controlled.

Reed, Rabe, and Mankinen (86) reviewed critically nine research reports on the outcomes of special programs for brain-damaged pupils, including those of Cruikshank, Silver and Hagin, Delacato, Kephart, and Orton. The reviewers declared the criteria for determining brain damage in these studies were either inadequate or nonexistent. They concluded that there was very little evidence that pupils with actual or "suspected" chronic neurological impairment need or benefit from the special teaching procedures extant.

CHEMOTHERAPY WITH THE BRAIN-DAMAGED

As usual, opinions on the values of drug treatment for dyslexic or brain-damaged pupils vary. Whitsell feels that they have only a limited place in the treatment of reading disabilities (118, p. 75), while many other practitioners are experimenting with chemotherapy extensively in these cases, as we shall see (41).

Smith and Carrigan (105) conducted one of the first large-scale medico-psychological studies of poor readers. Four types of readers were identified by a variety of psychometric, physiological, and personality tests. The groups differed in endocrine functions, metabolism, and the pattern of their test performances. Treatment by vitamin therapy and hormone medication produced a number of favorable changes in the behavior and test performances, but no changes in reading skills. Basic to their experiment was the theory that the treatments might modify the neurochemical balance of catalysts versus delimiting agents (acytelcholine versus cholinesterase) in brain action. The types of disabled readers that they identified were also characterized in terms of the probable relative balance of these neurochemical agents. The initial and the follow-up experiments seemed to support this theory, but the results were, as we have said, relatively inconclusive with respect to reading improvement.

More commonly, drug treatment is employed to reduce such symptoms as hyperkinesis, which has been described as "short attention span, poor concentration, impulsiveness, inability to delay gratification, irritability, explosiveness, perseveration and poor school performance," by Krippner et al. (65). These authors estimate that amphetamines (stimulants) are now being prescribed for 150,000–200,000 children. Many critics object to this treatment because of possible misdiagnoses, untoward side effects, and the neglect of nondrug alternatives, as behavior modification, perceptual-motor training, and megavitamin (massive vitamin) therapy. Krippner et al. studied forty-seven children, mean age 10-6, ages 7-6 to 19-4, referred to the clinic as hyperkinetic who were under medication. A nondrug control group also being seen for help in the clinic was composed of twenty-seven pupils, ages 7-5 to 17-3. There were no significant differences between the groups on the Graham-Ellis design test or the Peabody Picture Vocabulary Test. Drug cases tended to test poorly more often, and more nondrug cases tested above average. Differences were significant in favor of the nondrug cases in the Torrance Tests of Creative Thinking and the Rogers Personality Adjustment Inventory. More emotional problems were also evidenced by the drug group on the Purcell Incomplete Sentence measure. When queried, the parents of only five of the forty-seven children diagnosed as hyperkinetic said that the diagnosis was based on a medical or neurological examination. Krippner et al. wonder whether many of the drug cases were not simply experiencing emotional problems that may have been misdiagnosed as hyperkinesis. They felt it unlikely that brain damage was a possible basis for the pupils' emotional problems, for two tests that they administered failed to indicate any brain damage.

H. Charles (22) gave Deanol, a stimulant, to twenty-two students aged nine to thirteen over a period of fifteen weeks. They responded with significant gains in rate of reading but with no changes in vocabulary and comprehension. Since this pattern of some increase in rate without comparable gains in vocabulary or comprehension is readily stimulated by any of a number of training programs without drugs, the contribution of the drug to the changes in this study are not obvious.

McBride (72) claims that 3–5 percent of elementary children are brain-damaged and that two-thirds to three-quarters of these will respond favorably to stimulants. In support of this claim, he cites studies claiming improvement in 47–83 percent of the cases according to the medication chosen. The extent of undesirable side effects from the various drugs ranged from minimal with Deanol to 14 percent with other drugs. The use of tranquilizers, in contrast, yielded 55–60 percent improvement and 18-25 percent with side effects in other groups of children. Drug abuse is prevented, McBride says, by confining such chemotherapy to children under ten or eleven. He cautions that drugs do not provide complete answers to the problems of brain-damaged children, for such additional steps are essential as the relief of parental pressure; and observation by psychologists and teachers who will, presumably, cooperate in planning the educational experiences for these children.

Wunderlich (120) has compiled a review of the uses of various treatments for hyperactive children. He mentions such approaches as: stimulants and/or tranquilizers; megavitamin therapy—vitamin C to reduce allergies, as well as vitamins B_3, B_6, and calcium pantothenate; corticosteroids and occasionally antihistamines, which vary in their effects on different children; anticonvulsants, if the EEG is abnormal (also dilantin plus folic acids and vitamins in some such cases); elimination of foods that give rise to allergic reactions, as milk, chocolate, eggs, and the like; the elimination of simple sugars, of coffee, tea, or cola (because of the caffeine present); controlled air filtration with electrostatic precipitation to remove allergy-producing substances plus temperature control with air-conditioning; and finally allergic desensitization by injections following patch tests, as a last resort. Wunderlich, like McBride, would supplement chemotherapy with perceptual motor training in which he sees the visual-motor skill element as an important source of stress reduction; and with counseling for parents in behavior modification to improve their effectiveness in dealing with their children.

Speaking as a reading specialist, J. Wesley Schneyer (98) finds it difficult to interpret the reports on the role of drug therapy in learning problems because, he declares, it does not seem clear whether the "hyperactive child" syndrome is an entity or behavior resulting from a number of causes; the treatment reports often fail to control for such variables as reliability of diagnosis (see Krippner's comments above) severity of disturbance, age, sex, I.Q.; the dropouts from the treatment are seldom adequately described or explained; moreover, the effect of treatments seems temporary, for the syndrome tends to return. He concludes with the observation that some drugs may be useful in reducing anxiety and in improving attention and concentration for *some* children with *some* types of learning and behavior disorders, but the research results are neither specific nor conclusive, in his opinion. Other observers, like Schneyer, question the use of stimulants with central nervous system disorders or minimal brain damage because of equivocal results—results that may help or in some cases exacerbate hyperactivity. Some think that the stimulants help only when the pupil is underaroused but hyperactive, and are contraindicated when he is overresponsive, distractible, and hyperactive, a discrimination that requires a long series of observations, not simply an office examination.

If the statements regarding the present extent of use of drug therapy in children's learning problems are accurate, there should eventually be a considerable body of research data available to answer such questions as those raised by Krippner and Schneyer. We may well continue, however, to expect confusing results in these studies because of the current flaws in adequacy and accuracy of diagnosis, poor control of significant variables that affect the possible interpretation and application of results, and the perplexities inherent in the multiplicity of treatments and combinations of treatments in use. But certainly, in some respects, the future of drug therapy in learning problems holds some promise.

CEREBRAL DOMINANCE, LATERALITY, AND READING

The question of the significance of pupils' laterality characteristics in reading progress has been a subject of debate at least since the 1930s, remaining unresolved in the minds of some reading teachers and other specialists who persist in using tests of various types in the hope of proving some relationship. Those who continue to support a cause-effect relationship between various aspects of laterality offer some such argument as this:

> One hemisphere assumes dominance over the other in terms of language functions. Handedness and eye dominance or preference should be on the same side of the body as the dominant hemisphere. If there is not this consistent relationship among hemispheric dominance, eyedness, and handedness, reading disability arises. A left-hander and right-eyedness, for example, invariably shows early reading disabilities. Mixed dominance produces mirror reading, loss of place from line to line, and poor comprehension because of the failure of left-right eye-movements (27). The primary symptom in these cases is frequent reversals in reading caused by the confusing mirror images in both hemispheres (10, 78). It is very difficult for left-handed persons to suppress the reversed word image in their right hemispheres (the left being accepted as the usual center for language functions such as reading) because they use this area in a dominant way for nonlanguage activities (10). Regressions in eye movements while reading transmit letters in the wrong order to the right hemisphere (but apparently not to the left) and cause misreading (10). In fact, in some medical publications, lateral dominance problems are considered *the* cause of reading disability (77).

Every part of this concept of the role of laterality and cerebral dominance is untenable, in our opinion and that of many present-day medical, optometric, and psychological authorities both in the United States and elsewhere (37, 47, 63, 116, 121).   Let us consider the theory step by step and cite the contradictory evidence:

1. It is true that one hemisphere is responsible for language functions. As the neurosurgical study of Penfield and Roberts in Canada (79) shows, the speech or language centers are in the left hemisphere for 99 percent of right-handed individuals and for more than 90 percent of left-handed persons. In other words, handedness is unrelated to the hemispheric language center or the dominant hemisphere, for language is in the same hemisphere for practically all left- and right-handed persons.   Isom (56) confirms these facts by using comparisons of time of response to two successive sensory stimuli. When these are received by the nondominant hemisphere, they must be transferred to the dominant; response time is thus lengthened and the dominant hemisphere identified.

2. If handedness or eyedness is parallel to the nondominant hemisphere, or if these two characteristics are in opposite sides of the body, this condition, called mixed dominance, is supposed to result in reading disability. We shall offer a large number of studies of this question below and permit the reader to make his own judgment of the validity of this belief.

3. Lois Bing (13) and other vision specialists have carefully pointed out that the idea that eyedness is related to the dominant hemisphere is anatomically absurd.   The retinal nerve splits behind each eye and from each a portion of the nerve enters each hemisphere behind it and on the other side of the body.   In other words, visual stimuli are processed in both hemispheres.   In fact, the retina (or eye) does not function as a unit, for half of each field of vision of each eye is transmitted to one hemisphere, while the stimuli to the other half is sent on to the other hemisphere.   So-called eyedness, as measured by sighting tests and the like, which indicate preference for an eye in monocular activities, is not parallel to or determined by the dominant hemisphere.

Several vision specialists have tried to clarify the concept of eyedness or eye dominance.   Coren and Kaplan (28), for example, factor-analyzed thirteen tests of ocular dominance and were able to distinguish three types: *sighting dominance*—as in cone or hole-in-card tests; *ocular dominance*—as measured by tests of retinal rivalry in which the criterion is the frequency of response in each eye when different colored or striated targets are presented to each eye; *acuity dominance*—the relative number of errors for each eye in reading the Snellen test plus results in the dichoptic flash test that presents discrepant numerical stimuli simultaneously to both eyes in a very brief exposure. Sighting dominance accounted for 67 percent of the variance; ocular dominance for 16 percent and acuity dominance for 17 percent.   Coren and

Kaplan's proof of three dominance factors or types of dominance may explain the lack of correlation among dominance tests as reported in many studies. The results of the handedness tests did not load on any of these three ocular dominance factors, showing again the lack of relationship between handedness and "eyedness." Nathan Flax's review of fifty-eight sources (39) led him also to the conclusion that eye dominance, whether sighting, ocular, or acuity, was not at all related to reading disability. We shall cite a number of other relevant studies of "eyedness" and reading later. Humphiss (55) objects to all tests for eye dominance except those of retinal rivalry. The others, which compare the time or frequency of response to the different images before each eye, are too readily influenced by the child's reactions to the content or nature of the images, he believes. Using only a retinal rivalry test, he seemed to find that the pupils he tested showed no dominance at all at younger ages. He reasoned that this was due to the great flexibility in the personalities of young children, and that dominance became marked only as rigidity or perseveration developed with age. This, of course, is an interesting but unsubstantiated viewpoint of the development of ocular dominance.

4. Reversals, which are considered a primary symptom of reading disability or dyslexia by some, are not caused by mirror images of a word in both hemispheres. Word images, as some call them, are really neurochemical traces in the neurons of the brain. (See the Smith-Carrigan study (105) cited above.) They are not received or stored in two dimensions, so a reversal is thus impossible. How would one reverse laterally the traces of catalysts and delimiting chemicals that initiate or terminate the action of a nerve cell? Rather, reversals are universally common errors of almost all beginners in reading and foreign languages, regardless of age, tending to disappear as reading skill improves under ordinary instruction and without any special corrective steps. Moreover, reversals are specific to the type of material, in the beginning stages of learning, and differ for individuals from writing to reading to number work. Frequency of reversals is not related to any aspect of laterality or cerebral dominance, as we shall see. We shall cite a number of studies later that have explored their significance in reading.

Isom (56) has pointed out that laterality is a function of age, may and often does change in the early years, and is not completely established until the age of eleven or twelve. Lateral awareness, or R-L discrimination or knowledge, is also developmental. The child evidences recognition of R and L on himself at about five but cannot order objects in space in terms of R and L until about seven or eight. This physician believes that any deficiencies in this area among poor readers are in the development of lateral awareness, not in mixed laterality.

Perhaps the most readable way of presenting the research data on these various aspects is in Table 7-1, entitled "Relationships among Laterality, Lateral Awareness, and Reading." The table lists each study and indicates whether a positive difference between good and poor readers was found for each characteristic tested.

To us, the agreement among these studies—despite the variations in testing procedures, in control of variables that might affect the results, and in the care in matching groups of good and poor readers—is amazing. The proportion of studies refuting any relationship between these aspects of laterality and reading development ranges from 80 percent for reversals to 100 percent for left-handedness. It is equally amazing that the claims for significant effects of laterality upon reading persist in view of this overwhelming negative evidence here and in the reviews of Weintraub (116), Zangwill (121), and many others.

SUMMARY

The length and complexity of this chapter may justify a summary to aid the reader in organizing the facts presented here.

Definitions of Dyslexia   The definitions of dyslexia, which are as individualistic as their writers, tend to emphasize the hereditary nature of reading disability.

Signs and Symptoms   Although also extremely variable from author to author, these often include mention of brain damage as a basic cause plus contributing deficits as sound-symbol association, visual perception, mixed laterality, disorientation in directionality, WISC P. higher than V., and sequencing input.

Treatments   Dyslexia treatments parallel those used in reading clinics for reading disability in stressing the VAKT technique, perceptual-motor training, phonics, and the attempt to strengthen deficits in sequencing and processing visual and auditory stimuli.

Brain Function and Reading   Brain damage as a basic or frequent cause of reading disability is rejected by present-day knowledge of brain function and the effects of brain pathology upon reading ability. The claimed relationship is based on a narrow concept of localization of functions in the brain that is untenable today.

TABLE 7–1 RELATIONSHIPS AMONG LATERALITY, LATERAL AWARENESS, AND READING

AUTHOR	GRADE-AGE NUMBER	LEFT-HANDEDNESS	LEFT-EYEDNESS	MIXED EYE-HAND	KNOWLEDGE OF L-R	REVERSALS
Ayres (6)	Primary	None	None	None		
Balow and Balow (8)	552 in I–II	None	None	None		
Hillerich (53)	400 primary			None		None
Monk (74)	II	None			Yes	Yes
Malmquist (71)	399 I	None				
Rice (90)	200 primary 41 EMR				None	
Stephens et al. (108)	90 I			None		
Belmont and Birch (11)	200 9–10-year-old	None	None	None	None	
Boos (15)	273 VIII		None	None		
Cashdan et al. (20)	1227 8–10-year-olds			None		
Coleman and Deutsch (25)	123 V–VI	None	None	None	None	
Cohen (23)	120 I and IV			Yes in I, None in IV, None in I and IV	Yes in I None in IV	
Douglas et al. (35)	3253 at ages 6 and 11	None	None	None		
Monroe (75)	Elementary	None				
Shafer and Lilly (100)	100 VI	None	None	None		
Shearer (101)	347 7–10-year-olds	None		None	None	
Shepherd (103)	809 elementary	None				None
Smith (106)	Elementary	None				
Sparrow and Satz (107)	80 elementary	None	None	None	None	
Stevenson (109)	Elementary	None				None
Tinker (111)	134 elementary	None	None	None		None
Trieschman (112)	Elementary	None				
Chakrabarti and Backer (21)	99 college freshmen	None		–		
Alexander and Money (5)	13 with Turner's Syndrome				None	
Capobianco (19)	46 7–16 year-olds with learning disability	None	None			

(table 7–1, continued)

AUTHOR	GRADE-AGE NUMBER	LEFT-HANDEDNESS	LEFT-EYEDNESS	MIXED EYE-HAND	KNOWLEDGE OF L-R	REVERSALS
Forness and Weil (40)	13 brain-damaged	None	Yes	Yes		
Lindell (67)	Remedial pupils	None	None	None		
Rengstorff (89)	5546 mixed			Probably yes		
Sheperd (102)	40 EMR	None	None	None		
Silver and Hagin (104)	Mixed hospital clinic cases	None	None	None		
Warrington (115)	76 ages 7–15	None		None		
Rutter (94)	334 ages 9–12	None				
Isom (57)	150 elementary	None	None	None		
Lovell and Gorton (68)	100 ages 9–10				Yes	

Signs and Symptoms of Brain Damage These cluster around such behaviors as hyperactivity, distractibility, finger localization, early speech defects or delayed speech development, and possible deficits in motor coordination. Premature birth, epileptiform seizures, and unfavorable prenatal events may well be part of the birth history in these cases.

Treatment of Brain-Damaged Poor Readers This is usually planned to counteract the hyperactivity and distractibility by reducing the number of stimuli present in the child's environment. Other popular procedures include perceptual-motor training and multisensory reinforcement of learning, but these, too, are of questionable effectiveness.

Chemotherapy with the Brain-Damaged This has recently become relatively widespread, although its use can be criticized for superficial diagnoses; overemphasis to the exclusion of other recognized treatments such as parental counseling and behavior modification; and equivocal research results because of poor scientific design of studies and the confusion inherent in a multiplicity of treatments.

Cerebral Dominance, Laterality, and Reading Deviations in hand-eye dominance and laterality, as well as in lateral awareness, have persisted as suspected causes of reading disability and symptoms of brain malfunction. In the minds of some, these signs are supported by concepts of the linkage between cerebral dominance and laterality and equally untenable ideas about brain function in word recognition and reading. A sample of thirty-five research studies is cited to prove the rebuttal of any significant relationship of handedness, "eyedness," mixed eye-hand domi-

TABLE 7–2   A GROUP OF 100 "DYSLEXIC" CHILDREN

	NORMAL READERS	RETARDED READERS
Total group	55	45
Mean age	10.1	9.9
Grade	4.5	4.4
Abnormally slow in physical development	5	5
Abnormal EEG	10	2
Abnormal skull X-ray	2	0
Poor in neuropsychological exam.	13	10
Vision problems	13	5
WISC Full Scale	106.6	100.9
Verbal	104.3	99.7
Performance	107.8	102.3
Repeated one grade or more	21	22
WISC P. higher than V.	26 (n.s.d)	
No detectable problem	23	

nance, R-L discrimination or knowledge, and reversals in oral reading to progress in reading.

We close this chapter by adding our voice to those of Reitan (87) and Carter (19), who have emphasized the obvious need for a cooperative interdisciplinary effort to bring some sense of order to this chaotic field.

We are fully cognizant of the fact that the conclusions drawn in this opinionated review of dyslexia will be received very negatively by many individuals and groups. For this reason, it would be most desirable to introduce some objective data regarding children diagnosed as dyslexic, particularly when that diagnosis was obtained in an interdisciplinary approach. Two such reports have been found, and we shall summarize their data.*

A group of 100 children referred as dyslexic to the University of Florida Interdisciplinary Child Help Center for Learning Disabilities were the subjects of these studies. Practically all these children were referred on this basis by medical professionals over a two-year period. Extensive data on the physiological, neurological, intellectual, and reading traits of the entire group are presented in the article by Larsen et al., but we shall tabulate only the pertinent facts as they bear upon our discussion of dyslexia. (See Table 7-2.)

*J. Larsen, Chester E. Tillman, J. J. Ross, P. Satz, B. Cassin, and W. Wolkin, "Factors in Reading Achievement: An Interdisciplinary Approach," *Journal of Learning Disabilities*, 6 (December 1973), 636–44. Chester E. Tillman, "Dyslexia as a Diagnostic Label in a College Learning Center" (Paper presented at the National Reading Conference, Kansas City, December 1974).

The incidence of medical and neuropsychological (motor speed, finger localization, motor patterning, lateral awareness, and central nervous system integrity) problems was strikingly low. Other supposed signs or symptoms of dyslexia, such as slow physical development, abnormal EEG's or skull X-Rays, and WISC Performance higher than Verbal obviously failed to distinguish the normal from the retarded readers. Only the reading test scores in word recognition, oral reading, silent reading and, particularly, listening comprehension differed significantly and then only by design. Poor EEG's, in fact, were significantly more frequent among the normally achieving readers.

In our opinion, the data from these reports on an interdisciplinary study of 100 "dyslexic" children support our contention that this labeling of children is hardly justified when more than half of them are not even seriously retarded in reading; the diagnostic label is not supported by a very extensive evaluation; and the signs or symptoms supposed to indicate the condition fail utterly even to distinguish between the normal and the nonachieving readers. These reports do contain additional facts in contrasting the characteristics of boys and girls, of children with abnormal vision and slow physical development or with abnormal EEG's and poor performance on the neuropsychological tests, and repeaters versus nonrepeaters that will be pertinent to other interdisciplinary teams.

LEARNING PROJECT

Find an article for the general public on the subject of dyslexia in a magazine such as *Redbook, Instructor, Education Age, Reading Newsreport,* or *Psychology Today.* Read and critique the article in terms of the following:
1. The author's definition and description of dyslexia and its causes.
2. The evidence cited to support this interpretation.
3. The nature of treatments suggested.
4. The differences between these treatments and ordinary remedial instruction, if any.

REFERENCES

1. Abrams, Jules C., "Neurological and Psychological Influence on Reading," in *Perception and Reading,* Helen K. Smith, editor, Proceedings International Reading Association, 12, No. 4 (1968), 63–67.

2. Abrams, Jules C., "Dyslexia—Single or Plural," in *Psychology of Reading Behavior,* Eighteenth Yearbook National Reading Conference, 1969, 181–87.

3. Abrams, Jules C., "Learning Disabilities—A Complex Phenomenon," *Reading Teacher,* 23 (January 1970), 299–303.

4. Adams, R. B., "Dyslexia: A Discussion of Its Definition," *Journal of Learning Disabilities,* 2 (1969), 616–33.

5. Alexander, Duane, and Money, John, "Reading Ability, Object Constancy and Turner's Syndrome," *Perceptual and Motor Skills,* 20 (June 1965), 981–84.

6. Ayres, A. Jean, "Patterns of Perceptual-Motor Dysfunction in Children: A Factor Analytic Study," *Perceptual and Motor Skills,* 20 (April 1965), 335–68.

7. Balow, Bruce, "Perceptual-Motor Activities in the Treatment of Severe Reading Disability," *Reading Teacher,* 24 (March 1971), 513–25, 542.

8. Balow, Irving H., and Balow, Bruce, "Lateral Dominance and Reading Achievement in the Second Grade," *American Educational Research Journal,* 1 (May 1964), 139–43.

9. Bannatyne, Alex, "Psychological Bases of Reading in the United Kingdom," pp. 327–35 in *Reading Instruction: An International Forum,* Marion D. Jenkinson, editor. Newark: International Reading Association, 1967.

10. Bannatyne, Alex, "Mirror-Images and Reversals," *Academic Therapy,* 8 (Fall 1972), 87–92.

11. Belmont, Lillian, and Birch, Herbert G., "Lateral Dominance, Lateral Awareness and Reading Disability," *Child Development,* 36 (March 1965), 57–71.

12. Benton, Arthur L., "Dyslexia in Relation to Form Perception and Directional Sense," pp. 81–102 in *Reading Disability Progress and Research Needs in Dyslexia.* Baltimore: Johns Hopkins Press, 1962.

13. Bing, Lois, "A Critical Analysis of the Literature on Certain Visual Functions Which Seem to Be Related to Reading Achievement," *Journal American Optometric Association,* 22 (March 1951), 454–63.

14. Blau, Harold, Schwalb, Eugene, Zanger, Eugene, and Blau, Harriet, "Developmental Dyslexia and Its Remediation," *Reading Teacher,* 22 (April 1969), 649–53.

15. Boos, R. W., "Dominance and Control: Relation to Reading Achievement," *Journal of Educational Research,* 63 (1970), 466–70.

16. Boshes, Benjamin, and Myklebust, Helmer R., "A Neurological and Behavioral Study of Children with Learning Disorders," *Neurology,* 14 (January 1964), 7–12.

17. Bryant, N. Dale, Mirling, Bernard, and Patterson, Paul R., "Impaired Motor Development as a Characteristic of Reading Disability Cases," Report on Public Health Service Grant OM 225. Bethesda, Md.: National Institute of Mental Health.

18. Capobianco, R. J., "Ocular-Manual Laterality and Reading Achievement in Children with Specific Learning Disabilities," *American Educational Research Journal,* 4 (March 1967), 133–138.

19. Carter, Darrell, editor, *Interdisciplinary Approach to Learning Disorders.* Philadelphia: Chilton, 1970.

20. Cashdan, A., Pumfrey, P. D., and Lunzer, E. A., "Children Receiving Remedial Teaching in Reading," *Educational Research,* 13 (1971), 98–105.

21. Chakrabarti, J., and Backer, D. G., "Lateral Dominance and Reading Ability," *Perceptual and Motor Skills,* 22 (1966), 881–82.

22. Charles, H., "A Selected Drug as Determinant in the Reading Process," *Journal Reading Specialist,* 5 (1966), 154–55, 170.

23. Cohen, Alice, "Relationship between Factors of Dominance and Reading Ability," in *Reading Disability and Perception,* George D. Spache, editor, Proceedings International Reading Association, 13, No. 3 (1969), 38–45.

24. Cohn, Robert, "Neurological Concepts Pertaining to the Brain-Damaged Child," pp. 13–36 in *Speech and Language Therapy with the Brain-Damaged Child.* Washington: Catholic University Press, 1962.

25. Coleman, Richard I., and Deutsch, Cynthia P., "Lateral Dominance and Right-Left Discrimination: A Comparison of Normal and Retarded Readers," *Perceptual and Motor Skills,* 19 (August 1964), 43–50.

26. Conners, Keith C., "Cortical Visual Evoked Response in Children with Learning Disorders," *Psychophysiology,* 7 (1970), 418–28.

27. Connor, Marjorie, "Elementary Reading Teachers and the School Psychologist," *Reading Teacher,* 23 (November 1969), 151–55.

28. Coren, Stanley, and Kaplan, Clare P., "Patterns of Ocular Dominance," *American Journal of Optometry and Archives of American Academy of Optometry,* 50 (April 1973), 283–92.

29. Critchley, Macdonald, "The Enigma of Gerstmann's Syndrome," *Brain,* 89 (June 1966), 183–99.

30. Critchley, Macdonald, "Isolation of the Specific Dyslexic," pp. 17–20 in *Dyslexia, Diagnosis and Treatment of Reading Disorders,* A. H. Keeney and V. I. Keeney, editors. St. Louis: C. V. Mosby, 1968.

31. Critchley, Macdonald, *The Dyslexic Child.* Springfield: Charles C. Thomas, 1970.

32. Crosby, R. M. N., and Liston, R., "Dyslexia: What You Can Do—and Can't Do about It," *Instructor,* 36 (1969), 74–87.

33. Croxen, Mary E., and Lytton, Hugh, "Reading Disability and Difficulties in Finger Localization and Right-Left Discrimination," *Developmental Psychology,* 5 (September 1971), 256–62.

34. Dauzat, Sam V., "Good Gosh! My Child Has Dyslexia," *Reading Teacher,* 22 (April 1969), 630–33.

35. Douglas, J. W. B., Ross, J. M., and Cooper, J. E., "The Relationship between Handedness, Attainment and Adjustment in a National Sample of School Children," *Educational Research,* 9 (1967), 223–32.

36. Drake, Charles, "Reading, 'Riting and Rhythm," *Reading Teacher,* 18 (December 1964), 202–205.

37. Eames, Thomas H., "Vision and Learning," *American Journal of Optometry and Archives of American Academy of Optometry,* 26 (April 1959), 218.

38. Faigel, Harris C., "The Doctor and the Teacher," *Education Age,* 4 (January–February 1968), 38–39.

39. Flax, Nathan, "The Clinical Significance of Dominance," *American Journal of Optometry and Archives of American Academy of Optometry,* 43 (September 1966), 566–81.

40. Forness, S. R., and Weil, M. C., "Laterality in Retarded Readers with Brain Dysfunction," *Exceptional Children,* 36 (1970), 684–85.

41. Freeman, Roger D., "Drug Effects on Learning in Children: A Selective Review of the Past Thirty Years," *Journal of Special Education,* 1 (1969).

42. French, Joseph L., "Critical Review of a Standardized Road-Map Test of Direction Sense," *Journal of Educational Measurement,* 3 (Summer 1966), 197–98.

43. Friedman, Ronald, "Utility of the Concept of Brain Damage for the School Psychologist," *Journal of School Psychology,* 7 (1968–69), 27–32.

44. Fry, Edward, "Do-It-Yourself Terminology Generator," *Journal of Reading,* 11 (March 1968), 428.

45. Gallegher, James J., *The Tutoring of Brain-Injured Mentally Retarded Children.* Springfield: Charles C. Thomas, 1960.

46. Geneva Medico-Educational Service, "Problems Posed by Dyslexia," *Journal of Learning Disabilities,* 1 (1968), 158–71.

47. Goldberg, Herman K., "The Role of Patching in Learning," in *Reading Disability and Perception,* George D. Spache, editor, Proceedings International Reading Association, 13, No. 3 (1969), 58–60.

48. Goldstein, Kurt, *After Effects of Brain Injuries in War.* New York: Grune and Stratton, 1942.

49. Grassi, Joseph R., *The Grassi Block Substitution Test for Measuring Organic Brain Pathology.* Springfield: Charles C. Thomas, 1970.

50. Hallgren, B., *Specific Dyslexia.* Copenhagen: Munksgaard, 1950.

51. Hartlage, Lawrence C., "Differential Diagnosis of Dyslexia, Minimal Brain Damage and Emotional Disturbances in Children," *Psychology in the Schools,* 7 (1970), 403–406.

52. Hermann, Knud, *Reading Disabilities: A Medical Study of Word-Blindness and Related Handicaps.* Springfield: Charles C. Thomas, 1970.

53. Hillerich, R. L., "Eye-Hand Dominance and Reading Achievement," *American Educational Research Journal,* 1 (1964), 121–26.

54. Hughs, J. R., Leander, R., and Ketchum, G., "Electroencephalographic Study of Specific Reading Disabilities," *Electroencephalographic and Clinical Neurophysiology,* 2 (1949), 377–78.

55. Humphiss, Deryck, "The Measurement of Sensory Ocular Dominance and Its Relation to Personality," *American Journal of Optometry and Archives of American Academy of Optometry,* 46 (August 1969), 603–15.

56. Isom, John B., "Neurological Research Relevant to Reading," in *Perception and Reading,* Helen K. Smith, editor, Proceedings International Reading Association, 12, No. 4 (1968), 67–72.

57. Isom, John B., "An Interpretation of Dyslexia: A Medical Viewpoint," in *Reading Disability and Perception,* George D. Spache, editor, Proceedings International Reading Association, 13, No. 3 (1969), 1–7.

58. Johnson, Doris J., "Treatment Approaches to Dyslexia," in *Reading Disability and Perception,* George D. Spache, editor, Proceedings International Reading Association, 13, No. 3 (1969), 95–102.

59. Jordan, Dale R., *Dyslexia in the Classroom.* Columbus: Charles E. Merrill, 1972.

60. Kawi, A., and Pasamanick, B., "The Association of Factors of Pregnancy with the Development of Reading Disorders in Childhood," *Journal of the American Medical Association,* 166 (1958), 1420–23.

61. Kephart, Newell C., "Let's Not Misunderstand Dyslexia," *Instructor,* 78 (1968), 62–63.

62. Kephart, Newell C., "Learning Characteristics of the Brain-Injured Child," in

Clinical Studies in Reading III, Helen M. Robinson, editor. Supplementary Educational Monographs, 97 (1968), 136–42. Chicago: University of Chicago Press.

63. Ketchum, E. Gillet, "Neurological and/or Emotional Factors in Reading Disabilities," in *Vistas in Reading,* Proceedings International Reading Association, 11, No. 1 (1966), 521–26.

64. Knott, J. R., Muehl, S., and Benton, A., "Electroencephalography in Children with Reading Disabilities," *Electroencephalography and Clinical Neurophysiology,* 18 (1965), 513–33.

65. Krippner, Stanley, Silverman, Robert, Cavallo, Michael, and Healy, Michael, "A Study of 'Hyperkinetic' Children Receiving Stimulant Drugs," *Academic Therapy,* 8 (Spring 1973), 261–70.

66. Lerner, Janet W., "A Thorn by Any Other Name: Dyslexia or Reading Disability," *Elementary English,* 48 (January 1971), 75–80.

67. Lindell, Ebbe, *Report No. 7.* Lund, Sweden: Institute of Education, University of Lund, 1965, as quoted by Malmquist (71).

68. Lovell, K., and Gorton, A., "A Study of Some Differences between Backward and Normal Readers of Average Intelligence," *British Journal of Educational Psychology,* 38 (February 1968), 240–47.

69. Lovell, K., Shapton, D., and Warren, N. S., "A Study of Some Cognitive and Other Disabilities in Backward Readers of Average Intelligence as Assessed by a Non-Verbal Test," *British Journal of Educational Psychology,* 34 (1964), 58–64.

70. Lyle, J. G., "Certain Antenatal, Perinatal and Developmental Variables and Reading Retardation in Middle-Class Boys," *Child Development,* 41 (1970), 481–91.

71. Malmquist, Eve, *Las-och skrivsvaarighter hos born. Analys och behandlingsmetodik.* Lund, Sweden, 1967.

72. McBride, Robert R., "Psychochemicals and the Minimal Brain Dysfunction Child," *Academic Therapy,* 8 (Spring 1973), 303–15.

73. Meyers, Russell, "Aphasia: A Problem in Differential Diagnosis and Reeducation," *Quarterly Journal of Speech,* 23 (October 1937), 357–77.

74. Monk, Evelyn Silberbusch, "Reading Reversal, Right-Left Discrimination, and Lateral Preference," *Dissertation Abstracts,* 27 (May 1967), 4114B.

75. Monroe, Marion, *Children Who Cannot Read.* Chicago: University of Chicago Press, 1932.

76. Myklebust, H. R., "Psychoneurological Differences in Childhood," *Rehabilitation Literature,* 25 (1964), 12.

77. "Ophthalmologists Urged to Keep Eye Out for Nonreaders," *Medical New World* (December 23, 1966), 46–49.

78. Orton, Samuel T., *Reading, Writing and Speech Problems in Children.* New York: Norton, 1937.

79. Penfield, Wilder, and Roberts, Lamar, *Speech and Brain Mechanisms.* Princeton: Princeton University Press, 1959.

80. Penn, Julia M., "Reading Disability: A Neurological Deficit?" *Exceptional Children,* 33 (1966), 243–48.

81. Rabinovitch, Ralph D., and Ingram, Winifred, "Neuropsychiatric Considerations in Reading Retardation," *Reading Teacher,* 15 (May 1962), 433–38.

82. *Reading Newsreport,* "Kids Who Can't Learn," 2 (February 1968), 16–23.
83. *Reading Newsreport,* "Early Help for Dyslexics," 3 (May–June 1969), 32–6.
84. Reed, H. B. C., Jr., Reitan, R. M., and Klove, H., "Influences of Cerebral Lesions on Psychological Test Performances of Older Children," *Journal of Consulting Psychology,* 29 (1965), 247–51.
85. Reed, James C., "Lateralized Finger Agnosia and Reading Achievement at Ages 6 and 10," *Child Development,* 38 (September 1967), 213–20.
86. Reed, James C., Rabe, Edward F., and Mankinen, Margaret, "Teaching Reading to Brain-Damaged Children: A Review," *Reading Research Quarterly,* 5 (Spring 1970), 379–401.
87. Reitan, Ralph M., "A Research Program on the Psychological Effects of Brain Lesions in Human Beings," pp. 153–218 in *International Review of Research in Mental Retardation,* vol. 1. New York: Academic Press, 1966.
88. Reitan, Ralph M., and Klove, H., "Identifying the Brain-Injured Child," pp. 129–135 in *Clinical Studies in Reading III,* Helen M. Robinson, editor. Supplementary Educational Monographs No. 97. Chicago: University of Chicago Press, 1968.
89. Rengstorff, R. H., "The Types and Incidence of Hand-Eye Preference and Its Relationship with Certain Abilities," *American Journal of Optometry and Archives of American Academy of Optometry,* 44 (1967), 233–38.
90. Rice, J. A., "Confusion in Laterality: A Validity Study with Bright and Dull Children," *Journal of Learning Disabilities,* 2 (1969), 368–73.
91. Rosenthal, Joseph H., "Recent Advances in the Neurophysiology of Some Specific Cognitive Functions," *Academic Therapy,* 8 (Summer 1973), 423–28.
92. Rosner, Stanley L., "Word Games in Reading Diagnosis," *Reading Teacher,* 24 (January 1971), 331–35.
93. Rost, K. J., and Charles, D. C., "Academic Achievement of Brain-Injured and Hyperactive Children in Isolation," *Exceptional Children,* 34 (1967), 125–26.
94. Rutter, M., Yule, W., Trizard, J., and Graham, P., "Severe Reading Retardation: Its Relationship to Maladjustment, Epilepsy and Neurological Disorder," in "What is Special Education?" *Proceedings of the First International Congress of the Association for Special Education,* 1 (1966), 25–28.
95. Samuels, S. Jay, "Success and Failure in Learning to Read: A Critique of the Research," *Reading Research Quarterly,* 8 (Winter 1973), 200–39.
96. Samuels, S. Jay, "Reading Disability?" *Reading Teacher,* 24 (December 1970), 267, 271.
97. Schiffman, G. B., "Diagnosing Cases of Reading Disability with Suspected Neurological Impairment," in *Vistas in Reading,* Proceedings International Reading Association, 11 (1966), 513–21.
98. Schneyer, J. Wesley, "Research: Drug Therapy and Learning in Children," *Reading Teacher,* 24 (March 1971), 561–63.
99. Schubert, Delwyn G., "Diagnosis in Severe Reading Disability," in *Reading Disability and Perception,* George D. Spache, editor, Proceedings International Reading Association, 13, No. 3 (1969), 29–37.
100. Shafer, Sarah A., and Lilly, E. C., "Dominance in Relation to Achievement," *Academic Therapy,* 6 (1970), 177–85.

101. Shearer, E., "Physical Skills and Reading Backwardness," *Educational Research,* 10 (1968), 197–206.

102. Sheperd, G., "Selected Factors in the Reading Ability of Educable Mentally Retarded Boys," *American Journal of Mental Deficiency,* 71 (1967), 563–70.

103. Shepherd, Edwin M., "Reading Efficiency of 809 Average School Children: The Effect of Reversal on Their Performance," *American Journal of Ophthalmology,* 41 (June 1956), 1029–39.

104. Silver, A. A., and Hagin, R., "Specific Reading Disability: A Declination of the Syndrome and Relationship to Cerebral Dominance," *Comprehensive Psychiatry,* 1 (1960), 126–34.

105. Smith, Donald E. P., and Carrigan, Patricia M., *The Nature of Reading Disability.* New York: Harcourt, Brace & World, 1959.

106. Smith, Linda D., "Study of Laterality Characteristics of Retarded Readers and Reading Achievers," *Journal of Experimental Education,* 18 (June 1950), 321–29.

107. Sparrow, Sara S., and Satz, P., "Dyslexia, Laterality and Neuropsychological Development," pp. 41–60 in *Specific Reading Disability,* D. J. Bakker and P. Satz, editors. Amsterdam: Rotterdam University Press, 1970.

108. Stephens, W. E., Cunningham, E. S., and Stigler, B. J., "Reading Readiness and Eye-Hand Preference Patterns in First Grade Children," *Exceptional Children,* 33 (1967), 481–88.

109. Stevenson, Lillian P., "Eye-Hand Preference, Reversals and Reading Progress," in *Clinical Studies in Reading II,* Helen M. Robinson, editor. Supplementary Educational Monographs No. 77 (1953), 83–88. Chicago: University of Chicago Press.

110. Symmes, Jean S., and Rapoport, Judith L., "Unexpected Reading Failure," *American Journal of Orthopsychiatry,* 42 (January 1972), 82–91.

111. Tinker, Karen J., "The Role of Laterality in Reading Disability," in *Reading and Inquiry,* Proceedings International Reading Association 10 (1965), 300–303.

112. Trieschman, Roberta B., "Undifferentiated Handedness and Perceptual Development in Children with Reading Problems," *Perceptual and Motor Skills,* 27 (December 1968), 1123–34.

113. Wagner, Rudolph F., *Dyslexia and Your Child.* New York: Harper and Row, 1971.

114. Walsh, Mary W., "What is Dyslexia?" *Instructor,* 77 (1967), 54–57.

115. Warrington, Elizabeth K., "The Incidence of Verbal Disability Associated with Retardation in Reading," *Neuropsychologia,* 5 (1967), 175–79.

116. Weintraub, Samuel, "Eye-Hand Preference and Reading," *Reading Teacher,* 21 (January 1968), 369–73, 401.

117. Wepman, Joseph M., "The Modality Concept—Including a Statement of the Perceptual and Conceptual Levels of Learning," in *Perception and Reading,* Helen K. Smith, editor, Proceedings International Reading Association, 12, No. 4 (1968), 1–6.

118. Whitsell, Leon J., "A Clinic Team Approach to Reading Problems: Role of the Neurologist," in *Perception and Reading,* Helen K. Smith, editor, Proceedings International Reading Association, 12, No. 4 (1968), 72–77.

119. Woody, Robert H., "Diagnosis of Behavioral Problem Children: Electroencephalography and Mental Abilities," *Journal of School Psychology,* 5 (Winter 1967), 116–21.

120. Wunderlich, Ray C., "Treatment of the Hyperactive Child," *Academic Therapy*, 8 (Summer 1973), 375–90.
121. Zangwill, O. L., *Cerebral Dominance and Its Relation to Psychological Function.* London: Oliver and Boyd, 1960.
122. Zedler, Empress Y., "Management of Reading in the Educational Program of Pupils with Neurologically Based Learning Problems," in *Reading Disability and Perception,* George D. Spache, editor, Proceedings International Reading Association, 13, No. 3 (1969), 103–12.

In many quarters, schools are accused of having failed in their responsibility in teaching children to read. And the bare statistics of about a 50 percent failure ratio among lower class children seem to support this criticism. The American public school system is further attacked for clinging to strictly middle class mores and ideals and thus, as it were, denying academic success to those of different backgrounds. Yet when we examine this area of socio-cultural factors and reading, we find a large number of psychological and social conditions that tend to negate any real solutions to this problem.

Among the factors that tend to circumscribe the academic success of lower class pupils are differences in language development; a harmful interaction among poverty, unemployment, mobility, and untreated physical handicaps; and conflict between the cultural mores and values of pupils and those of the middle class teacher or middle-class–oriented school. Other deterrents to school progress are basic differences in child-rearing patterns, mother-child relationships, teacher prejudice, and fundamental parental attitudes toward reading and education.

As you survey these socio-cultural obstacles to success in the school as it is today, ask yourself such questions as:

1. Could some of these deterrents to school success be ameliorated by changes in the framework of our schools, as in curriculum, goals, values, rewards, and the like? How?

2. Do you feel that educators, in general, are failing in their responsibility for educating children? Or that, in some respects, the school is also the victim of circumstances, often beyond its control?

8
Socio-Cultural Factors

THE SOCIOCULTURAL FACTORS that affect reading success include a number of areas such as language development, racial or ethnic characteristics, familial relationships, and school relationships as well as socioeconomic status. Negative elements in each of these areas combine to influence the child's ultimate success in the classroom. The volume of research and recorded opinion regarding the significant aspects of these sociocultural factors is very great. But we shall attempt to touch upon each area and convey a few basic ideas that are relevant to reading instruction.

LANGUAGE DEVELOPMENT

Some writers would have us consider the language development of children as the most important element in their eventual reading success. They point out that the child's language is fostered or retarded by the environment provided from the moment of birth. Institutionalized infants develop much more slowly in both mobility and language because of the lack of stimulation from parents, and this interaction continues to be significant throughout the child's early years. Economically disadvantaged pupils are said to be deficient in verbal fluency, breadth of speech, and auditory vocabularies, diction, and articulation. Their grammar, word usage, sentence length, and variety of sentence patterns are also supposed to be poorer than those of middle-class children. Verbal deficits and low socioeconomic status are said to be linked in the causes of reading retardation (7, 78).

Just how language development occurs is still a matter of debate. One author offers three possible theories: operant conditioning in imitation of the adult and by reinforcement; cognitive development—a gradual evolution from composition to production of language based on concept acquisition and spontaneous experimentation and generalization about language; and an organismic development (à la Piaget) on a biological basis plus a state of readiness promoted by experiences (3). All these theories seem to acknowledge the parallelism between language and thought, although they recognize that some early thinking precedes actual language use. In another sense, all three of these theories recognize the interaction between the child's language development and his experiences.

A few studies seem to find delayed speech development among retarded readers, as in the work of Warrington (81) and Rutter et al. (70).

Mason (49), following the educational attainments of children with retarded speech development, found that 81 percent of such a group had problems in early reading stages sufficient to reduce their reading scores to a point below the normal controls. As may be expected, the greatest reading difficulties were experienced by the speech-retarded boys. With respect to actual speech defects such as articulatory disorders, the evidence is less consistent. Gaines (24) reviewed thirteen studies of speech and reading disabilities. Of seven reported by trained speech examiners, only three studies found a marked relationship with reading, with the others finding little or no significance in speech defects for reading success. Morris's large-scale British study (55) attributed a relationship between speech defects, retarded language development, and reading. In contrast, in six studies conducted by untrained speech examiners, five report a marked relationship with reading and spelling disabilities. The implication is clear that articulatory defects assume significance in reading failure mainly when they are viewed subjectively, as by the average teacher listening to the oral reading of her pupils. Speech diagnosticians, who evaluate them more scientifically, are not so apt to consider these defects a barrier to reading success, since they know that such errors often reflect developmental stages that speech maturation will probably eliminate. But to the teacher judging pupil oral reading, they are an interference to good performance.

The interactions of language, race, social class, and reading are the subject of many recent investigations. Some emphasize the language deficits among various racial minority groups, as the many confusions in word sounds, word meanings, and word usage among Indian children noted by Philion and Galloway (66) in British Columbia. Werner et al. (83) found that 88 percent of the reading-problem children in a large-scale study in Hawaii came from homes where Pidgin English was frequently spoken. Other studies claim that these minority children are deficient in the range of vocabulary, in the use of syntactic variations within sentences or endings signifying tense and number, and in general facility with words. It is claimed that these children tend to use a restricted code of fast speech, with poor articulation and with whole expressions telescoped into a word (as "Wa-cha-dn?"), and to be relatively nonverbal in the classroom.

Alexander Frazier (22), in an examination of underdeveloped language in children with poorer backgrounds, offers a three-part explanation: verbal destitution or less language; full language but nonstandard; and unconceptualized or unverbalized experience in areas important to school success. A number of writers, like Baratz (5), S. Alan Cohen (14), and others, react very negatively to the theory that lower-class children are verbally destitute (32). They point to the studies indicating that such children are not inferior in language structure—as in a British study (47) or in oral language production in an Indian group (23)—and they criticize severely the way that investigations supporting this view were conducted.   Just because low socioeconomic black children do not use all such words, they say, we cannot conclude they do not know or understand 50 percent of the beginning reader vocabulary.   For when given pictures of common objects, their recognition did not differ significantly from that of high socioeconomic children.   S. Alan Cohen and Thelma Cooper (13) cite seven contradictions of fallacies that they think they see in studies of the language of black children:

> 1. Urban black children tend to be less verbal because of the school's hostile atmosphere rather than because of a lack of verbal facility.
> 2. Studies of verbal interaction in the lower-class family show a good deal of communication rather than a lack.
> 3. Black English is a well-ordered, highly structured, sophisticated language system, not an inferior form of standard English.
> 4. The school actually requires the child to translate from black English to standard in order to communicate with his teacher, with a consequent breakdown.
> 5. This child's vocabulary may be less than in the middle class but certainly is sufficient for beginning reading.
> 6. Training intended to improve the oral language of these pupils does not affect power in reading, for we do not speak as we read.
> 7. Although there are a few sounds that are poorly articulated or auditorily discriminated by these pupils, these can be readily learned by training.

S. Alan Cohen claims that any differences in reading success for black pupils could be overcome by intensive, quality instruction, particularly at the critical primary reading stages.

Cohen's arguments and criticisms may be correct, but the point remains that, at the hands of the average teacher, the language deviations of minority children do contribute to reading failure.   These deviations from standard English have a significant impact, as in the study showing that blacks and whites interpret Southern speech, whether by black or white, as substandard. Black English is often interpreted as indicative of low intelligence or carelessness, and the speaker may be constantly corrected and criticized in the classroom.   Judgments of reading ability based on the pupil's oral reading—as they so frequently are—are almost automatically lowered when the reader uses substandard speech.   It is a moot question whether this type of child's language affects his intellectual development, his ability to learn to read, his comprehension in reading, or his ability to think with words.   But there is little doubt of its impact upon his relations with the average standard-English-speaking teacher.

The only comparable data available on a group of pupils who similarly experienced a language problem in dealing with the school are those that we have about the progress of immigrant children in our schools earlier in this century. Such children were, in general, also retarded in grade placement for their age twice as often as were native whites. But this handicap varied from one ethnic group to another. German and Russian children did not show this degree of retardation. Jewish children from these two countries were more successful than those from Poland, reflecting such factors as their origin in rural or urban backgrounds, motivation, ease of assimilation, and parental aspirations.

SOCIOECONOMIC STATUS

Barton and Wilder in the United States (6) and Joyce M. Morris in Britain (55) have made large-scale surveys of the relationships between reading achievement and socioeconomic status. Barton and Wilder found that the proportions of children below grade in classes of the lower-level vocations increased steadily from the first to sixth grade and reached about 50 percent by this time. The failure ratio was significantly greater than in middle-class groups in every grade. Morris found a correlation of .68 between the socioeconomic status of the school and reading achievement. In this population, as in the American studies, more boys were retarded than girls as early as age eight. Unlike our findings, British pupils in larger and urban schools and those in large classes excelled. As in the Barton-Wilder study, the failure ratio for British pupils increased with grade level to 50-60 percent. Of children poor in reading at age eight, only 13 percent reached the standard by the time that they began secondary school. Not all other studies agree in finding such marked relationships between socioeconomic status and reading, partly because they vary in their criteria for judging this characteristic (34). Callaway (10), for example, did not find father's occupation significant but did note that children with working fathers scored significantly higher in reading. Bell, Lewis, and Anderson (7) factor analyzed forty-three variables that might be related to reading and established one as low socioeconomic status as measured by the educational level of the father or mother.

Socioeconomic status may be judged by the income of the family or by their educational or vocational levels. These three traits are not identical and do not necessarily agree with each other or have exactly the same effects upon children's school success. But they do interact with race, particularly, to exert a significant effect upon such success (21). The interaction among poverty, unemployment, and frequent changes of school does tend to affect the children of the lower socioeconomic levels unfavorably. The daily physical hazards, poor health of mothers, malnourishment, and uncorrected visual, hearing, and dental defects, which are often characteristic of this group, also militate against school progress. Yet these handicaps are not universal for low socioeconomic children and may be ameliorated by favorable factors in the family relationships, as we shall see later.

One of the results of this group of sociological factors is to depress the children's intelligence and to produce a greater extent of mild mental retardation. But there is evidence that systematic increase in intelligence in individuals and in populations is possible through time, particularly as social environment improves (79). The national effort to improve housing, to eradicate poverty and unemployment, and to improve the poor schooling often provided these pupils offers some promise in view of these facts.

Di Lorenzo, Salter, and Hayden collated the findings of a large number of research studies in reading to identify the relationships of many reading skills with socioeconomic status (19). The correlations ranged from .17 for visual design memory and recall to .53 for reading letters and numbers. Of the others only auditory discrimination gave a correlation above .40, the level considered to indicate a moderate relationship. If reading letters and numbers at primary and preprimary levels reflects prereading knowledge, as we would suspect, it is not surprising to find it related to socioeconomic status. Accomplishment of this type may certainly reflect home conditions, as we shall point out later in considering family patterns of child-rearing. The positive relation between auditory discrimination and socioeconomic status is also an expected finding in view of the widespread evidence of inferiority in this area among linguistically and economically disadvantaged pupils. However, this finding cannot be interpreted as proof of the need for auditory discrimination training for low socioeconomic pupils. (See chapter 4 for discussion of this point.)

SCHOOL RELATIONSHIPS: WITH PEERS

We explore the peer relationships of poor readers at length in chapter 9, "Personality and Self-Concept Factors," and need only to summarize the evidence at this point. Peer relationships of poor readers—and particularly of those who are disadvantaged—are characterized by aggressiveness, inability to accept blame, rejection by the more successful peers, and withdrawal symptoms. Poor readers tend to recognize their lack of acceptance, as shown by negativism toward peers as well as adults and sometimes by their passivity toward their isolation. These relationships with peers are typical whether the group is disadvantaged, affluent, or mixed in socioeconomic status.

Of course, when a child is both a poor reader and economically disadvantaged in a group of more affluent peers, his social acceptance and peer relations are apt to be even worse. Being a disadvantaged poor reader and member of a small group differing from the rest in race, compounds the weak peer relations even further. A single child who differs from the group mode in one or several of these social handicaps is often accepted compassionately or sometimes even lionized. But a group of "different" children tends to form an identity apart from, and often rejected by, the majority, unless the teacher is sophisticated enough to capitalize upon the differences of the small group in achieving their acceptance.

SCHOOL RELATIONSHIPS: TEACHER-PUPIL INTERACTION

Disadvantaged pupils are faced by the fact that, in practically all aspects, the school promotes a way of life different from what they see and experience. The informal standards, as dress codes, behavior norms, reward systems, and the like are based on the middle-class culture and criteria. The formal curriculum assumes a homogeneous, static, patriotic, ethical society and supports the school's historical role of promoting the remodeling or retooling of foreign, immigrant, or lower-class children into the middle-class format. When this goal is failed, the results are attributed to a "culture deprivation" theory—"those kids just don't have any culture and are incapable of emulating ours." Even the compensatory or remedial programs are loaded with the same middle-class cultural content. In addition to comments of this sort, Thomas P. Carter (11) also points out that much of the formal school curriculum is not relevant to the knowledges or values acquired in extraschool life of the disadvantaged. Moreover, the instructional methods employed do not correspond to this type of child's concept of teacher-pupil behavior or perhaps to his learning style. In fact, the content of the school curriculum is often contradictory to the goals and values as seen by the child's family; and in ignoring his cultural background, the school rejects it as inferior. Some hope that the school can be an agent of change in the social adaptation of the disadvantaged (45), but, in our opinion, this is a vain hope for many reasons except for a minority of these youth. For example, disadvantaged pupils see a greater discrepancy between their personal goals and those of the teacher, as we might expect, than do middle-class pupils (29). They are also less apt to perceive the teacher as someone who wants to help them achieve what they think is significant. Acceptance and identification with the school's basic goals are very difficult for these pupils.

This estrangement is further fostered by the common negative practices of teachers in dealing with pupils who fail to meet their expectations. As a group, boys receive more negative remarks, are given fewer opportunities to participate in the reading lesson, and receive lower grades than do girls, in keeping with their tendency to disappoint the teacher's expectations in reading achievement and classroom behavior (2, 17, 26, 76). Even the children are aware of this discrimination (17). The sex of the teacher does not change this picture of teacher-expectation–pupil treatment, although men teachers tend to give slightly higher grades. Failure to meet teacher expectations results in much lecturing and criticism even among high-ability pupils, with consequent actual loss in reading comprehension for pupils and a tendency to pupil withdrawal from the conflict (64).

These negative, discriminative practices are apt to be even more prominent when pupils differ from the teacher in social class. Although often from lower-class origins themselves, teachers are apt to be upward-mobile, moving toward identification with what they believe is a better way of life. For many their professional identity is an entree to a higher social status, a way of escaping the life of the ghetto, as in the case of those of disadvantaged or nonwhite birth. Some of these fail to achieve the social service motif of the teaching profession and may even reject those pupils of obvious lower-class origin. "They ain't never goin' amount to nothin'," as one teacher engaged in a special program to help disadvantaged pupils remarked to this author.

The dramatic effect of teacher expectations upon pupil achievement has been explored in a number of research studies. When teachers are given correct or even false information regarding their pupils' potentials, most of the studies indicate that the pupils were led to achieve in the expected fashion (41, 61, 62, 69, 82). The Pygmalion effect of experimenter expectation upon the performances of animals, children, or other experimental subjects is very real and, unfortunately, functions in negative directions for children who are "different" from the teacher's ideal.

RACIAL OR ETHNIC DIFFERENCES

Racial discrimination is an ugly component of white middle-class culture. The late Whitney M. Young declared that the white family fails in its supposed function of teaching the young how to be human and civilized and how to get along with other people. The white family, he says, suffers from an almost tribal xenophobia in its fear of strangers or the foreign to a pathological degree (86). Moreover, Young accuses sociologists of carefully avoiding exploring racial relationships or seeking possible solutions to this social problem. There is little question of the accuracy of Young's remarks, for such studies as are available confirm the white family's role in promoting negative racist attitudes. Even kindergarten white children associate negative attitudes toward pictures of black children but not to pictures of their own race.

There are certainly differences among racial and ethnic groups that distinguish them from the middle-class majority and affect their success in learning. Jews, whites, and blacks tend to fall in that order in school achievement, and in a similar order in tested intelligence (67). Whether this fact produces a similar hierarchy in terms of positive self-concept is debated by various researchers, but logic seems to support this belief. Other comparisons among ethnic and racial groups (4) find Jewish pupils highest in verbal intelligence and math but low in visual reasoning and memory; Orientals high in math only and blacks generally lower in all areas except memory and perceptual speed (4). Other studies ranking grade twelve pupils by achievement scores yield an order of whites, Orientals, Indians, Mexican-Americans, Puerto Ricans, and blacks.

Blacks of junior high ages scored lower in several tests of symbol substitution (which may be tests of learning or perceptual-motor speed) and in reading, but higher in the Myklebust Picture Language Story test than did whites in one study (46), and lower in the Minnesota Percepto-Diagnostic test in another (30). Basic visual perceptual skills, in contrast, did not appear to be related to low socioeconomic status or to visual-motor skills among Head Start children. But, as in many other studies, low socioeconomic pupils did perform more poorly in form reproduction (28). At ages five to nine, black children were not differentiated in paired-associate learning tasks despite the lower I.Q.'s for the blacks (73). But, as we have pointed out elsewhere, the results of these comparative studies, particularly among racially or culturally different groups, are clouded by the question of the fairness of such tests for different populations. (See chapter 10 on Selecting and Interpreting Group Reading Measures.) Many of the tests used are built to middle-class criteria in content, directions, norms, and the like. Validity and reliability of the tests are significantly poorer when they are used for economically or culturally different groups. In a sense, many of the apparent differences found reflect cultural and experiential background rather than variations in potential for learning or deficits that cannot be changed by appropriate training.

Miles V. Zintz (87) has offered what we think is the most dramatic comparison of the effect of differences in cultural background upon beliefs

TABLE 8–1   CONFLICTS IN CULTURAL VALUES
IN THE MINORITY GROUPS IN THE SOUTHWEST
Adapted from Zintz (87)*

TRADITIONAL AMERICAN	INDIAN	SPANISH-AMERICAN
Man must harness Nature.	Nature will provide for man if he observes the law.	If it's God's Will.
All living is future-oriented.	Here and now is good; future will be good.	Rewards are in the next life (Heaven).
Climb the ladder of success.	Follow ways of old people.	Work a little, rest a little. Follow father's footsteps.
Success achieved by hard work.	Satisfy present needs. Don't be selfish or stingy in acquiring more.	Try to be satisfied with what one has.
Everybody save for the future.	One shares freely what he has.	Share within extended family.
Adhere to time schedules.	Time is always with us.	The clock walks—"Hasta manana—si Dios quiere."
Change is normal behavior.	Follow old ways with confidence.	Follow old ways. Life here is endured to win eternal life.
Scientific explanation for everything.	Mythology, fear of the supernatural and sorcery.	Fears, witches, and nonscientific medical practices.
One competes to win.	Remain submerged within the group. Do not seek leadership.	Accept the status quo.
Each individual shapes his own destiny.	Accept group sanctions. Conformity.	Obedience to will of God.

*Reprinted with permission of Miles V. Zintz and the International Reading Association.

and behavior (see Table 8-1).   He contrasts these cultural ideals in the minority groups of the Southwest, wherein he is a recognized authority.

FAMILIAL RELATIONSHIPS

We shall briefly touch upon the role of the family in the discussion of the self-concept in chapter 9.   Here we shall review a part of the mass of evidence regarding such characteristics of the disadvantaged family as child-rearing patterns, parental attitudes toward schooling and toward reading failure, general home conditions that influence the child's school success, and the significance of such factors as birth order and family mobility.

After an extensive examination of the literature, Edmund W. Gordon (27) considers that home conditions and general conditions of life are more important predictors of achievement than are any other of the variables studied in the Coleman Report and other research sources. We shall examine some of the evidence supporting this viewpoint.

CHILD-REARING PATTERNS

In the lower-class home, Thomas (80) notes that there are a number of distinctive features:

> 1. Fear of parental authority leads the children to relate to and be dependent upon their siblings and friends in preference to parents.
> 2. Girls are overprotected, while the discipline of boys is inadequate.
> 3. A strong mother-dominated atmosphere is common, particularly in view of the frequent absence of a father.
> 4. Parents tend to react to the child's behavior in terms of immediate consequences of the act, often with punitive action, without considering the child's intent.
> 5. Husbands are expected to impose restraints, not to be supportive of the children.
> 6. Child-rearing is the responsibility of the wife, in the father's mind.

Other negative aspects of child-parent relations are the fact that children seldom eat a meal with the parents and, in fact, group family activities are also infrequent. In contrast, the superior readers identified by Dorothy J. McGinnis (51) had parents who fostered independence, encouraged communication, did not hurry growth, and refrained from restricting their children unduly.

Since the primary parent-child relationship is so often with the mother, the nature and effects of this interaction upon language development, intelligence of the children, and school success has been frequently analyzed. It appears that the mother's language style tends to determine the child's ability to handle language abstractions, even more so than does his I.Q. Lack of verbal interaction in the lower-class home may lead to delaying the development of speech sounds, retardation in vocalization, and the mastery of speech sounds at expected ages. The models of the language of these mothers is characterized as meager, restricted, grammatically incorrect, and often so punitive and threatening as to repress the child's own speech (59). In contrast, middle-class mothers engage in active conversation with their children at meals, answer questions, and, through such affectionate display and the association with adults, foster practice in advanced patterns of language (36, 85).

Della-Piana and Martin (18) and Miller (53) have explored other aspects of this mother-child relationship and its effects on child development. In comparing the mothers of over- and underachievers after interviews, Della-Piana and Martin concluded that the mothers of overachieving girls gave more positive affect and warmth, in contrast to the negative feeling tone of mothers of underachieving girls. Miller found that middle-class mothers show an "active" teaching style, with specific and concrete directions when teaching their children a simple sorting task. Lower-class mothers used a "passive" style with little precision in their directions. The mother's teaching style was related .59 with the child's score on a readiness test in the middle-class group, and .59 and .63 with silent and oral reading test scores. Such relations were much lower in the lower-lower-class children. Middle class and upper-lower-class mothers were similar and were significantly different from the mothers of the lowest class of children, perhaps reflecting their educational levels and verbal abilities.

Relationships of child with mother or father are also distinctly different among achievers and nonachievers in reading. The parallelism between some of the relations of underachievers with the male parent to the general pattern of child-rearing in disadvantaged homes will be apparent. Glick (25) showed that poor male readers had a negative concept of parental behavior as hostile and anxiety-provoking. Few of these unfavorable impressions were present among good female readers as compared to poor female readers. School achievers had a solid relationship with their fathers or another adult male who was viewed as competent in the case of both boys and girls, according to Hirsch and Costello (38). Underachievers in contrast were dependent upon their dominant mothers, identified tenuously with both parents, but often saw their parents as incompetent. Mazurkiewicz (50) claims that male parents unconsciously lead their boys to reject reading as a feminine activity by failing to provide a positive model in this activity. Mutimer, Loughlin, and Powell discovered that underachieving boys considered their parents as the least significant members of the family, while achieving boy readers identified with their fathers (57). Achieving girls identified with their mothers, in distinction to underachieving girls, who interacted more with their siblings, as did the underachieving boys. In a comparison of the predictors of success in beginning reading of black and white children, Henderson and Long (37) found that having a father present in the home was significant for black boys but not for black girls.   Among whites, achieving girls were significantly closer to their mothers than to their fathers.   Achieving black girls, on the other hand, related more to their friends than to mothers.

To summarize these child-rearing patterns in homes of the disadvantaged or underachieving pupils, we may point out these features:

1. The mother-dominated home is characterized by a negative feeling tone, a passive teaching style, and a poor language model.
2. The impression of hostile, punitive, anxiety-producing discipline is often centered in the father.
3. The relationships of boys or girls with the feared and often absent father are weak.   When present, the father provides a poor model of reading practices.
4. The view of parents is one of incompetence or of less significance than friends or siblings.
5. The family lacks group activities, even including joining in regular mealtimes.

These interfamily relationships, which negatively affect reading success greatly, are further reinforced by some parental attitudes toward the school and its middle-class goals, as well as toward their children's progress in that institution.   According to Gurman (33) taping sessions with underachieving students and their parents separately yielded these central themes: meaning of grades—students believe that parents feel grades more important than individual development or quality of education. In contradiction, parents were not so concerned with grades as their sons thought but expressed hopes for inner contentment and well-roundedness for their children; student self-determination—boys felt that they were given too much freedom but little guidance and interpreted this as rejection; parents agree that they were ambivalent in allowing freedom but expected assumption of adult responsibility; need for adult models—students expressed a need for adult models but felt their parents inconsistent in words versus deeds. Parents admitted their own conflict between ethical norms and their observation of these; need for mutual openness—students had too little time for communication of their needs to parents; parents claimed that they did not know how to help and were afraid to be too close to their children for fear of exposing themselves; need for mutual trust—students felt that parents were "against" them and that they could not consult freely or trust their parents; parents felt that they could not trust or communicate with their sons. This is indeed a bitter picture of frustration and lack of communication that, unfortunately, is all too familiar to teachers, psychologists, and social workers, in general, in working with school underachievers.

MacDonald (48) in the United States and Johansson in Denmark (40) cite the direct effect of negative parental attitudes toward education, toward language development, and toward the importance of success in reading upon pupil school success in this field.   Preston (68) was amazed to find that half of the parents of reading disability cases had no sympathy or understanding of the impact of this failure on their children and that more than three out of four of these parents treated their failing children with contempt, reproach, or taunting!   Like many others engaged in medical or clinical services to the public, Hardy (35) is depressed by parental resistance to their children's needs for remedial or preventive services.   Finally, it has been observed that parents who conceive of themselves as vocational, marital, or educational failures tend to transmit their feelings of frustration and hopelessness to their children—with obvious effects (31).   It is no surprise that many believe parental aspirations, or their lack, are more significant in the child's reading success than is socioeconomic or cultural background.

GENERAL HOME CONDITIONS

Among other aspects of the home environment that have been examined for their relationship with the child's reading success are the literary atmosphere, supply of reading matter, fostering of study habits, prereading experiences, and family harmony.   The literary environment of the home is reflected in such things as the number of books, magazines and newspapers, the mother's reading habits, and use of the library.   In various studies, each one of these evidences of family interest in reading has been shown to be significantly related to reading achievement (34, 44, 63, 74, 75).

The impetus toward reading in these factors exerts a greater influence upon the reading success of the child than does the precise socioeconomic status of the family or even the child's I.Q. (34).   Favorable literary environment can be present in lower classes, as Peil shows that black mothers, despite lower income, tended to read more than low-income whites did, even when age and education were controlled.   Those black mothers who used the public library also bought more books for their children and influenced them to use the library also (63).   As in many other aspects of child-rearing, the patterns provided by the mother in reading in the disadvantaged home have marked impact upon the child's attitudes toward reading.   Promotion of reading by the children and providing a desk or other space for such activity are part of the background of able readers in other cultures such as the Japanese (71) as well as in the American (16).

In writing about the significance of prereading experiences as a foundation for reading, such early reading specialists as Marion Monroe and Bernice Rogers (54) did not emphasize the role of class structure in this factor. Middle-class authors then just did not stress class differences as such, although, of course, they recognized that the kinds of informational experiences they were discussing were a reflection of the educational socioeconomic status of the family. Wilma. H. Miller (52), in contrast, did not hesitate to compare practices in lower- and middle-class homes. Using a structured interview, she found that lower-class children were given few field trips and less dramatic play; they were read to less and were seldom taught the alphabet or beginning reading. No differences were disclosed with respect to manipulative materials such as crayons, paints, and scissors, or in incidence of use of the public library. These early experiences with books and language in printed form have recently been emphasized again as significant to the very early stages of learning to read. The values of learning the alphabet prior to reading experiences are, of course, highly questionable except in promoting a positive attitude toward the area of reading. As Miller showed, this specific type of learning may influence readiness test scores; but, because it can readily be supplied by the teacher, it is not highly related to actual reading achievement in the first grade.

Family harmony, as measured by the incidence of broken homes, separation, and divorce, has not been consistently found important in school success. Absence of a father figure, as seen so frequently in lower-class homes, is in this group not so much an indication of family disharmony as much as it is evidence of the looseness of structure of the family unit (43). It is an important facet of the child's background, as we have seen. The more subtle evidences of parental disagreements or conflict have also been shown to affect the child's personal and school adjustment. In contrast to matched parents of good readers, the parents of poor readers manifested these symptoms more frequently: more derogatory critical terms; describing their children as aggressive, distrustful, or dependent; parental disagreements in descriptions of their children; dissatisfaction with their spouses and their children; and denigrating their children's personalities (72). The bare statistics on marital status and harmony may not reflect these interfamily pathological symptoms or their unwholesome effects upon children and their reading abilities.

The significance of the family constellation in terms of birth order of the children (and what this may mean in school and family relationships) has been explored in a number of studies. The evidence has not been consistent, however, with some studies finding a relation of birth order to achievement (1, 58, 60) and equally as many reports denying any significance (12, 34, 39). The age of the parents and whether the family is presently complete influence these studies of the importance of birth order. Studies based on young families with primary or elementary school-age children tend to give negative results, while those involving older pupils or college students (1, 58) are more apt to find differences in favor of the first-born in both verbal intelligence and achievement. An older, large-scale study in Britain appears to confirm the tendency of first-born children to vary both positively and negatively from the average pattern of their siblings. Other relationships, too, are significant in the sex of siblings, for in small families of two children, reading achievement is enhanced if both are of the same sex and close in age (12). Many clinicians have observed the opposite effect when the older child is a successful female whose accomplishments cannot be matched by a younger male sibling.

In recent decades, the American family has been characterized by a marked degree of mobility, with some saying that about one-fifth of families change their place of residence each year. The possible effects of this mobility upon children's schooling has been a matter of concern among school personnel, for, particularly among middle- and upper-class families, the moves involve frequent changes of school. The mobility patterns of upper and lower class, urban or suburban families tend to differ, and school systems vary in methodology and quality of instruction—factors that affect the interpretation of the impact of the sheer number of school changes in a given period in the child's school life. Large-scale studies in both the United States and Canada (8, 9, 15, 20, 77, 84) have agreed in finding no significant differences in reading due to transiency or frequency of school changes. But when the socioeconomic status of the families is considered, the picture changes to indicate that achievement is definitely lower for mobile lower-class pupils than for middle- and upper-class mobile students (42, 56). For lower-class students, I.Q. and reading achievement declined as mobility increased, even though in this group most moves are within the same school system (42, 65). Middle-class suburban dwellers tend to move longer distances and, perhaps because of better than average intelligence, were not affected by the mobility (65, 77). Mobility is relatively frequent among military and middle-management personnel; but, because of their educational and intellectual advantages, it does not seem to depress their children's school progress.

This consideration of the sociocultural factors in reading disability has uncovered a host of negative influences upon pupil reading ability particularly in socioeconomically deprived or culturally different groups. We find such attitudes and practices as these: those that retard speech and language development, poor peer and teacher-pupil relationships, racial discrimination, harmful child-rearing habits, pathological behaviors between parents and between parents and children, negative parental feelings about the school, poor general home conditions and literary environment, and excessive mobility—all are significant deterrents to child success in reading. We must certainly admit that the school faces a massive group of social problems that it is ill-equipped to solve or even ameliorate in its attempts to promote reading ability in all pupils. Yet, as we shall see in the later discussion of various approaches to personality problems in reading disabilities in chapter 9, there are at least hopeful solutions to lessening the impact of these sociocultural factors.

LEARNING PROJECT

Drawing upon your readings and teaching experiences, what steps do you suggest that a school could adopt to deal with such problems as the following?
1. Low parental aspirations for children and poor attitudes toward schooling.
2. Lack of language and perhaps of cognitive development of pupils.
3. Teacher prejudice against racial and ethnic minority pupils or those of lower socioeconomic status.
4. Some of the basic conflicts between the WASP traditional values promoted by the school versus those of various minority groups.

REFERENCES

1. Altus, William D., "Birth Order and Scholastic Aptitude," *Journal of Consulting Psychology,* 29 (June 1965), 202–205.
2. Arnold, Richard D., "The Achievement of Boys and Girls Taught by Men and Women Teachers," *Elementary School Journal,* 68 (April 1968), 367–72.
3. Athey, Irene, "Theories of Language Development," in *Reading: The Right to Participate,* Twentieth Yearbook National Reading Conference, 1971, 118–27.
4. Backman, Margaret E., "Patterns of Mental Abilities: Ethnic, Socioeconomic and Sex Differences," *American Educational Research Journal,* 9 (Winter 1972), 1–12.
5. Baratz, Joan C., "Language and Cognitive Assessment of Negro Children: Assumptions and Research Needs," ERIC Document 020-518 (1968).
6. Barton, Allen H., and Wilder, David E., "Research and Practice in the Teaching of Reading: A Progress Report," Research Project A 388. New York: Bureau of Applied Social Research, Columbia University.
7. Bell, D. Bruce, Lewis, F. D., and Anderson, R. F., "Some Personality and Motivational Factors in Reading Retardation," *Journal of Educational Research,* 65 (January 1972), 229–33.
8. Bollenbacher, Joan, "A Study of the Effect of Mobility on Reading Achievement," *Reading Teacher,* 15 (March 1962), 356–60, 365.
9. Brockman, Sister Mary A., and Reeves, A. W., "Relationship between Transiency and Test Achievement," *Alberta Journal of Educational Research,* 13 (1967), 319–30.

10. Callaway, Byron, "Pupil and Family Characteristics Related to Reading Achievement," *Education,* 92 (February–March 1972), 71–75.

11. Carter, Thomas P., "Cultural Content for Linguistically Different Learners," *Elementary English,* 48 (February 1971), 162–75.

12. Cicirelli, V. G., "Sibling Constellation, Creativity, I.Q. and Academic Achievement," *Child Development,* 38 (1967), 481–90.

13. Cohen, S. Alan, and Cooper, Thelma, "Seven Fallacies: Reading Retardation and the Urban Disadvantaged Beginning Reader," *Reading Teacher,* 26 (October 1972), 38–45.

14. Cohen, S. Alan, and Kornfeld, Gita S., "Oral Vocabulary and Beginning Reading in Disadvantaged Black Children," *Reading Teacher,* 24 (October 1970), 33–38.

15. Cramer, Ward, and Dorsey, Suzanne, "Are Movers Losers?" *Elementary School Journal,* 70 (April 1970), 387–90.

16. Dave, R. H., "The Identification and Measurement of Environmental Variables That Are Related to Educational Achievement," doctoral dissertation, University of Chicago, 1963.

17. Davis, O. L., Jr., and Slobodian, J. J., "Teacher Behavior Toward Boys and Girls During First Grade Instruction," *American Educational Research Journal,* 4 (May 1967), 261–70.

18. Della-Piana, Gabriel, and Martin, Helen, "Reading Achievement and Maternal Behavior," *Reading Teacher,* 20 (1966), 225–30.

19. DiLorenzo, Louis T., Salter, Ruth, and Hayden, Robert, "Empirical Bases for a Prekindergarten Curriculum for Disadvantaged Children," paper presented at the Educational Research Association of New York State, 1968.

20. Evans, J. W., "The Effect of Pupil Mobility upon Academic Achievement," *National Elementary Principal,* 45 (1966), 18–22.

21. Filmer, H. T., and Kahn, Helen S., "Race, Socio-economic Level, Housing and Reading Readiness," *Reading Teacher,* 21 (1967), 153–57.

22. Frazier, Alexander, "A Research Proposal to Develop the Language Skills of Children with Poor Backgrounds," pp. 69–79 in *Improving English Skills of Culturally Different Youth in Large Cities, Bulletin 1964, No. 5.* Washington D.C.: Office of Education, 1964.

23. Fry, Maurine A., and Johnson, Carole S., *Oral Language Production and Reading Achievement among Select Second Grade Indian Children.* Tempe: Arizona State University, Educational Psychology Department.

24. Gaines, Frances P., "Interrelations of Speech and Reading Disabilities," *Elementary School Journal,* 41 (April 1941), 605–13.

25. Glick, Oren, "Some Social-Emotional Consequences of Early Inadequate Acquisition of Reading Skills," *Journal of Educational Research,* 65 (June 1972), 253–57.

26. Good, Thomas L., "Which Pupils Do Teachers Call On?" *Elementary School Journal,* 70 (October 1970), 190–98.

27. Gordon, Edmund W., "Introduction—Education for Socially Disadvantaged Children," *Review of Educational Research,* 40 (February 1970), 1–12.

28. Gordon, George, and Hyman, Irwin, "The Measurement of Perceptual-Motor Abilities of Head Start Children," *Psychology in the Schools,* 8 (1971), 41–48.

29. Gottlieb, David, "Goal Aspirations and Goal Fulfillments: Differences between Deprived and Affluent American Adolescents," *American Journal of Orthopsychiatry,* 34 (October 1964), 934–41.

30. Gredler, Gilbert R., "Performance on a Perceptual Test with Children from a Culturally Disadvantaged Background," in *Perception and Reading,* Helen K. Smith, editor, Proceedings International Reading Association, 12, No. 4, (1968), 86–91.
31. Grunebaum, M. G., et al., "Fathers of Sons with Primary Neurotic Inhibitions," *American Journal of Orthopsychiatry,* 32 (April 1962), 462–72.
32. Gunderson, Doris V., compiler, *Language and Reading: An Interdisciplinary Approach.* Washington D.C.: Center for Applied Linguistics, 1970.
33. Gurman, Alan S., "The Role of the Family in Underachievement," *Journal of School Psychology,* 8 (Fall 1970), 48–53.
34. Hansen, Harlan S., "The Impact of the Home Literary Environment on Reading Attitude," *Elementary English,* 46 (January 1969), 17–24.
35. Hardy, Martha Crumpton, "Parent Resistance to Need for Remedial and Preventive Services," *Journal of Pediatrics,* 48 (January 1956), 104–14.
36. Harmer, William R., "To What Extent Should Parents Be Involved in Language Programs for Linguistically Different Learners?" *Elementary English,* 47 (November 1970), 940–43.
37. Henderson, Edmund H., and Long, Barbara H., "Predictors of Success in Beginning Reading among Negroes and Whites," pp. 34–42 in *Reading Goals for the Disadvantaged,* J. Allen Figurel, editor. Newark, Del.: International Reading Association, 1970.
38. Hirsch, Jay G., and Costello, Joan, "School Achievers and Underachievers in an Urban Ghetto," *Elementary School Journal,* 71 (November 1970), 78–85.
39. Hodges, Allen, and Balow, Bruce, "Learning Disability in Relation to Family Constellation," *Journal of Educational Research,* 55 (September 1961), 412.
40. Johansson, Bror A., *Criteria of School Readiness.* Stockholm: Almqvist and Wiksell, 1965.
41. Jośe, Jean, and Cody, John J., "Teacher-Pupil interaction as It Relates to Attempted Changes in Teacher Expectancy of Academic Ability and Achievement," *American Educational Research Journal,* 8 (January 1971), 39–50.
42. Justman, J., "Academic Aptitude and Reading Test Scores of Disadvantaged Children Showing Varying Degrees of Mobility," *Journal of Educational Measurement,* 2 (1965), 151–55.
43. Kelly, F. J., North, J., and Zingle, H., "The Relationship of Broken Homes to Subsequent School Behaviors," *Alberta Journal of Educational Research,* 11, (1965), 215–18.
44. Ketcham, C. A., "Factors in the Home Background and Reader Self-Concept Which Related to Reading Achievement," in *Proceedings College Reading Association,* 7 (1966), 66–68.
45. Kvaraceus, William C., et al., *Negro Self-Concept: Implications for School and Citizenship.* New York: McGraw-Hill, 1965.
46. Lewis, F. D., Bell, D. B., and Anderson, R. F., "Reading Retardation: A Bi-Racial Comparison," *Journal of Reading,* 13 (1970), 433–36, 474–78.
47. Lovell, K., Shapton, D., and Warren, N. S., "A Study of Some Cognitive and Other Disabilities in Backward Readers of Average Intelligence as Assessed by a Non-Verbal Test," *British Journal of Educational Psychology,* 34 (1964), 58–64.
48. MacDonald, Dorothy P., "An Investigation of the Attitudes of Parents of Unsuccessful and Successful Readers," *Journal of Educational Research,* 56 (April 1963), 437–38.

49. Mason, Anne W., "Follow-up of Educational Attainments in a Group of Children with Retarded Speech Development and in a Control Group," in *Reading: Influences on Progress,* M. M. Clark and S. M. Maxwell, editors, Proceedings of the Annual Study Congress of the United Kingdom, 5 (1967), 37–44.

50. Mazurkiewicz, Albert J., "Socio-Cultural Influences and Reading," *Journal of Developmental Reading,* 3 (Summer 1960), 254–63.

51. McGinnis, Dorothy J., "A Comparative Study of the Attitude of Parents of Superior and Inferior Readers Toward Certain Child-Rearing Patterns," pp. 99–105 in *Philosophical and Sociological Bases of Reading,* Fourteenth Yearbook National Reading Conference, 1965.

52. Miller, Wilma H., "Home Prereading Experiences and First Grade Reading Achievement," *Reading Teacher,* 22 (April 1969), 641–45.

53. Miller, Wilma H., "When Mothers Teach Their Children," *Elementary School Journal,* 70 (October 1969), 38–42.

54. Monroe, Marion, and Rogers, Bernice, *Foundations for Reading.* Chicago: Scott, Foresman, 1964.

55. Morris, Joyce M., *Standards and Progress in Reading.* Slough, Bucks: National Foundation for Educational Research in England and Wales, 1966.

56. Morris, J. L., Pestaner, Mariana, and Nelson, A., "Mobility and Achievement," *Journal of Experimental Education,* 35 (1967), 74–80.

57. Mutimer, Dorothy, Loughlin, L., and Powell, M., "Some Differences in the Family Relationships of Achieving and Underachieving Readers," *Journal of Genetic Psychology,* 109 (1966), 67–74.

58. Oberlander, M., and Jenkin, N., "Birth Order and Academic Achievement," *Journal of Individual Psychology,* 1 (1967), 103–10.

59. Olim, Ellis G., Hess, Robert D., and Shipman, Virginia C., "Relationship Between Mothers' Language Styles and Cognitive Styles of Urban Pre-School Children," *Urban Child Study Center,* Chicago, 1965.

60. Otto, Wayne, "Family Position and Success in Reading," *Reading Teacher,* 19 (November 1965), 119–23.

61. Palardy, J. Michael, "What Teachers Believe—What Children Achieve," *Elementary School Journal,* 69 (April 1969), 370–74.

62. Palardy, J. Michael, "For Johnny's Reading Sake," *Reading Teacher,* 22 (May 1969), 720–23.

63. Peil, Margaret, "Library Use by Low-Income Chicago Families," *Library Quarterly,* 33 (October 1963), 329–33.

64. Perkins, H. V., "Classroom Behavior and Underachievement," *American Educational Research Journal,* 2 (January 1965), 1–12.

65. Perrodin, A. F., and Snipes, W. T., "The Relationship of Mobility to Achievement in Reading, Arithmetic and Language in Selected Georgia Elementary Schools," *Journal of Educational Research,* 59 (1966), 315–19.

66. Philion, William L. E., and Galloway, Charles G., "Indian Children and the Reading Program," *Journal of Reading,* 12 (April 1969), 553–60.

67. Powers, Jerry M., et al., "A Research Note on the Self-Perception of Youth," *American Educational Research Journal,* 4 (November 1971), 665–70.

68. Preston, M. I., "The Reaction of Parents to Reading Failure," *Child Development,* 10 (September 1939), 173–79.

69. Rist, R., "Student Social Class and Teacher Expectations, The Self-Fulfilling Prophecy in Ghetto Education," *Harvard Educational Review,* 40 (1970), 411–51.
70. Rutter, M., Yule, W., Trizard, J., and Graham, P., "Severe Reading Retardation: Its Relationship to Maladjustment, Epilepsy, and Neurological Disorder," in *What Is Special Education?* Proceedings of the First International Congress of the Association for Special Education, 1 (1966), 25–28.
71. Sakamoto, T., and Takagi, K., "A Study of Disabled Readers," *Science of Reading,* 11 (1968), 1–15.
72. Seigler, Hazel G., and Gynther, Malcolm D., "Reading Ability of Children and Family Harmony," *Journal of Developmental Reading,* 4 (Autumn 1960), 17–24.
73. Semler, Ira J., and Iscoe, I., "Comparative Developmental Study of the Learning Abilities of Negro and White Children under Four Conditions," *Journal of Educational Psychology,* 54 (1963), 38–44.
74. Sheldon, William D., and Carrillo, Lawrence, "Relations of Parents, Home and Certain Developmental Characteristics to Children's Reading," *Elementary School Journal,* 52 (January 1952), 262–70.
75. Sheldon, William D., and Cutts, Warren G., "Relations of Parents, Home and Certain Developmental Characteristics to Children's Reading," *Elementary School Journal,* 53 (May 1953), 517–21.
76. Slobodian, June, and Campbell, Paul, "Do Children's Perceptions Influence Beginning Reading Achievement?" *Elementary School Journal,* 67 (May 1967), 423–27.
77. Snipes, Walter T., "The Effect of Moving on Reading Achievement," *Reading Teacher,* 20 (December 1966), 242–46.
78. Spache, George D., *Good Reading for the Disadvantaged Reader.* Champaign, Ill.: Garrard Publishing, 1975.
79. Stein, Zena, and Susser, Mervyn, "Mutability of Intelligence and Epidemiology of Mild Mental Retardation," *Review of Educational Research,* 40 (February 1970), 29–68.
80. Thomas, Dominic, "Our Disadvantaged Older Children," in *Vistas in Reading,* J. Allen Figurel, editor, Proceedings International Reading Association, 11, No. 1 (1966), 349–52.
81. Warrington, Elizabeth K., "The Incidence of Verbal Disability Associated with Retardation in Reading," *Neuropsychologia,* 5 (1967), 175–79.
82. Weintraub, Samuel, "Research-Teacher Expectation and Reading Performance," *Reading Teacher,* 22 (March 1969), 555–59.
83. Werner, E. E., Simonian K., and Smith, R. D., "Reading Achievement, Language Functioning and Perceptual-Motor Development of 10 and 11 Year-Olds," *Perceptual and Motor Skills,* 25 (1967), 409–20.
84. Wickstrom, R. A., "Pupil Mobility and School Achievement," *Alberta Journal of Educational Research,* 13 (1967), 311–18.
85. Wyatt, Gertrud, *Language Learning and Communication Disorders in Children.* New York: Free Press, 1969.
86. Young, Whitney M., Jr., Remarks delivered to the American Sociological Association, Boston, August 27, 1968.
87. Zintz, Miles V., "Cultural Aspects of Bilingualism," in *Vistas in Reading,* J. Allen Figurel, editor, Proceedings International Reading Association, 11, No. 1 (1966), 353–61.

It is apparent that most reading treatment centers do not emphasize the significance of personality problems of poor readers. And yet it is equally obvious that a large proportion of such failing pupils do have crippling deviations from normal adjustments. In this chapter we attempt to help reading teachers reconcile their remedial practices to the existence of these emotional maladjustments. First, we review the kinds of maladjusted behaviors that are common among poor readers, in the hope that these facts will foster recognition of the deviations. Second, we contrast the emotional problems or behavior of good and poor readers, again to alert teachers to some of the maladjustments associated with reading failure. And, third, we look at those longitudinal studies that try to identify deviations in personality adjustment tending to precede or predict reading failures. The sum of the evidence about the personality problems of poor readers yields a number of symptoms that remedial therapists cannot fail to note or to treat if they wish to be successful.

9 Personality and Self-Concept Factors

The relatively recent and rapid development of research in the area of self-concept has tended to set it apart from the parent field of personality study. But, whether it is a separate field or not, the facts about pupil self-concept must be familiar to reading teachers. To discharge their remedial responsibilities adequately—and particularly if they hope to produce some permanent gains for their pupils—reading teachers must understand how self-concept develops, and what internal and environmental factors mould it, such as teacher-pupil interaction.

In reviewing these areas of diagnosis, try to answer these questions.

1. What types of emotional problems or maladjusted behaviors seem to be common among poor readers?

2. What are some of the obvious steps that teachers should take to lessen the effects of these personality problems upon their relationships with pupils?

3. How would you answer these same questions with respect to the construct of the self-concept?

ALMOST EVERYONE WHO HAS worked with or written about retard- ed readers has reacted to the personality problems that complicate treatment of the disability. Among the questions that these ele- ments of the reading case raise are whether reading retardation is caused by personal and social maladjustments; whether the reverse is true; or whether reading failure and maladjustment develop simultaneously and exacerbate each other. Some say that it does not really matter what interpretation is made, for the academic problem is paramount and the personality problems will diminish or disappear if the remedial reading treatment is successful. Judging by what one sees in reading clinics and special schools for the dyslexic, this viewpoint is rather widely accepted. Many treatment centers simply stress remedial correction of real or suspected skill or sensory deficits; and, if reading test scores rise, they are satisfied that they have followed the most practical treatment program. Those who examine the eventual reading success or school adjustment of pupils treated in this fashion, as given in the follow-up studies published by the centers, have some doubts about the direct, pragmatic approach. Our review of follow-up studies of ordinary remedial reading seems to indicate that the success of this type of treatment is often superficial and temporary. In many instances, when personality ele- ments are more or less ignored, the reading difficulties of treated pupils tend to reappear in the years following remedial reading treatment.

Because of these observations, some experts feel that poor readers' personality problems are more than just a concomitant of the disability. To these therapists, the reading disability is but another symptom of the pupil's basic maladjustment to life. Therefore, remedial reading is treatment for an isolated symptom and cannot produce a solution of the fundamental problem. Treatment should be intended to modify the pupil's total adjustment; or, if remedial reading procedures do seem a suitable medium for approaching the pupil, they should be employed only in a fashion that helps to solve the greater problem. Other types of therapy for the personality problems of the pupil should accompany any remedial reading efforts and form the major thrust of the entire treatment program, according to this viewpoint.

In the absence of definitive proof of the validity of these contrasting concepts of the proper treatment of emotionally disturbed retarded readers, it does appear desirable to study the personality traits of poor readers. Even when the reading teacher believes only in the efficacy of the common remedial approaches, if it can be shown that certain personality traits characterize poor readers, or differentiate poor from good readers, or are significant prognostic signs of future reading difficulties, such information is relevant to the teacher-pupil relationship.   For this reason, it seems desirable to review the literature bearing on these interactions of personality and reading.

PERSONALITY TRAITS ATTRIBUTED TO POOR READERS

Early writers in the field of reading disability appear to have been quite certain that poor readers frequently manifested such characteristics as these:

> dislike of reading, instability, poor attention, lack of motivation; timidity or aggressiveness; nervousness, self-consciousness; indifference, immaturity, withdrawal, compensatory mechanisms, defeatism, hypertension; apathy, feelings of inferiority, and mild paranoid reactions.

These are some of the traits mentioned by early leaders in the field of reading disability as Emmett A. Betts, Arthur I. Gates, Marion Monroe, Samuel T. Orton, and others.

As summarized in the review by Helen M. Robinson (42), disabled readers were characterized by restlessness, loneliness, introversive or withdrawal tendencies, inadequate school relations, and conscious self-control bordering on rigidity.   Recent writers speak of neurotic factors such as conflicts becoming internalized, and, at least in part, outside conscious awareness; severe inhibition of aggression and curiosity because of unconscious fear of the consequences; using not learning as a weapon to express resentment against parents or siblings; seeking failure (unconsciously) because success is equated with attainment of a forbidden goal; not allowing oneself to be competitive in school and thus insuring failure (1).

Most of these descriptive statements represent the subjective impressions of reading teachers, psychologists, and reading clinicians.   These observations, in many cases, have not been confirmed by testing the personalities of poor readers.   Thus there is no real evidence of their accuracy in reflecting the personality component of a reading disability other than that inherent in the experience of the observers.   Many studies, however, have tried to identify objectively the personality symptoms of poor readers.

Bell, Lewis, and Anderson (4) factor-analyzed forty-three test variables in the attempt to find those related to reading retardation.   One such factor was aggressive, negative, or passive attitudes.   In a similar factorial analysis study, Wilderson (62) studied children referred to a psychiatric clinic for school or community maladjustment or deficient academic performance.   He found seven psychiatric-reading factors that seemed to distinguish these fifty pupils, ages nine to fourteen.

1. Word and Meaning Deficiency—no psychiatric symptoms.
2. Character Disorder——WISC V. versus P., poor verbal memory, need for verbal relearning, tendency to lose place while reading.
3. Neurosis—motor symptoms, mannerisms, bizarre movements, obsessive symptoms, and poor word analysis.
4. Borderline Psychosis—hallucinations, delusions, disorganization, paranoid symptoms, memory disturbance.
5. Somatic Complaints—delayed onset of speech, disorder of articulation plus family history of psychological illness, special childhood and sleeping problems, visual vertical imbalance, lower right-eye acuity.
6. Reality Orientation—loose association, enuresis, reduced attention span, disturbance of food intake.
7. Passive-Dependence—separation anxiety, neurological symptoms, passivity, special childhood sleeping problems.

There are problems in interpreting this type of study, aside from the psychiatric terminology, for some traits were derived from test results and others from observation by those trained in a particular way of investigating and describing personality. Factor analysis simply indicates the relationships among groups of observations and tests and cannot yield information about symptoms not tested or observed. In other words, it reveals only the common groupings among all the facts analyzed. Thus the results represent, in a sense, the selection of tests and observations that the experimenter thinks are likely to be important, not the entire picture of the personality formation of retarded readers.

The influence of the tests or observations selected to study the personalities of poor readers is also shown in several of the studies of this type done by the present author. Using the Rosenzweig Picture Frustration Study, a cartoonlike projective test for reflecting the child's handling of situations depicting conflict between children or a child and an adult figure, Spache (50, 51, 52, 53) reports these findings:

1. As a group, retarded readers show significantly more hostility and overt aggressiveness toward others, and less ability to acknowledge or acept blame.
2. Their responses to the situation of adult-child conflict were characterized by resistance to adult suggestion, and lack of interest or passiveness toward solutions of conflict.
3. In contrast, in dealing with other children, retarded readers show less tolerance, fewer efforts to find solutions for conflict, and greater defensiveness than do normals.

4. A number of subpatterns or types manifest themselves in the responses of the poor readers:

   a. Hostile type—with strong feelings of frustration and hostility expressed against adults and other children. These children show lack of self-insight and self-blame and are unable to meet frustrating situations with constructive thinking (42 percent).

   b. Adjustive type—a more or less passive-acceptant orientation to others, with avoidance of overt hostility or aggressiveness and withdrawal or acceptance of the domination of others, both peers and authority figures (10 percent).

   c. Defensive type—resentful of others, particularly adults, suspicious, sensitive to criticism, unable to accept or acknowledge blame, and sometimes showing temper manifestations. These feelings are less strong against other children than toward adults (28 percent).

   d. Solution-seeking type—self-motivating, practical, ambitious, avoiding conflict or obvious aggression but rather making excessive attempts to find solutions to conflict. Readily acceptant of suggestions, even when these are too simplistic and obvious (18 percent).

   e. Autistic or withdrawn type—argumentative when pressed, unstable in interests, prone to daydreaming and fantasy, blocked in expressing feelings toward others or in finding constructive solutions to problems, detailistic in thinking, avoiding confrontation with others by projecting their frustration on the general environment in irritability or disorganization (10 percent).

   f. Another 10 percent of children show responses that do not form any consistent pattern; and the remainder, about 30 percent, are apparently normally adjusted, that is, relatively aggressive, cocky, and self-confident, particularly in dealing with other children, with moderate ability to accept blame or suggestion from adults but less of these traits when dealing with other children.

Other psychometric studies, with similarly limited significance, include that by Callaway, Jerrolds, and Tisdale (7), who, in using the California Test of Personality, found relationships with reading of the subscores in Family Relations, Community Relations, and School Relations: and that by Rankin (40), who discovered that reliability and validity indices of a reading test were higher for introverts than for extraverts. Rugel (43) used galvanic skin response as a measure of "anxiety" in the reading act and, contrary to expectations, did not find increases in this symptom as oral reading errors increased with the difficulties of the materials read. Unfortunately, this study neither proves nor disproves that reading can be an anxiety-producing experience for some pupils, since other studies indicate that the increase in oral reading errors, as used in the Informal Reading Inventory, is neither a valid measure of total reading ability nor a threatening situation for many children. The galvanic skin response does reflect the rise and fall of emotional feelings by measuring the electrical resistance of the skin.   Some time ago, Homer L. J. Carter (8) suggested this technique to distinguish emotionally disturbed readers from others.   He recommended the logical differentiation in treatments addressed to the correction of the emotionality or reading skills.   But the validity of this diagnostic step—particularly among the college freshmen whom Carter tested and for whom, through lack of practice, oral reading may well have been an anxiety-producing state—is still questionable.   We cannot assume that, simply because oral reading causes a rise in the feeling tone of the pupil, his primary problem lies in the area of personality adjustment.   The decision is much more complex, as we shall see.

These generalizations about the personality attributes of poor readers whether derived from testing or observation are not very significant in the absence of comparative data for successful readers.   As probably most teachers have observed, some pupils who exhibit some of these personality deviations learn to read well in comparison with almost any criterion of their potential.   Conversely, some pupils who are originally apparently admirably well-adjusted to life fail miserably in reading.   As noted in the research report by Spache cited above, about 30 percent of the severely retarded readers in his clinic sample seemed normally adapted.   Perhaps the comparison of the personalities of good and poor readers may clarify this question.

EMOTIONAL PROBLEMS—GOOD VERSUS POOR READERS

As we have implied, if it were possible to establish that, in general, poor readers show certain emotional and behavioral symptoms distinguishing them from good readers, it would be a very significant contribution to the treatment of reading disability.   Then teachers could be especially trained in ameliorating these symptoms with obviously dramatic results in correcting this widespread educational problem.   In Table 9–1 we examine comparative studies of good and poor readers to discover whether this solution has been found.

It is difficult to relate these diverse findings because of their bases in varying theories of personality and its measurement.   We receive the impression that, in general, poor readers show many more symptoms of maladjustment such as aggressiveness (particularly in boys), anxiety, negativeness, and withdrawal, similar to the results cited above by Spache in his typing of poor readers.   Negative teacher reactions to these problem children appear as part of the picture, as in the studies of Hake and Wolf.   The personality symptoms among poor readers are so varied and yet so manifestly indicative of poor personal and social adjustment that they create the implication that perhaps reading failure is just one more symptom of these pupils' failure to deal

TABLE 9–1. COMPARATIVE STUDIES IN PERSONALITY TRAITS—GOOD VERSUS POOR READERS

AUTHOR GRADE-NUMBER	GOOD VERSUS POOR READERS
Barsky (3): 42 versus 42 in V–VI	Poor males—significantly more antisocial aggressiveness in teacher and self-ratings; higher in self-assertion and leadership in teacher ratings. Poor females—higher in pro-social aggression (that is, conformity) than poor males.
Douglas, Ross, and Cooper (12): 1,687 males 1,566 females ages 6, 11, and 15	No significant differences in emotional disturbances.
Dudek and Lester (13): 80, ages 13–17	Poor readers evidenced anxiety about handling their aggressive impulses; tended to retreat into passivity, compliance and depression, in their Rorschach responses
Feshbach, Adelman, and Burke (14): 60 junior high pupils	Older, culturally disadvantaged boys manifested considerable anxiety. Their greatest problem was deviant manners, that is, profanity, physical aggression, dress, and avoidance of relationship with teachers
Hake (19): 86 in VI	Poor readers gave more negative responses to his test of pictures of ambiguous reading situations and were ranked lower in adjustment by teachers on author's rating scale. Good females tended to score more negatively on his test. No real differences between boys and girls, however.
Joseph and McDonald (25): college freshmen	On the Edwards Personal Preference Schedule, poor readers evidenced greater aggression, needs for order, and abasement. Good readers showed needs to achieve and for change and affiliation.
Knoblock (28): 33 versus 29 in II	In Rorschach responses, quality of sentence structure, flexibility, and perceptual flexibility were better for good readers. No difference in concrete or abstract approaches to the task.
Malmquist (33): 399 in I	Good readers superior in self-confidence, ability to make social contacts, persistence, concentration; low in dominance—high in submissiveness, and in stability versus nervousness. These factors significant in 23 percent of the cases of reading disability.
Noland and Schuldt (37): 20 in IV	Using device testing speed of response to flashing light, found poor readers worse in attention (accuracy) but not speed after continued trials.
Raygor and Wark (41): 228 poor versus 1,116 normals in XIII	Students who entered study skills center voluntarily were less verbal and less socially skilled, but the females were better adjusted socially.

TABLE 9–1. (Continued)

AUTHOR GRADE-NUMBER	GOOD VERSUS POOR READERS
Stavrianos and Landsman (56): 151 good males versus 160 poor males	In Rorschach responses, deficient readers gave fewer emotionally balanced and mature patterns of responses. Those with perceptual-motor dysfunctions showed no significant differences from others.
Tillman et al. (59): college students	Those high on *Intuitive*-Sensing scale tended to have higher reading scores in rate, comprehension, and vocabulary. No personality type associated with volunteering for help in college clinic or number of visits to clinic. Among special group admitted to college with minimal qualifications, *Feeling* versus thinking (in Judgment scale) associated with higher reading scores and higher grade point average. Used Briggs Type Indicator Indices scales.
Wolf (63): 80 personality disorders versus 80 normal siblings	Report card grades in "Effort" in grades II to IV (but not in kindergarten, and not in scholastic grades at any of these levels) were higher than normals.
Zimmerman and Allebrand (64)	Good readers have feelings of personal worth, belongingness, personal freedom, and self-reliance; poor, are discouraged and helpless in efforts to succeed.

adequately with school and life demands. There is certainly sufficient evidence here (and in many other studies that might have been cited) that the personality maladjustments of poor readers must be considered and treated, if at all possible, in remediation.

Another viewpoint of the role of personality problems in reading disability may be gained from those studies that have used their tests and observations to predict future difficulties. This type of study avoids the fallacious tendency to see cause-effect relationships in certain personality traits found in poor readers after their difficulties have become well established. Most of the research studies cited thus far have made this assumption that the unfavorable traits currently present among poor readers probably contributed to the genesis of disability. Few have recognized the equally plausible deduction that the symptoms of maladjustment might have appeared because of the reading failure. Longitudinal studies in which personality evaluation is proven significant in predicting future reading difficulties are probably the most significant assessments of the relationships. Not all the studies to be cited are truly longitudinal, but all have an element of prediction in their results.

PREDICTING READING FAILURE THROUGH PERSONALITY EVALUATION

Beginning at kindergarten-primary levels, we shall look for the implications of predictive studies. Ruth H. Solomon's (48) research indicated that, as we have seen in several studies cited above, the kindergarten child's Rorschach responses revealed certain personality traits that, in this case, were predictive of the reading success in primary grades. Kagan (26) reports that the children characterized as impulsive in the first grade made the most reading errors in a test at the end of the second grade. Ames and Walker (2) found that the variables of clarity, detailing, and accuracy of perception in the Rorschach responses of kindergarten children were significantly related to reading success in the fifth grade. The Rorschach index correlated .53 with reading; intelligence and reading, .57; and the multiple correlation of these two variables with reading was .73. The extent to which this study can be generalized is quite limited by the fact that the group of fifty-four studied was above average in intelligence and quite accelerated in reading by the fifth grade.

Neville, Pfost, and Dobbs (36) found that for pupils in a summer remedial program an initial high score on the Test Anxiety Scale was inversely related to improvement in reading comprehension, but irrelevant to vocabulary gains. Richard H. Bloomer (6) attempted to identify the pattern of reading skills achieved by pupils who were rejected by their classmates. He found that these pupils tested poorly in measures involving analysis and synthesis, as phonetically consistent words and phrases, letter cloze, and word cloze tests. In measures involving memory, as letter identification, letters in words, and nonphonetic words and phrases, the rejected pupils did as well as their peers. Chansky and Bregman (9) report that the Psychasthenia Score on the MMPI (obsessions, compulsions, phobias) was the best predictor of reading improvement among college students. This measure was a better predictor than were the college entrance intelligence test (ACE) and the Brown-Holtzman Survey of Study Habits.

These six studies in toto do not really clarify the problem of identifying the personality symptoms that will successfully predict future reading success. Three of them, both of those using the Rorschach and that with the MMPI (Minnesota Multiphasic Inventory), seem to indicate the obvious fact that the more signs of normality shown by the student the more likely he is to succeed or improve in reading. The symptoms identified in the three other studies—anxiety, impulsiveness, and poor social acceptance—offer a very limited picture of the personalities of pupils who fail in reading. In fact, the sum total of the clues that we can find in all of the thirty-two studies cited thus far is meager. We see that retarded readers may be distinguished by the symptoms of aggressiveness (in boys), negativeness, withdrawal patterns, impulsiveness, anxiety, and poor social acceptance. But we still do not know whether these personality deviations cause, or are caused by, reading disability, although the evidence seems to be in favor of the latter conclusion. Perhaps in the later discussion of the relationships between personality and various remedial approaches, we may find stronger clues to guide the treatment of reading disability.

SELF-CONCEPT AND READING

Judging by the volume of literature on the subject, and the many new tests and research reports, one might conclude that the self-concept is independent of the study of personality. There is little attempt on the part of those interested in this facet of human behavior to relate their inquiries to the mass of materials available on attitudes, feelings, emotions, and mental health. To us, investigation of the self-concept is just another way of exploring for explanations of human behavior; it is significant only in the context of basic personality types and personality mechanisms.

What Is Self-Concept?

A variety of definitions of the self-concept is offered, such as these:

> People discover who they are and what they are from the ways in which they have been treated by those who surround them in the process of growing up (Coombs, 10).

> Self-concept is: "the individual's understanding of the expectations of society and his peers; and the kind of behavior which the individual selects as a style of life" (Berg, 5).

> As an example of self-concept: "Teachers tend to see themselves as relatively well-educated, well-organized, and well-informed. Some observers note that teachers are quick to share their informational background, when the opportunity presents itself, even in casual conversation. . . . At the same time the average teacher is socially conscious and concerned about the people around her. She shows this concern frequently by active participation in school and community affairs mainly of nonpolitical nature. She contributes time and money to fund collections, school bond drives, community betterment projects, and the like. She probably secures more collegiate post-graduate training in her professional field and

spends more time at workshops, seminars, and demonstrations of new materials and techniques, as well as committee and staff meetings, than any other type of professional worker. The average teacher, it is said, also shows her social motif by contributing to indigent relations to a unique degree" (Spache, 49, 54).

Some writers distinguish between specific and global self-concepts or, in other words, between the way the individual conceives of himself generally as a member of society versus, for example, how he sees himself as a reader (58) or an athlete, a conversationalist, a student, and so on.

Another aspect of the self-concept is the individual's aspirations, as a student for achievement (55) or a worker for productivity (45). By some, this aspect of the self-concept is termed the "self-ideal," a comparison between the self as the individual sees it and how he wishes he could be. Another facet of the self-concept is the comparison that the individual makes of himself with others, the self-other perception.

In a very early presentation of his theory of self-consistency, Lecky (31) proposed that the ego-ideal or self-concept gradually crystallizes as we mature and tends to direct all our behavior. His point was that, in almost every way we behave, we try to be consistent with the self-image that we have.

As we review these explanations of the self-concept, it becomes apparent that, like personality, the self-image has many facets. We have a global self-concept as a kind of person, specific self-concepts as we function in social, physical, and mental activities (as well as a self-ideal or kind of person that we aspire to be), and a self-other perception or comparison of our traits and habits with those of others. It is also apparent that a great many life experiences contribute to moulding the self-concept as we mature from childhood to adulthood. This development is integrated with basic personality traits that appear early in childhood and also mature during the same period. In our opinion, there is a gradual amalgamation of the personality traits that may be genetically and physiologically based with the impact and shaping of our self-concepts by the relationships with the environment and other persons. Perhaps some idea of this development into a completely individualized person with specific views of himself and others may be revealed by reviewing some of the environmental factors that affect it.

What Affects Self-Concept?

Some of those defining self-concept have implied that it is largely formed by the actions of others toward oneself. These actions tell the person what he is like and thus provide the bases for his self-evaluations. But the impact of the actions of others is not the sole agent in forming the self-concept, as Coombs implies above, for the implications in these actions may be accepted or rejected. Mechanisms such as compensation, face-saving efforts, and disguised behavior may appear in an effort to counteract the messages conveyed by the actions of others. Negativism, temper tantrums, counteraggression, or passivity bordering on withdrawal may be employed by the individual in defending himself (and his self-concept) against these forces. Thus although, in a sense, our self-concept is constantly being modified by others in our immediate environment, these implications may be incorporated into the self-concept both negatively and positively, depending upon the strength of our self-concepts. We shall point out some of these compensatory and negative responses to the actions of others as we review the correlates of the self-concept, particularly as they affect reading success.

The Family Ketcham (27) and others have shown that such factors as the mother's use of the library, the number of magazines and newspapers in the home, and the father's occupational level—as well as many other facts reflecting the socioeconomic status of the home—enter into the child's concept of himself as a reader and his reading progress. The pupil's aspirations, reaction to grades, and the satisfaction of both parents and pupil with his grades are also positively related. Such attitudes as "college is for those who can afford it," "girls don't need college," "reading is feminine," and "only eggheads like to read," are, of course, negatively related to reading success, as is the amount of TV viewing of parents, which implies their lack of need for reading. Here, in the family setting, we see physical and attitudinal factors that help shape the child's attitudes toward reading, his recognition of a need for reading, and thus his self-concept as a reader.

Sexual Identity The development of self-concept involves a search for sexual identity, which gives rise to both positive and negative reactions to the kinds of behavior that are thought consistent with the ideal sex (17). We see that as early as primary grades boys and girls differentiate themselves in the subjects they tell about in class and in the language experience stories they compose. Girls want to talk about birthday parties, events at home, shopping, and the like, while boys offer stories of real or imaginary adventure, outdoor activities, and things that their father does with them. Striving for sexual identity is already beginning to manifest itself. One observer has noted the infrequency with which boys speak of their fathers' reading and the subsequent tendency to reject reading as a feminine activity. In striving to reach the male ideal, as they see it, boys are less conforming, more aggressive, and more difficult for teachers to mould to the proper attitudes and behavior in school. Poor male readers see themselves correctly as more antisocially aggressive than do good readers; more assertive, and more often as leaders than followers—all characteristics that seem consistent to them as part of the male role they want to play. And, as most studies show, girls grow toward prosocial aggression, conforming to school demands even when they do not succeed in reading, thus in turn playing the role that both they and society seem to think is appropriate (3).

White achieving girls are significantly further detached from their fathers than boys are; black achieving girls are more attached to their friends than to their mothers. White achieving boys show significantly higher self-esteem than white achieving girls. Among blacks, the father's presence in the home is a very significant predictor of success in beginning reading for boys, and relatively insignificant for black girls, when compared with measures of I.Q., readiness test, age, and teachers' ratings. Here again we see the attempt to relate to the adult or peer figure of the same sex for children of both races. When they do succeed in school, white boys are more significantly strengthened in their self-concept than are white achieving girls, who may simply see such success as a minor part of their conforming to the female pattern of behavior expected of them (22), although all the evidence of these trends is not in total agreement (15).

Peer Relationships

When children are asked to indicate which of their classmates they would like to work or sit with or otherwise relate to, poor readers tend to be isolated in the diagrammatic sociogram used to depict these interpupil choices (18). In self-ratings on a social distance scale, poor readers recognize and acknowledge their lack of acceptance by their peers (57). It is not quite clear whether these pupils withdraw from social contacts because they are threatened by the reading failure or the competition, or whether they recognize and accept isolation because of inability to identify with the more successful pupils. In any event, peer status is more closely related to reading achievement than is the socioeconomic status of the student body. Rejection by peers strengthens the low self-concept and withdrawal that many poor readers exhibit (38).

Race

Many contrasts of the development of self-concept and the factors influencing this development have recently been made (29, 35). In the primary grades, in racial groups black children seem to show lower self-esteem; and the boys receive lower teacher ratings (21). Some sociologists attribute this low self-concept to the black's lack of historical perspective—he is never really part of the overall culture and has lost his own African culture. They feel the implied inferiority of being black even as small children, these writers say (35), and also feel their family background as unworthy. Undoubtedly these feelings have been fostered in the past by the stereotyping of blacks in our literature. Cox (11) demonstrates this by an analysis of magazine advertisements of 1949–50 and 1967–68. Advertisements in widely sold magazines offered ads containing blacks in less than 1 percent in the earlier issues and have increased this representation to only slightly more than 2 percent. Blacks depicted as workers rating higher than skilled labor has grown from 6 percent to 71 percent in the advertisements; conversely, blacks as maids and cooks has dropped in this period from 75 percent to 8 percent. Blacks in school readers have made their appearance only in the past few years in the attempts to provide multiethnic books; and American Indians or other minority groups are still largely conspicuous by their omission even in American history books. The lack of a positive representation of blacks and other minority groups in our reading and instructional materials has undoubtedly promoted lower self-esteem for members of these groups. Except perhaps in sports and the entertainment field, there have been almost no models of successful adult members of their group for black and other minority children to try to identify with.

Soares and Soares (47) have offered an inventory for sampling pupil self-concept, and with this inventory, Powers et al. (39) claim to find that in older pupils, blacks test higher in self-image than whites do, even when they are attending recently integrated schools and are lower in grade-point average than the whites, and are particularly lower than the Jewish children. They concluded that the self-concept is more likely a product of a person's interactions within his own subgroups than of school or community environment.

Trowbridge (60) also showed that low socioeconomic pupils, both rural and urban blacks and whites, scored higher in self-concept than did middle-class children at all the ages of eight to fourteen.

Barbara Long (32) has strongly criticized these unusual results by citing many contradictory studies. In using such a self-rating scale, she insists, low socioeconomic children tend to extreme self-ratings around the central neutral point where high socioeconomic pupils cluster in their self-ratings. We are inclined to accept her argument in view of the frequent tendency for pupils with low self-concept to be defensive about their traits and abilities. Such pupils could readily have sensed the intent of the self-rating scale (as often happens in responses to such instruments) and responded with the picture of their self-images as they would like them to be, rather than as they actually exist. The great bulk of the evidence regarding the self-concepts of economically deprived minority groups implies that these are relatively low, in our opinion.

Shulman (45) has pointed out some interesting contrasts in blacks and whites in mentally handicapped adolescents who were being given vocational training. He used four measures of self-concept: an inventory, a structured interview, the subject's drawings, and his level of aspiration as expressed in his prediction of output versus his actual production. For blacks, the self-concept variables tended to relate positively with employability, a combined measure of productivity, and ratings in vocational development. But these same self-concept measures related negatively for whites. Blacks tended to give consistently high or low self-reports combined with high aspiration score. (See Barbara Long's comment on this tendency, above.) Employable whites tended to show high self-report in the inventory and interview but low level of aspiration. Shulman concluded that blacks tend to denigrate their own abilities but to relate their ability to their own aspirations; whites tend to bluff or to pretend and to be unrealistic in denying their own competence. These results are not directly relevant to the relationships of the self-concept to reading in these racial groups, but they are significant in deepening our concepts of the racial differences in self-concept.

Teacher-Pupil Interaction   Teacher-pupil relationships are more significant in pupil success in reading than are most other factors, as many recent studies show. The teachers' attitudes interact with the sex and race of pupils in terms of her expectations, her social class as compared to that of the pupils, and her ability to relate warmly and physically with them. Women teachers tend to relate more positively to girl students, perhaps because these tend to conform to the teachers' standards for behavior better than boys do in general. Positive, encouraging comments help these girls grow in self-concept, while the majority of disparaging, negative remarks confirm the unsuccessful boys' lower self-concept. Girls respond with a degree of identification with teachers naturally, while boys seek identifications elsewhere (21). These slower learners are quite aware of their limitations, as manifest in their ability to estimate their own achievement levels more accurately, particularly in reading, than even able students, who tend to underestimate their own accomplishments (55).

The manner in which the teacher operates in reading instruction and the social climate that she thus promotes are influences upon pupil success in reading and the development of their self-concepts. For example, in the San Diego study contrasting the outcomes of the language experience, individualized, and basal systems, those teachers employing the language experience had significantly higher scores in social climate (less authoritarian) than did other teachers (24). Virginia B. Morrison (34) has similarly shown that teacher-pupil interaction, mobility of pupils, more positive verbal, physical, and covert behaviors of the teacher, and less punitive actions result as a teacher moves from use of a single text to multilevel texts to individualized reading. Other positive results of the more flexible program are the development of pupil leadership and initiative, less negative interaction among pupils, and, of course, greater use of a wide variety of activities and materials. Unfortunately, these significant results are often ignored in the stereotyped evaluation of reading programs solely by reading test scores.

Parallel research reports on social climate, self-concept, and reading confirm these trends. Nancy St. John (44), analyzing teacher behavior in interracial classrooms, identified three climates: child-oriented, task-oriented, and fair or impersonal. Black children made greater gains in the child-oriented environment, while whites responded best to a task-oriented climate. Smith (46) showed that children given no reading instruction but who received a good deal of personal interaction gained as much in reading as those who pursued a basal program. When reading was taught according to the pupils' personal needs, the greatest gains in self-concept and oral reading were present.

Teacher-pupil relationships interact with race in many ways. Gottlieb (16) says that black high school students see greater discrepancy than do white students between their goals and those held by the teacher. Low socioeconomic, especially blacks, are the least likely to perceive the teacher as wanting to help them achieve their goals. Heath's observations (20) were that the blacks felt that when teacher style included listening to student responses, knowing her subject well, seeming to enjoy teaching, managing the class well, and speaking clearly, the teacher was better in relating to them. White high school students, in contrast, rated only the first and third of these teacher characteristics as significant to the teacher's ability to relate to them.

The implications of all these studies seem to support a dramatic relationship between self-concept and reading success. The evidence is stronger in this area of personality adjustment than in the earlier studies cited on the interaction of personality symptoms and reading success. The factors of family attitudes and aspirations, striving for sexual identity, peer relationships, race, and, above all, teacher-pupil interaction all impinge upon pupil self-concept and academic success. Not only is there interplay among these aspects, but also the sheer fact of reading success may raise or lower the pupil's self-concept and thus further align or alienate him from his teacher and the school's demands. Although we have not emphasized them here, in many classroom situations, such elements as the teacher's expectations for her pupils, her own self-concept of her proper role in instructing youth, the differences between personal and social standards of the social class to which the teacher belongs or aspires to belong and those of her pupils further complicate the educational process and its outcomes in pupil achievement (14, 30, 54). It is not surprising that Herbert (23) finds a direct relationship between high self-concept and high reading comprehension, or that Wattenberg and Clifford (61) declare that self-concept is more closely related to reading achievement than intelligence is.

LEARNING PROJECT

Choose one of the common symptoms of emotionally disturbed behavior frequently found among poor readers. List and prepare to defend a number of suggestions for the reading teacher who is facing such a problem. Include in your recommendations specific suggestions regarding the following.

1. Scheduling remedial sessions.
2. The length of such sessions.
3. The difficulty of the tasks.
4. The degree of teacher-pupil planning.
5. Records of pupil progress.
6. The selection of the pupils for small-group work.
7. The use of rewards both verbal and material.
8. The possibilities of behavior modification techniques.
9. The nature of the teacher-pupil relationship.

REFERENCES

1. Abrams, Jules C., "Learning Disabilities—a Complex Phenomenon," *Reading Teacher,* 23 (January 1970), 299–303.
2. Ames, Louise B., and Walker, Richard N., "Prediction of Later Reading Ability from Kindergarten Rorschach and I.Q. Scores," *Journal of Educational Psychology,* 55 (December 1964), 309–13.
3. Barsky, Marilyn, "The Relationship of Some Aggressive Characteristics to Reading Achievement in Fifth and Sixth Grade Males and Females," Paper presented at AERA meeting, February 1967.
4. Bell, D. Bruce, Lewis, F. D., and Anderson, R. P., "Some Personality and Motivational Factors in Reading Retardation," *Journal of Educational Research,* 65 (January 1972), 229–33.
5. Berg, Paul C., "Reading: The Learner's Needs and Self-Concepts," *Florida Reading Quarterly,* 4 (June 1968), 3–8.

6. Bloomer, Richard H., "Reading Patterns of the Rejected Child," *Reading Teacher,* 22 (January 1969), 320–24.
7. Callaway, Byron B., Jerrolds, W., and Tisdale, L., "Symposium of Scores on the California Test of Personality with Reading Achievement," *Education,* 93 (November–December 1972), 160–64.
8. Carter, Homer L., "Combined Oral Reading and Psychogalvanic Response Technique for Investigating Certain Reading Disabilities of College Students," *Journal of Applied Psychology,* 34 (August 1950), 267–69.
9. Chansky, N. M., and Bregman, M., "Improvement of Reading in College," *Journal of Educational Research,* 51 (1957), 313–17.
10. Coombs, Arthur W., "New Horizons in Field Research: The Self-Concept," *Educational Leadership,* 15 (February 1958), 315–19.
11. Cox, K. K., "Changes in Stereotyping of Negroes and Whites in Magazine Advertisements," *Public Opinion Quarterly,* 33 (1969–70), 603–606.
12. Douglas, J. W. B., Ross, J. M., and Cooper, J. E., "The Relationship between Handedness, Attainment and Adjustment in a National Sample of School Children," *Educational Research,* 9 (1967), 223–32.
13. Dudek, S. Z., and Lester, E. P., "The Good Child Facade in Chronic Underachievers," *American Journal of Orthopsychiatry,* 38 (1968), 153–59.
14. Feshbach, Seymour, Adelman, Howard, and Burke, Edward, "Empirical Evaluation of a Program for the Remediation of Learning Disabilities in Culturally Disadvantaged Youth: Some Issues and Data." Los Angeles: Office of Compensatory Education, State of California at Fernald School, University of California.
15. Glick, Oren, "Some Social-Emotional Consequences of Early Inadequate Acquisition of Reading Skills," *Journal of Educational Research,* 65 (June 1972), 253–57.
16. Gottlieb, David, "Goal Aspirations and Goal Fulfillments: Differences between Deprived and Affluent American Adolescents," *American Journal of Orthopsychiatry,* 34 (October 1964), 934–41.
17. Green, Richard, *Sexual Identity Conflict in Children and Adults.* New York: Basic Books, 1973.
18. Grice, Joan S., and Wolfe, Lee R., "Peer vs. Teacher Correction of Classwork and Selected Reading Criteria," pp. 218–27 in *Investigations Relating to Mature Reading,* Frank P. Greene, editor, Twenty-first Yearbook National Reading Conference, 1972.
19. Hake, James M., "Covert Motivations of Good and Poor Readers," *Reading Teacher,* 22 (May 1969), 731–38.
20. Heath, Robert W., "The Ability of White Teachers to Relate to Black Students and to White Students," *American Educational Research Journal,* 8 (January 1971), 1–10.
21. Henderson, Edmund H., and Long, Barbara H., "Correlations of Reading Readiness Among Children of Varying Background," *Reading Teacher,* 22 (October 1968), 40–44.
22. Henderson, Edmund H., and Long, Barbara H., "Predictors of Success in Beginning Reading among Negroes and Whites," pp. 34–42 in *Reading Goals for the Disadvantaged,* J. Allen Figurel, editor. Newark, Del.: International Reading Association, 1970.
23. Herbert, D., "Reading Comprehension as a Function of Self-Concept," *Perceptual and Motor Skills,* 27 (1968), 78.
24. Hoihjelle, Anne L., "Social Climate and Personality Traits of Able Teachers in

Relation to Reading Instruction," pp. 114–21 in *Claremont College Reading Conference,* Twenty-sixth Yearbook, 1962.

25. Joseph, M. P., and McDonald, Arthur S., "Psychological Needs and Reading Achievement," pp. 150–57 in *New Concepts in College-Adult Reading,* Thirteenth Yearbook National Reading Conference, 1964.

26. Kagan, J., "Reflection-Impulsivity and Reading Ability in Primary-Grade Children," *Child Development,* 36 (1965), 609–28.

27. Ketcham, C. A., "Factors in the Home Background and Reader Self-Concept Which Relate to Reading Achievement," pp. 66–68 in *Proceedings College Reading Association,* 6 (1966).

28. Knoblock, Peter, "A Rorschach Investigation of the Reading Process," *Journal of Experimental Education,* 33 (Spring 1965), 277–82.

29. Kvaraceus, William C., et al., *Negro Self-Concept: Implications for School and Citizenship.* New York: McGraw-Hill, 1965.

30. LaBenne, Wallace D., and Thorsen, Carl E., *Educational Implications of the Self-Concept Theory.* Pacific Palisades: Goodyear, 1969.

31. Lecky, Prescott, "Preventing Failure by Removing Resistance," pp. 152–60 in *Yearbook of the New York Society for the Study of Experimental Education,* 1938.

32. Long, Barbara H., "Critique of Soares and Soares 'Self-Perceptions of Culturally Disadvantaged Children,'" *American Educational Research Journal,* 6 (November 1969), 710–11.

33. Malmquist, Eve, *Las-och skrivsvaarighter hos born. Analys och behandlingsmetodik.* Lund, Sweden, 1967.

34. Morrison, Virginia B., "Teacher-Pupil Interaction in Three Types of Elementary Classroom Reading Situations," *Reading Teacher,* 22 (December 1968), 271–75.

35. Nelson, Jack L., and Besag, Frank P., *Sociological Perspectives in Education: Models for Analysis.* New York: Pitman, 1970.

36. Neville, Donald, Pfost, Philip, and Dobbs, Virginia, "The Relationship between Test Anxiety and Silent Reading Gain," *American Educational Research Journal,* 4 (January 1967), 45–50.

37. Noland, Eunice C., and Schuldt, W. John, "Sustained Attention and Reading Retardation," *Journal of Experimental Education,* 40 (Winter 1971), 73–76.

38. Porterfield, A. V., and Schlicting, H. F., "Peer Status and Reading Achievement," *Journal of Educational Research,* 54 (April 1961), 291–97.

39. Powers, Jerry M., Drane, H. Tupper, Close, Bonnie L., Noonan, Pat, Wines, Audrey M., and Marshall, Jon C., "A Research Note on the Self-Perception of Youth," *American Educational Research Journal,* 4 (November 1971), 665–70.

40. Rankin, Earl F., "Reading Test Reliability and Validity as a Function of Introversion-Extraversion," *Journal of Developmental Reading,* 6 (Winter 1963), 106–17.

41. Raygor, Alton L., and Wark, David, M., "Personality Patterns of Poor Readers Compared with College Freshmen," *Journal of Reading,* 8 (October 1964), 40–46.

42. Robinson, Helen M., "Personality and Reading," pp. 87–99 in *Modern Educational Problems,* Arthur E. Traxler, editor. Washington, D.C.: American Council on Education, 1953.

43. Rugel, Robert P., "Arousal and Levels of Reading Difficulty," *Reading Teacher,* 24 (February 1971), 458–60.

44. St. John, Nancy, "Thirty-Six Teachers: Their Characteristics and Outcomes for Black

and White Pupils," *American Educational Research Journal,* 8 (November 1971), 635–48.

45. Shulman, L. S., "The Vocational Development of Mentally Handicapped Adolescents: An Experimental and Longitudinal Study." Bureau of Education for the Handicapped, U.S. Office of Education. Michigan State University, 1967.

46. Smith, Phyllis W., "Self-Concept Gain Scores and Reading Efficiency Terminal Ratios as Function of Specialized Reading Instruction or Personal Interaction," pp. 671–74 in *Reading and Realism,* J. Allen Figurel, editor, Proceedings International Reading Association, 13, 1969.

47. Soares, Anthony T., and Soares, Louise M., "Self-Perceptions of Culturally Disadvantaged Children," *American Educational Research Journal,* 6 (January 1969), 31–45.

48. Solomon, Ruth H., "Personality Adjustment to Reading Success and Failure," pp. 64–82 in *Clinical Studies in Reading II,* Helen M. Robinson, editor. Supplementary Educational Monographs No. 77. Chicago: University of Chicago Press, 1953.

49. Spache, George D., "The Learner's Concept of Self," pp. 97–99 in Education for the Preservation of Democracy," *American Council on Education Studies,* Series I, Vol. 13 (April 1949).

50. Spache, George D., "Personality Characteristics of Retarded Readers as Measured by the Picture-Frustration Study," *Educational and Psychological Measurement,* 14 (1954), 186–91.

51. Spache, George D., "Appraising the Personality of Remedial Pupils," pp. 122–32 in *Education in a Free World,* Arthur E. Traxler, editor. Washington, D.C.: American Council on Education, 1955.

52. Spache, George D., "Personality Patterns of Retarded Readers," *Journal of Educational Research,* 50 (February 1957), 461–69.

53. Spache, George D., "Intellectual and Personality Characteristics of Retarded Readers," *Psychological Newsletter,* 9 (September 1957), 9–12.

54. Spache, George D., *Good Reading for the Disadvantaged Reader.* Champaign, Ill.: Garrard Publishing, 1975.

55. Spaights, Ernest, "Accuracy of Self-Estimating of Junior High School Students," *Journal of Educational Research,* 58 (May–June 1965), 416–19.

56. Stavrianos, Bertha K., and Landsman, Sylvia C., "Personality Patterns of Deficient Readers with Perceptual-Motor Problems," *Psychology in the Schools,* 6 (1969), 109–23.

57. Stevens, Deon O., "Reading Difficulty and Classroom Acceptance," *Reading Teacher,* 25 (October 1971), 52–55.

58. Stillwell, Lois, *Specific and Global Self-Concept.* 3921 Woodthrust Road, Akron, Ohio: the author.

59. Tillman, Chester, et al., "Summary of Five Studies of Reading Ability and Personality Types," Paper presented at the National Reading Conference, December 1, 1973.

60. Trowbridge, Norma, "Self-Concept and Socio-Economic Status in Elementary School Children," *American Educational Research Journal,* 9 (Fall 1972), 525–38.

61. Wattenberg, W. W., and Clifford, C., "Relationships of Self-Concept to Beginning Achievement in Reading," *Childhood Education,* 43 (September 1966), 58.

62. Wilderson, Frank B., Jr., "An Exploratory Study of Reading Skills Deficiencies and

Psychiatric Symptoms in Emotionally Disturbed Children," *Reading Research Quarterly*, 2 (Spring 1967), 47–74.

63. Wolf, Martin G., "Emotional Disturbance and School Achievement," *Journal of School Psychology*, 4 (Autumn 1965), 16–18.

64. Zimmerman, E., and Allebrand, G. W., "Personality Characteristics and Attitudes Toward Achievement of Good and Poor Readers," *Journal of Educational Research*, 59 (September 1965), 28–31.

part two

DIAGNOSIS
OF
READING
SKILLS

The author opens this discussion of group reading tests by contrasting the two goals of measurement of evaluation versus testing of progress. This distinction seems lost in the current emphasis upon informal and criterion-referenced instruments, he appears to believe. He questions the validity of these currently popular approaches to measurement, while remarking upon the comparative strengths and weaknesses of the alternative group tests of reading. Perhaps he is implying that no single approach to measuring pupil progress, whether informal or standardized, criterion or norm-referenced, really samples the major outcomes of an effective reading program. In discussing the measurement of reading gains, the author again points out the fallacies in using a single test or formula for such a purpose.

In attempting to retain some of the ideas of this chapter, use these questions to help you.

10 Selecting and Interpreting Group Reading Measures

1. What are some of the basic differences between testing and evaluation? Which of these concepts do most school systems accept, judging from their testing procedures? Why do you suppose this is so?

2. The author finds faults with teacher-made or commercial tests, standardized or criterion-referenced instruments. What alternative approaches to determining pupil progress in learning to read does he offer?

3. What are some of the problems in attempting to measure the total outcomes of any special program in reading? Can you suggest any tentative solutions to some of these problems?

THE PROBLEMS OF CLASSIFICATION and effective use of manpower during World War I gave a tremendous impetus to the use of commercial or standardized tests. Crude as they were, the instruments of that day provided a rapid and practical means of evaluating the abilities of large masses of the population. Then, as the war crisis subsided, the testing movement spread into our schools, with widespread use of tests becoming firmly established there. Standardized tests were almost completely accepted as capable of performing miracles in classification, grouping, selection, and measurement of capacity and achievement. A few critics may have doubted these results, but their criticisms were overwhelmed by the avalanche of paper.

TESTING AND EVALUATION

For about fifteen years, the use of reading tests in our schools continued to grow without very widespread criticism. Then, stimulated in part by a redefinition of the objectives of reading instruction by the National Committee on Reading in 1924 and by the attempt in 1933 to evaluate the less obvious outcomes of education in the Eight-Year Study, a reassessment of the values of current tests began. The conception of the purposes of tests shifted. What were once paper and pencil devices measuring specific skills or knowledge were now considered to be a series of educational situations providing opportunity for the evaluation of student behaviors in relation to recognized objectives (27). The use of standardized tests did not necessarily diminish as the concept of evaluation grew, for the majority of present-day teachers is still highly dependent upon such instruments (6). But our whole concepts of the basic purposes of testing and the adequacy of standardized tests for measuring the outcomes of our instruction were modified. Evaluation of the real purposes of reading instruction—attitudes, interests, and the personal and social effects of reading—was sought, rather than mere repeated testing of skills and information.

Furthermore, evaluation was to be concerned with the influence of the learner's characteristics and the learning conditions upon the outcomes of instruction (27). The traits of the learner are perhaps more significant in reading than in most curriculum areas. Reading performances are influenced by such factors as age, sex, mental ability, social class, cultural and linguistic background, and interests and motivation of the learner. Social acceptance by peers; physical development; educational, cultural, and vocational goals; work experience; and the attitudes of parents toward education also affect the pupils' reading behaviors. Wherever possible, the influence of these elements must be considered in attempting a realistic evaluation of the student's reading progress.

Other factors must also enter into our interpretation of pupils' reading performances. For example, a recent study (18) demonstrated the influence of the anxiety created by tests upon gains from a remedial program. Neville and his coworkers found that very high anxiety and very low anxiety about tests resulted in little gain in comprehension after a six-weeks' program. Children with high anxiety, in fact, lost in posttraining testing. Robinson (21) questioned the validity of common tests for advantaged and disadvantaged kindergarten children. As measured by the reliability of the test in each population, tests of auditory discrimination and vision varied greatly between these two groups. Several common readiness, intelligence, and prereading skill tests did not so vary, however.

Comparisons of the reliability of readiness and reading tests in different ethnic or racial groups are not always in agreement. Mishra and Hurt,* for example, find that the word meaning and listening tests of the Metropolitan Readiness test, in particular, as well as the total score, have lower reliability and lower predictive validity in a sample of Mexican-American children than are reported for the standardization population. Other studies tend to confirm these findings for these two subtests. As for the Metropolitan Reading test, other researchers criticize the Word Knowledge subtest as low in reliability for these bilingual pupils. One study claims that only 35 percent of the items of the Metropolitan Readiness and 21 percent of those of the Metropolitan Reading have acceptable levels of difficulty and validity in such a population.

However, variations in reliability and validity coefficients and in the actual difficulty of items may be expected from one sample to another. The size of the sample, the range of the scores, the range of grades tested, as well as the heterogeneity of the abilities of the group and other considerations affect these evaluations and are responsible for variations. More data on sizeable samples from ethnic or racial groups will be needed to draw firm conclusions regarding the functioning of these tests in the various populations. We can expect variations from one population to another without

---

*Shitala Mishra and M. Hurt, Jr., "The Use of Metropolitan Readiness Tests with Mexican-American Children," *California Journal of Educational Research* 21 (1970), 182–87.

becoming embroiled in the current argument that such tests discriminate against nonwhite, non-middle-class pupils, as they probably do. As diagnosticians and teachers, we ought to be concerned with finding tests that can be shown to function adequately for our purposes, rather than simply rejecting most common tests on political or civil rights grounds, however justified the criticisms may be.

Cawley (2) questions the use of the norms for various diagnostic tests with mentally handicapped children. His data seem to indicate that the subtests of various diagnostic batteries do discriminate between good and poor readers in a small mentally handicapped population. But he wonders about the pertinence of the norms. Should we compare such children on the basis of mental age or grade placement or what criteria? Do mentally handicapped pupils (or any other pupils) tend to perform in most reading skills at a level equal to their mental age?

Thorough and accurate evaluation also demands a detailed analysis of the learning conditions. Classroom methods or practices such as "individualized reading," "teacher-pupil planning," and "free reading" do not mean exactly the same conditions in different schools. For true comparability of experimental evaluations, Tyler suggests that a number of aspects of the learning conditions must be carefully noted and described (27). Among the more important of these are student motivation, self-insight, satisfactions, and standards of performance. The guidance available in developing new behaviors, the time allotments, the available materials, provisions for application, and the opportunities for student self-evaluation are also highly significant elements of the learning situation.

A sound evaluation program must be comprehensive, continuous, and articulated through the school system, as well as functional and practical. To be comprehensive and well-balanced in terms of both the learner and the curriculum, it will include (1) teacher observation, (2) health records, (3) anecdotal records, (4) work samples, (5) cumulative records, (6) classroom tests, (7) follow-up studies, (8) case histories, (9) studies by special consultants, as those in psychology and guidance, and (10) objective or standardized tests.

Continuity and articulation throughout the grades demand all-school planning, comparable and interrelated tests, frequent cross-sectional samples of the curriculum, and the learner's behaviors. To be functional, the program should give the specific information desired by both teachers and administrators, and should employ instruments that are simple to give, easy to score and interpret, as diagnostic as possible, and convenient to store or record.

To these basic principles, Russell adds the reminder that evaluation should certainly be related to the objectives of the reading program, promote change or clarification of these objectives, and be amenable to experimenta-tion with new methods of evaluation (22). The comprehensiveness of the evaluation program implies, as Russell cautions, that it must be introduced slowly and with adequate all-staff consideration and discussion if it is to become truly effective.

Thus evaluation has added broader, deeper, and more meaningful facets to the testing movement. It has redefined many of the terms of the field and brought a whole new viewpoint to the purposes of testing. Evaluation is concerned with the student's reading behaviors and performance in relation to instructional objectives, but it also stresses the interaction of these behaviors, the traits of the learner, and the learning conditions.

Roger Farr* has historically reviewed the development of reading tests and made some cogent observations. He retraces the imitation of intelligence tests in the construction of reading tests, which measure general behavior in reading as though it were true under all conditions. Early test makers revered the I.Q., considered it a permanent trait of the child; and makers of reading tests followed, and still follow, this philosophy in offering us instruments that define reading as an all-encompassing behavior. Farr describes the early tests that measured the ability to reproduce in writing, an approach still used today in Durrell's Analysis of Reading Difficulty kit, although the reproduction now is oral and the scoring is only quantitative. Following this type, we find tests of short paragraphs demanding inferential reading and, later, similarly construct-ed measures requiring the reader to identify the main idea by a single word, still used today in the Gates-MacGinitie series of reading tests. Later readers were asked to find a single word that was irrelevant in a short paragraph, or to choose a single word to fill a blank space, still present in the New Stanford and Gates-MacGinitie tests. Farr feels that test makers lost sight of the goal of measuring the quality of reproduction or of understanding; tests came to measure only the test developer's purpose, not those of the reader.

Arthur S. McDonald† has similarly criticized current reading tests for failing to evaluate versatility in task-oriented ways. He believes that we should determine effectiveness and efficiency under a variety of situations, trying to discover under what conditions and with what materials the reader is effective (is he able to satisfy the purpose for reading?) and efficient (is he able to accomplish the purposes with appropriate expenditure of time and energy,

---

*Roger Farr, "Measuring Reading Comprehension: An Historical Perspective," pp. 187–97 in *Reading: The Right to Participate,* Twentieth Yearbook National Reading Conference, 1971.

†Arthur S. McDonald, "Reading Versatility Twelve Years Later," pp. 168–73 in *Reading: The Right to Participate,* Twentieth Yearbook National Reading Conference, 1971.

and to vary his strategies and tactics of processing input according to different purposes and reading situations?). Rather, as McDonald observes, we overemphasize tests of rate, comprehension, and vocabulary, usually in one kind of material under one condition and call the results a measure of "reading."

It is apparent from the comments by Farr and McDonald that we have not yet begun to achieve true evaluation in testing in reading in our current testing programs. Perhaps the contemporary movement toward behavioral objectives and criterion-referenced tests may move us in that direction.

BEHAVIORAL OBJECTIVES AND CRITERION-REFERENCED TESTS

Currently there is wide interest in another approach to evaluation termed *behavioral objectives.* These objectives are simply detailed descriptions of the tasks or behaviors that should be acquired by pupils in learning to read. In many school systems, classroom teachers have been asked to frame the behavioral objectives in reading for their children. When the teachers understand what is desired in formulating such lists, they are stimulated to make a much more detailed analysis of all the components of each reading skill. For example, rather than talking vaguely about promoting auditory discrimination, behavioral objectives require the teacher to spell out exactly what sounds are to be discriminated; how the sounds will differ (pitch, loudness, duration, sequence); how the child can differentiate ordinary environmental sounds from those in words or syllables, as well as the final performances in identifying similarities and differences in the sounds of initial consonants, in rhyming, and in distinguishing medial sounds. In behavioral objectives each skill area is broken down into its smallest bits, and the child's performance for each bit is described precisely.

Advantages

Although many teachers felt that the requirement of their framing behavioral objectives was only busy work, there are obvious advantages to the experience. For perhaps the first time in their professional lives, teachers were asked to analyze and describe in detail their instructional practices. They could not assume that all necessary skills and subskills would be taught by faithfully following the basal reader manual. In fact, as their explorations deepened, many teachers discovered that some skills were not taught in their particular basal series and that they would have to supplement this source. Other teachers working with their colleagues discovered that the process of learning to read was much more complex and involved many more skills than they had ever realized. The variety and interrelatedness of subskills that underlie a common reading performance such as word recognition was another revelation for many classroom teachers. And in those school systems that have continued to use and refine their behavioral objectives, these gains in professional knowledge and instructional practices have been largely maintained.

A logical extension of the behavioral objectives movement has been the search for new and better tests of the hundreds of reading performances thus identified. No standardized reading tests in the market attempted to cover this multitude of skills, and new instruments were obviously needed. As a result, there appeared short, unstandardized tests keyed to behavioral objectives lists. These brief tests are called criterion-referenced tests. They differ from ordinary norm-referenced tests in that each samples only one kind of reading performance or one subskill at a time. Presumably as the child completed his practice in a subskill, the test would demonstrate his degree of mastery and his readiness for the next related subskill. Since the child's development would be assessed at every step of the reading process, teachers would be provided with the information needed to adjust their instruction to each child's needs. No norms are established for criterion-referenced tests, but rather some a priori standard is established, such as 80 percent correct of the items.

The Hackett Reading System, by Marie Hackett, is an example of a highly organized group of criterion-referenced tests. It is now published by Random House under the title "Criterion Reading." Three hundred and twenty skills, called Process and Outcome skills, are identified, and a test for each provided in the kit. The test materials are divided into large skill areas such as Sensorimotor Skills, Phonology, Word Analysis, Verbal Information, Syntax, and Comprehension. The 320 steps cover reading instruction of the first six grades, and separate but overlapping kits are provided for the various grade levels, each covering the relevant skills in the last five major areas of emphasis.

Each Process skill and the related Outcome skill is tested by separate one-sheet tests of six to twenty items. A performance level of 95 percent accuracy is required for a child to pass each test, which implies that in the tests of less than twenty items, of which there are many, the pupil must answer *all* items correctly. The system suggests that all the Outcome skill tests (which parallel the author's list of behavioral objectives) appropriate to the grade level be given as initial assessments. Those Outcome skills failed are then retested by the Process Skills tests, which are intended to evaluate the subskills underlying each Outcome skill. On the basis of the diagnostic testing in the

Process skills, children are identified in terms of needs for instruction; and a sequence of learning is presumably indicated.

Limitations

There are, of course, immediate questions about a criterion-referenced system and the justification of its rationale. There are implicit assumptions about test construction and the reading process such as these:

1. All children learn to read by building this series of skills in the order in which it is planned.

2. All children need training in these hundreds of skills to read successfully.

3. There are definite hierarchies of subskills that underlie each of the behavioral objectives.

4. These skills must be real since they can be described in the behavioral objectives.*

5. The identity and independence of the subskills has been established by such techniques as factor analysis.†

6. The tests are valid and reliable samples of the subskills.‡

7. Normal or acceptable norms of performance in each subskill test items can be established by a priori standards announced by the author.

8. Identifying deficiencies in subskills in this fashion and then teaching to eradicate these deficiencies has been shown to be the most practical way of conducting reading instruction.

As we remarked elsewhere, the logic of testing pupils and then teaching to eradicate what appear to be weaknesses may not be as sound as it appears. All readers do not use the same skills in the same manner or to the same degree in order to read well. For example, two children reading at the same level with comparable comprehension may differ greatly in their use of word analysis skills and contextual clues. One may be painstakingly analytic with words, while the other may depend almost solely on context for word recognition and meanings.

Studies of the interrelationships of word analysis skills to comprehension and the Holmes-Singer studies of subskills do not indicate that all these skills are essential. And we do not find that all the skills are possessed by all good readers and lacking among poor readers. In the Hackett system,

---

*Richard A. Thompson and Charles D. Dziuban, "Criterion Referenced Tests in Perspective," *Reading Teacher*, 27 (December 1973), 292–95.

†Ibid

‡Ibid

for example, we observed that some children can do all the Process skills and yet fail the Outcome test, or that some can read successfully on much higher levels than the assessment testing would place them. In other words, some children perform satisfactorily at different reading levels, even though they may lack ability in a number of the criterion skills. These observations argue against a stipulated hierarchy of skills for all children.

It is one thing to seem to identify hundreds of subskills that logically appear to function in the reading act. But it is another matter to build valid and reliable measures of these skills. Criterion-referenced tests tend to be very specific and brief. Because of this, their reliabilities are low, and children's performances might well vary considerably on them from day to day. Moreover, unless cumulative review tests are given, there is no evidence that the learning of the skills has been either real or permanent.

Behavioral objectives and the related criterion-referenced tests may have real values in deepening teachers' understanding of the reading process and children's difficulties in learning to read. But we question strongly whether they should be the basis of a detailed learning sequence that all children are required to pursue.

Some observers consider the trend toward behavioral objectives and criterion-referenced tests a regression in the progress of the field of testing. This detailistic, almost perfectionistic trend ignores the deeper insights inherent in evaluation. Social, environmental, linguistic, and classroom conditions, as well as the personal characteristics of the learner, all appear to be glossed over in this new development.

MacDonald and Wolfson* have made a strong case against behavioral objectives and hence against criterion-referenced tests. They point out that the performance of a behavioral objective (as evidenced in a criterion-referenced test) is deceptive as a criterion of learning, for the performance may be chance behavior; may not be displayed because of the conditions of the situation (for example, the child may block or not really make an effort); or the child may not retain the behavior in the future.

They further state that behavior suggests the possibility of transfer to life situations the abilities to reason, to value, and to act on relevant information. In contrast, behavioral objectives deal only with bits and pieces of subject matter. As we suggested above, MacDonald and Wolfson stress that higher levels of functioning (vide our example of comprehension) are not simply a sum of lower-level perceptions. Higher levels are dependent upon lower

---

*James B. MacDonald and Bernice J. Wolfson, "A Case Against Behavioral Objectives," *Elementary School Journal* 71 (December 1970), 119–28.

levels for developing new behavior. Thus, higher-level functioning, although dependent upon lower levels, has its own organizing behavior. We cannot, according to these authors, emphasize lower levels at the expense of higher-level functioning, as we do in following behavioral objectives.

Behavioral objectives emphasize learning as though it were solely training, MacDonald and Wolfson continue. They focus on the teacher's view rather than on the child's, for, under a system of behavioral objectives, all activities are teacher-selected, teacher-planned, and teacher-directed. The concept of an objective apart from its setting in the individual members of the class and their relationships ignores individual differences, as behavioral objectives do. Objectives are also inherent in the classroom activity, the materials, and the individuals who are manipulating them.

Finally, MacDonald and Wolfson accuse behavioral objectives of being based on a false definition of knowledge. The objectives assume that knowledge is certain when it is really uncertain and relative; that knowledge is absolute (vide the scoring of the criterion tests in the Hackett system); that knowledge is impersonal (the same program for all children) when it is really personal and functional.

As Arthur S. McDonald and Roger Farr claim, we have not really made any real progress toward the broader goals of evaluation as compared with testing, and certainly are not moving in this direction using behavioral objectives and criterion-referenced tests.

STANDARDIZED TESTS—THEIR VALUES AND LIMITATIONS

Dr. Arthur E. Traxler, formerly of the Educational Records Bureau, has probably had more personal experience with tests and testing programs than any other writer in this field. For more than twenty years he directed and guided the use of tests in hundreds of private and public schools. As he views them, standardized tests possess the values of objectivity, effective appraisal, diagnosis, and classification (26). Test results may be expressed in quantitative terms. Tests are usually carefully constructed and permit comparisons with the performances characteristic of a specific school grade level, as well as comparison among the pupil's skills. They also provide for the appraisal of the growth of individuals and groups, as well as for the effectiveness of the reading program. With respect to their diagnostic features, Traxler recognizes that these are not necessarily inherent in many tests bearing such a label, but that diagnostic information may be found in the clues provided by the test.

Values

Tests given at the beginning of the year provide records of improvement, guides to sectioning or placement, diagnosis of needs, and additional data for the cumulative record. In contrast, tests used at the end of the year permit measurement of growth and of the effectiveness of new procedures. Midyear tests provide intermittent measures of progress, rediagnosis, and a check on the accuracy of placement; they also function as a teaching device.

Other values often claimed for standardized tests include greater reliability than teacher-made tests and the availability of comparable forms. More time and care is given to the construction of standardized tests; hence their measures of pupil performance are apt to be more accurate and dependable than are many teacher-made instruments. Parallel forms permit repeated testing with reasonable assurance of comparability of tests and scores.

Limitations

But some of the limitations of standardized tests are freely admitted, even by their supporters. Traxler points out the inherently artificial nature of reading tests. "Reading is a process which flows past as you try to appraise it," he reminds us. And again, "no aspect of silent reading can be measured without interrupting the process" (26, pp. 111, 112). Test specialists often make logical but artificial analyses of the process and then build tests on the elements they believe that they have identified (5, 8, 12).

A quotation from Roger T. Lennon, who is director of the test division of a large publishing house, is quite pertinent to this view: (13)

> It is one thing, and a necessary thing, to make a careful analysis of reading ability, to spell out its various supposed components in detail, and to prepare extensive lists or charts of the specific skills or abilities to serve as statements of the desired goals or outcomes of the reading program. It is quite another thing to demonstrate that these manifold skills or abilities do, in fact, exist as differentiable characteristics of students; and still a third thing to build tests which are in truth measures of one or another of these skills, and not of some general, pervasive reading ability.

Measures of rate of reading commonly treat it as a constant or unitary trait, while the research literature clearly points out that most readers possess several characteristic reading rates. Even if we assume that the individual's various rates tend to cluster around a relative level, our rate tests vary considerably in the lengths of the samples and in their reliabilities (26). Since we have several reading vocabularies, rather than a single one, tests of general vocabulary are seldom meaningful except in terms of their adequacy in sampling our various vocabularies. Other writers offer the further criticisms that our reading tests place too much emphasis on memory, on vocabulary, and on speed in silent reading rather than on oral comprehension. Or, that most tests lack diagnostic adequacy for the individual pupil and are inaccurate in predicting classroom performances.

Interpreting Scores

Jackson sums up the basic problem in interpreting reading tests in these words: "Rather than being viewed as convenient symbols which summarize an individual's performance in a most crude fashion, test scores come to seem as something the individual 'has'" (12). The false impressions of accuracy conveyed by decimal scores (8.5 or 2.35, for example) have concerned many test critics. The pupil's score on a test is not *the* score or a *true* score. In successive attempts he would undoubtedly vary from this estimate. Enlightened test makers point this out clearly and indicate a range of scores somewhere within which the pupil's true ability probably lies. Sometimes the range extends six to twelve months either way from the score obtained. Differences between pupils' scores are probably not real unless their ranges are separated and do not overlap.

Grade scores are usually interpreted as indicating the grade level of the test material that the pupil can handle adequately; for example, 7.5 on a test of reading comprehension is supposed to mean that the pupil can read mid-seventh grade material as well as pupils of that grade placement. Actually this grade score merely shows that our pupil did as many items correctly as average seventh graders commonly do. It does not mean that our pupil has the reading background, interests, or skills to handle the usual reading materials of the seventh grade. Moreover, if our pupil is a sixth grader, his performance may not indicate accelerated reading, since it may be well within the limits of probable error in a score or within the range of the middle 50 percent of average sixth graders. Performances above or below the expected "normal" grade score must be well outside the chance limits, which widen grade after grade, before they can be considered significant.

These test standards or norms, as they are called, are often partly hypothetical, which is almost equivalent to saying that they are artificial. Tests sold for use in a particular grade may offer norms for several grade levels above or below that grade. Seldom has such a test actually been standardized except in the central grade level. The extrapolated grade scores outside the proper grade level for the test are derived by a logical extension of the increase or decrease in scores in other grades. But they do not represent actual scores of pupils; therefore, they cannot represent a norm or standard for real pupils.

Norms based on the "general" population are useful only for vague comparisons with imaginary average pupils. They usually fail to represent some significant segments of the population, such as regional, racial, or socioeconomic groups. Only perhaps in general surveys of school systems are these so-called national norms meaningful. And then only if the school system and community is similar in size, degree of industrialization, average income level, and so on, with the samples on which the "national" norms are based. Many of these general norms do not represent true samples of the entire school population but are merely collections of all the scores available to the publisher. Alert test users should look for norms on groups resembling their own pupils as closely as possible, or else they should collect scores on their own pupils and use these as local norms.

Reliability

The vaunted reliability of some standardized tests is just not present. Often comparisons between pupils are not justified (unless the differences are large) because the tests are not sufficiently dependable or the amount of probable error in a score is great. The claimed reliability of the test is spuriously inflated by the speed element in many brief tests. It is true that pupils do not seem to vary much from one form of such a test to another; therefore the test-retest yields fairly high coefficients. But it may well be that no pupil actually could vary much in successive attempts because the time allowed is short.

Misapplications

We certainly must mention some of the improper uses or even abuses of standardized tests by teachers and administrators. Tests constructed for other purposes are seldom justified for rating teachers' efficiency or as a basis for pupil promotion or marks, or for measuring most of the outcomes of instruction in an experimental or regular classroom situation. Too many variables affect pupil performances to use common reading tests for hiring and firing teachers, promoting pupils, or evaluating experimental conditions of learning. Reading tests cannot possibly measure more than a minute portion of the results arising from the influence of a certain teacher, a method of teaching reading, or a particular experiment. Nor can standardized reading tests alone measure what happens in the reading program or some version of it (17). After all, standardized reading tests are supposed to give only a crude estimate of a pupil's performance in a certain small portion of all of his reading behaviors.

Other common misapplications of standardized tests include the naive use of several different reading tests in successive testings, as though the tests were comparable. To mention only a few recent studies refuting this belief, McCall and McCall (15, 16) found major differences among first grade and diagnostic phonics tests in two comparative studies. Eller and Attea (7) point out variations in several scores of individual diagnosis batteries. Benz and Rosemier (1) point out the lack of comparability between two common group tests because of the differences in the skills measured. Evaluations of reading abilities or needs for instruction differ from test to test, and the scores cannot be compared or combined or, sometimes, even reconciled.

Another problem in test interpretation is the general practice of expecting pupils to achieve equal scores in all the subtests of a multipart test. Subtest scores or profiles are accepted at face value as indicating significant strengths and weaknesses, regardless of their respective validities and reliabilities. A low test score is interpreted as a signal for special instruction by the average teacher or reading clinician. There are several assumptions present in this common use of skills tests that, in our opinion, are highly questionable.

What logic justifies the assumption that, to be successful in reading, the individual must show an equal degree of development in most reading skills? Longitudinal studies of human intellectual or academic development do not support this assumption. Rather they indicate that with increasing age the discrepancies among skills and among cognitive abilities continually become greater. Multifaceted studies of reading skill development such as those by Holmes and Singer (10) do not support this belief. In fact, we find that when we test many reading skills, successful readers vary greatly from each other in their patterns of strengths and weaknesses.

More specifically, in the diagnosis of reading abilities we expect all pupils who are successful comprehenders to perform equally well in a half-dozen word analysis skills. Any pupil who varies from the expected flat or straight-line profile is immediately given corrective instruction. It is an axiomatic belief among teachers and reading clinicians that, after all, comprehension is dependent upon good word analysis skills (all of them). Let us cite but a single study that contradicts this almost universal delusion. Benz and Rosemier (1) analyzed the performances of high, average, and low comprehenders as identified by the Level of Comprehension part of the Gates Survey

Reading Test.   In the six word-analysis subtests of the Bond-Clymer-Hoyt Diagnostic Tests, these pupils tended to vary in keeping with their comprehension rating.   In other words, high comprehenders achieved higher mean scores on the word analysis tests than average comprehenders; average comprehenders, in turn, scored higher, *on the average,* than poor comprehenders.   But this expected pattern was true only in a group sense.   Inspection of the individual scores would reveal some high comprehenders who were weak in some word analysis tests, while, at the other extreme, some poor comprehenders would be found who were strong in some or even all the word analysis tests.   In fact, Benz and Rosemier found that only 57 percent of the variance in comprehension scores was related to performance in the combined six word analysis tests.   Obviously, there is *not* a close relationship between comprehension—the most important aspect of reading—and any one word analysis skill or, in this case, with all six word analysis tests combined.

We recognize, of course, that this type of interpretation of skills tests could be discussed further.   There is certainly some sort of relationship between word analysis skills and comprehension.   But our point is that this relationship varies among individuals and that a high degree of performance in any one or group of skills is not always essential for success in reading.   The direct application of subtest scores to corrective or remedial instruction is not so sensible as it appears.   Rather we should be using our diagnostic time and instruments to discover exactly how each pupil achieves his degree of success in comprehension and to determine *whether or not* his performance could be improved by further instruction in some particular fundamental skill.

MEASURING READING GAINS

Probably the most widely recognized function or purpose for which reading tests are employed is that of the measurement of gains.   Practically all reading programs, methods of reading, and experiments utilize gain on reading tests as their criterion of success.   While this may be a legitimate function of reading tests, many writers are very critical of the naive manner in which posttraining reading test results are interpreted.

Just what does it mean when a pupil makes more than normal progress in reading as evidenced by a test score?   Does this prove that the technique or method used with him was effective?   Many reports claim dramatic success for their approach when their groups show more gain in the test scores than might be expected during the elapsed time.   In our opinion, this type of interpretation makes several questionable assumptions about test scores.   Even if we presume that the tests measure the most significant outcomes of teaching, the posttraining scores do not prove what they seem to. Few present-day reading tests are so refined and accurate that they can actually reflect month-by-month progress. Rather the scores for each month are largely hypothetical, being derived by extrapolation of the actual scores obtained in two testings a year apart. No one really knows if this extrapolation of scores for each month is justified. Experiments that have used repeated testing at short intervals indicate that most of the year's gain in test scores occurs in the first few months rather than being distributed evenly throughout the year, as test norms imply.

Moreover, the dramatic impact of a new method or an impressive device helps to produce a learning spurt during the initial stages of its use. After the novelty has worn off, pupils probably make much less progress and, perhaps a year after the beginning of the experiment, may show no more total gain than other classes. Thus it is possible to produce for a brief space of time what appears to be more than normal progress by techniques or methods that are completely contradictory or even irrelevant. For example, we read accounts of dramatic reading gains when pupils are shifted from a visual method to a kinesthetic or phonic approach, or vice versa; when the change is from a textbook to a machine approach, or from a gray-haired teacher to a young blonde teacher, or vice versa. Other writers claim similar gains when pupils are shifted from a group approach to individualized or from basal readers to an individualized program. Many reports of reading programs of developmental, corrective, or remedial types completely ignore the fact that their results in a short training period may merely reflect the element of novelty or intrinsic motivation. The only proper method of evaluation in most of these experiments would be the use of continued follow-up and retesting extending over a period of several years.

There is a second major pitfall in the interpretation of posttraining test results, particularly in studies involving poor or retarded readers. Such studies usually deal with readers whose initial status is below the average of the normal population. These low scorers tend to score higher in any retest simply because of the phenomenon of regression to the mean, regardless of the nature of the training program. This tendency for low scorers to score higher in retesting (and for high scorers to score lower) is a well-established statistical fact.

Regression to the mean can and should be considered in any attempt to evaluate group or individual gain from a reading program by the use of the same test before and after training. One simple way of correcting gain scores was suggested by Diederich (6) by using the reliability coefficient of a test to determine the probable gain due to regression to the mean. In applying Diederich's procedure, follow these steps:

1. Find the difference between the pupil's initial score and the norm for his present grade level after training.

2. Multiply this difference by the reliability of the test. This figure represents an expected gain by regression to the mean.

3. Subtract this expected gain from the norm. This yields an estimate of the pupil's posttraining score that he might be expected to achieve by regression from the mean, a score that he might well achieve by chance, that is, an expected retest score.

4. Compare expected retest score with actual retest score.

5. Determine whether pupil has made gain significantly greater than expected by chance.

To illustrate, the pupil's initial score is 18; the norm for his grade level at the end of the training period is 26. The difference, 8, multiplied by the reliability of the test (.75) would be 6. This figure subtracted from 26 yields an expected retest score by chance of 20, an expected chance gain of 2 points. Only when the pupil's gain from pretesting to posttesting is greater than 2 points can we assume that he has made more than chance progress. Sakamoto and Takagi of Tokyo (23) have suggested similar correction procedures. Others are suggested by Harris (9).

Earl F. Rankin and his coworkers have explored this idea of correction for chance gains in a number of studies (19, 20, 25). They have refined this essential correction by explaining how to determine residual gain (gain after correction) and have distinguished it from crude gain, that from one test to another. Their formula for residual gain is

$$\text{Residual gain} = z - r_{12} z_1$$

in which z is the posttraining score, r_{12} is the correlation between pretest and posttest scores (the reliability coefficient), and z_1 is the pretraining score. To use this formula, pretest and posttest scores must be transformed into standard or z scores. These are found by dividing the difference of a score from the group mean by the standard deviation of the scores.* Residual or true gain is thus defined as that part of the posttest score that is independent of the initial score. The formula computes the error of estimate in a gain by correcting for the influence of the reliability of the initial score.

Residual gain offers a number of obvious advantages over crude gain, besides correcting for regression to the mean. It is more reliable than crude gain; it eliminates the spurious correlation between initial status and gain; it eliminates the influence of differences on the pretest gain, and it is a statistic

---

*See any standard text in educational statistics or Frank F. Gorow's *Statistical Measures: A Programmed Text* (San Francisco: Chandler, 1962) for assistance in computing the components of this formula.

that can be used in correlations and other studies. The use of residual gain would correct the findings of many studies by demonstrating that there is a significant correlation between gain and such variables as initial status, intelligence, personality variables, and some aspects of the instructional program.

Subsequent studies contrasting crude gain versus residual gain have supported Rankin's claims for the advantages of utilizing residual gain. Anita B. Dahlke (3) found that there were significant relationships between grade level, age, silent reading on the Diagnostic Reading Scales, potential level as measured by the same test, and the difference between silent and oral reading levels—and residual gain. Individual subtest scores in the WISC and the pupil's degree of retardation prior to remedial instruction were not significant predictors of residual gain. With a similar population of retarded readers, Chester E. Tillman (24) found negative or low correlation between crude and true or residual gain in three parts of the Diagnostic Reading Scales. True gain was significantly related to age, grade, certain personality variables, father's occupation, and initial status in all parts of the Diagnostic Reading Scales. These correlations varied somewhat in the word recognition, oral, silent, and listening parts of the Scales. Both of these studies employed a formula for computing true gain somewhat similar to that of Rankin, as suggested by Lord (9). The findings certainly appear to support the claims for the advantages of correcting test results for regression to the mean.

Many other ways of dealing with gains in minimizing regression to the mean and the relationship of initial status and gain are possible. Frederick Davis (5) has proposed a number of formulas for assessing gain among individuals or groups: He rejects the simple comparison of the score on a pretest with that on a posttest, or comparing the average score on a pair of pretests with that on a pair of posttests. The difference found systematically overestimates change for low pretest scorers and underestimates it for high pretest scorers. These errors of overestimation of gain would be particularly present in a group of children chosen for remedial work because of low initial scores. This regression to the mean and overestimation of gain is present among low initial scores because the errors in the measurement tend to be negative, that is, too low, while the reverse condition accounts for the regression downward of initially high scorers.

The effect of this regression toward the mean score can be minimized in a number of ways, according to Davis. If the group to be treated is selected on the basis of one form of a test, a second form of the same test would be used as the pretest before training, and a third form after it. Change is determined by the differences between the scores on the second and third tests. Similarly, for group comparisons, the mean scores on the second and third forms of the test are used to determine change. This approach tends to avoid spurious gains or losses owing to the effect of regression alone. In addition to these relatively simple approaches to the measurement of change, Davis offers other formulas for correcting for regression in terms of the reliability of the test and the range of scores, as in Rankin's formula, as well as more complicated ways of determining residual gain or estimates of the deviation from the expected scores of individuals or groups. For details of these approaches, see Davis's article in the Twenty-first Yearbook of the National Reading Conference (5).

LEARNING PROJECT

Assume that you are a classroom teacher about to begin the school year with a group of children who are unfamiliar to you. Divide a sheet of paper into two columns labeled "Information Usually Received" and "Information I Would Like to Have." Under the first heading, list the items of information you usually receive as a classroom teacher that help you understand the previous reading development of your new pupils. Under the second heading, list all the other types of information that would be helpful but are not usually given to you. Ignore the probable cost of obtaining such desired facts, and assume that your situation is an ideal one with all resources open to you.

1. What sort of precise information would you like to have about a pupil's skill development that does not ordinarily come to you?

2. Are there social and family facts that you would like to know, that do not normally appear in any school records? Such as what?

3. Some of the informational items not available through usual school records could perhaps be gathered by your own efforts. What might you do to obtain these desirable facts?

4. What can you suggest to improve the quality and quantity of the information flow from one grade to the next?

REFERENCES

1. Benz, D. A., and Rosemier, R. A., "Concurrent Validity of the Gates Level of Comprehension Test and the Bond-Clymer-Hoyt Reading Diagnostic Tests," *Educational and Psychological Measurement,* 26 (1966), 1057–62.

2. Cawley, J. F., "Reading Performance Among the Mentally Handicapped, A Problem in Assessment," *Training School Bulletin,* 63 (1966), 11–16.

3. Dahlke, Anita B., "The Use of WISC Scores to Predict Reading Achievement," doctoral dissertation, University of Florida, 1968.

4. Davis, Frederick B., *Educational Measurements and Their Interpretation.* Belmont, Calif.: Wadsworth Press, 1964.

5. Davis, Frederick B., "A Comparison of Psychometric Models Used in Measuring Change," pp. 134–40 in *Investigations Relating to Mature Reading,* Frank P. Greene, editor, Twenty-first Yearbook National Reading Conference, 1972.

6. Diederich, Paul B., "Pitfalls in the Measurement of Gains in Achievement," *School Review,* 64 (February 1956), 59–63.

7. Eller, William, and Attea, Mary, "Three Diagnostic Reading Tests: Some Comparisons," in *Vistas in Reading,* J. Allen Figurel, editor, Proceedings International Reading Association, 11, Part 1 (1966), 562–66.

8. Gustafson, Richard A., "Factor Analyzing the Iowa Tests of Basic Skills," *Psychology in the Schools,* 7 (July 1970), 226-27.

9. Harris, C. W., *Problems in Measuring Change.* Madison: University of Wisconsin Press, 1963.

10. Holmes, Jack A., and Singer, Harry, *The Substrata Factor Theory: Substrata Factor Differences Underlying Reading Ability in Known Groups.* Washington, D. C.: U.S. Office of Education, 1961.

11. Hunt, Lyman C., Jr., "Do We Have Diagnostic Measures of Reading Comprehension?" *High School Journal,* 39 (October 1955), 44–48.

12. Jackson, Philip W., "Determining Expectations for Reading in Grades Seven Through Nine," pp. 28–31 in *Evaluation of Reading,* Helen M. Robinson, editor. Supplementary Educational Monographs No. 88. Chicago: University of Chicago Press, 1958.

13. Lennon, Roger T., "What Can Be Measured?" *Reading Teacher,* 15 (March 1962), 326–37.

14. Lowell, Robert E., "Problems in Identifying Reading Levels with Informal Reading Inventories," pp. 120–26 in *Reading Difficulties: Diagnosis, Correction and Remediation,* William K. Durr, editor. Newark, Del.: International Reading Association, 1970.

15. McCall, Rozanne, and McCall, R. B., "A Comparison of First Grade Reading Tests," *Illinois School Research,* 2 (1965), 32–37.

16. McCall, Rozanne, and McCall, R. B., "Comparative Validity of Five Reading Diagnostic Tests," *Journal of Educational Research,* 62 (1969), 329–33.

17. McDonald, Arthur S., "Some Pitfalls in Evaluating Progress in Reading Instruction," *Phi Delta Kappan,* 45 (April 1964), 336–38.

18. Neville, Donald, Pfost, Philip, and Dobbs, Virginia, "The Relationship between Test Anxiety and Silent Reading Gains," *American Educational Research Journal,* 4 (January 1967), 45–50.

19. Rankin, Earl F., Jr., and Dale, Lothar H., "Cloze Residual Gain—A Technique for Measuring Learning Through Reading," pp. 17–26 in *Psychology of Reading Behavior,* Eighteenth Yearbook National Conference, 1969.

20. Rankin, Earl F., Jr., and Tracy, R. J., "Residual Gain as a Measure of Individual Differences in Reading Improvement," *Journal of Reading,* 8 (March 1965), 224–33.

21. Robinson, H. Alan, "Reliability of Measures Related to Reading Success of Average, Disadvantaged and Advantaged Kindergarten Children," *Reading Teacher,* 20 (December 1966), 203–208.

22. Russell, David H., "Evaluation of Pupil Growth in and Through Reading," pp. 284–301 in *Reading in the Elementary School,* Forty-eighth Yearbook, Part II, National Society for the Study of Education.   Chicago: University of Chicago Press, 1949.
23. Sakamoto, T., and Takagi, K., "A Study of Disabled Readers," *Science of Reading* (Tokyo) 11 (1968), 1–15.
24. Tillman, Chester Earl, "Crude Gain vs. True Gain: Correlates of Gain in Reading after Remedial Tutoring," doctoral dissertation, University of Florida, 1969.
25. Tracy, Robert J., and Rankin, Earl F., Jr., "Methods of Computing and Evaluating Residual Gain Scores in the Reading Program," *Journal of Reading,* 10 (March 1967), 363–71.
26. Traxler, Arthur E., "Values and Limitations of Standardized Reading Tests," pp. 111–17 in *Evaluation of Reading,* Helen M. Robinson, editor.   Supplementary Educational Monographs No. 88.   Chicago: University of Chicago Press, 1958.
27. Tyler, Ralph W., "The Essential Aspects of Evaluation," pp. 4–9 in *Evaluation of Reading,* Helen M. Robinson, editor.   Supplementary Educational Monographs No. 88.   Chicago: University of Chicago Press, 1958.

Complementary References

Ahmann, J. Stanley, and Glock, Marvin D., *Evaluating Pupil Growth.*   Boston: Allyn and Bacon, 1970.

Austin, Mary, Bush, Clifford L., and Huebner, Mildred H., *Reading Evaluation.*   New York: Ronald Press, 1961.

DeBoer, Dorothy L., editor, *Reading Diagnosis and Evaluation,* Proceedings Thirteenth Annual Convention, Part 4.   Newark, Del.: International Reading Association, 1970.

Farr, Roger, *Reading: What Can Be Measured.*   Newark, Del.: International Reading Association, 1969.

Farr, Roger, *Measurement and Evaluation of Reading.*   New York: Harcourt Brace Jovanovich, 1970.

Farr, Roger, and Anastasiouw, Nicholas, *Tests of Reading Readiness and Achievement: A Review and Evaluation.*   Newark, Del.: International Reading Association, 1969.

Guide to Tests and Measuring Instruments for Reading, ED 022-973.   Bloomington, Indiana: ERIC-CRIER.

Johnson, Marjorie S., and Kress, Roy A., *Informal Reading Inventories,* Reading Aids Series.   Newark, Del.: International Reading Association, 1965.

Robinson, Helen M., editor, *Evaluation of Reading.*   Supplementary Educational Monographs No. 88.   Chicago: University of Chicago Press, 1958.

Smith, Henry P., and Dechant, Emerald V., *Psychology in Teaching Reading.*   Englewood Cliffs, N.J.: Prentice-Hall, 1961.

Tyler, Ralph W., editor, *Educational Evaluation: New Roles, New Means,* Sixty-eighth Yearbook, National Society for the Study of Education, Part II.   Chicago: University of Chicago Press, 1969.

In this chapter, the author offers a check list for test evaluation of more than a score of questions to be answered regarding a test being considered for use. As you read these check points over, ask yourself the following questions and frame answers to them.

1. Is it really essential to make as critical an evaluation of a test as this? Why?

2. Which points of evaluation had you never thought of when considering the use of a test? Do these seem important?

3. Do not expect to remember all the evaluation criteria mentioned. Rather, use the chapter as a guide when you do the Learning Project at the end of the chapter.

11
A Check List for Test Evaluation

STANDARDIZED TESTS ARE IN WIDE USE in our schools and will probably continue to be one of the most popular measuring instruments, despite their limitations. For these reasons, we offer a check list for test evaluation to aid in making intelligent selections among the great variety of tests offered. The check list proposes and explains twenty questions that are, in effect, addressed to the author and publisher. These questions are crucial to the evaluation of validity, reliability, and norms of the instrument.

Presumably, the answers should be found in the manual or other technical data supplied by the publisher. Insofar as possible, the questions demand objective information about the test, rather than reflecting the personal opinions of the person applying the check list. Since reading tests vary in their nature, as group versus individual, scaled versus unscaled, timed versus power, and the like, some judgment in applying the questions to be certain that they are relevant to the type of test is essential. When the questions are relevant, we believe that the answers must be supplied by the publisher to each prospective user of the test. This opinion is supported by official statements of the American Psychological Association regarding essential practices in commercial test production.

We evolved the check list as part of our training of reading teachers and clinicians. We have observed that its users are often amazed and frustrated to discover that many test authors apparently do not seem to think it necessary to supply these essential facts. Some test authors apparently do not wish to expose the possible defects in their creations, while others do not seem to know what data ought to be given to a prospective purchaser. We have found that use of this check list increases sophistication in test selection and use. It may be disturbing to find that a test one has been using is defective or questionable, but promoting this insight or sophistication is, after all, this writer's primary goal.

CHECK LIST

(Note: If the test does not have items in a scaled series, omit the starred questions.)

General Validity

1. What is the apparent purpose of the test? What reading skills does the test claim to measure?

Are these the skills that we want to measure? Are they significant objectives in our reading program? Each test author makes assumptions about the way reading is or should be taught, for example, from two-letter to three-letter to four-letter words; from regular to irregular words; or from picturable, meaningful words to others. Is the test relevant to our procedures? (8)

2. How are the reading skills measured?

Does the test measure reading skills in a manner similar to the way that we are teaching children to handle them? Different ways of measuring rate of reading, or of testing for comprehension yield widely varying measures of ability. For example, measuring rate or comprehension in a large body of material does not give the same estimate as does a measure in successive short paragraphs of varying difficulty (13). What exactly does this test try to measure?

3. Can test be administered easily by the average teacher?

If the directions, timing, scoring, and interpretation are not feasible for the average teacher, how, then, can this test be used properly? Unless special personnel are available to administer the test, there is no purpose in using it, when administration is complex. The most direct way of answering this question of validity of the test in the hands of the average teacher is to have her give a trial administration to a few pupils. Be wary of tests that demand almost impossible tasks of the teacher, such as timing in seconds or recording hesitations or phrasing in oral reading.

Content Validity

4. Are test items reasonably similar to those actually used in a class-room?

Were the selections or other test items drawn from sources resembling those that we ordinarily employ in reading situations? Test materials should be feasible in suitability of vocabulary, appeal, difficulty of instructions to children, and the simplicity of the opening items and the format (8). The content of the test, particularly of reading passages, should be relevant to the grade-level curriculum, not to strange or unfamiliar topics. The arrangement of the test should be readily understood by pupils. Any reading test is a rather artificial sampling of the pupil's reading behavior. One way of reducing this artificiality is by emulating classroom materials and procedures. If this element is lacking or weak, it is virtually impossible to utilize the scores of the test in classroom procedures.

Construct Validity

5. Is speed an important factor in the test? Or, can the average pupil at the lowest grade tested attempt at least 40–50 percent of the items?

6. Is length of each portion yielding a score reasonably adequate?

When time limits for a test are short, there is apt to be a large speed element in the score. Thus the test may not be sampling whatever it claims to measure but may function only as a test of the speed of reaction of the pupil. Total scores based on a number of short subtests may be reliable, but the part scores probably should be used for group comparisons rather than for estimates of the development of specific subskills for individual pupils.

Traxler suggests that for adequate reliability a three-minute test of rate is the minimum, and a five-minute test is much preferable (13). Other reading skills, such as comprehension of a content area or ability in recognizing main ideas, require even longer periods of testing for adequate sampling. Above the intermediate grades, we doubt that more than three–four major reading skills can be tested in a forty-minute period, if evaluations are to be meaningful and accurate enough for discrimination among individual pupils.

We also suggest that the time limit on the test should permit the average pupil, at the lowest grade level for which the test is offered, to complete 40–50 percent of the items. There is considerable evidence that a test in which the average pupil can do 40–50 percent of the items is much superior to harder tests. This criterion also tends to insure a more adequate sampling of the skill being tested and to prevent judgments based on a pupil's success with only a few test items. To apply this criterion, inspect the norms at the lowest grade level at which the test is supposed to be used to find how many items a child scoring at this level is expected to do correctly. Is this about 40–50 percent of the total number of items in the test or subtest? (Do not be confused by the fact that the test may offer norms for grade levels below where it is commonly administered, that is, first- or second-grade norms for a third-grade test. Ignore these extrapolated norms.)

7. Is there proof that part scores measure different abilities?

Test makers are prone to label parts of tests with logical-sounding titles but often fail to prove that a specific reading skill is really being measured. In the area of comprehension, for example, test makers have failed to prove the very existence of many of the skills they claim to measure (2, 5, 6). When the test author offers separate scores on various reading abilities, we expect him to show that these subtests actually do measure different aspects of the same skill or different reading skills.

This judgment may be made by comparing the reliability coefficient for each subtest with the coefficients of correlation with each other subtest, if the author gives a table of intercorrelation of the subtests. When the reliability for a test is .15 or .20 higher than its correlation with any other test, we may assume that this test is probably measuring something different from the other subtests. When the coefficient of intercorrelation is almost as great as the reliability coefficient, it implies that the two subtests resemble each other or overlap as much as two successive administrations of either one of them. Ideally, intercorrelations among subtests for which scores are reported should be low, that is, about .40 or .50, while reliability coefficients should probably be better than .80, but this is not always the case.

*8. Does the test adequately discriminate between grade levels by using a reasonable number of items to measure a year's growth, such as at least 15–20 percent of the total number of items?

At first glance, some tests appear to use a large number of items, thus giving the impression that their sampling of the reading behavior is quite comprehensive. Closer inspection of the norms for each grade level may reveal that many of these items do not actually function at the grade levels for which the test is offered. This criterion can be applied by inspecting the norms to see how many items are supposed to be performed correctly by pupils at successive grade levels. Obviously, the more items covering each year's growth, the more realistic is the sample of reading performance. Without any proof of its appropriateness, we suggest a rule of thumb that the number of items supposed to represent a year's development should be at least 15–20 percent of the total number of items. In a very brief test, even this criterion may be meaningless in proving the discriminative power of the test.

*9. What is the effective range of the test, that is, the points between which pupils can score 40 percent to that point where they score 85 percent correct?

Very high or very low scores on a test may imply that it is too easy or too difficult for the pupil. Only when the pupil can perform a reasonable proportion of the items can the test be considered as appropriate for evaluation of his abilities. We suggest that the teacher find that point in the norms at which the average pupil can do 40–50 percent of the items. This is also the lowest grade level at which the test should be administered. At the other extreme, a pupil who does more than 85 percent of the items has probably not been evaluated accurately. That point in the norms at which pupils do 85 percent or more of the items correctly represents the highest grade level at which the test score should be used. This effective range of the test from the 40 percent to 85 percent success level may or may not agree with the suggestions of the test author regarding the grade levels at which the test may be used. But administering the test only within this effective range does tend to insure a more accurate evaluation of pupils' abilities.

Concurrent Validity

10. How does this test compare with other available tests in the scores it yields and the skills it claims to evaluate?

Tests that purport to measure the same skills may yield very different grade scores, as emphasized in this chapter. Some tests consistently yield much higher reading scores than do others. Some tests that apparently measure the very same skills yield very different grade level estimates for the same pupils (3, 4, 10). Read the test manual to find the author's comparisons with other tests. How do the mean scores for this test compare with those for other tests? Are they about the same at each grade level?

Compare the way that each skill is measured with the same kind of test in other tests available to you. Which approach seems likely to give an estimate that is more relevant to classroom performances? What correlations between this test and other comparable instruments does the author offer? Are these correlations reasonable (about .50 to .60), or is this test approaching the measurement of reading in its own peculiar way?

Reliability

11. Is the reliability of the total test above .90, and part scores above .75?

The reliability coefficient of a test reflects the precision of the instrument and the consistency of performances on the test. How high should reliability be for practical purposes? This depends upon the purpose of the testing. Lower reliabilities, as those under .80, will be relatively satisfactory for comparing group or class averages or for school evaluation surveys. Reliability close to or above .90 is essential for individual evaluation, or diagnosis or other important decisions (11).

Authors use different types of coefficients and report these in varying forms, for example, over one or several grade levels. For a single grade, reliability coefficients should be at least in the high .70s or low .80s for any study of individuals. For a several-grade range, reliability should be in the high .80s or above .90 for the same purpose.

Tyler (14) reminds us that reliability is an estimate of the breadth or adequacy of the sample of reading behavior.   Reliability is not an indication of the representativeness or the validity of the sample in testing true reading behaviors.   All that reliability tells us is the consistency with which the instrument measures whatever it is measuring.

Paul B. Diederich* has been most kind in responding to my request for suggestions on how a teacher can estimate the reliability of a test in her own class.   His letter is so clear on this point that, with his permission, we will quote it in its entirety.

> There is no good way to estimate in advance the reliability of the sort of reading test you describe.   Even if a single figure for reliability is given by the publisher, it is wise to distrust it.   Such figures are usually based on the administration of the test to large groups for the purpose of establishing norms, and such groups are likely to include a much wider range in reading ability than one would find in any one class.   The tests produced under the direction of Professor E. F. Lindquist at the University of Iowa usually report a range of reliabilities for groups of class size.   These can be trusted, but one still does not know which of these reliabilities applies to the group of students one has tested.   That depends primarily on the spread of reading ability within this group: i.e., the standard deviation of their scores.   A large standard deviation results in high reliability, since scores on a second test of the same sort would have to shift considerably in order to change the relative position of very many students.   Conversely, a small standard deviation results in low reliability, since slight changes in scores would alter the position of a good many students.   One has to bear in mind the basic meaning of the term *reliability* as applied to test scores.   It is an estimate of how close you would come to getting the same score for each pupil if you measured the same group again.   In more technical terms, it is an estimate of the *correlation* you would find between their present scores and their scores on a second test of the same kind.
>
> Consequently you have to wait until you have scores for any given class or group before you can determine the reliability of the test *for them*.   Then you should make a distribution of their *raw scores* (not grade-equivalent scores): i.e., the number of items answered correctly.   Just list all possible scores from high to low and put a tally (/) after each score for each pupil who made it.   Next, draw a line under the *top fifth* of scores and over the *bottom fifth*—both rounded to the nearest whole number.   For example, if you have 36 pupils, a fifth of this number will be 7 pupils.   But suppose the top 10 scores are the following: 42, 40, 38, 37, 36, 35, 34, 34, 34, 34.   I have underlined the top 7 scores ending with 34, and it does not matter that the next three scores are also 34; all you need is the sum of the top 7: i.e., 262.   Then suppose the sum of the bottom 7 is 92.   To get the standard deviation, subtract the bottom fifth from the top fifth (262 − 92 = 170), multiply this

---

*Personal correspondence from Paul B. Diederich, October 10, 1973.   Quoted with permission of the author.

number by 1.8 (170 × 1.8 = 306.0), and divide by the number of students (306 divided by 36 = 8.5, the standard deviation).

In an article by Darrell L. Sabers and Richard D. Klausmeier, "Accuracy of Short-Cut Estimates for Standard Deviation," *Journal of Education Measurement*, 8, 4 (Winter 1971), pp. 335–339, this formula proved most accurate:

Standard deviation equals

$$\frac{1.8 \text{ (Sum of top 5th of scores minus sum of bottom 5th)}}{\text{Number of Students}}$$

As you can tell from the foregoing illustration, this takes only a couple of minutes after you have the distribution of raw scores, which you ought to prepare anyway. It is easier than computing the average, since you do not have to add all the scores but only the top fifth and the bottom fifth—usually quite a small number.

Then you are in a position to compute the reliability of the test *for this group* by the Kuder-Richardson Formula 21. You may see this formula written in different ways, but the simplest way—accurate enough for this purpose—is the following:

Reliability equals

$$\text{ONE minus } \frac{\text{Mean times (number of items minus the Mean)}}{\text{Number of items times standard deviation squared}}$$

If you prefer letters to words, the formula is:

$$r_{xx} = 1 - \frac{M(n-M)}{n\,s^2} \quad \text{(in which M = Mean; n = number of items; s = standard deviation)}$$

I often have to remind my students that the most common error in applying this formula is to forget to subtract the fraction from ONE, because you get so involved in computing the fraction that, when you finally get it, you take it to be the reliability. What should alert you to the mistake is that it usually turns out to be a fairly small number like .22. If that were really the reliability, it would be terrible; no publisher could get away with publishing a reading test with a reliability that low. But it is not; the reliability is ONE minus this fraction, or .78. This is still not very high; in a controlled experiment one would want a much longer test with a reliability in the neighborhood of .90; but it is a realistic estimate of the reliability you are likely to find for a reading test that can be administered in 35 or 40 minutes. It is only fair to add, however, that this formula yields a *minimal* estimate of reliability, and it is only a rough estimate, but accurate as one can get without the elaborate computations.

To remind my students about subtracting from ONE, I ask them to think of the formula in these terms:

Reliability = ONE minus ERROR (random variation)

The fraction is then a quick way to compute the ERROR—the amount of random variation in the scores—and the reliability is ONE minus this amount. Incidentally, unless the distribution of raw scores looks odd, it makes very little difference if one uses the median (the middle score) instead of the mean in the formula, and it saves a lot of time.

P.S. Better not use my crude estimate of .15n for S.D. for the tests you describe.

For those readers who feel uncomfortable in handling the Kuder-Richardson Formula, as Dr. Diederich has suggested, a simpler approach to finding the reliability of a test in a particular population is possible. After having found the standard deviation of the raw scores for a group, use Tables 11-1 and 11-2 to estimate the reliability of the test in question.

Table 11-1 refers to easy tests in which the average raw score of your group is between 70 and 90 percent of the total items. This average score is found by simply adding all the scores and dividing by the total number of pupils. If the standard deviation of the scores that you found is about 10 percent of the items, read the estimate of reliability in the first line, under the column indicating the total number of items in the test. For example, if your standard deviation for an easy test is twelve items, and the test has forty items in all, the estimate of reliability is .62. Such a test would be reliable enough perhaps for comparing your average score with that from another class. But it would not be sufficient to make individual comparisons among children within your group, or useful in identifying their individual instructional needs. As we suggested above, general tests of overall reading ability, or tests of subskills should have reliabilities above .70 in your group, if you are to make comparisons among individuals. Moreover, even when the reliability of the test in your group is apparently sufficient to make comparisons among individuals, this comparison must consider the standard error of measurement inherent in the test, as we shall point out later.

12. Are reliability coefficients inflated by the speed factor?

The apparent reliability of a test can be spuriously inflated if the instrument is very brief or if the time allowed is very short. When the time interval is only a few minutes, a human being cannot vary greatly from one performance to the next. Hence the test appears to be very con-

TABLE 11-1   APPROXIMATE RELIABILITY OF EASY TESTS
(AVERAGE SCORE 70 PERCENT TO 90 PERCENT CORRECT)*

NUMBER OF ITEMS	(n)	20	30	40	50	60	70	80	90	100
If S.D. is .10n		.21	.48	.62	.69	.75	.78	.81	.83	.85
If S.D. is .15n		.68	.80	.84	.88	.90	.91	.92	.93	.94
If S.D. is .20n		.84	.90	.92	.94	.95	.96	.96	.97	.97

*From *Short-Cut Statistics for Teacher-Made Tests.* Copyright © 1960, 1964 by Educational Testing Service. All rights reserved. Reprinted by permission.

TABLE 11–2   APPROXIMATE RELIABILITY OF HARD TESTS
(AVERAGE SCORE 50 PERCENT TO 70 PERCENT CORRECT).*

NUMBER OF ITEMS	(n)	20	30	40	50	60	70	80	90	100
If S.D. is .10n		—	.21	.41	.53	.61	.66	.71	.74	.77
If S.D. is .15n		.49	.67	.75	.80	.84	.86	.88	.89	.90
If S.D. is .20n		.74	.83	.87	.90	.92	.93	.94	.94	.95

sistent (reliable) in some types of reliability coefficients (split-half or Kuder-Richardson). When items range from easy to hard, and the test extends beyond just a few minutes, the reliability estimate is not apt to be so false (11).

13. What is the standard error of measurement for the total score? for part scores?

Any test score represents an estimate of ability, not the absolute quantity or degree of skill possessed by the pupil. Repeated tests would vary above and below the first test score because of human variability and the lack of complete reliability of any test. This range of scores that would be found is indicated by the standard error of measurement. If this error is six months, the true or real score for the pupil is probably somewhere between a point six months above, and another six months below, the test score found. The chances are two to one that the true score is within this one-year range. To illustrate, a grade score of 4.6 on a test with a standard error of six months means that the pupil's performance is really somewhere between 4.0 and 5.2. It is not precisely at 4.6, as many teachers assume.

This standard error of measurement also becomes very significant when comparing subtest scores of an individual or one pupil's scores with those of another. Only when the two scores are two or more standard errors apart can we be fairly certain that there is a real difference between them. To reuse the earlier illustration, scores on that hypothetical test would have to be more than twelve months apart before we could be reasonably sure that there was a real difference between the two pupils or the pupil's performance on two parts of the test. Read the test manual to find the standard error of measurement, and use it in correcting your estimates of pupils' abilities and in making pupil comparisons.

When the author does not give the standard error of the score on his test, it may be possible to estimate it by means of Table 11–3. The standard error for a raw score varies with the size of the score and the length of the test.

TABLE 11–3   ESTIMATE OF STANDARD ERROR OF A RAW TEST SCORE*

The standard error is:
  0 when score is 0 or perfect
  1   a) when score is 1 or 2
        b) within 2 points of perfect score
  2   a) on tests of less than 24 items
      or b) when score is 3–7
      or c) within 3–7 points of a perfect score
  3   a) on tests of 24–37 items
      or b) when score is 8–15
      or c) with 8–15 points of a perfect score
  4 on tests of 38–89 items
  5 on tests of 90–109 items
  6 on tests of 110–129 items
  7 on tests of 130–150 items

*From *Short-Cut Statistics for Teacher-Made Tests.* Copyright © 1960, 1964 by Educational Testing Service. All rights reserved. Reprinted by permission.

When the raw score is very low or nearly perfect, the standard error is very small; and, as the test increases in length, the error tends to increase, as may be seen in the table. The error is expressed here in raw score, that is, the number of test items, not months or grade scores.

To translate the standard error into months of grade score, we need to look at the table of norms for a test in order to determine how many months of change is represented by each raw score. For example, a seventh grader's raw score is 18 on the 36-item Speed and Accuracy test of the Gates-MacGinitie Survey Reading Test.* According to our table, the standard error for such a score is 3 items, or, in other words, the true score is somewhere between 15 and 21. According to the authors' norms, our pupil has scored somewhere between 7.7 and 12.3 in grade level. (In this test, 3 points in raw score is equal to 23 months, at this level of performance.) We cannot assume that the pupil's score is precisely 10.0, as the authors' norms tell us, in speed of reading. If we use grade scores for comparisons between pupils, the difference would have to be six points in raw score or *46 months* to conclude that one pupil was different in speed from another, in this test.

The authors tell us that this test was standardized in grades seven to nine only. Since no tenth graders were tested, our pupil's score of 10.0 is hardly meaningful or real, in any event, except perhaps to indicate that his reading speed may be somewhat better than a ninth grade level.

Gates-MacGinitie Reading Test, Survey E (New York: Teachers College Press, Columbia University, 1965).

Norms

14. For what grades is the test offered? For what grades are norms offered?

In many current tests, norms are offered for scores at grade levels above or below those grades at which the test is supposed to be administered; that is, norms for the first and second grade are included in the manual for a third-grade test.   Unfortunately for their realism, these extrapolated or hypothetical norms are obtained by mathematical or graphic means, often not by actual testing of live pupils.   Seldom is a test constructed for some particular grades actually tried out on pupils above or below these levels.   Thus norms offered for these levels represent what pupils *might* do on the test, not what their actual performances are.   In other words, unless the author's data show that the test was standardized in grades above and below those for which he offers the test, norms for those other grades are, in our opinion, meaningless.   Read the author's description of the standardization population and thus determine for which grade level pupils his norms are meaningful.

15. Are norms given for part scores?

Some test makers are prone to divide their tests into part scores with impressive titles.   The titles imply that a number of important skills are being measured.   Yet, in some instances, the authors give no norms for these subscores or, even more realistically, warn the user against too much dependence upon their results because of brevity or lack of reliability.   If the author himself gives no norms to interpret a subtest score or warns against serious consideration of the score, the user certainly can decide for himself whether to bother giving a test for which there are no means of interpretation.

*16. Are various types of norms available, that is, grade scores, percentiles, or scaled scores?

Each of the common types of norms has definite limitations (12).   Grade scores are extrapolated from one grade level to the next and do not really represent month-by-month progress.   In all probability, most of the gain represented by monthly grade scores occurs in the first half of the school year, or appears as the initial spurt in learning under a new approach or method. For example, many of the recent experiments in reading discover that results are inconclusive because most of the gains occur in the first few months, regardless of the methods used (4).   In some tests, the educational ages and grade equivalents are in disagreement with current age-grade relationships in the schools.   The ages assigned to certain grade levels do not reflect the actual ages in current schools (7).

Percentiles do not have the same meaning at all levels.   For example, growth from the 1st to the 5th percentile represents as much gain as growth from the 50th to the 75th percentile. Percentiles cannot be combined arithmetically, as in finding an average. The percentile represents a ranking of the pupil in a certain population, not, as sometimes interpreted, the proportion of right answers that he has achieved.

Scaled scores and stanines permit more accurate comparisons and can be combined in various ways for statistical interpretations. But they are derived by complex processes and are not widely understood by classroom teachers. Thus, ideally, the test publisher should offer several types of norms so that the user may interpret the results with as much sophistication as he can muster.

17. Are norms based on broad sampling, that is, at least several states with populations of several hundred per grade?

Most present-day reading tests are based on an adequately broad or stratified sampling of the population. Their samples are probably large enough and of sufficient diversity to avoid reflecting provincial or narrow segments of the population that differ markedly from prospective users of the test. While stratified or specific types of norms are more useful than national norms in our opinion, both types should be reasonably large and diverse and accompanied by adequate descriptions of the population used (7).

· If the first thousand or two pupils in the standardization population represent a good cross-section of the general population, it does not add anything to the value of the test to add larger numbers. Some test publishers continue to collect scores (without changing the original norms) until the numbers become very impressive, they hope. These figures simply prove that sale of the test is successful, not that it is necessarily a good test.

18. Are equivalent alternate forms available? Are there any data regarding the practice effect of repeated testing?

Practically all group reading tests, and some individual tests, offer alternate forms for retest purposes. But, very few test makers give any information regarding the amount of gain in repeated testing that is due to the practice effect. Undoubtedly a practice effect is present in retesting, even with an alternate form. Repeated testings at short intervals, as it may occur in remedial teaching, is particularly affected by this factor. Semiannual or quarterly testing programs probably contribute to the pupils' sophistication with tests and may eventually produce cumulative gains that give a spurious estimate of ability. This information could easily be supplied by test publishers and would aid in more accurate interpretation of gains in scores. A clue to the effect of practice is given in a comparison of the means in a test-retest reliability study, if this is available.

19. Are various norms available, that is, geographical, sex, rural and urban, and various types of schools?

Interpretation of test scores for a certain group of pupils can be meaningful solely when the norms are based on a similar population (7). Schools and children differ in reading abilities according to socioeconomic status, geography, sex, and size and type of school. We cannot compare one type of pupil or school with another unless there are basic similarities of age, sex, opportunities for schooling, socioeconomic background, and other factors. As we have pointed out before, general or national norms are useful only in certain limited circumstances. When we are ignoring the characteristics of the learners or the differences in learning conditions, as in comparing one whole school system with another, we may find a use for general population norms. But evaluation of a single individual or class with an imaginary national average is hardly meaningful. Some writers insist upon separate norms for pupils of varying intelligence—as the retarded, normal, and gifted—because of the fact that intelligence is a significant variable in reading measures, particularly those of comprehension from the intermediate grades upward. Other critics, with some justification, seek separate norms for children of varying ethnic backgrounds and differing socioeconomic status, although this need can be met by assembling local norms. But offering these differentiated norms is not yet a widespread practice among test publishers.

20. When was the test copyrighted?

An aspect of norms that must be considered is implied in the copyright date of the test. Any group of norms reflects the performances of school children of a particular date and does not represent permanent standards applicable to different generations. Changes in the objectives of the reading program, changes in instructional practices, and, even more significantly, changes in society, such as the exposure of children to television, the mobility of the American family, the migration of rural population to urban areas, the gradual increase in the educational level achieved by the average American parent—all these factors have tended to alter the reading performances of school children over periods of time.

To illustrate specifically the inadequacy of reading test norms over a long period of time, we need only to review some of the comparative studies of achievement of pupils of different generations. In one collection of these studies by Spache,* it was demonstrated that, using the same tests, children of recent times read with less oral accuracy but with greater silent comprehension in keeping with the shift in emphasis in instruction during the past few

---

*George D. Spache, *Are We Teaching Reading?* (Gainesville: School of Education, University of Florida, 1956).

decades. In other reports, revisions of popular tests such as the Gates series indicated major changes in the reading and readiness abilities of American pupils between the date of original and revised versions. A recent British study by Bookbinder* of the Schonell Word Recognition Test demonstrates the inappropriateness for today's children of the primary norms of this test standardized almost thirty years ago.

Publishers, too, are conscious of the implications of the copyright dates of their tests, and they frequently try to update these. Sometimes revisions of tests involve actual rewriting of the items and restandardization. Sometimes only the titles of the tests are changed, or the manual of directions is rewritten, or a few more subtests are added without any actual rewriting of the content or restandardization of the norms. In all probability, when the interval between test revisions is a decade or less, restandardization of norms is not essential. But intervals of several decades probably do demand renorming, certainly of achievement tests, if not even of some measures of physical behavior or activities. For all these reasons, it will be essential for the purchaser of a newly revised test to make a detailed comparison of the contents and norms of the two versions to determine the current validity of the test and its norms.

It should not be necessary to point out that norms for a test standard-ized in another English-speaking country are not applicable to American school children. There are too many differences among the British, Canadian, Australian, and American societies and school systems to permit the easy interchange of measuring instruments without restandardization for each national population. Similarly, an American test cannot simply be translated into an Indian language or Spanish—as in testing our bilingual children—and be expected to function with validity in both language populations. Learning and even physical development vary because of climatic, racial, and social conditions sufficiently to make the use of a single standard of performance impossible. Besides, one cannot assume that a concept translated from one language to another is of similar difficulty to the readers of each language, unless their cultures are very similar, an improbable condition.

LEARNING PROJECT

The values of this Check List for Test Evaluation can be realized best, in our opinion, by the experience of applying it to a familiar or favorite test.
   1. Choose a test that you have used or are otherwise familiar with and apply the

---

*G. E. Bookbinder, "Variations in Reading Test Norms," *Educational Research,* 12 (1970), 99–105.

Check List for Test Evaluation. Using the Manual of Directions, the test itself, and any technical report supplied by the test publisher, seek the answers to the evaluative questions. Make written notes or comments regarding each of the twenty areas.

2. Bring your notes on a test evaluation, the Manual, test, and so on, to class. As you display and describe the test to the group, share your comments on its strengths and weaknesses.

3. Using the chapter "Interpreting Individual Diagnostic Reading Tests," in *Diagnosing and Correcting Reading Disabilities,* as a resource, try to find tests that exemplify the common flaws in test construction and standardization mentioned in the check list. You will probably not find all these flaws in any test critiqued in that chapter but will need to use several tests to illustrate your points.

4. The evaluative questions of the check list are not of equal importance or significance. A published test may exhibit several weaknesses and yet be reasonably serviceable for many situations. Illustrate this point in discussion with your group by defending the use of a particular test with relatively minor flaws.

5. If you feel that you have had sufficient experience with a certain test, prepare yourself to demonstrate how the test might be employed for diagnostic purposes and information beyond those implicit in the test and its scores. In effect, we are asking you to share your intuitions, hunches, and clinical observations about the real meaning of this test and its interpretation.

REFERENCES

1. Benz, D. A., and Rosemier, R. A., "Concurrent Validity of the Gates Level of Comprehension Test and the Bond-Clymer-Hoyt Reading Diagnostic Tests," *Educational and Psychological Measurement,* 26 (1966), 1057–62.
2. Davis, Frederick B., "Research in Comprehension in Reading," *Reading Research Quarterly,* 3 (Summer 1968), 499–543.
3. Eller, William, and Attea, Mary, "Three Diagnostic Reading Tests: Some Comparisons," in *Vistas in Reading,* J. Allen Figurel, editor. Proceedings International Reading Association, 11, Part 1, 1966, 562–66.
4. Emans, R., Urbas, R., and Dummet, M., "The Meaning of Reading Tests," *Journal of Reading,* 9 (May 1966), 406–409.
5. Gustafson, Richard A., "Factor Analyzing the Iowa Tests of Basic Skills," *Psychology in the Schools,* 7 (July 1970), 226–27.
6. Hunt, Lyman C., Jr., "Do We Have Diagnostic Measures of Reading Comprehension? *High School Journal,* 39 (October 1955), 44–48.
7. Lewerenz, Alfred S., "Needed Improvements in Test Norms," *California Journal of Educational Research,* 7 (January 1956), 2–5.
8. Mary Julitta, Sister, "Selection and Use of Standardized Reading Tests in Kindergar-

ten Through Grade Three," pp. 118–22 in *Evaluation of Reading,* Helen M. Robinson, editor.   Supplementary Educational Monographs No. 88.   Chicago: University of Chicago Press, 1958.

9. Morris, Ronald, *Success and Failure in Learning to Read.*   London: Oldbourne, 1963.

10. Murray, Carol-Faith, and Karlsen, Bjorn, "A Concurrent Validity Study of the Silent Reading Tests and the Gates Reading Diagnostic Tests," *Reading Teacher,* 13 (April 1960), 293–94, 296.

11. Psychological Corporation, "Reliability and Confidence," *Test Service Bulletin,* No. 44 (May 1952).

12. Psychological Corporation, "Methods of Expressing Test Scores," *Test Service Bulletin,* No. 48 (January 1955).

13. Traxler, Arthur E., "Values and Limitations of Standardized Reading Tests," pp. 111–17 in *Evaluation of Reading,* Helen M. Robinson, editor.   Supplementary Educational Monographs No. 88.   Chicago: University of Chicago Press, 1958.

14. Tyler, Ralph W., "The Essential Aspects of Evaluation," pp. 4–9 in *Evaluation of Reading,* Helen M. Robinson, editor.   Supplementary Educational Monographs No. 88.   Chicago: University of Chicago Press, 1958.

You may have been introduced to the use of an Informal Reading Inventory in some other course in reading. If so, this chapter will give an entirely new look at this popular practice. Through a brief review of the history, the development of the scoring criteria, and the manner of constructing and applying this device, the author offers a background for his critical evaluation.

Guide your reading by answering these questions as you go through the chapter.

1. Do you accept most of the author's criticisms of the I.R.I.? With which ones do you disagree? Which need more proof, in your opinion?

2. Are worksample or open-book tests a viable alternative to the I.R.I., as in measurement of such areas as contextual clues, summarizing, outlining, and using reference tools?

3. What other alternatives to the presently popular I.R.I. does the author offer? Are these adequate in revealing the diagnostic facts sought in such testing?

12
Informal Testing and Evaluation

I T IS APPARENT that some objectives of the reading program and many reading behaviors cannot be evaluated by any known tests. For example, teacher observation is essential for estimating pupil interest in reading assignments, resistance to distractibility, enthusiasm for reading, speed in assigned tasks, and dependence upon listening as a substitute for reading. Similarly, a great deal of information regarding pupil attitudes, working habits, reading skills, and needs in realistic reading situations can be obtained only through informal approaches to evaluation.

Informal evaluation is commonly used in four aspects of reading: interests, skills, effects of reading, and estimation of capacity for growth. Observations can be made of the pupil's vocabulary usage, comprehension, and interpretation as exhibited in discussion; of his choice and use of library resources; and of recreational and other applications of reading. Check lists are frequently used to record details of reading behaviors as in error tendencies in oral reading. Pupil-interest check lists have been made available by a number of writers (2, 16, 17).

Informal tests of silent and oral reading, of listening comprehension, of study skills, and of reading in content fields are finding increasing use in modern classrooms. Helpful models are offered by Anderson and Lindquist (1) and by Gray (13). More effective informal tests can be constructed if teachers examine sample tests and test items with the aid of textbooks on measurement (10), read the critical reviews of standardized tests collected by Buros (7), and become familiar with some of the principles of test construction, such as those presented by Wood (36).

Letton suggests that use of a parental interview to secure information regarding the books or magazines that children ask for or buy; the child's use of his leisure time; and whether he reads in private or engages in trading books, magazines, or comic books (24). Interesting reflections of parent-child relationships may be secured by inquiring about parental attitudes toward the child's use of books, their knowledge of his current reading, and whether there is an interchange of ideas about what the parent or child is reading. This is another way of exploring the subtle influence of family attitudes toward reading as a pastime and toward the child's reading progress.

Many other informal evaluation approaches will be used by the flexible teacher. Boning and Boning suggest the use of the sentence completion technique for investigating interests and attitude toward reading (6). Sociometric tests, perhaps using the Guess Who technics, and the child's personal writing under such titles as "The Story of My Life," "The Biggest Event in My Life," and "If I Had Three Wishes," help to reveal in greater depth the interplay of the child's personality and his reading (14, 30).

Capacity or potential for growth should be evaluated by many approaches. As several writers have pointed out, no simple comparison of mental age and reading test score gives an adequate picture of potential (34, 35). Jackson speaks in the same vein in emphasizing that capacity cannot be compared with achievement. Capacity is an inference rather than an entity. It is something that the student may realize rather than an easily measured trait that he now "has" (18). In our opinion, potential for growth differs from one reading skill to another, from one desired outcome of the program to another.

We have used measures of auditory comprehension to estimate potential reading level. A test of auditory comprehension measures, in a sense, the level of language complexity (the level of reading materials?) that the pupil can comprehend auditorily. As such, it probably measures the language usage and education of his family as much as anything else. But these are only minor factors in determining a pupil's ultimate or possible achievement (29). This approach yields a convenient figure but one that frequently underestimates the future. Intensive remedial work, modification of teaching method, or any major adjustment to an individual difference further stimulates the dynamic nature of capacity as estimated by listening or auditory comprehension. For these reasons, evaluation of potential must be based on numerous observations and estimates, including many of those mentioned above in Chapter 6.

LIMITATIONS

This discussion of informal methods of evaluation has dealt more with their types and advantages than with their limitations. Informal methods may well lack the qualities of objectivity, reliability, and careful construction claimed for standardized tests. But, to our way of thinking, the major pitfall in the use of informal measures lies in the dangerous assumption that they are final, complete, or highly accurate. No single instrument, informal or standardized, possesses these virtues. Each is but a type of observation or sample of behavior that is meaningful only in the context of repeated samples. Each adds a bit of information about the child's reading behaviors, his progress, or his future. If many of the informal instruments we have mentioned are used repeatedly and the results are thoughtfully analyzed, these measures can improve immeasurably the process of evaluation.

THE INFORMAL READING INVENTORY

The most widespread example of the use of informal approaches to measurement is the Informal Reading Inventory. Hundreds of teachers construct and use this instrument, and even the International Reading Association has furthered this practice with a bulletin to instruct teachers in the construction and use of the I.R.I., as it is called (19). Many other current books* are offering their own homemade versions of these inventories.

What is an I.R.I.? A good description is offered by Austin and Huebner (2) and by Johnson and Kress (19), paraphrased as follows:

To construct an I.R.I.—

1. Choose a word list from a basal reader, ten to fifteen words at primary, twenty to twenty-five at upper levels. Have child read this list. Failure to recognize one or more words at a grade level indicates the need for instructional materials below that level.

2. Choose passages from each level of a basal series not familiar to the child. Use one selection for oral reading at sight. If needed, use other selection for silent. As he reads orally, record carefully the errors he makes. Ask five to ten questions that you have previously prepared.

If the child makes more than one word recognition error (counting only omissions, insertions, substitutions, and requests for help) in twenty words of oral reading, the selection is too difficult for him, and he will need instructional materials below that level.

The commonest standards used in the I.R.I. are these:†

Independent Level—Less than one error per 100 running words
Not less than 90 percent comprehension
No finger pointing, head movements, or poor phrasing
Instructional Level—No more than one error per twenty words, that is, 95 percent accuracy in word recognition
At least 75 percent comprehension
No symptoms of difficulty

---

*Informal Evaluation of Oral Reading Grade Level (New York: Book-Lab, Inc. 1973); Margaret LaPray, Teaching Children to Become Independent Readers (New York: Center for Applied Research in Education, 1972); Thomas C. Potter and Gwenneth Rae, Informal Reading Diagnosis: A Practical Guide for the Classroom Teacher (Englewood Cliffs, N.J.: Prentice-Hall, 1973).

†As Powell and Dunkeld (32) have pointed out, these standards, especially for Instructional Level, are as much as 15 percent lower in percentage of errors or comprehension among some writers, usually without any supporting data on actual performances of children.

Frustration Level—More than ten errors per 100 words
Comprehension 50 percent or less
Many symptoms of stress
Hearing Comprehension Level—Comprehension of 75 percent of questions
based on selection read to him

      The arguments offered in support of the I.R.I. are numerous: standardized tests overestimate the child's instructional level (22); the I.R.I. is the most realistic measure of the child's probable classroom performances; the I.R.I. tests children on materials of known level, not a random sample of paragraphs; the I.R.I. determines the pupil's specific strengths and weaknesses and directs the teacher's instructional efforts. Other supportive statements point out that any teacher can construct an I.R.I.; moreover, it is easy to administer and to score, and its cost is low.

History of the I.R.I.

      Before contrasting the contrary arguments of those who do not recommend the I.R.I., a quick review of its history would be appropriate. Beldin (4) and Kender (22) have reviewed the development of the I.R.I. in great detail. The original study was that of Kilgallon, a student of Emmett A. Betts, who analyzed the reading of forty-one children in an effort to set up criteria for scoring such an instrument (23). Strangely enough, he established a priori criteria for accuracy in word recognition and comprehension, judging children as reading adequately if they met these standards; thus, in his opinion, reconfirming his criteria. His forty-one children read with only 93 percent accuracy in word recognition, but he decided that 95 percent was a better standard. Another interesting fact about this study, upon which most I.R.I. standards for instructional level are based, is pointed out by Powell (32). Kilgallon's testing procedure was to have the children read a passage *first silently and then orally!* Thus the standard for instructional level was based on a procedure different from that now employed in the average I.R.I. inventory, in which word recognition accuracy is based on a single oral reading at sight. However, Kilgallon's mentor, Emmett A. Betts, apparently accepted the study at face value; added his own definitions of independent, frustration and hearing comprehension levels; and presented this total concept of the I.R.I. in his textbook in 1946 (5).

      J. Louis Cooper (8) approached the establishment of criteria for an I.R.I. more objectively by testing about 1,000 children in the first six grades. His pupils were selected for their reading adequacy in terms of their gains on a silent reading standardized test. Presumably only those showing at least average gain in silent reading comprehension were tested in oral reading of selected basal reader passages at sight. There is the questionable assumption here that silent reading comprehension is synonymous with oral reading accuracy, an assumption that correlational studies of the overlap of these two different reading performances does not really support. Only at very primary reading levels are these two reading skills highly similar for the average pupil, and this similarity rapidly diminishes through the grade levels. It may be that this questionable selection procedure accounts for Cooper's very high standards of 98 percent in primary and 96 percent in intermediate grades in accuracy of reading orally at sight. Or it is possible that the basal reader passages used in the testing were very easy for the children, since no objective evaluation of their actual difficulty was attempted. Another possible explanation for Cooper's data is his acceptance of only 70 percent in comprehension at primary levels and 60 percent for intermediate pupils, standards that are obviously lower than most users of I.R.I.'s accept.

Most reading authorities agree upon these historical facts, accepting some of the arguments offered in support of the I.R.I., but at this point agreement ends. For the convenience of the reader, we have tried to tabulate and contrast the pros and cons, in Table 12–1.

To our knowledge, there is only one other study testing the validity of the I.R.I. standards, that by Powell and Dunkeld (32). Using 70 percent comprehension as a minimum and tabulating the errors children made when reading selections with at least this degree of comprehension, Powell found standards for oral reading that differ dramatically from those proposed by Kilgallon, Betts, or Cooper, or by most reading authorities who have imitated the early studies. He found 85 percent in word recognition accuracy in grades one and two; 91 percent in three to five, and 94 percent in grade six. Some critics have objected to Powell's use of comprehension as a basic criterion for selecting instructional materials (4). But, in our opinion, Powell's assumption that pupils cannot be assigned to instructional materials solely on their word-naming ability and regardless of their comprehension is quite defensible.

Critique of the I.R.I.

Some of the other studies that seem to contradict the standards offered for the I.R.I. bear mention. When Sipay (33) scored an I.R.I. with Betts's standards, a comparison with three silent reading tests indicated that these latter were overestimating the instructional levels as given by the I.R.I. However, when

TABLE 12–1 PROS AND CONS OF THE I.R.I.

PRO	CON
Easy to construct by selecting samples from a basal series.	Only true if we assume that almost any basal at any level is similar to most others.
Selections from a basal are the most realistic testing material.	Not true for reading programs of a nonbasal nature, that is, individualized, language experience, and so on.
Selections from basal reflect exact grade levels.	Basal readers vary widely in reflecting the usual materials of a grade level (25). See our data on the readability levels of basals later in this chapter.
If child makes more than five word recognition errors per 100 words, the selection is too difficult for instructional purposes.	Apparently an arbitrary standard, particularly if applied regardless of pupil's comprehension (22).
Child should show at least 75 percent comprehension at instructional level.	True; in basal-type materials pupils are apt to show at least this degree of comprehension.
Independent reading level is that at which child reads with 99 percent oral accuracy and 90 percent comprehension.	If we follow these standards, pupils cannot use materials in his areas of interest, or resource books, as dictionaries, encyclopedias, and the like.
Frustration level is that at which child reads with 90 percent oral accuracy and less than 75 percent comprehension.	Is relatively meaningless. Once the instructional level is established, any level about this is frustrating (according to current practice)!
Almost any teacher can frame appropriate comprehension questions.	Typical teachers' questions demand only recall of detail. Besides, without item analysis, how do we know that questions discriminate between good and poor comprehenders?
The I.R.I. provides a body of diagnostic information to the teacher.	Unless she collects and analyzes 75–100 errors, no accurate diagnosis of skills is possible.
The average teacher can administer, score, and interpret the I.R.I.	Very doubtful (22). Studies of teacher skill in recording an oral reading test indicate that she does not even hear a sizeable proportion of the errors. Also assumes teacher has broad knowledge of reading skills and the reading process.

he lowered the I.R.I. standard to 90 percent oral accuracy, there was no difference from the scores of one of the standardized tests. If a direct comparison between silent and oral reading scores is significant, Sipay is implying that the current I.R.I. standards are too high. Daniel (9) also found that a lower standard for I.R.I. gave much better agreement with teacher grouping arrangements than did the standard proposed by Betts.

Lowell (25) attacks the current I.R.I. criteria and procedure as arbitrary and variable, emphasizing the fact that the same standards are applied whether the pupils read silently, then orally (as for Kilgallon) or only orally at sight (as in present I.R.I.'s). Guszak (15) questions whether there is any real practical difference between giving the pupil reading materials at his instructional or independent level. He should also have emphasized the point that there are no objective data whatsoever to support Betts's independent level concept. Millsap (28) cites several studies indicating that experienced classroom teachers cannot identify the frustration level even when supposedly following Betts's hypothetical definition of this performance.

In a study of the Spache Diagnostic Reading Scales, Eller and Attea (12) found that 53 percent of the pupils could comprehend successfully in passages of a more difficult level than they could read orally with acceptable accuracy. This particular testing instrument denies Betts's demand for higher word accuracy in independent reading, and the procedure permits children to attempt to read passages silently at a higher level after having failed the oral test in terms of word recognition errors. The Spache test assumes that many children can read silently at levels above their oral levels—in particular, those pupils above very primary levels—and still show acceptable comprehension. Eller and Attea's study seems to indicate that this is a correct assumption for many children. If Betts's standards were followed rigorously, many children would be denied access to reading materials of a higher grade level than their instructional performance, regardless of pupil interest or demonstrated comprehension.

Kasdon (20, 21) has explored the effects of following Kilgallon's original procedure of having the child read silently first and then orally, in contrast to the current I.R.I. pattern of oral reading at sight. Using two standardized oral reading tests, Kasdon found marked differences according to the procedure used in estimates of reading level, as we might expect. Even the pattern of oral errors varied when reading silent-then-oral from oral at sight. Only speed of oral reading did not vary from one type of testing to another. Obviously the original standards for the I.R.I. are not an appropriate basis for present-day procedures in using this type of inventory.

To support his criticism of the I.R.I. standards, Powell compared the word recognitions error ratios of five individual oral reading instruments with the data of Kilgallon, Cooper, and his own study. We have adapted his table to express this comparison in terms of the percentage of accuracy expected in oral reading according to the standards of these sources (see Table 12–2).

The variations in the standards for the five standardized tests might be accounted for by variations in scoring procedures. In some the grade level of oral reading is determined by a combination of time and error scores, as in the Gilmore, Gray, and Gates-McKillop. In others, the actual number of reading errors committed by the pupils tested determines the final score, as in the Spache Scales, which use the mean number of errors plus one standard deviation as norms. In the Durrell, an arbitrary standard permitting no more than seven errors per selection is used. Despite these variations in the bases of scoring, the length of passages, and the differences in difficulty inherent in selections from several content fields, the parallelism between the Spache, Durrell, and Gilmore standards is apparent. Yet none of these commercial tests nor Powell's data resemble the extremely high standards offered by Kilgallon, promoted by Betts, and currently used in I.R.I.

Moreover, static norms for all grade levels, as promulgated by Betts and the others, obviously do not agree with the manifest trend from a relatively low level of accuracy in the first two grades to higher level performances in the intermediate grades.

One final research study is relevant to the construction of the I.R.I. in Della-Piana's study of commercial oral reading tests (11). He finds that the

TABLE 12–2 ORAL READING ACCURACY STANDARDS

LEVEL	KILGALLON	COOPER	POWELL	SPACHE	DURRELL	GILMORE	GRAY	GATES-McKILLOP
1¹	95	98		75	67	67	86	
1²	95	98	85*(83)	80		80	88	
2¹	95	98	85	88	88	83	91	
2²	95	98	85 (88)	86	89			50
3¹	95	98	91	90		88	91	
3²	95	98	91	92	92			67
4	95	96	91 (92)	93	92	91	90	75
5	95	96	91 (92)	94	94	92	91	84
6	95	96	94	94	95	93	89	84
7	95			94	94	95	90	84
8	95			94		95	89	84

*In his table Powell cites error ratios for his study that do not agree with the standards he himself suggests, but he does not explain the reason for this variation. We have indicated the standards implied by his error ratios in parentheses when they differ from his recommendations.

profile of oral reading errors of a child differ significantly from one oral reading test to another. A reader varies in types and proportions of errors (as well as in the oral reading score he achieves) from one selection of passages to the next. This variation is present in carefully selected and standardized paragraphs, which have been tried out before publication on hundreds of children. How comparable, then, are two sets of reading selections drawn from two different basal series in two teacher-made I.R.I.'s? How valid is a diagnosis of errors made from the oral reading of any single set of selections in an I.R.I.?

Another naive assumption inherent in the usual directions to teachers in constructing an I.R.I. is the belief that selections chosen from basal readers at certain grade levels really represent typical reading materials for a level. When we compare basal readers by readability formula, we find wide variations in their actual difficulty. Thus there is no guarantee at all that a selection drawn, say from a basal 2^2 reader, actually is representative of that school level.

Several years ago the author submitted all basal readers on the market to evaluation by readability formulas. While these formulas are not an absolute standard, they are the most objective way available to estimate the actual grade level of a book. Table 12–3 summarizes the data from this comparative study of basal readers. Twenty basal series in common use in schools were sampled in this survey. Each book was analyzed for readability level at five to ten points scattered throughout the book. This is a sufficient sampling to yield very accurate estimates of the overall reading level of each book.

It is apparent that basals offered by different publishers for the same grade level vary greatly in their actual reading level. There is more than one full grade difference between the easiest and the hardest basal offered for the various levels of the first grade, almost two years difference among readers for the second, third and fourth grades, and about a year-and-one-half difference at the fifth and sixth grades. How, then, does the teacher know that the

TABLE 12–3 READING DIFFICULTY OF BASAL READERS

LEVEL	N	RANGE	MEDIAN
P.P.	44	1.1 to 2.2	1.5
Primer	18	1.2 to 2.9	1.8
First	22	1.8 to 3.1	2.0
Second	30	2.0 to 4.2	2.6
Third	32	2.5 to 4.8	3.4
Fourth	17	3.5 to 5.1	4.4
Fifth	16	4.5 to 5.9	4.9
Sixth	16	4.5 to 6.0	5.3

selections she chooses from the basals available to her truly represent grade levels in reading?

Let us illustrate further the difficulty in producing an Informal Reading Inventory in which the reading selections truly represent various grade levels. We have selected two such Inventories constructed by recognized experts in the field of reading, one that was offered in the original edition of the Sheldon Basic Readers; the other by Mary C. Austin and Clifford L. Bush, the authors of a fine book on reading evaluation.* We have many other such Inventories on file that we could have chosen to analyze. But these two were thought to have been constructed more carefully, in all probability, because of their authorship.

We submitted each reading selection in the Inventories to the Spache or Dale-Chall readability formula to estimate its readability level. While such formulas do not measure interest or the complexity of the concepts offered, they do rate selections in terms of vocabulary difficulty and sentence length, two characteristics that are usually controlled in the preparation of basal reading materials. Moreover, these readability formulas were devised from the analysis of these two traits as present in large samples of books commonly used in schools. In effect, the formulas do indicate how a reading selection resembles or differs from common instructional materials, at least in these two characteristics, in a completely objective manner.

The readability levels of the selections in these two Inventories are compared with the expected level of readability according to grade levels (see Table 12–4).

Assuming that the reading selections were intended to represent the grade levels as noted in the second column of the table, we find many irregularities in the hierarchal arrangement. Theoretically, at least, paragraphs at higher levels should yield higher readability estimates than for those that are supposed to be easier selections. But this arrangement breaks down in the first grade; in the second half of the second grade; in the second half of the third grade; in the fourth grade; and in the sequence from fifth to sixth grades in the Sheldon Inventory. Similarly, the readability estimates do not show normal progression in difficulty from the second preprimer to the primer; from the primer to the first grade; between samples in both halves of the second grade; and from second to third grade; and between the two halves of the third grade, in the Austin-Bush Inventory.

Another point of comparison may be drawn between the selections of

---

*Mary C. Austin, Clifford L. Bush, and Mildred H. Huebner, *Reading Evaluation* (New York: Ronald Press, 1961).

TABLE 12–4 ANALYSIS OF TWO INFORMAL READING INVENTORIES
READABILITY LEVEL

READING LEVEL	GRADE LEVEL	SHELDON BASIC	AUSTIN-BUSH
Preprimer	1.3	1.5	1.5
Preprimer	1.3	1.5	1.7
Primer	1.5	1.5	1.8
Primer	1.5	1.7	1.7
First	1.8	2.2	1.8
First	1.8	1.8	1.7
Second	2.3	2.2	2.3
Second	2.3	2.6	2.6
Second	2.8	3.2	2.0
Second	2.8	2.8	2.6
Third	3.3	3.3	2.8
Third	3.3	3.3	
Third	3.8	3.7	3.4
Third	3.8	2.9	
Fourth	4.5	4.8	
Fourth	4.5	4.5	
Fifth	5.5	5.6	
Fifth	5.5	5.5	
Sixth	6.5	4.6	
Sixth	6.5	4.8	

both Inventories which, we suppose, are intended to represent materials of equal difficulty. One may agree that differences as slight as two–three months between selections are not very significant, except perhaps during the first grade. There are six such small differences between the Inventories. But what of the four-month difference in the first half of the first grade reading level; the twelve-month difference in the second half of the second grade; and the five-month difference in the first half of the third grade? In the second half of the second grade a Sheldon selection, according to readability estimates, resembles a low third reader, while the parallel selection offered by Austin-Bush is easier than most beginning second-grade texts. Both selections differ from the expected level of difficulty by four to eight months. Again, at the first half of the third grade, the Sheldon selection is of normal difficulty as measured by readability formula, while the Austin-Bush comparable (?) selection resembles materials commonly used in the latter half of the second grade.

Our comparison is intended to point out the unlikelihood that Informal Reading Inventories constructed by two different persons would be equivalent, scaled similarly, or interchangeable. When experts apparently cannot achieve these goals, what can we think of Inventories produced by ordinary classroom teachers?

Using the Spache and Fry formulas on thirteen fourth-grade basal readers, Rogers* found two distinct levels for these books. The more difficult fourth-grade readers had a range of readability samples from 3.5 to 6.0, with a mean of 4.5. Easy fourth-grade readers sampled from 2.8 to 3.9 with a mean at 3.2. Rogers did not average his samples to find a general readability level for each reader, as in the table above. But the similarity between his samples from the "more difficult" fourth-grade basal readers and our data for entire readers is marked.

Leibert† attempted a comparative study of the Informal Reading Inventory and the Gates Primary Reading Test in terms of pupils' performances in dealing with different formats of tests. Using the test words of the Gates, children were examined in three ways: recognition in isolation, as in the I.R.I.; marking the one word in four pronounced by the examiner; and circling the one word that best fit a pictured idea, as in the Gates. In paragraph reading, two conditions were used: the first, in which the children read the directions of the Gates paragraph items only; and second, normal reading of the paragraph and answering the directions, as in the Gates, plus oral rereading scored for accuracy.

Word scores were greater in both recognition type tests than in the recall from a list, as in the I.R.I. In paragraph reading, the pupils could answer all but three of the items of the Gates by reading only the directions. The author concluded that, judging from these results, children would achieve higher reading level estimates from either of the Gates tests than from the I.R.I. He generalized his results to offer the conclusion that standardized test scores really may represent the maximum rather than the instructional reading levels of pupils.

While the author's conclusions seem reasonable for the Gates word test scores, they cannot be generalized to other standardized reading tests unless substantiated by other comparative studies. The tendency of the Gates tests to give somewhat exaggerated reading scores is well-known, but this is not necessarily true for all other standardized tests.

---

*A. R. Rogers, "Comparing the Difficulty of Basal Readers," *Journal of the New England Reading Association,* 5 (1970), 35–37.

†R. E. Leibert, "Some Differences between Silent and Oral Reading Responses on a Standardized Test," in *Forging Ahead in Reading,* J. Allen Figurel, editor, Proceedings International Reading Association, 12, 1968, 472–77.

Since the Gates paragraph reading test is not sharply scaled in difficulty but is rather a measure of speed in comprehension, the fact that third-grade pupils could follow the directions for most items without reading the selections is merely evidence of the nature of the test. Given unlimited time, most pupils of third or higher grades can answer most of the relatively unscaled Gates items. Hence it cannot be accused of yielding false estimates of the levels of materials pupils can deal with, since that is apparently not its intention.

This study is useful in pointing out a partial reason for lower word recognition scores, or reading level estimates based on these, on the I.R.I. than on many other tests. But it has not clarified the frequent differences between the I.R.I. and other tests in the measurement of silent reading levels. As we implied earlier, this latter difference could well be due to the lack of proof of scaling in difficulty of the I.R.I. selections because their random sources are not known to be truly scaled. In contrast, many standardized tests are carefully scaled during their construction and thus are more truly representative of levels of materials that pupils of different grades can deal with.

We could also point out that, if the word lists of the I.R.I. were standardized, the difficulty of their present format would be immaterial. Reading estimates would be made comparable to those tests, using different formats by the act of standardization. To illustrate this point, fifth-grade children achieving five of twenty items correct on one test would receive the same grade scores as on another test in which fifth graders normally scored ten out of twenty items if they were standardized on comparable populations. Both performances having been established as normal fifth-grade achievement would be translated into the same estimate of reading level, regardless of the format of the testing procedure—hence, Leibert's argument that standardized tests give higher reading level estimates because the manner of testing in the I.R.I. is harder for the pupil is really irrelevant. The differences are due to the fact that, on the one hand, an untested, probably unscaled list of words in the I.R.I. is being compared with a scaled list yielding known performances at each grade level. Which estimate is likely to represent a valid estimate of reading ability?

To complain that standardized tests constantly give erroneous overestimates of pupil ability, when compared with the I.R.I., is absurd. For until the content is scaled and standardization of performances for each reading level is done for an I.R.I., we have no evidence that it represents the true reading levels of pupils. The performances of a pupil on an I.R.I. are almost meaningless, for they represent his reading of an unscaled list of words and paragraphs of unknown difficulty.

Peggy E. Ransom* compared I.R.I. reading levels with those determined by the cloze procedure. In this latter, the child is required to show comprehension by giving the exact word for each fifth or tenth word that is deleted. Using Betts's standards for the I.R.I., Ransom computed correlations between the pupil reading levels suggested by the two tests. She defined the child's functional or instructional level in cloze as that level where he could supply 30 percent of the deleted words; his independent level as a 50 percent level; and his frustration level as the 20 percent correct level. Ransom's comparison yielded a correlation of .835 at the instructional, .498 at the independent, and .811 at the frustration level.

As we shall point out later, Ransom's identification of instructional, independent, and frustration levels was not consonant with the recommendations of other researchers in this area. Her 20 percent cloze level would certainly indicate material too difficult for the pupils, for such a performance is equal to comprehension far below 65 percent. On the other hand, using 50 percent cloze as the independent level demands about 80 percent comprehension (not the 90 percent demanded by the I.R.I.). Using the 30 percent cloze level required only about 50 percent comprehension at the instructional level, which is far below the 75 percent demanded by the I.R.I.

Unfortunately, Ransom's report does not give the mean reading levels found by the two tests to enable us to note whether there were, as we would expect, significant differences between the reading level estimates. We shall point out later ways of determining pupils' reading levels by the cloze procedure, which will probably give more accurate estimates than Ransom's approach does.

It would seem from all these criticisms and contradictory studies that the I.R.I. is not a simple, practical instrument for diagnosis or evaluation that almost any teacher can construct. Its scoring standards are subjective and probably invalid; its basal reader source is questionable; its testing procedure differs from that used in the research on which it is supposed to be based. And no one has yet answered the questions of the effect of the nature of the reading selections upon the ratio or patterns of errors, or how the tester can be certain that two I.R.I.'s will yield comparable scores or diagnostic information.

The argument that there must be some merit to the I.R.I. for, after all, hundreds of teachers use the technique and gain information about their pupils' reading from it, is a meretricious defense. The fact that a practice may be widespread among a group of practitioners is no proof of its true values.

---

*Peggy E. Ransom, "Determining Reading Levels of Elementary School Children by Cloze Testing," in *Forging Ahead in Reading*, J. Allen Figurel, editor, Proceedings International Reading Association, 12, 1968, 477–82.

The practice of grouping pupils into three reading groups that remain almost unchanged throughout the school year is well-nigh universal in American classrooms.   Yet almost every reading expert who has analyzed this practice condemns its usual form.

We have introduced some evidence showing that the diagnostic information teachers obtain by using the I.R.I. is most likely to be false and misleading.   An instrument that has no statistical evidence of validity or reliability; that uses standards established by an administration entirely different from those currently employed; that demands standards of performance in oral reading differing from every large-scale study of actual pupil performances available; and that employs testing material of unknown difficulty cannot be expected to yield accurate information.

In our opinion, what probably happens as a result of use of the I.R.I. is that teachers underestimate the level of appropriate instructional materials, as well as the levels of recreational and supplementary materials that pupils could read with adequate comprehension.   As a result, pupils do make good progress in the assigned materials that are too easy, and their performances thus appear to confirm the indications of the I.R.I.   Placed in this fashion in very easy materials, pupils readily do the almost perfect word-calling that most teachers tend to equate with good oral reading ability.   The progress in reading levels or breadth of reading that might have been accomplished if different standards for placement were used are, of course, unknown to both pupil and teacher.

But there are many occasions when a teacher wishes to estimate the child's probable reading level and to get some ideas about his needs for skill instruction. Rather than the construction of another I.R.I. of unknown merit, we recommend the following:

1. Test the child in oral and silent reading in the basal readers being used with the reading groups.

2. Consider the child's oral performance adequate, if (a) he reads with no more than 15-20 errors per 100 words orally with at least 70 percent comprehension in the mid-first or the second grade; (b) he reads with about 10 errors per 100 words orally, with 70 percent comprehension, in the other grades.

3. Test the child's silent reading, if possible in the same story or on adjoining pages of the reader.   Expect at least 70 percent comprehension.

4. If you wish to make a diagnostic plan in skill development, make a list of the skills that he is supposed to know.   Collect about 75-100 oral reading errors in several testings.   List these and then categorize them according to the skill involved.

This approach assumes that the teacher has a copy of the selections the child reads on which she will mark his errors. It also assumes that she has prepared ten–twenty questions, depending on the length of the selection, of varied types, before the testings. She will, of course, use questions involving recall, memory, evaluation, inference, and interpretation, in relatively equal proportions.

The teacher will then assign the child to that highest reading level at which he performs adequately in both oral errors and comprehension. If the testing of silent reading comprehension includes higher level materials in order to establish his upper limit, consider these levels in assigning supplementary reading and in providing recreational reading materials.

Another approach to informal testing that is less complex and open to subjectivity than the procedure we have recommended is the use of the cloze procedure. Briefly it involves selecting new materials assumed to be representative of several grade levels. A tentative grade level can be assigned each selection by application of the Spache formula to primary level materials or the Dale-Chall formula to those assumed to be fourth grade level or higher.* The various selections will permit testing in successive levels later in individual testing.

Delete every tenth word in each selection, leaving blank spaces of similar size (five or six letters at least in width) for each deletion. Retype or ditto the material in this fashion, unless you have a copy of each selection for each child in your class. In that case, delete by pasting a small piece of paper over each tenth word or by concealing with opaque white typewriter correction fluid, beginning deletions with the second sentence. Dittoing would be less expensive and time-consuming.

Use selections of about 500 words so that the deletions will number fifty. Give the readings to the pupils, asking them to write a word for each blank space, on a separate paper. Have them arrange answers in two columns, making sure to skip a line when they cannot think of a good word for a blank. Allow ample time for all to attempt all items.

Score for the total number of words exactly like those deleted that they can supply. Synonyms are wrong; misspelled words are not. Multiply each score by two to find the percentage of correct answers. Compute the class average by adding the percentage scores and dividing by the number of pupils, separately for each selection. That selection on which the class averages 44

---

*George D. Spache, *Good Reading for Poor Readers* (Champaign, Ill.: Garrard Publishing, 1974); Edgar Dale and Jeanne S. Chall, "A Formula for Predicting Readability," *Educational Research Bulletin* (Ohio State University) 27 (January 21 and February 28, 1948).

percent correct is equal to their average reading grade level. This standard of 44 percent is equal to 75 percent comprehension in the usual types of questions. The basic steps for this procedure have been established in a series of studies by Earl F. Rankin.* Another report confirms Rankin's standards for intermediate grades in finding that 42 percent in cloze tests yields an accurate estimate of pupil reading levels among high school pupils.†

Tentative grade levels can be assigned to the selections that are easier and harder than that designated as at grade level by comparing the performances on these selections with the grade level of the reading abilities of your pupils. In other words, if the percentage of correct answers is about 44, consider that selection equal in difficulty to the average reading level of the group of children who read it with that degree of accuracy. For example, if you have a group of children reading at about fifth-grade level, consider that selection on which their average cloze percentage was about 44 as a fifth-grade selection. This group would probably have averaged more than 44 percent on the selection at grade level, in a fourth-grade class for example. Repeat this inspection procedure for the group of children reading, on the average, a year below grade level, choosing a selection on which they averaged 44 percent in cloze as representative of that level of reading ability. You now have at least three levels of reading selections (more if your class is large and has a wide range of reading levels) that you may use in informal testing.

In your future use of these selections, you will be making comparisons in silent reading comprehension with the performances of a group whose abilities are familiar to you. Your comparisons will not be based on norms established in schools unlike yours. Your estimate of comprehension (38 percent on cloze equals 65 percent, 44 percent equal 75 percent comprehension) will be objective and free from the vagaries of your own skill in framing valid questions that really measure comprehension of a selection.

LEARNING PROJECT

Obviously there is a place in reading instruction for simple informal tests that can add to the teacher's knowledge of pupil development. One of these is called an open-book test because it is actually based on the child's performances in certain specific skills needed to handle that aid.

---

*Earl F. Rankin, "Grade Level Interpretation of Cloze Readability Scores," in *Reading: The Right to Participate,* Twentieth Yearbook National Reading Conference, 1971, 30–37.
†Joe Peterson, Ed Paradis, and Nat Peters, "Revalidation of the Cloze Procedure as a Measure of the Instructional Level for High School Students" (Paper presented at the National Reading Conference, New Orleans, December 1972).

1. Choose a type of book for which multiple copies are available. You may use a dictionary, a social science, a science, a math, or any other kind of book.

2. Decide precisely what skill or skills, preferably not more than one or two, you would like to evaluate in a group of pupils.

3. Write out the objectives of your test. Then describe the reading task that you will sample, along with the questions that the pupils will answer or the steps that they will take in carrying out the task.

4. List the criteria that you will use in evaluating the pupil's performances, that is, what you think will be a performance indicating a reasonable degree of the skill for pupils of that age.

5. If you can, try this worksample test on a group of pupils for whom it is suitable. Then critique your own test for difficulty, for validity in sampling a specific reading behavior, and for its probable future usefulness.

REFERENCES

1. Anderson, Howard, R., and Lindquist, E. F., *Selected Test Items in American History,* Bulletin No. 6. Washington, D.C.: National Council for the Social Studies, 1957. (See this source for other model items in social sciences.)

2. Austin, Mary C., and Huebner, Mildred H., "Evaluating Progress in Reading Through Informal Procedures," *Reading Teacher,* 15 (March 1962), 338–43.

3. Beard, Richard L., "Reading Habits and Interests," *High School Journal,* 39 (January 1956), 207–12.

4. Beldin, H. O., "Informal Reading Testing: Historical Review and Review of the Research," pp. 67–84 in *Reading Difficulties: Diagnosis, Correction and Remediation,* William K. Durr, editor. Newark, Del.: International Reading Association, 1970.

5. Betts, Emmett A., *Foundation of Reading Instruction.* New York: American Book Co., 1946.

6. Boning, Thomas, and Boning, Richard, "I'd Rather Read Than – – –," *Reading Teacher,* 10 (April 1957), 196–99.

7. Buros, Oscar K., *Reading Tests and Reviews.* Highland Park, N.J.: Gryphon Press, 1968.

8. Cooper, J. Louis, "The Effect of Adjustment of Basal Reading Achievement," doctoral dissertation, Boston University, 1952.

9. Daniel, John E., "The Effectiveness of Various Procedures in Reading Level Placement," *Elementary English,* 39 (October 1962), 590–600.

10. Davis, Frederick B., *Educational Measurements and Their Interpretation.* Belmont, Calif.: Wadsworth Press, 1964.

11. Della-Piana, Gabriel M., and Herlin, Wayne R., "Are Normative Oral Reading Error Profiles Necessary?" in *Improvement of Reading Through Classroom Practice,* J. Allen Figurel, editor, Proceedings International Reading Association, 9 (1964), 306–309.

12. Eller, William, and Attea, Mary, "Three Diagnostic Reading Tests: Some Comparisons," in *Vistas in Reading,* J. Allen Figurel, editor, Proceedings International Reading Association 11, Part 2 (1966), 562–66.

13. Gray, William S., "The Measurement of Understanding in the Language Arts: The Receptive Language Arts," pp. 189–200 in *The Measurement of Understanding,* Forty-fifth Yearbook, Part I, National Society for the Study of Education. Chicago: University of Chicago Press, 1946.

14. Gronlund, Norman E., *Sociometry in the Classroom.* New York: Harper & Row, 1959.

15. Guszak, Frank J., "Dilemmas in Informal Reading Assessments," *Elementary English,* 47 (May 1970), 666–70.

16. Hanna, Geneva R., and McAllister, Mariana K., *Books, Young People and Reading Guidance.* New York: Harper & Row, 1960.

17. Harris, Albert J., *How to Increase Reading Ability.* New York: David McKay, 1970.

18. Jackson, Philip W., "Determining Expectations for Reading in Grades Seven Through Nine," pp. 28–31 in *Evaluation of Reading,* Helen M. Robinson, editor. Supplementary Educational Monographs No. 88. Chicago: University of Chicago Press, 1958.

19. Johnson, Marjorie Seddon, and Kress, Roy A., *Informal Reading Inventories.* Reading Aids Series. Newark, Del.: International Reading Association, 1965.

20. Kasdon, Lawrence M., "Silent Reading Before Oral Reading?" *Ohio Reading Teacher,* 2 (1967), 6–8.

21. Kasdon, Lawrence M., "Oral versus Silent-Oral Diagnosis," in *Reading Diagnosis and Evaluation,* Dorothy L. DeBoer, editor, Proceedings International Reading Association, 13, Part 4 (1970), 86–92.

22. Kender, Joseph P., "How Useful Are Informal Reading Tests?" *Journal of Reading,* 11 (February 1968), 337–42.

23. Kilgallon, Patsy A., "A Study of Relationships among Certain Pupil Adjustments in Language Situations," doctoral dissertation, Pennsylvania State College, 1942.

24. Letton, Mildred C., "Evaluating the Effectiveness of Teaching Reading," pp. 76–82 in *Evaluation of Reading,* Helen M. Robinson, editor. Supplementary Educational Monographs No. 88. Chicago: University of Chicago Press, 1958.

25. Lowell, Robert E., "Problems in Identifying Reading Levels with Informal Reading Inventories," pp. 120–126 in *Reading Difficulties: Diagnosis, Correction and Remediation,* William K. Durr, editor. Newark, Del.: International Reading Association, 1970.

26. Maginnis, George H., "The Readability Graph and Informal Reading Inventories," *Reading Teacher,* 22 (March 1969), 516–18, 559.

27. McCracken, Robert A., "Standardized Reading Tests and Informal Reading Inventories," *Education,* 82 (February 1962), 366–69.

28. Millsap, Lucille N., "A Study of Teachers' Awareness of Frustration Reading Level among Their Pupils in Basal Readers," doctoral dissertation, University of Oregon, 1962.

29. Moe, Iver A., "Auding Ability as a Measure of Reading Potential Among Pupils in Primary Grades," doctoral dissertation, University of Florida, 1957.

30. Northway, Mary L., and Weld, Lindsay, *Sociometric Testing.* Toronto: University of Toronto Press, 1957.

31. Powell, William R., "Reappraising the Criteria for Interpreting Informal Inventories," pp. 100–109 in *Reading Diagnosis and Evaluation,* Dorothy L. DeBoer, editor, Proceedings International Reading Association, 13, Part 4 (1970).
32. Powell, William R., and Dunkeld, Colin G., "Validity of the IRI Reading Levels," *Elementary English,* 48 (October 1971), 632–42.
33. Sipay, Edward R., "A Comparison of Standardized Reading Scores and Functional Reading Levels," *Reading Teacher,* 17 (January 1964), 265–68.
34. Spache, George D., "Classroom Techniques of Identifying and Diagnosing the Needs of Retarded Readers in High School and College," in *Better Readers for Our Times,* Nancy Larrick, editor, Proceedings International Reading Association, 1 (1956), 128–32.
35. Spache, George D., "Estimating Reading Capacity," pp. 15–20 in *Evaluation of Reading,* Helen M. Robinson, editor. Supplementary Educational Monographs No. 88. Chicago: University of Chicago Press, 1958.
36. Wood, Dorothy Adkins, *Test Construction.* Columbus: Charles E. Merrill, 1961.

part three

REMEDIATION

A number of interesting new ways of approaching reading instruction have appeared in the past decade. Some of these involve changes in our alphabet; some present the primary word analysis skill of phonics in a very colorful way. Others offer completely new patterns of sequences of skill development, presumably suitable for all or most children. Several proffer a detailed step-by-step learning system for each specific skill. In addition to all these approaches, we find innovative practices in the use of adults or children as tutors for pupils of various ages. Finally, a method of shaping pupil behavior that may supplant many of our older ideas about rewards and punishments is reviewed. As you read about these suggested changes in current practices, try to answer these questions.

1. Which approaches to instruction, in your opinion, seem to offer significant values in treating reading disabilities? Which would you try, if the opportunity were present?

2. Why do you suppose that some of these innovations can produce greater pupil interest and gain in reading development, at least in short-term trials? Would you expect these gains to persist in long-term application? Why or why not?

13
Innovative Approaches to Corrective Instruction

If there is such tremendous variation among individuals in so many dimensions of human makeup—both physiological and psychological—how, then, can we look for the method that will be the universal panacea for problems in the development of reading ability or of any other skill?

DESPITE THE CAUTION by Thomas J. Edwards (43, p. 361), cited above, the decade of the 1960s and the years following have witnessed a materials and methods explosion of tremendous size (94). In the search for answers to the problems inherent in attempting reading instruction for almost the total school-age population, dozens of new programs and approaches are being tried. Many of these are truly innovative only in the sense that some facet of the materials, the instructional procedures or the rationale is different from common current reading methods. To one familiar with the chronology of reading instruction, however, almost none is historically new. Perhaps, as William D. Sheldon has said, this old wine in new bottles simply reflects a pendulum swing away from the conservative middle of the basal approach toward either an ultraconservative philosophy as in phonic systems or toward a radical left of a potpourri of gadgets and devices (122). But we should not prejudge these innovations simply because we know "there is no one method that is so outstanding that it should be used to the exclusion of the others" (7). Rather, these approaches may, as the First-Grade Reading Studies indicated (7, 11), increase the effectiveness of current methods and materials when combined with the latter. The innovative programs reviewed here represent this author's selection of those for which there is, first of all, sufficient research evidence to warrant evaluation. Second, we include only relatively recent approaches in the belief that there has been adequate review of older innovative programs such as individualized reading. Third, we eliminated those that involve only changes in classroom organization, such as programmed learning, computer-assisted-instruction, Individually Prescribed Instruction, and the like. We discuss all these other systems in *Diagnosing and Correcting Reading Disabilities.*

Much of the research on these innovative methods and media has been concentrated in the primary grades rather than in emphasizing their values in corrective or remedial teaching. Most of the conclusions we can draw from this research regarding the probable effects of each new system upon various reading skills apply largely to young, beginning readers. Yet all this background material is relevant to corrective and remedial programs. First of all, the research does help to indicate what results are likely when each system is used with a nonreader or even an older student who functions at a primary reading level.   Because of their natures, the various approaches produce differential development of reading skills, some producing accelerated word recognition, others resulting in strong phonic skills, and others promoting writing and other language skills.   Knowing the particular strengths of each type, of approach will enable the reading teacher to make a more intelligent choice of method or medium that is relevant to each retarded student's needs.

Second, this background material is relevant to corrective or remedial work in helping the reading teacher to find a new and reasonably effective approach to learning to read for each failing student.   The student's gains may strongly reflect the Hawthorne effect of the novelty of the approach.   But it is of great psychological value for the student's self-concept of himself as a reader to find an approach that is fresh and untainted with previous failures.

MODIFIED ALPHABETS

The Initial Teaching Alphabet

In 1961, John Downing, formerly of the University of London, began what was intended to be a ten-year experiment in British schools with a new medium for the teaching of beginning reading.   A forty-four-symbol alphabet was adapted by Sir James Pitman from one originally designed by his grandfather, Sir Isaac Pitman, author of the Pitman shorthand method.   The plan was to present one symbol for each sound in English, thus simplifying the sound-symbol correspondence of the written language.

Rationale   The justification for the i.t.a. (Initial Teaching Alphabet) was as follows (22):

> 1. Beginning readers would not be hampered by trying to read various forms of the same letter, as A, a, *a*, **a,** or words as DOG, dog, *dog,* and so on.
> 2. Success in early reading would be promoted by the increased number of experiences with a regular phoneme-grapheme (sound-letter) correspondence.
> 3. Spelling and reading would be enhanced because of the use of the same symbol for all spellings of a sound.
> 4. If carefully designed, the new alphabet would produce word forms resembling conventional orthography; thus, having served its purpose in the early stages, it would promote the eventual transition into reading of T.O. (traditional orthography).

Number	Character	Name	Example	Traditional spelling
1	æ	ae	ræt	rate
2	b	bee	big	big
3	c	kee	cat	cat
4	d	dee	dog	dog
5	ЄЄ	ee	sЄЄt	seat
6	f	ef	fill	fill
7	ɡ	gae	ɡun	gun
8	h	hae	hat	hat
9	ie	ie	ieland	island
10	j	jae	jieant	giant
11	k	kae	kit	kit
12	l	el	lamp	lamp
13	m	em	man	man
14	n	en	net	net
15	œ	oe	bœt	boat
16	p	pee	pig	pig
17	r	rae	run	run
18	s	ess	sad	sad
19	t	tee	tap	tap
20	ue	ue	fue	few
21	v	vee	van	van
22	w	wae	will	will
23	y	i-ae	yell	yell
24	z	zed or zee	fizz	fizz
25	ᴣ	zess	houᴣeᴣ	houses
26	wh	whae	when	when
27	ꛯh	chae	ꛯhick	chick
28	th	ith	thaut	thought
29	ꜩh	thee	ꜩhe	the
30	ʃh	ish	ʃheperd	shepherd
31	ʒ	zhee	judʒ	judge
32	ŋ	ing	siŋ	sing
33	ɑ	ah	fɑr	far

Number	Character	Name	Example	Traditional spelling
34	au	au	aut	ought
35	a	at	appl	apple
36	e	et	egg	egg
37	i	it	dip	dip
38	o	ot	hot	hot
39	u	ut	ugly	ugly
40	ω	oot	bωk	book
41	ꙍ	oo	mꙍn	moon
42	ou	ow	bou	bough
43	oi	oi	toi	toy

FIGURE 13–1   The i.t.a. alphabet (From *Tw Bee or Not to Be,* by J. A. Downing. Reprinted by permission of Pitman Publishing Corporation and Cassell and Company Ltd.

Other justifications cited by Downing in his early writings were the failure of current methods with 15–20 percent of the population; the apparent success of a number of similar nineteenth-century American experiments with a phonetically regular set of symbols; and the difficulties of early learners in dealing with the phonetic irregularities of English.   Other uses of i.t.a. would be in the prevention of writing and reading disabilities among native or foreign-speaking students; in the treatment of reading disabilities; and in teaching literacy to adults (32).

Some users of i.t.a., after its introduction into our country in 1963 and the publication of an American version called I.T.A., were confused, to say the least, in their attempts to apply the system in American classrooms. i.t.a. is not a method of teaching beginning reading, as Downing has pointed out again and again.   It is simply an orthographic medium through which, presumably, children would learn to read with greater ease.   More specifically, i.t.a. (26) includes the following characteristics:

1. It is not a phonetic alphabet but is one for teaching beginning reading.
2. It is not a perfectly regular code for phonemes.   For example, several sounds are represented by a number of symbols; that is, *k* by *c* and *k; z* by two symbols; *l* by two; *a* by two; *ch* by four; *s* by four; *w* and *h* by three. There is no symbol for the schwa sound, double consonants are still present, and the ligatures are often simply common digraphs or vowel phoneme clusters (7, 76).   (See Figure 13–1.)
3. It is not a synthetic phonics method (as so often interpreted in America).

4. It is based on a British pronunciation of vowel sounds, which is, of course, different from American standard English (147).

Despite these limitations, some American authorities recognize the positive values of i.t.a. in permitting the beginner the rapid learning of a regular phonetic system. At the same time, as Constance M. McCullough has pointed out, there are the negative aspects of the false representation of the language as regular, the delay of experience with the true configurations of many words, the lack of environmental support because of few reading materials at the beginner's reading level in which his reading could be applied, the need to substitute, finally, T.O. in both reading and spelling, and the overemphasis upon auditory skills inherent in the approach (94).

The argument that one would learn to read faster and more readily in a language of regular grapheme-phoneme correspondence is too simplistic, according to S. Jay Samuels (113). If this were true, we would expect the smallest proportion of failures to learn to read in regular languages such as Spanish, Russian, Bohemian, and the like; a larger proportion of failure in less regular languages as Italian, Dutch, and German, or English, French, and Greek, and most of all in Chinese and Japanese. Yet the Japanese claim less than 1 percent failure,* the Germans 12–15 percent, the Americans, 15–20 percent, and the Finnish, about 20 percent, a reverse order in terms of regularity of the language. Success in beginning reading is certainly not assured by the regularity of the language, if we may judge by the literacy rates in such countries as Mexico and Spain, as typical examples where this proposition does not hold. Other sociological factors such as educational opportunity, the methods of instruction, and the national expenditures for education are much more significant in the total picture than is the nature of the language. Even when the instruction emphasizes a phonic approach in a perfectly regular language, as in the experiment in the Philippines by Tensuan and Davis (136), success in beginning reading is neither universal nor superior to that achieved in a more eclectic approach in that language.

The argument that beginners are confused by the variations in letter forms does seem to be confirmed by Rystrom's study (112). With tests of naming, matching, and identifying different forms of the same letter, he found an increase in accuracy from the kindergarten to the third grade, with most errors concentrated on reversals and rotations. He argues, like Downing, that early reading would be enhanced by elimination of these variations or by more training in discriminating among them. Unfortunately, his results indicate

---

*This Japanese report is hardly credible, however, in view of the fact that their children must learn a fifty-one letter alphabet as well as from forty-six to seventy-six ideographs during the first year.

simply that children improved in their discriminations, not that difficulty with these was a major handicap in learning to read or that improvement in discrimination was significantly related to reading progress.

The argument that dependence upon word forms in beginning reading is a major explanation of the failures, as offered by Downing and many other critics of current methods, seems contradictory to the attempt to make i.t.a. produce word forms resembling T.O. Even if we agree that the basals overemphasize word form as a clue to recognition, a very dubious claim, why should the new alphabet try to resemble these same word forms? Is this not a tacit admission that word form does play a significant part in word recognition? The justification for the parallelism in word forms in order to promote eventual transition from i.t.a. to T.O. is acceptable and logical. But, if word form is an undesirable clue, why bother to imitate the words in T.O.?

Methods and Materials

The methods and materials of the British and American versions of i.t.a. differ markedly, a point that beclouds the research reports greatly, as we shall point out later. The *Downing Readers,* for example, differ from the American *Early-to-Read i/t/a* (90) in these respects:

1. The system was designed as an adjunct to a basal reading program employing a whole word plus phonics method, or any other method.

2. British teachers were urged to use the material only as the children's individual differences indicated their ability to profit from this aid, not as a general system.

3. No manuals or workbooks were offered, for it was expected that teachers would adapt the materials to their own teaching style, creating any exercise material that they deemed necessary. This freedom from stereotyped directions and the use of teacher-made practice materials are common in British schools.

4. The language experience approach in i.t.a. was emphasized by many British teachers. But concern for spelling, mechanics, and the like was not to be emphasized for at least the first two years.

5. There was no set deadline for transition of the pupil to T.O. in reading or spelling. It would be introduced only after fluency in i.t.a. had been achieved, particularly for pupils of lesser ability. In other words, children would continue to use and read in i.t.a. as long as it appeared to be of assistance.

6. The goal of instruction in the British schools was not achievement in formal reading tests (which are used somewhat infrequently), but rather progress of the child in the discovery of the relationships between letters and sounds as manifest both in his fluency and breadth of reading and in his writing ability.

The American version of the i.t.a. was crystalized into what resembles a basal reading program with readers, teachers' manuals, and workbooks.

Observers have noted the emphasis upon individual sounds and forms that represent these sounds, that is, a synthetic phonics system, as contrasted with the language experience, discovery approach of the British classrooms (102). The American plan proposes that the transition to T.O. should be made as early as possible, perhaps for most by the second grade, and the materials are so written as to force transition at this time.

The experimental nature of the original i.t.a. studies seems to have been lost sight of in the American version. Mazurkiewicz responds to Zeitz's criticisms of the alphabet by claiming that correction of the ambiguities in the grapheme-phoneme correspondence does not seem warranted (147). In comparison, Downing suggests (28) that the alphabet should certainly be redesigned to resemble T.O. more, for the transition from i.t.a. to T.O. causes a plateau or regression in the child's progress. Moreover, duplications in several graphemes must be eliminated and others redesigned because they are difficult for children to write.

Critique

The research and the reactions of both British and American reading authorities to i.t.a. have been quite mixed. For clarification, it will be best to separate the reports from both countries, particularly since two different systems are really being reported on.

The American version of i.t.a. was employed in four of the large-scale First Grade Reading Studies, some of which extended their comparisons into the third grade. Edward B. Fry (49) found no significant differences in a half-dozen measures of silent and oral reading among the i.t.a., a basal reader system, and his own Diacritical Marking system, at the end of the first, second, or third grade. The children using i.t.a. wrote longer stories in the first grade, but with inferior mechanics and spelling; and even these minor differences disappeared in the later grades. As usual, girls excelled boys by the third grade regardless of method or medium.

Hayes and Wuest (62) report on a three-year study contrasting i.t.a. with basal, phonics, and language experience systems. Since i.t.a. pupils moved into a literary reader upon making the transition to T.O. in the first grade, only the results for that first year offer a meaningful comparison of i.t.a. and other approaches. They found i.t.a. pupils significantly superior to basal in word reading, word study skills, and spelling; but such pupils read fewer books than the basal. The i.t.a. pupils were superior to the basal in two oral word lists, and rate of oral reading. For the high and the average I.Q. group, i.t.a. produced better silent and oral achievement than did the basal or phonics programs. For the low I.Q. group, i.t.a. produced better silent and oral achievement in general than did any other approach.

Mazurkiewicz (90), one of the authors of the American version of i.t.a., has offered many reports on his system.   One report, by Tanyzer and Alpert on a First Grade Reading study (135), indicates that i.t.a. pupils were superior on all parts of the Stanford Achievement Test and three oral word reading tests to a basal system at the end of the first grade. The same pupils were inferior in vocabulary and spelling, however, to those trained by a phonics system. In a second study (90), Mazurkiewicz reports that in the second grade the i.t.a. pupils maintained their superiority in spelling and language usage but were only equal to the other systems in word meaning, paragraph meaning, and word study skills. In a matched pairs comparison, from among the original first-grade population of this study that Mazurkiewicz reports, the i.t.a. pupils were better in word meaning only, of all the Stanford tests. In fact, these pupils were inferior in spelling, somewhat poorer in word study and vocabulary, and superior on only one of the three oral tests. In this report, Mazurkiewicz describes his i.t.a. system as emphasizing the language experience at the very beginning stages, then basal readers as the nucleus of instruction, with strong emphasis upon writing and the language arts. These emphases upon writing and language experiences may have contributed to the superiority of the i.t.a. pupils in the number of running words and the number of polysyllabic words in their writing, although, as noted above, they do not seem to have helped the pupils' spelling to the same degree.

These particular American studies have been severely criticized by Warburton and Southgate (143) and by John Downing (27, 28, 33, 34). The first objection to their meaningfulness is that different reading materials as well as different methods were compared simultaneously, thus obscuring the results because of the interaction of the two variables.   All the British critics point out that such a comparison must be made on the basis of similar materials—one in i.t.a., the other in T.O.—before we can judge the values of the i.t.a. medium. In most of the British experiments reported later, this error was avoided.

Arthur Heilman (65) has argued that the efficacy of the i.t.a. could be tested only if the contrasting basal instruction included the same amount of early phonics instruction. In one sense, he is simply repeating the criticism that a researcher cannot compare two methods in two different media at the same time and isolate any results due to one medium. This is, of course, really an objection to the research on the American version of i.t.a., which, as we have said, strongly emphasizes a synthetic phonics approach, as well as using a new alphabet.

J. William Asher (3) has pointedly shown that Mazurkiewicz's comparison of matched pairs drawn from unequal groups is an indefensible procedure, for it results in producing supposedly matched groups that are inherently unequal. He also points out a number of further errors in statistics in the Mazurkiewicz reports.

Other minor studies with the American i.t.a. may be briefly summarized. These studies, of course, are open to the same criticisms of confusion of method and medium, since none used exactly the same materials in T.O. and i.t.a. Morris (97) claimed superiority for i.t.a. classes in word recognition and oral reading above classes using a kinesthetic or sentence method. At the end of a two-year study, Stewart (132) reported that i.t.a. children tended to score higher in word recognition and spelling but were inferior in comprehension. Chasnoff's results indicate significantly better scores in first grade for i.t.a. pupils in word reading, word study, and total score on the Stanford Achievement. No significant differences appeared in rate or accuracy of oral reading or when pupils read a T.O. version of the Stanford or the California silent reading tests. In an attempt to control the effect of practice in i.t.a., Chasnoff used a transliterated version of the standard reading tests in i.t.a. But his own analysis led him to believe that even this did not produce parallel or fairer tests of the children's progress in i.t.a. versus T.O. As his results indicate, pupils do not perform alike in exactly comparable i.t.a. or T.O. versions of the same material. A follow-up of the same children into second grade revealed no difference in their median scores, although i.t.a. pupils were significantly higher in mean scores in word study skills and spelling. These results may be interpreted to signify that while the average performance is similar in i.t.a. and T.O. pupils after two years, more competent pupils tend to score higher when trained in i.t.a., at least in spelling and word study skills (14, 15).

Evens (45) employed eye-movement photography rather than reading tests to contrast pupil progress in i.t.a. or T.O. At the end of the first grade, all differences were statistically in favor of the T.O. groups, that is, in fixations and regressions per 100 words, average recognition span, rate of reading, and duration of fixation. By the third grade, however, all of these differences disappeared. This was a small-scale study involving only thirty-eight children and certainly should be replicated on a larger group.

Holmes and Rose (72) tested the values of i.t.a. with forty classes of largely Mexican-American disadvantaged pupils. The i.t.a. pupils progressed through their reading materials somewhat more rapidly, but 14 percent of them and 19 percent of the T.O. pupils were still at preprimer or below levels at the end of the first grade. At that time, 37 percent of the i.t.a. were reading in first grade readers, while only 7 percent of the T.O. pupils had reached that point, although there were no differences on a silent reading test. The researchers noted that Spanish-speaking pupils did not make this accelerated progress, and that the superiority was present in the group of i.t.a. pupils only for the top half.   In the lowest quarter of ability, there were no differences on the Stanford Achievement battery.   In other words, i.t.a. tends to accelerate early reading progress among disadvantaged children who are not too handicapped, while neither basal nor i.t.a. was very effective with those suffering from language and socioeconomic hindrances.

Barclay (6) used i.t.a. with institutionalized, emotionally disturbed boys who had not yet learned to read at an average age of nine. The younger pupils in i.t.a. made about 30 percent better progress through their reading materials than did a T.O. group equated for age and I.Q.   At the same time, these pupils evidenced better adjustment and more favorable attitudes toward reading as they improved, as we might expect.   To be meaningful, this study should be repeated under conditions that introduce both groups to a new medium in which they have not experienced prior failure.   As it now stands, Barclay's study simply reproves that a basal method did not succeed with these difficult boys, whether tried once, or all over again a second time.

Shapiro and Willford (121) attempted to answer the question of whether i.t.a. should be begun in the kindergarten or the first grade. Selecting groups from a larger sample, a very questionable procedure, produced experimental groups equal in I.Q. (average 110), but not in teacher experience or instructional time.   Children who began i.t.a. in the kindergarten naturally were superior in several reading tests during the first and second grades to those pupils given no reading instruction at all in the kindergarten—all of which proves only that two or three years of reading instruction are better respectively than one or two years; it tells us nothing about the specific values of i.t.a.

In summaries of the major comparative studies (11, 40), performances only in word recognition appear to be superior for i.t.a. pupils at the end of the first grade. By the second grade, i.t.a. appears to promote better spelling and phonic skills only among average and bright pupils. Among low-ability pupils, the basal program was just as adequate. The minor studies agree in indicating some advantage for i.t.a. in the same skills of word study, (phonics) and spelling. No advantage other than somewhat faster progress in the readers in the early stages is present among disadvantaged, and then only if they are not further handicapped by bilingualism. Those studies that seem to show faster initial progress in the readers in i.t.a. raise an interesting question, in view of Chasnoff's demonstration of the inequality of identical materials in i.t.a. and T.O. How comparable in reading level are readers in i.t.a. and T.O.? What does it mean when some children progress faster in i.t.a. readers than others do in T.O. readers? Does i.t.a. help children to learn to read more quickly, or are the materials much easier than the parallel levels in T.O.? What is the value of this faster initial progress, if it does not produce significant results on different tests of reading performances after a year or two or three?

The British version of i.t.a. was used in one major American two-year study by Hahn (58). In both grades, he obtained similar results: no significant differences in a battery of silent and oral reading tests among i.t.a., language experience, or basal pupils. The i.t.a. pupils were superior to the basal in spelling, word study, and an oral word list, but inferior to the same in reading attitudes and writing mechanics. The language experience pupils read more books and wrote more stories than the other pupils.

John Downing has written many reports on the i.t.a. experiments in England (27, 30, 31, 35, 36). A summary of two of the more comprehensive studies will suffice to give an indication of the results. Downing claims that by the mid-second grade, i.t.a. pupils could not read as well in T.O. as in i.t.a. (Contrast this with the American pattern of pushing toward transition by the end of the first grade.) But these second graders could read T.O. as well as T.O. pupils! By the third grade, i.t.a. pupils averaged five months' acceleration in word recognition and accuracy of oral reading; used 45 percent more difficult words in their longer compositions; and showed spelling in T.O. equal to T.O. pupils. In one of his experimental groups i.t.a. pupils exceeded T.O. and T.O. spelling by mid-fourth grade, but this result did not appear in a second experimental group. In general, Downing feels that i.t.a. produces superior reading and spelling in T.O., particularly in word recognition and oral accuracy, but not in comprehension. These achievements are greatest among highest-ability students, while the lowest 10 percent show negligible differences after three years of i.t.a. He emphasizes that during transition to T.O. there is a setback in progress except in speed of reading among the highest 70 percent of i.t.a. pupils. Downing suggests that this plateau or regression could be avoided if those preparing i.t.a. materials were willing to make the many corrections and changes in the symbols that may be causing the difficulties encountered during the transition (28).

Swales (134) reports on a British study on the results of i.t.a. after three years. There were no significant differences in reading achievement from that of T.O. pupils, but there were fewer backward pupils in i.t.a. The marked variations in the results Swales found from one school to the next indicated to him that other factors than the new alphabet alone were affecting the results. This is the kind of observation of the influence of the teacher variable that one derives from any large-scale study of comparative methods. As in the American First Grade Reading studies, results varied more often from class to class within a method than from one method to another.

Reviewers of the British i.t.a. research have been cautious about accepting Downing's results at face value. Southgate (125), for example, has stressed the effects of teacher inspiration and the Hawthorne effect of a novel approach; the influence upon teacher skill of being trained in the new method as compared with the lack of such intensive in-service training among control teachers. Marsh (88) believes that when the differences in the ages and intelligence of the control and experimental groups in Downing's experiments are considered, about 70 percent of the differences in their reading performances may be accounted for. The remainder of the differences may reflect the Hawthorne effect plus whatever advantage the new medium has, Marsh says.

Warburton and Southgate (143) reviewed all the American and British research and pointed out numerous procedural errors in ten of eleven American studies in their confused comparison of different methods and different materials in the same attempt at evaluation. Responses of British teachers using i.t.a. (9 percent of all British schools) showed that only 2 percent had discontinued its use, and none of these because of dissatisfaction with its results. Their interviews with teachers and supervisors confirmed this highly positive evaluation of i.t.a. It should be noted that decisions regarding methods and materials are largely the teacher's prerogative in British schools, and thus reflect classroom teachers' judgments, not administrative pronouncements. Warburton and Southgate summarized the implications of their comprehensive reviews of the research as indicating that i.t.a. pupils learn earlier, easier, and faster; are inclined to be slower in rate and poorer in comprehension; but that these differences tend to disappear by the third year in i.t.a. instruction.

In view of the many flaws in the so-called research studies on the i.t.a., particularly in the American reports, it is difficult to make many conclusive statements at this time regarding its values. Downing does seem to have proved his point that early reading can be simplified for many children by employing a more consistent phonetic alphabet. Just how helpful this initial teaching alphabet is, however, remains to be demonstrated in experiments exactly parallel in methods (amount, emphasis, and kind of phonics training, for example) and in materials identical in content and vocabulary in i.t.a. and T.O. The present i.t.a. alphabet must also be revised in simplicity, consistency, and, perhaps, also in similarity to T.O. Unfortunately, however, the British government has withdrawn its support for the proposed ten-year experiment, and the American publishers of i.t.a. have denied the need for such improvements.

Other Alphabetic Systems

Attempts to modify our alphabet, as in i.t.a., have been a recurring phenomenon particularly during the past 100 years. The systems have taken the forms of devising a symbol for each sound, respelling phonetically, simplifying spelling by eliminating silent or double letters, using diacritical marks to indicate pronunciation, and others. Some of these systems were designed solely to simplify spelling, ignoring their implications for reading instruction, while others like i.t.a. were specifically intended to make learning to read easier. Most of the current schemes have had little or no supporting research and may be disposed of by brief descriptions.

The Ten-Vowel Alphabet   Leo G. Davis (21) would simplify things by using capitals for long vowels and lower case for the short vowels, by dropping silent letters and doubled consonants, and by respelling phonetically such sounds as hard *c*, the *z* sound of *s*, *ph*, and so on. For reading training he has transliterated the first and second McGuffey readers, and as a guide offers *The Davis Speller* (Carlton Press).

Laubach's Alphabet   Frank C. Laubach, known best for his literacy campaign, "Each One Teach One," offers another adaptation of the alphabet. He would insert a slanted line after each long vowel; spell other vowel combinations phonetically, as *yoo* for *you*; omit silent letters, and double vowels before *r*, as *haart* for *heart* (82).

Unifon   This system offers a forty-letter synthetic alphabet using only capital letters, but retaining eighteen of the original consonants. Speech combinations as *sh, ch, th,* and *ng* would have new symbols; as would long vowels and diphthongs; all silent and doubled letters would be dropped. Short vowel sounds would remain as at present. The instructional materials include several readers, word cards, a dictionary, and a teacher's manual. The method emphasizes taking dictation at the seat or chalkboard, using capital letters exclusively (85). A single experimental study is reported by Nold (101), which revealed no significant difference in groups of twenty-five experimental and control first graders in word knowledge, word discrimination, or reading comprehension.

Fonetic English   Offers itself as more logical, easier to learn, promoting faster progress in early reading, eliminating illiteracy, and a basis for a worldwide simple language! The system would accomplish these goals by a variety of phonetic respellings, dropping duplicated letters and silent letters (and even some sounded letters as *b* for *be*, *U* for *you*, and the like), representing the schwa sound only by *u*, spelling *a* followed by *r* or *a* as in *father* by *o* (as in *bother*). According to these writers, these *a* and *o* sounds are all the same—*hot, charm, rock, large,* and hence should be spelled the same. In all, the system simplifies the alphabet by using twenty-nine instead of twenty-six letters and making many changes by adding letters to respell phonetically (110).

Diacritical Marking System

Edward Fry's Diacritical Marking System would regularize orthography for beginning readers by adding diacritical marks at first, gradually eliminating them as the reader progressed. The system is similar to several used in early American readers of the last century, although it is somewhat simpler in using only the characters found on a standard typewriter. Using a basal reading system adapted to his markings, Fry found no real differences in the outcomes of his method in each of three successive years in comparison with the usual basal or i.t.a. (49). Nor were any relationships present because of age, sex, or I.Q. in the first two years. By the third grade, however, girls excelled boys regardless of method or medium.

First Steps to Reading English

In their 1957 materials for adult literacy, which are now adapted for beginning readers, Gibson and Richards (52) proposed a somewhat different alphabetic approach. Rather than modify the present letters, their system controls the appearance of letters in the reading materials. The first few pages are composed of words that can be formed of a small group of letters, and a few more letters are added each few pages.

Their rationale is that reading is based on letter discrimination; hence beginning material would be scheduled to use letters in the order of their discriminability. Readers would be trained in noting the characteristic differences among letters (54). Letters would be used to form words that were, first of all, meaningful and second, pronounceable. The order of presentation of letters (in words) has been established by the research of Gibson (54) and others (37). Further research has indicated that strings of letters are most readily learned when meaningful, then if pronounceable but not necessarily meaningful, and, poorest of all, if neither meaningful nor pronounceable (53, 137).

Despite all the emphasis upon letter discrimination, Gibson recognizes that reading is not a letter-by-letter sequence. She thinks that the unit of recognition is a spelling pattern—a cluster of letters with an invariant pronunciation (called phonograms by other authors). Meaning is less important, in Gibson's opinion, than pronounceability, even though she admits that real words are more easily perceived than are nonword pronounceable strings.

Although some aspects of Gibson's theories are supported by the research, the deemphasis upon the role of meaningfulness in word recognition is in conflict with a variety of other studies. Thomas, for example, has shown that words are recognized more accurately in tachistoscopic exposure than are pronounceable three-letter trigrams at primary ages (137). Many other laboratory and classroom reports confirm this fact. In several recent reports, S. Jay Samuels (114, 115, 117, 118) has redemonstrated the greater speed and accuracy of word recognition of pairs of words between which an association had been established.   In this type of experiment, the speed of reacting to the associations was even greater among children than among adults.   Similarly, when selections contain high association words (as dark–night, dark–light, dark–black) in the context, both rate and comprehension were enhanced among school children and college students.   Kolers (80) and others doubt seriously that the geometry of letters is crucial to their recognition.

The Gibson-Richards materials do control the appearance of letters in words in terms of their discriminability, but apparently no attention is paid to the variations in sounds represented by the letters.   For example, in the same unit introducing the letter *t*, it may represent the sound of *d,* or *t,* or be used in both *th* sounds; *s* appears with the sound of *s*, *sh*, and *z* within a page or two. Furthermore, these instructional materials are severely controlled in sentence patterns using repetitively only three common simple structures, the 1-2-4, 1-2-5, and 1-2-4-6 (subject-verb-complement; subject-verb-predicate nominative; subject-verb-complement-modifier).   Pictures on each line were used repetitively to promote associations for each new picturable word.   Structure words or nonpicturable words are largely avoided.   Finally, the repetition of the highly concrete vocabulary was at least one and one-half times as frequent as that in the repetitious basal readers.

A. R. MacKinnon (84) explored the use of the Gibson-Richards materials with Scottish children.   He contrasted the progress of groups using this with teacher direction, without teacher aid, and a control group using a basal.   His results tended to favor the experimental groups, and he attributed this to the control of letter introduction in the materials.   Unfortunately, his findings are relatively meaningless, for the differences in reading progress may have been the result of any of the three or four variables present—letter control, sentence pattern control, the highly concrete and repetitive vocabulary, the picture reinforcements, or simply the Hawthorne effect.

A very useful observation that MacKinnon made, however, was the spontaneous development of various word analysis techniques, both conventional and original, displayed by the children working independently of teacher direction.   He noted also their intensive use of the pictures to identify words, their trial and error in reading words, their spontaneous self-corrections, and finally their tendency to substitute familiar phrases or patterns of words in the context.   Progress of these children was excellent without constant teacher corrections and directions and might remind some reading teachers of the inner resources and motivation children would show if given the opportunity.

These various modified alphabets and alphabetic approaches will probably continue to appear in various guises from time to time. In fact, some of the most recent instructional systems discussed later in this chapter are but new versions of this ancient method. There is a persuasive logic in returning to the fundamentals—letters—from which words are composed, as a basis for teaching reading. The reason that such approaches falter is that reading is more than a letter-by-letter recognition, and the word is greater than the sum of its parts.

DECODING OR PHONIC SYSTEMS

Phonic systems carry the emphasis upon letter forms of the alphabetic systems one step further to include knowledge of the sounds represented by the individual letters. Historically, phonic systems are perhaps the oldest method in American reading instruction. Moreover, according to Wilder's opinion surveys (145), about two-thirds of the public favor phonic instruction over the whole word or any other method, perhaps because most of them believe they were taught by this method. Because of this nostalgic public approval and the long history of apparent success, new phonic programs (or rather old systems under new labels) constantly appear upon the instructional scene, reiterate their panacea-like claims, dominate reading instruction for a short period, and then are replaced by newer (?) schemes (126).

As Constance M. McCullough (94) has observed, current innovative phonics programs arose as an answer to basal reader approaches that did not stress sounding out words (enough to satisfy the critics). As in the past, some schools responded to the pressure by adopting such systems exclusively (for a period of time) or adding them to existing programs. As Arthur Heilman sees them (65), these phonic programs emphasize beginning reading only, saturate this instructional period with analysis of letter sounds, and produce a favorable effect upon word recognition test scores, only. Since primary reading tests deal primarily with word recognition, phonic systems appear successful, at least by this criterion. In contrasting the effectiveness of code (phonics) or meaning-emphasis approaches in the First Grade Reading studies, Dykstra (39) again points out the superiority of code methods in oral word pronunciation and silent word recognition. At the same time, he cites their inferiority to meaning-emphasis programs in accuracy of oral reading, spelling, silent reading comprehension, and rate of oral reading.

Phonics or decoding systems are of two types: analytic—in which letter sounds are taught as integral parts of words, and synthetic—in which the isolated letter sounds are stressed and taught, often prior to any great experience with whole words. Despite the lack of any sizeable amount of corroborating research, some programs begin with long or short vowel sounds, then teach consonant sounds, while others reverse this sequence.

When used as the basic tool for learning to read, phonics gives the child the impression that English is regularly spelled, that most words can be sounded out, that reading is sounding out words, and that, when the symbols are decoded into sounds, the act of reading is complete (94). Because of its heavy demand upon auditory imagery and auditory discrimination, a phonics program creates difficulties for children lacking these auditory characteristics, for those with hearing losses, particularly in high tones, and for those with foreign language or strong dialect backgrounds.

At the same time, there is ample research to indicate that ability to analyze words phonically is of great assistance at primary reading levels, or, in other words, when the words are sufficiently familiar to the reader that he can recognize them when he pronounces them. The crux of the dispute lies in the degree of emphasis that should be given this word analysis skill. Some light on this facet of the argument may be gleaned from the observations of Harris, Serwer, and Gold (61), who discovered negative correlations (-.61 and -.75) between the time spent on phonics and eventual word knowledge achievement, and time on phonics and reading comprehension.

Words in Color

Rationale Gattegno has offered a phonic program with the added use of color to aid the child in distinguishing common letter sounds. He identifies and assigns a color to forty-seven sounds, first to five short vowels, later to the consonants. Consonant substitution, or forming new words by varying the first letter, is also taught. The program is intended to cover an eight-week period, after which the child will, presumably, be able to decode any word and progress in reading.

Methods and Materials The program consists of twenty-one colored charts and several in black and white; a Phonic Code chart presenting the 270 letter combinations found in the forty-seven sounds identified by the author (in forty-seven colors); and a series of three workbooks, 1,020 word cards, worksheets, a Book of Stories, and a teacher's guide. At some time during the program, the color charts are abandoned and replaced by those in black and white. The method of instruction emphasizes a "dynamic" approach by teaching cursive writing; by forming all vowels by varying the shape of the letter *a*; and by intensive practice in enunciating clearly the separate sounds of each word being analyzed.   In summary, this is a synthetic phonics system with the added fillip of color.

Critique
The author's reports on his own research with illiterate adults in several countries are rather vague, as are his references to trials with migrant children, illiterate adults, first graders, and so on, in this country.   Other researchers, fortunately, give more specific details.   Dodds (23, 24) reports on a longitudinal study from kindergarten to third grade comparing Words in Color with a basal reader program.   After four years in Words in Color, he found no significant differences in vocabulary, comprehension, or spelling.   An early advantage in word recognition in the Words in Color group disappeared by the third grade (24).   Hill (67) found no significant differences among first graders following Words in Color, or a basal or another phonics system.   Hinds and Dodds (68) report higher scores on vocabulary and spelling, but not in comprehension, for a small primary group at the end of the second grade.   A second trial with illiterate adults again favored Words in Color in these skills, but the comparison is unjustified, since the adult groups were not equated in intelligence. Lockmiller and Di Nello (83) report no significant differences on a reading test of vocabulary and comprehension or on a comprehensive test of phonic skills in the second grade for pupils using Words in Color or a basal with a strong intrinsic phonics component.   The second graders in this study were retarded in reading.

Words in Color is not the first attempt to add the element of color to a phonics system, for Nellie Dale in 1899 indentified vowel sounds with red, voiceless consonants with blue, voiced consonants with black, and yellow for silent letters; and several similar British schemes are mentioned by Morris (97). Recently Jones added a color to each letter shape in what is called Colour Story Reading (73); in a comparison with i.t.a. and a basal, he found his superior for reading and spelling.   Just what was involved in the comparative methods is not available to us.

There is a question as to the exact contribution of color to learning to read in a synthetic phonics program.   Many earlier studies in spelling indicate that marking hard spots consistently in color was of no value (109).   In paired-associate learning, Underwood, Ham, and Ekstrand (139) found no advantage in colored backgrounds for the pairs of words to be learned.   In fact, the children learned the colors better than the words, demonstrating again the known tendency for the learner to make a selection among the cues offered him in a compound stimuli.   Otto (103) found the order of a list of paired associates more significant to learning than the printing of them in color; and Samuels (116) discovered that printing one of the pairs in red, the others in black, was helpful during the learning trials. But in the transfer test on all black words there were fewer correct responses to the items presented in red. It would appear that any initial advantage from the use of color in association with a letter or word disappears when the learner must read normal black-and-white words.

Heilman (65) raises this very point in referring to the fact that in using Words in Color the child never reads anything in color except the beginning colored charts, even in the reading materials supplied with the system. Perhaps Gattegno has recognized the impossibility of transferring the color learning, and this is probably the reason that it is discarded early in his program.

THE LANGUAGE EXPERIENCE APPROACH

Strictly speaking, the language experience approach is not an innovation, for it has been recognized as a stage in beginning reading since about 1900. But it is being used innovatively today as a total medium for teaching primary reading in many school systems. The language experience method is now being recognized as a complete approach based on the total process of the child's language development in speaking, writing, listening, and reading. Books and other instructional materials become adjuncts or resources to the program of overall language development rather than, as in most other methods, forming the heart of the system.

Rationale
As outlined by Lee and Allen, by Stauffer, and by other proponents (20, 66), the language experience bases learning to read upon the child's classroom and extraschool life experiences. Using these experiences, various work-centers in the classroom, pictures, books, and many other audio-visual materials, the child learns to talk about his ideas and experiences, write about them, and then read what he and other children have written.

Methods and Materials
The materials prepared by the children are used in a variety of language, dramatic, and reading skill development activities. Reading vocabulary, phonic skills, and mechanics of writing—as well as handwriting and the development of speaking, writing, and listening vocabularies—are promoted in multiple uses of the child-produced material. The program moves from small-group oral composition, written down by the teacher, toward individualized or interest-group composition written down by the children. Its purpose is much broader than a preparation for the reading of basal readers, as

some authors seem to think (12). The material composed by the children *is* the reading program; and, since it includes content from all the instructional areas (as social science, science, nature study, health, and so on), it is actually broader in scope and depth than are common readers at this level.

At the same time, because of its relatively individualized or small-group nature, the child's reading program is paced to his own development in thinking and the use of language. The charts and stories that he contributes are phrased only in familiar language patterns (or even in his own dialect) and deal with completely familiar concepts, an advantage available in no other type of program. Since the language experience method is one of total language development keyed to the child's rate of progress, it has been especially useful for children in classes for the mentally retarded (146), for the language-handicapped low socioeconomic groups (104, 105, 120, 124), or for bilingual or variant dialect groups (56, 123). Other writers have pointed out the peculiar advantages of this approach for the functionally illiterate, or potential school dropouts who are retarded in reading (42), although as yet there is little research justification for its use in these special groups. Keith (74) conducted a 200-day program with bilingual pupils. One group followed the language experience approach in both Spanish and English with a special emphasis upon the Spanish-American–Anglo heritage of the group. This group excelled pupils following the basal method in word discrimination and was also superior in this skill to a control group given a special oral language program in English. There were no differences among the groups in word meaning or paragraph reading at the end of the program. The implications of this study are obscure, however, for the superiority of the language experience group could have been due to the use of that method, or to the bilingual instruction, or to the emphasis upon their cultural heritage in their chart stories.

The author served as a consultant to a project in five middle schools of Tampa, Florida. The seventh- to ninth-grade pupils were taught the content of the usual science, social science, English, and mathematics through the language experience medium, since most of them were unable to utilize the appropriate textbooks. Each day the teacher and the pupils collated all that they knew about a topic from visual aids, experience, demonstrations, and discussion. These facts were written on the blackboard as phrased by the pupils, then duplicated, and read and discussed the following day. At the end of the first year of the project, the pupils showed significantly greater gains in reading, language usage, study skills, and social science than in previous years. There were also decreases in absences and school dropouts during the school year.

The approach to learning to read better from one's own writings has particular advantages for corrective or remedial instruction, in our opinion. What the student can talk and write about, he can surely read. Thus the threat of failure ever present in book reading is absent, and the student is free to progress successfully in accordance with his other verbal skills. He will, of course, use some books and other resources as sources of facts to be incorporated into his own writing and reading. But these will be largely self-selected for their relevance to his own interests, not thrust upon him by the dictates of a structured reading program. Thus the language experience approach may be more closely attuned to the learner's interests and language development than is any other system of learning to read.

Critique   The criticisms of the language experience approach include a lack of repetition of basic vocabulary; introduction of words of only temporary value; memorization of the charts rather than true reading; restriction of the content of the reading material to children's knowledge and experiences; and lack of organization and sequential development in the children's writings (12). Others claim that it has inherent weaknesses in sequential skill development, that it is difficult to conduct in large classes, and, finally, that there is much incidental or opportunistic learning rather than systematic instruction (66). Supporters of language experience refute all these criticisms when the approach is supervised in a planned in-service training program in which teachers are trained and assisted by the available guides and manuals (1).

Exemplifying the renaissance of interest in the language experience approach was its inclusion in six of the large-scale First Grade Reading studies. In their three-year study of the language experience versus a basal reader approach Stauffer and Hammond (129) report that, at the end of the first grade, the language experience pupils were superior in most of the formal measures used in all the First Grade Reading studies, including word reading, paragraph reading, oral accuracy, three word lists, writing mechanics, and number of running words in compositions. Their language experience girls also excelled the basal pupils in a test of spelling.

Kendrick and Bennett (75) reported their results in terms of HSE (high socioeconomic) and LSE (Low socioeconomic) groups, as well as separately for boys and girls. At the end of the first year, both HSE and LSE basal boys excelled in paragraph reading. Among the language experience groups, HSE girls were superior in arithmetic; LSE boys, in attitude toward reading. Both sexes in both HSE and LSE groups were superior to basal pupils in the number of running words in their compositions. In this study, measures of speaking, unique to the Kendrick-Bennett study, indicated superiority for the basal pupils in number of different words, total number of words, mean sentence length, and sentence complexity. A difference in a measure of listening also showed basal low socioeconomic girls to be superior. The language experience pupils excelled only in the ratio of the number of different words to their total number of words in speaking tests.

McCanne's study (91) contrasted basal, language experience and Teaching English as a Second Language by an aural-oral approach among Spanish-speaking first graders. In his population he included his own tests of understanding spoken English (no differences according to method) and oral vocabulary (better for basal and TESL). For these Spanish-speaking pupils, McCanne concluded that either of the two experimental methods would be desirable for developing language skills, when used as a supplement to the basal program.

McCanne's basal pupils were superior in word and paragraph reading, vocabulary, and attitude toward reading at the end of the first grade. His language experience group excelled only in the number of running words.

Harris, Serwer, and Gold (61) conducted their first-grade study of the basal, the language experience, the same plus a strong audio-visual program, and a heavy phonics program among disadvantaged, largely black, inner-city children. The only differences were in superior performances for the basal pupils in paragraph reading and attitude toward reading, although the groups in his experiment all tended to score higher than comparable classes in the same schools (Hawthorne effect?) but still below national norms.

Hahn's language experience pupils were superior in word reading and vocabulary only to the matched i.t.a. and basal pupils (58). There were no other differences among the groups. Vilscek's (141) language experience pupils were superior at the end of the first grade in word reading, paragraph reading, and vocabulary; in word study (phonics); in two of the three word lists; and in attitude toward reading, when compared with pupils in a broad basal program. At the end of the second grade, Kendrick and Bennett (75) again used unique tests of speaking and writing. In the total of words used in speaking, language experience pupils excelled in all groups and sexes, while in the number of different words, the basal pupils were superior. In their writing test, low socioeconomic basal boys were superior in number of different words and total words, while high socioeconomic girls were best in average sentence length, at the end of the second grade.

In the standardized tests, HSE basal pupils were superior in word meaning (girls only), in paragraph meaning, in attitude toward reading (girls only), in writing mechanics (boys only), and in number of books read (girls only). Among LSE pupils, the language experience-trained pupils were superior in science, social science, and (the boys only) in number of running words, number of different words, and in spelling in their compositions.

Hahn's second-year results (58) showed superiority for the language experience pupils in ten of the fourteen standardized tests, excepting vocabulary, arithmetic computation, arithmetic concepts, and oral reading. At this time, these pupils also excelled in number of running words and books read. Basal pupils were superior only in writing mechanics.

Vilscek's second-grade language experience pupils were found to excel in tests of spelling, arithmetic concepts, science, and social science in comparison with the basal pupils (142).

Stauffer and Hammond (130) employed their own measures of originality of content, consistency in story sequence, and total of polysyllabic words in the children's writing. The language experience children were consistently superior in all these measures during the three consecutive years of this study. Other three-year results from Stauffer and Hammond indicate superiority for language experience pupils in paragraph meaning (girls only), spelling, science, social studies concepts, oral rate and accuracy; in two oral word lists; in writing mechanics, number of running words, and number of different words. Basal boys continued to show superiority in arithmetic computation. At the conclusion of their third year, Harris and Morrison (60) report no significant differences in test scores among the four methods contrasted. They note, however, that teachers who had used the language experience method, alone or with audio-visual aids, and had learned how to use it effectively after a year or so, tended to continue with this approach in conjunction with their former basal method. The authors noted also that these teachers were more permissive, less rigid, and more creative as a result of their experience with the language experience approach. Harris and Coleman concluded that when audio-visual aids were added to the language experience method to a significant degree, the method would probably be more effective.

In summarizing these one- to three-year studies, there do appear certain distinct advantages for the method for certain pupils. Pupils are apparently helped to grow in writing ability in the length of their compositions and in their spelling in these creative efforts. The development of a broader informational background as in science and social science is fostered by the second or third year of training. Reading development, as in word or paragraph reading and vocabulary, is at least as great as in basal programs. Among high socioeconomic pupils, the basal seems to produce better development of reading skills, and yet the language experience does not show any strong advantage for economically deprived pupils in this same area.

The language experience approach does appeal to teachers who try it for a period of years, particularly as an adjunct to their basal program, as Harris notes (60). Perhaps the effect that the method has on the classroom climate, as in reducing the authoritarian nature of the pupil-teacher relationship observed by Hoihjelle (70), explains this attitude of the teachers.

A good, controlled study by Cramer (18) contrasts the effect of the language experience approach, particularly on spelling and children's writing. Language experience children who were encouraged to write, without constant correction, achieved equally well on tests of irregularly and regularly spelled words and were superior to basal pupils in those spellings as well as in number of running words and number of different words in their compositions. Basal pupils achieved better spelling of regular than irregular words but were inferior in accuracy in both types to the language experience pupils.

OTHER CURRENT APPROACHES

There are a number of other systems of beginning reading hovering around the fringe of the field. Some of these are innovative; others represent a renaissance of old, but not forgotten, approaches. Among those revived from the past is the Montessori method. This includes several current concepts, for example, the impressions of letters and sounds as introductory to reading; motor education, which, to Montessori, meant everyday movements, care of the body and person, manual work, and gymnastic and rhythmic exercises. Montessori used sandpaper letters, groups of letters and words of different sizes and colors; consonant and vowel groups in black sandpaper on white background in vertical script, as well as word cards. Then later phrases, sentences, sentence games in actions or following directions, and, finally, books were used. Theoretically, Montessori sequenced these experiences in a learning order and encouraged self-correction, an early version of programming and learning by discovery. A fact often forgotten by American practitioners of her method is that Montessori proposed teaching reading only after the child reached the age of six years. To our knowledge, there are no published research studies demonstrating the values of this approach.

Two approaches have made much use of neurological jargon to justify their rationale. One of these offered by Delacato (27) emphasizes that failure in any language difficulty such as reading is due to lack of the child's development of cortical hemispheric dominance or complete one-sidedness in handedness, eyedness, and foot preference. The program takes children through a schedule of creeping and crawling and other exercises that will presumably establish the necessary sidedness by stimulating a reorganization of neural connections. Glass and Robbins (55), after reviewing critically twelve studies of Delacato's treatment methods, found them all completely inadequate in statistical controls. Not one study, they say, can be considered to support the claims made for this therapy for improving reading performances. Having carefully learned the treatment, Robbins (107) applied it to second graders in comparison to a group given nonspecific patterning training (as contrasted with Delacato's emphasis upon use of exercises to produce one-sidedness) and a traditional control group. The results did not support Delacato's postulated relationship between neurological organization and reading achievement; moreover, the special program did not enhance reading development in any way or affect the development of laterality. But those who are impressed by the pseudo-scientific basis of Delacato's treatment continue to seek its panacea effect.

A second neurologically based method, or so it is claimed, has been termed the "Neurological Impress Remedial Reading Technique (64). All this amounts to is having the teacher and the child read aloud together or the child repeat aloud after the teacher. It sounds just like the method used in the Dames' schools of England several centuries ago. In this age of technology, however, the system has been quickly adapted by using tapes in place of the Dame or teacher. Hollingsworth (71) utilized tapes in a classroom wireless system for thirty sessions with eight pairs of children and found no significant gains in vocabulary, comprehension, accuracy, or speed. Hite (69) claimed that in ninety days a retarded reading primary-age group made from two to five months' gain in word recognition, but there were no differences when the taped lessons were used with or without worksheets from a control group given only seatwork exercises. Railsback (106) used such an approach with functionally illiterate adolescents in which the subject listened to tapes while looking at the identical material in printed form. Gains per instructional month of forty hours averaged a half year or more in test scores, although the author feels that the program could be greatly improved.

The Impress Method has been further expanded technologically by the use of records, as in *The Talking Page,* manufactured by Rank of England, similar combinations of records or tapes, and by parallel reading materials in America (*Decoding for Meaning* by Macmillan Company and many others); and even by adding a computerized talking typewriter as in O. K. Moore's *Responsive Environment Program.* The method is intriguing enough to warrant some careful comparative research to discover what, if anything, it will add to reading instruction.

Another technological approach to reading is manifest in the filmstrip program espoused by McCracken (93), in which one entire reading period each day was spent reading a frame of a filmstrip. The frame presented the same page of the reader used in the second reading lesson of the day. No recreational reading or language activities were allowed to intrude on the program, although the workbooks accompanying the reader were utilized in the afternoon reading lesson. McCracken offers statistical evidence that all the children learned to read, as evidenced by the lowest score of 1.9 at the end of first grade, on a reading test ten years old. No comparisons with other groups were made, and the above-average intelligence of his groups was ignored in interpreting his results. Ungaro (140) reports a similarly almost meaningless experiment using, like McCracken, filmstrips identical with the reader and teacher-composed stories, plus two reading lessons a day. He then compared his experimental classes with last year's classes taught by the same teachers, claiming that more of the filmstrip-trained group were above grade level then last year's groups. Since his classes were split in half for one reading lesson for each half, there is no way of evaluating the relative effects of class size, filmstrip method, or Hawthorne effect.

Methods for Parents

Recognizing that parents could play a part in stimulating their children's reading achievement has led several entrepreneurs to devise home-teaching methods. One of these, written by a physical therapist whose association with Delacato apparently qualified him as a reading specialist, has offered a system of cards in large red letters containing common words, simple sentences, short stories, and the alphabet (25). The kit was sold through advertisements in the Sunday magazine section of many newspapers as a "simple, joyous approach" to teaching toddlers to read. No evidence that teaching children to read at two, three, or four would be either successful or desirable for the average child was offered by the author, although he buttressed his sales pitch by quoting part of the research on early readers by Dolores Durkin (38), omitting to quote, of course, her observation that children taught to read during preschool ages by their parents do *not* maintain the temporary acceleration.

The idea that young children can and should learn to read under parental tutelage is held by a number of writers (131), and other materials are available for this purpose, as the Allen kit (2), which employs a system like the Impress method, and a programmed primer by the Grolier Society (47). Suffice it to say, that there is as yet little evidence of any permanent educational value in beginning reading instruction during preschool years, and even less evidence that such instruction contributes to child development or the child's social or emotional needs.

Pupil Teams and Pupil Tutors

Donald D. Durrell, formerly of Boston University, has been prominent in promoting the use of pupil teams or pairs of pupils in a helping relationship. Less capable students seem to respond with improvement when matched with a superior student of the same age. Other studies have suggested that arrangements of pairs of pupils or groups up to as large as four show comparatively good results (77). When teacher aides are not feasible and the class is relatively large, pupil teams or very small groups can reinforce the teacher's efforts. These arrangements are most successful when the skills emphasized can be improved by repeated practice, as in dictionary use, spelling, sight vocabulary, and word analysis. And, as we shall point out, some attention to the attitudes and human relations skills of the tutor or leader of the group will also be profitable.

Pupil tutors may be drawn from older pupils as well as from within the same class, with profit for both, as many recent studies show (78, 96). When given at least four hours tutoring per week by high school pupils, Cloward's (17) intermediate pupils showed improvement in reading; so did the tutors themselves. Similarly, Frager and Stern's sixth graders improved in morale, attendance, and self-concept as a result of tutoring kindergarteners in pre-reading skills (48). Five sessions of counseling were given the sixth graders either in pupil-tutor relationships or principles of learning, but these types of training did not produce different effects among their respective kindergarten pupils, although the tutored groups excelled nontutored controls.

Other studies indicate that with a modicum of training, even inter-mediate-grade pupils show growth in techniques of maintaining rapport (99) and that specific training procedures can be validated (100).

Lambert's study (81) cautions us that the desired effects of pupil teams are not always apparent immediately. Some teams or groups develop the necessary esprit and cohesion slowly and only after a period of what appears to be rivalry and disorganization. But, once these problems of group organization have been worked out, the pupils involved do show academic gains.

Operant Conditioning

Operant conditioning, as we now see it in schools, is a systematic approach to learning borrowed from the fields of animal and experimental psychology. Basically the approach involves analyzing the learning into small steps, repeated frequently, with immediate reinforcement or reward until the desired behavior becomes fixed. Transfer of this learning theory into the classroom has taken the forms of programmed instruction and systems approaches, computer-assisted instruction, and, more recently, behavior modification.

Programmed instruction was the first application of operant condition-ing introduced to schools in the 1950s. Learning of a specific skill such as sight vocabulary was arranged in minute steps called frames, with each frame involving the learner in an active response such as inserting a single letter or a word in a context. The pages of the material were so arranged that the learner's response was immediately confirmed by an answer in the margin or on the back of the page. Several types of programming became available, as linear (in which the learner moved simply from one frame to the next) and branching (which directs the learner to another page for repeated or corrective frames in case of an error). Programmed instructional materials took the form of a worksheet of a half-dozen frames, an entire workbook, or combinations of a film, filmstrip, or tape with accompanying worksheets or workbooks. Some programs necessitated a "teaching machine," which held the work pages, covered the learner's answer when he moved the roll of paper forward to receive the reinforcement, and recorded his answers on a disposable roll, so that the program itself was reusable.

Ellson, Harris, and Barber (44) experimented with a variety of programmed procedures, some of which involved a tutor in a coaching and supportive role. They soon discovered that the value of the tutor varied greatly and also that the training was more effective when used as an adjunct to regular classroom instruction than when independent of the normal reading program. As a result of these experiments, Ellson and his coworkers dispensed with the mechanical scroll used earlier and devised a number of materials that in effect programmed both the learner and the tutor in reading activities directly paralleling the materials of the basal reader program. These instructional materials have had extensive trial, and the one-to-one relationship makes a contribution to the development of the learner (92, 144).

Programmed instruction eventually broadened into what are now called systems approaches. Fundamentally, a systems approach supplies the teacher with almost all the instructional materials she is apt to need in following a reading program as it is defined by the authors of the system. Some systems consist of a multitude of worksheets, perhaps supplemented by cassettes and headsets, or skill books, or practice exercises, and even graduated supplementary reading materials. Record keeping may be performed by the pupil and/or the teacher or, in some instances, by a computer that reports each day's performances to the teacher. Any of these instructional materials used in each system is usually programmed and sequenced in terms of the authors' objectives for the learners. Progress may be measured by regularly spaced tests or in terms of the amount of time consumed by the pupil on each unit or, in a few cases, by graphs or charts of the units of work completed.

Computer-assisted instruction is, in effect, a complicated extension of programmed instruction. It sometimes involves not only a computer containing the program but also a variety of other devices that can respond to the child's typing or writing at the basic machine, correct auditorily his errors, provide corrective exercises, and record his progress. When first offered to schools, as by Atkinson and Hansen (5), their complex group of electronic devices was suggested as sufficient for a complete reading program for the first grade. More recently, this claim has been modified, stimulated perhaps by the implications of Ellson's research, to the offer of the training as only part of an instructional program that would need to be reinforced by ordinary classroom instruction (4).

There is little doubt that programmed instruction is effective, at least in the factual or mechanical aspects of reading. To cite only a few examples of the comparative studies, Feldhusen, Lamb, and Feldhusen (46), Bloomer (9), and Crimmins (19) found superior results in programmed learning when compared with basal systems in several different reading skills. At the kindergarten level, McNeil (95) obtained good results for boys in a seventeen-day prereading skills program. However, in the first grade, where they were not isolated from the girls, the boys' superiority disappeared after four months. Malpass (86, 87) had contradictory results in two experiments with mentally retarded pupils, while Blackman and Capobianco (8) found no advantages in programmed instruction for severely retarded adolescents.

Hamill and Mattelman (59) used a programmed approach for second–third graders in an inner-city school with no advantages apparent beyond the basal, while Rodgers and Fox (108) found that the programmed material gave greater word-naming ability, no difference in word discrimination, and inferior comprehension at the end of the first grade. Ruddell (111) contrasted reading development by a basal versus a program versus both of these approaches modified by an additional language structure training. Citing only his results for the basal versus the program, the latter was superior in producing word recognition on a standardized test and in a list of irregular words, but not in paragraph or sentence meaning, vocabulary, phonic skills, or a regular word list, at the end of the first grade. In the second grade, the basal was superior to the program only in paragraph and sentence reading.

Above the primary grades, the research in support of programmed materials is rather inconclusive. In the New York City experiment (41), in a fifth-grade study (13), and in vocabulary development in junior high school (50), no advantages appeared for programs versus traditional methods.

It is fairly obvious that operant conditioning, programmed instruction, or computer-assisted instruction must define learning to read in terms suitable to the nature of the devices employed. Reading has to be defined as a step-by-step procedure in practicing what amounts to a sound-symbol rela-tionship, a word-picture association, or a word discrimination task in order to fit the limitations of the media. As exemplified in the programs currently offered, the material cannot often relate to the normal speech or auditory experiences of the learner, to his experiential background, or to the modality strengths or weaknesses of the learner. The necessity for a step-by-step procedure demands a preplanned sequence of words and word elements that may or may not be relevant to these characteristics of each learner.

The preplanned sequence inherent in this approach to learning almost precludes teacher-pupil interaction or teacher-planned instruction keyed to her assessment of pupil needs or any flexibility in the emphasis upon a particular learning modality. Changes in instructional method or the content of the reading program are impossible unless programming is relegated to a very minor role in the total program. Other objections are these:

1. Despite publisher's claims, this is not an individualized approach, for it is practically the same program for all the children.
2. Learning to read tends to become atomized into disjointed bits and apparently unrelated skills, not a moving process of interpretation that involves the use of many skills almost simultaneously;
3. Reading training is apt to be divorced from the supportive areas of speaking, listening, and writing, with which it has a symbiotic relationship.

As one expert on programmed instruction has phrased it, programmed or computer assisted instruction cannot deal with the highly significant factors of the learner's aptitudes and personality variables or with the all-important teacher-pupil interaction. Yet it appears that, particularly in the more mechanical reading skills, this approach may serve as an adjunct to teacher instruction.

Behavior Modification

Arising from the same sources as programmed learning, behavior modification has recently made its impact felt in school situations. This system of pupil management employs many of the same principles in trying to move pupils toward a desired social behavior by a system of sequenced steps followed by reinforcement or reward until the desired behavior is habituated. Reinforcers may take the form of verbal praise, commendation, or encouragement; or of material rewards in the form of candy, toys, or other commonly desirable objects or tokens that may be exchanged for these rewards or used to secure certain privileges.

While relatively new to educators, behavior modification has already been used successfully in institutions for the mentally retarded or emotionally disturbed and similar situations. Some instructional systems employed in contracts with schools have combined behavior modification techniques with programmed materials in an effort to stimulate the academic progress of disadvantaged pupils. It was assumed that the combination of behavior modification techniques with a programmed systems approach would produce normal or better-than-normal progress and thus enable these pupils to overcome their academic retardation. The Office of Economic Opportunity, which sponsored many of these performance contracts, has commented upon their lack of success in recent newspaper releases. Hardly any of the programs produced the gains promised or resulted in progress in reading achievement equal to that in average schools.*

These results, however, should not be interpreted as indications of the failures of behavior modification techniques, for there were obviously many other possible explanations of the poor outcomes of the performance contracts. Behavior modification can help improve reading achievement, as a number of studies show. For example, massive verbal praise or rewarding good behavior, promptness, and regular attendance with tokens to be exchanged for grades and letters of recommendation were very effective with retarded readers of high school age in two recent research reports (16, 89), and other studies confirm these results (128, 138).

Although the basic principles are widely recognized, there will be need for research in exploring the relative merits of verbal versus material reinforcement for different types and social classes of children; in determining how long and how often the schedule of reinforcements must continue to achieve permanent results; and just how this approach to pupil management can be combined with counseling and guidance as well as instructional approaches. Behavior modification has moved beyond operant conditioning and programmed instruction in recognizing that simple knowledge of correctness in a task may not be sufficient motivation for many learners. Real and meaningful rewards or punishment, such as loss of tokens or privileges, extend the motivational or behavior-shaping effect beyond that inherent in programmed instruction.

Teacher Aides

Among the many current efforts to improve instruction in the classroom is the movement to employ teacher aides. The motivation for this practice is often mixed and conflicting, with some schools trying to relieve the teacher of petty

---

*Robert B. Ruddell has edited a critique of performance contracting, *Accountability and Reading* (Urbana, Ill.: National Council of Teachers of English, 1973).

responsibilities, while others try to train their aides to function effectively in small-group instruction. Some school systems seem doubtful of the values of having relatively untrained adults assisting in the classroom; they limit the use of aides to mechanical, nonprofessional activities only, and then, perhaps for only a small part of the school day. Other systems have accepted the idea wholeheartedly and, in effect, flood the classroom with more assistants than perhaps the teacher knows what to do with.

Arthur W. Schoeller and David A. Pearson (119) report results from an experiment in Milwaukee with trained teacher aides. After ten hours of preservice training, aides were placed in ten centers supervised by parttime reading teachers. The pupils responded with significant gains in word recognition and phonic skills and an average gain of 3.6 months in oral reading after three months of instruction. Other favorable results were improved attitudes toward reading and better work habits. Another experiment with kindergarten pupils demonstrated that use of an aide not only helped in readiness skills but also stimulated persistence and attention span in several nonreading tests (63). Goralski and Kerl (57) showed that intelligent use of a single aide in the kindergarten produced more growth in readiness than the teacher did alone, or a teacher assisted by as many as two to five aides.

These and other studies seem to indicate that trained teacher aides can make a real contribution to the professional work of the teacher. With some understanding of the goals and proper procedures to be followed, and with instructional materials selected by the teacher in terms of the pupil's individual needs, the teacher aide can function effectively particularly in corrective and remedial situations.

LEARNING PROJECT

Outline a plan for using behavior modification with a pupil retarded in reading to produce a specific change in an aspect of his reading behavior.

1. Describe the specific skill that you intend to modify and what you will consider a successful performance.

2. What type of reinforcement will you use and under what conditions? Tokens, candy, praise, or what?

3. What will your reinforcement schedule be—immediately after each successful performance; after several performances; once a day, or what?

4. Explain why you chose this particular type of reinforcement and justify its suitability in terms of the pupil's characteristics, such as sex, age, interests.

5. Estimate the length of time needed to bring about the desired change in the pupil's performance in the skill.

6. Do you believe that the treatment program you have outlined will be successful?

REFERENCES

1. Allen, Roach Van, *Language Experiences in Reading.* Chicago: Encyclopaedia Britannica, 1966.

2. Allen, Robert L., and Virginia I., *Reading Along with Me.* New York: Teachers College Press, 1966.

3. Asher, J. William, "Comment on Spelling Achievement Following i.t.a. Instruction," *Reading Teacher,* 22 (November 1968), 153–56.

4. Atkinson, R. C., "Instruction in Initial Reading under Computer Control: The Stanford Project," *Journal of Educational Data Processing,* 4 (1967), 175–92.

5. Atkinson, R. C., and Hansen, Duncan N., "Computer-Assisted Instruction in Initial Reading: The Stanford Project," *Reading Research Quarterly,* 2 (Fall 1966), 5–26.

6. Barclay, G. L., "i.t.a. with Emotionally Disturbed Children," in *Modern Educational Developments: Another Look,* Proceedings Educational Records Bureau Conference, 30 (1966), 135–46.

7. Birnie, J. R., "Inconsistencies in i.t.a. and TO—An Examination of Four Popular Children's Readers," *Reading,* 1 (1967), 19–25.

8. Blackman, L. S., and Capobianco, R. J., "An Evaluation of Programmed Instruction with the Mentally Retarded Utilizing Teaching Machines," *American Journal of Mental Deficiency,* 70 (1965), 262–69.

9. Bloomer, Richard H., "A Progressive-Choice Technique of Organizing Reading Materials," *Elementary School Journal,* 65 (December 1964), 153–58.

10. Bond, Guy L., "First-Grade Reading Studies: An Overview," *Elementary English,* 43 (May 1966), 464–70.

11. Bond, Guy L., and Dykstra, Robert, "The Cooperative Research Program in First-Grade Reading Instruction," *Reading Research Quarterly,* 2 (Summer 1967), 5–142.

12. Burns, Paul C., "A Re-Examination of the Role of Experience Charts," *Elementary English,* 36 (November 1959), 480–83, 532.

13. Calder, Clarence R., Jr., "Self-Directed Reading Materials," *Reading Teacher,* 21 (December 1967), 248–52.

14. Chasnoff, R. E., "Two Alphabets," *Elementary School Journal,* 67 (1967), 257–64.

15. Chasnoff, R. E., "Two Alphabets: A Follow-up," *Elementary School Journal,* 68 (1968), 251–57.

16. Clark, C. A., and Walberg, H. J., "The Influence of Massive Rewards on Reading Achievement in Potential Urban School Dropouts," *American Educational Research Journal,* 5 (1968), 305–10.

17. Cloward, R. D., "Studies in Tutoring," *Journal of Experimental Education,* 36 (1967), 14–25.

18. Cramer, Ronald L., "An Investigation of First-Grade Spelling Achievement," *Elementary English,* 47 (February 1970), 230–40.
19. Crimmins, Leonora A., "And Now There Are Ten," *Elementary English,* 43 (November 1966), 771–73.
20. Crutchfield, M. A., "In Practice: The Language-Experience Approach to Reading," *Elementary English,* 43 (March 1966), 285–88.
21. Davis, Leo G., *New England Orthography.* New York: Carlton Press.
22. Delacato, Carl H., *Neurological Organization and Reading.* Springfield, Ill.: Charles C. Thomas, 1966.
23. Dodds, William G., Jr., "A Longitudinal Study of Two Beginning Reading Programs: Words in Color and Traditional Basal Reader," *Dissertation Abstracts,* 27 (1967), 4163A–4164A.
24. Dodds, William G., Jr., "Words in Color and Basal Readers: A Follow-up of Two Beginning Reading Programs," *Ohio Reading Teacher,* 3 (1968), 8–11.
25. Doman, Glenn, *How to Teach Your Baby to Read.* New York: Random House, 1964.
26. Downing, John A., *The Initial Teaching Alphabet Reading Experiment.* Chicago: Scott, Foresman, 1965.
27. Downing, John A., "Conflicts and Confusions in i.t.a. Experiments," in *Vistas in Reading,* J. Allen Figurel, editor, Proceedings International Reading Association, 11, Part 1 (1966), 268–72.
28. Downing, John A., "A Closer Scrutiny of Research Data on i.t.a.," *Education,* 88 (April–May 1966), 308–12.
29. Downing, John A., "Can i.t.a. Be Improved?" *Elementary English,* 44 (December 1967), 849–55.
30. Downing, John A., *Evaluating the Initial Teaching Alphabet.* London: Cassell, 1967.
31. Downing, John A., "Initial Teaching Alphabet: Results after Six Years," *Elementary School Journal,* 69 (February 1969), 242–49.
32. Downing, John A., "The Effectiveness of i.t.a. (Initial Teaching Alphabet) in the Prevention and Treatment of Dyslexia and Dysgraphia," paper presented to the World Mental Health Assembly, Washington, D.C., November 1969.
33. Downing, John A., "Cautionary Comments on Some American i.t.a. Reports," *Educational Research,* 13 (November 1970), 70–72.
34. Downing, John A., Cartwright, Daphne, Jones, Barbara, and Latham, William, "Methodological Problems in the British i.t.a. Research," *Reading Research Quarterly,* 3 (Fall 1967), 85–100.
35. Downing, John A., and Jones, Barbara, "Some Problems of Evaluating i.t.a.: A Second Experiment," *Educational Research,* 8 (1966), 100–14.
36. Downing, John, and Latham, William, "Research Notes: A Follow-up of Children in the First i.t.a. Experiment," *British Journal of Psychology,* 39 (November 1969), 303–305.
37. Dunn-Rankin, P., "The Similarity of Lower-Case Letters of the English Alphabet," *Journal of Verbal Learning and Verbal Behavior,* 7 (1968), 990–95.
38. Durkin, Dolores, "Early Readers—Reflections After Six Years of Research," *Reading Teacher,* 18 (October 1964), 3–7.

39. Dykstra, Robert, "The Effectiveness of Code and Meaning-Emphasis Beginning Reading Programs," *Reading Teacher,* 22 (October 1968), 17–23.
40. Dykstra, Robert, "Summary of the Second-Grade Phase of the Cooperative Research Program in Primary Reading Instruction," *Reading Research Quarterly,* 4 (Fall 1968), 49–70.
41. Educational Records Bureau, *Final Evaluation Report of Project Read in New York City Schools.* Greenwich, Conn.: The Bureau, 1971.
42. Edwards, Thomas J., "The Language Experience Attack on Cultural Deprivation," *Reading Teacher,* 18 (April 1965), 546–51.
43. Edwards, Thomas J., "The Progressive Choice Method," pp. 215–62 in *Disabled Reader,* John Money, editor.   Baltimore: Johns Hopkins, 1966.
44. Ellson, W. G., Harris, Phillip, and Barber, Larry, "A Field Test of Programmed and Direct Tutoring," *Reading Research Quarterly,* 3 (Spring 1968), 307–68.
45. Evans, R. M., "Eye-Movement Photography as a Criterion for Measuring Differences between Students in i.t.a. and t.o. Reading Instructional Programs," *Illinois School Research,* 4 (1968), 52–55.
46. Feldhusen, Hazel, Lamb, Pose, and Feldhusen, John, "Prediction of Reading Achievement under Programmed and Traditional Instruction," *Reading Teacher,* 23 (February 1970), 446–54.
47. *First Steps in Reading.*   New York: Grolier Society, 1962.
48. Frager, Stanley, and Stern, Carolyn, "Learning by Teaching," *Reading Teacher,* 23 (February 1970), 403–405, 417.
49. Fry, Edward B., "Comparison of Beginning Reading with i.t.a., DMS and t.o. after Three Years," *Reading Teacher,* 22 (January 1969), 357–62.
50. Geiger, Evangeline Drury, "An Investigation of Three Methods of Teaching Vocabulary at the Junior High School Level," doctoral dissertation, University of California, Berkeley, 1967.
51. Gibson, C. M., and Richards, I. A., *First Steps in Reading English.*   New York: Pocket Books, 1957.
52. Gibson, Eleanor J., *A Basic Research Program on Reading.*   Research Project No. 639.   Ithaca: Cornell University, 1963.
53. Gibson, Eleanor J., "Learning to Read," pp. 315–34 in *Theoretical Models and Processes of Reading,* Harry Singer and Robert B. Ruddell, editors.   Newark, Del.: International Reading Association, 1970.
54. Gibson, Eleanor J., Bishop, Carol H., Scheff, William, and Smith, Jesse, "Comparison of Meaningfulness and Pronounceability as Grouping Principles in the Perception and Retention of Verbal Materials," *Journal of Experimental Psychology,* 67 (February 1964), 173–82.
55. Glass, Gene V., and Robbins, Melvyn P., "A Critique of Experiments on the Role of Neurological Organization in Reading Performance," *Reading Research Quarterly,* 3 (Fall 1967), 5–52.
56. Goodman, Kenneth S., "Dialect Barriers to Reading Comprehension," *Elementary English,* 42 (December 1965), 852–60.
57. Goralski, Patricia J., and Kerl, Joyce M., "Kindergarten Teacher Aides and Reading Readiness in Minneapolis Public Schools," *Journal of Experimental Education,* 37 (1968), 34–38.

58. Hahn, Harry T., "Three Approaches to Beginning Reading Instruction—ITA, Language Experience and Basic Readers—Extended into Second Grade," *Reading Teacher,* 20 (May 1967), 711–15.

59. Hamill, D., and Mattleman, Marciene, "An Evaluation of a Programmed Reading Approach in the Primary Grades," *Elementary English,* 46 (March 1969), 310–12.

60. Harris, Albert J., and Morrison, Coleman, "The Craft Project: A Final Report," *Reading Teacher,* 22 (January 1969), 335–40.

61. Harris, Albert J., Serwer, Blanche L., and Gold, Lawrence, "Comparing Reading Approaches in First Grade Teaching with Disadvantaged Children, Extended into Second Grade," *Reading Teacher,* 20 (May 1967), 698–703.

62. Hayes, Robert B., and Wuest, Richard C., "A Three Year Look at i.t.a., Lippincott, Phonics and Word Power, and Scott, Foresman," *Reading Teacher,* 22 (January 1969), 363–70.

63. Hayden, Robert R., Murdoch, Robert L., and Quick, Custer A., "Teacher Aides Improve Attention Span," *Elementary School Journal,* 70 (October 1969), 43–47.

64. Heckleman, R. G., "Using the Neurological Impress Method Remedial Reading Technique," *Academic Therapy Quarterly,* 1 (Summer 1966) 235–39, 250.

65. Heilman, Arthur W., "Phonic Emphasis Approaches," pp. 56–71 in *First Grade Reading Programs,* Perspectives in Reading, No. 5. Newark, Del.: International Reading Association, 1965.

66. Hildreth, Gertrude H., "Experience-Related Reading for School Beginners," *Elementary English,* 42 (March 1965), 280–84, 289.

67. Hill, Frank Grant, "A Comparison of the Effectiveness of Words in Color with the Basic Readiness Program Used in the Washington Elementary School District," *Dissertation Abstracts,* 27 (May 1967).

68. Hinds, Lillian R., and Dodds, W. G., "Words in Color: Two Experimental Studies," *Journal of Typographic Research,* 2 (1968), 43–52.

69. Hite, Sister Rebecca, "Reading via Tape for the Inhibited Reader," *Academic Therapy Quarterly,* 2 (1966), 23–27, 63.

70. Hoihjelle, Anne L., "Social Climate and Personality Traits of Able Readers in Relation to Reading Instruction," *Claremont College Reading Conference,* Twenty-sixth Yearbook (1962), 114–21.

71. Hollingsworth, Paul M., "An Experiment with the Impress Method of Teaching Reading," *Reading Teacher, 24 (November 1970), 112–14, 187.*

72. Holmes, Jack A., and Rose, Ivan M., "Disadvantaged Children and the Effectiveness of i.t.a.," *Reading Teacher,* 22 (January 1969), 350–56.

73. Jones, J. K., "Comparing i.t.a. with Colour Story Reading," *Educational Research,* 10 (1968), 226–34.

74. Keith, Mary T., "Sustained Primary Program for Bilingual Children," pp. 262–77 in *Reading Goals for the Disadvantaged,* J. Allen Figurel, editor. Newark, Del.: International Reading Association, 1970.

75. Kendrick, C. M., and Bennett, Clayton L., "A Comparative Study of Two First Grade Language Arts Programs—Extended into Second Grade," *Reading Teacher,* 20 (May 1967), 747–55

76. Key, Mary Ritchie, "The English Spelling System and the Initial Teaching Alphabet," *Elementary School Journal,* 69 (March 1969), 313–26.

77. Klausmeier, Herbert J., Wiersma, William, and Harris, Chester W., "Efficiency of Initial Learning and Transfer by Individuals, Pairs, and Quads," *Journal of Educational Psychology,* 54 (June 1963), 160–64.

78. Klosterman, Sister Rita, "The Effectiveness of a Diagnostically Structured Reading Program," *Reading Teacher,* 24 (November 1970), 159–62.

79. Kolers, Paul A., "Reading and Talking Bilingually," *American Journal of Psychology,* 79 (September 1966), 357–76.

80. Kolers, Paul A., "Reading Is Only Incidentally Visual," pp. 8–16 in *Psycholinguistics and the Teaching of Reading,* Kenneth S. Goodman and James T. Fleming, editors. Newark, Del.: International Reading Association, 1969.

81. Lambert, Phillip, et al., "A Comparison of Pupil Achievement in Team and Self-Contained Organization," *Journal of Experimental Education,* 33 (Spring 1965), 217–24.

82. Laubach, Frank C., "Progress Toward World Literacy," in *New Developments in Programs and Procedures for College-Adult Reading,* Ralph C. Staiger and Culbreth Y. Melton, editors, Twelfth Yearbook National Reading Conference (1963), 87–99.

83. Lockmiller, Pauline, and Di Nello, Mario, "Words in Color vs. a Basal Reading Program with Retarded Readers in Grade 2," *Journal of Educational Research,* 63 (March 1970), 330–34.

84. MacKinnon, A. R., *How Do Children Learn to Read?* Toronto: Copp, Clark, 1959.

85. Malone, John R., "The Larger Aspects of Spelling Reform," *Elementary English,* 39 (May 1962), 611–16.

86. Malpass, Leslie F., et al., "Automated Instruction for Retarded Children," *American Journal of Mental Deficiency,* 69 (November 1964), 405–12.

87. Malpass, Leslie F., et al., *Comparison of Two Automated Teaching Procedures for Retarded Children.* Cooperative Research Project No. 1267, Office of Education, Department of Health, Education and Welfare, 1963.

88. Marsh, R. W., "Some Cautionary Notes on the Results of the London i.t.a. Experiment," *Reading Research Quarterly,* 2 (Fall 1966), 119–26.

89. Martin, Marian, et al., "Teaching Motivation in a High School Reading Program," *Journal of Reading,* 11 (November 1967), 111–21.

90. Mazurkiewicz, Albert J., "ITA and TO Reading Achievement when Methodology Is Controlled—Extended into Second Grade," *Reading Teacher,* 20 (May 1967), 726–29.

91. McCanne, R., "Approaches to First Grade Reading Instruction for Children from Spanish-Speaking Homes," *Reading Teacher,* 19 (May 1966), 670–75.

92. McCleary, Emily K., "Report of Results of Tutorial Reading Project," *Reading Teacher,* 24 (March 1971), 556–59.

93. McCracken, Glenn, *The Right to Learn.* Chicago: Regnery, 1959.

94. McCullough, Constance M., "Balanced Reading Development," pp. 320–56 in *Innovation and Change in Reading Instruction,* Sixty-seventh Yearbook National Society for the Study of Education, Part 2 (1968).

95. McNeil, John D., "Programmed Instruction versus Usual Classroom Procedures in Teaching Boys to Read," *American Educational Research Journal,* 1 (March 1964), 113–19.

96. McWhorter, Kathleen T., and Levy, Jean, "The Influence of a Tutorial Program upon Tutors," *Journal of Reading,* 14 (January 1971), 221–24.

97. Morris, J. L., "The Teaching of Reading Using a Phonetic Alphabet," *California Journal of Educational Research,* 18 (1967), 5–22.

98. Morris, Ronald, *Success and Failure in Learning to Read.* London: Oldbourne Book Co., 1963.

99. Niedermeyer, F. C., "Effects of Training on the Instructional Behavior of Student Tutors," *Journal of Educational Research,* 64 (1970), 119–23.

100. Niedermeyer, F. C., and Ellis, Patricia, "Remedial Reading Instruction by Trained Pupil Tutors," *Elementary School Journal,* 71 (April 1971), 400–405.

101. Nold, J. T., "The Effect of UNIFON on Teaching Beginning Reading: A Pilot Study," *Illinois School Research,* 4 (1968), 38–40.

102. Ohanian, Vera, "Control Populations in i.t.a. Experiments," *Elementary English,* 43 (April 1966), 373–80.

103. Otto, W., "Interlist Similarity, Order of Presentation and Color in Children's Paired Associate Learning," *Psychonomic Science,* 9 (1967), 531–32.

104. Packer, Athold B., "Ashton-Warner's Key Vocabulary for the Disadvantaged," *Reading Teacher,* 23 (March 1970), 559–64.

105. Platt, Penny, "Teaching Beginning Reading to Disadvantaged Children from Pictures Children Draw," pp. 84–90 in *Reading Goals for the Disadvantaged,* J. Allen Figurel, editor. Newark, Del.: International Reading Association, 1970.

106. Railsback, Lem, "Use of Automated Aural-Oral Techniques to Teach Functional Illiterates Who Are Upper Age Level Adolescents," pp. 207–11 in *The Psychology of Reading Behavior,* Eighteenth Yearbook National Reading Conference (1969).

107. Robbins, Melvyn Paul, "The Delacato Interpretation of Neurological Organization," *Reading Research Quarterly,* 1 (Spring 1966), 57–78.

108. Rodgers, P. R., and Fox, C. E., "A Comparison of McGraw-Hill Programmed Reading and the Scott-Foresman Basic Reading Program," *Illinois School Research,* 4 (1967), 45–47.

109. Rogers, Don C., "Teaching the Hard Spots in Words," *Chicago Schools Journal,* 8 (1926), 256–59.

110. Rohner, Traugott, *Fonetic English Spelling.* Evanston, Ill.: Fonetic English Spelling Association, 1966.

111. Ruddell, Robert B., "Reading Instruction in First Grade with Varying Emphasis on the Regularity of Grapheme-Phoneme Correspondences and the Relation of Language Structures to Meaning—Extended into the Second Grade," *Reading Teacher,* 20 (May 1967), 730–39.

112. Rystrom, Richard, "Evaluating Letter Discrimination Problems in the Primary Grades," *Journal of Reading Behavior,* 1 (Fall 1969), 38–48.

113. Samuels, S. Jay, "Cross-National Studies in Reading: The Relationship between the Sound-Letter Correspondence in Language and Reading Achievement," in *Reading and Realism,* J. Allen Figurel, editor, Proceedings International Reading Association, 13, Part 1 (1959), 846–53.

114. Samuels, S. Jay, *Word Associations and the Recognition of Flashed Words.* Project 6-8774, Office of Education, Department of Health, Education and Welfare, 1968.

115. Samuels, S. Jay, "Effect of Word Associations on Reading Speed, Recall and Guessing Behavior on Tests," *Journal of Educational Psychology,* 59 (1968), 12–15.

116. Samuels, S. Jay, "Relationship between Formal Intralist Similarity and the von Restorff Effect," *Journal of Educational Psychology,* 59 (December 1968), 432–37.

117. Samuels, S. Jay, "Effect of Word Associations on the Recognition of Flashed Words," *Journal of Educational Psychology,* 60 (1969), 97–102.

118. Samuels, S. Jay, and Wittrock, Merlin C., "Word Association Strength and Learning to Read," *Journal of Educational Psychology,* 60 (1969), 248–52.

119. Schoeller, Arthur W., and Pearson, David A., "Better Reading Through Volunteer Reading Tutors," *Reading Teacher,* 23 (April 1970), 625–30, 636.

120. Serwer, Blanche L., "Linguistic Support for a Method of Teaching Reading to Black Children," *Reading Research Quarterly,* 4 (Summer 1969), 449–67.

121. Shapiro, Bernard J., and Willford, Robert E., "i.t.a.—Kindergarten or First Grade," *Reading Teacher,* 22 (January 1969), 307–11.

122. Sheldon, William D., *New Approaches to Primary Reading.* Bulletin No. 133. Boston: Allyn and Bacon.

123. Shuy, Roger W., "Some Considerations for Developing Beginning Reading Materials for Ghetto Children," *Journal of Reading Behavior,* 1 (Spring 1969), 33–44.

124. Smith, Mildred Beatty, "Reading for the Culturally Disadvantaged," *Educational Leadership,* 22 (March 1965), 398.

125. Southgate, Vera, "Approaching i.t.a. Results with Caution," *Reading Research Quarterly,* 1 (Spring 1966), 35–56.

126. Spache, George D., "Innovations in Reading Instruction," pp. 53–60 in *Recent Developments in Reading,* Helen M. Robinson, editor. Supplementary Educational Monographs No. 95. Chicago: University of Chicago Press, 1965.

127. Spache, George D., "The Materials Explosion," in *Vistas in Reading,* J. Allen Figurel, editor, Proceedings International Reading Association, 10, Part 1 (1966), 571–72.

128. Staats, Arthur W., and Butterfield, William H., "Treatment of Non-Reading in a Culturally Deprived Juvenile Delinquent: An Application of Reinforcement Principles," *Child Development,* 36 (1965), 925–42.

129. Stauffer, Russell G., and Hammond, W. Dorsey, "The Effectiveness of Language Arts and Basic Reader Approaches to First Grade Reading Instruction—Extended into Second Grade," *Reading Teacher,* 20 (May 1967), 740–46.

130. Stauffer, Russell G., and Hammond, W. Dorsey, "The Effectiveness of Language Arts and Basic Reader Approaches to First Grade Reading Instruction—Extended into Third Grade," *Reading Research Quarterly,* 4 (Summer 1969), 468–99.

131. Stevens, George L., and Orem, R. C., *The Case for Early Reading.* St. Louis: Warren H. Green, 1967.

132. Stewart, Rebecca W., "ITA After Two Years," *Elementary English,* 42 (October 1965), 660–65.

133. Stolorow, L. M., *Essential Principles of Programmed Instruction.* Technical Report No. 8. Urbana: Training Research Laboratory, University of Illinois, 1965.

134. Swales, T. D., "The Attainments in Reading and Spelling of Children Who Learned to Read Through i.t.a.," *British Journal of Educational Psychology,* 37 (1967), 126–27.

135. Tanyzer, Harold J., and Alpert, Harvey, "Three Different Basal Reading Systems and First Grade Reading Achievement," *Reading Teacher,* 19 (May 1966), 636–42.

136. Tensuan, Emperatriz S., and Davis, Frederick B., "The Phonic Method versus the Combination Method in Teaching Beginning Reading," pp. 175–88 in *New Developments in Programs and Procedures for College-Adult Reading,* Twelfth Yearbook National Reading Conference, 1963.

137. Thomas, H., "Children's Tachistoscopic Recognition of Words and Pseudowords Varying in Pronounceability and Consonant-Vowel Sequence," *Journal of Experimental Psychology,* 77 (1968), 511–13.

138. Tyler, Vernon O., Jr., and Brown, G. Duane, "Token Reinforcement of Academic Performance with Institutionalized Delinquent Boys," *Journal of Educational Psychology,* 59 (June 1968), 164–68.

139. Underwood, B. J., Ham, M., and Ekstrand, B., "Cue Selection in Paired-Associates Learning," *Journal of Experimental Psychology,* 64 (1962), 405–409.

140. Ungaro, Daniel, "The Split-Vu Reading Program: A Follow-Up," *Elementary English,* 42 (March 1965), 254–57, 260.

141. Vilscek, Elaine, et al., "Coordinating and Integrating Language Arts Instruction in First Grade," *Reading Teacher,* 20 (October 1966), 31–37.

142. Vilscek, Elaine, et al., "Coordinating and Integrating Language Arts Instruction," *Reading Teacher,* 21 (October 1967), 3–10.

143. Warburton, F. W., and Southgate, Vera, *An Independent Evaluation of i.t.a.* Edinburgh: Chambers, 1969.

144. White, Jean, "The Programmed Tutor," *American Education,* 7 (December 1971), 18–21.

145. Wilder, David E., "Social Factors Related to the Public Awareness, Perception and Evaluation of the Teaching of Reading," unpublished paper, February 8, 1965.

146. Young, Virgil M., and Young, Katherine A., "Special Education Children as the Authors of Books," *Reading Teacher,* 22 (November 1968), 122–25.

147. Zeitz, F. "ITA and the Below-Average Child: With Reply by Mazurkiewicz and Rejoinder," *Reading Teacher,* 19 (April 1966), 515–18.

Complementary References

Ashton-Warner, Sylvia, *Teacher.* New York: Simon and Schuster, 1963.

Bitner, A. R., Dlabel, J. J., Jr., and Kise, L. K., editors, *Readings on Reading.* Scranton: International Textbook, 1969.

Carter, E., and Dapper, A., *School Volunteers: What They Do and How They Do It.* New York: Citation Press, 1971.

Dale, Ruth, *How to Make a Book.* New York: Citation Press, 1970.

Danish, Steven J., and Hauser, Allen L., *Helping Skills: A Basic Training Program.* New York: Behavioral Publications, 1973.

Downing, John A., *The i.t.a. Reading Experiment.* Chicago: Scott Foresman, 1964.

Featherstone, Joseph, *The Primary School Revolution in Britain.* New York: New Republic.

Fry, Edward B., *The Emergency Reading Teacher's Manual.* Highland Park: Drier Educational Systems.

Gattegno, Caleb, *Words in Color.* Chicago: Encyclopaedia Britannica, 1962.

Hafner, Lawrence E., and Jolly, Hayden B., *Patterns of Teaching Reading in the Elementary School.* New York: Macmillan, 1972.

Hall, Mary Anne, *Teaching Reading as a Language Experience.* Columbus: Charles E. Merrill, 1970.

Holdaway, Don, *Independence in Reading: A Handbook on Individualized Procedures.* Auckland: Ashton Educational, 1972.

Lee, Doris M., and Allen, Roach V., *Learning to Read Through Experience.* New York: Appleton-Century-Crofts, 1963.

McManama, John J., *An Effective Program for Teacher-Aide Training.* Englewood Cliffs, N.J.: Educators Book Club.

Niedermeyer, Fred C., *Parent-Assisted Learning.* Inglewood, Calif.: Southwest Regional Laboratory, 1970.

Orem, R. C., *A Montessori Handbook.* New York: Putnam, 1965.

Orlick, Gloria, *Reading Helpers.* Brooklyn, N.Y.: Book-Lab.

Smith, Nila B., *American Reading Instruction.* Newark, Del.: International Reading Association, 1965.

Snow, Lawrence, *Using Teacher Aides.* Highland Park, N.J.: Drier Educational Systems, 1972.

Spache, Evelyn B., *Reading Activities for Child Involvement,* 2nd edition. Boston: Allyn and Bacon, 1976.

Spache, George D., and Spache, Evelyn B., *Reading in the Elementary School.* Boston: Allyn and Bacon, 1973.

Spitzer, Lillian K., *Language Experience Approach to Reading Instruction: An Annotated Bibliography.* Newark, Del.: International Reading Association, 1967.

Stauffer, Russell G., *The Language-Experience Approach to the Teaching of Reading.* New York: Harper, 1970.

Umans, Shelley, *New Trends in Reading Instruction.* New York: Teachers College Press, Columbia University, 1963.

Vilscek, Elaine E., editor, *A Decade of Innovations: Approaches to Beginning Reading.* Proceedings Twelfth Annual Convention, Vol. 12, Part 3. Newark, Del.: International Reading Association, 1967.

Wittick, Mildred Letton, "Innovations in Reading Instruction for Beginners," pp. 72–125 in *Innovations and Change in Reading Instruction,* Helen M. Robinson, editor. Sixty-seventh Yearbook National Society for the Study of Education, Part II. Chicago: University of Chicago Press, 1968.

The major premise of this chapter is that most of the visually handicapped children in our schools are not discovered by present common vision screening methods. Despite a fine sight conservation program in many school systems, which serves adequately about 10 percent of the pupils with low vision, other children equally handicapped are excluded from help by the narrowness of the selection procedures. Many criticisms of the vision screening techniques used to find visually handicapped pupils are possible. Among these are the nature of the vision test used, its lack of relationship to academic success, the peculiar interpretation of the research that claims to validate this test, and the false impressions regarding child vision that the test conveys. Alternative screening approaches and ways of incorporating teacher observation in the screening are recommended. Typical behavioral symptoms of visually handicapped pupils are described, and basic classroom adjustments to alleviate and reduce vision problems are illustrated.

14 Identifying and Helping the Visually Handicapped Child

As you read this discussion of visually handicapped children, frame your answers to these questions.

1. What method of visual screening is familiar to you? Can you justify this technique or are some of the criticisms offered here pertinent to that system?

2. How do children show the existence of a vision problem by some of the ways they behave, in your experience?

3. What are some of the ways that a classroom teacher can help children with visual problems succeed in academic work?

READING SUCCESS of the visually handicapped child is closely linked to the school's methods of vision screening. Unless screening procedures are efficient, many school children are predestined to reading failure because of their visual handicaps. With appropriate screening and identification, visually handicapped children can be helped by a number of adjustments in the physical environment of the classroom. It is our purpose here to examine present methods of vision screening and their efficiency in identifying the visually handicapped child, and to point out constructive classroom steps intended to aid such children toward reading success.

AN OPHTHALMOLOGICAL APPROACH

Special provisions for visually handicapped children were present in many school systems as early as 1925. They usually took the form of sight-saving or sight conservation classrooms composed of pupils of subnormal acuity or those who were partially blind or extremely myopic. The pupils were supplied with special writing instruments (broad-point pens); nonglare paper; soft heavy pencils; broad, soft chalk; books in oversized type; better than usual lighting conditions, and a program that emphasized near-point work, to mention only some of the basic treatments usually available.

For their original limited purpose, the sight-saving classes and their equipment were appropriate. More recently, as the technology of vision has progressed, additional devices such as contact lenses, alone or with additional glasses, special high-magnification spectacles, simple reading machines that enlarge the page of print, and other visual aids have proved useful.

Despite the apparent progress in this particular service to visually handicapped children, one authority estimates that only 10 percent of such pupils ever receive appropriate low vision aids, even though 70 percent could be aided by such devices.*

However, the selection of pupils for these classes has always been based upon an extremely narrow concept of the vision process. The medico-legal criteria for admission to sight-saving classes have been (1) visual acuity

Portions of this paper have been presented in various articles by the author. See Spache (15, 16, 17, 18, 19).
*Matthew J. Burns, "Our Stake in the Future of Health Care," *Optical Index,* 47 (June 1972), entire issue.

between 20/70 and 20/200 in the better eye; (2) serious, progressive eye defects; or (3) diseases of the eye or body that seriously affect vision (6).

It is apparent that only one major aspect of vision is considered important in these selection criteria, namely, visual acuity. Certainly the effort to conserve the vision of children handicapped in this manner is laudable. But is is also obvious that all other visually handicapped children whose reading progress might be thus hindered are systematically excluded from this special care. Moreover, since schools were led to believe that the sight-saving classes served most or all the children in need of special vision services, other visually handicapped children seldom receive any help or attention.

Our criticism of the present selection procedures of the sight conservation programs is based on the fact that they serve only a small proportion of the pupils that vision specialists consider handicapped. A United States Public Health Service survey, "Vision and Its Disorders," published in 1967, estimated that the number of children under fifteen with visual problems would be 75 million by 1975. Even the most optimistic statisticians do not claim that more than a small portion of this handicapped group is served by our sight conservation programs.

The restricted function of sight-saving services has arisen from the dependence upon an ophthalmological or medical concept of vision. In medical hands, vision examinations tend to stress the anatomical, pathological, and refractive aspects of vision. Frequently, visual functions such as binocular coordination, fusion, depth perception, near-point acuity, and slight vertical or lateral imbalances are not considered very significant; tests for them may even be omitted in routine examinations. Few ophthalmologists consider any of these functions as possible of improvement through training, despite the existence of a medical branch of their field, orthoptics, which employs such training procedures. Thus, first, by a narrow definition of vision in terms only of acuity at far-point, and, second, by literally ignoring the possible effects of other visual defects that might be ameliorated, most of the visually handicapped children have received only cursory attention in our schools.

WHAT IS WRONG WITH PRESENT METHODS OF VISION SCREENING?

Vision screening in most schools is still dominated by the ophthalmological overemphasis upon the importance of visual acuity at far-point. The Snellen Chart, which measures only clear vision at 20 feet, remains the most widely used instrument in this procedure. It is essential, then, that we examine the history of this test and the studies that claim to show its validity.

The Snellen Chart was designed in 1862 to present several lines of letters graded in size to correspond to their appearance at varying distances from the viewer.   Each line contains six or eight capital letters in vertical position or several capital *E*'s tilted in various directions.   The mathematical theory is that the top line containing the largest capitals or *E*'s can be distinguished readily by any person with normal far-point acuity at a certain distance such as 100 feet. The second line presumably can be seen by the normal person at 90 feet, the next at 80 feet, and so on down the chart.   The capital *E* chart is used with young children or illiterates who are unfamiliar with the alphabet, and the responses are given by indicating the direction of the tilt of the *E*.   Interestingly enough, we know of no scientific research by the authors of the chart that tried to demonstrate its validity and reliability.   For the first fifty years or more of its use, the fact that it appeared to detect nearsightedness seems to have been sufficient proof of its values for vision specialists.

Writing on this subject in 1940, this author collated these criticisms of the Snellen Chart (15):

1. It is highly questionable whether the reading of letters is a real test of visual acuity.   Many comparative studies indicate that other targets than capitals or *E*'s are superior tests of visual acuity.   Moreover, the letters on each line are not equally discriminable; errors tend to concentrate on certain of the letters, as *B* and *R*, which are more difficult to discriminate than some others.   When two errors on a line is considered a failure, this variation in difficulty of the various letters becomes highly significant. Moreover, in some lines this makes some letters harder to discriminate than the larger letters in the line above (4).

2. The test does not measure the clearness of vision at reading distance. Since there is little relationship between acuity at far-point and near-point, it is quite possible for children to pass the Snellen test and yet experience considerable difficulty in dealing with the printed page.   A person, for example, may have good far-point acuity and poor near-point acuity.   Thus the test by the Snellen tells the examiner nothing about an individual's ability to perform in school at a desk, or in industry in near-point tasks (10).

3. Only 20 to 40 percent of the children are identified (according to the standard used) who really need the aid of a vision specialist.   In addition, a large number of the children who pass the Snellen are found to have significant visual defects when examined professionally (1, 7, 13) by either ophthalmological or optometric standards.

4. Failure on the test is interpreted by most schools as a prognostic sign of future school difficulties.   But, as we have shown in other chapters on vision and reading in this collection, the loss of good far-point acuity is more probably an outcome of near-point work in school and is more common among children who *succeed in school* than among those who fail.   There is strong evidence to support the view that gradual increase in

myopia represents a successful adjustment to the near-point tasks of school and civilized life, rather than a significant visual defect.

5. The Snellen test is administered to each eye separately with the other eye covered, as though we functioned as one-eyed individuals in most of life's tasks. Thus the visual acuity present when both eyes are used, as in reading and other tasks, is not measured, despite the fact that it may differ from that found for the separate eyes. The Snellen ignores the normal binocular coordination present in practically all tasks involving vision and makes no attempt to test for difficulties in this type of functioning. It is purely a measure of acuity of the independent eyes at distance, which, as we have pointed out, is both unimportant and irrelevant to school success.

The test could be used to measure farsightedness, which, if persistent, becomes a handicap to reading success; but it is seldom so employed in school practice. Nor does it detect astigmatism, a defect resulting in blurred images, since the viewer can temporarily force his eyes to read small enough type to pass the test, even when his refractive error is so great as to make sustained reading difficult and uncomfortable. Nor does it make any attempt to measure a number of other visual functions known to be related to reading success.

6. Many of those who have used the Snellen test with groups of children have discovered that the test type is not sufficiently varied. Pupils can and do memorize the lines of letters while awaiting their turn to be tested. Some sort of targets that could not be memorized would be more realistic.

These criticisms do not represent solely the opinion of this author. For example, 66 percent of a large number of ophthalmologists surveyed in the New England area agreed that the Snellen was inadequate for school screening purposes (8). At the same time, these criticisms are strongly denied by other medical vision specialists. Those supporting the use of the Snellen base their arguments largely upon a research study conducted by the Children's Bureau of the U.S. Department of Health, Education and Welfare in 1949–50. The St. Louis study (2), as it is called, included 609 sixth-grade and 606 first-grade pupils who were tested with the Snellen, the Massachusetts Vision Test, the Keystone Telebinocular, the Bausch and Lomb Ortho-Rater, and the American Optical Company Sight-Screener. The last three of these are batteries of eight or nine vision tests administered by placing test cards or slides in a stereo-scope. The Massachusetts Vision test measures only four vision skills, one of the tests being an abbreviated Snellen Chart.

Each of the commercial screening batteries was repeated to determine its test-retest reliability, and the results of each test were compared with an examination by an ophthalmologist. But the reliability of this medical examina-tion was never determined. It was assumed that whatever the doctor did (and this might have varied from one office to another) was a perfectly accurate procedure with no false diagnoses or errors of any kind. In view of the fact that the examinations were conducted by a group of physicians who varied in their clinical experience and, perhaps, their standards of normal vision, this arbitrary ruling out of any possibility of human error is absurd. These ophthalmological examinations served as the criterion of success for all the other vision tests. All other tests were judged in terms of their agreement with the criterion examination conducted by the physicians.

One of the two major conclusions of this study was that none of the screening tests or combinations of tests showed very high agreement with the criterion, and therefore none was judged high in screening efficiency. The second conclusion was that the Snellen test used alone—although it, too, was not very efficient—was as good as any of the batteries of tests. We shall review the validity of these conclusions by a closer examination of the procedures used in this study, as Kelley (9) has done.

The screening devices were, in effect, being judged by their ability to refer children for visual care. In other words, if the test failed to refer children who were later found to have conjunctivitis or *any other disease* or pathological condition (which the test made no attempt or pretense to detect), the screening procedure was considered inadequate. Thus every case of disease or pathology discovered by the ophthalmologists in which the child had not failed the visual skills tests was judged to be a failure of the screening test. The reasoning that would justify this type of comparison is certainly obscure and would account for the fact that most of the screening tests were judged to be underreferring children for visual care.

A second line of strange reasoning was employed in the St. Louis study in judging the efficiency of the screening procedures. Many children were referred because of a failure in a particular visual skill; but, under their concepts of vision, the ophthalmologists judged these children as untreatable or not really requiring treatment. These referrals, in which a visual deviation was detected, were considered overreferrals by the ophthalmologists, and another indication of the inefficiency of the screening tests. In other words, when the tests correctly performed their intended function of referring children who deviated from normal, they were penalized if the physicians decided not to treat the children for those defects or judged that the defects were not important.

These overreferrals, as the physicians called them, were considered more important than failure to detect children who did need visual care, as determined by the ophthalmological examination. In their opinion, the Snellen test was considered the most efficient test because it made fewer overreferrals, yet it failed to detect *25 percent* of the pupils needing care. In contrast, the other batteries of tests missed only 6–8 percent of the visually handicapped children. Underreferrals, or failures to detect cases needing visual care, were obviously regarded as relatively unimportant. For a supposedly scientific study, this reasoning—which penalized those tests that performed their intended function and praised those tests that failed to find children needing attention—is certainly unusual. If overreferrals for a professional examination are undesirable, how do these physicians justify their support for the tuberculosis and glaucoma screening programs that they sponsor, in which overreferrals, that is, no evidence of defect, is present in more than 90 percent of the individuals screened?

In this section we have tried to represent the research evidence regarding common vision screening procedures in schools that employ the Snellen Test. We think it obvious that this is a pointless approach yielding no significant information regarding our pupils. Moreover, use of this faulty procedure lulls teachers into believing that most of their children have no visual condition that might interfere with their reading progress. As a matter of fact, it is estimated that 25 to 50 percent of school children need visual correction (13). Continued use of the Snellen test in school vision screening programs is indefensible (12, 14, 16, 17, 18).

Some school systems are improving their screening by interdisciplinary planning. Advisory committees of parents, teachers, optometrists, and ophthalmologists are formed to plan an effective approach to screening, reporting to parents, and follow-up. Sometimes these plans lead to use of one of the commercial batteries of tests that we mentioned earlier, since these are more efficient, although by no means complete, visual examinations (13). Other schools have adopted the modified clinical testing program devised for the Orinda study (1). Since certain of the tests in this abbreviated clinical examination require a professional vision specialist, its adoption introduces other problems than use of the commercial batteries that can be administered by a teacher or a parent. Among the schools that have evolved a satisfactory vision screening program in this planned manner are New Haven, Connecticut (20); Euclid, Ohio; Peoria, Illinois; Orinda, California; and Brevard County in Florida, to mention only a few examples. Some of these schools have profited from the financial and personal assistance of the Sight-Conservation Committees of local Lions Clubs in implementing their plans.

Unfortunately, attempts to improve vision screening in this fashion sometimes encounter the resistance of local physicians or county health officers. In some states, vision screening is defined as the responsibility of county physicians or nurses; for example, it is conceived of as a medical function, like a medical examination before school entrance. Even though most of the actual testing is usually performed by classroom teachers or parents, with only the aid of the school nurse, who could not possibly personally administer all the tests, some of these medical personnel are obstructionist in their attitudes toward improvements in vision screening. The present writer has had the experience of having a complete plan for the county of Alachua, Florida, quashed by an enraged county health officer (who never did any testing in schools anyway). This unpleasant problem has been solved by some school systems by officially incorporating vision screening into the annual academic achievement testing, thus making it a purely internal school function.

Obtaining the fullest cooperation among the members of the committee planning the vision screening program is of paramount importance. Optometrists and ophthalmologists have different concepts of the nature of vision and different standards for normal and abnormal performances. These must be reconciled, as they were in the Orinda project, and a common ground for referral of children agreed upon. A simple solution to the whole problem is not found, as Rosen emphasizes (14), by buying one or the other of the commercial screening batteries. They are not equivalent in effectiveness, for some, like the Snellen test, give excessive underreferrals (the Massachusetts Vision Test, for example); while others, like the Keystone Telebinocular series, tend to overreferrals. Some batteries are no more than an imitation of the Snellen, as the New York School Vision tester of Bausch and Lomb, and exhibit all the same limitations. Some batteries omit important visual functions as depth perception at near-point, and other measures. Thus, it is apparent that the parents, vision specialists, and educators must give considerable thought to the planning of the program of vision screening if it is to be maximally effective.

Although the efficacy of teacher observation in detecting visual problems is decried in some studies (1), we believe that it can be a valuable adjunct to the vision screening program. Gertrude Knox (11) has made a careful study of the significant symptoms that can be observed by the teacher and are likely to be confirmed as true indications of visual malfunctioning by professional examination. We shall describe the postural and behavioral traits of children that enable the teacher to recognize these symptoms. One of the common characteristics of children who are approaching myopia and experiencing difficulty with far-point vision is the tendency to facial contortions or forward thrusting of the head in attempting to read at a distance. Children will often thrust their heads forward and squint with both eyes in the attempt to achieve clear vision. Occasionally the squinting will be done with only one eye, or the child will tilt or turn his head to favor one eye.

Tilting of the head while working at the desk—another significant symptom, according to Knox—tends to cause children to lose binocular vision, to force one eye toward a lateral or vertical imbalance, and to suppress vision in that eye.   Instead of tilting the head, some pupils achieve the same goal of removing one eye from the visual task by squinting, by closing the eye, by resting the head on their hand in such a manner that one eye is covered or pushed closed, or by resting the head on the desk while reading or writing.   In some cases, the pupil tilts the book or paper to produce one-eyed functioning. Some of these adjustments may indicate the child's attempt to avoid strong contrasts in lighting or glare in his visual field.   Since this possible cause is easily corrected, the true significance of the behavior is readily determined. Practically all the research on vision and reading indicates that loss of binocular function often seriously affects reading success.

Tension during close work is frequently a manifestation of a visual problem.   It may be shown by short attention span, a strained expression of the face, twisting and other repeated bodily movements, or rigidity of the posture.   Some children show their tension in near-point reading by having to reinforce their vision by whispering the words or using their finger as a pointer, because their eye-aiming skills are poor.

Other symptoms of probable vision defects that may be observed by the teacher are difficulties in body movements, as clumsiness; frequent turning aside from near-point work to a far-point focus; frequent miscalling or misspelling of words actually known by the pupil; recurring errors in letter formation in handwriting or in reproducing drawings; ineffectual throwing and catching a bean bag or ball; and strong tendencies to inaccuracy in copying at the desk from chalkboard materials.   Losing place while reading either on the same line or vertically from one line to another may be another symptom, if it occurs repeatedly during the child's reading.

These observations of behavioral symptoms of probable visual handicap are subjective, of course.   Single instances of a symptom might be seen in the total behavior pattern of almost any child.   Only when a symptom or two is repeated in similar situations can the teacher assume that it is a basis for referral for a visual examination.

CLASSROOM ADJUSTMENTS TO VISION PROBLEMS

In addition to participating in the planning of the vision screening program and, probably, performing a good part of the eventual testing, classroom teachers may make a number of other contributions to the amelioration of children's vision problems.   In the early school years, most children are farsighted and can see more clearly at distance than at desk work. They can read more comfortably from the chalkboard or a chart than they can from the pages of a book. Many primary classroom procedures such as great use of the chalkboard, books printed in oversized type, primer typewriters, manuscript writing, and large-scale reproductions of the page of the basal reader are adjustments to the visual condition of many primary children and are amply justified.

At the same time, many other classroom procedures should be adapted to the needs of those children who are handicapped by other visual conditions. For example, about 7 percent of first graders are nearsighted and cannot readily profit from the far-point emphasis on chalkboard and display chart work. When these pupils are identified, they must be given the freedom to sit or move closer to the distant work area when they wish to. Children with fusional, coordination, or accommodative defects find great difficulty in shifting focus from desk to chalkboard. They have problems in achieving focus or clear-cut impressions of words, and in copying from the book to the paper. These children will be discovered by an adequate screening program (not by the Snellen, of course) and by careful teacher observation in the manner that we have described earlier. Until the teacher can secure specific suggestions from the vision specialist, these children may sometimes be aided by kinesthetic methods of learning to read and write, by books in oversized type such as those used in sight conservation classes, by using manuscript writing, and by typing their worksheets or other desk work on the primer typewriter. Buff-colored manila paper, soft, large pencils, and soft, large chalk should be substituted for the common classroom equipment for these and the myopic children.

Some time ago, Paul Fendrick (3) studied the relationship of the reading success of visually handicapped children to the method of instruction employed. His research indicated that these children fail in greater numbers when taught by a method emphasizing visual impressions of words than when taught by a phonic method. As we might expect, these children needed to form concepts of words through phonic and kinesthetic cues if they were to overcome their visual handicaps.

In addition to these fairly obvious changes in materials and methods there are a number of physical adjustments in the classroom that will benefit the normal as well as the visually handicapped pupils. Darell Boyd Harmon (5) has made intensive studies of the effects of seating arrangements, lighting, decoration, and brightness contrasts upon academic achievement and health. Among the essential physical adjustments that he recommends are avoiding strong contrasts in reflection, both on the walls of the room and on the child's working surface. The difference in the reflection qualities of areas of the wall or desk should be minimal. This implies that working surfaces should be light-colored or natural wood finish, walls should be in grayed or muted colors, and chalkboards should be yellow-green, not black.

The child's working surface for reading, writing, and drawing should be 20 degrees off the horizontal (not flat) to insure proper balance of the child's body and to avoid energy-consuming muscular stresses. Flat working surfaces tend to draw the child's body and head into a tilt so that he works monocularly and thus begins to lose binocular coordination.

The working surface should be placed so that the greatest source of light, as the windows, falls outside his binocular field. In other words, the major light source should be outside his visual field, which extends about 50 degrees to each side of his forward line of sight. The field of vision can be roughly estimated by imaginary lines from his head to the far corners of his desk. No major source of light should be within this area, for the child will be subject to glare.

The child's desk and seat must be adjusted so that when he faces the desk with arms folded upward vertically toward the shoulders, his elbows will just slide on to the top of the desk. This tends to make the distance from his eyes to the working surface equal to approximately the length of his forearm and fist. Another way of estimating this proper distance from the paper or book is, after placing his fist against his mouth, to slide the elbow forward onto the desk top. The desk and seat should be so adjusted that the pupil can sit at this distance from the working surface without tilting his head or body. Occasionally some children seem to be more comfortable when their heads are somewhat closer to the work. Whether this is merely habit or a natural adjustment to the child's own visual condition should be confirmed by a professional vision specialist.

The adequacy of the lighting on common work areas of the classroom as the desks and the chalkboard, particularly in older school buildings, should be evaluated. This service will usually be performed by a local utility company, upon request, if the school system does not possess the necessary equipment. Insufficient light reduces visual acuity and is a source of strain and fatigue. It also contributes to irritability and consequent behavior problems among children.

We have attempted to alert the reader to the inadequacies in present methods of visual screening and in the current provisions for visually handicapped children. We are properly concerned about the one or two out of every five pupils whose visual conditions limit their academic success. But correction of these conditions is possible, as we have tried to indicate, by the actions of concerned teachers and parents.

LEARNING PROJECT

Make a list of some of the steps that the classroom or remedial teacher can take to alleviate, or prevent the development of, vision difficulties among pupils. Be sure to include changes in the areas of lighting, seating, reading materials, writing materials, ·pupil posture, teacher observation check lists, instructional method, furniture arrangement, and the like.

REFERENCES

1. Blum, Henrich L., Peters, Henry B., and Bettman, Jerome W., *Vision Screening for Elementary Schools—The Orinda Study.* Berkeley: University of California Press, 1959.
2. Crane, Marian M., et al., *Screening School Children for Visual Defects.* Washington, D.C.: Children's Bureau Publications, No. 345, 1954.
3. Fendrick, Paul, *Visual Characteristics of Poor Readers.* Contributions to Education No. 656. New York: Teachers College, Columbia University, 1934.
4. Garrett, Henry E., and Schneck, M. R., *Psychological Tests, Methods and Results.* New York: Harper, 1933.
5. Harmon, Darell Boyd, *The Coordinated Classroom.* Grand Rapids: American Seating Company, 1950.
6. Hathaway, Winifred, *Education and Health of the Partially-Seeing Child.* New York: Columbia University Press, 1960.
7. Hirsch, Monroe J., and Wick, Ralph E., *Vision of Children: An Optometric Symposium.* Philadelphia: Chilton, 1963.
8. Jackson, Walter M., "Visual Screening in City Schools," *Optometric Weekly,* April 16, 1953.
9. Kelley, Charles R., *Visual Screening and Child Development: The North Carolina Study.* Raleigh: Department of Psychology, College of Education, North Carolina State College, 1957.
10. Kempf, Grover A., Jarman, Bernard L., and Collins, Selwyn D., "A Special Study of the Vision of School Children," *Public Health Reports,* 43, Part 2, No. 27, 1713–39.
11. Knox, Gertrude, "Classroom Symptoms of Visual Difficulty," master's thesis, University of Chicago, 1951.

12. Peters, Henry B., "Vision Screening with a Snellen Chart," *American Journal of Optometry and Archives of American Academy of Optometry,* 38 (September 1961), 487–505.
13. Robinson, Helen M., "Visual Screening Tests for Schools," *Elementary School Journal,* 53 (December 1953), 217–22.
14. Rosen, Carl L., "The Status of Vision Screening: A Review of Research and Consideration of Some Selected Problems," pp. 42–48 in *Psychology of Reading Behavior,* George B. Schick and Merrill M. May, editors, Eighteenth Yearbook National Reading Conference, 1969.
15. Spache, George D., "A Comparative Study of Three Tests of Visual Acuity," *Journal of Applied Psychology,* 24 (April 1940), 207–12.
16. Spache, George D., "Facts about Vision Significant to the Classroom Teacher," pp. 65–74 in *Twenty-first Yearbook* Claremont College Reading Conference, 1956.
17. Spache, George D., "Vision and Success in Reading," *Journal of the American Optometric Association,* 32 (June 1961), 886–88.
18. Spache, George D., "Classroom Reading and the Visually Handicapped Child," in *Changing Concepts of Reading Instruction,* J. Allen Figurel, editor, Proceedings International Reading Association, 6 (1961), 93–96.
19. Spache, George D., "What Teachers and Parents Should Know about Vision and Reading," pp. 169–78 in *New Directions in Reading,* Ralph C. Staiger and David A. Sohn, editors. New York: Bantam Books, 1967.
20. Sweeting, Orville J., "An Improved Vision Screening Program in the New Haven Schools," *Journal of the American Optometric Association,* 30 (May 1959), 675–77.

Complementary References

Ames, Louise Bates, Gillespie, Clyde, and Streff, John W., *Stop School Failure.* New York: Harper & Row, 1972.
Graham, Clarence, et al., *Vision and Visual Perception.* New York: John Wiley & Sons, 1965.
Kidd, Aline H., and Rivoire, Jeanne L., editors, *Perceptual Development in Children.* New York: International Universities Press, 1966.
Smith, Henry P., and Dechant, Emerald V., *Psychology in Teaching Reading.* Englewood Cliffs, N.J.: Prentice-Hall, 1961.

As one reads the literature on visual perception testing and training programs, it soon becomes apparent that there is a great deal of freedom in labeling the supposed components of this ability. We have made a small step toward bringing some system into this confusion by grouping many terms used to describe training procedures into related categories, and by listing some of the activities commonly employed in each category.

Following this attempt to clarify the terminology, fifteen treatment programs of widely varying nature are described in terms of the activities employed. No real evaluation of these programs is offered at this time, since the research data on the outcomes of such programs are presented in the next chapter. The simple purpose of this chapter is to familiarize the reader with some of the terms and programs commonly employed in the improvement of visual perception in the hope of fostering reading achievement.

15
Visual Perception Training Activities

As you read the descriptions of these perceptual training programs, consider these questions.

1. In the light of your own experiences in teaching reading, which of these programs would seem to be logically related to word recognition? to comprehension?

2. Is it conceivable that some of these activities, which do not seem closely related to progress in reading (such as the outdoor, gross muscle experiences), could be making some contribution to the child's academic progress? How?

THERE ARE GREAT PROBLEMS in interpreting the research on visual training programs and experiments that we shall report on later. One difficulty is the vagueness with which many authors allude to their actual training procedures. Some are satisfied to say simply that they conducted "visual perception training," as though all readers would immediately know what had transpired. After all, they reason, everybody knows that visual perception training (no matter what its nature?) is good for children.

Another difficulty in evaluating these experiments is the fact that a wide variety of training activities is often employed. Sometimes as many as eight or ten types of exercises are used with the children, often with no apparent relationship between the diagnostic measures and the remediation techniques. Many authors use a single visual perception test, not even a battery of such; then they prescribe and implement this superficial diagnosis with many corrective measures. How does one analyzing this shotgun treatment approach sort out the merits of different training activities? Or are we supposed to believe, as the authors apparently do, that almost any combination of corrective procedures is equally effective? Perhaps we are naive in believing that one experimenting in the area of visual perception has an obligation to describe and justify his treatment techniques. How else can we determine the merits of any of the programs in helping us to improve children's reading?

Insofar as we can, we shall attempt to describe common visual training procedures used in the experiments cited in the next chapter in our discussion of the results of such training. A great many terms are used by the different experimenters, often to describe or categorize the very same activity. For example, an activity, Angels-in-the-Snow, which involves moving the arms and legs at command while lying on the back is considered training in Body Image and Differentiation by one author (8). Factor analysis of a series of such activities indicates that Angels-in-the-Snow is closely related to those labeled Organization of Movements in Space by Dunsing (3), such as chalkboard exercises (which the first author calls Perceptual-Motor Match). Each experimenter in visual perception seems to have his own concepts of the purpose of each of the activities he prescribes. Hence, in listing and describing visual perception training programs (Table 15-1), we shall have to group them more or less arbitrarily into what we consider to be logically related types. Alternative descriptive terms are also noted for each category. We shall, of course, utilize the results of Dunsing's factor analysis, which did show some inherent relationships among some of these training activities.

The reader should be cognizant of the tendency to use a great variety of

TABLE 15–1   VISUAL PERCEPTION TRAINING PROGRAMS

CATEGORIES	ACTIVITIES
Body schema—knowledge of the body and its parts and control of its functions (self-concept, motor planning and mobilization, body image).	Jointed dolls, Simon Says, rhythmic movements to music, movement games, trunk and leg lifts, Angels-in-the-Snow, skipping rope, verbal identification of body parts, imitation of movements.
Balance—control of body and its parts (laterality, directionality, postural flexibility, movement training).	Walking beam, creeping obstacle course, walking obstacle course, stepping games, balance disc, trampoline.
Hand-eye coordination—the integration of visual information with motoric responses of the hand (perceptual-motor match, organization of movements in space).	Templates, chalkboard exercises, coloring, cutting, pasting, jacks, marbles, bean bags, darts, ball throwing, catching and bouncing, nail pounding, ring toss, rhythm bands, Lummi sticks, hoops, jump board, bead stringing, paper and pencil activities, tracing, dot patterns or pictures, pick-up sticks.
Ocular control—developing controlled, effective movements of the eyes (distance, size, and shape in space).	Marsden swinging ball, finger play, straight line and rotary pursuits tasks with flashlights or eyes, walking beam (when used while fixating on wall target).
Form-perception—recognition of visual shapes and symbols	
Three-dimensional:	Puzzles, nested cubes, pegboards; same with rubber bands, parquetry, mosaic tiles, pattern boards, block designs, clay.
Two-dimensional:	Ditto masters for tracing, reproducing, matching, or assembling forms; desk templates; drawing.

terms interchangeably in speaking of types of training. For example, the terms *body schema, body image, body ego,* and *body experience* are often used to describe the child's awareness of his body. Body image and body ego are personality-related terms and really refer to emotional attitudes toward one's own body. These concepts are often sampled in various projective tests of drawing. Body experience refers more directly to tactile and kinesthetic experiences. Body schema, which is the term that we prefer, incorporates the knowledge of the size, shape, configuration, and functioning of body parts.

Kinesthetic, muscular, and tactile experiences do contribute to this concept, it is quite true, but, like Getman (5) and Layton,* we think that the visual sense is dominant in the formation of the child's concept of his body schema.

Similarly, the term *balance* is alternated with other terms as *laterality, directionality,* and others to mean the child's ability to control his body and its parts, as well as to associate movements with the verbal terms indicating direction as *up, down, forward, backward,* and the terms indicating sidedness, as *left foot, right hand,* and so on.   Balance implies that the child can move his body and its parts consciously to accomplish certain goals, or move them in answer to directions or in imitation of the movements of another person.   It is not, as some critics think, a simple matter of the ability to balance oneself, as on the walking beam.

Hand-eye coordination and form perception are rather well understood generally.   Ocular control, on the other hand, is often conceived of as eye-movement training.   In a sense, it is such training but is scheduled to enable the child to deal effectively with objects in space by being able to maintain or change fixation, to follow movement by visual fixations, and to coordinate his eyes in a purposeful task, an ability that is not commonly present even by kindergarten age.

Several authors have developed relatively complete training programs that include a number of these activities.   G. N. Getman and a group of fellow optometrists, Elmer R. Kane, Marvin R. Halgren, and Gordon W. McKee, evolved what is probably the earliest, well-developed visual perception program, although it was not offered to the public until 1964.   The current manual, *Developing Learning Readiness* (5), outlines seven subprograms as follows:

1. Body image—bodily movements and manipulation of a jointed doll
2. General coordination—practice in the coordination of head, arms, torso, and legs to gain skill in movement
3. Balance—using the walking beam
4. Eye-hand coordination—ditto masters and desk templates
5. Eye-movements—to improve ocular fixation, sweep, and scanning by eye movement charts, masks, sighting exercises
6. Form recognition—chalkboard exercises and templates, desk templates, ditto masters
7. Visual memory—filmstrips, charts, and games to improve recall and visualization

---

*Arthur Layton, "Body Imagery in Perceptual Learning," *American Journal of Optometry and Archives of American Academy of Optometry,* 49 (October 1972), 840–46.

Another program in wide use was evolved by G. N. Getman and Newell C. Kephart and is described in Kephart's book, *The Slow Learner in the Classroom* (6). It includes these features:

1. Chalkboard training—scribbling, finger painting, drawing and copying geometric forms, using templates
2. Sensory-motor training—using the walking board, trampoline, Angels-in-the-Snow, rhythmic activities, and various stunts and games
3. Ocular control—ocular pursuit training and activities with the Marsden ball (swinging ball)
4. Form perception—using puzzles, stick figures, and pegboards

As we might expect, the increased interest in visual perception has brought forth a flood of guides to training programs and of commercial kits. Many of these are mentioned and described in the Complementary References for this chapter. These guides and kits vary greatly in their recommendations for training that is intended to be reflected in academic success. Some offer fairly comprehensive training programs based on the author's extensive experiences in a related discipline, as the guides by Barsch, Cratty, Oxendine, and Bentley. These authors write from the viewpoint of their training in psychology or physical education. Others of the guides we list emphasize how-to-do such training rather than presenting the background information and research of the field, as in the case of those by Arena, Behrmann, Braley, Magdol, Orem, and Van Witsen. Lorena Porter's book, *Movement Education for Children,* is offered by the Association of Elementary-Kindergarten Nursery Education, another interested group. Frostig's manual for a training program is based on her perceptual test and her experiences in a treatment center. It consists largely of worksheets offering training in eye-hand coordination, figure-ground perception, perception of form constancy, position in space, and spatial relationships (4).

The commercial kits likewise vary in the depth of their treatment or approach. Some make no pretense of providing a comprehensive program and offer simply one type of aid, such as records for movement or rhythmic training, puzzles for form perception, ditto master worksheets, printed patterns for tracing, or the materials needed for various games or single activities as rubber squares, blocks, and so on.

Another treatment approach to visual perceptual problems is that offered by Delacato's theory that all language and perception deficits arise from lack of neurological organization and failure to develop complete one-sidedness in relation to the dominant cortical hemisphere. According to Delacato, dysfunction of the midbrain is indicated if the child does not creep in a cross-lateral pattern, that is, using the knee and hand on opposite sides of the body simultaneously. Cortex functioning is judged by the child's walking in cross pattern with the opposite hand and foot moving forward at the same time. Cerebral dominance is estimated on the basis of tests of handedness, footedness, eyedness and posture. Training in creeping, walking, and posture during sleep are given at the lowest level of neurological organization indicated by the tests to induce neurological development and complete one-sidedness. Since music is presumably reacted to by the nondominant hemisphere, the child must be shielded from any musical experiences to keep this cerebral hemisphere inactive, according to Delacato. This unique theory of remediation has been examined in a number of the studies that we cite in the later discussion of the outcomes of visual perceptual training.

Valett has offered both a series of tests and detailed suggestions for remediation in his handbook (11). The areas that he includes relevant to visual perception are gross motor development, sensory-motor integration, and perceptual-motor skills. The thirty-six training programs he offers in these three areas have not, to our knowledge, ever been tested for their efficacy or relevance to progress in reading. Rather, they represent a conglomeration of games, stunts, and activities known to physical educators, with some ideas similar to other programs such as the Frostig.

Silver, Hagin, and Hersh (9) have used a theory of stimulating deficit perceptual areas in their hospital populations. At first, accuracy of perception within a sense modality is promoted, then two or more modalities are related in intersensory training, and finally an attempt is made to transfer the abilities trained to a verbal level. Among the areas stressed are the visual, auditory, tactile, and kinesthetic modalities and body image. This multisensory or VAKT approach has been extended to the teaching of word recognition by some other remedial theorists.

Still another approach to perceptual problems is termed the Ortho-molecular Treatment and consists of massive doses of vitamins and minerals. The theory is that children exhibiting difficulties have markedly atypical metabolism with respect to these chemicals. Thus it is believed that, by providing the brain with large amounts of the B vitamin group and certain minerals, it may be possible to assist their perceptual functioning. A high protein, low carbohydrate diet is also used to facilitate the utilization of the vitamins and minerals and to provide a better biochemical balance (1). Those physicians who employ this approach avoid the use of the amphetamines or tranquilizers that other medical treatment approaches suggest.

A program exemplifying the tendency to mix exercises from several sources and to combine activities of proven and unproven merit or relevance to reading is that employed by the Reading Research Foundation of Chicago, and described in the materials it distributes. Briefly the program includes these activities:*

Creeping—frog crawl, frog jump, cross-pattern, lateral creeping to the side

Walking—cross pattern, upon command, lateral walking and gliding

Turns and steps

Balancing—walking beam

Body imagery—assuming positions by name

Rope jumping—cradle, front, back

Maze walk—to command

Eight count—eight body positions with stepping, arm raising, and lowering

Motor planning—creeping or walking in the shape of an alphabetic letter; walking between markers to command

Use nonsense syllable or short vowel sound as cue in place of terms such as *right, left, backward, forward,* varying cue sound each day or so

Another comprehensive program was offered in the Coronado School District Visual-Perceptual Training Program† for primary children who exhibited learning problems associated with visual perception and sensorimotor problems. Several tests and optometric evaluation were used to determine pupil needs in each area of the program. Its emphases may be outlined as follows:

Perception—tachistoscopic training for visual memory, parquetry, cubes, trampoline

Visual coordination—Marsden ball, beads and strings for pursuits and fixations, Polaroid vectograms, tracking books and red/green glasses, metronome

Motor skills: gross—hopping, skipping, balance beam, trampoline, rhythms with metronome, jump rope, throwing, and catching

Motor skills: fine—chalkboard exercises, templates, mazes, tracking books and glasses, ball push games

---

Perceptual Motor Training—Basic Exercise Guide Chicago: Reading Research Foundation).

†Stuart J. Mandell, *An Identification and Remediation Visual Perceptual Training Program* (Coronado, Calif.: Coronado Unified School District, 1972).

As is not uncommon, the Coronado program included auditory perception training activities such as tapes, listening games, buzzer board, and rhythmic clapping. To facilitate sensory integration, the La Barge Vision Trainer,* which introduces visual, auditory and motor activities, and the Rosner Auditory Analysis program† were also employed. However, unlike many other experiments in this area, the Coronado study reported pretesting and posttesting results for every one of the visual and motor skills considered significant, as well as the results in terms of gains in reading, spelling, and teachers' judgments. These results will be reported in detail in the next chapter, which discusses the outcomes of visual perception experiments.

With tongue in cheek, the present author outlined the probable future development of treatment for children suffering from perceptual difficulties (10). Borrowing freely from these various programs, we recommended training exercises for each subtype of problem child and for each kind of perceptual deficit. As in the other programs described above, some of the training procedures we recommended might seem logical, while others are completely untested and seem to bear little logical relationship to the difficulty that they are supposed to eradicate. Our satirical program of remedial and corrective steps was assembled simply to demonstrate that almost anyone can prescribe for these children with some semblance of logic, perhaps without having any proof of the true values of the recommended procedures, at this stage in the development of our knowledge in this area.

As we have suggested earlier, a number of physical educators have entered actively into the field of visual perception training. The April 1970 issue of the *Journal of Health-Physical Education and Recreation,* the official journal of the national association of physical educators, and the conference report, *Foundations and Practices in Perceptual Motor Learning—A Quest for Understanding,* are examples of the concern of this group with perceptual programs. As we might expect, the programs recommended by various authors differ considerably. Among the components frequently stressed are these:

1. Body size, control, and spatial requirements—maneuvering the body between upright aluminum rods (which topple easily) with eyes open or closed: same through copper tubing or large plywood squares, triangles, or circles, or a maze made from upright folding mats; duck walk, rabbit hop, crab walk, elephant walk, and similar activities; bilateral body

---

La Barge Electro Therapist (Rapid City, N. Dak.: MKM, Inc.).
†J. Rosner, *Rosner Auditory Analysis Program* (Pittsburgh, Pa.: Learning Research and Development Center, University of Pittsburgh).

movements upon command; bilateral tracing of letters in the air, while verbalizing directions; exercises in arresting motion and in relaxing while resting on the back upon command.

2. Sensory modalities
   a. auditory—listening for the sound of a ball rolling down one of several chutes; detecting by ear the landing of a bean bag on an extended tarp above one's head; aiming a ball at a metal target with eyes closed; simple rhythmic activities
   b. tactual—traveling over inclined hollow boxes.
   c. proprioceptive—bouncing on a bedspring, with eyes closed; rolling a golf ball down an inclined plane into a bucket, with eyes closed; crawling across a swinging bridge, with eyes closed; bouncing on a trampoline
   d. visual—standing behind a plexiglass screen and indicating by hand where an object thrown toward the screen will land
   e. motor fitness—adaptations of the Kraus-Weber physical fitness tests, as sit-ups, push-ups, back arch, and the like

A British program designed by A. E. Tansley,* headmaster of a school for children who are educationally subnormal or maladjusted, is now offered for most children suffering difficulties in learning to read. The author suggests a number of informal tests of sensory integration, visual and auditory perception, and lateral dominance in diagnosing the pupil's needs for treatment. He also employs certain standardized tests of form perception, intelligence, psycholinguistic abilities, reading, and other areas. We shall discuss these diagnostic procedures in other contexts and presently simply review some of the treatment procedures Tansley recommends, as follows:

Form perception—jigsaw puzzles, sorting forms, using forms to represent objects, arranging parts of a cardboard human figure, free play with paint, clay, wet sand, mosaics, blocks, and the like

Hand-eye motor coordination—tracing simple mazes, joining dots, drawing within printed paths, chalkboard drawing at command, discriminating reversed drawings and models

Visual copying—copying geometric figures with matchsticks, tracing over same figures with finger, copying figures or patterns from chalkboard, copying mosaics

Visual memory—reproducing figures and patterns used in copying, from memory; giving names to figures to aid recall

Completion and closure—finishing incomplete figures and patterns by pointing out missing part, or completing the figure; identifying verbally incomplete drawings of objects or actions

---

*A. E. Tansley, *Reading and Remedial Reading* (London: Routledge and Kegan Paul, 1967).

Visual rhythm—extending and drawing given sample of a repetitive pattern, while describing it

Visual sequencing—repeating the arrangement of two or three pictures as demonstrated; same with two–five geometric forms; encouraging children to verbalize placement; useful also for auditory memory by having child name sequence after observing it

Temporal sequencing—arranging pictures, diagrams in temporal order, that is, house in various stages of erection; increases gradually from four to ten pictures

Visual discrimination—discriminating similar figures in groups of five, explaining reasons for choice and rejections

Auditory sequencing and rhythm—repeating short sentences, jingles or rhymes; executing simple commands; marching, dancing, scribbling or finger painting in time to rhythms; sound blending; telling sequence of events in story read or heard; drawing series of patterns from memory; selecting figures as named from a group; verbalizing dot and dash patterns in imitation of teacher; repeating same patterns by tapping while verbalizing; drawing dots and dashes to represent auditory pattern, repeating same by tapping; similar training with sequences and rhythms using percussion instruments

As the reader will note, the terms describing the nature of these various training activities are used according to the author's own definitions. The looseness of these definitions permits specific activities to be categorized under different headings, despite their similarity. In Tansley's program, this is evident in the inclusion of body schema activities under the rubric of form perception, drawing from memory under auditory sequencing, and in the labored distinction between form perception and visual discrimination. On the positive side, there is the distinct effort to promote verbalization or, as some might call it, intersensory integration, in many of these visual-auditory training activities. Thus Tansley tries to bring these fundamental motor and sensory activities closer to the verbal level of letter and word recognition.

Some programs, such as that employed in the Learning Disabilities classes of Pinellas County, Florida, broaden the approach in an attempt to deal with what they believe are the learning modalities of their pupils. Using the questionable Slingerland test as the sole diagnostic test, pupils are classified as visual, auditory, or motor learners. The justification offered for the use of this unvalidated instrument is that it does give some clues to the apparent modality that should be used in teaching the child. This line of thinking by these learning disability teachers assumes that the clues offered by the Slingerland test really mean what they seem to mean, justifying intensive emphasis upon one modality. Then, after a period of training focused on the supposed learning channel appropriate for a pupil, the progress in reading and related skills is taken as further evidence of the soundness of this program.

We are not questioning whether the training programs have some merit, for, as we describe them, the reader will recognize some intrinsic logic. Any of them applied in a one-to-one or small-group arrangement would probably induce some acceleration in learning because of the personalized attention and the newness of the many teacher-made and commercial materials, as well as the Hawthorne effect. This apparent success does not prove the validity of the diagnostic testing, the accuracy of the identification of the pupil's learning modality, or even the relevance of the type of training to any particular modality.

For the learner deficient in visual areas:

visual reception—emphasizing phonics and many auditory aids; practicing with symbols, pictures, numbers, and letters in identification, likenesses and differences, matching; flash cards; categorizing pictures; following directions; measuring quantities; using TV schedules and various directories.

visual association—picture and word cards; grouping pictures from sports, catalogs; finding missing parts of common objects; multiple-choice pictorial representation of simple arithmetic problems; correcting sentences containing an incorrect homonym; crossing out wrong number or letter in series.

visual memory—rearranging scrambled letters of alphabet; alphabetizing words; writing cursively in the air; rearranging picture sequences; jigsaw puzzles from pictures, from catalogs, and the like; rearranging known sight words in meaningful sentences; practice in recalling the sequence of a small group of word cards; rearranging a series of directions in correct order, same with letters of a word, a jumbled sentence, pictures, and so on.

visual closure—missing parts, completing puzzles, words, sentences, pegboards; dot-to-dot exercises; anagrams; tracing figures in a confusing background.

For the learner deficient in auditory areas:

auditory reception—identifying everyday sounds; developing auditory figure-ground discrimination; identifying classmates' voices, footsteps; identifying emotional tones and intonation.

auditory memory—learning to recognize word clues to position, as *next, before, middle;* tapping or clapping in response to cues; teaching child to group numbers in a long sequence; integrating visual dots with tapping; reciting game rules; passing directions from one child to another;

playing sequence stories, with each child repeating given sentence and adding another.

auditory association—demonstrating opposites, asking child to supply such; developing time and space relationships between routines, days, seasons; temporal relationships present in words, as *before, after a while;* temporal relationships in telling time; recalling sequence of events in personal experience; assembling a meaningful sentence from a few given words; rearranging sentences in proper sequence; stressing the vocabulary of time and position in space; learning the first order and complete relationships in analogies; grouping within categories; incomplete sentences.

verbal language expression—prompting, confirming, and reinforcing child's ability to label or name things, describe surroundings, interpret pictures and experiences; promoting role-playing, puppetry, plays, and the like; assembling picture-word vocabulary file; trips to community points of interest followed by discussions; stimulating oral experience stories by pictures, personal events, book reports; stimulating more expressive and descriptive words; solving simple social problems orally.

For the learner deficient in motor areas:

mathematics—aid child by folding paper, wide spacing, color coding, manipulative materials, much practice in measuring and estimating.

reading—using markers or fingers to keep place; role-playing; using tape recorder, typewriter; cutting and pasting; providing writing materials such as those used in sight conservation classes; tracing on acetates; using writing models; developing gross motor coordination by games, as hopscotch, bean bags, drawing races at the chalkboard; clay, rice, and beans to make pictures on an outline; charades, pantomime; sewing activities; developing fine motor coordination by coloring, beads, blocks, pegboards, dot-to-dot pictures.

position in space activities—climbing; walking rail; completing pictures; assembling large-scale human figure; self-portraits; Simple Simon games; learning to associate words with directions; Angels-in-the-Snow; crab walk, frog squat, and the like; symmetrical activities of limbs upon command; eye-hand coordination exercises, as scribbling, ball play, marbles, buttoning, and the like; eye-foot coordination with balls, bean bags, jump rope, hopping; rhythmic practice with music.

The reader will note that this program is more of a corrective effort to improve weak input channels of a modality than it is an attempt to enable the learner to capitalize on his preferred modality. This is an emphasis different from most programs oriented to pupil modalities that try to help the pupil use those abilities that he already has to the utmost in learning to handle symbols. The research we have cited elsewhere on teaching through the child's preferred modality is not very positive. But neither do we have any strong evidence that strengthening a weak modality is more logical or effective. We do not really know whether it is possible to improve the factors presumably operating in each modality in such a manner that the learning of symbols will be accelerated. We do not know the relative relevance of each of these factors to reading or mathematics, or whether they are real and independent. Certainly, shotgun programs employing a wealth of new, attractive materials (thanks to the Federal grants) do seem to help some of these children. But, as we have pointed out, these results could be the result of any of several aspects of the way the program is conducted, rather than the validity of the diagnosis or the modality factors presumably strengthened. Maurice Kaufman* has prepared a critical review of a number of the programs that we have described here. His reviews include the Winter Haven program, Getman's *Developing Learning Readiness,* the Frostig approach, and the parallel *Patterns and Pictures* of the same author, all of which we described and evaluated earlier. His review of the validity research on these programs is scanty, however, and he has apparently not found many of the studies that we cited in discussing their outcomes. But his reviews are more detailed in their descriptions and may well be read for that purpose.

A commercial kit evaluated by Kaufman is the *Fairbanks-Robinson Program*—Level 1.† Briefly described, this approach includes these features:

> Tracing, cutting, and coloring activities to develop circular, straight line, and rhythmic movements; left to right; top to bottom; form recognition; size, shape and constancy; attention to details
> Figure-ground discrimination
> Spatial relationships in a two-dimensional plane

Still another such kit is the Erie Program,‡ which includes four boxes of training materials as follows:

> Visual perceptual—gameboards and eight tactile pieces
> Perceptual bingo—form matching at first with color aids, later without
> Visual-motor template forms—worksheets with templates
> Perceptual card and dominoes game—like Old Maid and Dominoes, using forms from which letters are constructed

---

*Maurice Kaufman, *Perceptual and Language Readiness Programs.* Reading Aids Series (Newark, Del.: International Reading Association, 1973).

†Jean S. Fairbanks and Janet Robinson, *Fairbanks Robinson Program* (Boston: Teaching Resources, 1969).

‡*Erie Program Perceptual-Motor Exercises* (Boston: Teaching Resources, 1969).

Like the present author, Kaufman could find no studies supporting the validity of these programs in terms of contributions to readiness or reading.

We alluded earlier to several programs in which optometrists have played a leading role. These vision specialists also make many contributions to perceptual training programs in applying their visual training techniques to problem cases. For example, many children who are exhibiting difficulties in maintaining their place while reading and hence losing inflection and relationships among words can be helped by an appropriate plus lens. This lens is convex and locates objects further away in space, thus enabling the child to organize the spatial relationships among words while reading. Other readers who show troubles in maintaining consistent left-to-right saccadic movements or in achieving accurate return sweeps to the next line can be assisted by the optometric visual training programs.* Other pupils manifest poor near-point of convergence in that they cannot maintain binocular fixation on an object at three–four inches from the face; difficulty in shifting fixation from near to far to near targets; unstable binocular fixation when following a moving object in the near-point area. It is interesting to note that accuracy in rotations and saccadic movements is positively related to success in reading when these are observed while the child is standing on a balance beam, but show little relationship if measured while the child is seated. Here again we see the interrelationship among visual functions, body balance, or posture.

Other symptoms may be the inability to achieve near-point fixations on several targets successively; slow recovery of binocular fixation on an object moved outward to four or more inches from the face, in that the diverged eye does not rapidly converge to binocular fixation; and unequal participation of both eyes in the reading act. Many of these symptoms may be improved by the use of near-point lenses and simple training programs that can be followed in the office or at home with the aid of inexpensive training materials.

The optometrist who is knowledgeable in the area of child vision care will use his clinical analysis to search for these symptoms and to suggest treatment for these interrelationships among vision, posture, learning, corrective lenses, and visual training. He is also anxious to clarify his findings to school personnel, as shown by the participation of optometrists in the Winter Haven project, the Getman program, the Kephart and the Barsch syllabi, the activities of the Yale Clinic of Child Development, and the Gesell Institute, as well as in many school programs throughout the country.

---

*J. Baxter Swartwout, "Educational Visual Training Programs," *Academic Therapy,* 7 (Fall 1971), 85–92.

LEARNING PROJECT

Select those visual perceptual training activities that you think might definitely effect reading progress for some pupils. Explain how you might incorporate them into the classroom program, in terms of (a) scheduling; (b) selecting pupils for training; (c) using pupil aides to supervise the activity; (d) ways of obtaining the necessary equipment. Justify your selection of activities by pointing out the ability that you believe it would develop, and the results that you expect to see.

REFERENCES

1. Cott, A., *Orthomolecular Treatment.* New York: American Schizophrenia Association, 1971.
2. Delacato, Carl H., *Neurological Organization and Reading.* Springfield, Ill.: Charles C. Thomas Co., 1966.
3. Dunsing, Jack A., "Perceptual-Motor Factors in the Development of School Readiness: An Analysis of the Purdue Perceptual-Motor Survey," *American Journal of Optometry and Archives of American Academy of Optometry,* 46 (October 1969), 760–65.
4. Frostig, Marianne, *Frostig Move, Grow, Learn.* Chicago: Follett Publishing, 1969.
5. Getman, G. N., Kane, Elmer R., Halgren, Marvin R., and McKee, Gordon W., *Developing Learning Readiness.* Manchester, Mo.: Webster Publishing, 1964.
6. Kephart, Newell C., *The Slow Learner in the Classroom.* Columbus: Charles E. Merrill, 1960.
7. Krippner, Stanley, "Perceptual Training and Reading Remediation for Children with Learning Disabilities," in *Issues in Urban Education and Mental Health,* Lillie Pope, editor. Brooklyn: Book-Lab, 1971.
8. Roach, Eugene G., and Kephart, Newell C., *The Purdue Perceptual-Motor Survey.* Columbus: Charles E. Merrill Co., 1966.
9. Silver, A. A., Hagin, R. A., and Hersh, M. F., "Reading Disability: Teaching Through Stimulation of Deficit Perceptual Areas," *American Journal of Orthopsychiatry,* 37 (1967), 744–52.
10. Spache, George D., "Diagnosis and Remediation in 1980," in *Reading Disability and Perception,* George D. Spache, editor, Proceedings International Reading Association, 13, Part 3 (1969), 135–51.
11. Valett, R. E., *The Remediation of Learning Disabilities.* Palo Alto: Fearon Publishers, 1967.

Complementary References

"Approaches to Perceptual-Motor Experience," *Journal of Health-Physical Education and Recreation,* April 1970, entire issue.

Arena, John J., *Teaching Through Sensory-Motor Experiences.* San Rafael, Calif.: Academic Therapy, 1969.

Barsch, Ray H., *A Perceptual-Motor Curriculum.* Volume 1—*Achieving Perceptual-Motor Efficiency.* Seattle: Special Child Publications, 1967.

Barsch, Ray H., *Enriching Perception and Cognition.* New York: Bruner-Mazel, 1968.

Behrmann, Polly, *Activities for Developing Visual Perception.* San Rafael, Calif.: Academic Therapy, 1970.

Belgau, Frank A., and Basden, Beverley V., *A Perceptual-Motor and Visual Perception Handbook of Developmental Activities for Schools, Clinics and Preschool Programs.* La Porte, Tex.: Perception Development Research Associates.

Bentley, William G., *Learning to Move and Moving to Learn.* New York: Citation Press, 1970.

Benton, Arthur L., *Right-Left Discrimination and Finger Localization.* New York: Hoeber, 1959.

Braley, William T., Konicki, Geraldine, and Leedy, Catherine, *Daily Sensorimotor Training Activities.* Freeport, N.Y.: Educational Activities.

Carter, Darrell, editor, *Interdisciplinary Approach to Learning Disorders.* Philadelphia: Chilton, 1970.

Cratty, Bryant J., *Development Sequence of Perceptual Motor Tasks.* Freeport, N.Y.: Educational Activities.

Cratty, Bryant J., *Motor Activity and the Education of Retardates.* Philadelphia: Lea and Febiger, 1969.

Cratty, Bryant J., *Movement Behavior and Motor Learning.* Philadelphia: Lea and Febiger, 1967.

Cratty, Bryant J., *Movement, Perception and Thought.* Freeport, N.Y.: Educational Activities.

Cratty, Bryant J., and Martin, Sister Margaret Mary, *Perceptual-Motor Efficiency in Children.* Philadelphia: Lea and Febiger, 1969.

Crawford, J. E., *Children with Subtle Perceptual Motor Difficulties.* Pittsburgh: Stanwix House, 1966.

Durbin, Mary Lee, *Teaching Techniques for Retarded and Pre-Reading Students.* Springfield, Ill.: Charles C. Thomas, 1967.

Frostig, Marianne, *Frostig Move, Grow, Learn.* Chicago: Follett Publishing, 1969.

Goodfriend, Ronnie Stephanie, *Power in Perception for the Young Child.* New York: Teachers College Press, 1972.

Gordon, Ira J., Guinagh, Barry, and Jester, R. Emile, *Child Learning Through Child Play.* New York: St. Martin's Press, 1972.

Green, Edward J., and O'Connell, Joan A., editors, *An Annotated Bibliography of Visual Discrimination Learning.* New York: Teachers College Press, 1970.

Hackett, Layne, *Movement Exploration and Games for the Mentally Retarded.* Palo Alto: Peek Publications, 1970.

Hackett, Layne, and Jenson, Robert, *Guide to Movement Exploration.* Palo Alto: Peek Publications, 1967.

Kephart, Newell C., *Slow Learner in the Classroom.* Columbus: Charles E. Merrill, 1960.

Magdol, Miriam Sper, *Perceptual Training in the Kindergarten.* San Rafael, Calif.: Academic Therapy, 1971.

Manual of Perceptual-Motor Activities. Johnstown, Pa.: Mafex Associates, no date.

Manual of Primary Perceptual Training—South Euclid-Lyndhurst Public Schools. Johnstown, Pa.: Mafex Associates, 1971.

Motor Perceptual Development Handbook. La Porte, Tex.: Perceptual Development Research Associates, 1967.

Orem, R. C., *Learning to See and Seeing to Learn.* Johnstown, Pa.: Mafex Associates, 1972.

Oxendine, Joseph B., *Psychology of Motor Learning.* New York: Appleton-Century-Crofts, 1968.

Porter, Lorena, *Movement Education for Children.* Washington, D.C.: American Association of Elementary-Kindergarten-Nursery Education, 1969.

Robb, Margaret D., editor, *Foundations and Practices in Perceptual-Motor Learning: A Quest for Understanding.* Washington, D.C.: American Association for Health, Physical Education and Recreation, 1971.

Smith, Helen K., editor, *Perception and Reading.* Proceedings International Reading Association, 12, No. 4 (1968).

Spache, George D., editor, *Reading Disability and Perception.* Proceedings International Reading Association, 13, No. 3 (1969).

Spache, George D., and Spache, Evelyn B., *Reading in the Elementary School.* Boston: Allyn and Bacon, 1973.

Teaching Through Sensory Motor Deficiencies. Johnstown, Pa.: Mafex Associates, 1969.

Valett, Robert E., *The Remediation of Learning Disabilities.* Palo Alto: Fearon, 1967.

Van Witsen, Betty, *Perceptual Training Activities Handbook.* New York: Teachers College Press, 1967.

Vernon, Magdalen D., *Perception Through Experience.* New York: Barnes and Noble, 1970.

Young, Francis, and Lindsley, Donald B., editors, *Early Experience and Visual Information Processing in Perceptual and Reading Disorders.* New York: National Academy of Sciences, 1971.

AUDIO-VISUAL AIDS

Films and Filmstrips

Kirshner, A. J., *The Kirshner Body Alphabet.* Johnstown, Pa.: Mafex Associates. A filmstrip offering body posture training to simulate the letters of the alphabet. Manual and student workbook, manikin, and posters available.

Learning to Move Series. New York: McGraw-Hill. Available in two sets of fourteen films each. The films provide stimuli to help children develop body awareness.

Look at It Series. New York: McGraw-Hill. Set A of eight films deals with visual tracking; B of thirteen films, with learning forms; and set C, eleven films on visual memory.

Motility Training, Controlled Reader Set MT. New York: Educational Development Labs. Twenty-five filmstrips for visual training and discrimination. Other strips at Readiness level extend the variety of skills taught.

Progressive Visual Perceptual Training. Freeport, N.Y.: Educational Activities. Training in seeing, recalling, and reproducing. Five strips for primary, five for intermediate levels.

Reading Readiness. Glenview, Ill.: Educational Projections. Collection of sixty strips includes a number on visual discrimination and L-R progression.

Reading Readiness. Chicago: Eye Gate. Set of ten strips includes some on visual and auditory discrimination.

Visual Perception Skills—Primary. Freeport, N.Y.: Educational Activities. Seven color filmstrips to promote facets of perception—memory, constancy, discrimination, visualization, and the like.

Visual Tracking Films. Glenview, Ill.: Psychotechnics. Films and worksheets for group practice in form and letter discrimination.

Records

Basic Concepts Through Dance. Freeport, N.Y.: Educational Activities. To promote body image, limb, and bodily control and awareness, as guided by a pair of records.

Classroom Rhythms. New York: Educational Record. Series of three albums to involve children in rhythmic bodily movements.

Dynamic Balancing Activities. Freeport, N.Y.: Educational Activities. Balance and body image activities on the balance beam, guided by two records.

Finger Play. New York: Educational Record. A pair of albums to help children develop finger coordination.

Hand Rhythms. Dansville, N.Y.: Instructor. Record offers twelve activities to aid manual dexterity, rhythms, hand and arm coordination.

Motor-Perceptual Learnings. Glendale, Calif.: Bowmar. Eight action-provoking records for nursery and kindergarten children for motor training.

Perception Development Research Associates. Big Spring, Tex.: Perception Development. Offer many individual training items, as swinging ball, bean bags, trampoline, crawl-through box, beam, visual tracking light, balance disc, bat and ball, peg boards, and the like. Some have records or tapes giving directions for sustained self-directed activities.

Perceptual Motor Development Program. Freeport, N.Y.: Educational Activities. Ten records to promote awareness of own body in relation to space, balance, agility, relaxation, muscular control, and the like. Available separately also.

Preschool activities. Dansville, N.Y.: Instructor. Record offers thirty rhythmic activities.

Schivera, Howard, *Sound-Sight Skills.* Freeport, N.Y.: Educational Activities. Six albums, ten activity books for paper-and-pencil hand-eye activities in content field materials. Offered for grades one to four.

Wilson, Robert H., Humphrey, James H., and Sullivan, Dorothy D., *Teaching Reading Through Creative Movement.* Freeport, N.Y.: Educational Activities, 1970. Manual for use of two records and eight workbooks for beginning reading. Uses A (audio—story), M (movement—act out story), A-V (audio-visual—children read while listening to story).

Miscellaneous

Cheves Visual-Motor Perception. Boston: Teaching Resources. Form and color puzzles largely to promote perception.

Developmental Learning Materials. Chicago: Developmental Learning Materials. Offer wide variety of simple games and devices: pictures, spatial relations, pegboards, puzzles, sequences, parquetry, and so on.

Dubnoff School Program 1. Boston: Teaching Resources. Two levels of paper and pencil perceptual motor exercises.

Dubnoff School Program 2. Boston: Teaching Resources. Spatial and directionality orientation activities, pattern cards and peg boards.

Durbin, Mary Lee, *Teaching Techniques for Retarded and Pre-reading Students.* Springfield, Ill.: Charles C. Thomas, 1967. Devices and techniques to improve eye-hand, perceptual, language and vocabulary, cognitive processes. For educable mentally retarded, trainable, delayed in readiness and disadvantaged(?).

Erie Program—Perceptual Motor Teaching Materials. Boston: Teaching Resources. Visual-perceptual exercises with templates, form and color discrimination, and so on.

Fairbanks-Robinson—Perceptual Motor Development. Boston: Teaching Resources. Worksheets and puzzles to develop hand-eye coordination, visual discrimination, form constancy, spatial relations, and the like. Modeled after Frostig Program.

Fitzhugh Plus. Galien, Mich.: Allied Education Council. Programmed workbooks in shape matching, figure completion, and shape identification.

Frostig, Marianne, and Horne, David, *The Frostig Program for the Development of Visual Perception.* Chicago: Follett Publishing. Largely paper-and-pencil workbooks to promote the facets of visual perception identified in Frostig Test. Basically offered as a remedial program for perceptually handicapped.

Frostig, Marianne, Miller, Ann-Marie, and Horne, David, *Pictures and Patterns.* Chicago: Follett Publishing. Includes body awareness, visual-motor coordination, figure-ground, perceptual constancy, and position in space activities; related worksheets. Offered at three levels for kindergarten–primary children.

Getman, G. N., *School Skill Tracing Board.* Harristown, Pa.: Pathway School. An individual training device in coordination, tracing, and form perception, by exercises on large designs on paper.

Getman, G. N., Kane, Elmer R., Halgren, Marvin R., and McKee, Gordon W., *Developing Learning Readiness.* Manchester, Mo.: Webster. Program includes balance beam, templates, doll models, filmstrips, duplicating masters, teacher's manual, and eye movement charts for a six-part training sequence in eye-hand-coordination and perception.

Gould, Lawrence N., *The Detect Series.* Chicago: Science Research. Detect Visual—using tachistoscope to improve visual discrimination and memory. Detect Tactile—experiences with textured forms, numerals, and letters.

Grimm Rocking Balance Platform. Freeport, N.Y.: Educational Activities. A small platform for balancing, rocking, and other activities.

Groffman Visual Tracing Program. Davenport, Iowa: Keystone View Division, Mast Development Co. Two hundred line patterns for tracing to improve perceptual ability.

KELP. Manchester, Mo.: Webster. Kit includes a number of spatial, form discrimination and auditory perception materials for kindergarten and first grade levels.

Leavell Language-Development Service. Davenport, Iowa: Keystone View Division, Mast Development Co. Drawing exercises in a chiroscope (a device for overcoming suppression of vision in one eye) offered to correct or promote eye dominance (in the binocular act of reading?)

Learning Squares. Freeport, N.Y.: Educational Activities. Rubber foam 10 × 10 squares containing letters, numbers, figures, and the like. For floor games.

McLeod, Pierce H., *Readiness for Learning.* Philadelphia: Lippincott, 1970. Subtitled "A Program for Visual and Auditory Perceptual Training." Includes motor training activities, visual training and listening activities outlined for six to ten weeks; then another six to ten weeks, same areas, more advanced tasks. Finally, letter and word knowledge using workbook, with visual-motor, letter knowledge, and word study by visual discrimination and tachistoscope.

Maney, Ethel S., *Reading Fundamentals Program.* Elizabethtown, Pa.: Continental Press. Offers ditto masters for seatwork in visual discrimination, visual-motor skills, and reasoning at several primary levels.

Parkinson Program for Special Children. Chicago: Follett Publishing. Matching, sorting games and worksheets offered for any problem children.

Parquetry Blocks. Rochester: Visual Needs. Blocks, with templates, if desired, for varied activities.

Pathway School Program. Boston: Teaching Resources. Exercises in hand-eye coordination.

Peabody Language Development Kit. Circle Pines, Minn.: American Guidance Services. An overall oral language development program emphasizing auditory, visual motor and factual approaches, reasoning, and verbal expression.

Perception Plaques. Princeton: Creative Playthings. Wooden squares portraying faces differing in some detail. Child is to make similar pairs.

Perceptual Concepts Series. Dansville, N.Y.: Instructor. Charts and ditto masters for Positions in Space, Shape Constancy, and Figure Ground.

Perceptual Testing and Training Materials. Winter Haven, Fla.: Winter Haven Lions Research Foundation. Guide test, called Perceptual Achievement Forms, and templates for training program in form perception and hand-eye coordination.

Sage, Michael, *Words Within Words.* Philadelphia: Lippincott, 1961. Workbook of sight words to be completed by child, to achieve closure.

Shape Up. New York: Educational Games. A game of matching geometric shapes.

TTC Delacato Stereo-Reading Service. Van Nuys, Calif.: Teaching Technology. Reading exercise cards viewed through a stereoscope. Presumably overcomes laterality confusions and improves reading.

Thinker Puzzles. San Rafael, Calif.: Academic Therapy. Form discrimination of shapes and letters. Three sets each with twenty interlocking pieces.

Thurstone, Thelma G., *Learning to Think Series.* Chicago: Science Research. Four workbooks to improve motor coordination, reasoning, quantitative and spatial thinking, and memory.

Thurstone, Thelma G., and Lillie, David L., *Beginning to Learn: Fine Motor Skills.* Chicago: Science Research. Cutting, tracing, templates, coloring, and the like.

Thurstone, Thelma G., and Lillie, David L., *Beginning to Learn: Perceptual Skills.* Chicago: Science Research. Likenesses and differences, size comparisons, noting details, discriminating reversals.

Visual Games. Princeton: Creative Playthings. Puzzle sets involving sequence of events.

Visual Perception. Troy, Mich.: Educational Corp. of America. Offer single tape and related materials including worksheets to improve eye-hand coordination, tracking, and visual accommodation. Each at several levels of difficulty.

We Study Word Shapes. Rockville Center, N.Y.: Dexter and Westbrook. Emphasizes word shapes, word beginnings, and directionality in beginning word recognition. For K–I, workbook.

Wright, Geneva, *Road Game.* Johnstown, Pa.: Mafex. Part I offers two sets of worksheet materials for eye-hand coordination; Part II extends these to basic shapes.

Zweig-Bruno Stereo-Tracing Exercise. Van Nuys, Calif.: Teaching Technology. Tracing exercises to promote hand-eye coordination to be used in Stereo-reader (a stereoscope).

For the Teacher

Early Recognition of Learning Disabilities. Washington, D.C.: National Audiovisual. 30-minute 16 mm. color film portraying the problems of children with learning disabilities.

Focus on Behavior: A World to Perceive. University Park: Pennsylvania State University. 30-minute film on the role of perception in handling information, and effect of personality on perception.

Initial Perceptual Training. New York: New York University. A brief 7½-minute film on sensory stimulation of sight, touch, weight, and sound.

Integrated Motor-Perceptual Training. New York: New York University. A 6-minute film depicting training in coordination of perceptual and motor coordination in a variety of ways.

Motor Training. New York: New York University. Devices and special exercises to stimulate the passive child (mentally retarded), mazes, ladders, swings, balance beam, and so on, in an 11 minute film.

Movement Exploration. Freeport, N.Y.: Educational Activities. A 16 mm. color film, 22 minutes, demonstrating a variety of motor activities.

One Who Can't. Chicago: Marketing Services. Three 20-minute films on a learning-disabled child.

Perceptual Training. Chicago: Cenco. A series of three films 6–9 minutes each on levels of perceptual-motor training.

Visual Perception Training in the Classroom. David Horne. A 20-minute b & w filmstrip on the use of the Frostig training program.

Visual Perception and Failure to Learn to Read. Los Angeles: Churchill Films. A 20-minute film on the Frostig program.

The variability in definitions of visual perception, and in the types of activities and programs that we described earlier, may lead the reader to anticipate conflicting results from these programs. And, indeed, it is difficult to draw many consistent conclusions from these outcomes. For convenience—and what we hope is clarity—we here categorize the reports of training programs according to their effects upon the development of visual perception, readiness, and reading.

Despite the claimed relationships with reading, one large group of studies almost ignored this interaction and was satisfied to report gains in some visual perception test. Apparently the authors of these studies were so impressed with their pretest to post-test gains that they assumed something of significance must have happened. Without exploration of the ultimate effects upon reading, however, these studies tell us nothing about the effectiveness of their training programs. Another group of reports includes those emphasizing visual discrimination of letters, words, and forms, and paired associate learning tasks. This group intended to affect reading and, on the whole, was successful. A third group stressed gain in readiness or reading from visual motor training programs and, again, showed some degree of success.

A small group of researches unsuccessfully employing still other types of training activities in the hopes of influencing reading is also reported. Finally, those experiments using the Frostig program, alone or with other training efforts, are critiqued as a separate collection.

As you try to achieve some overall impressions of the outcomes of perceptual training programs, ask yourself these questions.

1. How would you estimate the relative merits of programs in visual discrimination versus those in visual motor skills versus other types?

2. Why do you suppose that among some very similar programs, some appear successful in affecting pupil reading, while others do not? What factors in the selection of pupils for training, in the training activities employed, in the age and socioeconomic status of the pupils, or in other variables do you think produce these divergent results for similar programs?

16
Outcomes of Visual Perception Training Programs and Experiments

W E MAY WELL EXPECT training programs in visual perception to be varied as much as the theoretical and operational definitions of this ability that we reviewed in chapter 1. We may also expect, because of these variations in definitions and training procedures, that it is very difficult for even objective reviewers of the field to find much that is logically consistent and pragmatic in terms of significance for early reading. The fact that many current tests of perception were constructed solely for the possible detection of the condition of brain damage—and that the extension of their use to predict reading difficulties was a late and often questionable afterthought—is disturbing to many who review the field. Finally, the proliferation of jargon such as *minimal brain damage, dyslexia, suspected brain damage, perceptually handicapped,* and the like, evokes mixed reactions among onlookers. Edward Fry has offered us a "terminology generator" of thirty of these combining terms which, with tongue in cheek, he recommends as a source of about 1,000 of such almost meaningless phrases (32), if we feel the need for new descriptors.

For all these reasons, it is no surprise to find experienced reading clinicians like Bruce Balow of the University of Minnesota (4) rejecting any direct relationship between brain damage or tests for the same and reading achievement; and decrying any intrinsic merit in any type of perceptual motor training activities specifically intended to produce reading improvement. Joseph W. Denison* likewise rejects much of the current research on visual perception, auditory perception, and intersensory integration. He favors an approach that would identify the modality—visual, auditory, or kinesthetic—for which the child exhibited a preference or aptitude, as well as classroom experiments testing the validity of teaching reading to each child through his preferred modality. He recognizes, of course, that his view is still largely theoretical and relatively untested.

Although the modality concept is persuasive, it is an oversimplification of learning in reading, in our opinion. Teaching experiments keyed to the apparent learning modality of the child, as Denison recognizes, have not been consistent with the theory, for a number of reasons. One of these reasons may be, as Birch and Lefford (8) and many others hold, that learning to read, even when one modality is overemphasized, is dependent upon previous

*Joseph W. Denison, "Perceptual Influences in the Primary Grades: An Alternative Consideration," *Journal of School Psychology,* 7 (1968–69), 38–46.

sensory experiences in other modalities also. For example, a word or letter is not just a visual image, for it has auditory and kinesthetic components, which help determine its recognition and recall. And it may evoke a great variety of stored memories derived from sensory experiences of several types as well. A few moments in free association to words such as *salty, dream, deep* calls forth a number of sensory associations from the average person. These associations play a meaningful role in recognition, recall, and meaning in context, as many studies show. A word is not just an abstract symbol to be learned by its shape or length, its constituent sounds, or the kinesthetic impressions derived from writing it, however helpful these may be in discriminating and naming it. In our opinion, a word is one of a group of related memories derived from impressions from many sensory experiences. These memories strongly influence the learnability of words, their retention, and the ease with which the reader deals with them in context. Identifying the child's learning modality and using it for initial presentation of words may be economical of instructional time. But recognition must also be based upon a group of associated sensory memories; otherwise word recognition becomes a look and guess or word-calling practice.

Other criticisms of perceptual training are made by Helen M. Robinson and Stephen E. Klesius.* Both feel that much of the research attempting to prove the values of such training is poorly conceived and that many of the tests are questionable, as we have pointed out. While the training programs may produce gains in tests of visual perception, they do not consistently influence reading or readiness test performances, Robinson emphasizes. Moreover, she does not agree with Denison that teaching to the modality of the child is necessarily a better road to early reading success. Citing her own study,† she believes that reading instruction apparently keyed to the favored learning modality of the child, as offering a phonic approach to good auditory–poor visual learners, is no more successful than using a contraindicated sight word method with such pupils. Conversely, poor auditory–good visual learners were not more successful under a sight word approach than under a phonics system in her study.

Klesius identified eleven studies that he considered fairly sound in their research techniques. Five yielded positive results; five resulted in no effect

---

*Stephen E. Klesius, "Perceptual-Motor Developments and Reading—A Closer Look." pp. 151–59; and Helen M. Robinson, "Perceptual Training—Does It Result in Reading Improvement?" pp. 135–50 in *Some Persistent Questions on Beginning Reading,* Robert C. Aukerman, editor (Newark, Del.: International Reading Association, 1972).

†Helen M. Robinson, "Visual and Auditory Modalities Related to Methods for Beginning Reading," *Reading Research Quarterly,* 8 (Fall 1972), 7–39.

upon reading achievement; one was inconclusive. It should be noted that three of the positive studies were conducted with retarded readers or low socioeconomic groups; while the five negative experiments dealt with primary children of normal reading ability and average to middle-class socioeconomic status. Is there perhaps an implication in Klesius's review, as in the Spache study (79), that perceptual training is relevant to reading improvement only among those children who experience difficulties in the early reading program? Or that the training is relatively pointless for brighter children, for those who are middle-class or, in other words, for those who usually succeed in our beginning stages?

However, despite their impressions that perceptual training programs have not consistently been shown to influence reading achievement, Balow (4) and Klesius* see these other values: their developmental appropriateness for disadvantaged children as prevention of failures; as remedial treatment for *some* children with learning disabilities; as a supplement, not a substitute, for individualized competency-based reading instruction; and as a substitute for free play and game-oriented physical education programs. Other values that they feel may well be present are the relaxation of tension, the opportunity for freedom of movement (particularly desirable for boys), and, consequently, the improvement of attention as a result of these activities. Perhaps a detailed review of a relatively large number of perceptual training experiments may help the reader to reconcile these almost contradictory expert opinions and to decide whether some types of training may be educationally significant for some types of pupils in some kinds of reading programs.

VARYING OUTCOMES OF VISUAL PERCEPTION PROGRAMS

Gains in Perception Only

A number of programs in perceptual training have not attempted to relate their efforts to the effect upon reading achievement, but rather have been satisfied to demonstrate that they could produce gains on perception tests. These authors may be correct in assuming that there is some sort of relationship between reading improvement and gains in visual-motor skills, but such relationships do not guarantee, as they assume, that any and all kinds of training will be reflected in better reading scores, as we shall see later.

---

*Klesius, op. cit.

Bateman (6), Wiseman (92), and Boger (9) worked with mentally retarded children in programs of visual motor tasks. After a summer camp program, Bateman reported gains in Beery's perceptual test for those with I.Q.'s above 50; Wiseman found that a six-months' individualized program produced superior results on the same test. Boger and Wiseman both report gains in I.Q. for their mentally retarded children, even on such highly verbal instruments as the Stanford-Binet. Cruikshank (20) found that his gains among brain-injured children in the perceptual area tended to disappear during the second year of the training program. In a two-year study, alternating a year of tutoring with no tutoring and rotating his mentally retarded groups, Gallagher (33) also found that the marked growth on the Graham-Kendall perceptual test during the year of tutoring decreased during the no-tutoring year. Control groups made slow but equivalent growth in this measure of perception and eventually equaled the tutored groups. No real gains were found on the Strauss-Werner Marble Board for tutored or control groups in the two-year period. It appears from these five studies that, although gains in perception can be stimulated for mentally retarded or brain-injured children, these gains may prove no greater than those produced by maturation. Or, in other words, such gains are not permanent acceleration of perceptual development.

Other researchers who worked with normal children often selected their cases on the basis of a poor performance on some perceptual test. In their three-year project, Gaunt and Hayes (34) first used the Bender, dropped it as too difficult for first graders, and shifted to the Thurstone Pattern Copying, adding the Metropolitan Readiness in the third year. Pretesting and posttesting on the Frostig after a year's small-group work on a wide variety of visual motor tasks and printed materials indicated gains in that instrument greatest for initially low scorers. Among black children, the training apparently helped them to overcome their initial inferiority in the Frostig and to equal the scores of white children after one year's training. She does not seem to have used a control group or to have determined the effect of the training on readiness or reading achievement.

A seven-weeks' group program for the kindergarten children directed by Painter (66), using the Kephart and the Barsch procedures, produced greater gain on the Beery test than occurred among controls.

A summer training program of Wingert (91) increased scores on the Frostig significantly but did not influence the readiness test score. He concluded that if the readiness test is really a measure of that ability, then the Frostig is not; and his visual-motor program was apparently pointless in increasing readiness.

Bosworth* used the Winter Haven forms for a pretest, then gave training in multisensory activities and copying forms to twenty-eight kindergarten children. The control group followed the usual kindergarten program. The trained group, as may be expected, showed greater gains on the Winter Haven posttest than did the controls. Ferinden et al. (27) carefully selected eleven children, ages seven to eleven, training them in visual-motor coordination, tactile discrimination, visual memory, auditory discrimination, distance judgment, spatial relations, kinesthetic movement, and figure-ground perception. Just how he determined that these children needed all these training activities is not very clear, but they did show significant improvement on the posttest with the Bender.

First graders were exposed to perceptual programs of the Kephart or Getman type in experiments by Brown (11), LaPray and Ross (48), Emmons (25), O'Connor (62), and Slacks (77). Brown, LaPray and Ross, and Emmons reported gains in some measure of visual perception, while O'Connor and Slacks did not. None of the studies was able to show significant gains in reading achievement as a result of the training. Moreover, O'Connor and Slacks failed also to show gains in readiness test performances. In similar experiments, in terms of the nature of the training program, Fisher (28) with kindergarten pupils, Litchfield (49) with learning disability cases, McRaney (55) with pupils from the three primary grades, and Myerson (60) with first graders, all failed to find any gain in perceptual skills. Fisher and McRaney were also unsuccessful in producing gains in readiness. In all four studies, dealing with pupils above kindergarten status, no gains in reading achievement were accomplished.

We may summarize these perceptual training programs that seem to have had the improvement of some type of perceptual development as their primary goal in Table 16–1.

Collectively, this group of studies seems to imply that it is often possible to stimulate, at least temporarily, whatever is measured by popular perception tests. Among mentally retarded and brain-injured children these gains are only temporary and no greater than the effects of maturation. Among normal children, the permanence or reality of the test gains are unknown, and in these studies the relevance of the training to reading achievement or readiness was not demonstrated.

It is puzzling to try to understand how the diagnoses and prescriptive treatments were determined in these studies. Two courses of action appear to

---

*Mary H. Bosworth, "Prereading: Improvement of Visual-Motor Skills" (Doctoral dissertation, University of Miami, 1967).

TABLE 16–1 A SUMMARY OF INCONCLUSIVE PERCEPTUAL TRAINING EXPERIMENTS (EXCLUDING THE FROSTIG PROGRAM)

AUTHOR	POPULATION	TYPE OF PROGRAM	GAINS IN PERCEPTION	GAINS IN READINESS	GAINS IN READING	COMMENT
Bateman (6)	Mentally retarded	Visual motor	Yes			
Wiseman (92)	Mentally retarded	Individualized visual motor	Yes			Gains in I.Q. also
Boger (9)	Mentally retarded	Visual motor	Yes			Gains in I.Q. also
Cruikshank (20)	Brain-injured	Form perception and visual motor	Yes			Gains tended to disappear in second year
Gallagher (33)	Mentally retarded brain-injured	Form perception	Yes			Gains tended to disappear in second year
Gaunt (34)	Underachieving first graders	Visual motor and some Frostig	Yes			
Painter (66)	Kindergarten	Kephart program and Barsch rhythmics	Yes			
Wingert (91)	Kindergarten	Visual motor and auditory	Yes	No		
Bosworth*	Kindergarten pupils poor on Winter Haven	Multisensory and form perception	Yes			
Ferinden (27)	Eleven perceptually handicapped	Visual motor, tactile, auditory, spatial, and so on.	Yes			
Brown (11)	First graders	Kephart and Getman	Yes		No	
LaPray and Ross (48)	First graders	Kephart and Getman	Yes		No	
Emmons (25)	First graders	Kephart and Getman	Yes		No	
Braley (10)	Four-year-olds	Visual motor, body image	Yes		No	
Fisher (28)	Kindergarten	Individualized visual motor	No	No		
O'Connor (62)	First graders	Kephart	No	No	No	Gains in "internal awareness"
Slacks (77)	First graders	Kephart	No	No	No	
Litchfield (49)	Learning disability, primary pupils	Visual motor	No	No	No	
McRaney (55)	Primary pupils	Visual motor	No	No	No	

*Mary H. Bosworth, "Prereading: Improvement of Visual-Motor Skills," Doctoral dissertation, University of Miami, 1967.

(Continued on page 408)

TABLE 16-1 (Continued)

| AUTHOR | POPULATION | TYPE OF PROGRAM | PERCEPTION | GAINS IN | | COMMENT |
				READINESS	READING	
Myerson (60)	First graders	Kephart	No		No	
McBeath (52)	Kindergarten poor in Frostig	Getman-Kephart vs. modified Frostig vs. both		No		
Roach (70)	Remedial upper-middle class, eight years or older	Getman-Kephart			No	
Goins (37)	First grade	Tachistoscopic training in form perception			No	
Jensen and King (45)	Kindergarten	Tracing textured word forms, or matching; arranging plastic letters			No	
Lloyd (50)	First grade	Howard-Dolman chiroscope	No	No	No	Some gain in spatial relations
Yarborough (93)	Primary	Howard-Dolman chiroscope	No	No	No	Some gain in spatial relations
Collins and Bidle*	First graders	Motor fitness	Yes	No		Gains in readiness and motor test but same for both groups
Fisher and Turner†	Black kindergarten	Kephart	No	Yes	No	Six months' training better than full year
Falik‡	Kindergarten	Kephart	No	No	No	No differences still in second grade
Sullivan§	Remedial in fourth–twelfth	Kephart			No	

*Wayner Collins and Rae Bidle, "Motor Fitness Training and Reading Readiness: A Causal Relationship," Illinois School Bulletin, 8 (Fall 1971), 13–15.

†Maurice D. Fisher and Robert V. Turner, "The Effects of a Perceptual-Motor Training Program upon the Academic Readiness of Culturally Disadvantaged Kindergarten Children," Journal of Negro Education, 41 (Spring 1972), 142–50.

‡L. H. Falik, "The Effects of Special Perceptual Motor Training in Kindergarten on Reading Readiness and on Second Grade Performance," Journal of Learning Disabilities, 2 (August 1969), 395–400.

§Joanna Sullivan, "The Effects of Kephart's Perceptual Motor Training on a Reading Clinic Sample," Journal of Learning Disabilities, 5 (November 1972), 545–51.

have been present: one basing diagnosis on a single measure of perception followed by a logical training program seeming to emphasize the facet of perception measured in the pretest.   The other type of program appears to use a single pretest followed by a diverse training program stressing sometimes a half-dozen or more (à la Ferinden et al.) types of activities that may or may not be related to the nature of the pretest.   And in view of the present status of perceptual tests, these training activities may not even be related to the pupils' needs, for these needs are hardly identified by most of the perception tests in current use.   To be specific, how did Ferinden and his coworkers determine that their eleven children needed eight kinds of training in order to improve on the Bender?   We might also ask whether the researchers ever discovered which of the training activities was responsible for the gain on the Bender.   And what did improvement on the Bender do for these pupils who were presumably suffering from a learning disability?   Or is this a group of studies assuming that any kind of training program, which seems to result in improvement on the posttest in some kind of perception, must be good for the children?

Gains in Reading Performances

Experiments in perceptual training that seem related to reading assume a variety of modes, including practice with words and letters, with geometric forms and visual motor tasks, and with paired associates learning trials, as well as programs combining several of these approaches.   Seigmar Muehl and Ethel M. King, alone and in collaboration, have conducted a number of experiments in visual discrimination emphasizing letters and words among kindergarten children.   Although such experiments sample only a minor aspect of perception, current interest in prereading training in letter names and the like suggests that a review of some of these studies is relevant.   The objective of the Muehl-King research seems to have been to discover the effects of various types of training upon children's learning to read words. One such experiment (43) indicated that children learned words best when meanings were emphasized by establishing an association among the word, its sound, and an illustrative picture.   Training in recognizing the letters composing the criterion words was the next most effective procedure.   Practice with geometric forms or in matching identical words (which are favorite workbook exercises) were least effective.   Two of Muehl's studies in teaching letter names indicated that such learning interfered with the learning of words composed of the same letters (49, 50).   In summarizing their research, Muehl and King (59) conclude that the most effective prereading visual discrimination training should follow a sequence of matching letters, then words; then letter discrimination and letter names; then the sound, the picture, and the word form in simultaneous presentation. These authors feel that such training is very specific; that is, it does not transfer from geometric forms to words, or from other word training to the test words. Popp's study with one-, two- and three-letter trigrams (67) seems to agree in indicating the specificity of transfer from training materials (*d-t, b-t,* and so on) to criterion performances in letter discrimination. One of the experiments by Staats, Staats, and Schutz (80) is parallel to these other studies. Kindergarten children were trained in recognizing words (identical with test words) or in letters composing these words. They were not taught the letter names but were simply asked to discriminate same or different letters in groups of three. Those taught words were superior in the posttest to those trained in discriminating letters, who were no more successful than a control group given no training. Staats and her coworkers concluded that letters were not used as a clue to discriminating among the words, although they noted that there were large individual differences among the children regardless of the type of training.

Using symbols like capital letters and their transformations by reversal or inversion, Joanna P. Williams (89) gave discrimination training in matching, copying, and tracing such forms. There appeared to be no differences in the effectiveness of the three types of practice. Williams also noted that the more the criterion test items differed from the training items, the more frequent were the children's errors. She generalizes that the effectiveness of prereading visual discrimination training is related to its degree of similarity to the criterion performance; that is, to avoid the rotations and reversals that are common in early reading, children should receive specific training in those types of discrimination, not in copying or tracing forms. Using tachistoscopic exposures of a filmstrip, Wheelock (88) tried to train kindergarten children in recognizing capital letters. The children simply indicated whether two letters were the same or different and were not taught letter names. Success on the final test of discriminating sixteen capital letters was significantly related to socioeconomic status, for lower socioeconomic children tested poorer in the pretests on capitals and readiness and the final test. These children, though, showed greater gain in learning than did the higher socioeconomic children, possibly as a result of their regression to the mean.

There are some generalizations that may be drawn from these studies of visual discrimination training in words and letters, despite their variations in procedures and findings. It appears that the success of prereading training intended to facilitate word recognition should emphasize meaningfulness of words rather than word form or its sound or both, and training in discriminating among letters without stressing letter names. Training in copying or tracing geometric forms or discriminating among words by shape alone does not appear to be effective in these studies.   However, the individual differences among children's abilities to recognize words after different types of training implies that some sort of pretraining trials should be conducted to match children's aptitudes to type of visual discrimination training.   This pretesting would also be essential to determine which children, for reasons of socioeconomic deprivation or whatever, need and will benefit from training.

Paired associates experiments are a very popular type of research in educational psychology.   Briefly, they usually involve forming an association between pairs of words, letter groups, or symbols.   The subjects are usually practiced in some mode or other until they demonstrate mastery of the entire group.   Errors during learning trials and the number of trials needed for mastery are major criteria in judging the subjects' performances.

Giebink and Goodsell (35) tried to show that good readers needed fewer trials to form an association between either geometric forms or Japanese characters and English verbs.   Among seventy-two primary children, all of whom were poor in Bender scores, good readers did perform in the expected fashion.   But this study conflicts with many others that find varying degrees of relationship between associating a symbol and a word according to the nature of the tasks or symbols.   It was harder for Giebink and Goodsell's children to form an association between geometric forms and verbs because they tended to give names to the forms, and this association interfered with the intended performance.   Jenkins (44) found that in learning Japanese words several associated pictures were better than one, or better than attempting to associate with a printed English word.   Varying the type face, color, slant, and so on, of the Japanese words, saying the word when it was presented, or naming the picture did not facilitate learning.

Schoer's study tended to show that when vertical lists of paired words were to be learned, they were easiest when there was a meaningful relationship in the vertical list *(talk–from, speak–kept, whisper–toward)*.   Sound relationships were next most facilitating *(I–drop, eye–move)*, and structural similarities were least effective *(age–move, ago–drop)*.   Schoer considers his research as refuting those who would claim structural similarities (spelling patterns) as preeminent clues to learning.   His study was conducted with fifth graders, however, and may not reflect what happens in the very initial stages of learning to read (76).   Three paired associate experiments dealt with the effects of color in learning letter combinations or paired words.   Underwood et al. (83), using colored backgrounds for three-consonant trigrams, found that the subjects learned the colors better than they learned the associated trigrams.   Samuels (75) presented one word in each list in red, the others in black.   During learning trials, the color seemed to help in forming the paired association; but, in the posttest transfer to all words printed in black, there were fewer correct responses to the colored item. Samuels questions strongly whether the use of colors to help identify words or their constituent sounds is sound. Using three letter combinations from the Greek alphabet, Otto (65) also found that printing some of them in color did not help learning. As in Samuels's study, the color apparently functioned during learning trials, for learning was poorer without it; but ultimate learning on the criterion test was not aided by the use of color.

Hendrickson and Muehl (42) found that kindergarten children were not aided in discriminating directionality of letters as *b* and *d,* by being trained to respond by pushing a button with the corresponding hand, that is, left hand for *d,* right hand for *b.* Verbal instructions and arrows indicating the directionality of the letter were more effective in facilitating the discrimination. There is a great need for more studies of this exploration of the values of training in directionality, so common in perceptual training programs, for visual discrimination in reading. Caldwell and Hall's experiment (13) in training to judge forms having the same shape and orientation versus discrimination among forms of the same shape with different orientation is relevant here. A final test on discriminating among *b, d, p,* and *q* indicated no merit at all for the second type of training. In fact, this group did more poorly than the control group, which had had no directionality training whatsoever.

Elkind, Horn, and Schneider (24) reason that the child must learn decentration (freedom from being dominated by features of continuity, proximity, and closure) in order to read. He must use logic in rearranging mentally a stimulus array, organize wholes and parts, and explore perceptually (scan an array to note features). In keeping with this concept of the reading act, these experimenters gave nonverbal exercises in simple series, scrambled words, coding, and the like, for a half-hour per week for fifteen weeks to inner-city children. A control group followed a reading program in the Bank Street readers, a series purported to be written especially for ghetto, black children. The trained children were significantly better in posttests of word form, word recognition, and word association, but only equal to the controls in comprehension. Elkind, Horn, and Schneider think that perception arises from internalized actions based on sensorimotor training; they recommend such training, while rejecting the values of visual discrimination and of mental associations for word recognition.

It is difficult to summarize this group of studies of visual discrimination training, for they seem to have more definite negative results than positive. They tell us that color in letters or background, letter names or letter discrimination, matching geometric forms, and matching identical words all seem to contribute little to word recognition in controlled experiments. In contrast, meaningful associations given by pictures; by verbalizing a symbol (provided it is not a tangential relationship derived from children assigning some name to the symbol); and by sound or clang associations or meaningful relationships among words *(speak–say–talk),* all seem to aid in learning words. Manipulating letterlike or wordlike forms that strongly resemble words also seems more effective than simple activities with common geometric forms. Discrimination among letters commonly confused because of reversals or rotations is helped more by training that specifically counteracts these errors (in forms or symbols resembling these letters and by visual or verbal cues to the directionality of these letters) than by general practice with the usual geometric forms. Perhaps it is possible to say that these studies reinforce the axiom that training transfers to word recognition best when the training materials strongly resemble words or discriminative behaviors in the word recognition act.

Gains in Readiness or Reading

If we assume that gains in a readiness test indicate a better chance for the child to succeed in beginning reading, there are a number of studies that have produced this result. Beaupre and Kennard (7) explored the values of several perceptual training programs, as (a) one modeled on the Delacato approach; (b) a motor education program; (c) a physical education program designed by a local teacher; (d) the Frostig training plan; (e) counseling; and (f) the regular kindergarten schedule. Groups varied from six to twenty-two pupils. The motor education training produced the greatest gains on the Metropolitan Readiness test. Of the five other programs, only the Frostig failed to produce significant gains in readiness.

Jay D. Mack has generously made available to this writer a copy of the report of the Coronado Unified School District perceptual training program.* Two groups of primary grade children, numbering twenty-one and twenty-two, received visual and auditory perception training for periods of six and three months respectively. The children were selected by a battery of optometric and perception tests, and their training was keyed to individual needs. The thirty-five teachers of these children were given in-service training, training rooms, and equipment plus a consultant to conduct the program. Pretesting and posttesting utilized common optometric tests and those in the Rosner Perceptual Survey,† as well as standardized tests of

---

*Stuart J. Mandell, *An Identification and Remediation Visual Perceptual Training Program* (Coronado, Calif.: Coronado Unified School District, 1972).

†J. Rosner, *Rosner Perceptual Survey* (Pittsburgh: Learning Research and Development Center, University of Pittsburgh).

reading (Spache Diagnostic Reading Scales and Co-op Primary Reading Test) and spelling (Wide Range Achievement Test), as well as teachers' judgments as recorded on report cards.

The majority of the children showed marked improvement in visual efficiency in oculomotor skills of tracking, near-far fixation, and accommodation; in binocularity as shown in fusion, and freedom from suppressions; in freedom from visual performances that would normally demand referral, as in near-point visual acuity, the cover test at near and far, and static retinoscopy. In the perceptual motor area, the majority of children showed marked improvement in measures of general orientation, body schema, gross and fine motor skills, and spatial relationships. About half the group showed gains in auditory decoding skills. Roughly 60 percent of those pupils whose reading test measures were below normal in pretesting showed normal gains and reading at grade level in the posttesting. In spelling, about half of the children made normal progress, reaching grade level by the end of the project. Despite these successful results, though, the authors of this report recognize that they have not necessarily proven the values of such a training program. They realize that some of the results could, of course, be attributed to the individualized attention given to these children with learning problems. We may applaud the modesty of the claims made by the directors of this study, but we doubt that the Hawthorne effect could have been responsible for some of the effects, as in the various visual skills tested. Testing was done by a project teacher and an optometric consultant in all areas. Although the significance of the testing and the goals of the training were probably clarified for the teachers, their lack of professional knowledge of visual skills and hence of exact expectations in terms of improvement may well have prevented teachers' expectations from influencing the results, as is so often the case in experiments of this type. The same interpretation of the results in reading and spelling may not be true, however.

Gould, Henderson, and Scheele (39) included motor activities to strengthen body-image; visual training in ocular motility with the Marsden ball (following a swinging ball with the eyes to improve binocular coordination); the chalkboard exercises recommended by Getman; tachistoscopic training in visual discrimination, and auditory training in following directions. Using 262 kindergarten children as experimental subjects, with 226 controls, these authors found significantly higher scores in the subtests of the Metropolitan Readiness for the trained pupils, particularly for boys.

The variety of training activities in this last study, while perhaps desirable, precludes evaluation of the various parts of the program. The best implication that we can draw from this and from the Beaupre-Kennard study is that a number of visual-motor activities seem to contribute to readiness test scores. The visual training component does seem significantly related to readiness and reading, as confirmed in the studies of Baskin (5) with older, mentally handicapped children; of Cox and Hambly (18) in the primary grades; at the junior high school for underachievers, as reported by Cox and Stewart (19); and in both first and ninth grade with underachievers by Halgren (40).

Keim (46) employed only the Winter Haven template program in addition to the usual kindergarten schedule. The experimentals, who were selected by the Bender as having visual-motor deficiencies, surpassed the controls on the matching and copying subtests of the Metropolitan Readiness; and the great majority (60 percent) showed improvement on the Bender. Keim was disappointed in the Winter Haven training, even though it did produce the predictable gains in measures of form discrimination, hand-eye coordination, and visual-motor skill. Perhaps, like many of its users, he thought that the templates would have a panacealike effect upon other facets of readiness measured by the Metropolitan, such as auditory vocabulary, number readiness, and so forth.

These templates, chalkboard exercises, and some follow-up paper and pencil worksheets were employed in the Spache, Andres, and Curtis (79) extended readiness program. The visual discrimination training given to those pupils in need of it (plus auditory discrimination or auditory vocabulary programs for others) did produce significant results in visual discrimination tests of copying and matching, as might logically be expected. Results in the first-grade reading tests favored the experimental groups among white boys and black children of lower mental ability. Moreover, Dunsing's follow-up study indicates that this facet of readiness, as measured by the chalkboard exercises, is a good predictor for second- and third-grade reading achievement (23). To this point, we seem to have found some merits for some varied programs in visual-motor and oculo-motor education, particularly those utilizing the template and chalkboard exercises, for gains in certain types of readiness skills and for reading achievement.

The Getman-Kephart program of training in visual-motor skills, or some version of it, involves training in laterality or body-image; directionality; binocular and monocular motility and control, as well as the Winter Haven templates. In McBeath's dissertation (52) a comparison was made of a modified Frostig, the Getman-Kephart, and a combination of both in kindergarten. After sixty-four days none of these three experimental groups exceeded the controls in readiness testing. The experimentals were selected because they tested below the 25th percentile on the Frostig Battery. Our earlier analysis of this battery indicated some doubts regarding its relevance to readiness or reading achievement. Thus we cannot be certain that McBeath's experimental groups were really handicapped in significant visual-motor skills, and therefore might be expected to gain from training of various types in this area.

Wimsatt (90) used the Kephart visual-motor training program for kindergarten children for an entire year, while the controls had only the usual physical education periods. The experimental group showed significantly greater scores on the Monroe Reading Aptitude test than did the control kindergarteners.

An eleven-weeks' training in the Getman-Kephart visual-motor program did produce significantly more gain in readiness for a group of thirty-eight kindergarten pupils, according to Rutherford (74). The gains were greater for boys, but, as we would expect, generally were not significant in the number readiness subtest of the Metropolitan. Roach (70) concluded that use of this particular training program for remedial children of upper-middle-class origin who were older than seven to eleven produced no significant gains at the end of eight or nine weeks or in retesting six months later. Dunsing's factor analysis of the Purdue Perceptual Motor Survey Test (23), which is somewhat parallel to the actual training program recommended by Getman and Kephart, sheds some light on the values of various components of this visual-motor training. The ocular pursuits tests showed the greatest growth from kindergarten to second grade, with some regression in the third grade. They were a fair predictor of reading achievement in the first grade and of arithmetic in the fourth grade. Form reproduction, as measured by the Winter Haven Perceptual Achievement test, improves rapidly until second grade and then appears to cease development. The walking beam test, typical of exercises of this type, often included in body-image training, was also a very good predictor of reading achievement up to the second grade.

It appears that a perceptual training program emphasizing visual-motor skills of laterality, directionality, and form reproduction, as well as ocular control and body image, needs more research to sort out its effective components. Several of these types of training seem limited to usefulness probably only in the kindergarten to second-grade span. Some, such as the template, chalkboard exercises, and (at least in the hands of professional optometrists), the ocular motility and control training seem more relevant to reading than do other elements of the program. For the convenience of the reader, we shall summarize these experiments in visual discrimination or perceptual-motor training in Table 16–2.

The results of these visual-motor programs do not, in our mind, contradict the implications of the earlier section dealing with the paired associates, letter, and word discrimination training. The general training, as in the Kephart or Getman programs, in body image, directionality, form tracing,

TABLE 16–2   A SUMMARY OF APPARENTLY SUCCESSFUL PERCEPTUAL TRAINING PROGRAMS

AUTHOR	POPULATION	TYPE OF PROGRAM	OUTCOMES
A. Emphasizing Visual Discrimination			
King (47)	Kindergarten	Letters, words, form perception	Combination of meaning, sound, and picture test. Letter training next best, geometric forms and matching words poorest.
Muehl (57, 58)	Kindergarten	Letters composing words versus words	Letter names interfered with learning words composed of them.
Muehl and King (59)	Kindergarten	Letters, words, forms	Training sequence best: matching letters and words; letter discrimination and letter names; sound, picture and word together.
Popp (67)	Beginning readers	One-, two-, and three-letter trigrams	Letter discrimination training effective.
Staats (80)	Kindergarten	Letters versus words	Letter discrimination (no names) inferior to words.
Williams (89)	Kindergarten	Matching, copying, tracing forms	Give training to overcome specific confusions, not just copying or tracing.
Wheelock (88)	Kindergarten	Tachistoscopic presentation of capital letters	Lowest scores but greatest gain for low socioeconomic.
B. Emphasizing Perceptual-Motor Training			
McCullouch (54)	Kindergarten	Visual motor plus some Frostig	Gains in readiness.
Turner and Fisher (82)	Kindergarten disadvantaged pupils	Kephart	Gains in readiness and perceptual motor.
New Jersey (61)	Primary	Perceptual-motor plus usual reading instruction	Control group better after one year, no differences after second or third years. Some benefits for slower learners in reading or readiness.
Weisman and Leonard (87)	Low socioeconomic K to I	Perceptual-motor (Frostig, Kephart, Cratty)	Gains in reading persisted a year later.
Beaupre and Kennard (7)	Kindergarten	Contrasted six programs	Visual motor best, Frostig poorest in producing gains in readiness.

TABLE 16–2 (Continued)

AUTHOR	POPULATION	TYPE OF PROGRAM	OUTCOMES
Gould, Henderson, and Scheele (39)	Kindergarten	Getman plus auditory and tachistoscope	Gains in readiness particularly for boys.
Keim (46)	Kindergarten poor on Bender	Winter Haven plus usual kindergarten	Gains in matching and copying forms on readiness test and on Bender.
Spache et al. (79)	First grade	Winter Haven, chalkboard plus selected seatwork	Low mental ability and low socioeconomic pupils excelled controls in reading.
Wimsatt (90)	Kindergarten	Kephart versus physical education activities	Experimentals higher in readiness.
Rutherford (74)	Kindergarten	Getman-Kephart	Experimentals, particularly boys, higher in readiness.
Coronado (Mandell)	Primary	Getman plus auditory	Gains in visual skills, reading, spelling, and perceptual-motor skills.
Morgan*	Third-fourth	Winter Haven chalkboard	Gains in reading comprehension.

*Mavis Welch Morgan, "The Effect of Visual Perceptual Training upon Subsequent Scholastic Progress of Children with Specific Visual Disabilities," Master's thesis, University of Nevada, August 1966.

or hand-eye coordination, ocular control and motility, and the rest is relevant to readiness and reading, if we may believe the results of our own research (79) as well as the others. These types of training do benefit low socioeconomic or low intelligence children. The training does facilitate their early learning in reading, while it does nothing for most middle and upper-class children. Perhaps what we are discussing is a matter of the development of the child in visual-motor skills, orientation to direction and his own body and hand-eye coordination. It is almost axiomatic that children who are deprived by reason of socioeconomic status are lacking in the foundational sensorimotor experiences common to other children. Some of this group, not all, distinctly benefits from visual-motor training to the point where they can compete reasonably in learning to read with middle-class children whose homes and background have supplied this type of experience. The training is not generally good for lower-class deprived children but must be related to observation of their specific needs. The Roach-Kephart Perceptual Motor Survey, which we reviewed in the section on perception tests, is a possibility for diagnosis. But we feel that it is even more practical to use the training steps themselves as diagnostic cues, thus beginning each type of training at that point where the child's performances indicate need. Following this procedure with lower-class and middle-class children will clarify the desirability of any training or indicate whether we may proceed with visual discrimination training as indicated in our earlier review of the relevant studies.

No Gains in Reading

Several studies have tried other training plans and found them fruitless. But they must be reviewed because the practices employed are often included in multi-approach programs. Goins's (37) study of perceptual tests was followed by a schedule of tachistoscopic training in form discrimination for first graders with no positive effects. Despite these negative results and those in other studies cited by Goins, tachistoscopic training persists in such programs as that of Gould, Henderson, and Scheele (39) cited above.

Molly C. Gorelick (38) followed training in noting likenesses and differences in forms or pictures with a programmed word recognition schedule. No differences in learning in immediate word recognition recall were observable after the programmed work for experimental or control groups of first graders. A delayed test ten days after all the training did favor the children trained with forms. The picture-trained group at this time was even inferior to the untrained control group, which led Gorelick to conclude that the picture training seemed to interfere with word recognition learning.

Jensen and King (45) offered training in tracing textured word forms, matching word forms, and rearranging plastic letters. A posttest in reading four words, probably parallel to those used in the three types of practice, yielded no significant differences among the groups. Jensen and King's study could have ended inconclusively for any of a half-dozen reasons. With the growing attention to visual-kinesthetic and letter emphasis programs, this study again cautions us against indiscriminate acceptance of what appear to be logically related activities in these two areas.

Among the devices offered for some sort of perceptual training is the Howard-Dolman chiroscope, or the Leavell Language Development Service, as it is sometimes called. Based on a mixed-up theory of cerebral dominance, the instrument and its program presumably correct language difficulties by hand-eye coordination practice in drawing designs presented to only one eye through a viewing device. The student then draws the image as though seen in the visual field of the other eye. Thus, presumably the child learns to process images with the other eye and other hemisphere of the brain (which, unfortunately for the theory, does not happen since any image perceived in either or both eyes is always processed in both cerebral hemispheres). However, the chiroscope is well known in optometric circles as a device for overcoming the suppression of vision in an eye and restoring binocular function. The Howard-Dolman instrument is also recognized as a test for stereopsis (binocular function). Two studies by Lloyd (50) and Yarborough (93) used the device in the hope of affecting perception in reading. Both found no impact upon reading achievement or readiness, but Lloyd observed some gain in a non-language intelligence test measuring spatial relationships, and Yarborough noted that her experimental groups gained in hand-eye coordination, as we might expect. Lloyd also found that the trained children improved much more in reducing errors on the Howard-Dolman test, an expected behavior. Neither author was able to determine the effect upon cerebral dominance, if any.

The tendency to specificity of training intended to improve perceptual performances and the frequent lack of transfer of such training except to obviously parallel readiness or reading performances is again emphasized in the work of Macoby (51). He found that motor training alone produced no change in form reproduction. While visual-motor training may contribute to some aspects of readiness, as shown in the Beaupre-Kennard study mentioned above, each specific type of training does not necessarily transfer to all the facets of readiness, as evidenced in Keim's study and Dunsing's factor analysis.

THE FROSTIG PERCEPTUAL TRAINING PROGRAM

As we have noted, the authors of the Frostig have offered a five-part training schedule, the use of which is supposed to be based on the results of the corresponding subtests. Like the test, the program has had wide use, and some scientific evaluation. We shall attempt to summarize these evaluative studies in Table 16–3.

Even a casual reading of the results with the Frostig training program elicits several patent conclusions. The program produces gains on the Frostig Test in nine out of twelve studies in which retests were given. But no significant differences appear in readiness as a result of the Frostig training in seven out of nine studies exploring this value. Even the Hawthorne effect of a special treatment did not seem to help these results. Fourteen of the sixteen reports trying to find an effect of the Frostig on reading are also negative. In one positive study, the Frostig was combined with two other visual-motor programs; hence its contribution to the gains in reading is unknown.

TABLE 16–3 SCOREBOARD ON THE FROSTIG PERCEPTUAL TRAINING

SOURCE, GRADE, N OF CASES	GAINS ON FROSTIG TEST	GAINS ON READINESS TEST	GAINS ON READING TEST	FROSTIG VERSUS OTHERS
Alley (1): 108 disadvantaged kindergarten	Significant	Significant		8 months Frostig versus no Frostig
Arciszewski (3): 34 first grade	Significant		Not significant	Phonics program
Beaupre & Kennard (7): ca. 75 kindergarten		Not significant		Five other programs all superior to Frostig
Buckland (12): 16 first-grade classes	Not significant		Not significant	Listening to stories and discussion
Cohen (15): 155 first grade	Significant		Not significant	
Cohen (16): 120 first grade			Not significant	
Faustman (26): 14 kindergarten classes			Significant	Kephart programs plus Winter Haven plus Frostig
Fortenberry (29) first grade			Not significant	Frostig plus usual readiness
Jacobs (43): Pre-kindergarten, kindergarten, and first grade—300		Not significant		
Jacobs (43): Pre-kindergarten to third—300		Not significant	Not significant	
Pumfrey & Anthony (68): 24 physically handicapped	Not significant			Frostig program keyed to initial Frostig test versus total Frostig vs. none
Rosen (72)	Significant		Not significant	
Wingert (91): 54 kindergarten	Significant	Not significant		
Gamsky and Lloyd:* 20 kindergarten classes			Not significant	Lowest in Frostig were lowest in reading after training

*Neal R. Gamsky and Faye W. Lloyd, "A Longitudinal Study of Visual Perceptual Training and Reading Achievement," *Journal of Educational Research*, 64 (July–August 1971), 451–54.

TABLE 16–3 (Continued)

SOURCE, GRADE, N OF CASES	GAINS ON FROSTIG TEST	GAINS ON READINESS TEST	GAINS ON READING TEST	FROSTIG VERSUS OTHERS
Pryzwansky: 559 kindergarten*		Not significant		
McCullouch (54): kindergarten		Significant		Frostig plus a visual-motor program
McBeath (52): kindergarten		Not significant		Modified Frostig versus Getman-Kephart versus both
Wiederholt and Hammill: 70 low-income first grade†	Significant (if the Frostig was completed)	Not significant	Not significant	Gains on the Frostig not significant for initially low scorers
Belmont et al.: 30 in first, low in readiness‡			Not significant	Frostig plus the Kephart
Swanson: 63 black second graders poor in word recognition§			Significant	Frostig or Frostig plus regular program better than regular alone
Sherk: 75 disabled readers‖	Not significant		Not significant	Remedial plus Frostig versus remedial alone
Linn: 30 in kindergarten#	Significant		Not significant	
Mould: 21 perceptually handicapped**	Significant		Not significant	Experimentals gained in oral but neither of groups in silent
Bennet: Four second-grade classes††	Significant		Not significant	Experimental gained in nonlanguage I.Q.

*Walter B. Pryzwansky, "Effects of Perceptual-Motor Training and Manuscript Writing on Reading Readiness Skills in Kindergarten," *Journal of Educational Psychology*, 63 (April 1972), 110–15.

†J. Lee Wiederholt and Donald D. Hammill, "Use of the Frostig-Horne Visual Perception Program in the Urban School," *Psychology in the Schools*, 8 (July 1971), 268–74.

‡I Belmont, H. Flegenheimer, and H. G. Birch, "Comparison of Perceptual Training and Remedial Instruction for Poor Beginning Readers," *Journal of Learning Disabilities*, 6 (June 1973) 230–35.

§R. G. Swanson, "A Study of the Relationship between Perceptual-Motor Skills and the Learning of Word Recognition," *Dissertation Abstracts*, 29 (1968), 2158-A.

‖John K. Sherk, "A Study of the Effects of a Program of Visual Perceptual Training on the Progress of Retarded Readers," *Dissertation Abstracts*, 28 (1967), 4392-A.

#S. H. Linn, "From the Classroom: Visual-Perceptual Training for Kindergarten Children," *Academic Therapy Quarterly*, 4 (Summer 1967), 255–58.

**R. E. Mould, "An Evaluation of the Effectiveness of a Special Program for Retarded Readers Manifesting Disturbed Visual Perception," *Dissertation Abstracts*, 26 (1965), 228.

††R. M. Bennet, "A Study of the Effects of a Visual Perception Training Program upon School Achievement, I.Q. and Visual Perception," *Dissertation Abstracts*, 29 (1968), 3864-A.

Two other validity studies of the Frostig concepts of perceptual training are available. Frostig et al. (31) report that kindergarten children trained by their method gained significantly more on the test than did the controls; this, in their opinion, proved that the children were better prepared to succeed in reading. In view of the research we have reviewed here, such an assumption is very doubtful. Raven and Strubing (69) used the Frostig spatial relations and the hand-eye coordination segments in two groups, while a third group practiced coloring pictures. After this training, a science unit emphasizing spatial relationships was taught for two days. Both Frostig groups did better on a posttest on directionality in forms. As Cook and Hall (17) point out, the study simply proves that two doses of spatial relations, one in the Frostig, the other in the science unit, increases such learning more than one exposure does. In addition, the study was faulty in that the groups were not equated on the initial Frostig, in the authors reporting results on less than the entire group of subjects, and in their ignoring the effects of intelligence upon the results.

THE DELACATO PROGRAM

Using a great many neurological terms to justify the rationale, Delacato (21) offers an approach to cure all language difficulties by developing complete sidedness in the child. Communication is possible only when neurological organization permits sidedness, according to this author; hence, any disturbances in communication skills must reflect the need for this organization. This Delacato proposes to do by retraining the brain through creeping and crawling exercises patterned to induce homolateral and cross-lateral skills. The program has been adopted by many schools, and some of these have assayed an evaluation. Glass and Robbins (36), reviewing twelve such studies, found all of them poorly designed and not scientifically controlled. Three trials of the Delacato program were conducted also by O'Donnell (63) on disabled readers, seven to ten years old, with crossed or uncertain lateral dominance; by McCormick et al. (53) on first graders; and by Stone and Pielstick (81) with kindergarten children. Only McCormick claims any positive results, and Stone* has strongly criticized his study for lack of control of many variables, faulty interpretation of the data, ignoring regression to the mean or the Hawthorne effect, and improper use of his statistics. In contrast, O'Donnell rotated teachers from the Delacato group to that receiving ordinary

---

*Mark Stone, "Problems with Research Design in Studies of Sensory-Response Patterns in Remedial Reading," *Journal of the Association for the Study of Perception,* 8 (Spring 1972), 8–15.

physical education activities. There were no significant differences in any of four reading tests, in visual-motor integration or in measures of lateral dominance, after twenty weeks of training, including weekends also. Stone and Pielstick detected no effects upon the Peabody Picture Vocabulary intelligence test or the Lee-Clark readiness, although the experimentals did improve significantly on the Frostig, after eighteen full weeks of the Delacato treatment.

Robbins (71) studied the program under Delacato and applied it to second graders, in a comparison with a group given unpatterned physical activities and a control group with no training. The results did not support the neurological organization theory nor its relationship to reading, nor did it even improve the development of laterality. Like the American Academy of Pediatrics (22), Robbins rejects completely both the theory and the suggested treatment. Offering another medical opinion on Delacato's theories, Whitsell* considers them as not validated and as inconsistent with accepted neurological principles. As for the treatment, he considers it purely experimental—perhaps even potentially harmful—and, hence, not recommended for general use.

PERCEPTUAL-MOTOR TRAINING AND OPTOMETRY

Perhaps because of the leadership of G. N. Getman, the nationally known optometrist, and the fact that several established visual training procedures have been incorporated in many perceptual-motor training programs, many American optometrists have reacted very positively to this approach to learning problems. Obviously, it was not a great step from common visual training in ocular motility, binocular coordination, stereopsis, orientation to distance and shape in space, and other such visual skills to accepting some of the other types of perceptual-motor activities. As a result of this trend, many optometrists who include visual training in their practice have widened their procedures to include perceptual-motor tasks.

We can illustrate this development by briefly reviewing an example of some of the materials offered in the Optometric Extension Program, an organization disseminating in-service training matter to optometrists. Steven B. Greenspan,† who is a practicing optometrist and a frequent speaker on this

---

*Leon J. Whitsell, "Delacato's Neurological Organization: A Medical Appraisal," *California School Health,* 3 (Fall 1967), 1–13.

†Steven B. Greenspan, "Research Studies of Visual and Perceptual-Motor Training," *Optometric Extension Program,* 44 (October 1971 to August 1972).

subject at optometric conventions, has offered a series of articles reviewing research studies of visual training and perceptual-motor training. He cites approximately 100 studies in all, the majority of which have also been discussed earlier in this chapter.

Greenspan's articles open with a review of some thirteen case studies or other reports from optometric practice. All these reports claim gains in intelligence, perceptual-motor skills, readiness and reading for most of the individuals treated. But as Greenspan carefully points out, many of these claims exhibit a number of flaws in the conduct of the training. Some authors do not describe their training procedures in detail, some use no statistical tests to determine the significance of the observed gains; some failed to give comparable pretests and posttests. Many of the reports used no control subjects, and even some who compared treated and untreated groups made little attempt to control the Hawthorne effect upon posttraining testing of the fact that special attention had been given to the experimental pupils. Most of the case studies were probably subject to a halo effect, the influence of the investigator's expectations upon the subject's responses. In other words, although the results seem favorable to the use of perceptual-motor training, few of these case studies or group case reports could be considered scientifically controlled experiments. Case reports may provide clues to diagnosis and treatment, but, as this author recognizes, they do not constitute sound scientific evidence.

In a second article of this series, Greenspan describes some fifteen studies in which standard visual training procedures were employed alone or in conjunction with or in comparison to remedial reading activities. These reports included groups of pupils ranging from the first grade to college freshman. Among the visual functions for which training was offered were oculomotor rotations and pursuits, binocular function, rapid recognition as by tachistoscopic work, accommodation-convergence ratio, saccadic fixations, near-point of convergence, strabismus, and hand-eye coordination.

In general, these studies, including several we have already referred to (18, 19, 36), indicated that standard visual training techniques produced significant gains in reading and visual skills. Several comparative studies with retarded readers at first, ninth, and thirteenth grade levels demonstrated that, when visual training was carefully related to the pretraining visual skills of the pupils, programs as brief as eight to twelve weeks produced greater reading gains than ordinary remedial reading methods produced in the same period of time. Combinations of visual and reading training were also highly successful. One study, using carefully defined behavioral objectives and visual performances as criteria of improvement of strabismus, resulted in 73 percent of successful treatments and improvement in binocular vision, stereopsis, and reduction of deviation of the eyes from parallel posture to 5 percent or less of the time, in a group of 149 subjects. Follow-up on eighty-one of these cases of strabismus three to seven years later indicated that 89 percent of these remained long-range successes. Apparently even major visual defects that would interfere with reading success and perception may often be ameliorated through carefully selected visual training procedures.

The remainder of Greenspan's eleven articles are devoted to brief reviews of experiments in perceptual-motor training, such as we have offered earlier. Most of the studies referred to have already been cited and the remainder do not alter the general picture of the values of this training as we have tried to offer it. We have referred to Greenspan's review of the literature on visual training–perceptual-motor skills and reading simply because of its emphasis upon the role of optometrists in the area of visual perception. Because of the overlapping nature of visual training and perceptual-motor programs, it is obvious, we believe, that educators who attempt to work in the area of perceptual-motor development should maintain close professional relationships with those optometrists who are engaged in visual training practice.

The length and complexity of this chapter, as well as the many conflicting or inconclusive studies cited, confirm our impressions of this area. It is like a glass of Alka-Seltzer with new tests and new programs shooting off at tangents to be replaced with still newer tests and programs as the first sputter out into nothingness.

LEARNING PROJECT

The chapters on visual perception, its tests and programs, and their outcomes leave many readers relatively confused about the whole subject. Perhaps a class discussion of this area under the leadership of your instructor may help to clarify matters. Among the points that may be discussed are these:

1. What is visual perception, and just how does it affect reading?

2. Is there perhaps some stage in reading development at which visual perception is more significant? Or is it more closely related to a certain body of reading skills than to others?

3. What does the term *perceptually handicapped* mean? What exactly does such a handicap do to a beginner's efforts to learn to read? How may the presence of such a handicap be established in a particular case? Are there any recognized, consistent symptoms that characterize these cases?

In your discussion, be careful not to be diverted into talking about associative learning problems, those involving auditory perception or suspected brain damage, and so forth (as so many who write in this field do). If there is such a condition as a perceptual handicap, your group should be able to answer the three discussion questions above without introducing these other areas.

REFERENCES

1. Alley, G., et al., "Reading Readiness and the Frostig Training Program," *Exceptional Children,* 35 (September 1968), 68.
2. Anderson, R. W., "Effects of Neuro-Psychological Techniques on Reading Achievement," doctoral dissertation, Colorado State College, 1965.
3. Arciszewski, Raymond A., "A Pilot Study of the Effects of Visual Perception Training and Intensive Phonics Training on the Visual Perception and Reading Ability of First Grade Students," paper presented at American Educational Research Association, New York, February 18, 1967.
4. Balow, Bruce, "Perceptual-Motor Activities in the Treatment of Severe Reading Disability," *Reading Teacher,* 24 (March 1971), 513–25, 542.
5. Baskin, Jacquelyn White, "Teaching Reading to Older Mentally Handicapped Pupils," *Chicago Schools Journal,* 39 (February 1958), 152–53.
6. Bateman, B. D., "A Pilot Study of Mentally Retarded Children Attending Summer Day Camp," *Mental Retardation,* as quoted by Keith E. Beery, *Developmental Test of Visual-Motor Integration.* Chicago: Follett Publishing, 1967.
7. Beaupre, R. G., and Kennard, Ann, "An Investigation of Pre- and Post- Metropolitan Readiness Test Scores for Differing Motor Education Programs," *Illinois School Research,* 5 (1968), 22–25.
8. Birch, Herbert G., and Lefford, Arthur, "Intersensory Development in Children," *Monographs of the Society for Research in Child Development,* 28 (May 1963), 3–48.
9. Boger, Jack H., "An Experimental Study of the Effects of Perceptual Training on Group I.Q. Scores of Elementary Pupils in Rural Ungraded Schools," *Journal of Educational Research,* 46 (Spring 1952), 43–52.
10. Braley, William T., "Longitudinal Study of the Effects of Sensorimotor Training in Pre-school," Dayton Public Schools, 1970, as quoted by Klesius.
11. Brown, Roscoe, "Effect of Perceptual-Motor Education on Perceptual-Motor Skill and Readiness," in *Perceptual-Motor Efficiency in Children,* Bryant Cratty, editor. Philadelphia: Lea and Febiger, 1969.
12. Buckland, Pearl, "The Effect of Visual Perception Training on Reading Achievement of Low Readiness First Grade Pupils," doctoral dissertation, University of Minnesota, 1969.
13. Caldwell, E. C., and Hall, V. C., "The Influence of Concept Training on Letter Discrimination," *Child Development,* 40 (1969), 63–71.
14. Cohen, Ruth R., "Remedial Training of First-Grade Children with Visual Perception Retardation," *Educational Horizons,* 45 (1966–67), 60–63.
15. Cohen, Ruth R., "Remedial Training of First-Grade Children with Visual Perceptual Retardation," doctoral dissertation, University of California at Los Angeles, 1966.

16. Cohen, S. A., "Studies in Visual Perception and Reading in Disadvantaged Children," *Journal of Learning Disabilities,* 2 (October 1969), 498–507.
17. Cook, Harold, and Hall, Vernon, "The Effect of Achievement in a Science Unit on Visual Perception Units vice versa and/or the Effect of Achievement in a Science Unit on Achievement in a Science Unit," *American Educational Research Journal,* 6 (January 1969), 136–41.
18. Cox, Brian J., and Hambly, Lionel R., "Guided Development of Perceptual Skill of Visual Space as a Factor in the Achievement of Primary Grade Children," *American Journal of Optometry and Archives of American Academy of Optometry,* 38 (August 1961), 433–44.
19. Cox, Brian J., and Stewart, Colin, "The Effect of Certain Specific Factors in Optometric Care upon the Scholastic Performance of Underfunctioning Students in Junior High School in Their Response to Remedial Teaching," *Canadian Journal of Optometry,* 20 (December 1957), 31–42, 42–46, 53.
20. Cruikshank, William M., *A Teaching Method for Brain-Injured and Hyperactive Children: A Demonstration-Pilot Study.* Syracuse: Syracuse University Press, 1961.
21. Delacato, Carl H., *Neurological Organization and Reading.* Springfield: Charles C. Thomas, 1966.
22. "The Doman-Delacato Treatment of Neurologically Handicapped Children," *Journal of Pediatrics* (May 1968), 750–52.
23. Dunsing, Jack D., "Perceptual-Motor Factors in the Development of School Readiness: An Analysis of the Purdue Perceptual Motor Survey," *American Journal of Optometry and Archives of American Academy of Optometry,* 46 (October 1969), 760–65.
24. Elkind, D., Horn, J., and Schneider, G., "Modified Word Recognition, Reading Achievement and Perceptual Decentration," *Journal of Genetic Psychology,* 107 (1965), 235–51.
25. Emmons, Coralie, "A Comparison of Gross Motor Activities of the Getman-Kane and Kephart Perceptual-Motor Training Programs and Their Effects upon Certain Readiness Skills of First Grade Negro Children," in *Dissertation Abstracts,* 29 (1968), 1969–A.
26. Faustman, Marion N., "Some Effects of Perception Training in Kindergarten on First Grade Success in Reading," in *Perception and Reading,* Helen K. Smith, editor, Proceedings International Reading Association, 12, No. 4 (1968), 99–101.
27. Ferinden, William E., Van Handel, Donald, and Kovalinsky, Thomas, "A Supplemental Instructional Program for Children with Learning Disabilities," *Journal of Learning Disabilities,* 4 (April 1971), 193–203.
28. Fisher, David M., "Effects of Two Different Types f Physical Education Programs and Their Effects upon Skills Developed and Academic Readiness of Kindergarten Children," doctoral dissertation, Louisiana State University, 1970.
29. Fortenberry, Warren Dale, "An Investigation of the Effectiveness of the Frostig Program upon the Development of Visual Perception for Word Recognition of Culturally Disadvantaged First Grade Students," doctoral dissertation, University of Southern Mississippi, 1968.
30. Foster, J. J., "Effect of Mobility Training upon Reading Achievement and Intelligence," doctoral dissertation, University of California at Los Angeles, 1965.

31. Frostig, Marianne, Lefever, Welty, and Whittlesey, John, "Disturbances in Visual Perception," *Journal of Educational Research,* 57 (November 1963), 160–62.

32. Fry, Edward, "Do-It-Yourself Terminology Generator," *Journal of Reading,* 11 (March 1968), 428.

33. Gallagher, James J., *The Tutoring of Brain-Injured Mentally Retarded Children.* Springfield, Ill.: Charles C. Thomas, 1960.

34. Gaunt, Jean Campbell, and Hayes, Patricia Collis, *An Investigation of Visual-Motor Disabilities in First-Grade Children.* Project Public Law 89-10, FY 67-69. Clearwater, Fla.: Pinellas County Public Schools, 1969.

35. Giebink, John W., and Goodsell, Linda L., "Reading Ability and Associative Learning for Children with a Visuomotor Deficit," *American Educational Research Journal,* 3 (May 1968), 412–20.

36. Glass, Gene V., and Robbins, Melvyn P., "A Critique of Experiments on the Role of Neurological Organization in Reading Performance," *Reading Research Quarterly,* 3 (Fall 1967), 5–52.

37. Goins, Jean Turner, *Visual Perceptual Abilities and Early Reading Progress.* Supplementary Educational Monographs No. 87. Chicago: University of Chicago Press, 1958.

38. Gorelick, Molly C., "The Effectiveness of Visual Form Training in a Prereading Program," *Journal of Educational Research,* 58 (March 1965), 315–18.

39. Gould, Lawrence N., Henderson, Edward, and Scheele, Raymond L., "The Vision-Motor Perception Program in the Brentwood Public Schools," in *Improvement of Reading Through Classroom Practice,* J. Allen Figurel, editor, Proceedings International Reading Association Conference, 9 (1964), 271–75.

40. Halgren, Marvin R., "Opus in See Sharp," *Education,* 81 (February 1961), 369–71.

41. Hall, Vernon C., Caldwell, Edward, and Simpson, Given, "Variables Affecting the Performance of Young Children in a Letter Discrimination Task," unpublished paper.

42. Hendrickson, Lois N., and Muehl, Siegmar, "Effect of Attention and Motor Response Pretraining on Learning to Discriminate *b* and *d* in Kindergarten Children," *Journal of Educational Psychology,* 53 (October 1962), 236–41.

43. Jacobs, J. N., Wirthlin, L. D., and Miller, C. B., "A Follow-up Evaluation of the Frostig Visual-Perceptual Training Program," *Educational Leadership Research Supplement,* 26 (1968), 169–75.

44. Jenkins, Joseph R., "Effects of Incidental Cues and Encoding Strategies on Paired-Associate Learning," *Journal of Educational Psychology,* 59 (December 1968), 410–13.

45. Jensen, N. J., and King, Ethel M., "Effects of Different Kinds of Visual-Motor Discrimination Training on Learning to Read Words," *Journal of Educational Psychology,* 61 (1970), 90–96.

46. Keim, Richard P., "Visual-Motor Training, Readiness and Intelligence of Kindergarten Children," *Journal of Learning Disabilities,* 3 (May 1970), 256–59.

47. King, Ethel M., "Effects of Different Kinds of Visual Discrimination Training on Learning to Read Words," *Journal of Educational Psychology,* 55 (December 1964), 352–53.

48. LaPray, Margaret, and Ross, Ramon, "Auditory and Perceptual Training," in *Vistas*

in Reading, J. Allen Figurel, editor, Proceedings International Reading Association, 11, Part 1 (1967), 530–32.

49. Litchfield, Ticknor B., "A Program of Visual-Motor-Perceptual Training to Determine Its Effects upon Primary Level Children with Learning Deficiencies," ERIC/CRIER Ed 043-994. Suffern, N.Y.: Ramapo Central School District, 1970.

50. Lloyd, B., "The Effect of Programmed Perceptual Training on the Reading Achievement and Mental Maturity of Selected First Grade Pupils: A Pilot Study," *Journal of Reading Specialist,* 6 (1966), 49–55.

51. Macoby, E. E., "What Copying Requires," paper presented at American Psychological Association, Washington, D.C., September 1967.

52. McBeath, Pearl M., "The Effectiveness of Three Reading Preparedness Programs for Perceptually Handicapped Kindergartners," doctoral dissertation, Stanford University, 1966.

53. McCormick, C. C., Schnobrich, Janice N., and Footlik, S. W., "The Effect of Perceptual-Motor Training on Reading Achievement," *Academic Therapy Quarterly,* 4 (1969), 171–76.

54. McCullouch, Lovell, "Physical Education Perceptual-Motor Training Program for Kindergarten Children," Ripon, Wis.: Ripon Public Schools, 1969, as quoted by Klesius.

55. McRaney, Kenneth A., "A Study of Perceptual-Motor Exercises Utilized as an Early Grade Enrichment Program for the Improvement of Learning Activity and Motor Development," *Dissertation Abstracts,* 31 (1970), 3935-A.

56. Muehl, Siegmar, "The Effects of Visual Discrimination Pretraining on Learning to Read a Vocabulary List in Kindergarten Children," *Journal of Educational Psychology,* 51 (August 1960), 217–21.

57. Muehl, Siegmar, "Effects of Visual Discrimination Training on Learning to Read a Vocabulary List in Kindergarten Children," *Journal of Educational Psychology,* 51 (August 1961), 215–21.

58. Muehl, Siegmar, "The Effects of Letter-Name Knowledge on Learning to Read a Word List in Kindergarten Children," *Journal of Educational Psychology,* 53 (August 1962), 181–86.

59. Muehl, Siegmar, and King, Ethel M., "Recent Research in Visual Discrimination: Significance for Beginning Reading," in *Vistas in Reading,* J. Allen Figurel, editor, Proceedings International Reading Association, 11, Part 1 (1967), 434–39.

60. Myerson, Daniel, "A Reading Readiness Program for Perceptually Handicapped Kindergarten Pupils of Normal Vision, Final Report," ERIC/CRIER Ed 013–119. University of California, 1967.

61. New Jersey State Department of Education, *A Study in Visual-Motor Perceptual Training in the First Grade,* Trenton, New Jersey, 1965, as quoted by Klesius.

62. O'Connor, Colleen, "The Effects of Physical Activities upon Motor Ability, Perceptual Ability and Academic Achievement of First Graders," in *Dissertation Abstracts,* 29 (1968), 4310-A.

63. O'Donnell, P. A., "The Effects of Delacato Training on Reading Achievement and Visual-Motor Integration," doctoral dissertation, Stanford University, 1969.

64. Olson, Arthur V., "School Achievement, Reading Ability and Specific Visual Perception Skills in the Third Grade," *Reading Teacher,* 19 (April 1966), 490–92.

65. Otto, Wayne, "Interlist Similarity, Order of Presentation and Color in Children's Paired Associate Learning," *Psychonomic Science,* 9 (1967), 531–32.

66. Painter, G., "The Effect of a Rhythmic and Sensory-Motor Program on Perceptual-Motor-Spatial Abilities of Kindergarten Children," *Exceptional Children,* 33 (1966), 113–16.

67. Popp, Helen M., "The Measurement and Training of Visual Discrimination Skills Prior to Reading Instruction," *Journal of Experimental Education,* 35 (1967), 15–26.

68. Pumfrey, P. D., and Anthony, D. A. S., "The Use of the Frostig Programme for the Development of Visual Perception with Children Attending a Residential School," Personal communication from the authors, 1972.

69. Raven, Ronald J., and Strubing, Herbert, "The Effect of Visual Perception Units on Achievement in a Science Unit; Aptitudinal and Substantive Transfer in Second Grade Children," *American Educational Research Journal,* 3 (May 1968), 333–42.

70. Roach, Eugene G., "Evaluation of an Experimental Program of Perceptual-Motor Training with Slow Readers," in *Vistas in Reading,* J. Allen Figurel, editor, Proceedings International Reading Association, 11, Part 1 (1967), 446–50.

71. Robbins, Melvyn P., "The Delacato Interpretation of Neurological Organization," *Reading Research Quarterly,* 1 (Spring 1966), 57–78.

72. Rosen, Carl L., "An Experimental Study of Visual Perceptual Training and Reading Achievement in First Grade," *Perceptual and Motor Skills,* 22 (1966), 979–86.

73. Rosen, Carl L., "An Investigation of Perceptual Training and Reading Achievement in First Grade," *American Journal of Optometry and Archives of American Academy of Optometry,* 45 (May 1968), 322–32.

74. Rutherford, William L., "Perceptual-Motor Training and Readiness," in *Reading and Inquiry,* J. Allen Figurel, editor, Proceedings International Reading Association, 10 (1965), 294–96.

75. Samuels, S. Jay, "Relationship between Formal Intralist Similarity and the von Restorff Effect," *Journal of Educational Psychology,* 59 (December 1968), 432–37.

76. Schoer, Lowell, "Effect of Similarity in Structure, Meaning and Sound on Paired-Associate Learning," *Journal of Educational Psychology,* 58 (August 1967), 189–92.

77. Slacks, Rosemary, "The Effect of Physical Activities upon Perceptual Abilities, Reading Ability and Academic Achievement," master's thesis, University of Texas, 1969.

78. Spache, George D., "The Perceptual Bases of Reading," pp. 178–90 in *Reading Instruction: An International Forum,* Marion D. Jenkinson, editor. Newark, Del.: International Reading Association, 1967.

79. Spache, George D., Andres, Micaela C., Curtis, H. A., et al., *A Longitudinal First Grade Reading Readiness Program.* Cooperative Research Project, No. 2742. Tallahassee: Florida State Department of Education, 1965.

80. Staats, Carolyn K., Staats, Arthur W., and Schutz, Richard W., "Effects of Discrimination Pretraining on Textual Behavior," *Journal of Educational Psychology,* 53 (February 1962), 32–37.

81. Stone, M., and Pielstick, N. L., "Effectiveness of Delacato Treatment with Kindergarten Children," *Psychology in the Schools,* 6 (1969), 63–68.

82. Turner, Robert V., and Fisher, Maurice D., "The Effect of a Perceptual-Motor

Training Program upon the Readiness and Perceptual Development of Culturally Disadvantaged Kindergarten Children," ERIC/CRIER Ed 041-633. Richmond, Va.: Public Schools, 1970.

83. Underwood, B. J., Ham, M., and Ekstrand, B., "Cue Selection in Paired-Associate Learning," *Journal of Experimental Psychology,* 64 (1962), 405–409.

84. Vernon, Magdalene D., *The Psychology of Perception.* Baltimore: Penguin Books, 1962.

85. Vernon, Magdalene D., *A Further Study of Visual Perception.* Cambridge: Cambridge University Press, 1962.

86. Vernon, Magdalene D., compiler, *Visual Perception and Its Relation to Reading: An Annotated Bibliography.* Newark, Del.: International Reading Association, 1966.

87. Weisman, Eva A., and Leonard, Mary R., "A Multi-Disciplinary Approach to the Development of Verbal and Reading Skills," Baltimore Public Schools, 1969, as quoted by Klesius.

88. Wheelock, Warren H., "An Investigation of Visual Discrimination Training for Beginning Readers," in *Perception and Reading,* Helen K. Smith, editor, Proceedings International Reading Association, 12, No. 4 (1968), 101–5.

89. Williams, Joanna P., "Training Kindergarten Children to Discriminate Letter-Like Forms," *American Educational Research Journal,* 6 (November 1969), 501–14.

90. Wimsatt, William R., "The Effect of Sensory Motor Training on Learning Abilities of Grade School Children," doctoral dissertation, University of Minnesota, 1966.

91. Wingert, Roger C., "Evaluation of a Readiness Training Program," *Reading Teacher,* 22 (January 1969), 325–28.

92. Wiseman, Douglas E., "The Effects of an Individualized Remedial Program on Mentally Retarded Children with Psycholinguistic Disabilities," doctoral dissertation, University of Illinois, 1965.

93. Yarborough, Betty Hathaway, "A Study of the Effectiveness of the Leavell Language-Development Service in Improving the Silent Reading Ability and Other Language Skills of Persons with Mixed Dominance," doctoral dissertation, University of Virginia, 1964.

part four

ORGANIZATIONAL ASPECTS

As one visits reading or learning disability centers, one receives the impression that there is often a hiatus
between diagnosis and treatment procedures. Areas explored in diagnostic techniques may not appear to
be treatment areas; or conversely,
multi-faceted treatments are used on
the basis of the simplest of diagnostic
work-ups. In other places, we see
what is essentially the same treatment, such as phonics, visual motor,
programmed systems or the like
being applied to practically all the
cases. These are but a few examples
of an obvious dichotomy between diagnostic findings and remedial treatments. Many others are specifically
pointed out in this chapter.

In very brief style, this chapter reviews ways in which treatment procedures may be more closely related to
the indications found in the usual
areas of diagnosis. Considered
alone, these suggestions are oversim-

17 Integrating Diagnosis with Remediation

plified and should be supported by reading the much fuller treatments offered in
the earlier chapters of this book and its accompanying textbook. But this segment
serves the purpose of a quick review of some of the practices and malpractices in
remediation that we have emphasized elsewhere.

In reading this overview, consider such questions as the following.

1. What are some of the common faulty practices which militate against permanent, ultimate success in remediation?

2. Have you ever observed these or other inconsistencies in diagnosis and
remediation? What were they?

DESPITE REFINEMENTS IN DIAGNOSIS and remediation in reading in the last twenty or so years, there is still a widespread lack of integration between these two processes. There is evidence in numerous reports of remedial work that the procedures used are not directly related to the detailed diagnostic findings. In many instances, it seems that these two processes are carried on by different persons between whom there is a distinct lack of communication. One cause of lack of relevancy between diagnosis and remediation is the presence of biased or prejudiced thinking resulting in limited diagnostic efforts or in stereotyped remedial programs. A second cause may lie in the differing emphases in the training of clinicians, who are apt to do the diagnosis, and of remedial or classroom teachers, who are prominent in remedial work. But, whatever the reasons, the incoordination between diagnosis and remediation is a relatively common phenomenon, as we shall attempt to show.

There is evidence of bias or a priori thinking in the diagnostic statistics reported by many clinics and teachers. In investigation of the incidence of personality disturbances among retarded readers, a clinic in Boston reports 39 percent of the cases as having significant emotional problems. A clinic just outside of Chicago reports 50 percent; the St. Louis clinics find 4–6 percent, while we at the University of Florida feel that at least 70 percent of our reading cases (25) show emotional maladjustment. Certainly these differences reflect the breadth and depth of the diagnostic procedures used by these various clinics rather than any real differences in the extent of personality problems in various geographic areas.

In other diagnostic steps, such as the measurement of vision or reading skills, there are similar contradictory reports. One clinic in New York claims that 95 percent of all retarded reading cases are the result of difficulties in the convergence-divergence ratio in vision, while another clinic near Chicago apparently finds that most retarded readers are in dire need of visual training. Two other clinics spend three or four days in extensive medical examinations, although they admit that only a very small proportion of their cases show related organic defects. The report from a group of public school clinics in a

Adapted from George D. Spache, "Integrating Diagnosis with Remediation in Reading," *Elementary School Journal,* 56 (September 1955), 18–26, by permission of the University of Chicago Press. © 1955 by the University of Chicago.

large midwestern city finds that 96 percent of the cases lack skill in word analysis; it concludes, logically enough, that poor training in word analysis is the primary cause of reading retardation. These four clinic reports are typical examples of the circular reasoning present among many diagnosticians. They reason backward from effect to cause, assuming that, if a certain characteristic is found common among retarded readers, it must be a cause of the reading failure. As in the case of those who stress lack of word analysis as a cause, these diagnosticians assume that, since these children are weak in an educational tool, the cause of the reading failure must be in the reading methods or training. This is about as sensible as concluding that since all retarded readers are deficient in the school-trained skill of reading, the cause of the failure must lie somewhere in the school. These diagnosticians fail to try to discover the reasons *why* this methodology or training, which is very beneficial to many children, has failed with the retarded readers. In our opinion, these exaggerated reports reflect a diagnostic prejudice that practically dictates the remedial approach, making diversified remedial programs, keyed to the true causes, almost impossible.

Lack of direct thinking that would promote better integration between diagnosis and remediation is also shown in the tendency to stereotyped remedial programs. For example, all the cases in a clinic in the Far West seem to be given the kinesthetic approach to reading without reference to their capacities to learn by other methods. Certain proponents of psychotherapy (2, 6, 17) act as though remedial work in reading was synonymous with nondirective therapy. Apparently some of these authors want to use play therapy for all types of emotionally disturbed retarded readers, despite the fact that the cases exhibit a variety of personality adjustments (25) for some of which the nondirective approach would probably be inappropriate.

In those programs using mechanical devices extensively, there is a trend to employ such devices with little attention to the exact characteristics of each case. These atomistic training courses leave unanswered such questions as the kinds of remedial cases for which such a program is most or least effective. Apparently no training distinctions are made between slow readers with good comprehension and vocabulary—who might conceivably profit from mechanical acceleration—or cases with multiple difficulties in reading background, comprehension, vocabulary, and word analysis skills. In the widespread mechanistic programs for adults, there is similar lack of discrimination between adults who are merely slow readers and those who are deficient in a number of reading skills. Other facts that must be known before the success of mechanical programs can be considered real are the optimum length, intervals, and intensity of such training. Should this training be continued for a few hours, for a few weeks, or for indefinite periods? It appears from some research that the values of this approach tend to disappear after a very short period of exposure (9). One other serious objection to the stereotyped use of mechanical devices has been explored by Traxler (34) in pointing out the extent of individual differences in fluency, in speed of associative thinking, and, hence, in potential for growth in rate. For the past two years we have been following this type of research with only modest success in attempting to find a means of identifying those cases likely to profit from rate training. Frankly, practically nothing is known about techniques for careful selection of cases for training in speed. As long as such training continues to be successful with only a moderate proportion of cases, as is generally true, there will be a crying need for better diagnostic criteria, rather than for wider use of this method. In our opinion, the use of mechanical training with large numbers of retarded readers is another example of the lack of clear-cut relationships between diagnosis and remediation in many places.

Finally, there is one other body of evidence of poor communication between clinicians and remedial teachers shown in a great number of reports on purely formal remedial reading programs. In many places, there are reading cases differing widely in etiologic and prognostic details who are offered formal reading instruction exclusively. In reports from some clinics, groups of teachers taking university courses in remedial reading are merely matched with an equal number of retarded readers. All that seems important is that the case load per teacher is equalized. All that the teacher has to have, apparently, is a modicum of training in reading methods in order to be ready to do successful remedial work with almost any retarded reader. Actually, we still do not clearly know what kinds of cases should or should *not* be given direct reading training. Nor is it entirely clear what types of emotionally disturbed poor readers profit from the usual remedial work (25). Furthermore, apparently in an effort to widen the disparity between diagnostic implications and the remedial therapy, many training programs are carried out largely by visual methods practically identical with those used in the early training of the retarded reader—the same methods by which the student failed to learn to read successfully. Moreover, we often see emphasis upon visual methods in reading used with visually handicapped students despite the evidence of Fendrick (7) and others of the doubtful values of this approach in such cases. No real attempt is made to explore and relate the organic or learning capacities of the student to various basic methods of teaching reading, despite the available diagnostic techniques (15).

IMPLEMENTING DIAGNOSTIC FINDINGS

In attacking this problem constructively, it is possible to point out a significant number of ways in which the facts found in common diagnostic procedures may be better implemented by closely relevant remedial or therapeutic steps. We shall first name the characteristics of the retarded reader commonly evaluated because of the research evidence that may play a part in the causation of reading failure. Following each diagnostic step, we shall point out the most widely used related remedial procedures and their probable inadequacies. Finally, we shall suggest alternative remedial efforts that may not be widely known. It is our hope that the use of these additional remedial procedures will strengthen a more direct relationship between the causes found by diagnosis and the corrective steps used to relieve reading disability.

Vision

Testing of vision is probably the most common diagnostic step used in this country. Among the visual characteristics that are found to contribute to reading difficulties are deficiencies in visual acuity, hyperopia (farsightedness), astigmatism, and binocular incoordination resulting in abnormalities in fusion or the phorias, or in marked monocular preference. One other defect, aniseikonia, seems to be important, but its measurement is probably too difficult for most teachers or clinicians. Myopia, or nearsightedness, is also commonly tested, but there is great doubt that it contributes to reading difficulty except in rare cases. With the instruments now available, such as the Ortho-Rater, Keystone Telebinocular, the Binocular Reading Test (23), and a few others, diagnosis that is relatively complete and reasonably accurate is possible.

The initial remedial step when visual irregularities are diagnosed is usually to refer the case to a local "eye specialist" who, presumably, will make any corrections that are necessary. At the risk of offending many competent vision specialists, it must be pointed out that simple referral does not relieve the reading teacher of further responsibility in this diagnostic detail. As in every area that involves dealing with human beings, there are conflicting philosophies of remediation. For example, many medically trained specialists have, in our opinion, little training or time to engage in orthoptic or visual training corrective measures. It would seem that in many parts of our country, visual training is better understood and more widely used by optometrists than by ophthalmologists. This type of training is certainly not the panacea that some reading clinics and some optometrists seem to think it is; but there is a great deal of evidence that many of these visual handicaps can be relieved, if not entirely eradicated, by this calisthenic approach alone or in combination with other corrective efforts (4, 12, 21, 32).

It may be only a reflection of personal experience, but it also seems that many vision specialists are not aware of the peculiarly intensive demands in near-point work imposed on the student by high school or college. Perhaps this is the reason that some visual practitioners do not make corrections that relieve the symptoms of distress or even actually aid the older student in his near-point task of reading or studying.

In our opinion, it is the responsibility of the reading diagnostician to recheck the visual functioning of the retarded reader to determine whether the distress or handicap imposed by visual abnormality has been relieved as much as it is humanly possible to do. This does not imply that the reading teacher is to attempt to judge the accuracy of the optical prescription or the competence of the visual specialist. Rather the reading diagnostician should continue to explore the possibilities of further aid to the visually handicapped student by consultation with several eye specialists who may represent different schools of philosophy of remediation.

Other possible remedial steps to aid this type of case are the use of reading materials especially prepared for those of limited vision, as listed by Matson (14) and Galisdorfer (10); instructing the student in manuscript writing because of its greater visibility (11); and teaching the student better visual discrimination of forms by the use of such training materials as those of Durrell and Sullivan (5) or Thurstone (33). Four possible sources of further aid for the visually handicapped student are state commissions for the blind, the two national vision societies,* and local service clubs such as the Lions, who, we understand, are participating in a nationwide interest in visual problems. Help in financing such steps as visual treatments, mechanical aids, and the hiring of readers is often found in these sources. One further effort of the reading teacher that we have found desirable is in the training in efficient reading or study methods of those persons who read to the blind or extremely visually handicapped.

---

*National Society for the Prevention of Blindness, 1790 Broadway, New York, N.Y. 10019.
American Foundation for the Blind, 15 West 16th Street, New York, N.Y. 10011.

Hearing

Ordinarily auditory acuity and discrimination are explored in the diagnostic procedures. The ability of the poor reader to hear sounds of normal intensity, or sounds at various pitches, or to recognize similarities and differences in speech sounds are usually evaluated in this auditory testing. The common remedial steps are to refer the auditorily handicapped cases to an otologist and to avoid auditory or phonic methods of teaching. Because of the assumption that such cases cannot employ phonic approaches to reading, we seldom see any attempt to improve the situation by auditory training even though teaching materials are available (5). Actually we do know that discrimination often can be improved, particularly if hearing is reinforced by such devices as the Ambco Hearing Amplifier.* In the absence of actual hearing losses, poor auditory discrimination may be treated like any other undeveloped skill and repaired by appropriate teaching.

Intelligence

Measurement of intelligence today usually includes evaluation of verbal and nonverbal capacities. Remedial procedures are often predicated on the results of the intelligence testing, and we often see the mentally retarded being given the kinesthetic approach to reading, particularly if nonverbal intelligence appears to be significantly greater than verbal. This assumption is as yet unfounded, first, because several studies show that most retarded readers (and, in fact, most children) score higher in nonverbal than in verbal (16, 26); second, because there is very little evidence that the kinesthetic approach is peculiarly suited to mentally retarded poor readers.

There are several additional steps which, if employed, would further a more direct relationship between diagnostic estimates of intelligence and subsequent remediation. The use of the Learning Methods Test (15) will usually reveal which of four approaches to reading are desirable in each case. Briefly, the procedure in this test includes four teaching lessons, each based on a different reading method with testing of immediate and delayed recall. Thus far, there is no indication in the research data being compiled in use of this test that level of intelligence or differences in verbal and nonverbal abilities bear any direct relationship to the reading method best for each

*Ambco Hearing Amplifier, A. M. Brooks Company, 1222 West Washington Boulevard, Los Angeles, Calif.

individual. When verbal ability is significantly lower than nonverbal, it may be interpreted as indicative of poor cultural, linguistic, or reading background. If this interpretation is made, then remedial efforts will take the form of providing numerous firsthand and vicarious experiences as well as extensive reading of simple, realistic materials.

Furthermore, we suggest disregarding mental age as a guide to maximum level of potential growth. Many children exceed their own mental ages in reading achievement, while many others fail to progress to this point even under excellent instruction. We prefer to measure potential for growth in comprehension level by estimating the highest level at which the individual can show adequate comprehension when standardized paragraphs are read to him. We have found this method of estimating potential for growth feasible with children of the first six or seven grades. For testing from the seventh grade to college freshman level, there is available an Auditory Comprehension Test (24) that, when used in conjunction with a parallel measure of silent reading comprehension, yields similar estimates of potential. Faulty integration of diagnosis and remediation is fostered, in our opinion, by overdependence upon mental age or mental test performances as the critieria of potential or of the reading method to be employed, as we have pointed out in some detail in chapter 6.

Reading Skills

Rate   Present status and the prognosis for growth are commonly measured in the skills of rate, comprehension, vocabulary, and word analysis. Remedial procedures to improve rate are usually of two major types—timed reading with comprehension checks, or mechanized programs. We have already indicated some objection to indiscriminate mechanized procedures and shall merely point out several other doubtful assumptions that underlie such methods. Use of this type of training for speed ignores the fact that the eye movements, phrasing, and so on, shown by the reader are often merely a reflection of the difficulty of the reading materials. Even good readers show the same irregularities when reading very complex matter, as Anderson has shown (1). It seems more logical to implement the diagnosis of slow reading by providing simpler materials in which these irregularities do not appear, or to attack the problem more directly by trying to improve the poor vocabulary, word recognition, or word analysis skills that may be directly causal.

We also consider the other type of approach—timed reading or reading under pressure—inadequate for many slow readers. Extended practice with selections from the various content fields, as we commonly see, leaves the student ignorant of the basically different reading demands of each field. Such practice leads the student to expect naively a significant rate increase in all kinds of reading. We doubt that there is a general rate improvement that, as both timed reading and mechanized programs seem to assume, transfers automatically from reading in one content field to another.

More real and permanent growth in rate can be accomplished by teaching the student *how* and *when* to use rapid reading by direct instruction in reading for ideas, scanning for single facts without actual reading, and skimming by reading only headings, topic sentences, and summary sentences. The student achieves flexibility in rate (which, after all, is the real aim of rate training) only by learning to vary his speed and reading techniques according to his purpose, the difficulty, the style, and his familiarity with the content of the reading matter. This type of rate improvement is best accomplished by instruction in intelligent use of the rapid reading techniques suggested above in the types of content and reading situations in which they are appropriate.

Vocabulary   Common remedial steps to overcome poor vocabulary include training in word recognition, in word meanings, and in word relationships such as synonyms and antonyms. Other remedial approaches include urging use of the dictionary and giving the student word lists or lists of affixes and roots to learn. Except at primary levels, there is serious doubt of the values of programs stressing words as contrasted to those stressing tools for vocabulary growth (3). In view of our lack of knowledge of the words actually essential for reading success at upper elementary or higher levels, it is presumptuous for remedial teachers to offer any particular word list or "all-inclusive" list of affixes or roots for student learning. We do not know accurately how great the whole mass of our language is, how rapidly it is increasing, or how to make a cross-sectioning sample that will meet the needs of any particular student. We do not know how to anticipate the vocabulary needs of each individual. Perhaps the most we can do is to offer small lists of technical terms that seem to be important in circumscribed areas of study. The general vocabulary needs of each individual are still beyond our measurement or prediction skills.

If we accept this premise, then remediation will stress training in tools for vocabulary growth rather than in words or word relationships. Remedial work will include these features:

1. Practice with dictionary use for meanings, pronunciation, usage, derivation, and spelling
2. Practice with concentrated, small groups of affixes and roots in analytic attack upon words in context rather than synthetic juggling of lists of words

3. Training in the use of the context to derive meanings by such approaches as inference, direct explanation, structural cues, figures of speech, and tone or mood

4. Instruction in personalized use of a card file to study the new words that each individual meets in his work-type reading

Comprehension

In remedial training to improve comprehension, we usually see two types of programs. These include a drill program in simple varied materials stressing main ideas, details, or conclusions, and the like; or the use of basal reading materials supplemented by recreational reading. In both programs, there is an assumption that repeated practice in answering certain types of questions results in more intelligent reading and growth in the level of the material that can be read. Above primary levels, we believe that there is much more to the act of reading than this semimechanical process of reading and answering questions. There is considerable evidence that general training does not transfer to each content field and that specific, insightful training is necessary for each basic reading situation (19).

Rather than general drill in comprehension, the student should be taught how to read for differing degrees of comprehension. This type of instruction is available in a few present materials (30, 31) and is stressed by this author (27). The training to produce intelligent reading includes at least five major points:

1. Planning each reading and its purpose in relation to the whole area of study, the demands and general purposes of the instructor, and the specific purposes of the readers.

2. Teaching the student different ways or rates of reading and their effect upon comprehension.

3. Instructing him in a systematic approach to difficult materials such as Robinson's (18) Survey QRRR or even a better study procedure that will promote thorough retention.

4. Training in critical reading, as in social science and propaganda materials. This involves practice in identifying the facts given, evaluating the ideas offered, and detecting bias, omission, distortion, and the like.

5. Having the student practice in applying his reading skills in the various content fields. He must understand the demands of reading in literature of various types (as in social science, mathematics, and science): the nature of the material, the types of thinking demanded, the kinds of interrelationships present, and appropriate rates for accomplishing his various purposes. Fortunately for those attempting this type of approach, there are available several recent manuals that offer numerous suggestions as to procedures and materials (20, 28, 35).

Word Analysis Skills   Diagnostic steps in this area usually include an evaluation of the pupil's ability to make a systematic but varied attack upon unknown words met in context. Despite the recognition that word analysis skills must eventually function during the fluent act of reading, there is a tendency to retrain these skills atomistically and in learning situations that do not involve contextual reading. We see many remedial programs stressing letter phonics, or letter combinations, or formal syllabication, and so forth, which deal only with isolated words.

It is true (as some clinic reports cited earlier show) that one of the most prominent disabilities of retarded readers at all levels is in effective word attack or word analysis. Students may know and understand phonic principles or syllabication rules but seem to make no transfer or use of this theoretical knowledge when actually reading. A simple experiment that we carried on at the college level confirms this inability to apply principles of word analysis. We found practically no statistical relationship between the ability to quote the essential parts of syllabication rules and the ability to do syllabication. This lack of relationship between formal knowledge of word attack principles and success in word analysis in contextual reading at this level is widely recognized by diagnosticians. Yet most of the teacher-made or commercial materials that we see persist in using a synthetic approach involving drills on sounds or word construction rather than on word analysis in context. If we agree that most retarded readers need training in word analysis in the act of reading, and that formal training does not transfer readily, then there is a need for remedial training in varied methods of word attack *while reading,* rather than for programs stressing sounds, isolated words, and the like.

Personality

Many diagnosticians are making some effort to detect the extent and severity (and perhaps the nature) of emotional problems affecting reading performances. There is undoubtedly a growing recognition of the absolute necessity of evaluating by some objective means the influence of personality upon reading. Yet despite this increasing exploration of emotional concomitants, we see most retarded readers being referred to the remedial teacher for formal reading instruction. A few diagnosticians may refer children with severe emotional problems for play therapy, if such facilities are available. Other diagnosticians, as we have mentioned earlier, apparently wish to refer all retarded readers for psychotherapy. There are a number of questions to be answered before we know which of these three courses of action should be taken.

We still do not know what personality patterns are peculiarly characteristic of retarded readers. We are not certain of what kinds of maladjustment problems we are attempting to treat. Most studies of the personalities of retarded readers are based on personal experience or opinion. Those few studies available employing objective measures of personality have dealt with small groups or economically restricted samples (22, 29, 36). One recent exploratory study (25) points out at least five major personality types in an unrestricted sample of 125 retarded readers. Based on the Rosenzweig Picture-Frustration study, the patterns found in relatively large subgroups are the aggressive, defensive, adjustive, solution-seeking, and autistic or withdrawn. Specific suggestions for therapeutic approach to each type are offered in this study, but these suggestions are based largely on opinion rather than on controlled research. We still do not know exactly what kinds of therapy to use or how to relate these to the particular personality problems that we may eventually identify as common to poor readers. Lack of integration between diagnosis and remediation is evidenced in this area also.

In the near future, there are numerous remedial or therapeutic approaches that we must explore by controlled research. We should investigate the emotional relationships in the family of the retarded reader and the possibilities of therapy for the parent as well as the child. If—as seems true in certain types of emotionally disturbed readers (6, 25)—parental perfectionism or inconsistency is a predisposing factor, we must find means of extending guidance to the parent also. We should make wider use and careful evaluation of a number of approaches that have shown some merit in isolated studies. The values of bibliotherapy, play therapy, and ordinary remedial instruction used alone, or together, or successively in varying arrangements (14) still need extended research. Using the child's original stories or his verbal or artistic interpretation of other stories to gain insights into his feelings and attitudes will be another profitable approach. Various types of group therapy used alone or in conjunction with the usual remedial instruction need further investigation (8). These groups may range from bull sessions providing an opportunity for verbalizing feelings about reading through varying degrees of permissiveness to semidirective discussions of reading techniques. We also need to discover the types of individuals among high school and college students for whom directive, semidirective, or permissive kinds of psychotherapy may provide a better answer than formal skill instruction. We must explore all the possibilities of counseling and guidance procedures in the remedial reading program   In our reading clinic at the University of Florida, we found an individualized approach in testing and remedial instruction, with approximately one-fourth of the time spent in personalized, semidirective counseling, to be the most effective procedure despite a case load of almost one thousand each year (28). We feel strongly that the tendency to formal, group instruction at high school and college levels must be modified to something approximating the counseling approach used with younger pupils.

In summarizing, may we repeat the suggestion that despite our advances in diagnostic and remedial techniques, there is evidence of a lag in coordination of these processes. We have tried to point out a number of ways in which diagnosis may be made more truly effective in finding the real causes of reading failure and in which remedial work can be made directly relevant to our diagnosis.

LEARNING PROJECT

Try to borrow a number of case studies from a reading center; review them to observe the integration between diagnosis and remediation. Identify what seem to be the major causes of the subjects' difficulties and the relevance of the treatment to these causes. Try to discover the answers to these questions:

1. Were all major areas of diagnosis explored and treated in each case?

2. Are the most common areas of emphasis in reading development, such as skills, the usual basic treatments in most cases?

3. Are treatment procedures other than those to improve reading skills considered most important in some cases?

4. Does there appear to be a relatively static procedure or two for treating most reading disability cases?

5. Are a number of diagnostic tests used for which there does not appear to be any directly relevant follow-up in remediation?

If such case studies are not available to you, you might examine those in such sources as these:

Bond, Guy L., and Tinker, Miles A., *Reading Difficulties: Their Diagnosis and Correction.* New York: Appleton-Century-Crofts, 1967.

Crosby, R. M. N., *The Waysiders.* New York: Delacorte Press, 1968.

Della-Piana, Gabriel M., *Reading Diagnosis and Prescription: An Introduction.* New York: Holt, Rinehart & Winston, 1968.

Fernald, Grace M., *Remedial Techniques in Basic School Subjects.* New York: McGraw-Hill, 1943.

Heilman, Arthur W., *Principles and Practices of Teaching Reading.* Columbus: Charles E. Merrill, 1967.

Pollack, M. F. W., and Piekarz, Josephine, *Reading Problems and Problem Readers.* New York: David McKay, 1963.

REFERENCES

1. Anderson, I. H., "Research in the Psychology of Reading," *Journal of Exceptional Children,* 4 (January 1938), 57–60.
2. Axline, Virginia Mae, "Play Therapy—A Way of Understanding and Helping 'Reading Problems,'" *Childhood Education,* 26 (December 1949), 151–61.
3. Colvin, Cynthia, "A Re-examination of the Vocabulary Question," *Elementary English,* 28 (October 1951), 350–56.
4. Davis, Louise Farwell, "Visual Difficulties and Reading Disabilities" in *Recent Trends in Reading.* Supplementary Educational Monographs No. 49. Chicago: University of Chicago Press, 1939.
5. Durrell, Donald D., and Sullivan, Helen Blair, *Ready to Read.* New York: World Book, 1941.
6. Ephron, Beulah Kantor, *Emotional Difficulties in Reading.* New York: Julian Press, 1953.
7. Fendrick, Paul, *Visual Characteristics of Poor Readers.* Contributions to Education No. 656. New York: Teachers College, Columbia University, 1934.
8. Fisher, Bernard, "Group Therapy with Retarded Readers," *Journal of Educational Psychology,* 44 (October 1953), 354–60.
9. Freeburne, Cecil M., "Influence of Training in Perceptual Span and Perceptual Speed upon Reading Ability," *Journal of Educational Psychology,* 40 (October 1949), 321–52.
10. Galisdorfer, Lorraine, *A New Annotated Reading Guide for Children with Partial Vision.* Buffalo: Foster and Stewart, 1950.
11. Grill, E., "Manuscript Writing and Its Value to a Sight-Saving Child," *Educational Method,* 9 (April 1930), 407–12.
12. Lancaster, Julia E., *A Manual of Orthoptics.* Springfield, Ill.: Charles C. Thomas, 1951.
13. Mahus, Hilda, "Learning and Therapy," *American Journal of Orthopsychiatry,* 23 (April 1953), 416–21.
14. Matson, Charlotte, and Larson, Lola, *Books for Tired Eyes.* Chicago: American Library Association, 1951.
15. Mills, Robert E., *The Learning Methods Test.* The author: 1512 East Broward Boulevard, Fort Lauderdale, Florida.
16. Monroe, Marion, and Backus, Bertie, *Remedial Reading: A Monograph in Character Education.* Boston: Houghton Mifflin, 1937.
17. Potter, Muriel, "The Use of Limits in Reading Therapy," *Journal of Consulting Psychology,* 14 (August 1950), 250–55.
18. Robinson, Francis P., *Effective Study.* New York: Harper, 1946.
19. Shores, J. H., "Skills Related to Ability to Read History and Science," *Journal of Educational Research,* 36 (1943), 584–93.
20. Simpson, Elizabeth A., *Helping High-School Students Read Better.* Chicago: Science Research Associates, 1954.
21. Smith, William, *Clinical Orthoptic Procedures.* St. Louis: Mosby, 1950.
22. Solomon, Ruth H., "Personality Adjustment to Reading Success and Failure," pp. 64–82 in *Clinical Studies in Reading II.* Chicago: University of Chicago Press, 1953.

23. Spache, George, *The Binocular Reading Test.* Mast-Keystone, 1941.
24. Spache, George, "The Construction and Validation of a Silent and an Auditory Work-Type Comprehension Reading Test," *Educational and Psychological Measurement,* 10 (Summer 1950), 249–53.
25. Spache, George, "Appraising the Personality of Remedial Pupils," pp. 122–32 in *Education in a Free World,* Arthur E. Traxler, editor. Washington, D.C.: American Council on Education, 1955.
26. Spache, George, "Intellectual and Personality Characteristics of Retarded Readers," *Psychological Newsletter,* 9 (September 1957), 9–12.
27. Spache, George D., and Berg, Paul C., *The Art of Efficient Reading.* New York: Macmillan, 1966.
28. Spache, George D., and Berg. Paul C., *Instructor's Guide for The Art of Efficient Reading.* New York: Macmillan, 1955.
29. Stewart, Robert S., "Personality Maladjustment and Reading Achievement," *American Journal of Orthopsychiatry,* 20 (April 1950), 410–17.
30. Strang, Ruth, *Study Type of Reading Exercises.* New York: Bureau of Publications, Teachers College, Columbia University, 1935.
31. Strang, Ruth, *Study Type of Reading Exercises—College Level.* New York: Bureau of Publications, Teachers College, Columbia University, 1951.
32. Taylor, Earl A., *Controlled Reading.* Chicago: University of Chicago Press, 1937.
33. Thurstone, Thelma Gwinn, *Learning to Think Series.* Chicago: Science Research Associates, 1949.
34. Traxler, Arthur E., "The Relation between Rate of Reading and Speed of Association," *Journal of Educational Psychology,* 25 (May 1934), 357–65.
35. Triggs, Frances O., *We All Teach Reading.* Mountain Home, N. C.: The author.
36. Vorhaus, Pauline G., "Rorschach Configurations Associated with Reading Disability," *Journal of Projective Techniques, 16 (March 1952), 3–19.*

This is the presentation of a hypothetical but fairly typical research report, offered for your critical reading. The numbers in the margin refer to specific criticisms that are offered at the end of the report. As you read the report, try to anticipate what criticisms are being signaled by the marginal numbers. Then compare your questions with those proposed in the review of the report by this author.

Milton H. Hodge, professor of psychology at the University of Georgia, has compiled a glossary of terms often found in research reports.* We reproduce this glossary in the chart below to aid the reader in understanding our hypothetical research report and those he will read in the future.

18
Reading the Research

A KEY TO SCIENTIFIC RESEARCH LITERATURE

WHAT HE SAID	WHAT HE MEANT
It has long been known that . . .	I haven't bothered to look up the original reference but . . .
Of great theoretical and practical importance . . .	Interesting to me
While it has not been possible to provide definite answers to these questions . . .	The experiment didn't work out, but I figured I could at least get a publication out of it.
The operant conditioning technique was chosen to study the problem . . .	The fellow in the next lab already had the equipment set up.

*Milton H. Hodge, "A Literary Guide for Psychologists," American Psychologist 17 (1962), 154. Copyright 1962 by the American Psychological Association. Reprinted by permission of the publisher and author.

Three of the Ss were chosen for detailed study . . .	The results on the others didn't make sense.
Typical results are shown . . .	The best results are shown . . .
Agreement with the predicted curve is:	
excellent	fair
good	poor
satisfactory	doubtful
fair	imaginary
It is suggested that . . . It is believed that . . . It may be that . . .	I think.
It is generally believed that . . .	A couple of other guys think so too.
It is clear that much additional work will be required before a complete understanding . . .	I don't understand it.
Unfortunately, a quantitative theory to account for these results has not been formulated.	I can't think of one and neither has anyone else.
Correct within an order of magnitude . . .	Wrong.
Thanks are due to Joe Glotz for assistance with the experiments and to John Doe for valuable discussion.	Glotz did the work and Doe explained what it meant.

WHEN WE FIRST CONSIDERED this attempt to increase the critical faculties of reading teachers who read or write research reports, we thought of selecting a particularly poor published report to illustrate our points. But it would be kinder, we now feel, to use a hypothetical report that exhibits many of the defects commonly present in some of these so-called research efforts. Perhaps this may make the presentation seem unrealistic to some readers, but it is possible to offer a report of an experiment that is typical of what we often find in our professional journals.*

---

*Any similarity in names or places to actual persons or school systems is purely accidental.

A COMPARISON OF THE LANGUAGE EXPERIENCE APPROACH WITH BASAL READING PROGRAMS

We have been quite unhappy with the reading progress of our primary children for some time. Although we have tried several basal reading programs at various times, none seemed to produce the results we would hope for. Some teachers favored one reading series above the others, while other teachers had different preferences. But no teachers using a certain system have consistently produced readers who scored higher than the others. Finally, at the suggestion of our principal, Eugene Smith, we decided to undertake a careful comparison of the merits of these various reading systems. Because it was new to the school, we also included the language experience method in our comparison, particularly since some of our primary teachers expressed the desire to try this new approach.

(1)
(2)

(3)

(4)

(5)

(6)

(7)

(8)

(9)

(10)

Our school, the Mark Brown Elementary School, has five classes at each grade level and three half-day kindergartens, although kindergarten is not required for admission to the first grade. Mr. Smith chose three first-grade classes, one to use the Circle readers; one, the Star series; and one, the language experience. Our pupils are drawn largely from the families of business people, who live in the school district, plus some Mexican-American children of the domestics. These pupils were simply assigned at random to a first-grade class upon admission to the school. Our population is much the same from year to year, and these classes were typical of our first grades. All pupils were tested in readiness three weeks after entering school, and the average scores for the three classes were very similar.

Two of the three teachers have been teaching in the first grade for ten to twelve years, while Mrs. Brown, who would use the language experience approach has had about the same total experience teaching in the sixth grade. Mr. Smith chose these three teachers because, in his opinion, they were efficient workers and successful classroom teachers.

Our district policy is to admit only pupils who attain the age of six by December. All the pupils therefore were six years old or within three or four months of this age, except for a few repeaters in each class, and those whose sixth birthday occurred later than December in the previous year. We do not give intelligence tests until the third grade, but we judged these classes to be similar in ability on the basis of their ages and readiness scores.

In our planning conference, Mrs. Adams and Miss Casey were asked to follow the teachers' manuals for their basal programs, the Circle and Star series, respectively. The language experience approach was thoroughly discussed with Mrs. Brown by Professor T. E. Jones of our local university. All

(11) three teachers were familiarized with the experimental plan and urged to make their strongest effort in their teaching of the various reading systems.

(12) Our daily program includes about 90–120 minutes for reading per day. (13) Our teachers are familiar with the basic principles of grouping and commonly divide their pupils into three groups according to their progress and ability. In (14) the first grade, these groups are usually formed after the readiness program provided for in the basal series is completed. A teacher will work with two of (15) the groups early in the morning session, and a third group later that morning. (16) In the afternoon, a period of free reading, library visits, individual or small-group help, or additional seatwork in word recognition and phonics is conducted.

Since the approach to reading in the language approach does not employ readers, the procedures for Mrs. Brown's class differed from the other (17) two. More time was given to handwriting and letter formation to prepare pupils to write their own stories; and to word recognition because of the (18) greater number of words appearing in the stories than in the usual preprimer. (19) Mrs. Brown did have a list of basic words and tried to keep the group stories within this list in order to provide a basal reading vocabulary, but other words, of course, occurred that had to be learned. In the beginning of the year, the (20) entire class would participate in composing and reading a group story in the morning session. Following this group session, the children played word games with small word cards, in small groups, to speed up their learning of vocabulary and copied the group story from the chalkboard. As differences in their progress became apparent, the pupils were eventually divided into three (21) groups. One group moved into the reading of preprimers and primers after a few weeks; a second took several months to reach this point and continued to (22) work with the group story charts each day for this period. A third group (23) needed much more practice in letter formation in order to write, and more basic word drill to learn the basic vocabulary. This group was not ready for the introduction to preprimers until about February, and even then made slow (24) progress. The afternoon sessions of Mrs. Brown's class were spent in activities similar to those in the morning, stressing word recognition, hand-writing, and small-group chart or book reading under her direction.

Toward the close of the school year, we administered the Cosmopolitan (25) Reading tests and compared the results for the three experimental classes and the two other first grade classes not in the experiment. The Cosmopolitan test (26) has three parts, one of matching one of four words to a picture; a second, of underlining a word on a line of four as it is pronounced by the teacher; and a third of choosing one of four words printed below an incomplete sentence in (27) which one of the words would fit. Since the vocabulary in the language

TABLE 18–1 RANGES AND CLASS AVERAGES IN
READING TESTS

TEACHER	WORD-PICTURE (30 ITEMS) RAW SCORES	G.E.	WORD RECOGNITION (35 ITEMS) RAW SCORES	G.E.	COMPRE-HENSION (25 ITEMS) RAW SCORES	G.E.	WORD RECOGNITION (50 ITEMS)	NO. OF PUPILS
Adams (Circle)	7 to 30		10 to 35		5 to 19			
	27.5	2.3	24.3	2.4	14.6	1.7	—	28
Casey (Star)	15 to 30		18 to 34		10 to 17			
	24.2	2.0	17.5	1.8	18.3	2.1	—	30
Brown (L-E)	14 to 30		17 to 33		9 to 18			
	24.4	2.0	20.2	2.0	18.0	2.1	33.0	29
Class A	14 to 28		14 to 30		11 to 18			
	25.3	2.1	18.3	1.9	16.5	1.9		27
Class B	13 to 25		14 to 29		10 to 19			
	22.4	1.8	18.6	1.9	16.0	1.9		29

(28) experience stories was broader than that of the basal materials, Mrs. Brown made up an additional test of fifty items in which the children underlined one of the four words as she said it. This test sampled the words used in many of the group stories and did not duplicate the similar subtest in the Cosmopolitan battery. (See Table 18-1.)

(29) These results helped us to decide to use the Circle series hereafter for our primary grades. The system obviously produces significantly better word recognition than the other two approaches. In the sentence comprehension area, we will make a stronger effort in the use of the Circle readers, adding

(30) whatever seatwork in sentence reading will strengthen this skill.

CRITIQUE

There are at least thirty points in this research report on which we might comment. We have indicated these items by marginal numbering to enable the reader to relate our remarks to the content of the research report.

(1) From the very beginning of the study, there is the assumption that there will be real differences in the effectiveness of the two basal systems, without any analysis of the actual variations in the methods, content, and rationale of these systems. If such differences were to appear—and they do in the final test data—the lack of detailed analysis of the systems will conceal the probable

reasons for the variations and leave the school without any constructive results. It is certainly more significant to discover how and why the outcomes with basal systems differ, rather than whether they differ. We shall try to tease out the how and why in a later analysis of the test data, but this line of inquiry should have been planned in the study.

The same criticism of the comparison of the basals with the language experience approach is not so acute, for there are obvious differences in rationale, content, and method that may produce different outcomes. But, if the study is to contribute to more successful teaching of reading, both methods must be analyzed to identify and to compare their emphases upon various skills and the respective results. Methods and systems of teaching are not simply equivalent or better or worse, for each tends to produce a different pattern of skill development that we must discover in order to improve our reading instruction. Because they are so labeled, the basal readers are assumed to be comparable in difficulty. This is a very questionable assumption, since many studies (5, 6) show that readers offered for the same grade level may vary greatly in their readability and in their interest factor with obvious effects upon learnability and comprehension.

(2)   The description of the population implies a mixture of largely middle-class children and an unknown proportion of pupils who are probably lower in socioeconomic status and perhaps bilingual. The number of the Mexican-American children may have been so small as to be relatively unimportant in the results. But, on the other hand, if such children are present, should we not try to isolate the results of the different reading systems with them? Or, do we just assume that what is best for the middle-class pupils is also true for the Mexican-American? Certainly some provision should have been made to determine the specific results with the minority group, if only by careful observation, for the methods and the tests may have yielded different results for them (1).

(3)   Assigning pupils at random or alphabetically as they enroll does not necessarily produce equated groups. Their equivalence must be tested in terms of the factors likely to influence the results.

(4)   If the school population is drawn from the same area each year, and the area is not sharply deteriorating or changing in work opportunities, we may generalize our research results from one year to another. Arriving at this judgement by general impressions is, however, hardly a scientific approach.

(5)   Equating groups in the first grade by readiness scores is a common procedure, and, since many such tests are heavily loaded with the intelligence factor, this method does give some picture of the situation. But at least the mean scores of the groups should be reported, and the name of the test, as well as statistical evaluation of the significance of any differences, so that the reader may be certain of the accuracy of this statement and of the equivalence of the groups. We are not certain, however, that the groups were equated in intelligence, an important factor in classes of this size. This information would have been helpful, even though, as Reed has shown (4), equating by group mean I.Q.'s usually ignores the variations in verbal versus nonverbal intelligence.

(6) (7)   Years of teaching experience and supervisors' opinions of the teacher's effectiveness are not very significant factors in a study of this type. But, in this case, the teacher asked to employ the unfamiliar language experience approach was also lacking in any experience in first-grade teaching. With two such unfavorable factors, it would be surprising to find this method as effective as are the other familiar systems taught by teachers with first-grade experience. We know, for example, that teacher knowledge of primary reading skills, such as phonics, is related to their grade-level teaching experience. Mrs. Brown's sixth-grade teaching may well have handicapped her in this particular area, for it is not probable that she had done much instruction in this skill; moreover, she had no manual to guide her (although there are some available).

(8)   Like most present-day schools, this one assumed that admission age is significant in early reading success; it actually ignored the more important factors of kindergarten experience and mental age, although this latter was probably assessed in the readiness tests. The number of children with kindergarten experience in each experimental class, at least, should have been equated, unless we assume that the influence of this preschool training was measured by the readiness test. Children with kindergarten training do tend to have greater success in reading but do not always score higher in any readiness test. Few readiness tests, if any, actually sample all the outcomes of kindergarten. Thus both these factors should have been considered in equating the classes.

(9)   The teachers selected to try the basal systems should not only have been urged to follow the respective manuals, but should also have been supervised to insure this procedure. Teachers are prone to give their own interpretations to the directions of the manual, varying from it as they think best. As a result,

their statements regarding the system that they employ cannot be accepted at face value, for they may well give very different emphases to important skills than the authors of the series intended. Without supervision, we have no way of knowing whether we are comparing the two basal systems employed, or the versions that Mrs. Adams and Miss Casey used.

(10)   Like most reading methods, there are a number of versions of the language experience approach that differ considerably.* We shall have to examine the detailed description of Mrs. Brown's daily procedures before we can determine just which version Professor Jones taught her. This casual approach to introducing a teacher to a new teaching method by a few conversations illustrates another common defect in many similar research reports. Few teachers can really learn how to use an unfamiliar system effectively in such a fashion. Before we can make a valid comparison of methods as intended here, extended in-service training and classroom practice under supervision must be given to teachers using an unfamiliar method. In fact, this teacher training should probably extend over at least a semester before we can be fairly sure that we are making a fair comparison between systems, and not just contrasting teachers' instructional skills with an unfamiliar, poorly understood approach.

(11)   Apparently all three teachers attended the planning conferences to learn the details of the experimental study. In our opinion, this was most unwise, for it is well known that individuals who know that they are in an experiment (both teachers and pupils) tend to behave differently from what they would in ordinary situations. They tend to respond to the challenge or excitement with greater effort or even better reading if they realize that is the purpose of the experiment. The fact that a comparison of methods was intended should not have been disclosed to the teachers. Rather, each should have been simply assigned an approach, provided she was familiar with it and willing to use it, and then given adequate supervision to insure her following it accurately.

Teacher attitudes or feelings about a reading method seriously influence the class results. Many, many research contrasts of methods indicate more differences in class outcomes from one teacher to another using the same method, than between classes under different methods. If sufficiently motivated and inspired, it seems that a teacher may achieve outstanding results with almost any method in a short-term experiment. This teacher variable can

---

*See the chapter on the language experience approach in *Reading in the Elementary School* by George D. and Evelyn B. Spache (Boston: Allyn and Bacon, 1973).

be partially controlled by avoiding the stimulation of the knowledge that one is involved in a comparative experiment. Another control can be introduced by alternating teachers and methods in repeated trials, pooling the results of each method from all the teachers. And, as we have suggested, supervision of each teacher's procedures in following each method is another control of the teacher variable. Failure to control this teacher variable invalidates many short-term, small-scale experiments like this.

This Hawthorne effect, as it is called—of the response of subjects to being included in an experiment—is well known. Ideally, neither teachers nor pupils, nor experimenters nor subjects, should be aware that the treatment is an experimental one or that the results are likely to be influenced in the direction expected. If control groups are to be employed (as the two first grades here that received no experimental method), they, too, should be ignorant of the intended comparisons or the variations in methods among classes.

As McCracken (3) has pointed out, the Hawthorne effect may be either positive or negative depending upon the feelings of the teachers and pupils. In this study, we are not told whether the teachers were familiar with either of the basals tested or whether they had any preferences. And, for that matter, we do not know whether the teachers even wanted to be included in the experiment.

(12) (13) (14)   The instructional time per day can be a significant factor in children's reading success. Individual tutoring, use of paraprofessionals, coaching at home by parents, or even extending reading instruction into such areas as language arts, handwriting, and spelling (as some systems do) affect the outcomes. If these variations were avoided in this study, the amount of instructional time appears to be normal and comparable among the methods.

As for the grouping practices, these, too, could have affected the program. Grouping that becomes almost permanent, with few or no changes in response to variations in progress, can limit the ultimate progress of pupils. If grouping degenerates into teacher-directed pacing through materials, end-of-the-year test results may well be limited in range. Pupils may lack the breadth of reading experience that would permit them to move as far and as fast as they are capable of doing, and few high test scores will be obtained.

If we take the statement regarding the formation of groups after completion of the readiness materials at face value, we recognize that these teachers, like so many, do not understand readiness. It cannot be assumed that all children are ready for reading instruction just because they completed the readiness workbook. This assumption contravenes the idea of individual differences and the fact that readiness is a multifaceted group of behaviors. Proceeding in this fashion almost guarantees that some children will be inducted into reading with little chance of success because of foundational lacks in physical, social, or emotional factors. If schools must take this route, at least, they should report the outcomes separately for the ability groups to give the study real meaning.

(15) (16)　　The description of the two or three instructional periods during the day reveals that they resembled common practices. It is possible, of course, that there were distinct variations from one teacher to another within this common framework. Some comparison of the types and amount of supplementary materials, and of the seatwork, the library use, and free reading provisions, would be most desirable. We are not certain that all three teachers conducted parallel programs in these aspects, or in their time and emphasis upon skill development in seatwork and small-group instruction. These factors may have both positive and negative effects upon the test results, as we shall try to point out later. Frequent supervision of the classes would have insured comparability of the daily procedures, in all probability.

(17) (18)
(19) (20)　　The description of Mrs. Brown's program does show some variations naturally from the basal reader classes. The greater emphasis upon writing has been shown to contribute to reading success, and the word recognition drill may also prove significant in the evaluation. Some observers of the language experience, perhaps including Mrs. Brown, are disturbed by the wide variety of words that occur in the chart stories. They assume that, as in a basal reading system, the child is expected to learn all these words permanently, and drill accordingly, despite the fact that many such words have only temporary significance or, because of their interesting format and meanings, are readily learned for the time being. Others try to limit the chart vocabulary to some list of words derived from some basal reader, thus tending to destroy the spontaneity of the material, and contradicting the basic rationale of the language experience approach, as Mrs. Brown did. The casual reader may well accept this study as a comparative study of basal systems versus "the" language experience approach, as understood by Mrs. Brown.

(21) (22)
(23) (24)　　The further description of Mrs. Brown's program reinforces the observation that she followed the version of language experience that conceives of it as only an introduction to basal reading rather than as a different and complete method of teaching reading. When children move into basal readers as soon as the teacher judges them to be ready, there is no real contrast between two

methods. Rather, the study is comparing two basals with a basal plus a brief period of experience with chart stories. As a matter of fact, some basal systems normally include chart story reading as part of their program. We don't know whether this could have been true for the Circle and Star systems, too. These variations in definition of the approach cloud the results of this and many other such reports purporting to be comparisons of basal systems with language experience or individualized reading methods.

(25) (26)   The Cosmopolitan Test resembles many others used in primary grade testing in its emphasis upon testing word recognition in several ways. The sentence reading test would probably be labeled as a measure of comprehension, which, in a superficial sense, it does sample. But this subtest is also loaded with the task of word recognition in that the child must be able to recognize and discriminate among the four words offered before he can choose one to fit the sense of the sentence. The intercorrelations of these three subtests would probably indicate considerable overlap because of the common factor of word recognition. The important question is whether these tests sampling word recognition almost exclusively are really adequate to measure the outcomes of this study. Will these tests reveal any comparative strengths or weaknesses in the methods being explored? Or do we assume that word recognition is the sole goal of any first-grade reading program?

A second question regarding the tests is present in their relevance to the teaching method employed. Apparently Mrs. Brown was doubtful regarding this point, as shown by her attempt to devise an additional, more relevant word recognition test. This is a very real problem, for most, if not all, reading tests seem to be constructed to measure the results of the common basal system, tending to ignore the nuances present in other approaches. For example, simply because of the writing experience in the language experience approach, we might well expect variations in breadth of reading and writing vocabulary, in the content of the reading and writing of these children, and in their spelling ability, as well as in the length and quality of their compositions. It is possible that the sources of the content of their materials would be wider than in basal systems, with consequent learning in such areas as nature study, social science, and the like greater than that for the other children. None of these probable outcomes were sampled in the testing plan.

We do not know whether Mrs. Brown's version of the language experience will produce these variations normally to be anticipated in such a system. But, if her system did, we would never learn it from the tests selected for evaluation. Like so many other studies, this report assumes that ordinary reading tests will measure all the important outcomes.

(27) Mrs. Brown's attempt to devise a separate word recognition test to sample the broader reading vocabulary of her pupils was laudable. But how will the test be interpreted? What sort of performance on this test should we expect of her pupils? Should they have learned all the words or only about 50 percent or what? Unless this test was also given to all the other classes, we do not even know whether the pupils taught by the language experience approach did, in fact, acquire a broader sight vocabulary, although we could probably assume so.

It seems obvious that all pupils involved in an experiment should be administered all evaluative instruments employed to determine the outcomes. But, as in this study, this logic is not always recognized, and we are left wondering about the true significance of the study. Some studies do not even administer the evaluative instruments to the entire experimental populations, often deeming it sufficient to sample from the groups to save time and money, perhaps. Again, this incomplete testing fails to reveal what really happened in the entire experimental population, for we cannot assume that test results on a smaller sample accurately reflect the performances of the whole group.

Other faulty evaluation procedures—not present in this study but not uncommon—are the use of different reading tests in pretesting and posttesting, or of using several tests for posttesting. Results from different reading tests are not comparable in raw scores or grade scores. Nor may they be combined by averaging or some other technique. Tests employ many ways of assessing reading progress, almost as many ways as there are authors, and each has its own peculiar meanings. Mrs. Brown's special test of word recognition, for example, cannot be compared or combined with the other apparently similar tests because of its unusual vocabulary, if for no other reason. Nor can measures of oral and silent reading be compared or averaged or contrasted as measures of the outcomes of an experiment, as some reports do. The two ways of reading are not just different samples of the same behavior, but rather measures of two vastly different processes. Even the three word recognition tests used here are not directly comparable because of their variation in inherent difficulty. The word picture matching test is probably easier than the word recognition subtest of the Cosmopolitan battery or that prepared by Mrs. Brown (2). Using grade scores from each Cosmopolitan subtest would tend to equate the results for the difficulty of each, but grade scores, of course, were not available for Mrs. Brown's test.

(28) Let us examine the tabulation of the posttesting scores, noting the apparent facts obtained, the implications, and the unanswered questions, as follows:

1. The word picture test is easier than the word recognition test or the comprehension test.

2. All three standardized tests were harder than Mrs. Brown's special word recognition test.

3. The scores for Mrs. Adams's group using the Circle Readers are greater in the standardized word picture and word recognition subtests than any of the other classes. Apparently this system produces greater skill in sight vocabulary than the other approaches, if we assume that these differences are significant both statistically and educationally.

4. But, at the same time, the sentence reading scores for the Circle system are lowest among the five classes. What factor in this system promotes sight recognition without producing sentence comprehension? Is it the fact that, in contrast to the others, the Circle system places strong emphasis upon letter sounds, thus producing the pattern that many other studies have shown us to be expected of such an emphasis? Only a comparative analysis of the content of the daily lessons, not the test results, will reveal why this system produces such effects (and why the other systems do not).

5. What is the significance of the wider range of scores in each subtest for pupils using the Circle readers? Is the approach so difficult for this population that it produces many more low scores than the other systems? Were these low scores present among the middle-class pupils, or do they reflect the performances largely of the Mexican-American minority? For what kind of pupils is this system successful or unsuccessful in stimulating word recognition development?

6. Do the results justify discarding the language experience approach? The word picture and comprehension scores for Mrs. Brown's language experience class were equal to those derived from the Star system, and their scores in all three tests were equal or superior to those found for the two nonexperimental classes. Moreover, by averaging 66 percent on the special vocabulary test, her pupils evidenced learning of a broader vocabulary than did the other classes, who probably were never introduced to these words and are not likely to have learned many of them without instruction. In the comprehension test, Mrs. Brown's group excelled the Circle reader class, as did indeed all the other classes too. If breadth of sight vocabulary as well as sentence comprehension are major goals of first-grade reading, is the language experience approach really less effective than the Circle system or any of the others?

7. Without testing statistically the significance of the differences between the various raw or grade scores, we cannot be certain that there are real differences, particularly in view of the small numbers of pupils involved. All the apparent variations in group means may be well within the probable errors of the means. Each mean represents a probable range of possible means, not an absolute score; and we are not sure whether the errors of the means overlap. The same uncertainty applies to the interpretation of the grade score means. The Circle system may be better than all the others, particularly in the word recognition subtest, but we do not really know.

Furthermore, even if we accept the differences at face value, how significant are they educationally? The Circle system exceeds the others by only two to four months in grade score in word recognition, while it is inferior in sentence comprehension by the same amount. Logically, if we judge the Circle system superior in producing word recognition, we must judge it inferior in stimulating sentence comprehension, for the differences are similar in each area. Besides, are differences between small groups as little as two to four months decisive results?

(29) (30)   We have grave doubts that the conclusions of the authors of this report are justified. There is evidence that the Circle system produces a different pattern of skill development than the other systems do, but there is no real explanation of the reasons for this difference or how it may be altered. It may not be at all feasible, as they suggest, to strengthen the development of the relatively weak sentence comprehension that this system appears to produce, without changing the program drastically. Obviously, some present components of the Circle system would have to be supplanted by the planned emphasis upon sentence comprehension. Then the pattern of skill development that would be produced is highly questionable, and the superiority claimed for this system might well be lost. Moreover, the failure to follow up these pupils into later primary grades leaves us ignorant of the ultimate outcomes of these reading systems, which might be more significant than the present findings.

The presentation and critique of this hypothetical research report is intended as a simple introduction to the critical evaluation that, we think, reading teachers should make of such studies. This review and the research article itself could have been much more complex and formal. But we were not attempting to provide a wide background in educational statistics and research design. We did not intend to offer a substitute for study in these areas in order to sharpen the ability to read and plan research, but merely to illustrate how a simple research report of the type we are offered frequently might be analyzed.

LEARNING PROJECT

You have critiqued this research report yourself and also shared in the criticisms offered by the present author. It may now be apparent that there are a number of crucial points during the planning and execution of even a simple research study, points at which particular pains must be taken to insure the validity of the study. Review your criticisms and those of the author; then make a list of these very important stages in research work. Do not forget to include such basics as the assumptions that are used to justify the study; selection of the population; equating experimental and control groups; equating other variables or controlling them; control of the actual day-by-day procedures; control of the Hawthorne effect, and many more.

REFERENCES

1. Hernandez, Norma G., "Variables Affecting Achievement of Middle School Mexican-American Students," *Review of Educational Research,* 43 (Winter 1973), 1–39.
2. Leibert, R. E., "Some Differences between Silent and Oral Reading Responses on a Standardized Test," in *Forging Ahead in Reading,* J. Allen Figurel, editor. Proceedings International Reading Association, 12 (1968), 472–77.
3. McCracken, R. A., "An Observation of Hawthorne Effect in an Experiment in the Teaching of Reading in First Grade: A Hypothesis," in *Reading and Realism,* J. Allen Figurel, editor. Proceedings International Reading Association, 13 (1969), 582–85.
4. Reed, J. C., "The Deficits of Retarded Readers: Fact or Artifact," *Reading Teacher,* 23 (1970), 347–52, 393.
5. Rogers, A. R., "Comparing the Difficulty of Basal Readers," *Journal of the New England Reading Association,* 5 (1970), 35–37.
6. Spache, George D., see "Informal Testing and Evaluation," chapter 4 of this book.

Dr. Arthur S. McDonald, of Halifax, Nova Scotia, delivered this paper at the University of Chicago Reading Conference of 1964. In our opinion, it is one of the best exercises in critical reading for reading teachers in the literature. In very simple style, McDonald explains many of the phenomena that bias the results of a large number of experiments in reading, and those that limit the extent to which such experiments can be generalized to other school situations. He also exposes certain flaws in the procedures used to evaluate pupil progress or the outcomes of an experiment, procedures commonly presented in our professional literature.

You were introduced to critical evaluation of research reports in the preceding chapter. If you can combine the concepts gained there with the technical terms and ideas expressed here, your future reading of such articles will be more meaningful.

19
Evaluation of Innovations in Reading Instruction

By Arthur S. McDonald

As you learn about these biasing forces in experiments, ask yourself such questions as these:

1. Which of these common flaws in research design and evaluation are new to you? Can you understand them well enough to recognize them in the future in your reading?

2. Do you agree with the author that the failure to control such variables as the Hawthorne effect, the placebo, or the experimenter bias tends to destroy the significance of a research study? If you disagree, be prepared to offer your rebuttal arguments.

EACH INNOVATION IN READING INSTRUCTION has published reports of research showing dramatic results. Indeed, several new systems approach the panacea stage in their claims for insuring the success of every child in learning to read well, painlessly, and enjoyably. Since each new method asserts its superiority over all existing systems (including yesterday's innovation), educators face the task of careful evaluation.

In preparing this paper, the writer has assumed that you are not interested in inventing novel systems of teaching reading. (Any who are so inclined are probably already at work following the "principles" suggested by George D. Spache in his talk this morning.) Therefore, this paper discusses the main principles and problems of evaluating systems of reading instruction.

As a first step, you must have an adequate base of knowledge about the reading process, the psychology of learning, and the strengths and weaknesses of present instructional programs. Furthermore, an up-to-date familiarity with completed reading research is essential. And you must have an understanding of the basic principles of research design, methods of controlling critical variables, and statistical evaluation. In any evaluation—whether based on reports of research carried out by someone else or on research which you are conducting—knowledge, experience, and professional competence are limiting factors.

BIASING FORCES IN EXPERIMENTAL DESIGN

A majority of published studies reporting the effectiveness of various reading instructional programs are seriously vitiated by inadequate experimental designs. These designs have failed to take into account forces which invalidate research and experimentation. The most common and pernicious of these forces are discussed below.

1. Hawthorne Effect.

Desmond L. Cook has defined this as "an awareness on the part of the subject of special treatment created by artificial experimental conditions," pointing out

Arthur S. McDonald, "Evaluation of Innovations in Reading Instruction," pp. 95–101 in *Recent Developments in Reading,* H. Alan Robinson, editor. Supplementary Educational Monographs No. 95. Chicago: University of Chicago Press, 1965. © 1965 by the University of Chicago. Reprinted by permission of the publisher and author.

that it affects the *subject* and *not* the experimenter.[1] Cook found that pupils as young as fourth graders recognize significant departures from normal routine.[2] Thus, even nine-year-olds who are subjects of investigation realize their special role and are vulnerable to the Hawthorne effect.

2. Placebo Effect.

This is a special form of the Hawthorne effect which accompanies the use of novel materials, special equipment, secret methods, and so on. In the educational realm, a placebo may be defined as a mechanical or electronic instructional or psychological agent, material, or treatment used with or without some form of ritual but always with the suggestion or implication of its power and helpful effects. Unlike the Hawthorne effect, the placebo effect will not be attained unless the experimenter believes in the placebo.

A "placebo response" is a response of the agent or treatment which cannot be ascribed to the agent or treatment itself but which must be the result of other aspects of the situation. A placebo effect, then, is the apparent effectiveness of an instructional approach or treatment resulting from the faith of both the subject and the experimenter in the efficacy of the method, aided by its face validity.

It has been shown that the mere act of using placebo agents with the appropriate ritual accentuates their effect. Albert Kurland has reported that tranquilizers are often used in far too small a dosage to have beneficial pharmacologic effects.[3] In fact, it has been reported in the press that meprobamate (the Miltown of story and jest), long believed to be a tranquilizer, has been removed from the U.S. Pharmacopeia. Research demonstrated that it was not a tranquilizer (according to medical definition) but rather a sedative of less power and effectiveness than the barbiturates. (This comment is not intended to deprecate the medical or pharmacological professions but to illustrate the pervasiveness of placebo responses.)

The type and strength of a placebo effect depends on the circumstances under which the placebo is given and on the method of measuring the outcomes of its use. The nature of the subject and the situation in which the activity is carried out are important determiners of the effect. Vague means of measuring results and heavy reliance on subjective evaluation strongly favor placebo responses.

---

[1]Cook, "The Hawthorne Effect in Educational Research," *Phi Delta Kappan*, XLIV (December, 1962), 118.

[2]Cook, "The Hawthorne Effect and Reading Research," in *Improvement of Reading through Classroom Practice*, International Reading Conference Proceedings, ed. J. Allen Figurel (Newark: Del.: International Reading Association, 1964), IX, 251.

[3]Kurland, "Placebo Effect," in *Drugs and Behavior*, ed. Leonard Uhr and James G. Miller (New York: John Wiley & Sons, 1960), pp. 156–65.

Thus, placebo responses are particularly likely in reading programs in which the instructors rely heavily on specially prepared books, instructional materials, or special instrumentation (believing themselves in the beneficial effects of the materials). They are also likely in systems which have adopted "new breakthrough methods" which the practitioners believe cannot be measured by existing devices or techniques.

3. Experimenter Bias.

As used here, this term does not apply to unprofessional manipulation of data to produce the results the experimenter wants. Rather it applies to influence from the experimenter of which he is unaware. Subjects often know what an experimenter wants them to do, even though he may believe he is being quite objective or neutral in his behavior. Martin T. Orne has shown how powerful a set the realization "this is an experiment" can be for students. He asserts that the student sees his task as finding out the true purpose of the experiment in order to respond in a manner which will support the hypotheses being tested. Orne points out that a very important source of cues for the subject is in the experimental procedure itself. For instance, if a new kind of test is given before and after some type of instruction, even the dullest pupil is aware that some change is expected. Orne emphasizes that response to the experimental situation (which he calls "demand characteristics") is not merely conscious compliance.[4] Instead, the demand characteristics of the experimental situation help define the role of "good subject." The subject does his best to fit the role in his responses.

Robert Rosenthal found that data obtained by twenty-four assistants of twelve experimenters, who trained the assistants but did not tell them the results they expected, correlated significantly with the experimenters' expectancy of findings.[5]

Thus, the three forces discussed above—as embodied in the novel and dramatic nature of components of the instructional system—heightened willingness to respond because of knowledge of desired results, teacher-student faith and psychological interaction, suggestibility, feeling of importance ("I've been selected for special treatment"), and so on. These three forces appear to account for more than two-thirds of all reported results of successful results of innovations in reading instruction. George D. Spache has observed that by dramatic use of novel methods or impressive equipment "it is

---

[4]Orne, "On the Social Psychology of the Psychological Experiment, with Particular Reference to Demand Characteristics and Their Implications," *American Psychologist,* XVII (November, 1962), 778.

[5]Rosenthal et al., "The Effect of Experimenters' Bias on the Data Obtained by Their Research Assistants," *American Psychologist,* XVII (June, 1962), 328.

possible to produce for a brief space of time what appears to be more than normal progress by remedial techniques or methods that are completely contradictory or even irrelevant to the causes of the reading retardation."[6]

Thus, in evaluating results of new systems of teaching reading, it is essential to ascertain whether the investigators used experimental designs which would eliminate or minimize the Hawthorne and placebo effects and experimenter bias. Since these forces are so commonly overlooked—even in a complex and sophisticated research—it is probable that the investigator ignored them if no mention is made of procedures employed to mitigate them. Caution should be used in utilizing findings of research which has overlooked these forces. Outcomes will be spuriously favorable and benefits greatly overstated.

CAN THE RESEARCH FINDINGS BE GENERALIZED?

One purpose of educational research is the development of generalizations which can be used as a basis for application in a wide variety of teaching situations. In evaluating reports of research, you should make certain that the findings are really capable of being generalized so that they may be applied to your situation. For reasons to be discussed later, this is particularly important for evaluating innovations in reading instruction.

Learning is a highly personal activity. Most reports of instructional outcomes describe what happened when teacher T_1 used method M_1 with students SS_1 in classroom climate C_1 (perhaps with additional assistants AA_1). When teacher T_2 uses method M_1 with students SS_2 in classroom climate C_2 (certainly without additional assistants), he may find method M_1 no better than the method he was using before or perhaps even less effective. This latter outcome will be probable if the teacher is constrained to use the new method. On the other hand, should the teacher be convinced of its excellence and should the method lends itself to operation of the biasing forces, he will probably find the innovation "beneficial."

Harry F. Silberman for example, found that taped presentations of a program to teach first graders to read trigrams were not as effective as were the "live" presentations by the original experimenter.[7] Donald E. P. Smith and others found that, at the college level, students progressed better with

---

[6]Spache, *Toward Better Reading* (Champaign, Ill.: Garrard Publishing Co., 1963), p. 325.

[7]Silberman, *Experimental Analysis of a Beginning Reading Skill* (Santa Monica, Calif.: System Developmental Corp., 1964).

programs adapted to their personality patterns.[8]   Reviewing the research on new systems of teaching very young children to read, Joanna P. Williams found that all successful experiments used some form of individualized instruction.[9]

Although pupil behavior shows marked similarities, on the basis of age level, in different sizes of communities, there are significant differences in a number of aspects between urban and rural, industrial and resort, and urban and exurban environments.   Such differences limit the generalization of findings obtained in one kind of setting.   Class size, type of school, and the training and experience of the teacher are other factors which must be considered in evaluating the appropriateness of an instructional innovation for another setting.   Experiments which are carried on solely in campus laboratory schools, private schools, or in college psychology classes have limited possibilities of generalization.   The use of assistants—not usually available to the classroom teacher—or the restriction of class size to a fraction of the average also casts doubt on the application of findings to other classrooms across the country.

EVALUATING PROGRESS IN READING PROGRAMS

Four of the most common procedures used to evaluate progress in reading programs are the following:

1. Comparison of pre- and post-test scores on equated forms of standardized reading tests and/or informal tests, and comparison of test performance with the performance expected statistically (for example, "Bobby grew two years in reading during this school year.").
2. Use of national average yearly gains on a standardized group reading test as a basis for comparing test gains made in the local reading group.
3. Comparison of test-retest results of the experimental group using a new program with the test-retest performance of a control group.
4. Use of subjective questionnaires and interviews designed to "tap deeper changes and inner growth."

The first two methods are most commonly used in classroom and reading clinic descriptive reports.   The third and fourth are usual in published reports of research and experimental studies.   The fourth is quite usual with the "new breakthrough approaches" for which established tests and statistical evaluations are "outdated, inadequate, and straitjacketing."

---

[8]Smith et al., "Reading Improvement as a Function of Student Personality and Teaching Method," *Journal of Educational Psychology*, 47 (January 1956), 47–59.
[9]Williams, "Reading Research and Instruction," *Review of Educational Research*, 35 (April 1965), 147–54.

If properly used, these methods can yield valuable information, but they are subject to several types of error. Educators conducting investigations or reading reports of investigations should be aware of these errors and should note how they were mitigated (if they were.)

These sources of error include the following:

1. Failure to correct for regression to the mean. On a second testing, persons scoring low on the first test tend to move upward, and vice versa. (After all, if a student misses *all* the questions on the first test, he has probability on his side—he cannot get a lower score and his guesses cannot always be wrong.) Frederick P. Davis has given formulas to correct for this source of error.[10]

2. Treatment of reading grade scores as actual indications of month-by-month growth. Reading grade scores are extrapolated from one grade level to another rather than obtained by longitudinal study. Furthermore, principles of learning would suggest that learning takes place unevenly. Spache has pointed out that experiments using repeated testing indicate that reading growth is not evenly distributed throughout the year.[11]

3. Assumption that standardized reading tests provide reliable and valid measures of all the most important aspects of reading. Albert J. Kingston has recently warned against this assumption and has made suggestions for alternative bases of evaluation.[12]

4. Spurious scores obtained from the use of a single test over a wide range of educational levels. (Although extreme heterogeneity aids reliability, it weakens validity.) Such scores are usually too high for those at the lower levels and too low for those at the upper levels.

5. Experimenter-made tests to measure unique definitions or conceptual models of reading. Such results cannot be compared or generalized with other data; hence, they are not sufficient to evaluate outcomes of instruction. To meet this criterion, these special tests would have to be compared with existing measures of reading and a method of equating results prepared. An alternative would be to establish, by rigorous research, the defensibility of the new definition of reading and the viability of the conceptual model together with the appropriateness of the new tests for assessing the results of the new program.

6. Use of test questions for checking reading comprehension, which can be answered by many children from background knowledge (that is, without reading the selection).

7. Use of inappropriate norms to interpret test data, failure to allow for interform differences in equated forms, or the use of an inappropriate test.

---

[10]Davis, "The Assessment of Change," in *Phases of College and Other Adult Reading Programs,* Tenth Yearbook of the National Reading Conference, Emery P. Bliesmer and Albert J. Kingston, editors (Milwaukee: National Reading Conference, Inc., 1961), pp. 93–95.

[11]Spache, *op. cit.,* pp. 325, 359–60.

[12]Kingston, "Is Reading What the Reading Tests Test?" in *The Philosophical and Sociological Bases of Reading,* Fourteenth Yearbook of the National Reading Conference, Eric L. Thurston and Lawrence E. Hafner, editors (Milwaukee: National Reading Conference, Inc., 1965), pp. 106–9.

8. Failure to select a really comparable control group and failure to control for essential variables.

9. Reliance on subjective questionnaires with low reliability and validity for evaluation.

10. Failure to use any control groups at all. Experimenters use this approach with startling innovations and defend it on the ground that their specially devised methods of evaluation support the "revolutionary" rationale of the system.

IMPLICATIONS

Adequate evaluation of innovations in reading instruction requires the following:

1. Careful delineation of instructional objectives in operational form. This should include specification of how these objectives are to be measured, that is, what will be the evidence of progress in learning.

2. Specification of the limitations of the system of instruction. (What types of students is this system designed to teach? What kinds of learning problems will remain unaffected by it or show only Hawthorne, placebo, and experimenter-bias reactions? What kinds of student background are assumed? What is the nature of special training, if any, which the teacher must have?)

3. Evidence that the new program can be applied in daily teaching situations with the same effectiveness as in the experimental situation. This evidence should also indicate whether the experimental teaching personnel added instructional procedures from their previous methods of teaching to the new system so that the evaluator can judge whether he is dealing with a pure system or a combination.

4. Controls for biasing forces. (Cook suggests that placebo treatment be used to control the Hawthorne effect.[13]) Use some form of special instrumentation or special instructional material—perhaps stamped "A New Approach to Reading"—at specially scheduled times with all students in the control groups. Teachers of the control groups should believe that they are working with experimental groups, and they should be comparable in ability with those teaching the true experimental groups.

5. Use of more than one kind of measurement in assessing differences in performance between and within groups.

6. Demonstration of the direct relationships of the conclusions and implications to the research findings.

7. Detailed explanation of how the results, conclusions, and implications can be put to practical use by the classroom teacher.

8. Avoidance of any program that suggests that the innovation will work with all children under all conditions and with all teachers.

---

[13]Cook, *op. cit.*

9. Evidence that the experimenter took measures to safeguard against errors resulting from suggestion and experimenter bias. Cook has observed that awareness of the Hawthorne effect is a helpful beginning,[14] and Donald L. Cleland suggests randomization.[15] Nash advocates as close an approach to the "double-blind" technique of medicine as practicable be built into the research design.[16] This becomes increasingly important as the innovation departs more and more widely from current reading programs.

10. Sufficient information of a design and statistical nature that it can be replicated.

If a new system of reading instruction is to be evaluated as producing more than a non-specific Hawthorne or placebo response, its research reports must demonstrate that its effects are stronger, last longer, and are qualitatively different from those produced by biasing forces, or that it affects students in different ways than would be expected from placebo and Hawthorne reactions. Unfortunately, research reports on innovations in reading instruction often fail to do these things to an adequate degree.

LEARNING PROJECT

Select a report on an experiment in the field of reading, as complex as you can readily understand. You may easily find such an article in *Elementary English, The Reading Teacher, Journal of Reading, Reading Research Quarterly, Elementary School Journal, Journal of Educational Psychology,* **and others of these types. Be certain that the article is a report of an actual experiment, not an opinion statement or a popularized rehash of someone else's study.**

Read it as critically as you can, noting both positive and negative aspects of the study. Examine particularly such facets as the clarity of the planning and execution, the validity of the evaluation procedures, and their relevance to the goals of the experiment. Consider also whether the results could be generalized to other situations and whether a replication of the experiment in some other setting would be likely to yield the same indications. Evaluate the significance of the entire experiment as a research study, as well as the educational significance of the findings.

---

[14]*Ibid.*

[15]Cleland, "Needed Improvement in Research Design in Reading," in *Improvement of Reading through Classroom Practice,* International Reading Association Conference Proceedings, ed. J. Allen Figurel (Newark, Del.: International Reading Association, 1964), 9, 244–49.

[16]Harvey Nash, "The Design and Conduct of Experiments on the Psychological Effects of Drugs," in *Drugs and Behavior,* ed. Leonard Uhr and James G. Miller (New York: John Wiley & Sons, 1960), pp. 128–55.

Index